ASIAN ART MUSEUM OF SAN FRANCISCO

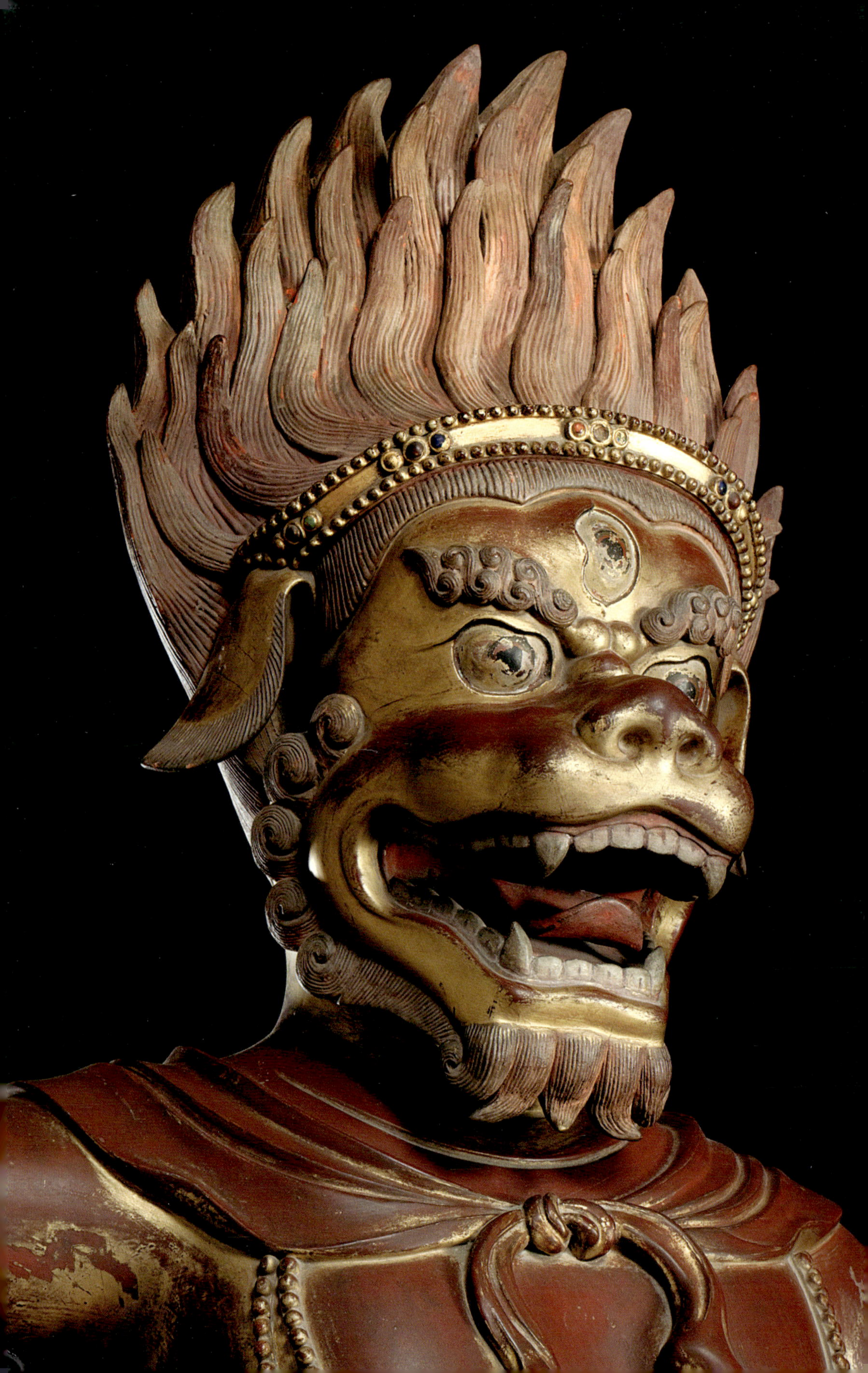

ASIAN ART MUSEUM OF SAN FRANCISCO

COLLECTION HIGHLIGHTS

JAY XU, DIRECTOR

Asian
Art
Museum

Published by
Asian Art Museum
Chong-Moon Lee Center for Asian Art and Culture
200 Larkin Street
San Francisco, CA 94102
www.asianart.org

Printed and bound in Italy
21 20 19 18   4 3 2 1 First edition

Library of Congress Cataloging-in-Publication Data
Names: Asian Art Museum of San Francisco, author.
Title: Asian Art Museum of San Francisco : collection highlights.
Description: First edition. | San Francisco, CA : Asian Art Museum, Chong-Moon Lee Center for Asian Art and Culture, 2018. | Includes bibliographical references and index.
Identifiers: LCCN 2017038832 | ISBN 9780939117840 (pbk. : alk. paper)
Subjects: LCSH: Art, Asian—Catalogs. | Art—California—San Francisco—Catalogs. | Asian Art Museum of San Francisco—Catalogs.
Classification: LCC N7262 .A882 2018 | DDC 709.5—dc23
LC record available at https://lccn.loc.gov/2017038832

Produced by the Publications Department, Asian Art Museum of San Francisco
Edited by Clare Jacobson, Head of Publications
Editorial assistance by Ruth Keffer, Copy Editor

Designed by Bob Aufuldish, Aufuldish & Warinner
Proofread by Melissa Stein
Indexed by Theresa Duran

Asian Art Museum of San Francisco: Collection Highlights is generously supported by Ann Tanenbaum in memory of Mary M. Tanenbaum.

Detail photographs: Front cover: Buddha dated 338, see pp. 132–33; Back cover: *Shimmering of Heated Air (Kageno)*, see p. 307; p. ii: The Buddhist deity Simhavaktra, a *dakini*, see pp. 110–11; p. v: Moon jar, see pp. 222–23; p. vi: The Hindu deity Vishnu, see pp. 66–67; p. viii: Ritual vessel in the shape of a rhinoceros, see pp. 120–21; p. xii: Dish with design of horse and cheetah, see p. 7; p. 22: The hero Rustam and the demoness, from a manuscript of the *Shahnama* (Book of Kings), see pp. 44–45; p. 58: Sarong, see p. 90; p. 94: The Buddhist deity Guhyasamaja, see p. 101; p. 112: Daoist celestial worthy, pp. 170–71; p. 210: Reading desk with "ten symbols of longevity" motif, see p. 226; p. 236: The bodhisattva Samantabhadra (Fugen Bosatsu), see p. 250; p. 312: Cup with calligraphic inscriptions, see pp. 16–17; p. 316: The Hindu deity Shiva, see pp. 36–37

Distributed by:
North America, Latin America, and Europe
Tuttle Publishing
364 Innovation Drive
North Clarendon, VT 05759-9436 U.S.A.
Tel: 1 (802) 773-8930; Fax: 1 (802) 773-6993
info@tuttlepublishing.com
www.tuttlepublishing.com
Asia Pacific
Berkeley Books Pte. Ltd.
61 Tai Seng Avenue #02-12
Singapore 534167
Tel: (65) 6280-1330; Fax: (65) 6280-6290
inquiries@periplus.com.sg www.periplus.com

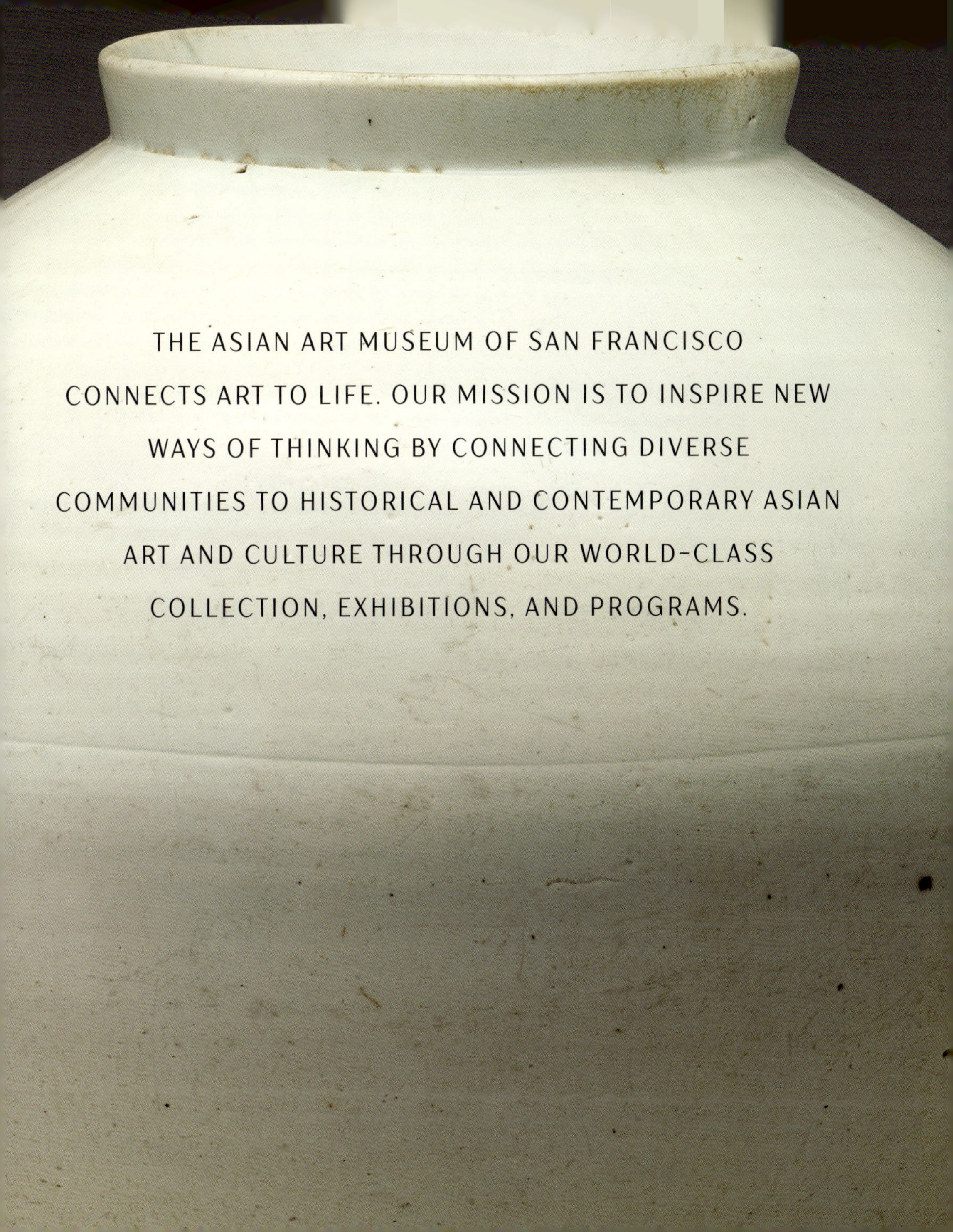

THE ASIAN ART MUSEUM OF SAN FRANCISCO CONNECTS ART TO LIFE. OUR MISSION IS TO INSPIRE NEW WAYS OF THINKING BY CONNECTING DIVERSE COMMUNITIES TO HISTORICAL AND CONTEMPORARY ASIAN ART AND CULTURE THROUGH OUR WORLD-CLASS COLLECTION, EXHIBITIONS, AND PROGRAMS.

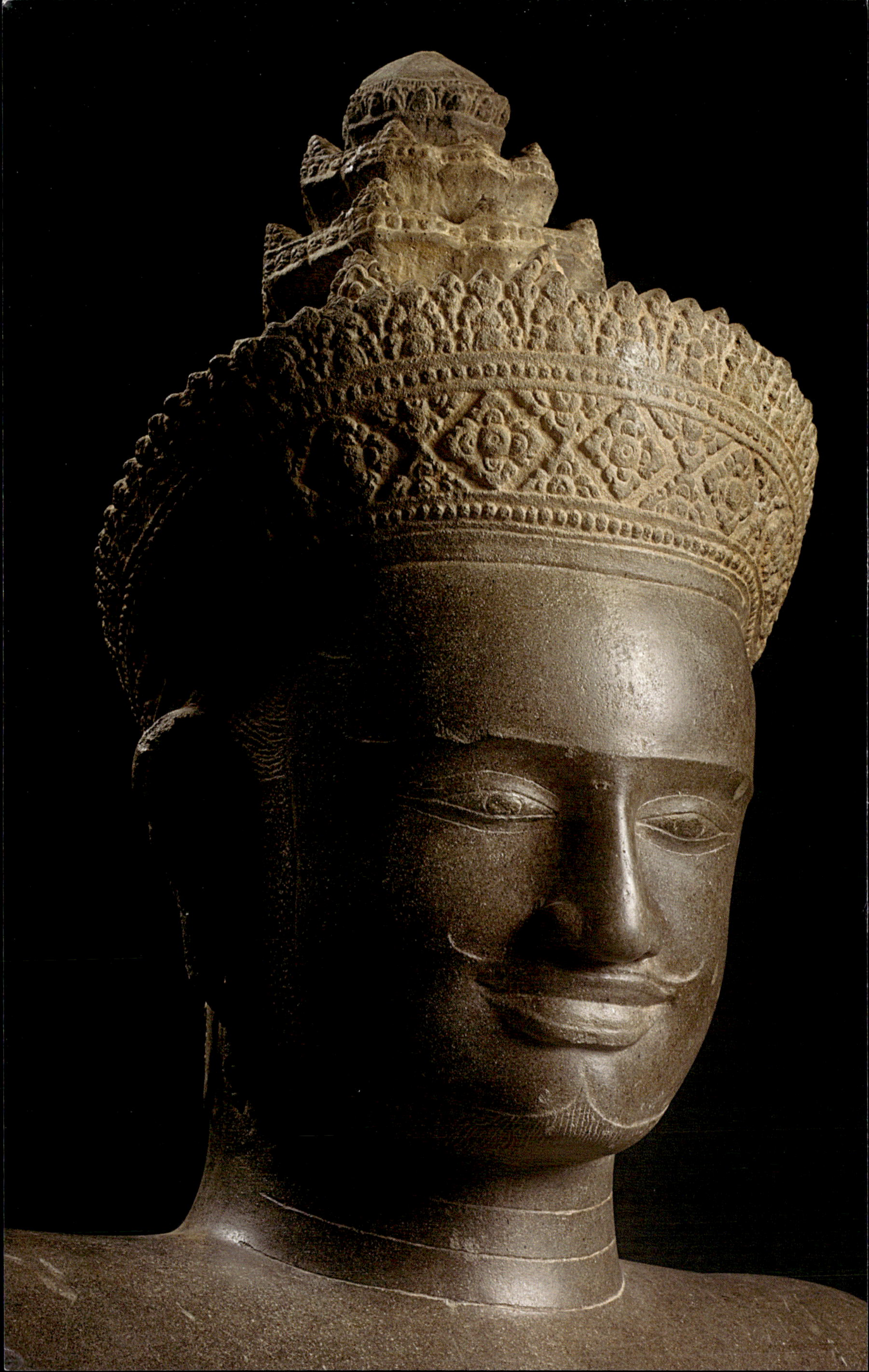

CONTENTS

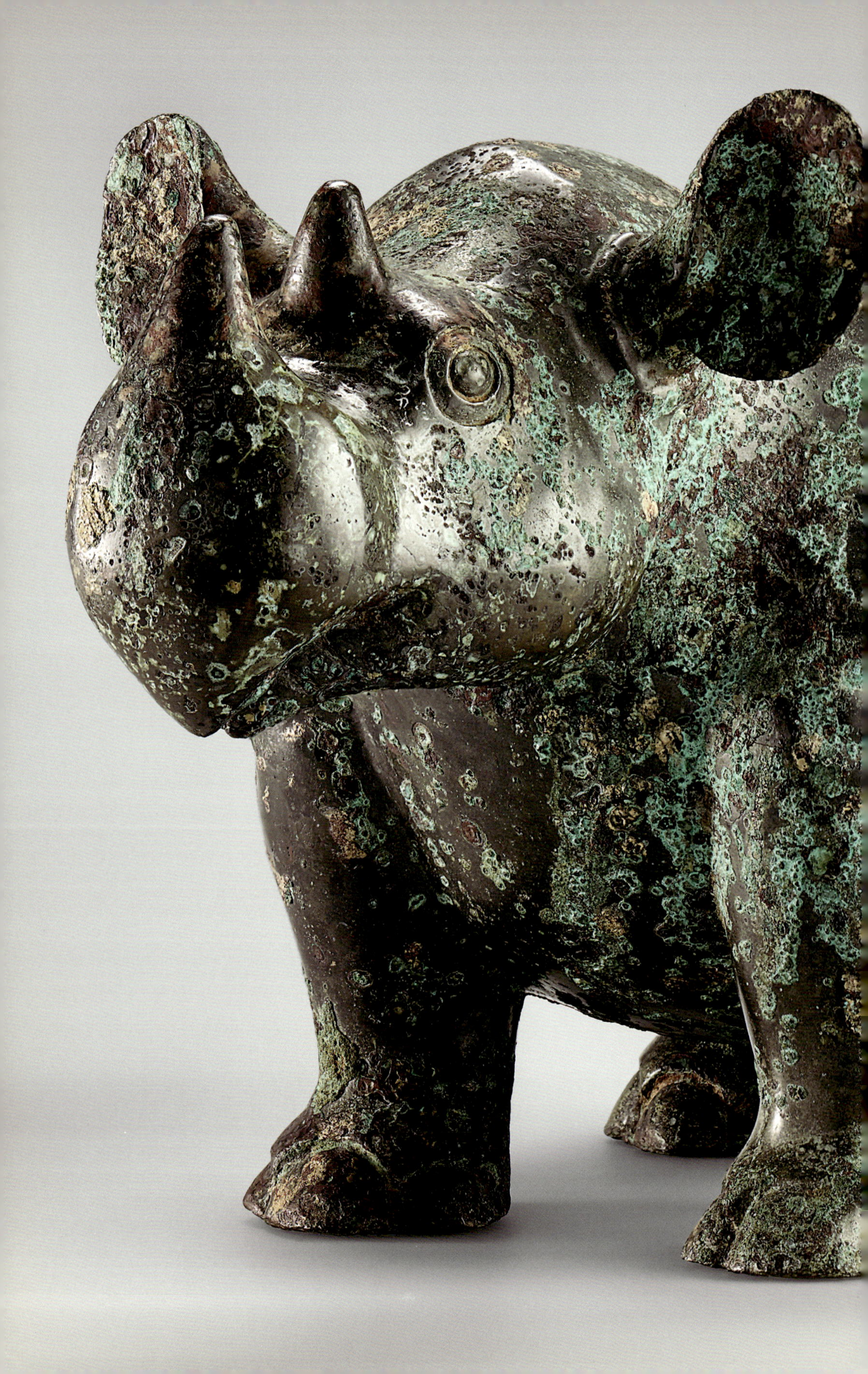

DIRECTOR'S FOREWORD

JAY XU

In a fundamental sense, an artwork is a living thing. It first serves to express the intentions and aesthetic sensibilities of the people who created it or commissioned it. From that point on, it takes on new meanings for everyone who comes in contact with it. In this way, even ancient artworks acquire relevance to our lives today. The Asian Art Museum of San Francisco contributes to the continuity of art through its role in preserving and researching Asian art and promoting its understanding and appreciation. Our collection offers many diverse stories to be told, and we celebrate these in this publication of *Collection Highlights*.

In recognition of the variety of readings that art enables, we have engaged diverse voices to express their unique perspectives on works in our collection. These include our own curators as well as artists, educators, collectors, and others who share our dedication to art. These writings inform us with well-researched critiques and knowledgeable insights. They also serve as invitations to readers to come up with their own interpretations. *Collection Highlights* is thus an entry point for readers' explorations.

This volume provides a broad survey of the breadth and depth of our collection, yet it cannot be comprehensive. Our museum—with more than 18,000 artworks dating from 6,000 years ago to today—is vastly richer than what is represented on these pages. We hope that the works included here will entice readers to further investigate the museum through our gallery displays and our online collection.

As artworks are always alive and changing, so too an art collection is a living organism, constantly growing and building on its strengths. This book includes many recognized masterworks that are the foundation of our museum. It also highlights more recently acquired historic works and significant pieces made by living artists. We hope the selections in this volume will awaken an understanding of the art, culture, and history of Asia and, in doing so, inspire a wider audience to discover the creative expression in works both ancient and modern.

The organization of *Collection Highlights* follows a journey roughly from west to east—from the Persian World and West Asia to South Asia,

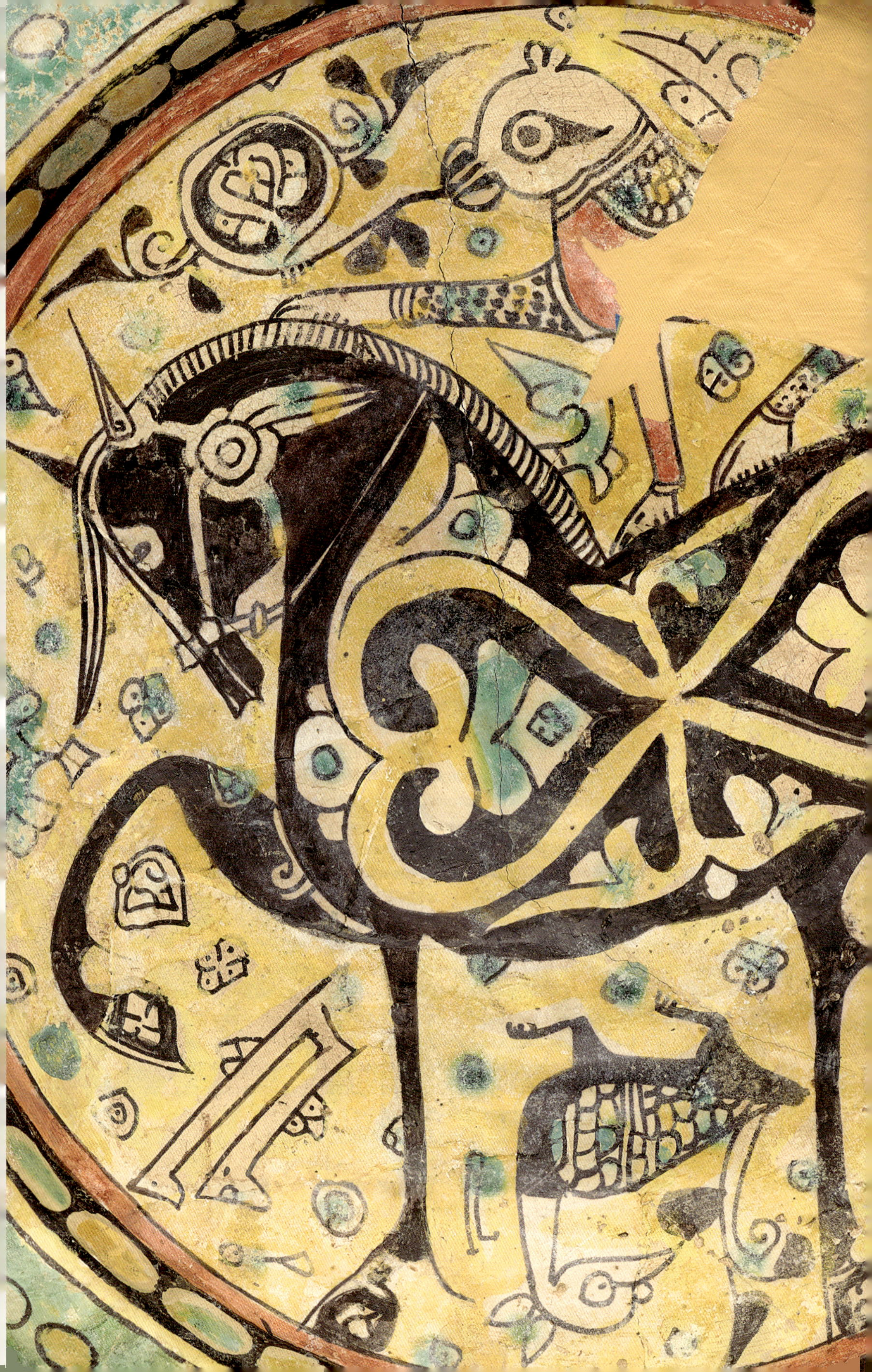

THE PERSIAN WORLD AND WEST ASIA

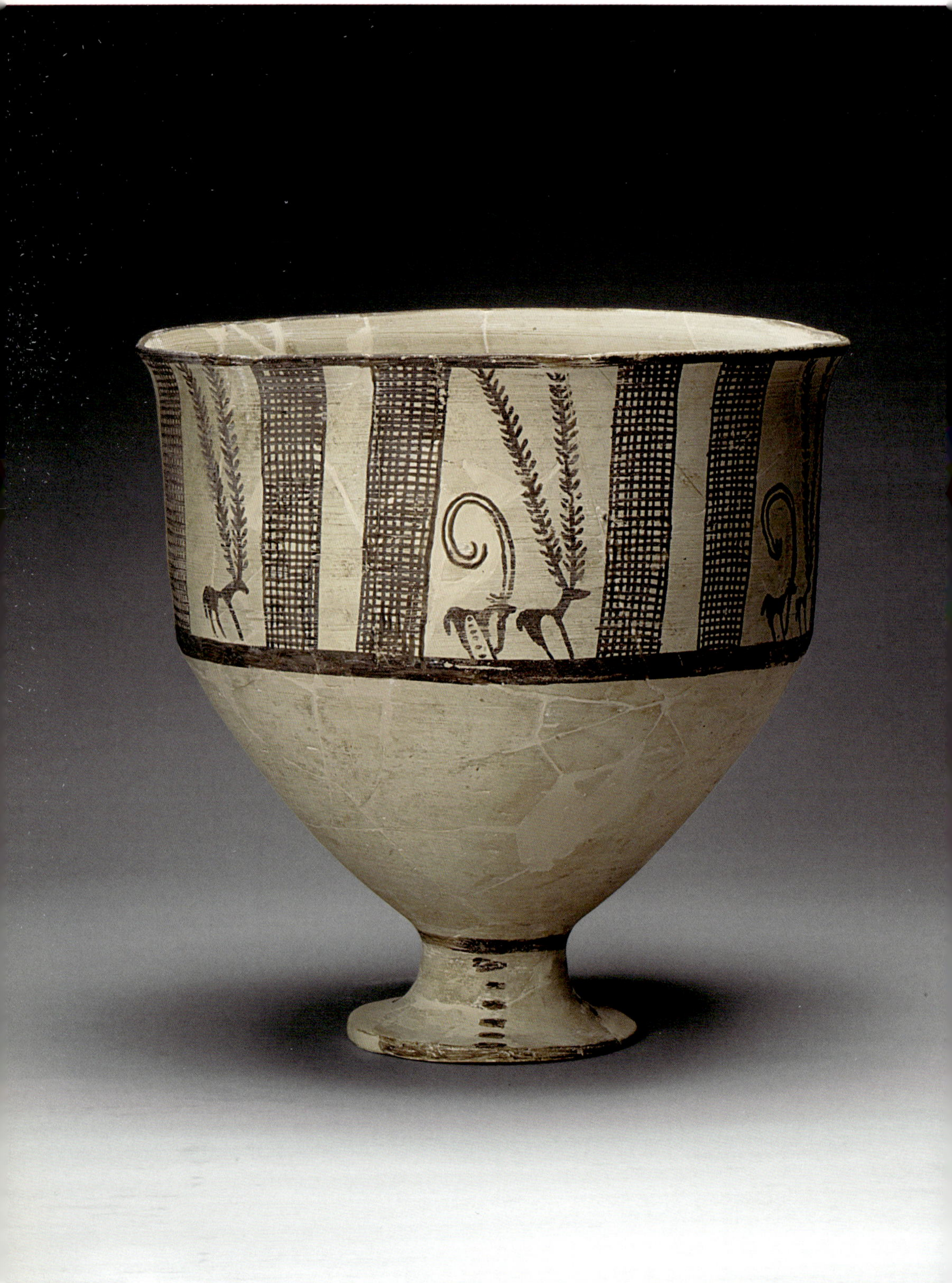

LARGE-FOOTED CUP WITH DECORATION OF WILD GOATS

approx. 4000–3500 BCE
Iran; Tepe Sialk
Earthenware with painted decoration
H. 30.5 cm × Diam. 25.4 cm
The Avery Brundage Collection, B60P469

Long-horned goats and ibexes and simple geometric patterns adorn this elegant cup. It is an example of the sophisticated (and often large) pottery made in central and southwestern Iran during the fourth millennium BCE and decorated with human figures, birds, animals, and geometric patterns. The animals here are at once stylized (their bodies are simplified and horns exaggerated) but also realistic (articulations on an ibex's horns are represented, as is the goat's long tuft of chin hair or "goatee"). The potter's economically artful brushstrokes convey the energy and agility of these creatures, indigenous to the Iranian highlands for millennia.

Vessels of this type were excavated from the region of Tepe Sialk in central Iran. The site is near Kashan, a leading ceramics center in later centuries (see page 11). Excavations at Sialk, one of the most important prehistoric ancient sites, show that the area was occupied for several thousand years, from approximately 4500 BCE through about 800 BCE.

The concentric rings visible on this cup's body indicate that it was made using a potter's wheel. There are differing opinions about when and where the potter's wheel was invented. But, as this example shows, Persian potters were using this mechanical device approximately six thousand years ago. Prior to the wheel, potters shaped vessels from coils of wet clay, which resulted in limited shapes and sizes and, typically, thick walls. The potter's wheel, whose descendants continue to be used today, was a major technological development in human history.

—*QA*

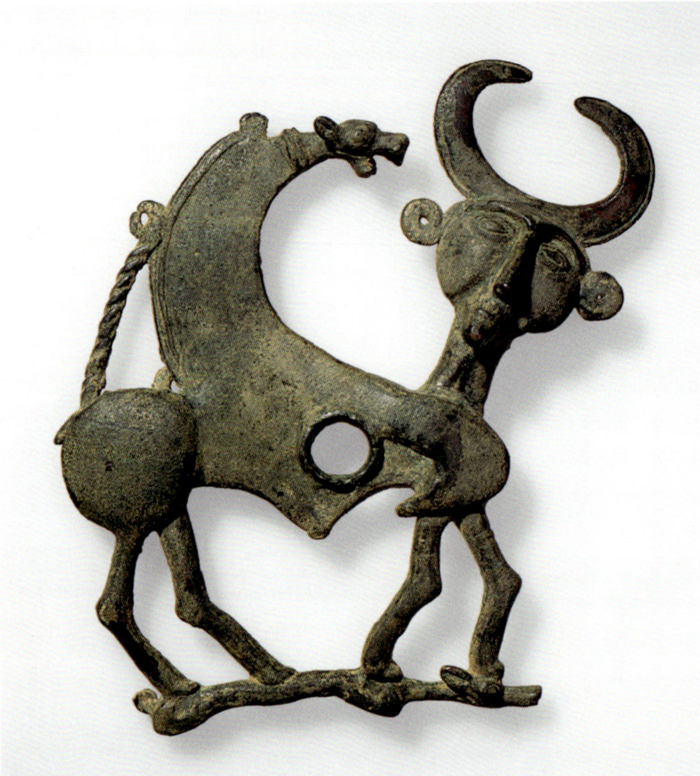

CHEEKPIECE OF A HORSE BRIDLE IN THE FORM OF A MYTHICAL CREATURE

approx. 800–700 BCE

Iran; Luristan region

Bronze

H. 17.8 cm × W. 17.5 cm × D. 2.9 cm

The Avery Brundage Collection, B60B17+

A winged sphinx with a horned human head tramples an antelope-like creature on this magnificent horse fitting. This is one of a pair of cheekpieces for a horse; it would have been connected to its matching counterpart (now in the Louvre in Paris) by a metal rod that passed through the circular hole and served as the bit. Horses were likely domesticated in Iran by the third millennium, or about five thousand years ago. By 1600 BCE, horses drew light chariots in war and were used for hunting and racing. By around 1000 BCE, when cavalry had replaced the chariot as the main mobile force in armies, the horses of the imperial Assyrian armies (who then controlled most of ancient Mesopotamia and parts of Egypt) came from the plains of western Iran, where they bred well.

Bronze harness fittings have been found in sizeable quantities in graves from Luristan, a region of open plains intersected by the Zagros Mountains. Their dynamic forms and rich decorative repertoire is unlike any other from elsewhere in West Asia at this time. Many feature real or mythical animals and human figures, but the precise significance of the imagery is unclear. Bronzes from Luristan entered Western collections by the early 1920s as a result of extensive robberies of ancient sites by local people, before scientific excavations were undertaken at those locations and stemmed the outflow of illegally acquired objects.

—*QA*

BOWL WITH GEOMETRIC DECORATION

800–900
Iraq; Basra
Earthenware with overglaze copper- and silver-oxide decoration
H. 7.6 cm × Diam. 26.7 cm
The Avery Brundage Collection, B60P478

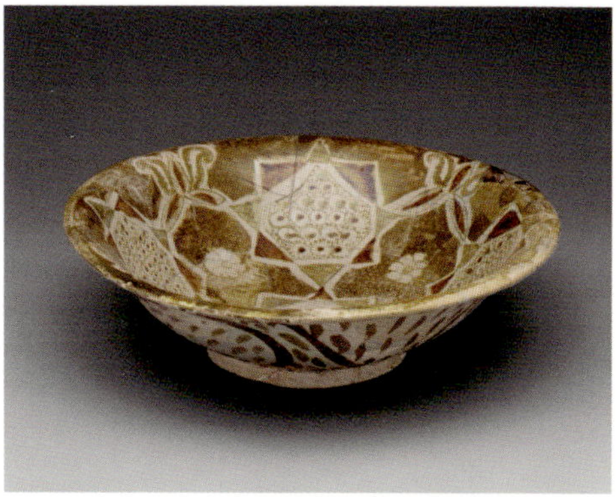

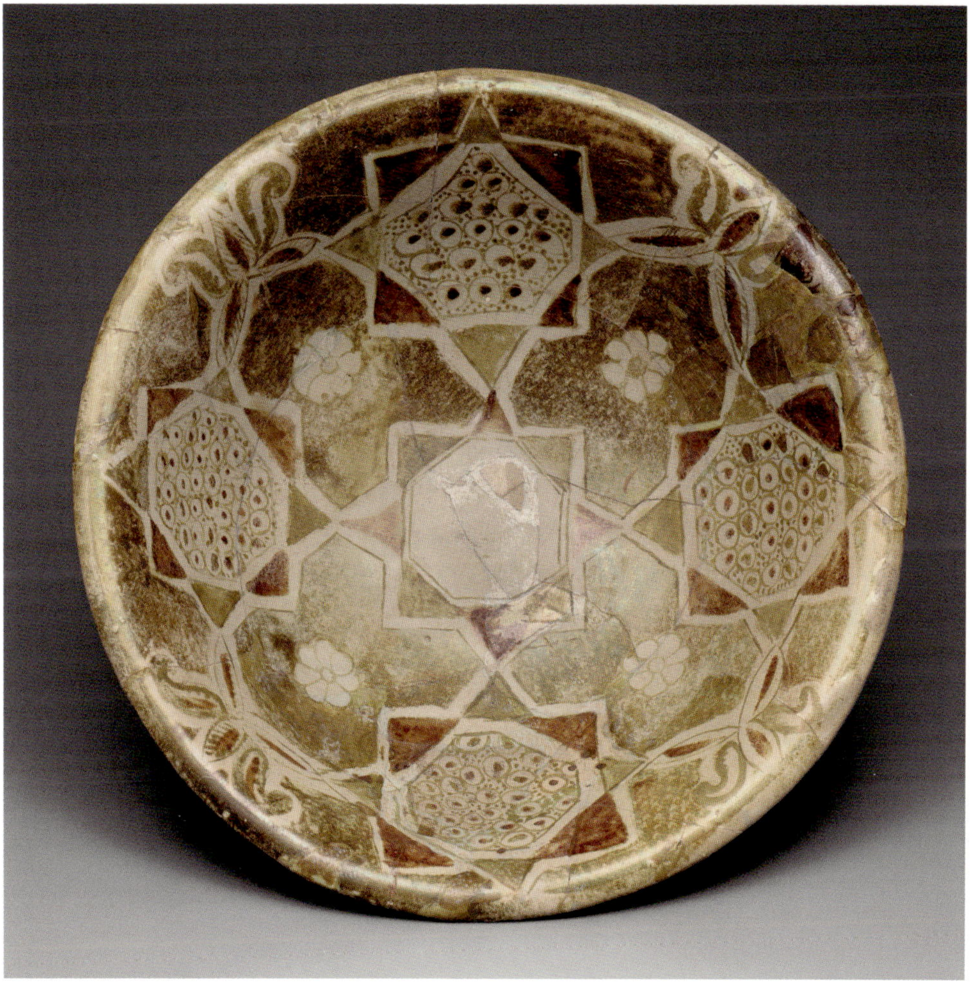

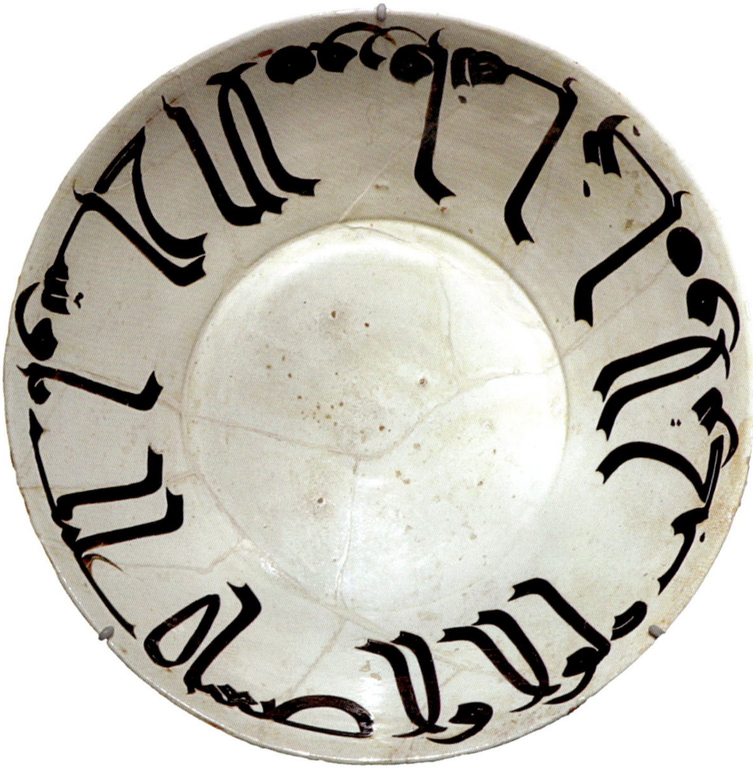

BOWL WITH ARABIC INSCRIPTION

approx. 900–1000
Northeastern Iran
Earthenware with slip decoration under clear glaze
H. 11.7 cm × Diam. 40.3 cm
The Avery Brundage Collection, B60P1862

Calligraphy, or beautiful writing, has transformed this bowl into something quite exceptional. A dynamic rhythm of positive and negative space results from the artistically elongated letters of the Arabic-language inscription (read here in a clockwise direction): "Take the middle road in [your] affairs; indeed, it is a salvation. Don't ride a too-gentle mount or a too-obstinate one."[1] With its spare, black-and-white aesthetic, this bowl exemplifies that such "epigraphic slipware" from the Samanid period (819–1005) are some of the most visually powerful ceramics produced in the Islamic world. Yet they are made from the simplest of materials: earthenware covered and decorated with a watery clay mixture called "slip."

These ceramics come from various centers of production in Iran, including Nishapur and Afrasiyab (now known as Samarqand). They appear to have been made for local use, since they are not found in excavations west of central Persia. The inscriptions are usually Arabic proverbs or maxims. The Samanid rulers fostered a highly sophisticated, multicultural society comprising different ethnic and cultural groups including Persians, Arabs, and Turks. They maintained older Persian artistic and literary forms while adding new Islamic elements, including the Arabic language.

The bowl's large size and deep, conical shape suggests that it was used for serving food. One can only imagine the delight with which diners experienced the bowl's words—advising moderation in life—as they were slowly revealed as the food was consumed.

—*QA*

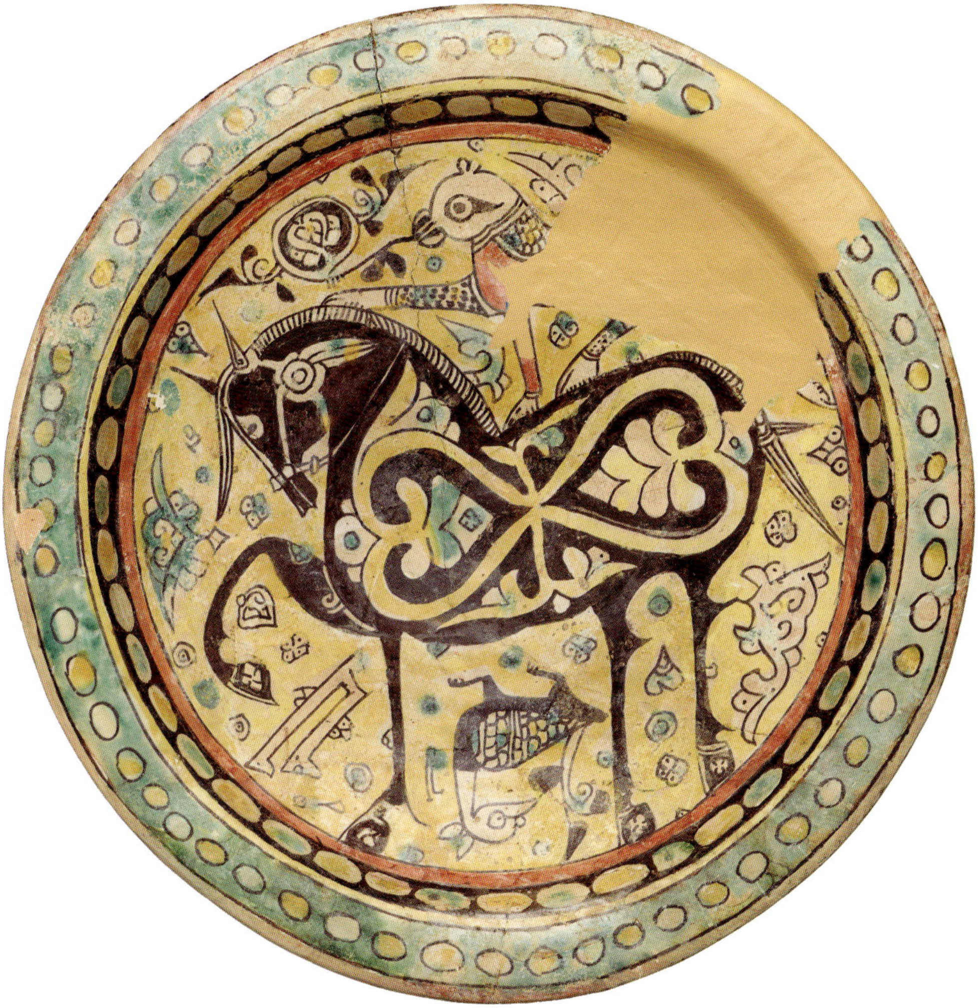

DISH WITH DESIGN OF HORSE AND CHEETAH

approx. 900–1000

Northeastern Iran; Nishapur

Earthenware with painted slip decoration under glaze

H. 5.1 cm × Diam. 35.2 cm

Museum purchase, B68P7

WALL PANEL

approx. 1100–1115

Afghanistan; Royal Palace of Mas'ud III, Ghazni

Ghaznavid dynasty, reign of Mas'ud III (1099–1115)

Marble

H. 74.3 cm × W. 43.2 cm × D. 10.2 cm

Gift of Shawn and Brook Byers and Peter Marks in honor of Avery Brundage's Centennial, B87S3

This panel—originally painted in lapis lazuli blue, red, and gold—was one of more than five hundred such panels decorating the walls of a courtyard of the Royal Palace of Mas'ud III in Ghazni in eastern Afghanistan. Together, the painted panels must have created a splendid effect, like "a brocaded surface."[2] The marble is not smoothly polished because it was originally not meant to be seen under the paint.

A portion of an inscription in Persian—praising the patron Sultan Mas'ud III, his ancestors, and their achievements—appears here, and continues on the other surviving panels (which are mainly in Rome today; only two are in American collections). This panel is one of the earliest examples on which the Persian language was used instead of Arabic for a monumental inscription. From the research of Italian archaeologists who excavated this site, we learn that until the Ghaznavid period (977–1186), marble was an uncommon building material in this region where brick and stucco were typically used for architecture and its decoration. A marble quarry was found near Ghazni, which was the source for the materials used for the palace decoration and other monuments in the area. A close study of tool marks on similar panels revealed that the carving techniques used here are related to ancient local stone-carving methods, like those on Buddhist sculpture from the region of Gandhara in northwest Pakistan (see page 24).

Mas'ud's palace was probably burned during the succeeding Ghurid dynasty's conquest of Ghazni in 1151. About a hundred years later, Ghazni and the palace were further damaged by the Mongol armies of Genghis Khan. Its ruins were excavated between 1957 and 1966 by Italian archaeologists, before the site suffered additional deterioration and looting during the Soviet invasion and the Afghan civil war.

—*QA*

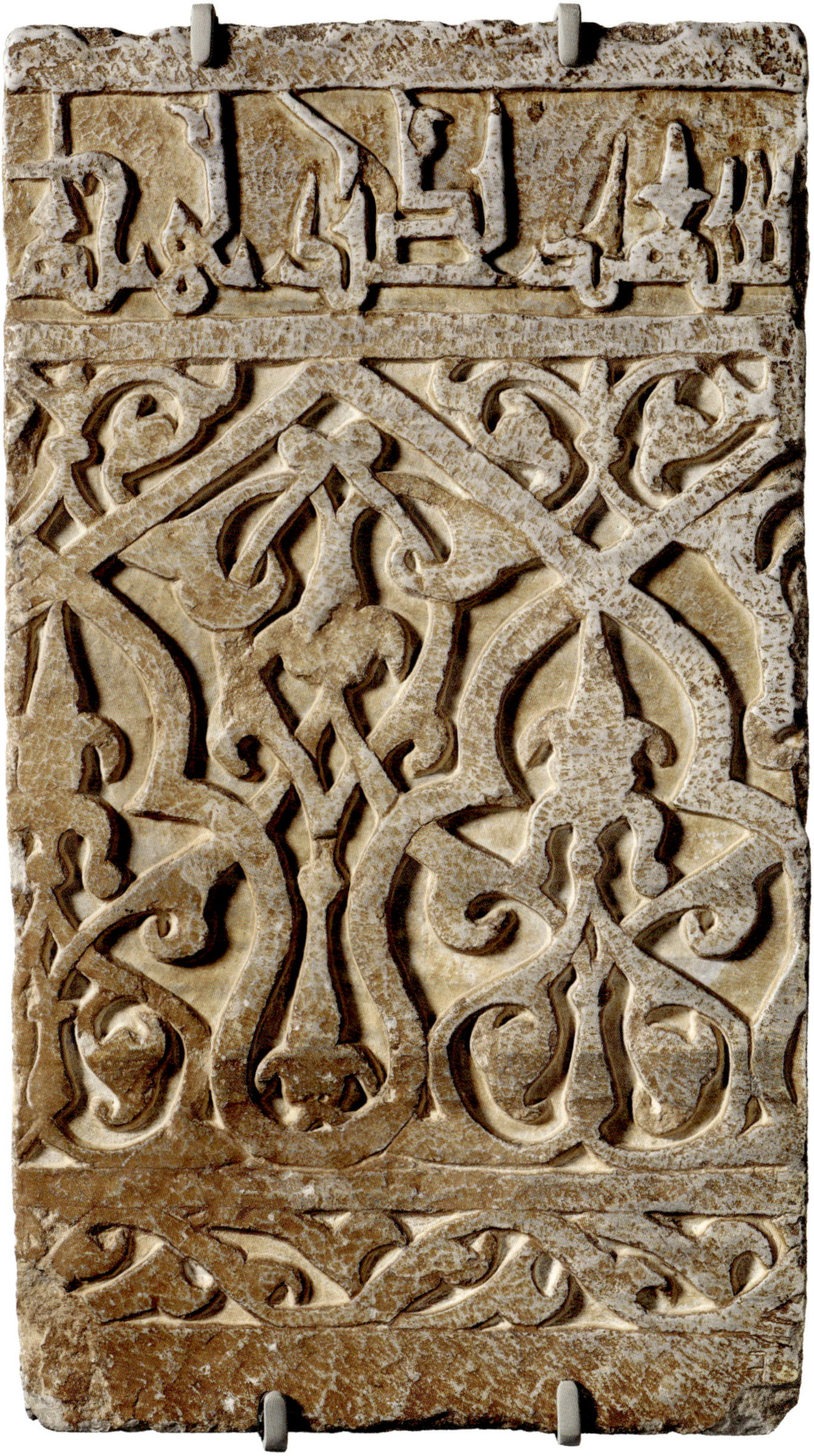

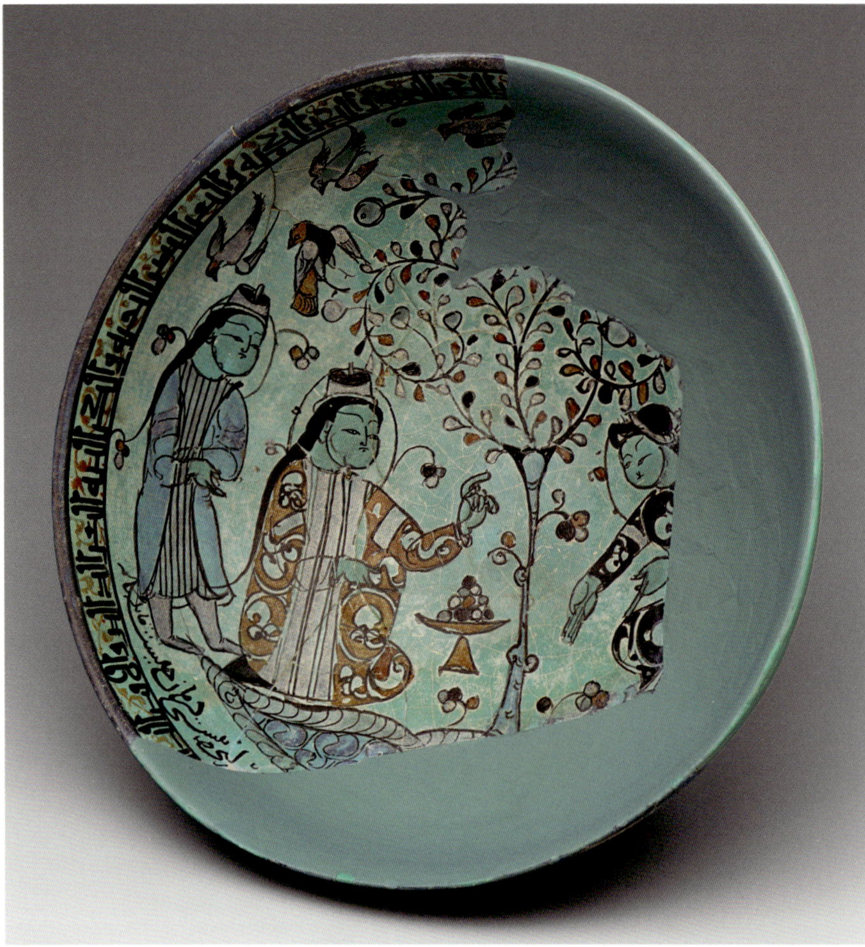

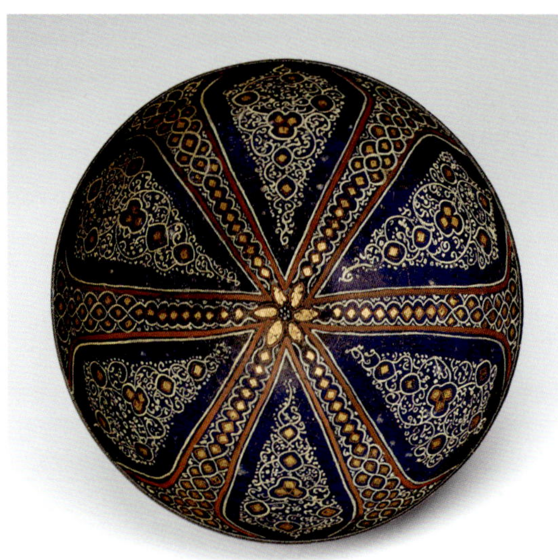

BOWL WITH FIGURES

—

1187

By Abu Zayd al-Kashani (Iranian)

Iran; Kashan

Composite-body ceramic (fritware) with underglaze painting and overglaze enamel decoration (minai ware)

H. 10.2 cm × Diam. 20.3 cm

The Avery Brundage Collection, B60P1874

—

For a relatively short period during the twelfth-thirteenth centuries, Persian potters produced a distinctive type of ware that became known as minai ("enameled"). These elegant, lightweight, and thin-walled dishes, such as the bowl here, were painted in a rich palette of colors. They were typically decorated with scenes of people engaging in leisure activities in pleasant outdoor settings, with poetic verses on their inner and outer rims. The painted lines, color range, imagery, and calligraphy on minai ceramics call to mind the art of illustrated books; in fact, some vessels included scenes that are identifiable from Persian literature, especially from the *Shahnama* (Book of Kings).

While ceramics (or fragments thereof) tend to survive through the centuries in reasonably large numbers, we almost never know who made them. This bowl is a rare exception. Its maker, the potter Abu Zayd al-Kashani, not only signed his name on the outer rim but also added the date. His inscription reads, "Written at the start of Muharram in 583 of the Hijri year. Long life to the owner. The reciter is the writer. [A]bu [Zayd]."[3] Clearly, Abu Zayd was proud of his achievement. Our bowl is one of seven known minai examples by Abu Zayd. Based on signatures and dates that he left on thirty-some other ceramic works made over a period of thirty-four years, we know that he worked in Kashan, a major ceramics production center in central Iran. He specialized in lusterware, a type of ceramic decorated with metallic glazes (see page 13) that was visually different from minai, but technically related.

In the early twentieth century, Western collectors of Persian ceramics found the colorful figural imagery on minai ware very attractive. Art dealers, eager to satisfy their customers, often provided "intact" examples for the market, which were carefully repainted or completed with numerous pottery shards (occasionally more than a hundred), most of which were old but not always original to the piece. Over the last few decades, museum conservators have taken these minai vessels apart, retained their original matrix and paint, and filled in the missing sections with blanks, as we see on this bowl.

—*QA*

BOWL

—

approx. 1275–1400

Iran; probably Kashan

Composite-body ceramic (fritware); cobalt glaze with inglaze painting and overglaze enamel and gold-leaf decoration (lajvardina ware)

H. 10.2 cm × Diam. 20.3 cm

The Avery Brundage Collection, B60P1871

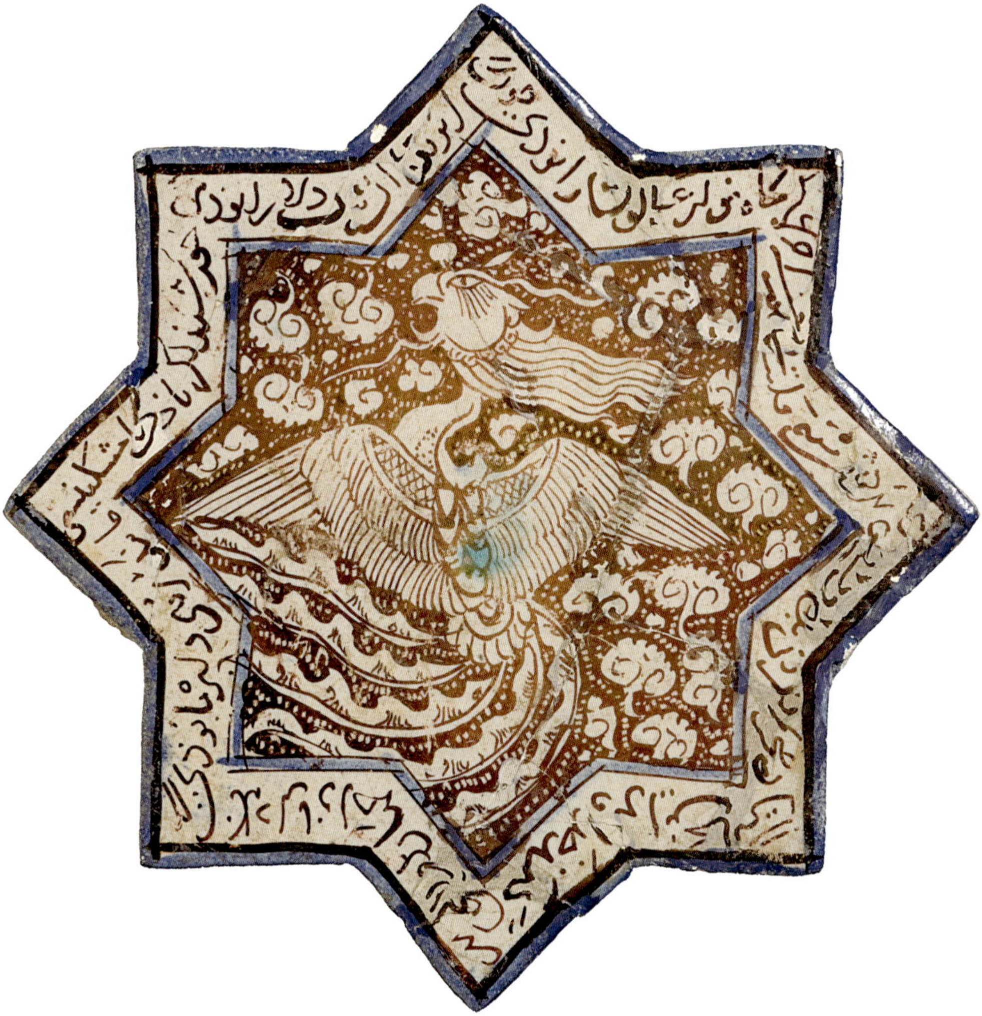

STAR-SHAPED TILE WITH PHOENIX DESIGN

1292–1293
Iran; probably Sultanabad
Composite-body ceramic (fritware) with overglaze copper- and silver-oxide decoration
H. 1.3 cm × Diam. 20.3 cm
The Avery Brundage Collection, B60P2148

A proud phoenix, surrounded by Chinese-style clouds and enclosed within a band of Persian poetry, spreads its elaborate plumage and takes center stage on this tile. The lyrical poem describes the qualities of the beloved, "whose face is like the sun, if only the sun were adorned with musk." Dated or signed works are rare in Islamic art, but this tile has the year 691 (of the Islamic calendar, 1292–1293 CE) inscribed in its upper right corner.

Originally a Chinese imperial motif, the phoenix was often combined with a dragon to represent the empress and emperor. As a decorative motif brought from China by the Mongols and used by their successors in Iran, the Ilkhanids, the phoenix lost its original associations and was merged with the simurgh, a Persian auspicious mythical bird.

A new type of engagement between China and the Middle East took place during the early 1200s. This brought into being, among many other types of changes, objects like this tile. Under the leadership of the fearless Genghis Khan, the Mongols, a nomadic Central Asian people, conquered vast territories. By the late 1200s, the sons and grandsons of Genghis had established powerful dynasties in China (Yuan dynasty, 1271–1368), the Islamic world from Afghanistan to Iraq (Ilkhanid period, 1256–1353), western Central Asia and southern Russia (Golden Horde, ca. 1227–1502), and eastern Central Asia and Inner Mongolia (Chaghatay dynasty, ca. 1227–1363). These kingdoms effectively connected a huge landmass into a single empire—for the first and only time in history.

The Mongol invasions had a devastating effect on the conquered lands. But their rule had an unexpectedly creative cultural impact. The Mongol practice of enslaving craftsmen from subjugated cities and relocating them to new urban centers brought together talented people from diverse backgrounds. This resulted in new forms of artistic and creative expressions that combined regional continuities with fresh inspirations from different cultures.

The tile here is in many ways typical of pre-Mongol Persian ceramics production from Kashan, the region's most important ceramic center. Such star-shaped tiles, which fit like puzzle pieces with cross-shaped tiles, ornamented walls inside public and private buildings, including mosques, schools, tombs, and palaces. Similar tiles, with the new Chinese-inspired motifs of the phoenix and dragon, were found at Takht-i Sulayman (built in the 1270s), the only surviving Ilkhanid palace.

—*QA*

MIHRAB-SHAPED PANEL

approx. 1350

Iran

Ilkhanid period (1256–1353)

Limestone

H. 81.3 cm × W. 50.8 cm × D. 12.7 cm

Gift of the Connoisseurs' Council, 2015.71

Mihrabs—which mark prayer direction on the Mecca-facing (*qibla*) wall in a mosque—have a long history in Islamic architecture. They commonly appear as recessed niches with pointed arches supported by columns and enclosed by bands of inscription. Mihrab-shaped panels like this one were typically commemorative, serving as tombstones or place markers, for example in shrines or mausoleums. As there is no deceased individual's name here, this panel was likely not a tombstone.

The panel's decoration presents a lot of information on a compact surface that together speaks of the glory of Allah (God). Different aspects of divine majesty are described in the Arabic inscriptions set within the angled square and verses from the Qur'anic Throne Verse (Chapter 2, verse 255) in the bands around the arch. The hanging lamp in the center represents, at one level, a practical lighting device that is seen in mosques, mausoleums, and schools (*madrasas*). At a symbolic level, as it appears here, it refers to God's presence as described in a Qur'anic verse in chapter 24, "The Light" (see translation below). A viewer would recognize this quotation even if the verse itself was not inscribed on the panel. The beauty of this panel's inscriptional content is further enhanced with four different calligraphic scripts, geometric and vegetal patterning, and *muqarnas* (decorative vaulting), which are seen widely on secular and religious artworks.

Qur'anic verse referencing the lamp: Chapter 24, "The Light" (Sura al-Nur), verses 35–36

Allah is the Light of the heavens and the earth;
The likeness of His Light is as a niche wherein is a lamp
(the lamp in a glass, the glass as it were a glittering star)
kindled from a Blessed Tree, an olive that is neither of the East
nor of the West
whose oil would shine, even if no fire touched it;
Light upon Light, Allah guides to His Light whom He Will [...]
[Such niches are] in mosques which Allah has ordered to be raised
and that His name be mentioned therein;
exalting Him within them in the morning and the evenings.

—*QA*

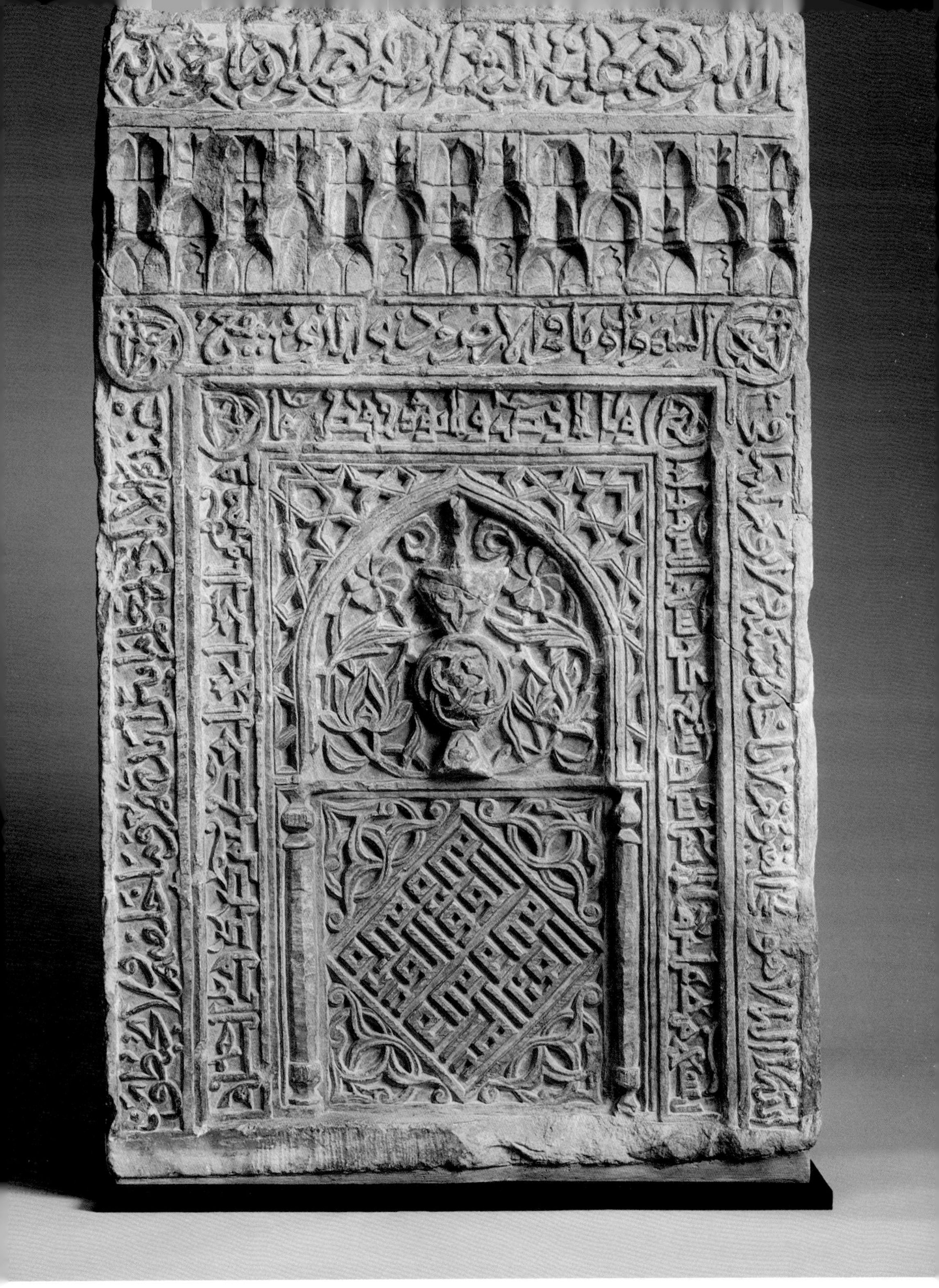

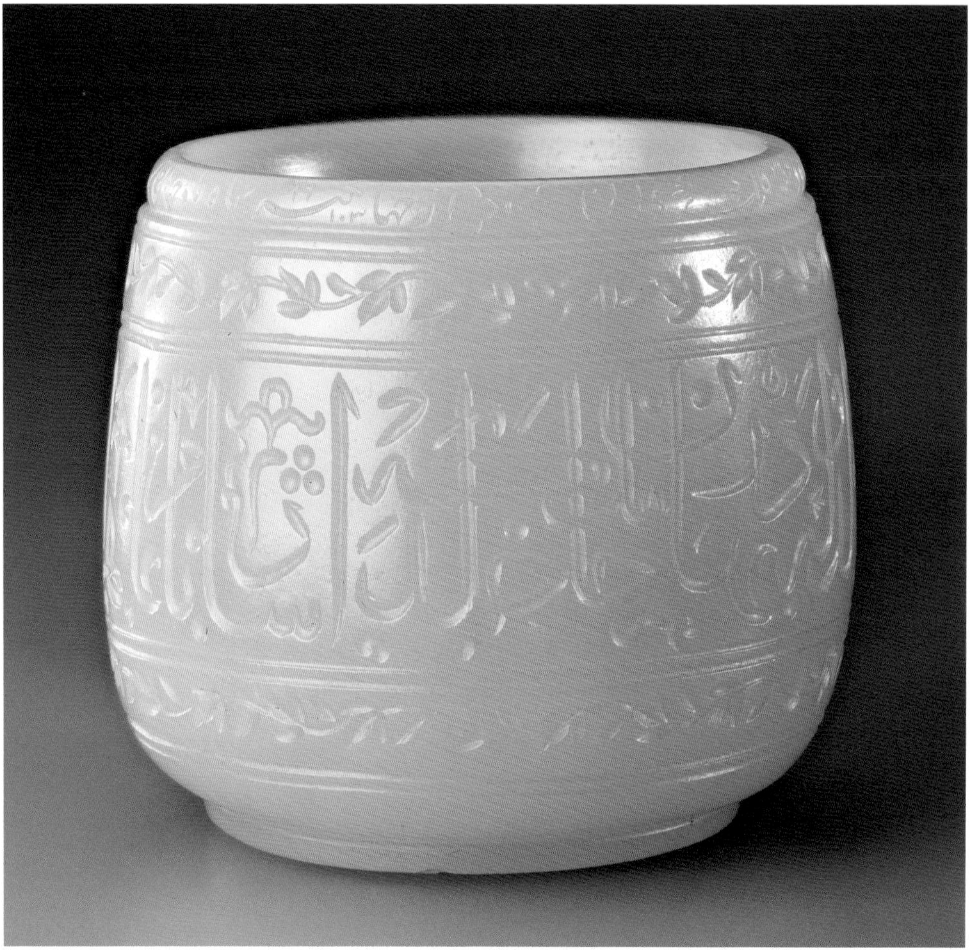

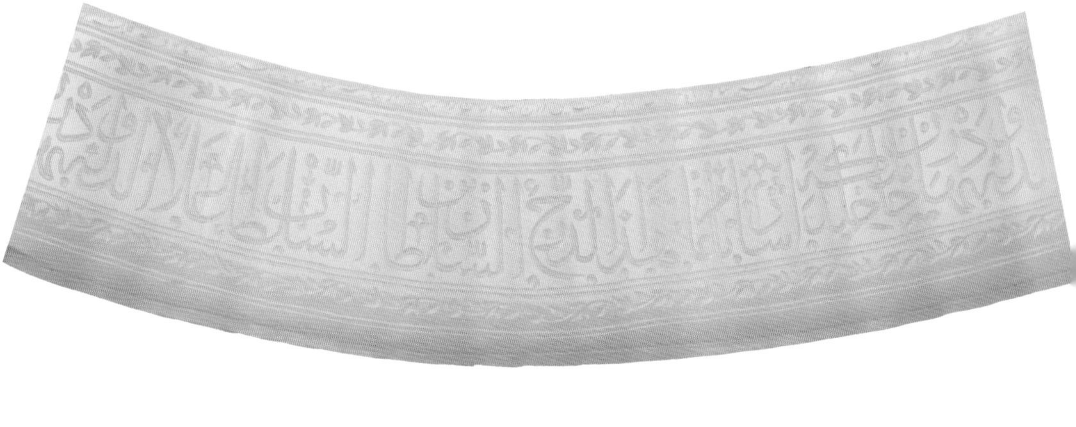

MASTERPIECE

CUP WITH CALLIGRAPHIC INSCRIPTIONS

1440–1460
Probably Uzbekistan; Samarqand
Timurid period (1370–1507)
Nephrite
H. 3.5 cm × Diam. 3.2 cm
The Avery Brundage Collection, B60J619

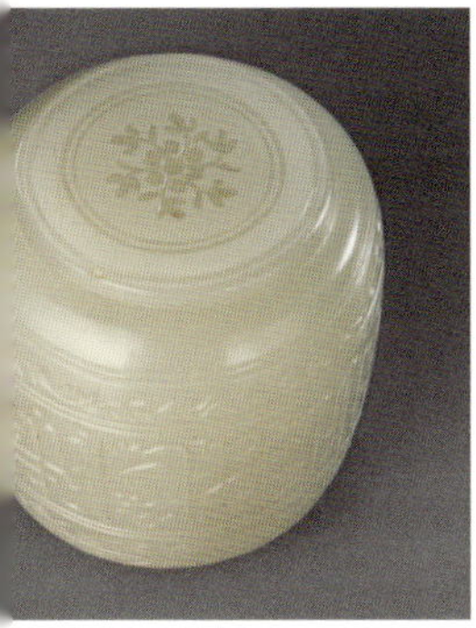

This small drinking cup is rare, one of only two known artworks in white jade from the Timurid period. Elegant jade objects gained popularity under the powerful Timurids (1370–1507), who ruled parts of modern Iran, Afghanistan, and Uzbekistan. The Timurids, important patrons of art and literature, were considered models of cultural sophistication throughout the Islamic world. Their love for exquisite artworks, including jades, was continued by their descendants, the Mughal emperors of India (1526–1858).

Names of artists or owners on artworks are relatively uncommon in Islamic art. The two royal inscriptions on this cup make it a unique object. 'Ala ud-Daulah (d. approx. 1460), whose name is part of the main inscription around the cup's body, was the great-grandson of the Timurid dynasty's founder, Timur (1336–1405). Little is known about 'Ala ud-Daulah's life and career. He may easily have been forgotten in time, but through this elegant inscription his memory as a cultured patron lives on. The second royal inscription, barely visible on the rim, belongs to Indian Mughal Emperor Jahangir (1569–1627), who owned this cup 150 years after it was made. His name and date (1621 CE) are incorporated into a poetic verse. The Mughals, fifth-generation descendants of Timur, left their Central Asian ancestral home for India and regarded their Timurid heritage with a sense of connection and loss. By collecting masterpieces of Timurid art (see page 18) and inscribing their names on them, Mughal emperors affirmed their links to the cultural and political legacy of their ancestors.

The main decoration on this cup is inscribed in Arabic. Elegant calligraphy, which ornaments the written word and the knowledge that it represents, is the highest form of art in Islamic culture. Many skills are required to produce a beautiful inscription: a calligrapher needs command over different styles of writing, impressive hand-eye control, and an artistic eye to lay out the text into a balanced composition so that the words fit within the given space and remain readable.

The challenge must have been great for the artists of this cup. Jade is an extremely difficult substance to manipulate and cannot be carved with cutting tools like chisels. Rather, it is ground down using a manual rotary tool and an abrasive wet paste. To use such a technique with the curving letters of the Arabic and Persian scripts on a small, rounded object like this cup demands talent and precision.

—*QA*

PAGE OF CALLIGRAPHY

1505–1545
By Mir Ali Haravi (d. approx. 1550)
Iran or Uzbekistan
Ink and colors on paper
H. 21.6 cm × W. 13 cm
Gift of the Todd G. Williams Memorial Fund and the Society for Asian Art, B87D6

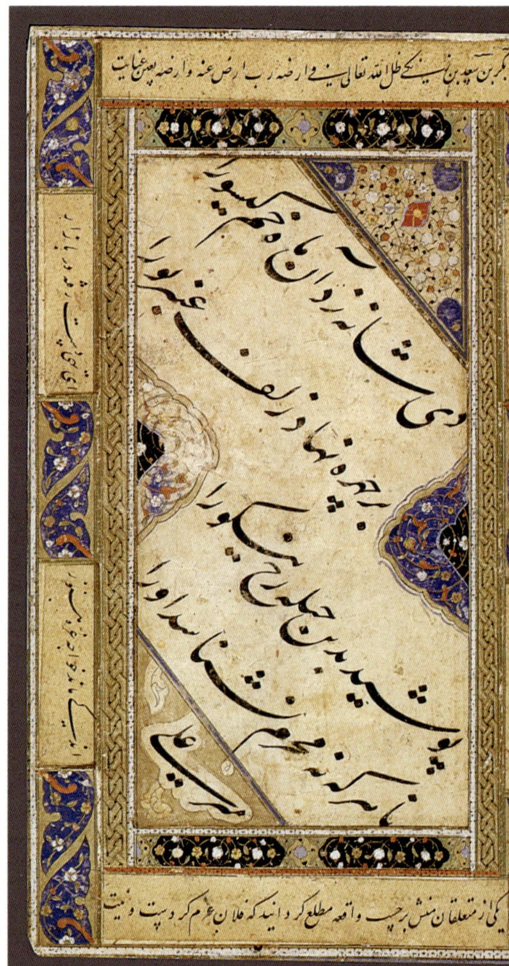

From Islam's early history in the 600s until today, calligraphy has held the highest status among the arts in Muslim culture. These lines of poetry were written by the famous and prolific Persian calligrapher Mir Ali Haravi, who signed his work in the lower left triangle. Mir Ali was a master of the *nasta'liq* script, which developed in Iran around 1350 and became the choice artistic script throughout the Persian-speaking sphere, from Delhi to Istanbul. *Nasta'liq*, like other Perso-Arabic scripts, is governed by an internal system of proportions and rules within which its sinuous lines, sense of rhythm, and relationship between words enable calligraphers to exploit the script's aesthetic potential. By 1500, *nasta'liq* had developed into the "large" and "small" variants, which appear here in the central composition and border text, respectively.

Calligraphers originally created works such as this example as exercise sheets. These were collected several decades later and gathered into albums, a format that become very popular in Iran, India, and Turkey onward from the 1500s. The calligraphy pages were often further embellished with elaborate borders and other decoration when compiled in an album, and they typically alternated with paintings. Mir Ali's work was highly prized by the Mughal emperors of India and is included in several imperial albums.

—*QA*

THE HERO RUSTAM KILLS THE WHITE DEMON, FROM A MANUSCRIPT OF THE *SHAHNAMA* (BOOK OF KINGS)

approx. 1580
Iran; perhaps Shiraz
Opaque watercolors on paper
H. 25.1 cm × W. 20.6 cm
From the Collection of William K. Ehrenfeld, M.D., 2005.64.162

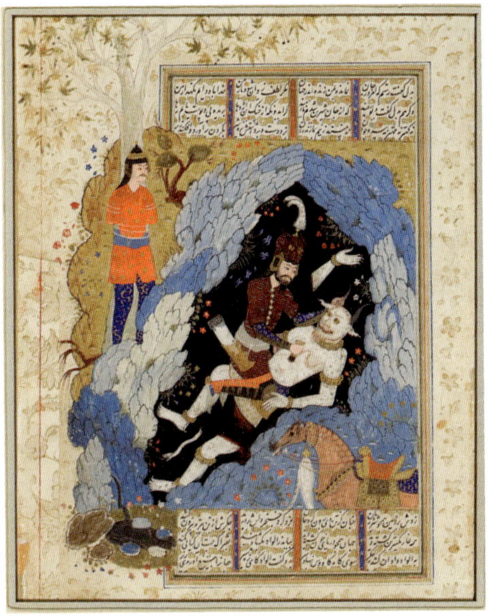

The *Shahnama* (Book of Kings), written by the poet Firdausi in approximately 1010 CE, is a literary classic relating the mythical and historical past of pre-Islamic Persian kings. The story of Kay Kavus, perhaps the most inept and capricious of the fifty rulers featured in this epic, occupies a substantial section of the text. Among other impetuous actions during his reign, Kavus undertook a wrongful and disastrous war against the kingdom of Mazandaran, which was famed for its riches—and its powerful demons (*divs*). To stop the looting and destruction of Mazandaran's cities, its king ordered the White Demon to blind Kavus and his men and keep them imprisoned in a cave. Upon receiving this news, the epic's hero Rustam journeyed from Iran to rescue Kavus. Blood from the White Demon's liver was the only cure for restoring his compatriots' sight, and defeating the demon became the seventh (and last) of Rustam's major trials (see also page 44).

The poet describes how Rustam's local guide, Ulad (seen here tied to the tree at upper left), led the hero to the White Demon's cave while it was asleep. The text and painting on this page describe the fierce battle inside the cave between the two formidable and evenly matched opponents. Rustam eventually gained the upper hand, and we see here the end of their combat. The White Demon's arm and leg have been severed, and Rustam makes the final assault, thrusting his dagger to extract the demon's liver.
—*QA*

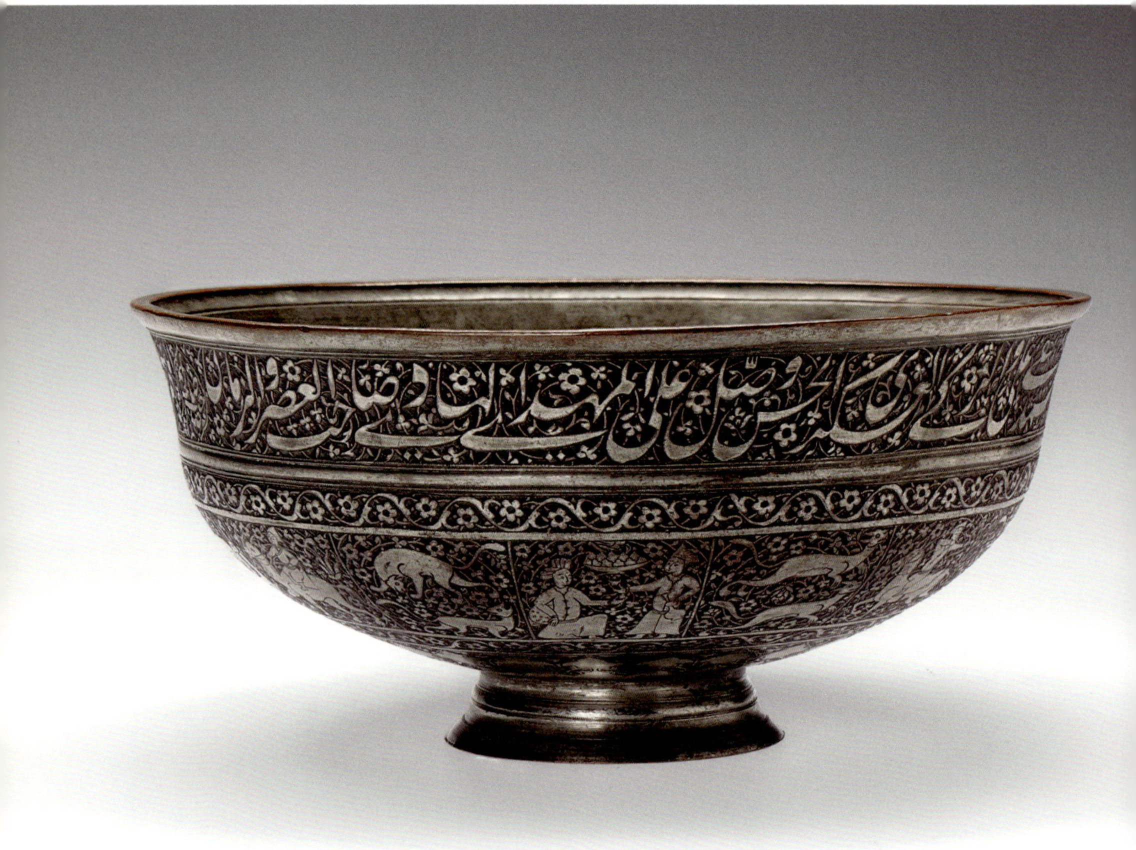

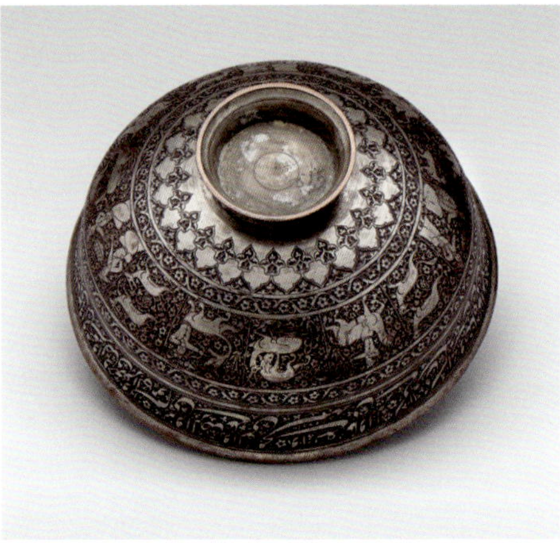

FOOTED BOWL WITH INSCRIPTIONS AND FIGURAL SCENES

1600–1650

Iran

Safavid period (1501–1722)

Copper; cast, engraved, and tinned with inlaid black compound

H. 13.3 cm × Diam. 29.5 cm

Gift of the Boards of the Asian Art Museum in honor of Valerie Pechenik, 2015.60

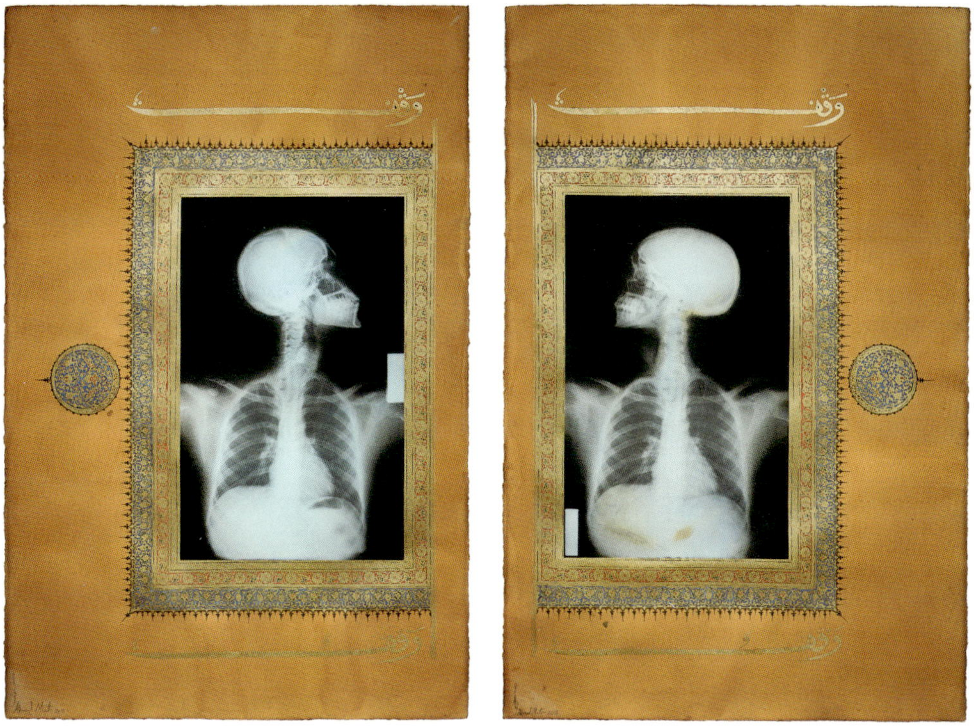

ILLUMINATION WAQF

2013

By Ahmed Mater (Saudi Arabian, b. 1979)

Diptych; gold, ink, and colors on offset lithographic prints

H. 153.7 cm × W. 102.9 cm (each print)

Museum purchase, 2014.15.a-.b

Ahmed Mater's diptych is in the format of pages from a Qur'an manuscript with decorated borders and margin ornamentation. But the borders frame, instead of verses from the Qur'an, torso-length human X-rays. Those familiar with Islamic art would recognize that the human figure is rarely, if ever, seen in a religious context. Yet, the artist's delicate illumination in gold and blue and the use of the word *waqf* (meaning "charitable donation") on the page reference traditional Islamic art, and Qur'an manuscripts in particular. Mater plays with multiple meanings of the word "illumination": as the precise painted ornament on the page that adds light to God's word, as the making visible of the interior human body with X-ray technology, and as the lighting up of the soul through the words of God.

—*QA*

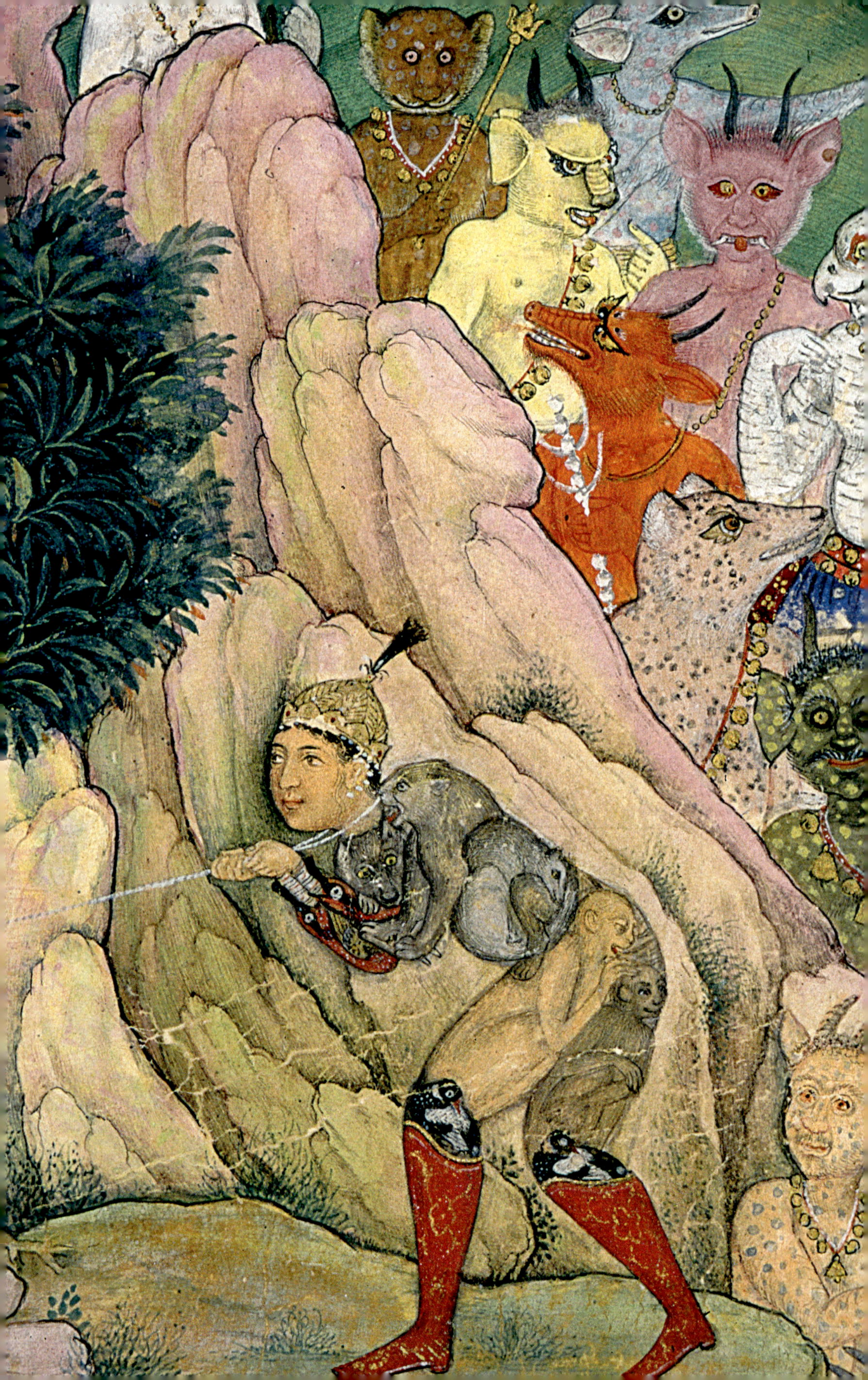

SOUTH ASIA

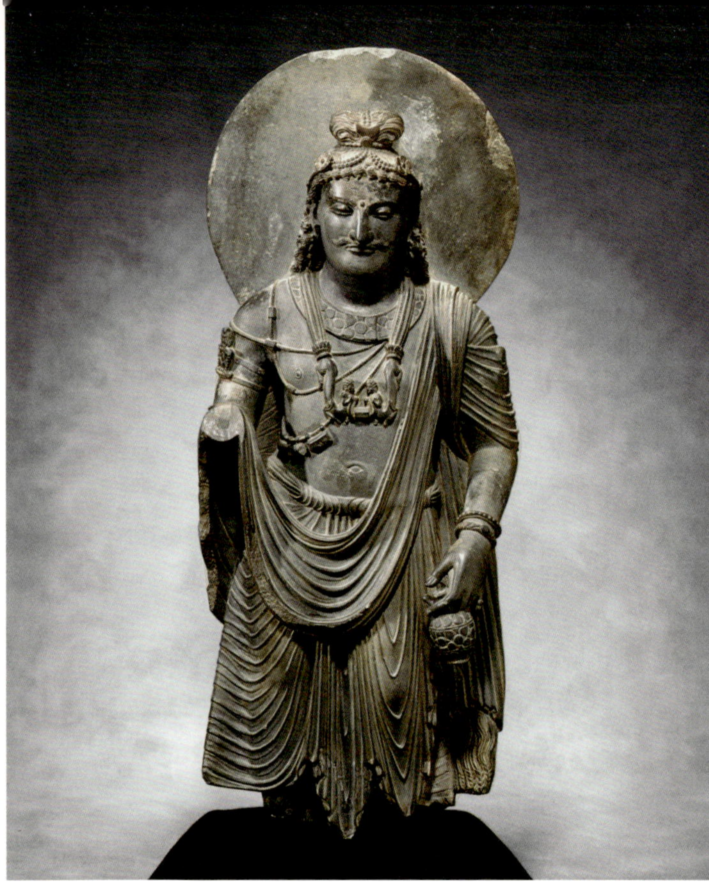

THE BODHISATTVA MAITREYA

approx. 200–350
Pakistan; former kingdom of Gandhara
Stone (schist)
H. 104.1 cm × W. 41.9 cm × D. 22.9 cm
The Avery Brundage Collection, B60S597

For centuries after followers of Alexander the Great (356–323 BCE) had established kingdoms there, areas of today's Afghanistan and Pakistan were in touch with the cultures of the wider Greco-Roman world. The physiques, facial features, drapery, and jewelry of the Buddhist sculpture of these areas recall, sometimes closely and sometimes more distantly, the traditions of the eastern Mediterranean.

A bodhisattva such as this might at first glance remind us of Apollo or some other Greco-Roman god. In fact, though, the artists of ancient Gandhara created works in a distinct, and rather consistent, style that for scholars is distinguishable from Hellenistic and speaks also of more local cultural connections. The splendid necklace, for example, with half-human beasts and the lion-shaped ear ornaments call to mind ancient Persian and Central Asian jewelry.

Bodhisattvas are usually represented as noble figures wearing the garments and adornments of a prince. In later Buddhist art, certain attributes were associated with particular bodhisattvas and allowed them to be identified. In the period when this sculpture was made, however, the identifiers may not have been standardized. The bottle that this figure holds in its left hand probably—but not certainly—indicates that the figure is the bodhisattva Maitreya.

Maitreya is a powerful spiritual being who currently resides in a heaven, waiting till the time is right to be born on earth in human form and become the next Buddha. Many Buddhists eagerly anticipate the distant day of Maitreya's coming. They hope to be reborn then to hear the great teachings expounded by a living Buddha.
—FMcG

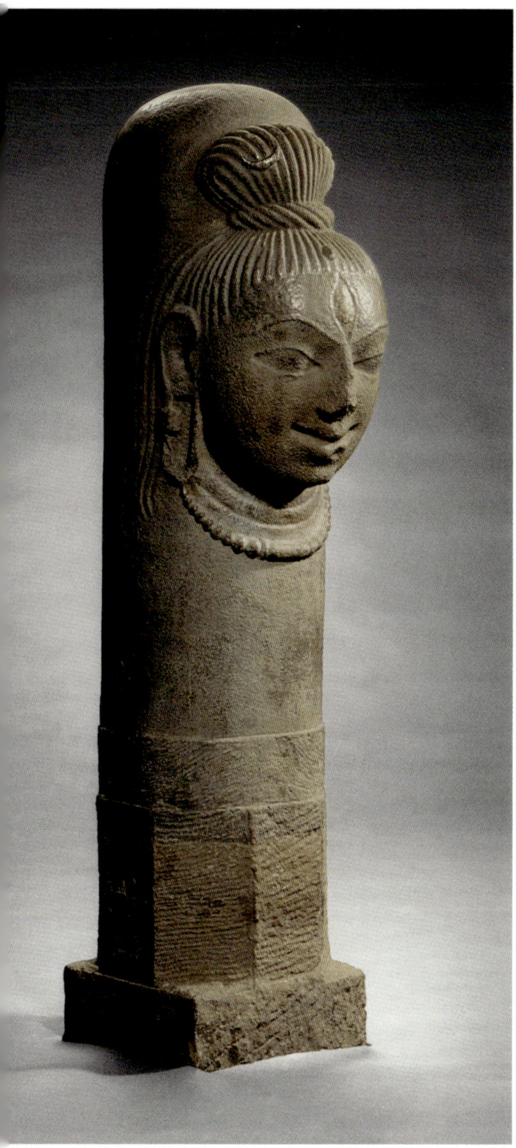

ONE-FACED LINGA

approx. 400–450
India; Madhya Pradesh state
Sandstone
H. 147.3 cm × W. 25.4 cm × D. 36.8 cm
Museum purchase, B69S15

Temples devoted to the Hindu god Shiva enshrine in their innermost sanctum a linga, the rounded cylindrical emblem of the god. The linga can be understood as both an abstract sign of Shiva's cosmic energy and as a phallus-like evocation of the potency he conserves through the discipline of yogic practice.

While most lingas are plain, some, like this one, include the face of Shiva (or sometimes multiple faces). For Hindu worshipers the key interaction with a deity embodied in an image is the meeting of eyes—seeing and being seen (*darshana*). Through this reciprocal seeing the deity confers blessings on the worshiper and the worshiper glimpses, however imperfectly, the divine.

This one-faced linga is notable not only for its early date but also for its aesthetic refinement. The great scholar Stella Kramrisch once described it in these words,

> The relation of the rounded pillar to the head is of great purity..., the curvature of the top supplying the theme for the form of the head. The roundness of the forehead carries the third, vertical, eye, which though only incised becomes a significant feature of the god's physiognomy. Straight strands of hair are pulled tight on the domed head and gathered on the top, while long strands fall in low relief behind the distended ears. Below the chignon, the cablelike twisted hair, and below the face, the bead necklace firmly attach [visually] the...head to the cylindrical shape of its ground.[1]

—*FMcG*

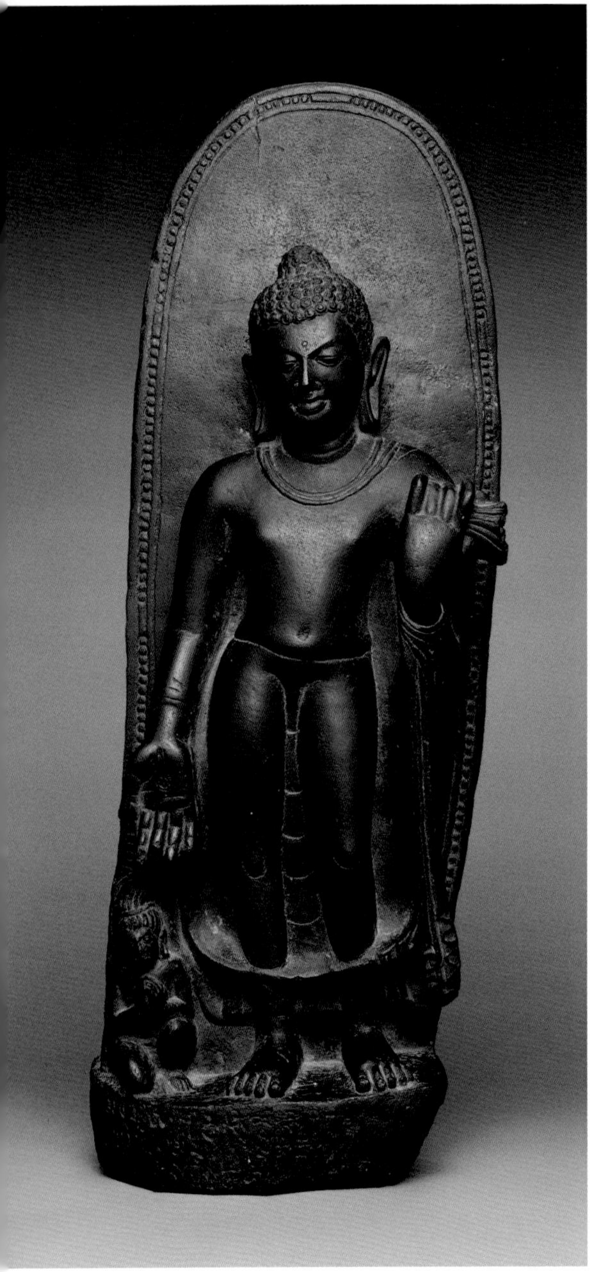

STANDING BUDDHA WITH DEVOTEE

500–700

India; Sultanganj, Bihar state

Stone (hornfels)

H. 61 cm × W. 22.9 cm × D. 11.4 cm

The Avery Brundage Collection, B60S571

In 1861 a British engineer overseeing the construction of a railway from Kolkata to Varanasi reported that during the digging of the railbed a huge metal Buddha image was uncovered. "The right foot of the copper image was met with ten feet under the surface. The news spread rapidly and by the next morning several thousands of natives had arrived, and others could be seen coming in all directions....After the image had been taken from...the excavation and some of the dust removed...the image was immediately surrounded, many of the Hindoo women kissed it making very curious remarks."[2]

A photo of the excavation was published several years later, and in it can be seen not only the colossus but also two smaller stone images. This sculpture is one of them. Seldom do we know so precisely where an ancient Indian artwork comes from.

The museum's artwork is important for other reasons too. In style it is close to the famous Sarnath Buddha images of the Gupta dynasty (fourth–fifth centuries) and testifies to the adoption of classical Gupta styles in eastern India. Also, it bears significant inscriptions. One names the donor and says that the donor "is making this religious gift by the oblations offered at the new and full moon unto the ancestors and all beings. The purpose is attaining superior knowledge." It may be that the donor himself is represented by the small figure kneeling in reverence beneath the Buddha's beneficently extended right hand.

Another inscription, on the back of the image together with a drawing of a stupa, records a standard Buddhist statement that infuses and vivifies the image with the Buddha's teaching.

—*FMcG*

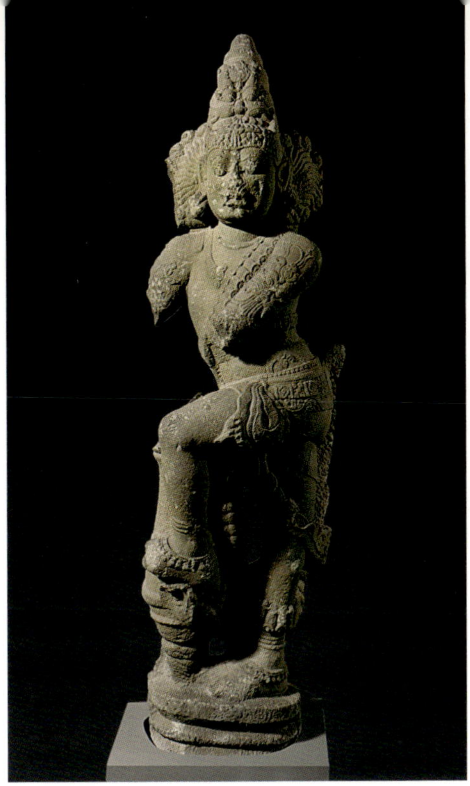

DOOR GUARDIAN

approx. 875–950
India; probably Kanchipuram region, Tamil Nadu state
Stone (hornfels)
H. 176.5 cm × W. 43.2 cm × D. 25.4 cm
The Avery Brundage Collection, B60S425

Decades of detective work were required to trace the history and context of this sculpture. In 1957 the Dutch art historian Johanna van Lohuizen-de Leeuw realized that this figure was one of a pair of male door guardians from a tenth-century south Indian temple and that its mate was in a collection in Switzerland. In succeeding years she and other scholars pieced together the story of how these sculptures and more than fifteen others, all from the same lost temple, had been shipped from south India to a Paris art dealer in the late 1920s. They were sold to collectors and museums in France, Great Britain, Canada, and the United States, and the fact that they had once belonged together was obscured. Only in 2012 did another art historian, Padma Kaimal, assemble and analyze all the evidence and sketch what could be known of their original context.

Most of the figures represented fearsome goddesses known as *yoginis*. Several others (including one in the Asian Art Museum collection) could be identified as among the "seven mothers," powerful embodiments of female energy. All these goddess figures, of which there may originally have been dozens, would have been arrayed around the outer walls of a *yogini* temple, facing inward "to generate visual and emotional echoes back and forth."

This guardian and its companion would have flanked the temple's entry, "twisting to address their protective energies to the portal between them by squaring their wide shoulders to confront intruders....Their bulging eyes, raised and furrowed brows, and bare fangs convey a clear warning to all who would approach. Each raised a flexed, brawny leg across his body....Extreme yet effortless twists like these signaled the guardians' yogic strength, another warning."[3]

—*FMcG*

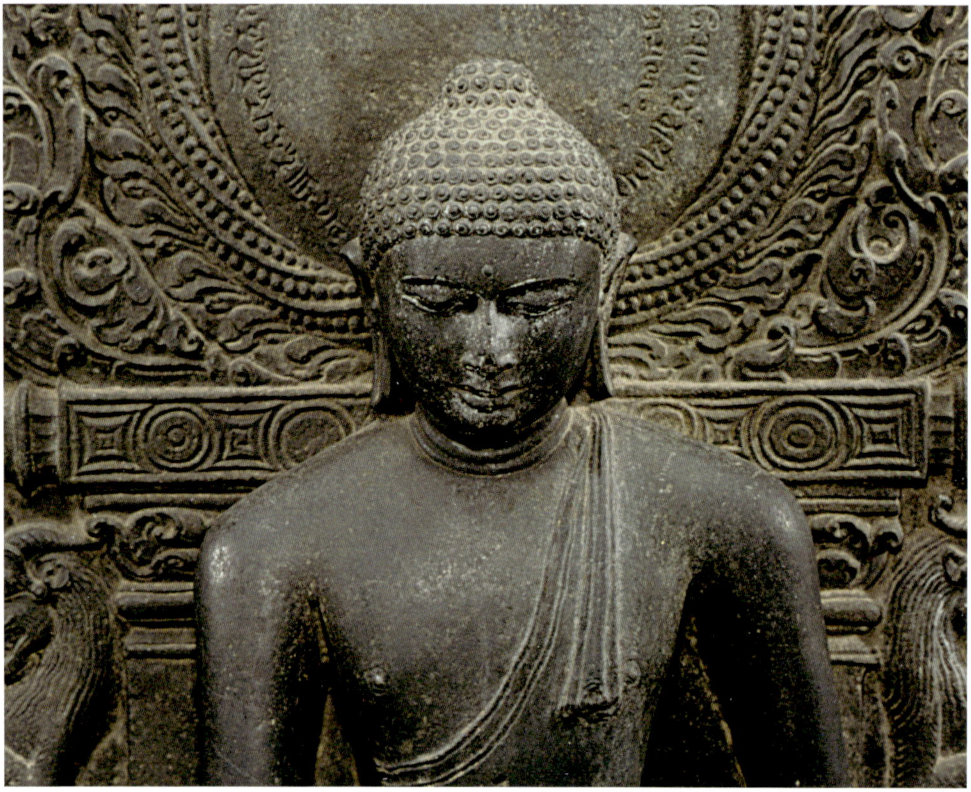

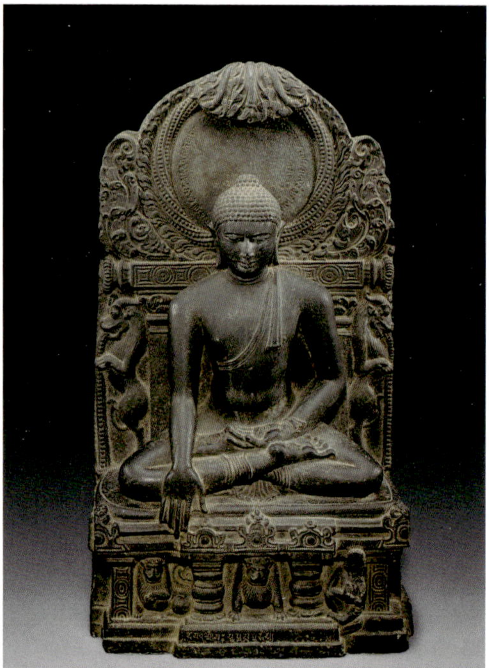

MASTERPIECE

THE BUDDHA TRIUMPHING OVER MARA

approx. 850–950

India; probably Kurkihar, Bihar state

Basalt

H. 83.8 cm × W. 44.5 cm × D. 24.1 cm

The Avery Brundage Collection, B60S598

After many lifetimes of spiritual and intellectual preparation, the Buddha-to-be neared the achievement of Enlightenment, and thus of buddhahood, as he sat meditating under a tree. The demon Mara, an embodiment of violence and uncontrolled passions, approached at the head of a monstrous army, intending to put a stop to the Enlightenment.

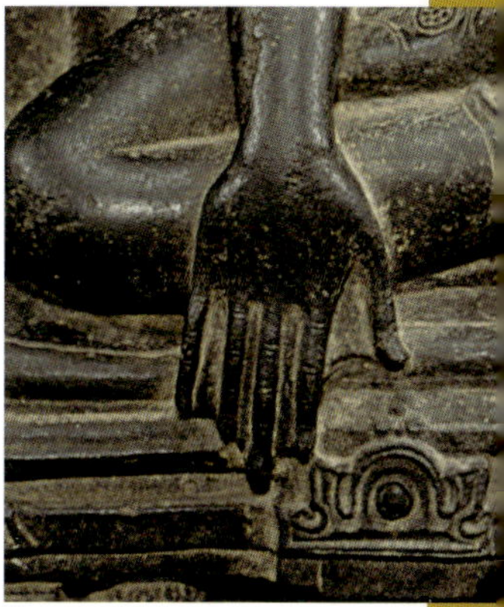

Mara and the Buddha-to-be repeatedly challenged each other's power and past accomplishments. Finally, the Buddha-to-be said,

> *'Mara, who is witness to your having given donations?' Said Mara, 'All these,' and he stretched out his hand in the direction of his army. Then Mara said, 'Who is witness to your having given donations?' The Buddha-to-be replied, 'I have no animate witnesses present. However, the great seven-hundred-fold donation I gave in my immediately previous existence will be testified to by the solid earth.' And drawing forth his right hand from beneath his priestly robe, he stretched it out towards the mighty earth. And the mighty earth thundered 'I bear you witness' with a hundred thousand roars. And the followers of Mara fled away in all directions.*[4]

This sculpture was made in northeastern India, very near where these events are supposed to have occurred. Buddha images seated with the right hand reaching down at the knee to touch the earth memorialize the victory of the Buddha-to-be over the forces embodied in Mara and his overcoming the last obstacles to attaining buddhahood.

The inscription on the base says that the sculpture was donated by the senior monk Prajnaprabha. The inscription on the halo gives the standard statement of Buddhist belief that is intended to animate the image with the Buddha's message. It reads, "The Buddha has explained the cause of all things that arise from a cause. He, the great monk, has also explained their cessation."

—*FMcG*

PLAQUE WITH SCENES OF THE LIFE OF THE BUDDHA

1000–1200
India; Bihar state
Stone (pyrophyllite)
H. 16.5 cm × W. 12.7 cm × D. 5.1 cm
Gift of the Connoisseurs' Council, 1991.224

The spiritual quest of the Buddha, and his subsequent career of teaching, took place some twenty-five hundred years ago in the Bihar region of northeastern India, an area that became famous as the Buddhist holy land. This small, portable plaque shows a number of episodes of the life of the Buddha and recalls the locations where they occurred.

The plaque also suggests the complexity of cultural relationships among various parts of the Buddhist world in the period 1000–1200. Plaques quite similar in arrangement, symbolism, size, and material have been found in northeastern India, Sri Lanka, and Tibet. Many were also found in Myanmar, and some scholars have assumed that all (or most of) the plaques of the type were made there. Some plaques have inscriptions on the back in Tibetan (including this one) or Chinese, however. The easiest way to explain this fact would be to say that the plaques were made in northeastern India for the many Buddhist pilgrims of various nationalities who came to worship at the holy sites there and carried the plaques home as sacred objects.

Myanmar art of this period had strong connections with the contemporary Buddhist art of northeastern India. Also, Myanmar pilgrims were significant patrons of Buddhist art and architecture in northeastern India, and their tastes and preferences may sometimes have made themselves felt. It is also possible that Indian or Indian-trained artists worked in Myanmar in this period, so clearly the question of where such plaques were made will never be easy to answer.

The central Buddha is shown seated beneath a tree, touching the ground to call the earth to affirm his fitness for achieving Enlightenment. This image is surrounded by representations of important events in the weeks after the achievement of Enlightenment and of seven scenes of the Buddha's life. The most easily recognizable scene is of the Buddha's death, at the top.

The Tibetan inscription on the back gives the sacred formula *om ah hum*.
—*FMcG*

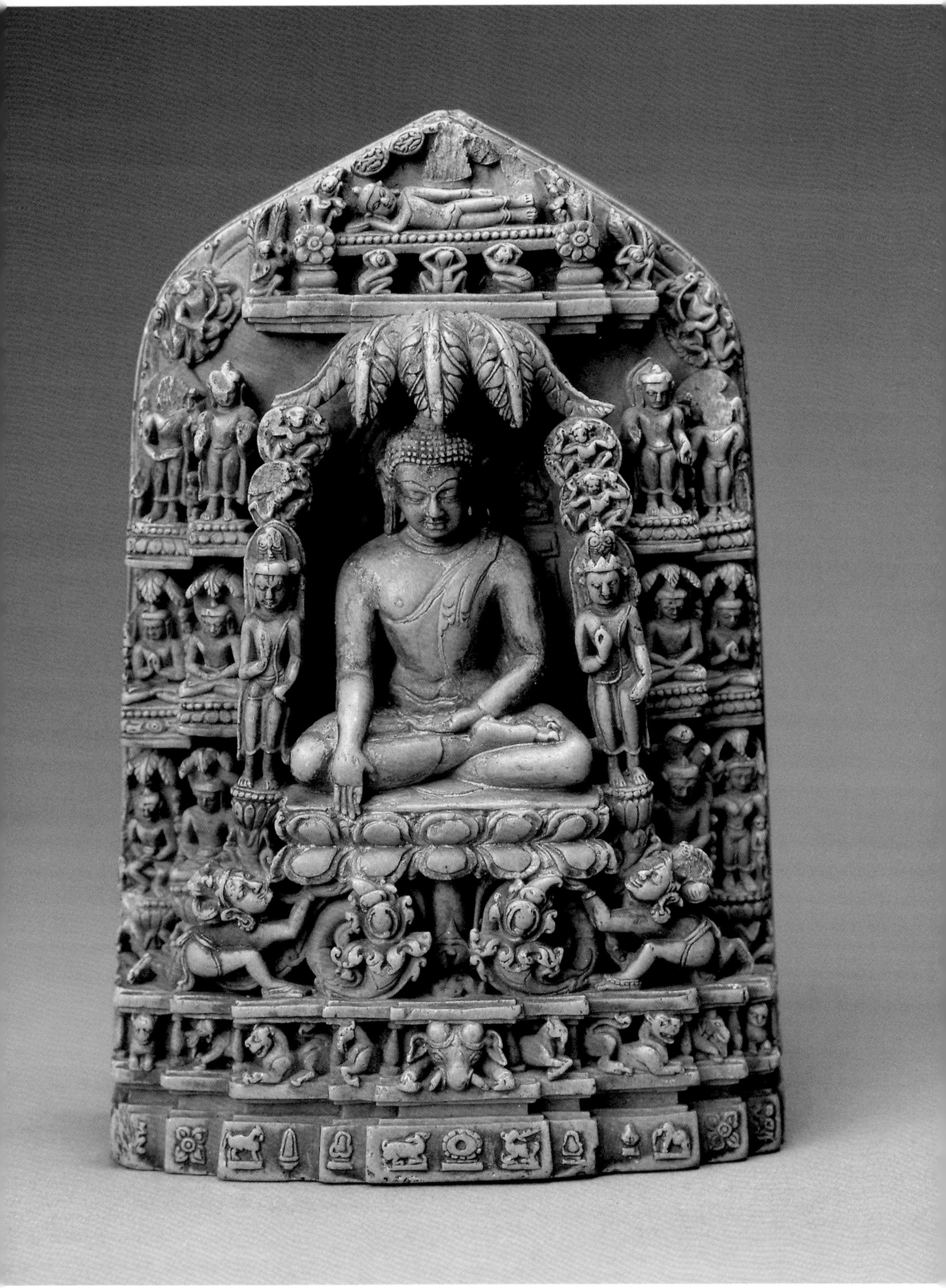

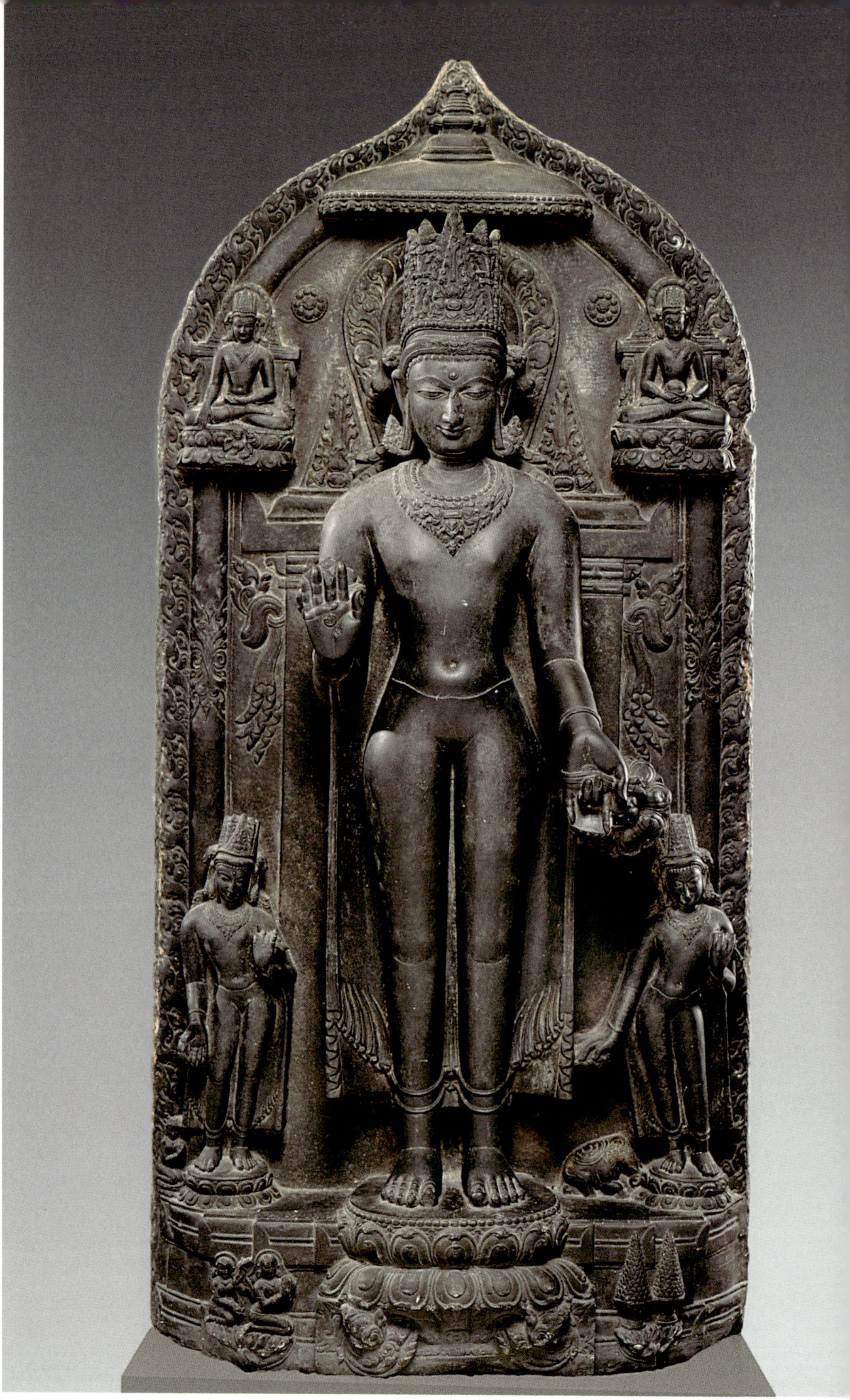

STANDING CROWNED BUDDHA WITH FOUR SCENES OF HIS LIFE

approx. 1050–1100
India; southern Magadha region, Bihar state
Stone
H. 104.1 cm × W. 50.8 cm × D. 17.8 cm
The Avery Brundage Collection, B65S11

The young prince who was to become the Buddha rejected the luxuries of royal life and embraced simplicity. Why then is he shown here wearing a crown and jewelry over his monk's robes? According to the scholars Susan and John Huntington, "The crown and jewelry emphasize the aspect of the Buddha as a universal sovereign, drawing a visual analogy between the attainment of buddhahood and coronation as a king. The royal adornments evoke the Buddha's majesty, kingly qualities, and omniscience."[5]

The large standing Buddha in the center is surrounded by four others, two standing and two seated, representing four of a common set of eight scenes of the Buddha's life. For example, to our left of the main figure is shown the episode when the Buddha, having gone to one of the heavens to preach to his deceased mother, descends to earth again and is reverently greeted by an eminent nun. Though these four smaller figures refer to moments in the Buddha's life story, they wear crowns, which the Buddha did not do during his earthly career. This suggests that the real emphasis is not on the Buddha as a human teacher but as an exalted, transcendent being.

The importance of pious women in Buddhism is suggested by the depiction of the nun and the presence of two small female figures on the base. It is possible that they represent the donors of the image.

Much of the stone sculpture of eastern India in the tenth and eleventh centuries is expertly carved and highly finished, but here the artist has reached a level of extraordinary refinement and suavity. The lustrous smoothness of the Buddhas' bodies and the plainness of the back slab are heightened by the contrast of the intricately detailed jewelry and decoration. These qualities reiterate that what we see is meant not as the representation of this-worldly events and beings but as a vision of otherworldly perfection.
—*FMcG*

THE BUDDHIST DEITY VAJRA TARA

1075–1200

India; perhaps Nalanda, Bihar state, Magadha region

Basalt

H. 100.3 cm × W. 59.7 cm × D. 22.9 cm

The Avery Brundage Collection, B63S20+

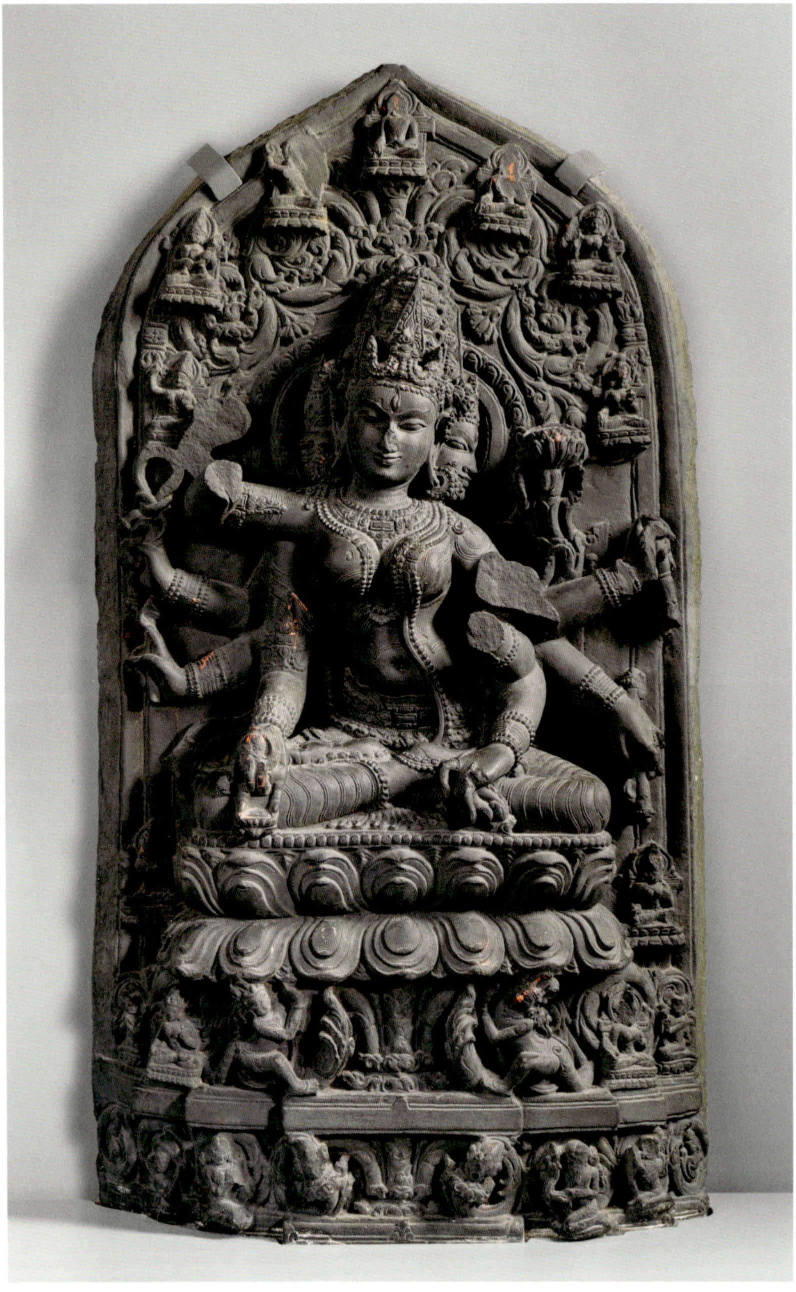

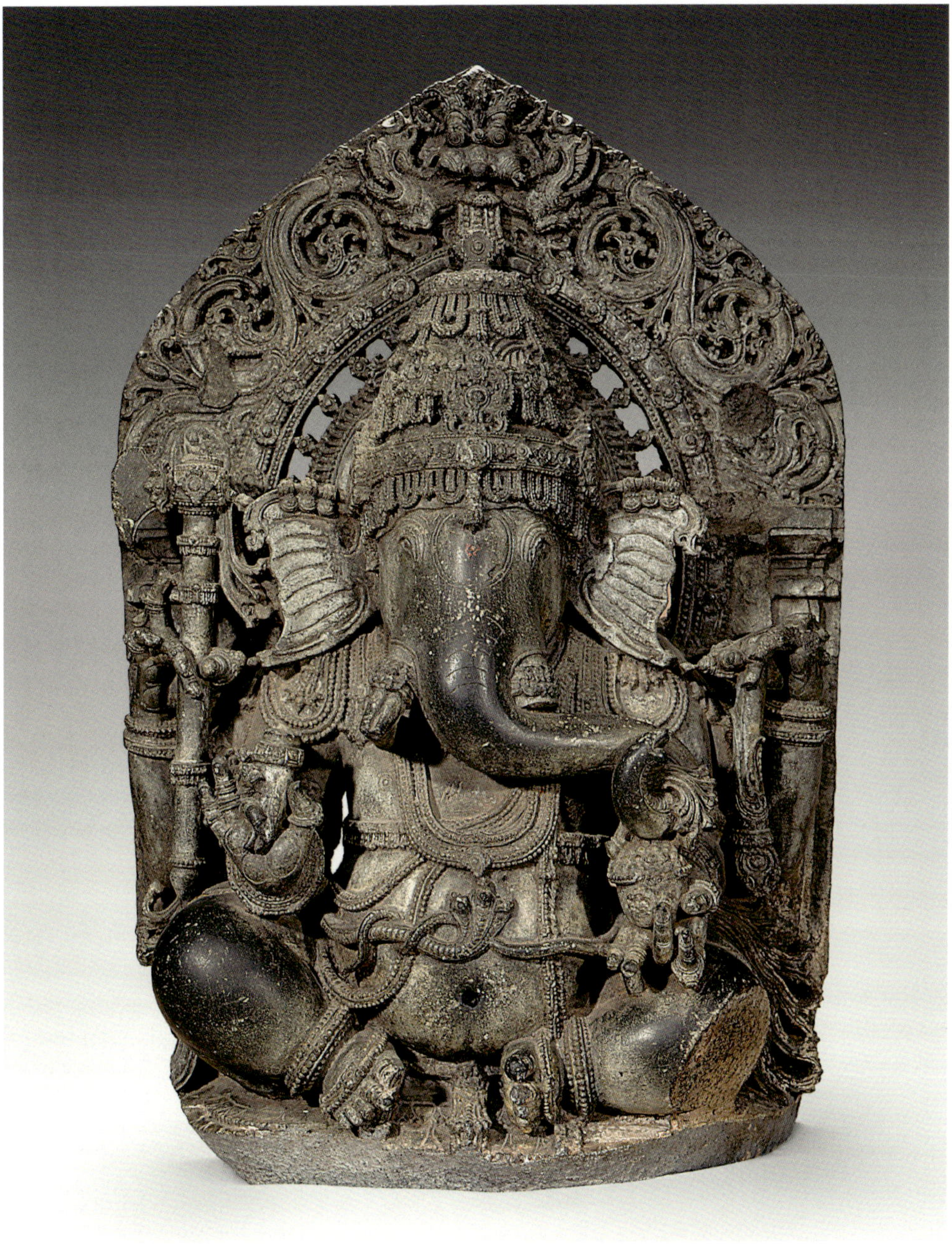

SEATED GANESHA

1200–1300

India; Karnataka state

Stone (schist)

H. 94 cm × W. 61 cm × D. 31.8 cm

Gift of the de Young Museum Society Auxiliary, B68S4

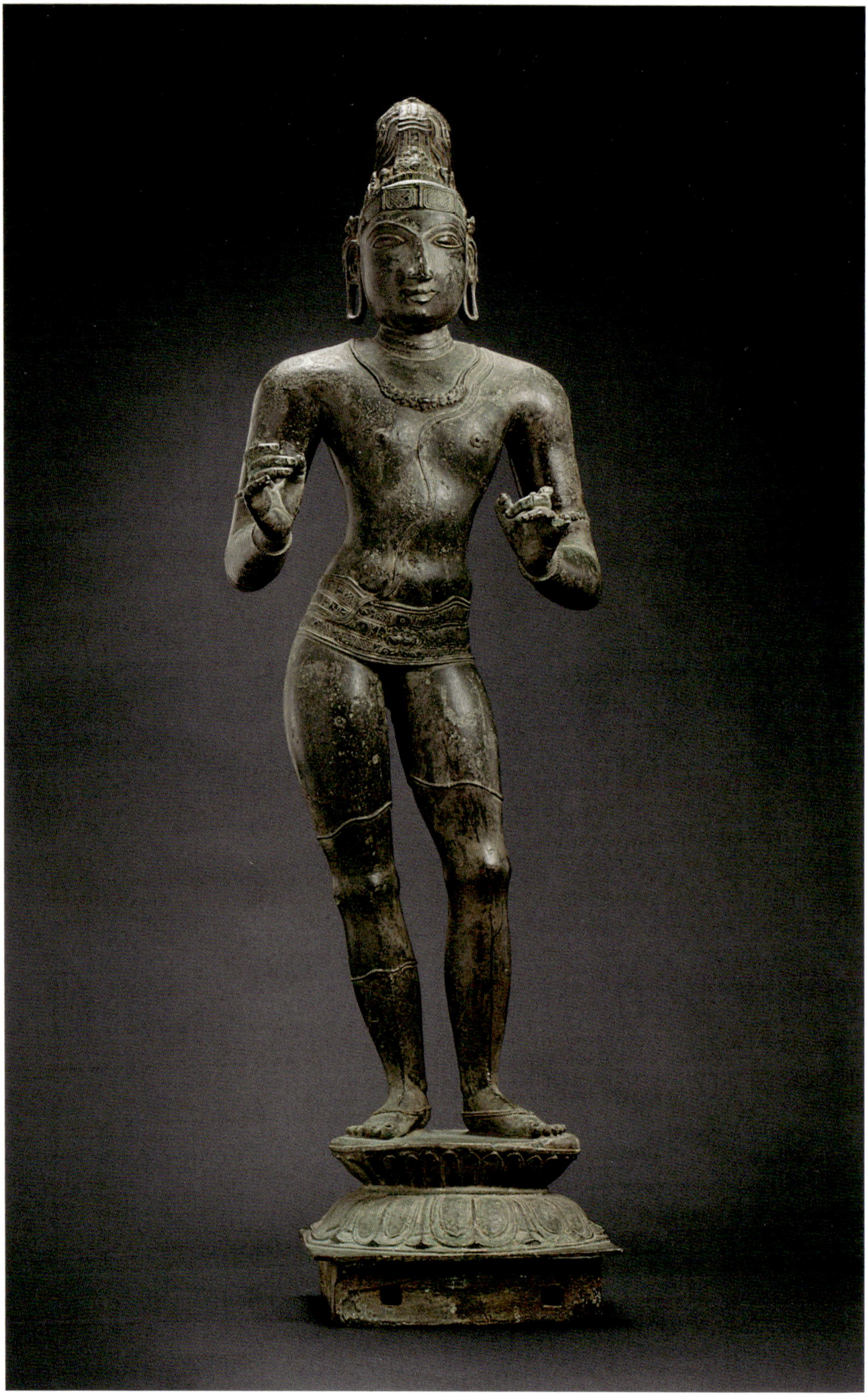

MASTERPIECE

THE HINDU DEITY SHIVA

approx. 1300–1500
India; Tamil Nadu state
Bronze
H. 95.2 cm × W. 29.8 cm × D. 25.4 cm
The Avery Brundage Collection, B69S14

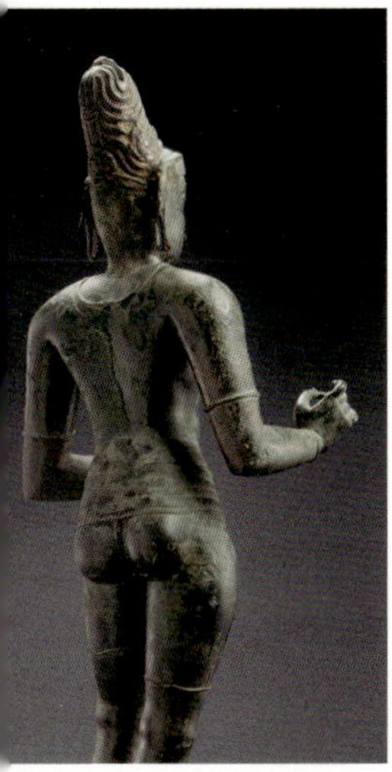

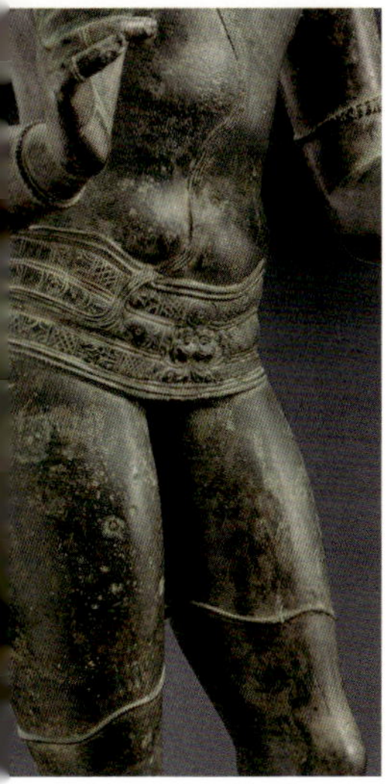

Pure gold, first being,
living in grove-encircled Pulamankai,
he is my own; he is music, he is
like the light of the morning sun.[6]

Hindu deities such as Shiva are usually envisioned as supremely beautiful. Their beauty, even sensuousness, manifests their perfection and power. In many Hindu traditions the magnetic attraction of the Divine for the individual soul is seen as similar to the attraction of lover for lover.

Shiva is usually represented with four or more arms and characteristically has a vertical third eye in his forehead. Here, however, he is identified only by his ascetic's dreadlocks, which are tied up with a tiny crescent moon and river goddess Ganga on either side.

Similar figures of earlier centuries would have had somewhat more naturalistic proportions and treatment of details. Here, though, the sculptor has chosen to exaggerate the broadness of the shoulders and the narrowness of the waist, and to treat lines such as the jeweled chain on the lower right leg and the sacred thread across the chest in a hyperelegant manner.

A noted scholar wrote of this image that it "brilliantly represents South Indian bronze casting. Although its stylistic precursors, the renowned bronze sculptures created [somewhat earlier] under the Chola kings…are often considered to exemplify the peak moment of such art, one could argue that post-Chola sculptures such as this also mark peaks."[7]

The lotus pedestal is placed on top of a square base with two holes pierced through it to hold wooden or metal posts inserted for carrying during ceremonial processions. For such a procession, the image would have been decked with elaborate textiles, jewelry, and flowers. The deity's beauty would have been hidden from ordinary sight, but glowingly vivid in the mind's eye of the worshiper.

—*FMcG*

HEIRLOOM TEXTILE WITH REPEATED DESIGN OF A WOMAN AND HER ATTENDANTS (DETAIL)

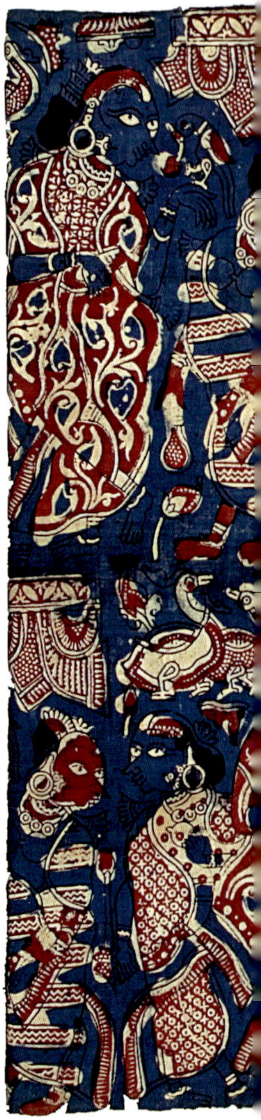

—

approx. 1325–1405

India; Gujarat state, made for the Indonesian market

Cotton, resist and mordant dyed, with block printing

H. 94 cm × W. 431.8 cm

Museum purchase with exchange funds from the gifts of Avery Brundage, Ed Nagel, Mr. and Mrs. John Bunker, Elizabeth Fullerton Crocker and various other donors, 2004.81

—

International textile trade has been a key contributor to India's wealth and economic prosperity from ancient times to today. Cotton is indigenously grown in many parts of India, and fine Indian cotton textiles were a major export item from early recorded history, as is documented in the Greek-language, Roman text *Periplus of the Erythraean Sea* (approx. 100 CE). Trade of Indian textiles continued steadily over the centuries and eventually extended from Europe to Southeast Asia. This textile, produced in Gujarat, western India, was collected in the Toraja region of Sulawesi, one of the Sunda islands of the Indonesian archipelago. Along the centuries-old trade routes of Southeast Asia, precious textiles from India were exchanged for rare spices as well as forest and sea products.

This cloth was block printed and resist and mordant dyed on hand-spun cotton. The design, repeated over two rows, depicts an elaborately dressed woman with a parrot, accompanied by attendants. Above the figures are parasols and geese. The subject and the drawing style both relate to the painting traditions of the Jain religious community of western India. Because of India's hot and humid climate, along with the practice of reusing old fabrics, relatively few early textiles survive from India itself. But carefully preserved heirloom textiles from regions outside India, such as this example, provide evidence for long-standing trade relationships. Such textiles enabled cultural exchanges across vast distances and evinced the high value of textiles as imported luxury goods.

—*QA*

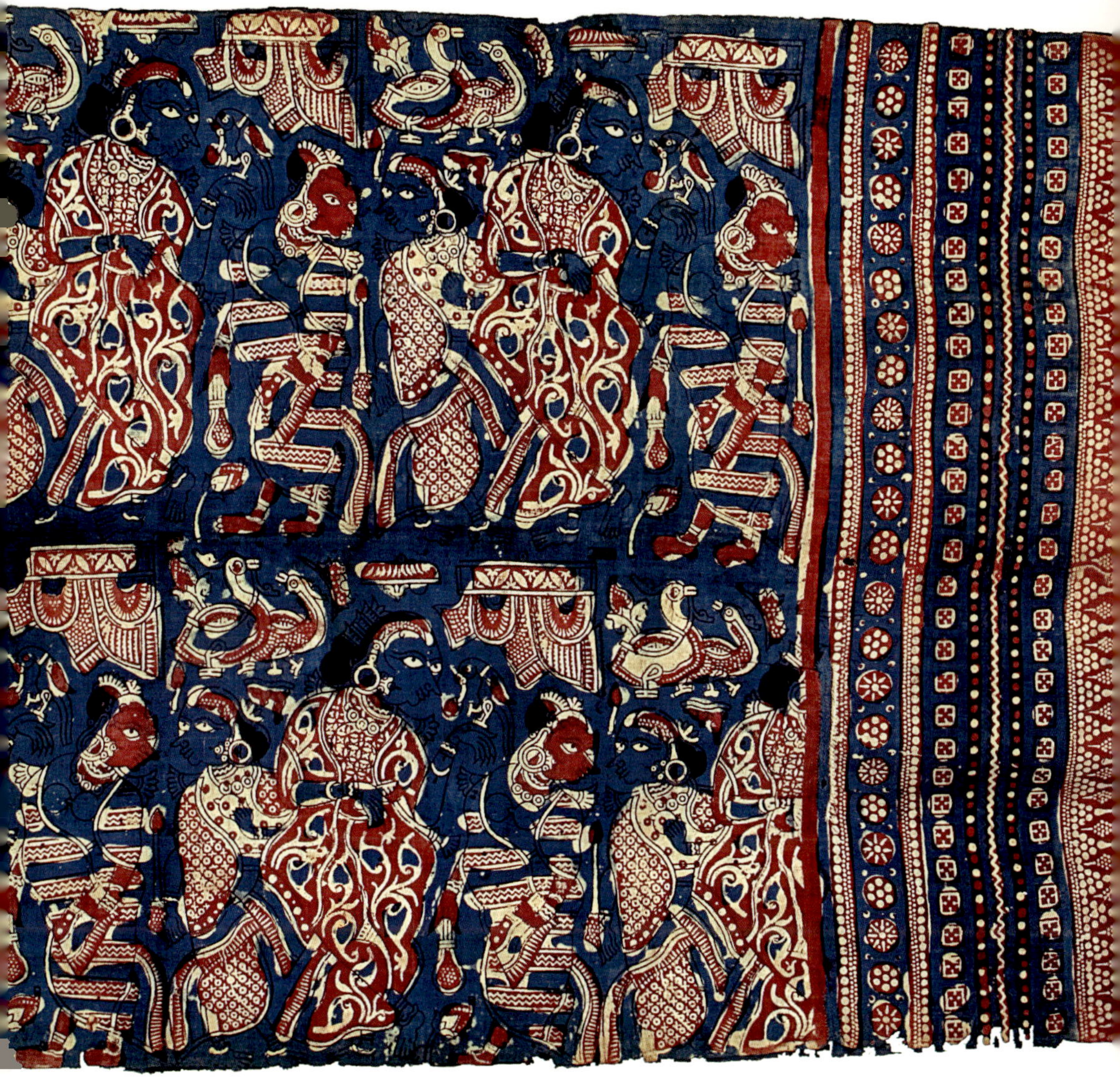

MINIATURE HINDU SHRINE WITH VISHNU SLEEPING ON THE COSMIC OCEAN

1500–1700

India; vicinity of Shrirangam, Tamil Nadu state

Ivory with traces of pigments

H. 21.6 cm × W. 12.7 cm × D. 3.8 cm

Acquisition made possible by Michel D. Weill bequest and C. Barry Randell bequest, B82M4

The universe has been destroyed. In the interval before it is recreated, nothing is left but limitless ocean. On this ocean floats Vishnu, lying on a serpent, asleep. The universe now persists, like a dream, within the sleeping god. When the time is right, he will put forth from his navel the god Brahma, who will reconstruct the universe, and the cycle will begin again.

The story of Vishnu's profound dream is a major narrative in Hinduism, presenting Vishnu as the deity preserving the cosmos from eon to eon. This particular form of Vishnu on the cosmic ocean is the central image of one of the most important Hindu temples in southern India, the Shri Ranganatha Temple at Shrirangam. This miniature shrine is an abbreviated representation of that vast temple. Its general form recalls the temple's towers, and the dome shape in its upper part recalls the dome-shaped superstructure of the temple's central building. In front of the dome-shaped element in both the miniature and the real building is an arched panel with a standing half-figure of Vishnu in a special form as the ultimate supreme deity.

Above the reclining Vishnu are the mythical serpent's multiple heads. Below are another standing Vishnu flanked by his consorts, a pair of door guardians, and other figures.

—*FMcG*

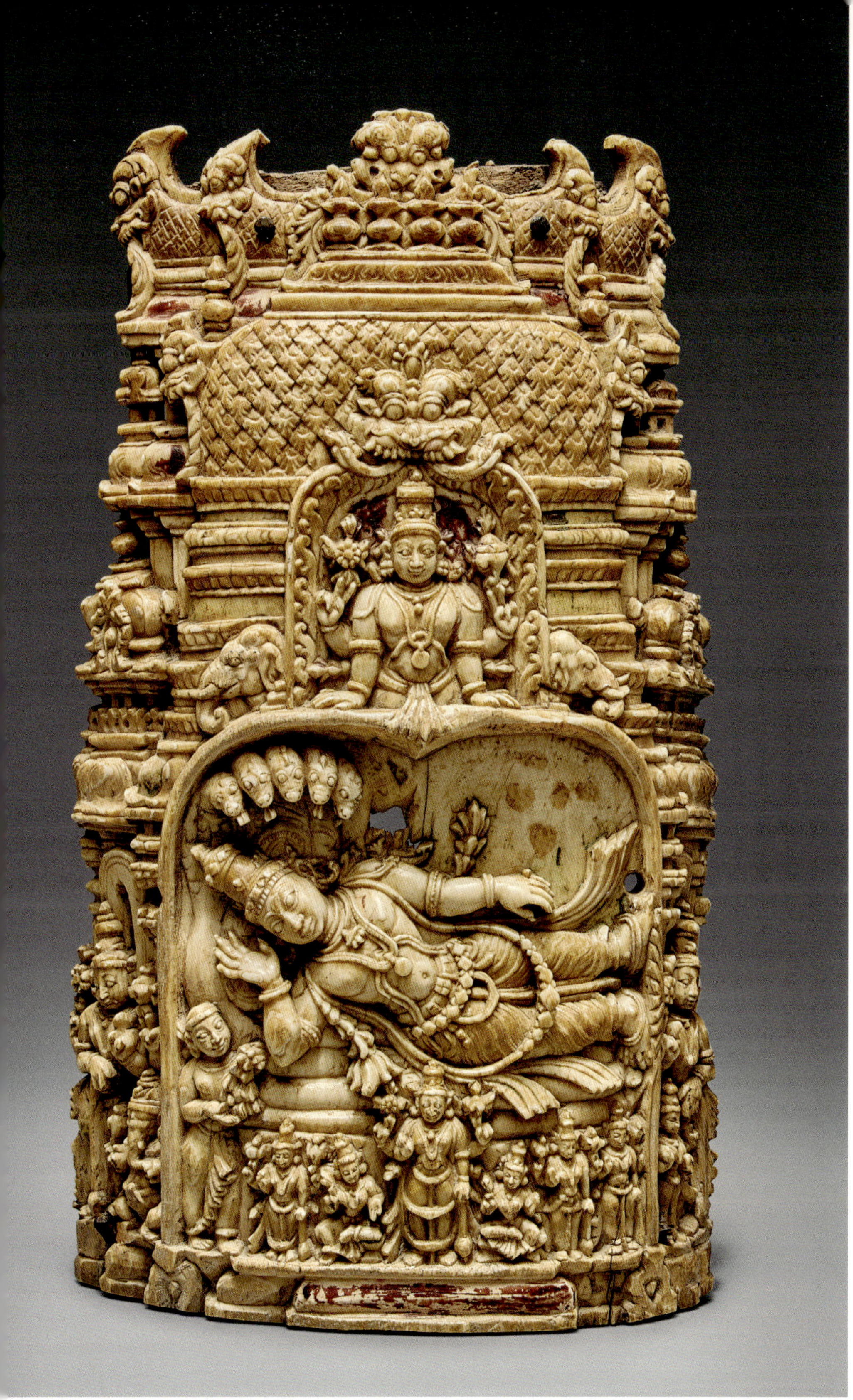

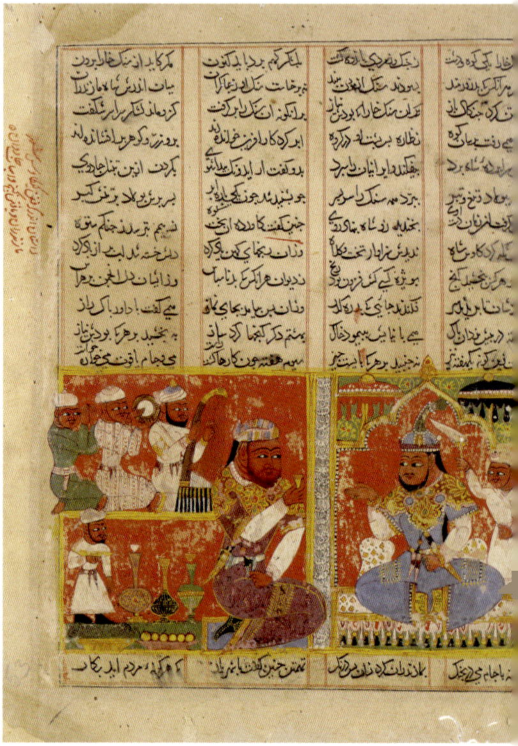

THE HERO RUSTAM CONVERSES WITH KAY KAVUS, KING OF IRAN, FROM A MANUSCRIPT OF THE *SHAHNAMA* (BOOK OF KINGS)

probably 1450–1500
India
Sultanate period (1206–1526)
Opaque watercolors on paper
H. 31.7 cm × W. 26.1 cm
Museum purchase, City Arts Trust Fund with additional funding from Stuart Harvey and the Levi Strauss Foundation, 1989.30

In the nearly fifty thousand verses of his literary masterpiece, the *Shahnama* (Book of Kings), the Persian poet Firdausi describes the myths and embellished history of Iran from the beginning of time to the Arab conquest in the seventh century. The epic—centered on stories of about fifty historical and legendary kings, as well as heroes and villains—features the moral consequences of the actions of people in power as one of its key themes.

The page here comes from a chapter about the impetuous and arrogant king Kay Kavus, who embarked on the conquest of Mazandaran, among several ill-advised exploits in the course of his reign. Mazandaran was a land known for its immense wealth, powerful sorcerers, and demonic beings, into which no other Iranian king had ventured. After overcoming numerous challenging and life-threatening odds (see page 19), Kay Kavus's Persian army succeeded in defeating the king of Mazandaran. In this painting we see the victorious king (at right) enjoying the riches of the Mazandaran court and its treasury. The scene is festive, with attendants serving food and wine and musicians providing entertainment to Kay Kavus and the epic's hero, Rustam (see also page 44). Here, Rustam advises Kay Kavus to return to his kingdom in Iran and leave Mazandaran to its local people.

Written in elegant poetic form, the *Shahnama*'s engaging tales about just and flawed kingship, adventure, and heroism resonated with audiences in many different places and cultures. Most Iranians and Iranian diaspora communities today continue to identify with stories from the *Shahnama*, which are recited, copied, and performed. For centuries, the epic was popular in the historically Persian-speaking world (modern Iran, Afghanistan, parts of India, and even Turkey).

This page was originally in a book with more than 350 pages, and it is among the earliest Persian-language manuscripts to survive from India. Its artistic elements—the bold color scheme, arrangement of figures in compartments and tiers, the figures' scale, facial features, and clothing—resemble contemporary Hindu and Jain paintings. These distinctive qualities suggest that this copy of the *Shahnama* was made by an artist trained in Indian (and not Persian) painting traditions.

—*QA*

CUP IN THE SHAPE OF A GOURD

1625–1650
India
Mughal period (1526–1858)
Nephrite
H. 7.6 cm × W. 20.3 cm × D. 13.5 cm
The Avery Brundage Collection, B60J485

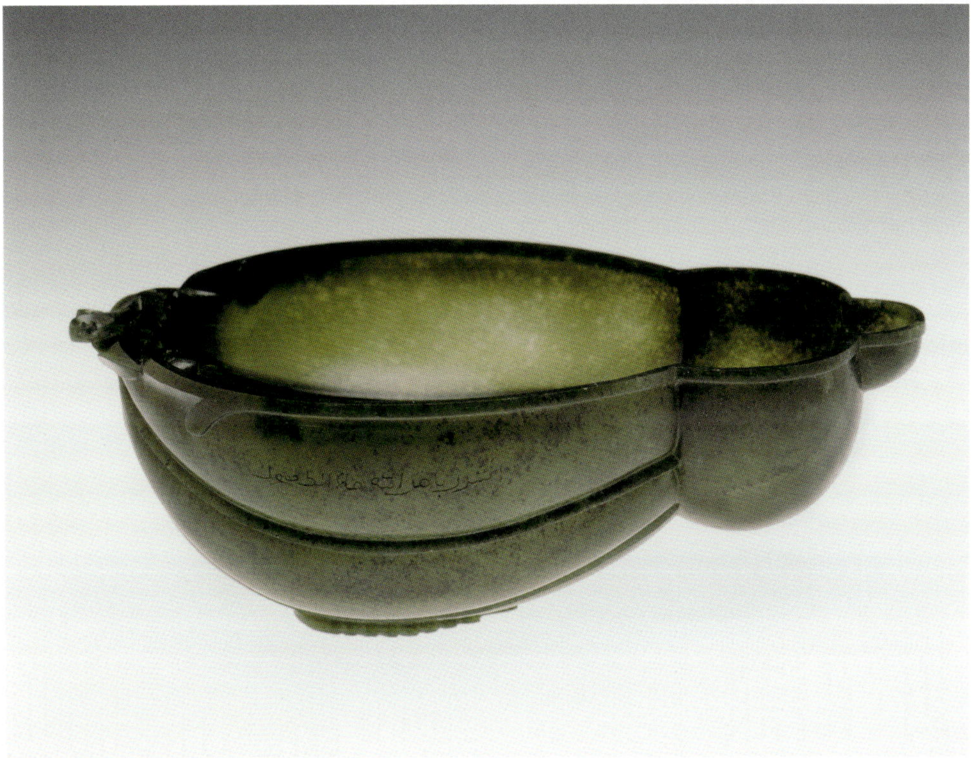

THE HERO RUSTAM AND THE DEMONESS, FROM A MANUSCRIPT OF THE *SHAHNAMA* (BOOK OF KINGS)

—

approx. 1610

By Bishandas (Indian)

Opaque watercolors on paper

H. 34.3 cm × W. 21.9 cm (image)

Museum purchase with exchange funds from the gifts of Avery Brundage, Ed Nagel, Mr. and Mrs. John Bunker, Elizabeth Fullerton Crocker and various other donors, 2004.24

—

The *Shahnama* (Book of Kings)—a literary masterpiece that weaves together the mythical and actual history of ancient Iran—contains many stories about the courageous and immensely strong hero Rustam. In the course of his unusually long life, he was a key advisor to numerous kings and was called upon whenever things got difficult. Among the popular episodes about Rustam are his seven labors—a series of trials that he undergoes alone with his faithful horse Rakhsh, on his journey to rescue the army of king Kay Kavus in Mazandaran (see pages 19 and 42).

After having survived near-death experiences in his first three trials, Rustam came upon a beautiful meadow with rivers where a delicious feast was laid out. He was amazed at his good fortune and sat down to enjoy the meal; seeing a lute nearby, he sang a song. Rustam did not know that he had disturbed a demons' banquet, and that they had disappeared when they heard him approach. His song attracted the attention of a demoness, who transformed herself into a beautiful young woman and came to join him. Praising god at this additional stroke of luck, he offered her a glass of wine, but on hearing the name of god, she turned back into her ugly self. Rustam caught the demoness with his lasso as she tried to escape and killed her. This was his fourth trial.

This painting shows the moment of the story where Rustam, recognizable by his distinctive lion-headed helmet and tiger-skin cloak, captures the demoness. The picture includes the key details of the story's setting and action: the pretty meadow with its river, Rustam's horse Rakhsh grazing peacefully, and the interrupted party of demons who look over from behind the rocky outcrop. The artist has cleverly portrayed the demoness with a beautiful human face and a body composed of many animals, appropriately reflecting her magical powers as she turns from her assumed human form back into her demonic self. Composite figures of this type became very popular in Indian painting in later centuries, and this is one of the earliest of such depictions. This painting is ascribed at the bottom margin to the Indian artist Bishandas. But paintings like this one were typically a result of collaboration, made in workshops that employed artists with individual specialties. It is likely that different artists contributed the landscape features and the group of delightful demons seen here.

—*QA*

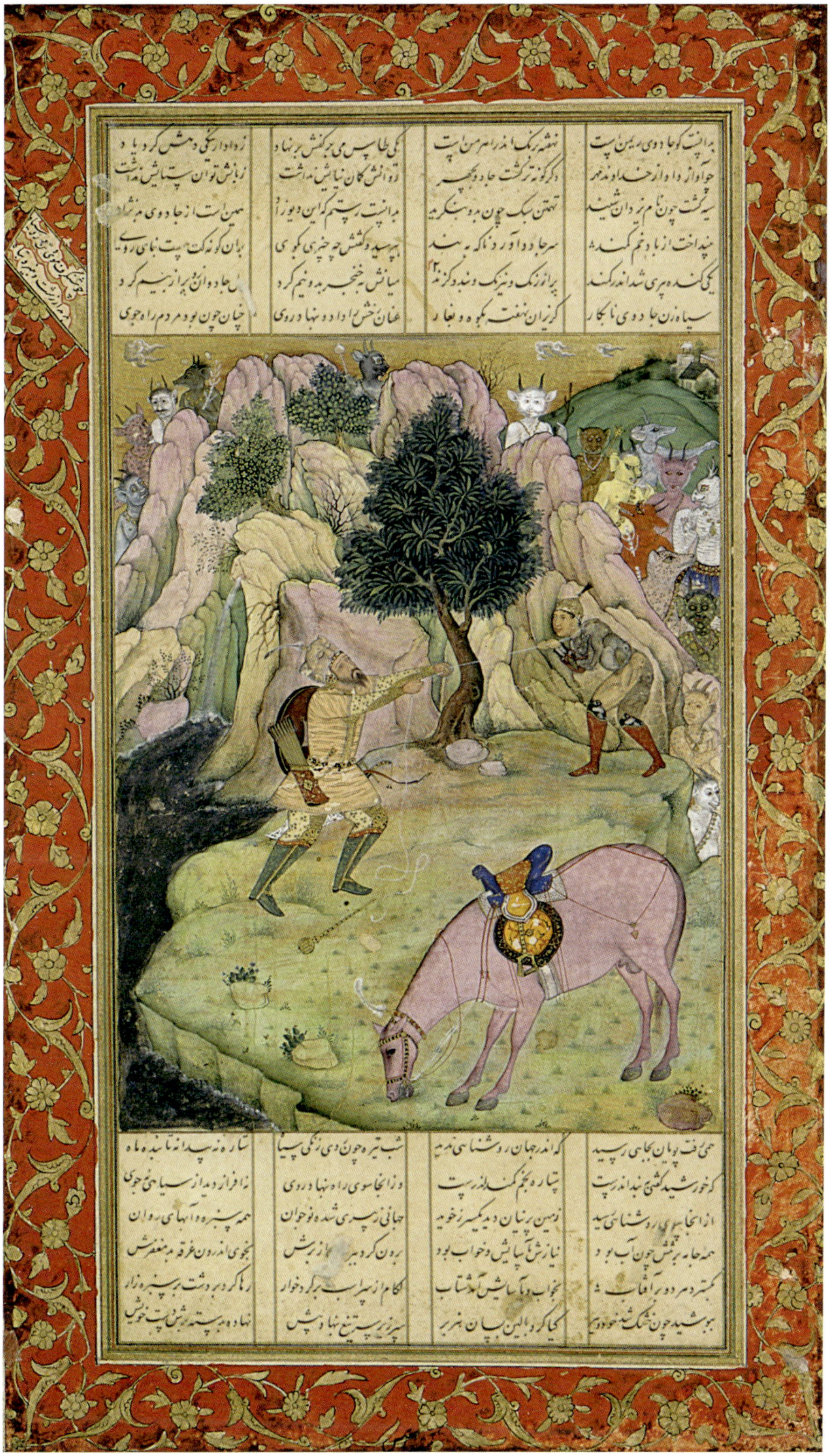

BOX, PROBABLY OWNED BY MAHARAJA RANJIT SINGH

approx. 1660–1700

India or Pakistan; Gujarat state or Sindh province

Sandalwood, ivory, tortoiseshell, and velvet

H. 30.5 cm × W. 39.4 cm × D. 27.9 cm

Gift of the Kapany Collection, 1998.61

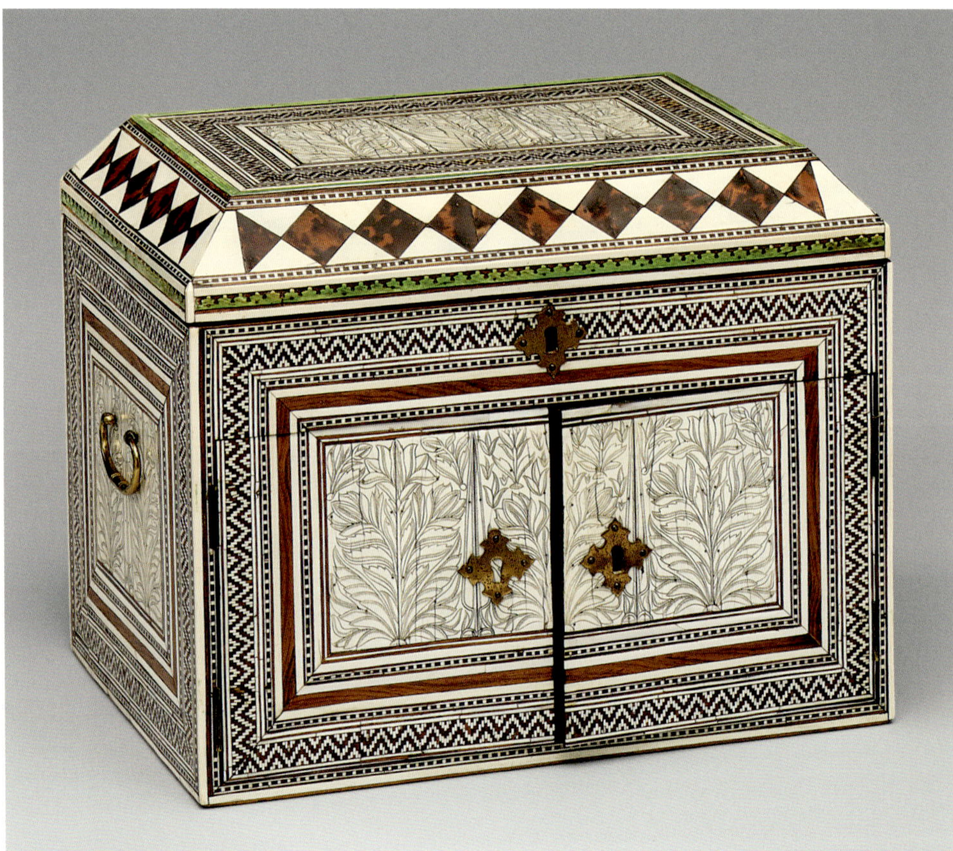

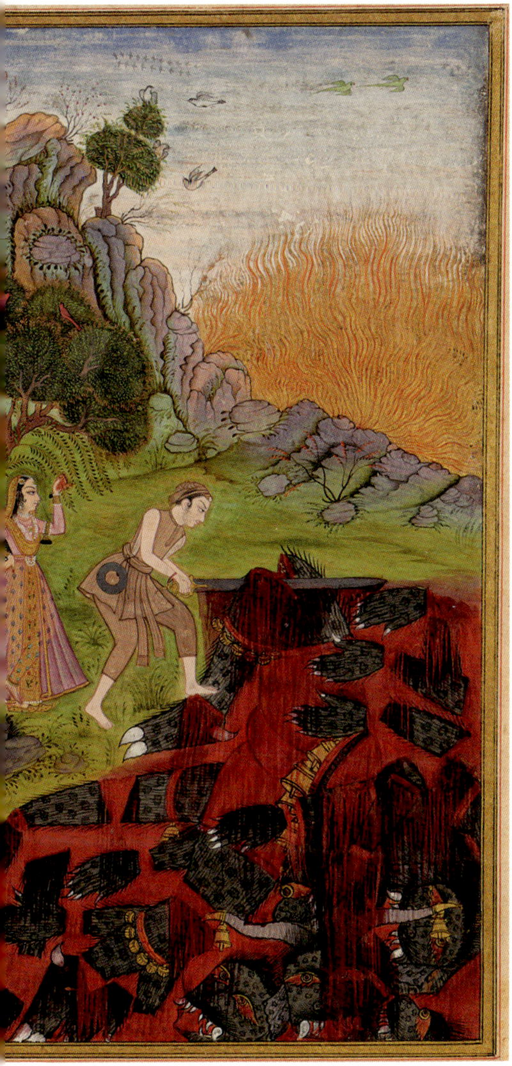

PRINCE MANOHAR BURNS THE TREE OF IMMORTALITY AND DESTROYS THE DEMON, FROM A MANUSCRIPT OF *GULSHAN-I ISHQ* (ROSE GARDEN OF LOVE)

approx. 1700
India; Deccan region
Ink, opaque watercolors, and gold on paper
H. 26.4 cm × W. 14.3 cm (image)
Museum purchase, 2015.38

This page from the *Gulshan-i Ishq* (Rose Garden of Love), a complicated romance about several pairs of lovers, comes from the section describing the hero Manohar's rescue of the princess Champavati. She had been kidnapped by a carnivorous, five-headed and ten-armed demon. Defeating it was a near-impossible task for the hero, for as long as the tree of immortality bore fruit, the demon would continually come back to life.

The painting shows the final stage of Prince Manohar's success against the demon. He and Champavati had found, and burned, the tree of immortality that gave the creature its incredible powers (see the raging fire at the upper right). This left the demon vulnerable, and Manohar took advantage of that to ultimately kill it.

In seeming contradiction to the drama unfolding around her, Champavati stands under a tree, appearing relaxed and detached. She holds a branch, adopting the form of a *shalabhanjika*, an ancient nature divinity representing female regenerative powers, which has a long history in Indian art. A delicately painted rocky outcrop with birds and trees (upper left) appears to match with Champavati's mood and contrasts with the vignettes of violence and destruction of the defeated demon and the raging fire.

The *Gulshan-i Ishq* romance was written in Deccani Urdu (a local dialect of southern India) by the poet Nusrati, who was active at the Bijapur court of Sultan Ali Adil Shah II (reigned 1656–1672). The story is based on the north Indian sixteenth-century Sufi romance *Madhumalati*, and Nusrati's new composition dates to 1567. This text was popular in the Deccan during the eighteenth century, and several illustrated manuscripts of the *Gulshan-i Ishq* are known.

—*QA*

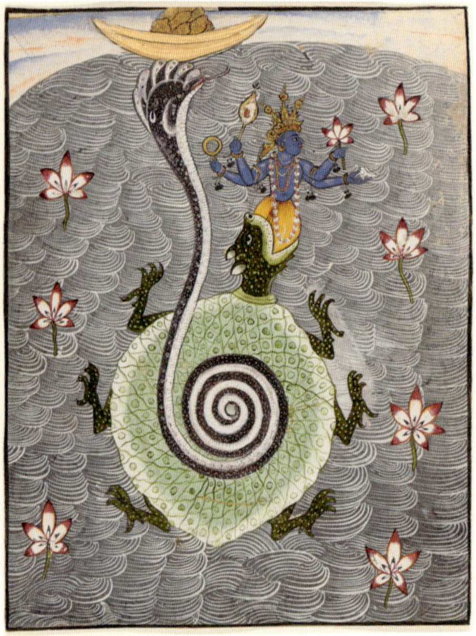

TORTOISE (KURMA) AVATAR OF VISHNU

approx. 1690

India; Rajasthan or central India

Opaque watercolor and gold on paper

H. 25.7 cm × W. 20 cm (image)

Museum purchase, Mortimer-Harvey Fund, 2016.127

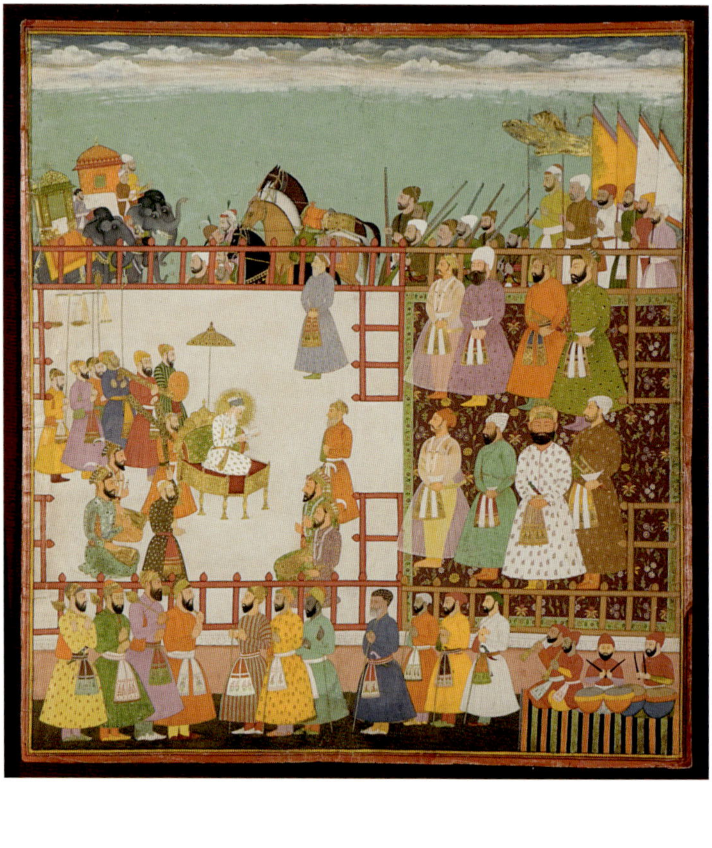

THE MUGHAL EMPEROR AURANGZEB HOLDING AUDIENCE

—

approx. 1710–1720

India; Udaipur, Rajasthan state, former kingdom of Mewar

Opaque watercolors and gold on paper

H. 55.8 cm × W. 52 cm (image)

Gift of the Connoisseurs' Council, 2006.4

—

In this painting, an aged king, dressed in white, sits on his throne, his bowed head framed by a halo. The sixth Mughal emperor Aurangzeb (ruled 1658–1707) was known for his pursuit of austerity. There is both frailty and power in this depiction; while the diminutive, white-haired king is near the end of his life, he is surrounded by enduring emblems of sacred and royal authority that draw on a number of traditions.

The retinue of men behind Aurangzeb hold peacock feathers whose use as emblems of royalty dates to the pre-Islamic Achaemenid Empire in Persia (553–330 BCE). The throne of Aurangzeb's father, Shah Jahan, was referred to as the "peacock throne" because of the jeweled peacocks that adorned it and invoked the celestial symbolism attached to the bird. One of the men behind Aurangzeb holds a scale that represents Mughal justice, and another holds the *khamsa* or "hand of Ali," a symbol found in many West Asian cultures and believed to ward off the influence of the evil eye. Another of Aurangzeb's attendants holds the trident associated with the Hindu god Shiva; this too is a protective symbol believed to possess the capacity to destroy evil. Aurangzeb is bent over a piece of paper with some writing on it that begins with *bismillah*, Arabic for "In the name of God."

This painting depicts Aurangzeb holding court in Mewar, a Hindu Rajput principality that had rebelled against him in 1680–1681 and supported his son, Prince Akbar, who had attempted to seize the throne from his father. Aurangzeb had subdued the rebellion and Mewar had surrendered to Mughal administration. It was the last of the powerful Rajput kingdoms to do so, and the Mewar rulers prided themselves on this.

In Indian popular culture, Aurangzeb is seen as a Muslim king who persecuted Hindus. This image of Aurangzeb comes from British colonial depictions of Mughal kings as either sectarian or syncretic; these images of kings were later adopted by Indian nationalists, themselves the products of British education. However, Mughal-Rajput relations cannot simply be seen through a Muslim/Hindu division. The Mewar Rajputs, for instance, collaborated with Prince Akbar, and many Rajput-Mughal alliances brought about mutual gain. This painting reveals how the sacred power of the king drew on the symbolism of multiple traditions, all of which enriched an empire that was a composite rather than a monolithic entity.

—Taymiya R. Zaman is an associate professor in the Department of History at the University of San Francisco

KRISHNA ATTEMPTS TO PLACATE HIS ANNOYED BELOVED RADHA

—

approx. 1720–1730

India, Andhra Pradesh state

Opaque watercolors and gold on paper

H. 26 cm × W. 16 cm (image); H. 27.5 cm × W. 19.4 cm (overall)

Acquisition made possible by the George Hopper Fitch Bequest, 2016.121

—

An inscription on the back specifies the subject of this painting: "The Lord is placating the cross Radha." The lord referred to is the great Hindu deity Krishna, and Radha is his mortal beloved. One of the important texts on the loves of Krishna is the Gitagovinda of the twelfth-century poet Jayadeva. These intensely emotional and erotic poems (sometimes interpreted allegorically) were, by the sixteenth century, widely known in southern India as well as in the poet's homeland of eastern India. The poems treat the complicated love relationship of Krishna and Radha. She often feels angered by Krishna's flirting and lovemaking with other young women. He uses every means to assure her of his love and soothe her hurt feelings. For example, the poet has Radha say,

Dark Krishna...
How can you deceive a faithful creature tortured by fevers of Love?
Damn you, Keshava! [Krishna]...
Don't plead your lies with me!
Later Krishna responds, as he might be doing in this painting,
Your useless silence tortures me, frail Radha.
Sing sweet lyrics in the mode of love!
Tender girl, destroy my pain with your eyes!
Beautiful Radha, don't be indifferent!
Don't elude me! I am deeply devoted to you.
Lovely fool, I am here as your lover.[8]

This striking painting, with its vigorously outlined and shaded volumes, combines boldness and delicacy. The bodies and other forms have a real sense of physical presence, while details such as the nearly transparent drapery falling from the female figure's leg or the pale blue garlands hanging between bright white ones have a subtle, diaphanous quality.

Recent research suggests that this painting and several related groups of paintings were created in the town of Tirupati in the southern Indian state of Andhra Pradesh. The painting traditions of southern India, often characterized by figures with full, emphatically modeled bodies, strong facial features, and large, rounded eyes, are less well known than those of the north, and southern paintings are much less numerous in museum collections.

—*FMcG*

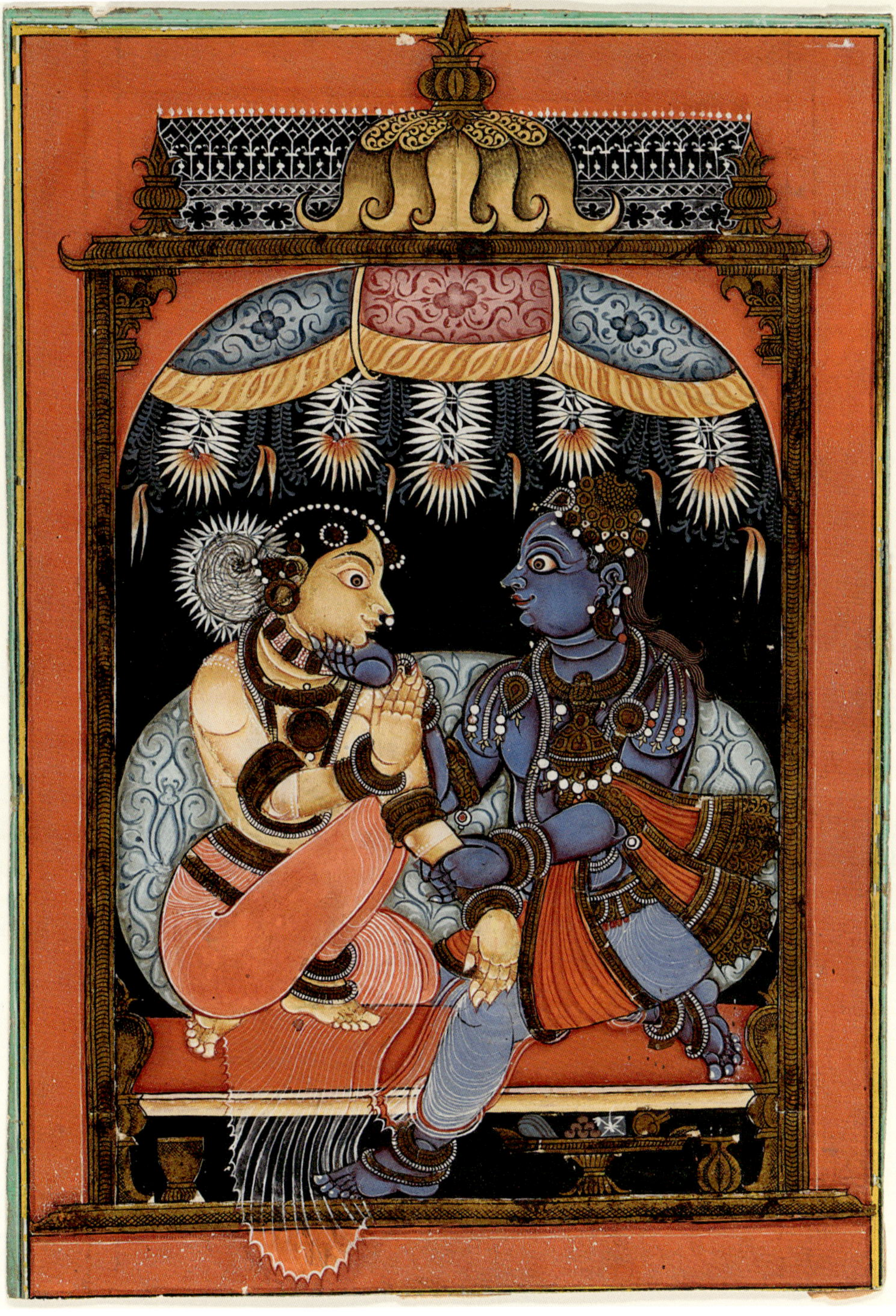

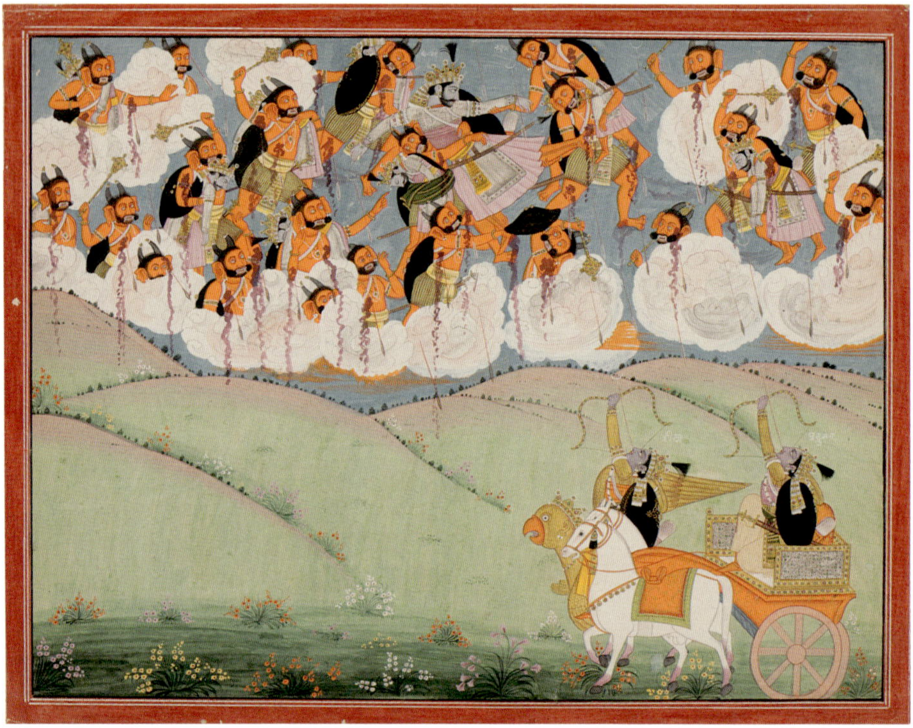

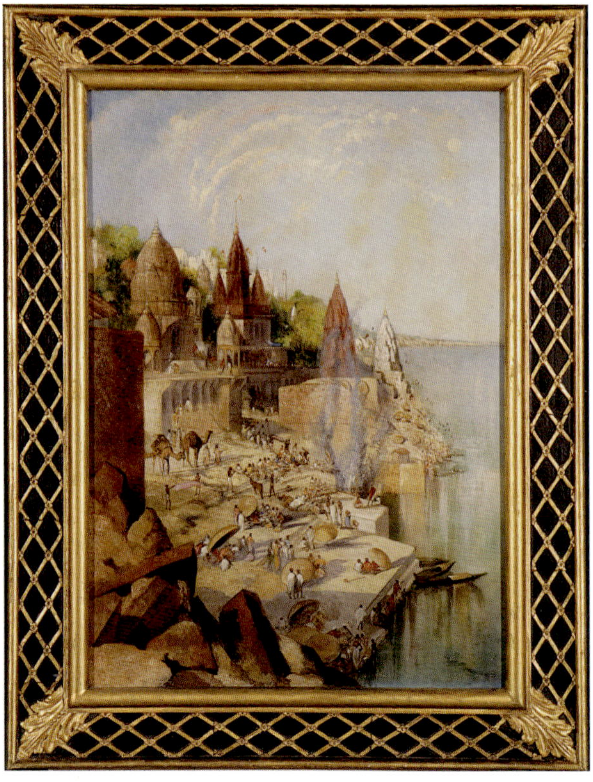

KRISHNA AND PRADYUMNA RESCUE ARJUNA, FROM A HARIVAMSHA MANUSCRIPT

—

approx. 1820

India; Kangra or Guler, Punjab Hills

Opaque watercolors and gold on paper

H. 36.8 cm × W. 47.3 cm

Acquisition made possible by the George Hopper Fitch Bequest, 2013.1

—

This painting comes from a manuscript of the Hindu religious text Harivamsha (Lineage of Hari [Vishnu]), an appendix to the Sanskrit epic Mahabharata. Among its other subjects, the text describes events from the life of Krishna, an incarnation (avatara) of the god Vishnu and a key figure in the Mahabharata. Krishna is identifiable, at bottom left, as the blue-skinned figure riding on his part-bird, part-human mount, Garuda. In this episode of the story, he is in the role of a fearless warrior and savior who rescues the brave Arjuna (the Mahabharata's hero and an incomparably skilled archer) from the clutches of a demon. Demons are typically no obstacle for Krishna, but Nikumbha here poses a problem: the demon can continually multiply himself, making it nearly impossible to defeat him. The odds appear to be stacked against Krishna and his son, Pradyumna (shown here riding on a chariot behind Krishna).

The painting captures the demon's rampage and the challenge that Krishna and Pradyumna face. The artist conveys here the story's action, tension, and successive moments in narrative time. To use a modern analogy, this painting appears to be a film scene unfolding in slow motion. The pink-robed Arjuna is shown nine times in the sky as he is manhandled by the bleeding demon, who we see twenty-three times. The story's psychological drama is enhanced by the use of color and landscape features contrasting the peaceful earthly zone with the chaotic heavenly realm. Amid all this tension, Krishna's skill and composure is expressed through his determined pose and expression. The viewer will have no doubt about who will emerge in control of the situation.

In Indian (Hindu, Buddhist, and Jain) traditions, books were typically not bound. Instead, individual pages of a text were gathered between wooden covers and protected by cloth wrappings. This page would have been one of more than a hundred that originally comprised the manuscript.

—*QA*

CREMATION GHAT AT BENARES (VARANASI)

—

1861

George Landseer (British, 1834–1878)

India

Oil on canvas

H. 59.1 cm × W. 42.2 cm (image)

From the Collection of William K. Ehrenfeld, M.D., 2005.64.194

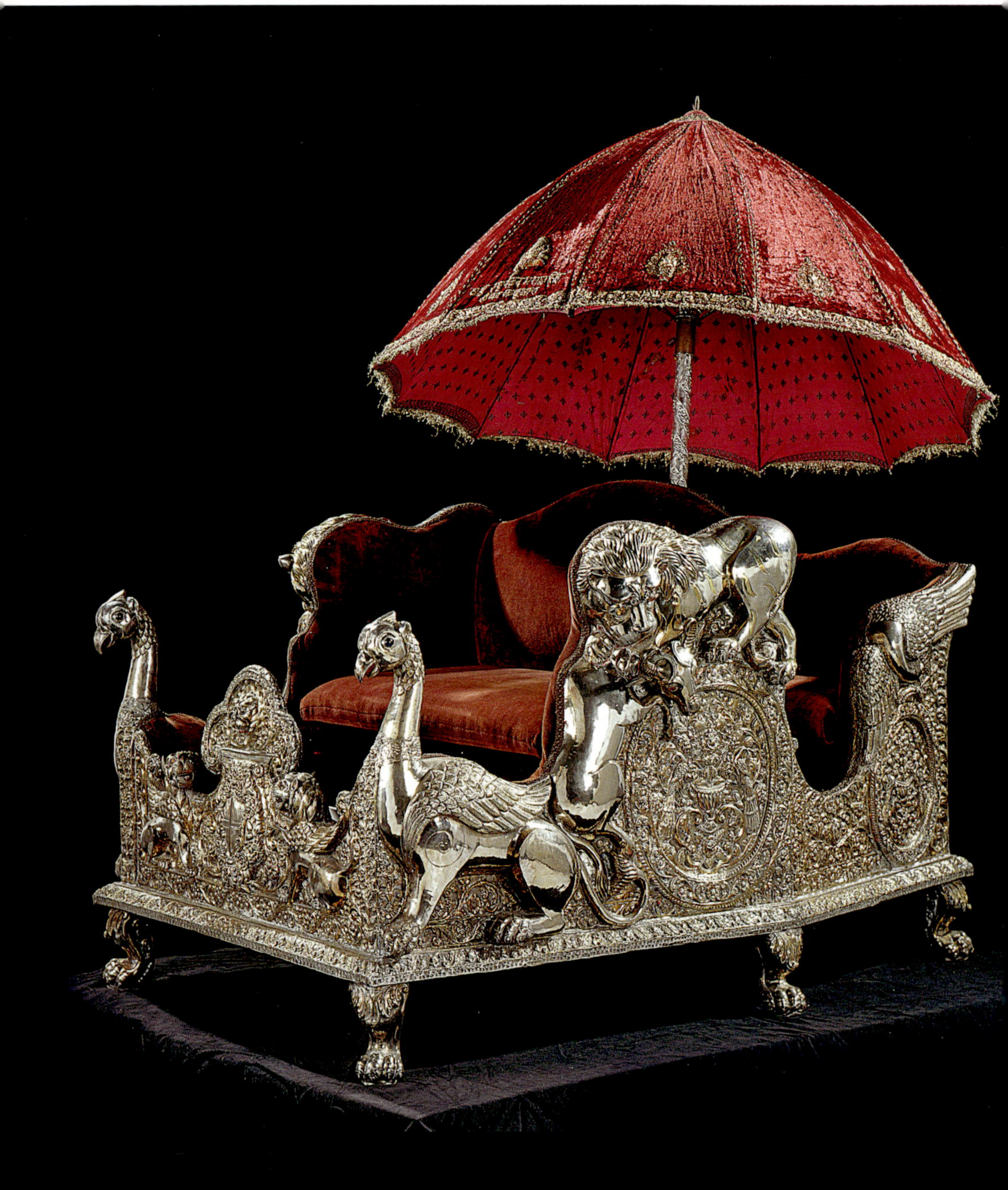

ELEPHANT THRONE (HOWDAH)

approx. 1895–1920
India; perhaps Chhattisgarh state, former princely state of Surguja
Wood with partially gilded and painted silver, velvet, and wicker
H. 177.8 cm × W. 125 cm × D. 159.4 cm (including parasol)
Acquisition made possible by Nancy B. Hamon in honor of Johnson S. Bogart, 2001.12.a-.c

Elephants, indigenous to India, were closely associated with kingship in South Asia and carried many kings through battles, hunts, and ceremonial processions. While a single rider could mount a bare-backed elephant, a box-seat (howdah) strapped onto the animal's back provided a more comfortable ride for multiple passengers. The expensive material (gilded sheets of silver) and elaborate decoration of this elephant seat indicate that it was made for a royal patron.

The decorative motifs here combine Europeanized designs with local imagery, reflecting the tastes of many Indian patrons during the colonial period. The coat of arms on its front and flower-filled urns on its sides, for example, are European in style. The lions, peacocks, and hunting scenes (seen on the sides, in the medallions, and on the back of the howdah) have a long history in the Indian artistic repertoire. The designs probably came from pattern books, and it is likely that this howdah was made at a workshop that specialized in custom-designed luxury furnishings.

Together, the materials and decoration of this howdah make it a splendid statement of royal luxury, which is ironic for a work produced during India's colonial period. After 1858, when India became a colony of the British Empire, Indian rulers were incorporated into an uneasy and complex system of governance. They lost their autonomy and instead became "princes" under the authority of Queen Victoria of England and her successors. In such a context, public displays of kingship by Indian royalty—such as impressive elephant processions—took on more complicated overtones. Elaborate ceremonies allowed Indian rulers to visibly assert their legitimacy and to maintain dynastic traditions, but they were also reminders of a now-lost glorious past.

—*QA*

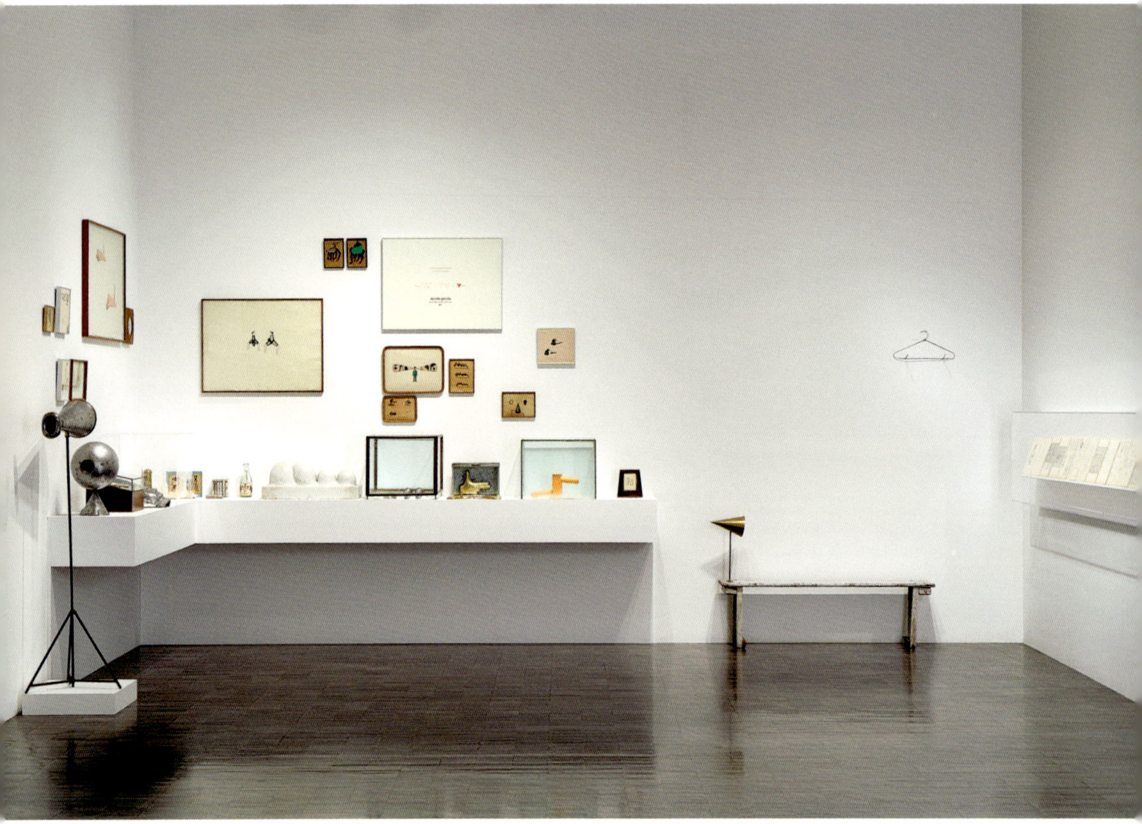

MUSEUM SHOP OF FETISH OBJECTS

2012

By Shreyas Karle (Indian, b. 1981)

Mixed media installation

Dimensions variable

Museum purchase, 2015.41.1-.32

Shreyas Karle's *Museum Shop of Fetish Objects* is a mixed-media installation designed to mimic a museum exhibition comprising three-dimensional objects, framed drawings, and prints. This work was originally exhibited at the National Gallery of Modern Art in Mumbai as part of the 2012 exhibition *Project Cinema City* to mark the centennial of Indian cinema. In this piece, Karle explores themes of melodrama, love, sex, religious devotion, and unbridled machismo common to Indian cinema, especially the popular movies of Bollywood. He does this in an oblique way by creating fantastical, satirical, witty, and absurd objects and drawings, composed of poor materials that appear in less-than-pristine condition.

In this work, as in much of the artist's oeuvre, Karle relies on tongue-in-cheek cultural and visual puns and an unspoken connection to Dadaism and the surreal. The objects in the installation include a milk bottle with a label that reads "*ma ka doodh*" ("mother's milk"), an allusion to Bollywood film dialogues where macho heroes refer to drinking mother's milk as a source of their strength and kindheartedness. The sculptural elements are diverse but consistently ambiguous: a "multireligious" brass pendant depicting the silhouettes of a church spire, a temple tower, and a mosque dome; a pair of spectacles made from conical *kulfi* ice cream molds; and a silicone "he-she object" and accompanying illustrations of its use for male and female pleasure.

—*KGO*

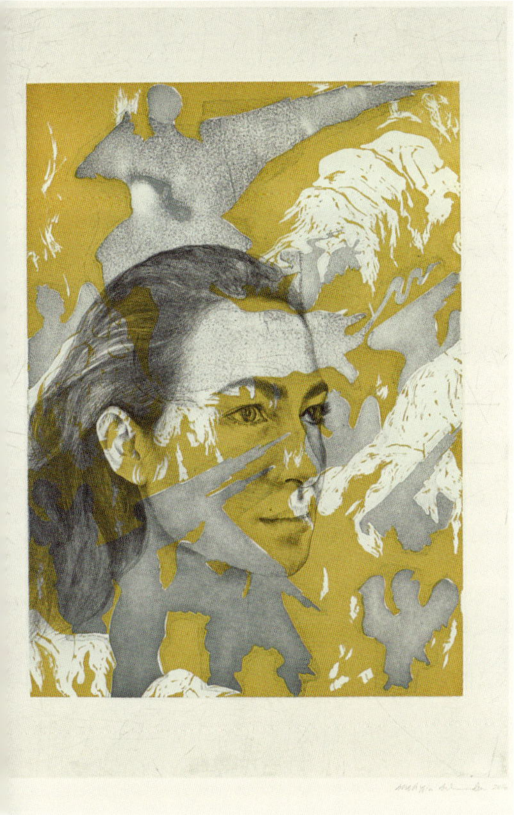

PORTRAIT OF THE ARTIST

—

2016

By Shahzia Sikander (American, b. Pakistan, 1969) and Ayad Akhtar (American, b. 1970)

Suite of four etchings and one text; ink and colors on paper

Etchings: H. 56.2 cm × W. 43.2 cm (each image); text: H. 56.2 cm × W. 43.2 cm

Museum purchase, 2016.171.1-.5

—

Shahzia Sikander, an artist who lives and works in New York, explored how the creative process is both exciting and intimidating in a collaboration with the poet, playwright, and novelist Ayad Akhtar. In this suite of four etchings, entitled *Portrait of the Artist* in a nod to James Joyce, Sikander blends portraiture of herself and Akhtar with imagery related to the Mi'raj—the mystical night journey of the Prophet Muhammad. The Mi'raj recounts the journey from the Great Mosque in Mecca to the Temple Mount in Jerusalem and the Prophet's ascension to heaven for an encounter with God. Variously interpreted as literal or metaphorical, the Mi'raj is a powerful theme in Islamic art and literature. For Sikander and Akhtar, this mystical journey is an important touchstone for artistic imagination. Akhtar expresses this idea in his text:

> For what else is Mi'raj if not the fulfillment of any artist's deepest longing: to have made a journey into the great unknown—to have seen the unseeable—and to return to the world as we know it with the capacity to express the inexpressible?

Sikander draws on imagery from Central Asian, Persian, and Indian miniature painting in her art. These visual quotations—seen in the silhouetted white figure of Muhammad on the mythical winged creature Buraq, in the Archangel Gabriel, and in the celestial beings (*peris*)—are inspired by historical Mi'raj paintings in the collections of the British Library and the Topkapı Palace Museum. Sikander's imagery also references eminent literary sources. The illustrated manuscripts of the *Khamsa* by twelfth-century Persian poet Nizami, the fifteenth-century Persian *Mi'rajnama*, and Qur'anic literary traditions all play a role for Akhtar and Sikander, as do Ernest Hemingway's *The Sun Also Rises* and James Joyce's *A Portrait of the Artist as a Young Man*.

—KGO and QA

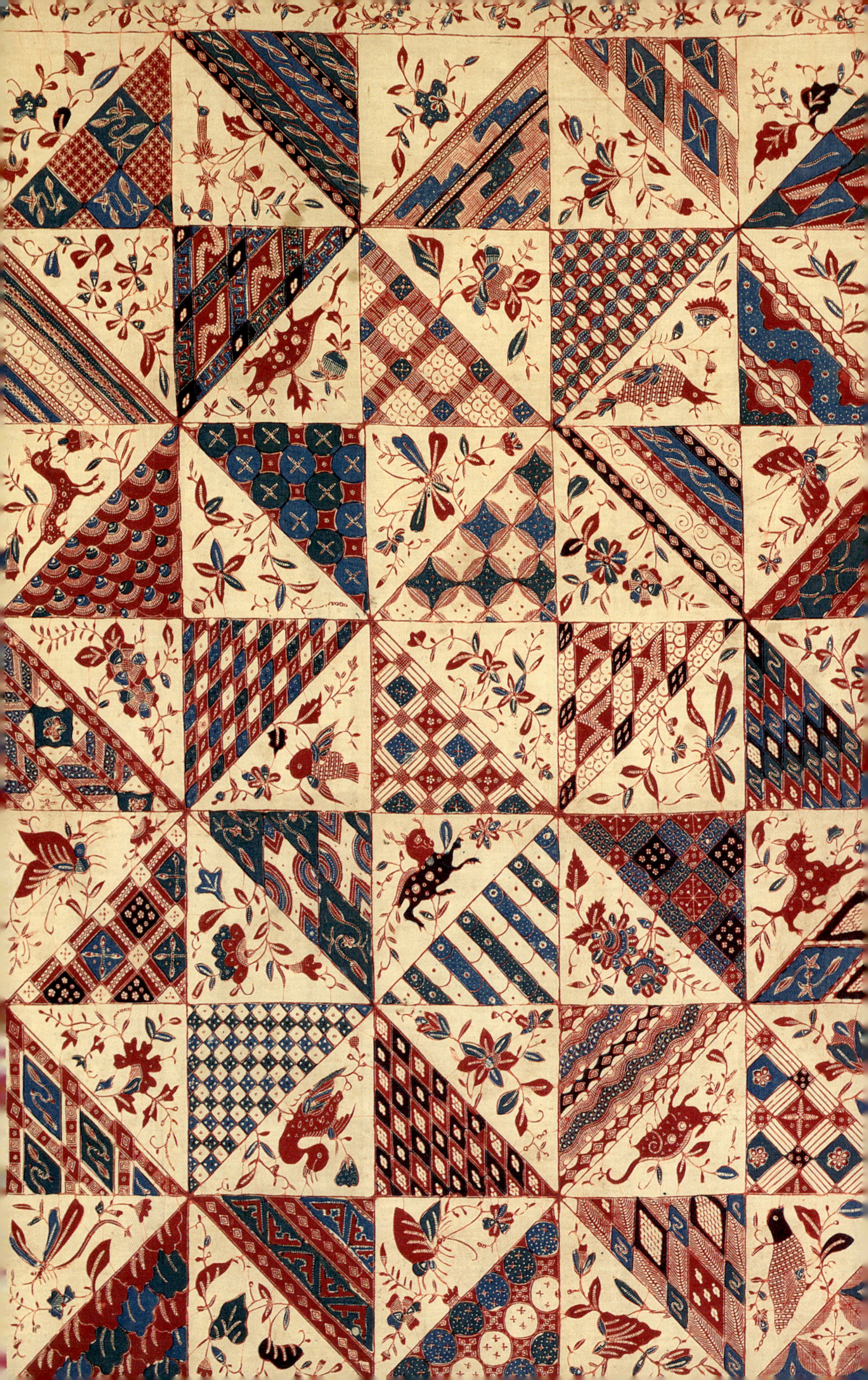

SOUTHEAST ASIA

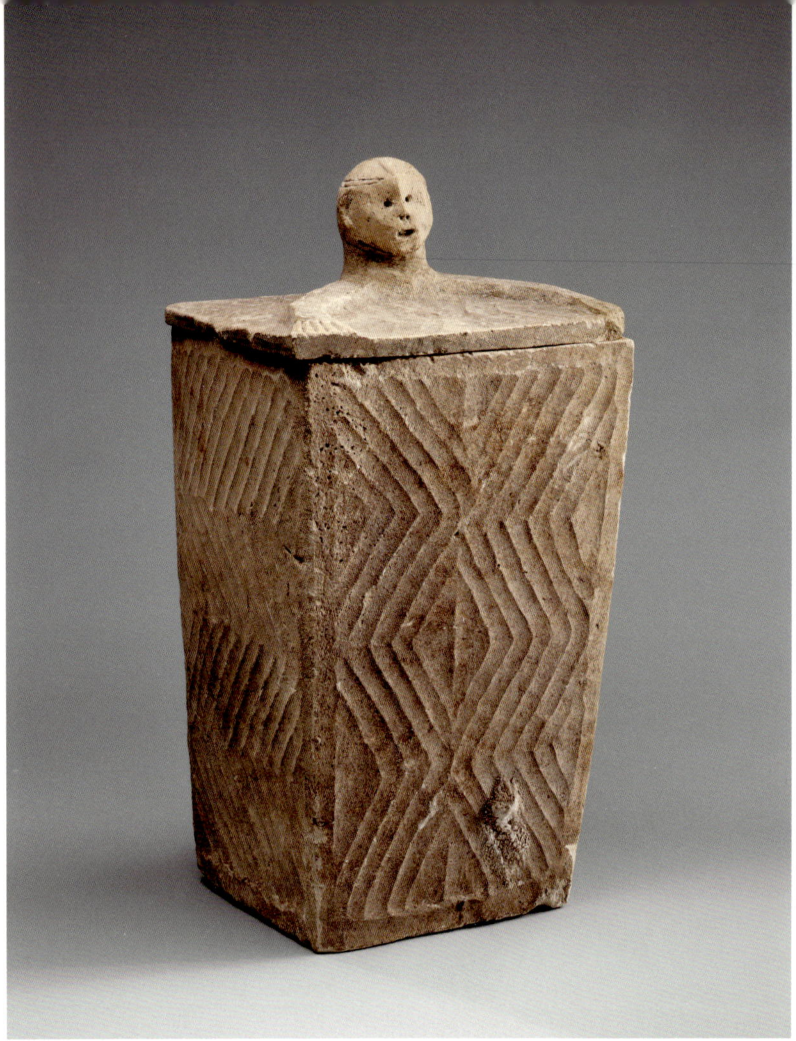

BURIAL URN

approx. 600
Philippines; Mindanao
Limestone
H. 71.1 cm × W. 33 cm × D. 33 cm
Gift of Marion Greene, 1991.323.1

The head of a lone figure peeks out from this limestone container, his flattened arms resting on the lid. Who is it? We don't know. We do know that human bones probably once were stored in this urn, discovered in a cave in Cotabato province of Mindanao in the southern Philippines. The rather small size of the jar suggests that only the bones of the deceased were placed within; the body had decomposed during an initial burial in the ground. This is part of a long-standing tradition of secondary burials found in ancient societies throughout Southeast Asia. A tradition of jar burials existed in the Philippines from the early Neolithic period around 1000 BCE and continues in some parts of Southeast Asia to the present day.

Philippine burial urns generally come in two shapes: circular or square in section. Typically, they are adorned with simple motifs such as zigzag, diamond, and other geometric patterns. A common decoration on the lid is a three-dimensional human head and arms. In this example, the face is quite detailed. The eyes and nostrils were drilled. The headband with a triangular element above the forehead may have indicated the status of the deceased.

—*NR*

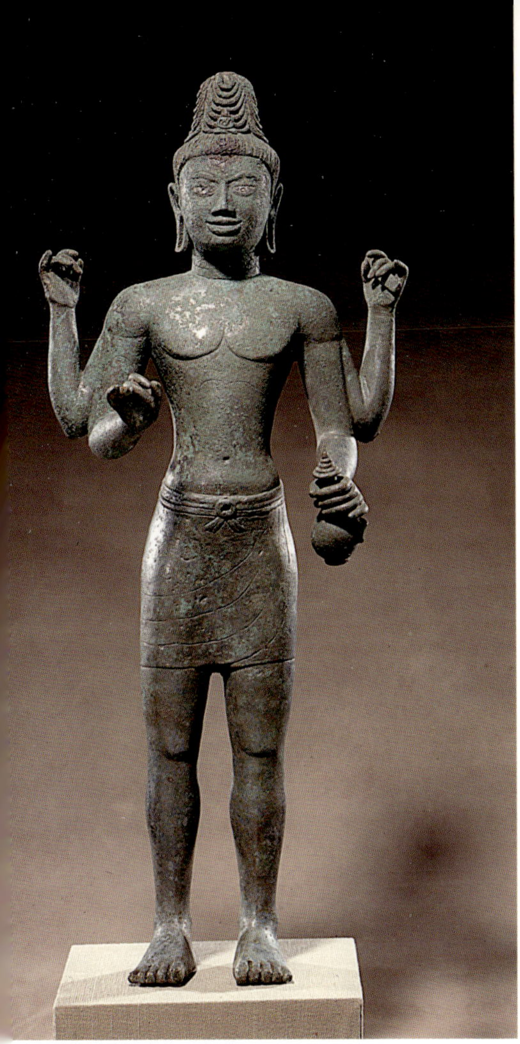

THE BODHISATTVA AVALOKITESHVARA

approx. 675–725

Thailand; Plai Bat Hill, Buriram province

Bronze

H. 69.9 cm × W. 29.2 cm × D. 14.6 cm

The Avery Brundage Collection, B65B57

In 1964 a group of stunning bronze Buddhist sculptures was discovered at a mysterious location in northeastern Thailand that was at first identified as "Prakhon Chai." It was not until 2002 that the actual find spot, Plai Bat Hill, was made known by the scholar who had written the first substantial article on the sculptures. The group largely consisted of standing images of bodhisattvas, but Buddha images were included as well. The styles suggest that some of the sculptures were two centuries older than others. No one knows why they were buried together, and there is little evidence about the ethnicity or language of the people who made them.

Shortly after the discovery, Avery Brundage, the Asian Art Museum's founding donor, acquired this and four other figures from the group from a dealer in London. Scholars believe this to be the earliest of the larger sculptures from the site, based on certain features: its square stance, somewhat severe facial features, sharp definition of the chest muscles, and hairdress of loosely looped braids.

This figure can be identified as the bodhisattva Avalokiteshvara by the small Buddha image at the front of the hairdress.

—*FMcG*

THE BUDDHIST DEITY CHUNDA IN HER SIXTEEN-ARMED FORM

800–1000

Indonesia; Central Java

Bronze

H. 22.5 cm × W. 14 cm × D. 9.2 cm

Gift of Dr. and Mrs. David Buchanan, 2006.48.a-.c

Here Chunda, a Buddhist goddess of wisdom, sits with two of her hands in the gesture of turning the wheel of the Buddha's doctrine. Her fourteen other hands hold many of her characteristic symbolic implements, including an ax, a discus, a conch, a water vessel, and a palm-leaf book. Multiarmed deities like this one indicate the popularity of esoteric Buddhism in Indonesia from the late 800s.

Buddhism flourished in Central Java from the late 700s to the early 900s. This period was marked by the construction of dozens of small temples as well as elaborate world-famous monuments like Borobudur. During this era bronze images of Buddhas and bodhisattvas were produced in great numbers.
—*NR*

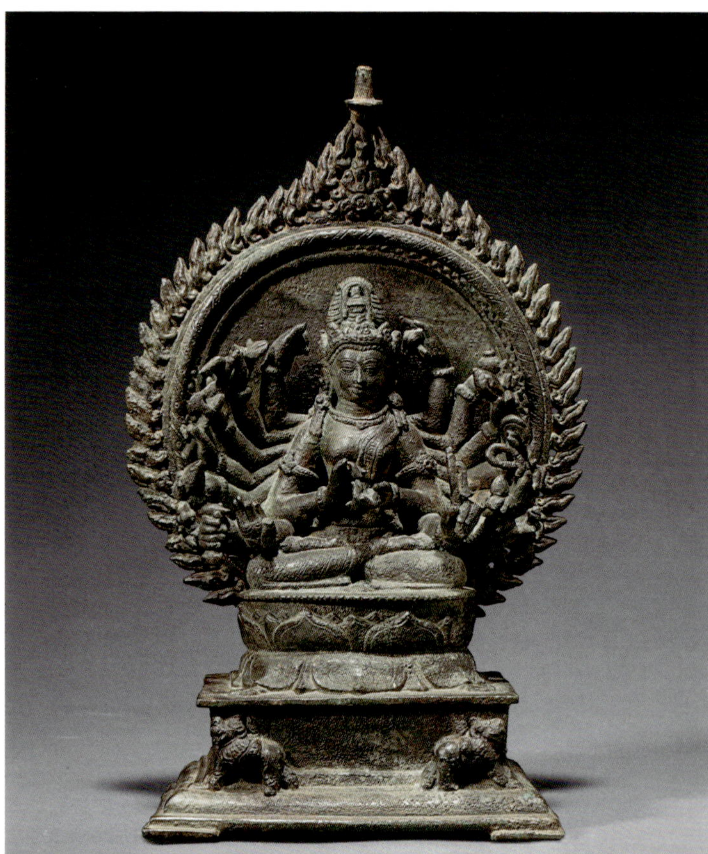

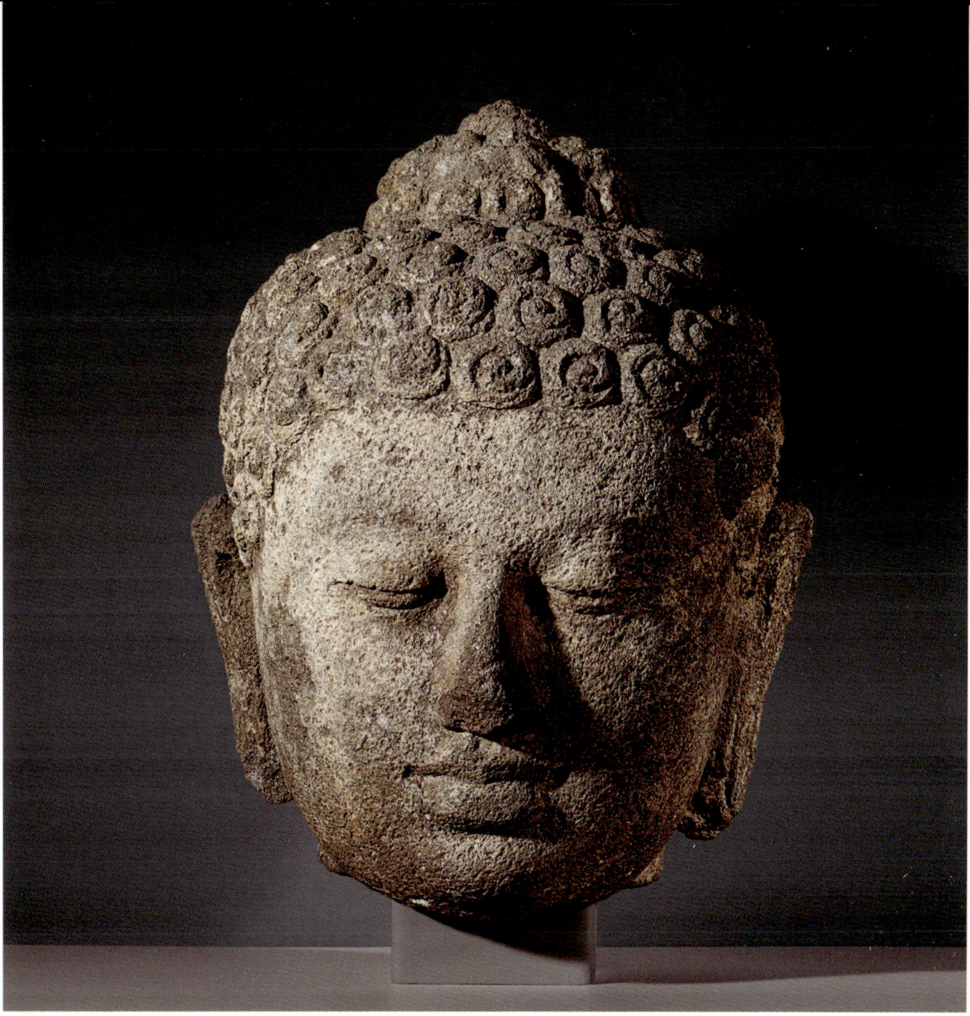

HEAD OF A BUDDHA IMAGE

800–850

Indonesia; Borobudur, Central Java

Stone

H. 31.8 cm × W. 25.4 cm × D. 22.9 cm

The Avery Brundage Collection, B60S379

This stone head bears the recognizable marks of a Buddha: a protuberance on the top of the head, a small circular dot on the forehead, and a monk's shorn hair grown back in tight curls.

The monument from which this head may have come, Borobudur, is one of the largest and most complex surviving monuments of the Buddhist world. It is a massive step pyramid with five square levels surmounted by three circular ones. The circular levels support seventy-two small stupas, and a large stupa crowns the entire structure. In niches along the square levels, and inside the small stupas, were a total of 504 seated Buddha images, with heads much like this one.

—*NR*

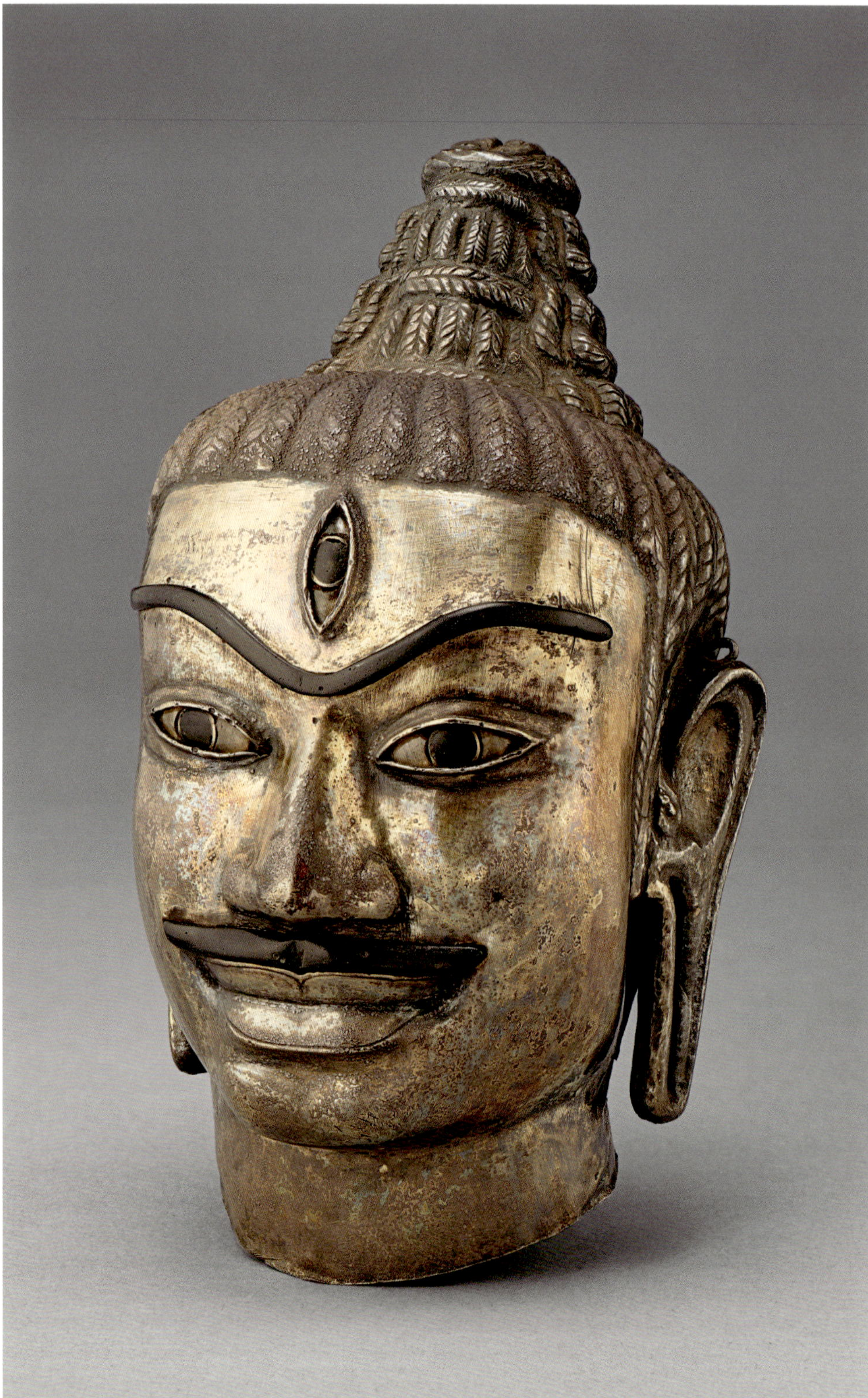

HEAD OF SHIVA, FROM A LINGA COVER

approx. 800

Central or southern Vietnam; former kingdoms of Champa

Gold and silver alloy with gold, glass, and ebony

H. 11.4 cm × W. 6.4 cm × D. 7.6 cm

Gift of the Christensen Fund, BL77B1

The Hindu deity Shiva was sometimes represented in human form, and sometimes as a cylindrical emblem called a linga. A linga was usually a sort of stone pillar, sometimes with a removable metal covering or sheath. This head would originally have been attached to such a covering and would have given the linga the appearance of having a head on one side. An earlier Indian stone linga with a head is shown on page 25.

For more than five hundred years small kingdoms or principalities of the Cham people flourished along the coast of what is now central and southern Vietnam, building impressive Hindu and Buddhist temples. Their artists and artisans created sculpture and luxury objects of stone, bronze, and precious metals, as well as, no doubt, of perishable materials that have not survived. This head, painstakingly formed of sheets of an alloy of almost equal parts gold and silver and inlaid with glass and other materials to increase its vividness, exemplifies Cham metal sculpture at its most technically refined and expressively powerful.

—*FMcG*

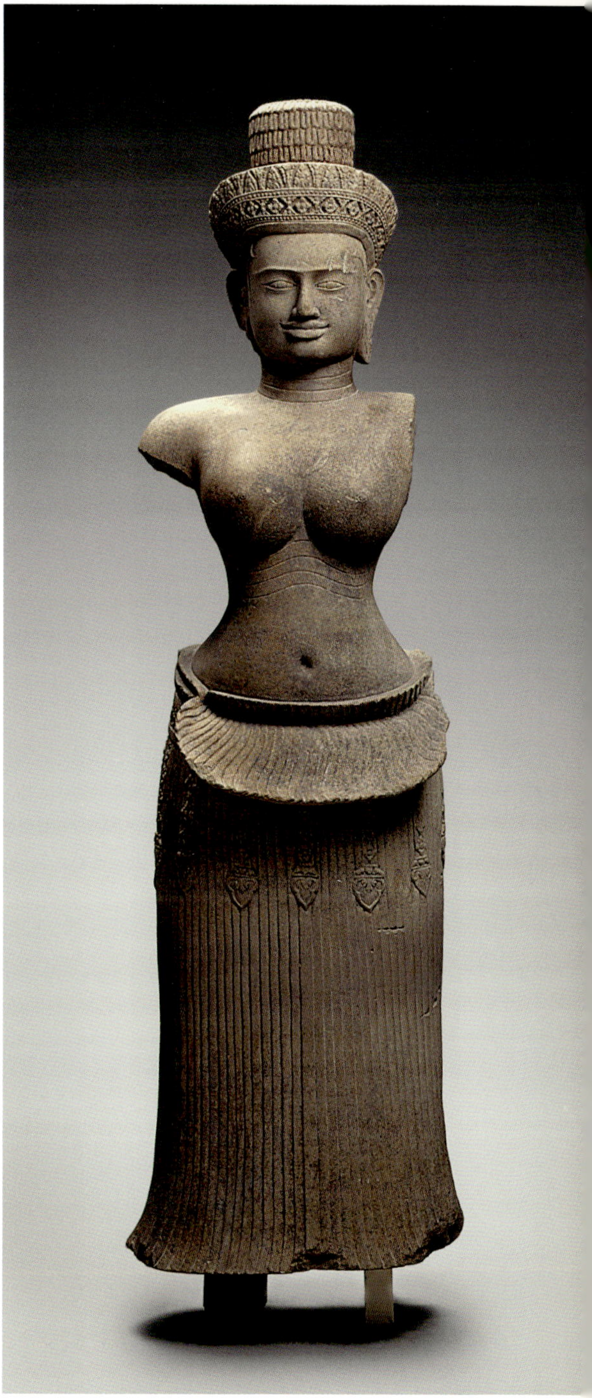

FEMALE HINDU DEITY

approx. 890–925

Cambodia, former kingdom of Angkor

Sandstone

H. 132.1 cm × W. 29.5 cm × D. 22.9 cm

Museum purchase with additional funding from G.F. Jewett, Jr. and family, B68S19

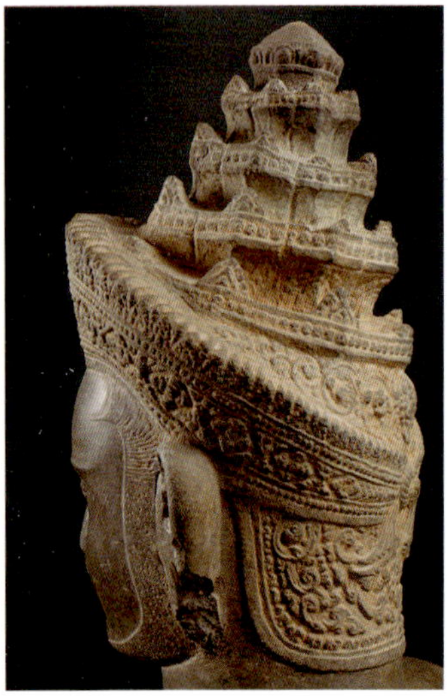

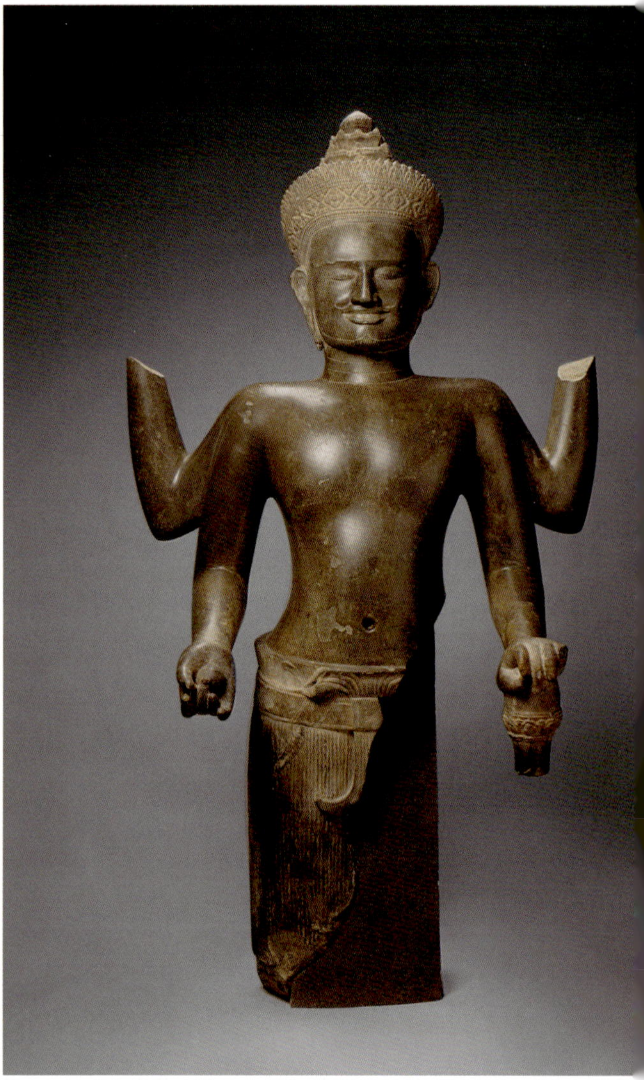

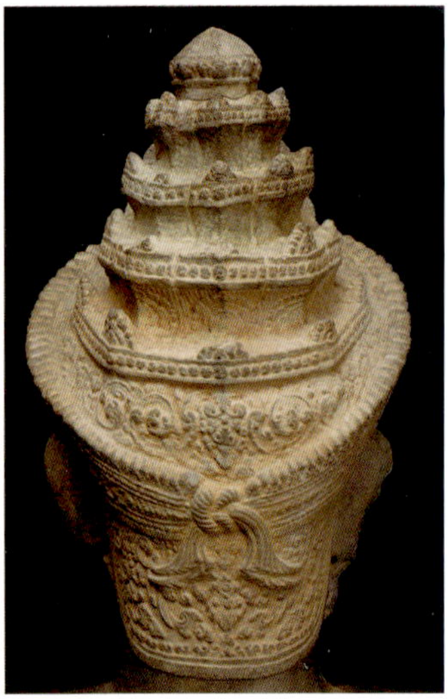

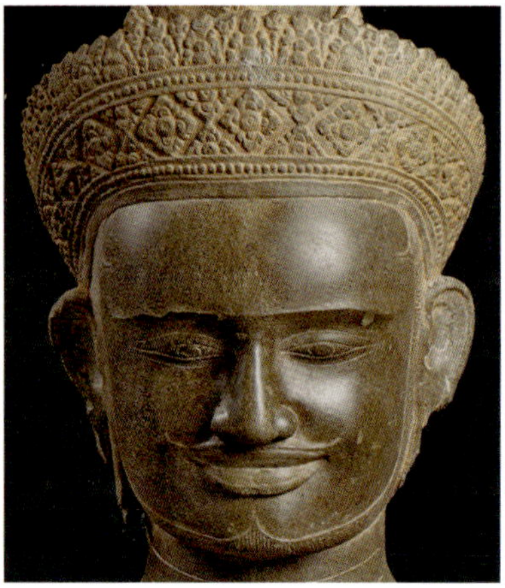

MASTERPIECE

THE HINDU DEITY VISHNU

940–965
Cambodia; former kingdom of Angkor
Sandstone
H. 142.2 cm × W. 83.8 cm × D. 48.3 cm
The Avery Brundage Collection, B65S7

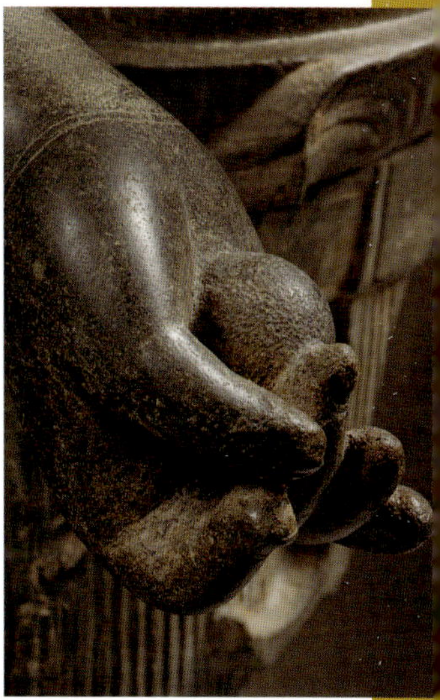

> *Victorious is Vishnu, whose four arms carry the disk, the earth, the conch, and the club as the four guardians of the cardinal directions.... Homage to this supreme soul...whose triple voices proclaim the Supreme and Imperishable. May Vishnu grant prosperity to all creatures.*[1]

This passage from a tenth-century inscription (contemporary with this sculpture) from the great kingdom of Angkor suggests the importance of the major Hindu deity Vishnu in ancient Cambodia.

The sculpture can be identified as Vishnu by its crown, its four arms, and the remains of the attributes it carried. In its surviving right hand is a round shape representing the earth; its left hand rests on the handle of a club symbolizing might in battle, the shaft of which has broken away. The missing attributes—the war discus, associated with the sun, and the conch shell, associated with the world's waters—would have emphasized how encompasses fundamental natural forces.

Vishnu (together with one of his incarnations, the princely hero Rama) was often associated both in India and Southeast Asia with powerful, righteous kingship. Such a large, imposing, and meticulously crafted image as this would have been commissioned from the royal workshop and would have been enshrined in a temple under court patronage. Two centuries later, a king of Angkor who associated himself with Vishnu built the world's largest temple dedicated to Vishnu, the monumental Angkor Wat.

The style of this sculpture is slightly old-fashioned for its period. Royally sponsored sculptures of the Angkor kingdom were often a bit conservative in style. A hundred years ago the development of ancient Cambodian sculpture was not at all well understood, and dating sculptures was difficult. Few works had inscribed dates or could be firmly associated with the dates of historical events. Over many decades, French scholars studied the smallest details of crowns, garments, and other features of sculptures and eventually succeeded in working out how such details evolved from one period to the next. As a result, it is now usually possible to determine the period of a particular sculpture with some confidence, although the preference of some ancient patrons for new sculptures in old-fashioned styles sometimes clouds the picture.

—*FMcG*

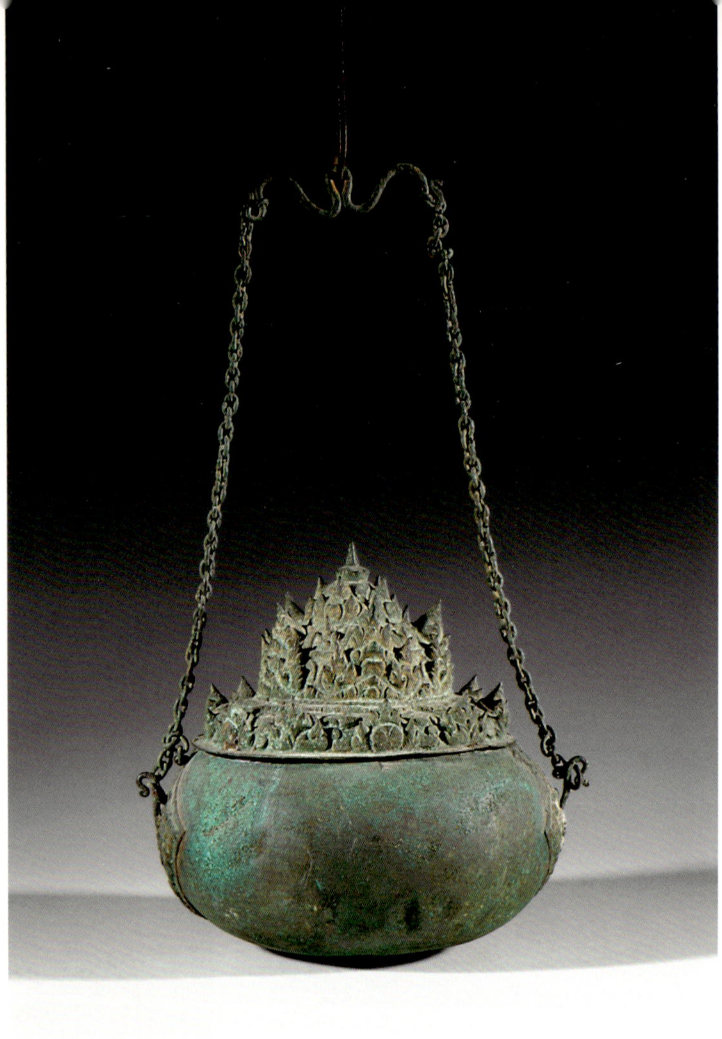

HANGING CONTAINER WITH MOUNTAIN-SHAPED LID

1000–1500

Indonesia; East Java

Bronze

H. 20.3 cm × Diam. 17.8 cm

Gift of Mr. Johnson S. Bogart, 2010.348.a-.b

On the lid of this hanging container, concentric circles of lotus petals and buds form a shape resembling mountains surrounding a central peak. This balanced, symmetrical motif may depict Mount Meru. In both Buddhist and Hindu mythology, this sacred mountain is considered the center of the universe, surrounded by rings of mountains and oceans.

Several containers of this type have been found in Eastern Java. It is thought that they may have contained holy water, a substance necessary for religious rituals. In Bali today holy water is an essential element of ritual worship, both at home and in the temple.

—*NR*

THE GIANT KUMBHAKARNA BATTLES THE MONKEYS, FROM THE RAMAYANA

—

approx. 1075–1125

Northeastern Thailand; former kingdom of Angkor

Sandstone

H. 88.9 cm × W. 188 cm × D. 15.2 cm

The Avery Brundage Collection, B66S7

—

> *Kumbhakarna wrought havoc upon the armies of the immensely powerful monkeys. As they were being slaughtered, those heroic monkeys fled. Seeing that the monkeys had broken ranks, the monkey general Angada said "Turn back, leaping monkeys! Stand fast! Let us fight!"*[2]

Stories from the Indian epic Ramayana have been familiar in Cambodia and other countries of Southeast Asia for well more than a thousand years.

Here is a scene from the later part of the story. The beloved wife of the hero Rama has been abducted by Ravana, the mighty king of the demons. Rama, together with his allies the monkeys, lays siege to rescue her. During the ensuing struggle, Ravana's giant brother Kumbhakarna (the largest figure) takes on the monkey warriors. They attack by the thousands, but for all their wrestling and biting and clawing they cannot overcome him. Kumbhakarna maims hundreds of monkeys and devours hundreds more. Some of the monkeys take fright and begin to run away, but the monkey prince Angada (shown here wearing a helmet-like crown) urges them to marshal their courage and resume the attack. They do so, and the carnage continues without resolution till Rama himself (possibly the figure with the head broken off at left) joins in and, using his most powerful weapons, is finally able to cut Kumbhakarna to pieces.

The unknown artists who created this relief were unusually skilled and effective in conveying the fury and confusion of a great battle. The relief would have been positioned over a door of a temple. The face and head of the central figure were entirely restored before this relief entered the Asian Art Museum's collection. The restored area has been toned dark to distinguish it from original areas.

—*FMcG*

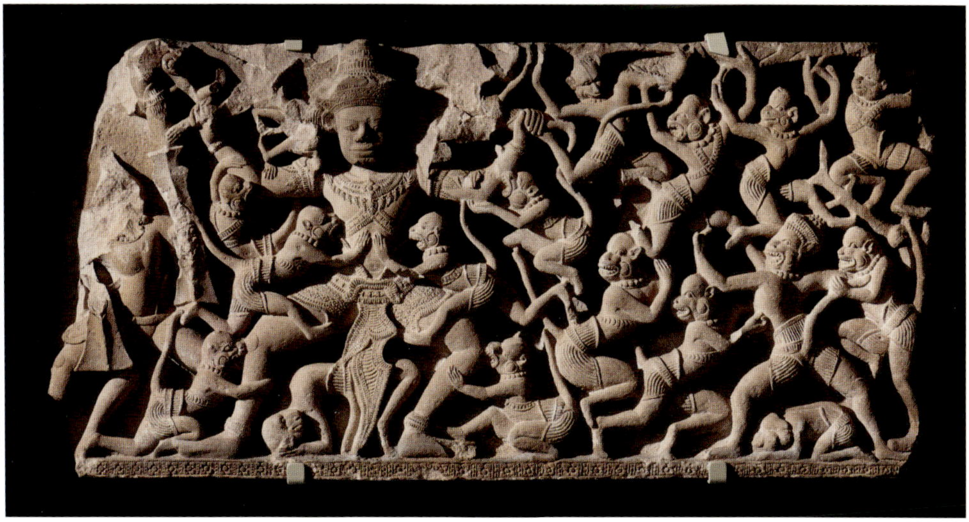

A MYTHICAL CREATURE WITH A WARRIOR IN ITS MOUTH, A WORSHIPING CELESTIAL, AND A FEMALE DANCER

approx. 1075–1125

Vietnam; Thu Thien temple, Binh Dinh province, former kingdoms of Champa

Sandstone

H. 94 cm × W. 100.3 cm × D. 19.7 cm; H. 57.2 cm × W. 34.3 cm × D. 38.1 cm;

H. 71.1 cm × W. 34.3 cm × D. 20.3 cm

Gift of the Christensen Fund, BL77S1, BL77S2, and BL77S3

These three sculptures were once attached to the sanctuary wall of a brick temple in the territories of Champa in today's Vietnam. Old photographs of the temple show how they were arranged, with this mythical creature and a mirroring one positioned to the right and left of a large shallow niche, with a dancer at the back of each creature. Above were arrayed a group of ten worshiping celestials. (The photo here matches, as closely as possible, the original placement.) Other sculptures from the ensemble are today in the collections of the Art Institute of Chicago and the Norton Simon Museum in Pasadena.

When a description of the temple was published in 1909 the large niche was empty and the main image of a deity was no longer in place. Because the rulers of Champa built both Hindu and Buddhist temples, it was not clear to which religion this temple belonged. Eventually, though, the likelihood that it was Buddhist was supported by the identification of a nearby stone Buddha image that probably once held the central place in the sanctuary.[3]

When the temple was in use the ensemble of sculptures behind the Buddha image—the paired mythical creatures supporting dancers and the group of worshiping celestials projecting from the wall above, all dimly lit in the shadowy space—must have been an imposing sight.

The people of Champa spoke a language related to Indonesian and were entirely distinct from the Vietnamese, against whom they struggled—ultimately unsuccessfully—for centuries. Their states declined and the construction of great temple complexes ceased. The people's culture changed too, as the old religions of Hinduism and Buddhism weakened and some of the Cham, like most of their Indonesian cousins, embraced Islam.

—*FMcG*

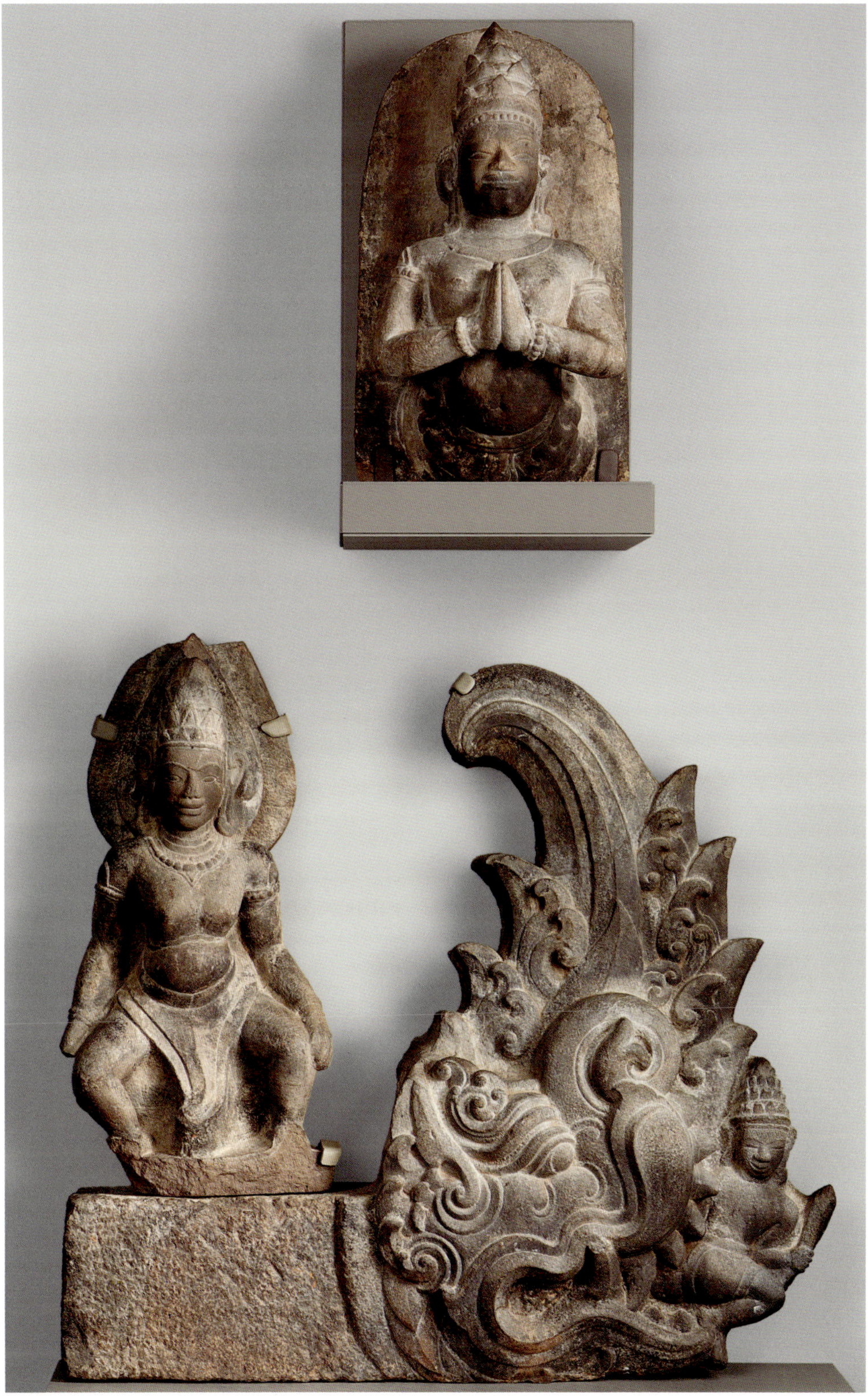

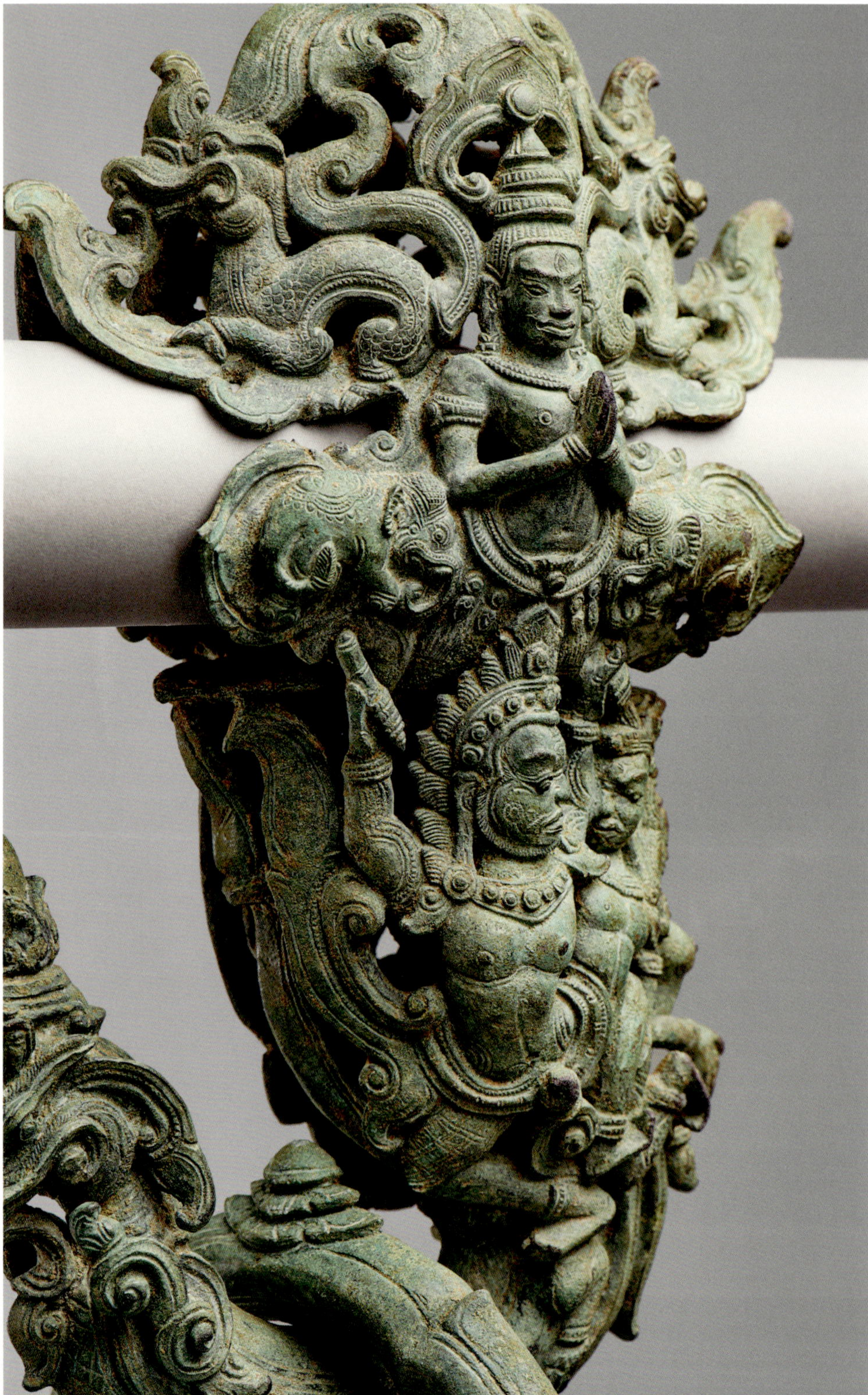

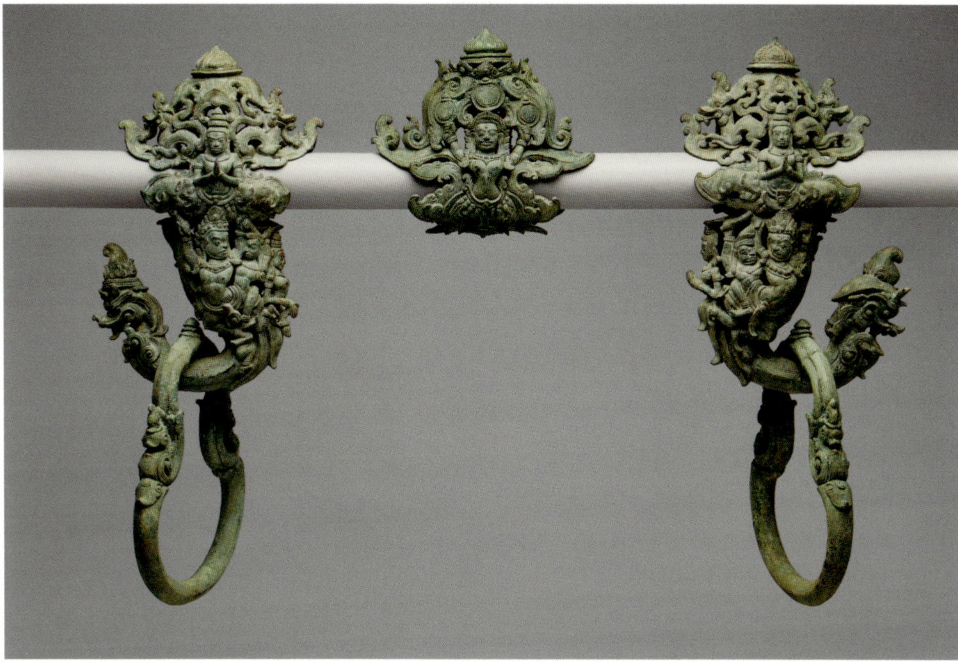

PALANQUIN FITTINGS

approx. 1200–1220

Cambodia

Bronze

L. 52.1 cm (one hook and ring overall)

Museum purchase, the Avery Brundage Collection, 1992.346.1-.5

These fittings decorated a palanquin, in this instance a sort of portable hammock, in which nobles of the ancient Angkor kingdom of Cambodia were carried from place to place by bearers. The hooks and rings were attached to a pole, and the hammock was hung from them. The central fitting had no function other than ornament.

A Chinese envoy to Angkor in 1296–1297 wrote:

> Palanquins are made of pieces of wood that bend in the middle and point upward at either end. They are carved with floral designs and girdled with gold or silver.... One foot down from each end of the palanquin pole is a hook nailed into the wood. A large cloth is tied to the hooks with a rope. A person sits in the cloth and is carried by two people, one at either end.

The elaborateness of palanquin fittings was governed by the status of the noble. According to the Chinese envoy,

> The insignia and retinues of these officials vary by rank. The most senior are those with a palanquin with gold poles and four parasols with gold handles. Next in rank are those that have a palanquin with gold poles and two gold-handled parasols [and so on].[4]

The hooks are decorated with figures locked in intense combat. One figure holds a short weapon in one hand and grasps another figure's hair with the other. The outer tip of each hook is adorned with an elaborate serpent head. On the upper part is a figure with hands in a gesture of worship, flanked by a pair of elephants. On top are dragons and cloud-like motifs reminiscent of those in Chinese art.

The central fitting is decorated with similarly ornate cloud-like motifs. A female mythical figure holds round implements, probably mirrors, in each hand. It is possible that this figure is related to the Chinese goddess Dian Mu, "Lightning Mother," who wields a pair of mirrors to flash lightning through the sky.

—*FMcG*

LOTUS-SHAPED BOWL

1165–1225
Cambodia, former kingdom of Angkor
Gold and silver alloy
H. 10.2 cm × Diam. 21 cm
Gift of the Connoisseurs' Council, 1990.201

This exceedingly rare object is important for three reasons. First, few ceremonial vessels of gold or silver (or, in this instance, an alloy of the two precious metals) from the ancient Cambodian kingdom of Angkor survive.

Second, the shape and decoration of the bowl have interesting implications. The overall shape resembles a lotus. Lotus-shaped bowls of metal or ceramic were also made in this period in both China and the kingdoms of Champa in what is now Vietnam. The expert artisans of these various areas could have been familiar with each other's work from seeing imported objects, but it is also possible that artisans themselves might have emigrated from one country to another.

The bowl's lotus has eight petals, and the eight-petaled lotus is highly significant in Hindu and Buddhist thought. Its center is related by analogy to the symbolic center of the cosmos, and the eight petals to the eight directions of space arrayed around it. Inside the bowl, at the bottom center, is another eight-petaled lotus, which is in turn surrounded by eight more lotuses, multiplying the cosmic resonances.

Third, the bowl bears a significant, but enigmatic, inscription in Old Khmer, the ancestor of the modern Cambodian language. Several scholars who have attempted to understand the inscription have arrived at somewhat varying readings and interpretations. All find that a figure named Tribhuvanadityavarman ("Protected by the Sun of the Three Worlds") is mentioned, and he is probably, but not certainly, a king. A king of this name, who was originally a usurper, is thought to have ruled in Angkor for a period in the 1160s and 1170s. The inscription on the bowl seems to include a date equivalent to 1222, long past the reign of this known king. Was there another king or local ruler of this name at the later period? The history of Angkor in both the 1170s and the 1220s is poorly documented, and so far these questions remain unanswered. This inscription may turn out to be a valuable clue.
—*FMcG*

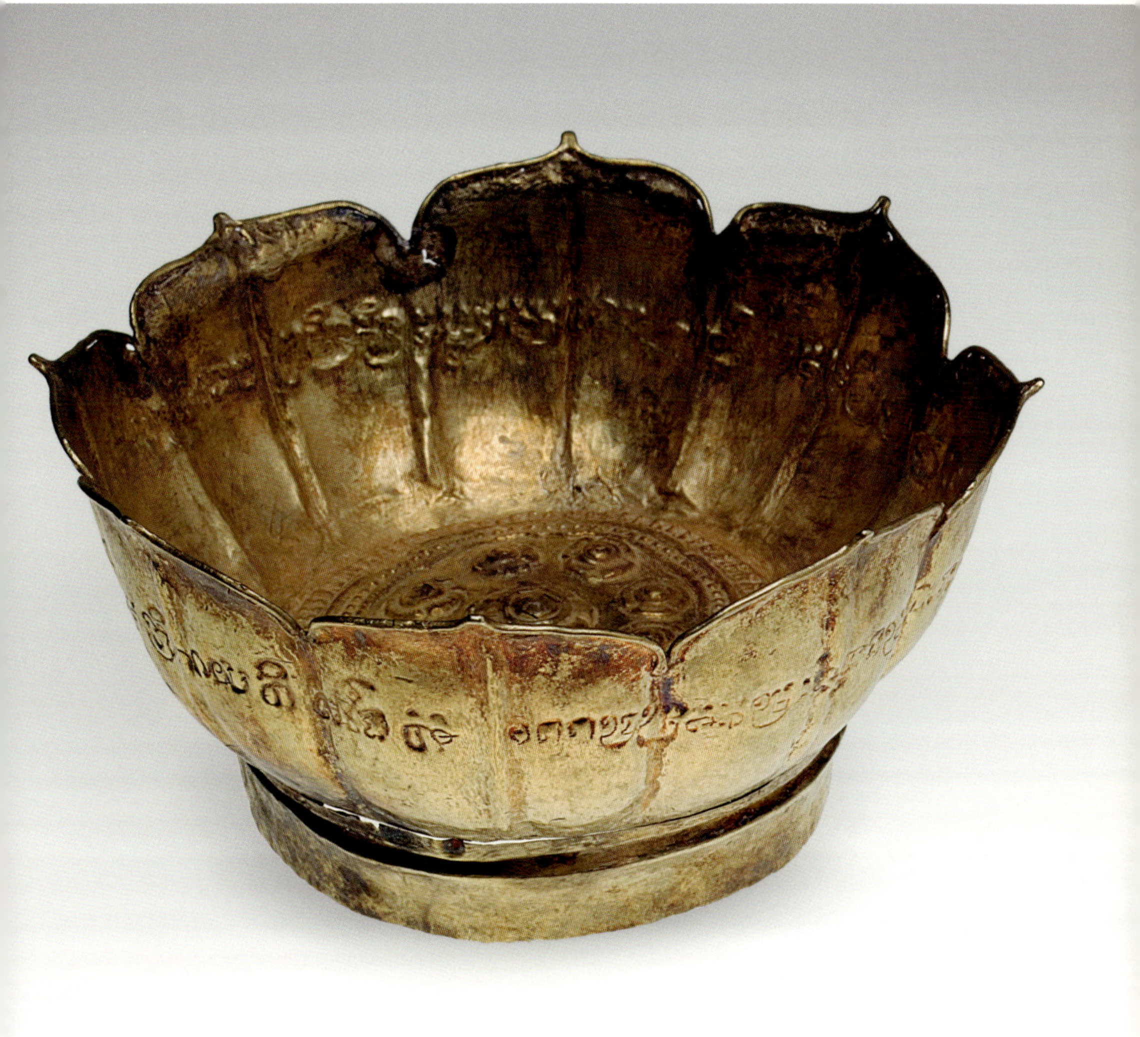

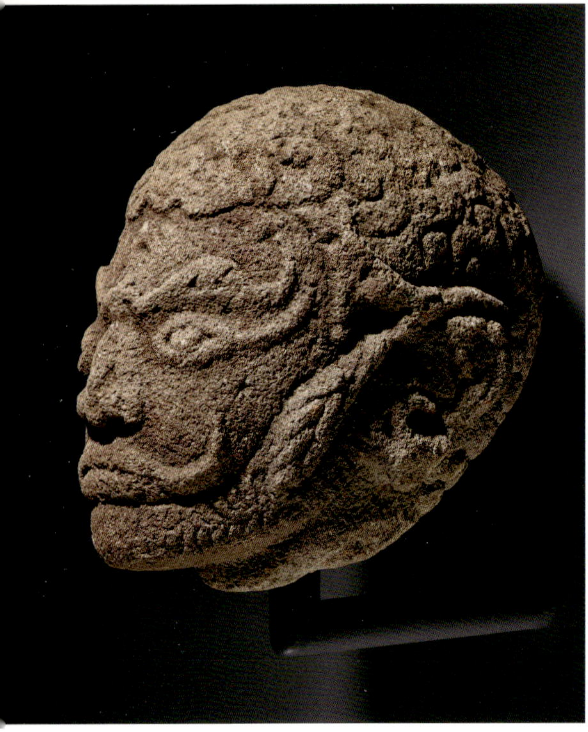

HEAD OF A MYTHOLOGICAL FIGURE

1400–1500

Indonesia; perhaps Candi Sukuh or Candi Ceto, Central Java

Stone

H. 45.7 cm × W. 21.6 cm × D. 29.2 cm

Gift of the Christensen Fund, BL77S4

As Islam was adopted across Java, many of the remaining Hindu practitioners moved up onto the slopes of volcanos. They built new temples there to continue to worship. Across central and eastern Java one finds traces of these structures. Perhaps the best known is Candi Sukuh.

Statues from this temple (and the neighboring temple, Candi Ceto) depict the human form in a markedly stylized manner. Here, the head seems to have been regularized into an egg shape, and the upturned curves of mouth, eyes, and eyebrows have been made to echo each other. This head has ornaments, or perhaps flower buds, looped over the ears and extending toward the face.

—*NR*

DAUGHTERS OF THE DEMON MARA

1470–1480

Southern Myanmar (Burma); Ajapala's Temple, Bago (Pegu)

Terra-cotta with glaze

H. 44 cm × W. 33 cm × D. 7.6 cm

Museum purchase, B86P14

As the Buddha sat meditating during the period of his Enlightenment, the demon Mara, a personification of evil and death, sent his daughters to tempt him. Trying to suit any taste, they magically appeared as women of various ages and occupations. The Buddha, of course, resisted all. The daughters depicted here are said by an inscription in the Mon language to be assuming the form of women who have not borne children.

This plaque comes from a ruined fifteenth-century temple complex in the old Mon kingdom of Bago (Pegu). Built under royal patronage, the complex included shrines dedicated to various events during and immediately after the Buddha's Enlightenment.

—*FMcG*

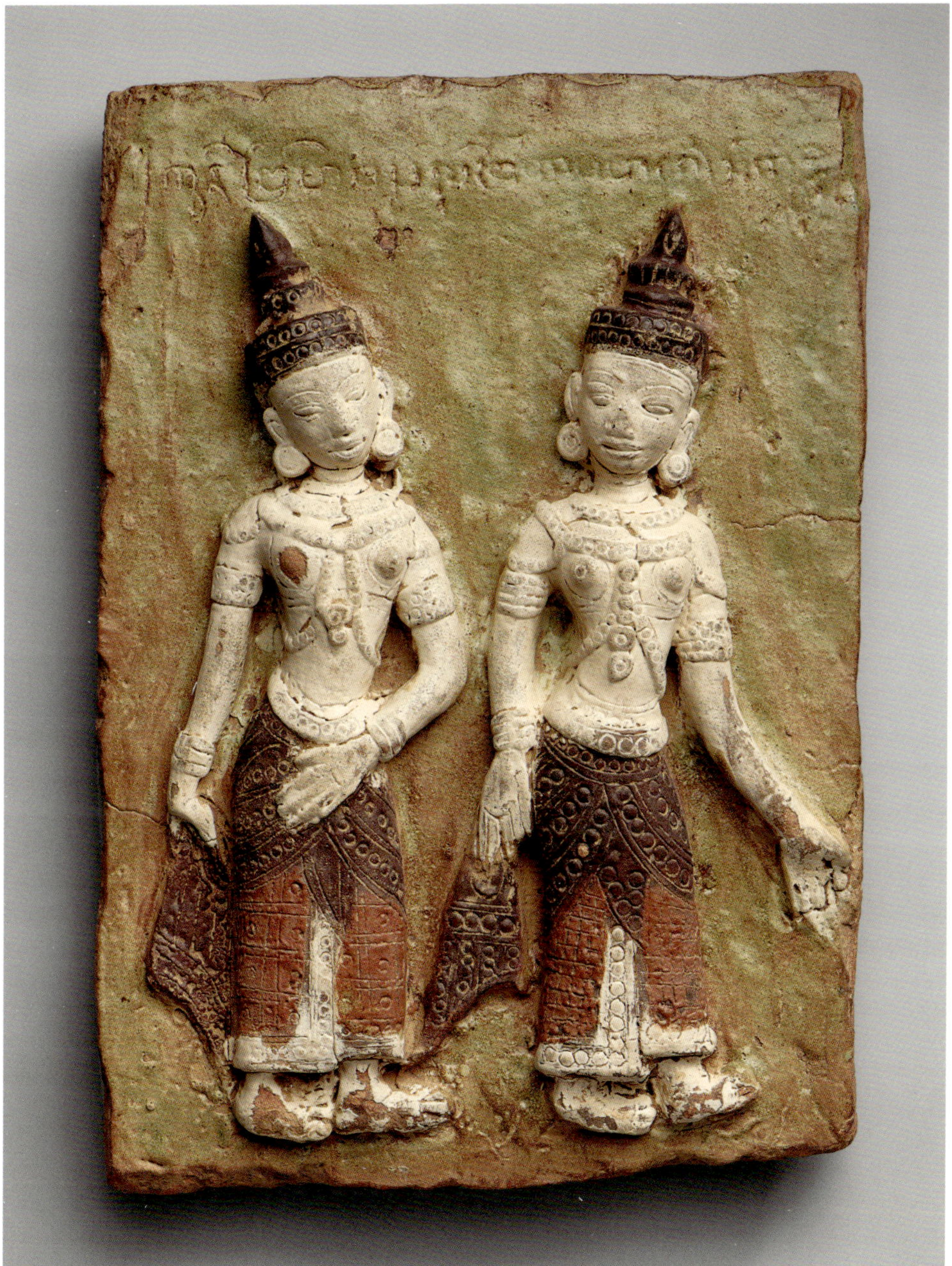

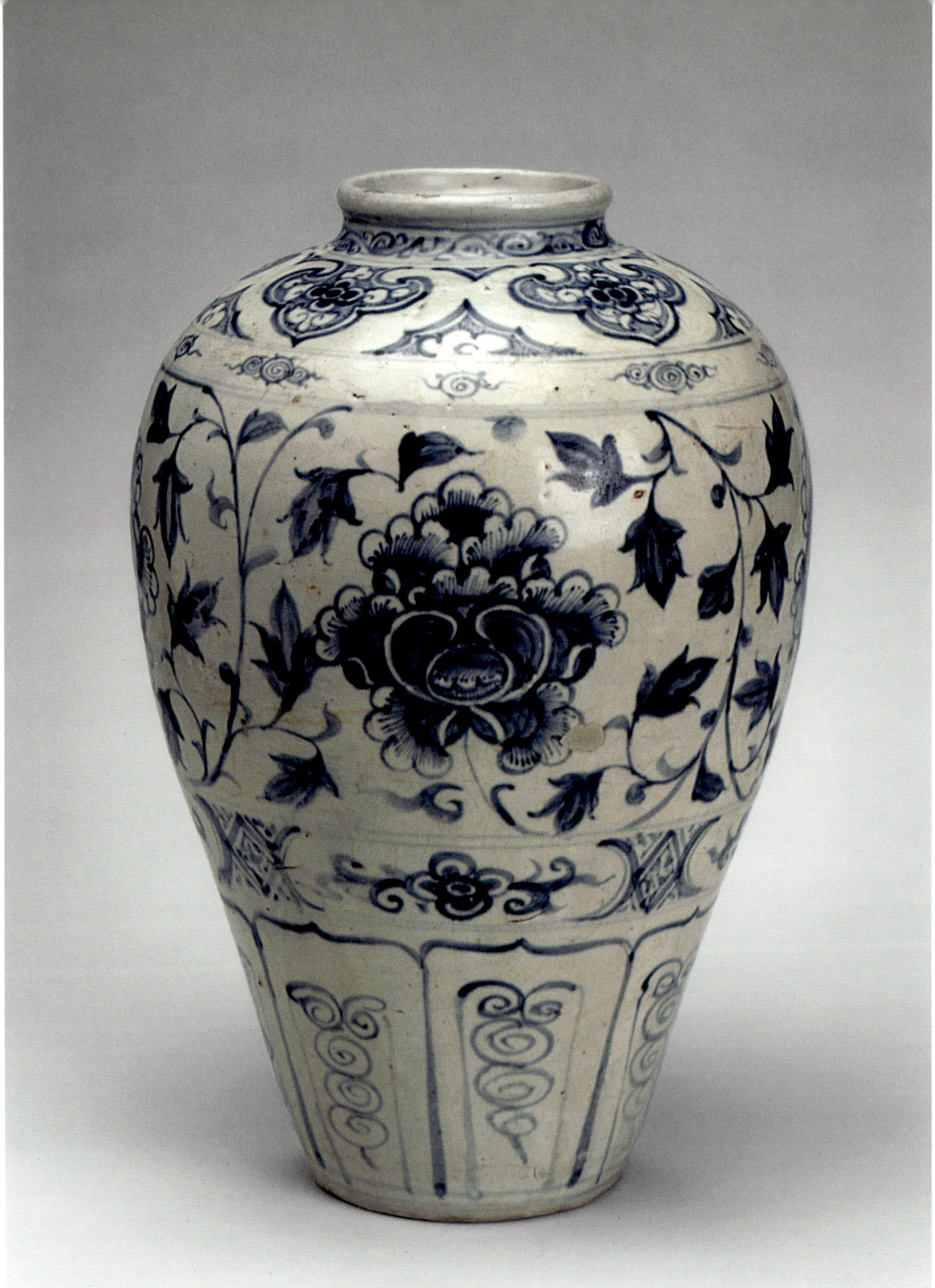

VASE

1400–1600
Northern Vietnam
High-fired ceramic with cobalt decoration under glaze
H. 39.4 cm × Diam. 26.4 cm
Gift of Betty Alberts, Forrest Mortimer, C. David Bromwell, David Buchanan, Marjorie W. Bissinger and the Connoisseurs' Council, 1992.347

MALE AND FEMALE ANCESTRAL FIGURES

1400–1600

Indonesia; Bali

Bronze

H. 37.5 cm × W. 12.7 cm × D. 8.9 cm; H. 38.7 cm × W. 11.4 cm × D. 9.5 cm

Gift of the Connoisseurs' Council and Shawn and Brook Byers; and museum purchase, B86B6.a-.b

Most Balinese sculpture is of stone or wood; bronze sculptures like these are uncommon. The purpose of these figures is not entirely certain. It seems likely, though, that they represented deceased ancestors and were used in a funeral or memorial ritual.

The people of Bali embraced a form of Hinduism more than a thousand years ago. However, they adapted it by mixing in local beliefs in which reverence for ancestors had an important part. The Balinese have maintained this sort of Hinduism to the present, while most of the rest of Indonesia, over many centuries, has converted to Islam.

—*NR*

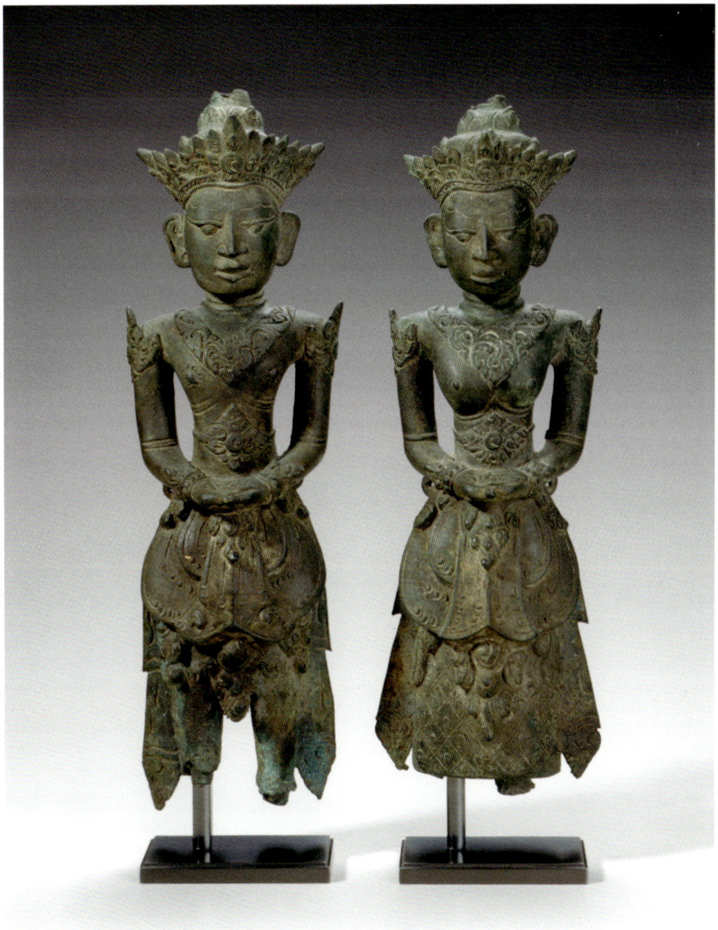

DAGGER HANDLE IN THE SHAPE OF A DEMON

1750–1850
Indonesia; Bali
Ivory
H. 13.3 cm × Diam. 4.4 cm
Acquisition made possible by William M. Brooks with additional funding from Betty and Bruce Alberts, Fred Levin and Nancy Livingston, Joan and M. Glenn Vinson Jr., Hok Pui and Sally Yu Leung, and an anonymous friend of the Asian Art Museum, 2010.1

This exquisitely carved object was once the handle of a Balinese kris (dagger). Krisses have long played important roles in Balinese society, and, in precolonial Bali, most men possessed at least one. Krisses were weapons that could be used in hand-to-hand warfare, but were also sacred heirlooms, spiritually powerful objects, and markers of status. The most significant part of a kris was its blade. Undoubtedly some of the power ascribed to krisses derived from the mysteries of their production. Metalworkers, especially producers of weapons, have long held special status in Indonesia, in part because of alchemy involved in transforming ore into tools and weapons.

Royal krisses often had handles made of precious materials, such as ivory or gold encrusted with gems. The handles frequently depict demonic figures, sometimes referred to as ogres (*raksasa*), and sometimes the wind god Vayu, father of the Pandava brother Bhima, a hero of the epic the Mahabharata. Comparison with other Balinese imagery suggests that this handle may represent one of two lesser-known characters, the *raksasa* Ratmaja or Bagaspati, a noble who was cursed to transform into a demonic form.

The figure's left hand seems to grasp a swath of cloth, perhaps a corner of one of his sashes. His right arm swings across his chest and clasps a segmented round object, framed by the elongated thumbnail of the figure's hand. Long, sharp fingernails, especially thumbnails, are associated with superhuman strength.

—*NR*

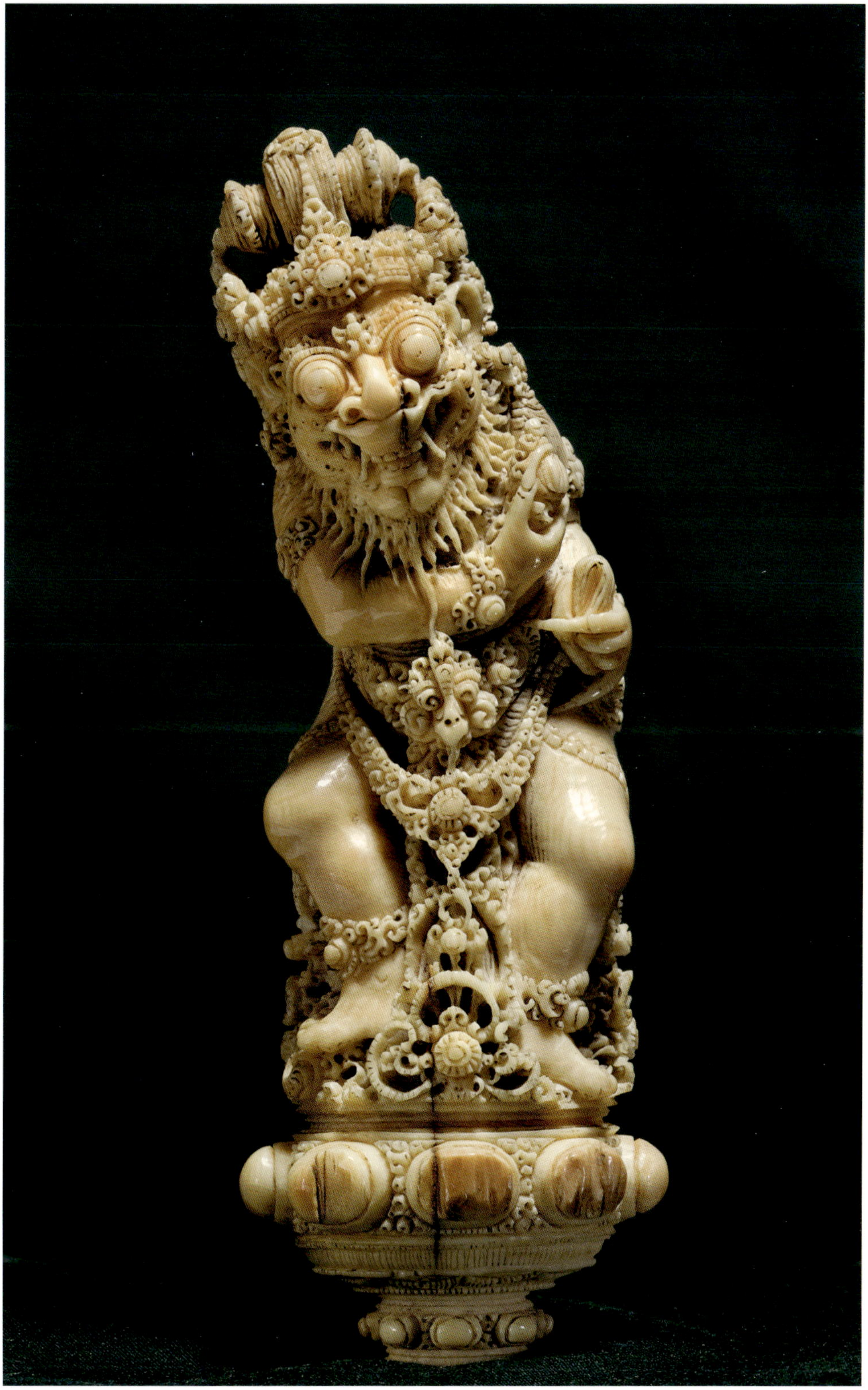

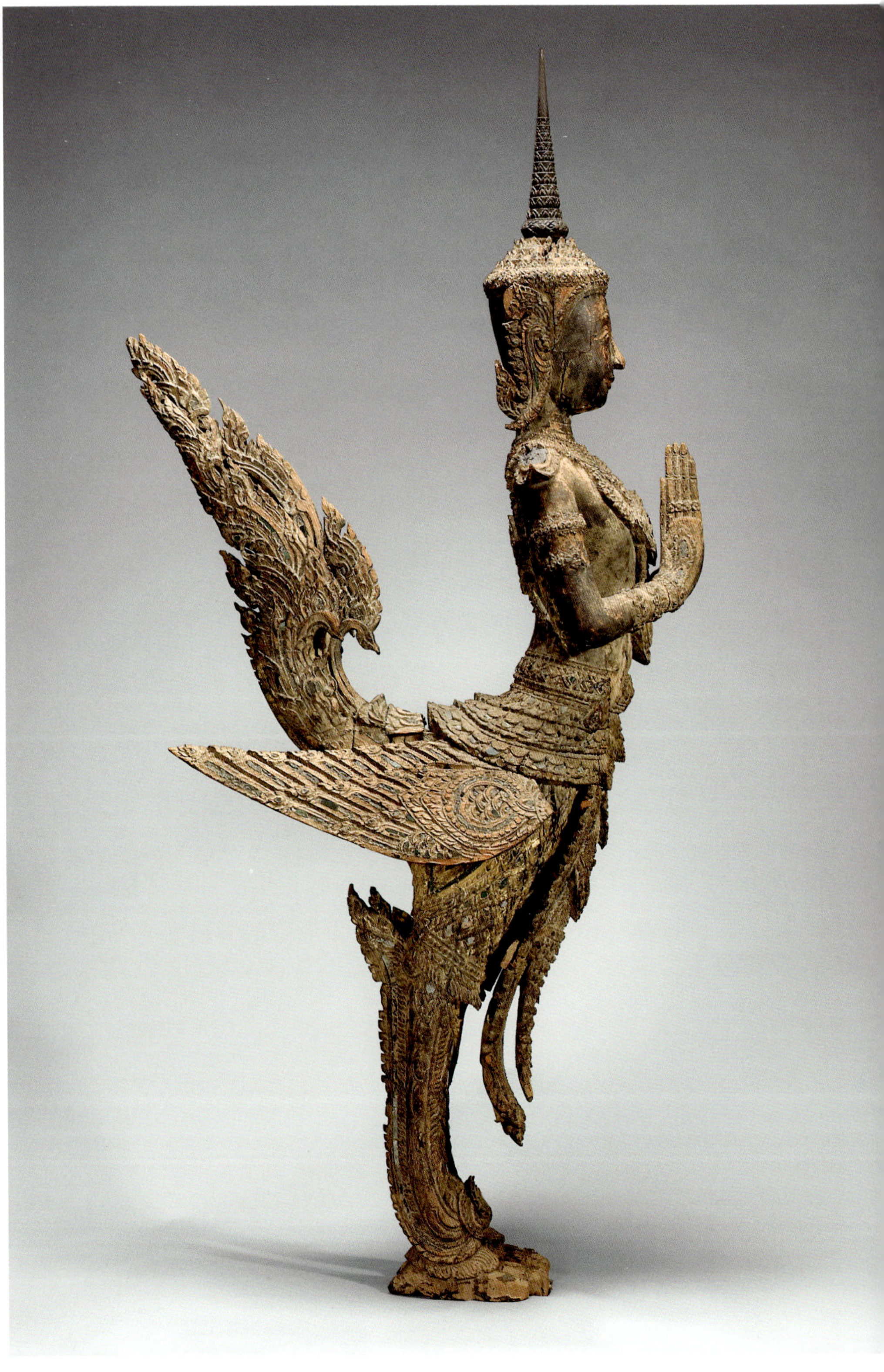

MYTHICAL BIRD-MAN

approx. 1775–1850

Central Thailand

Wood with remnants of lacquer, gilding, and inlaid mirrored glass

H. 125. 7 cm × W. 29.9 cm × D. 57.1 cm

Gift from Doris Duke Charitable Foundation's Southeast Asian Art Collection, 2006.27.24

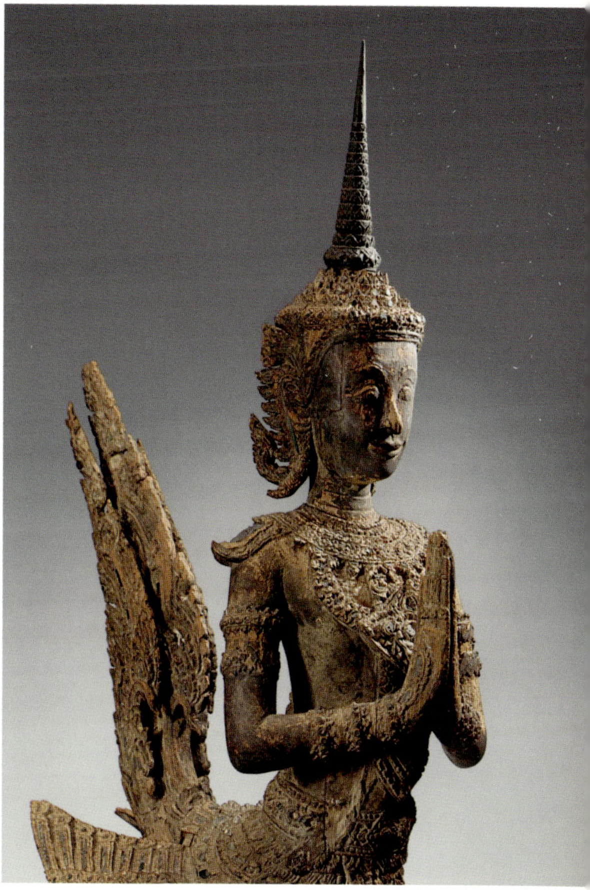

Adorning the columns along the freeway outside of Bangkok's Suvarnabhumi International Airport, mythical bird-men welcome people to Thailand. They clasp both hands in a similar manner to this wooden sculpture, in a traditional Thai salutation. Mythical beings commonly appear as decorative elements in Thai Buddhist temples and royal palaces and pavilions. They are portrayed in sculptural form as well as depicted in paintings. Among the most popular beings are bird-men (Thai: *kinnon*) and bird-women (*kinnari*). While the upper torso has a human form, the lower is in a bird shape; they have human hands and bird wings. They are creatures that reside in the Himavanta Forest that surrounds the base of Mount Meru, the center of the universe in Hindu and Buddhist mythologies.

Wooden figures of bird-men such as this one seem to have been produced for many centuries. A mention of one such image in the description of the coronation of King Rama IV in 1851 reports that it contained a relic of the Buddha. Photographs of King Rama IV's and King Rama V's cremation structures (known as "Meru platforms") show that similar bird-men adorned the ornate constructions. Sculptures and other materials related to funerals are considered inauspicious, so they are usually not kept. Only a handful of them have survived. Some are stored with other funeral implements in the National Museum, Bangkok.

—Pattaratorn Chirapravati is Professor of Southeast Asian Art History, Visiting Professor and Head of Studies, Arts and Humanities, Yale-NUS College, Singapore.

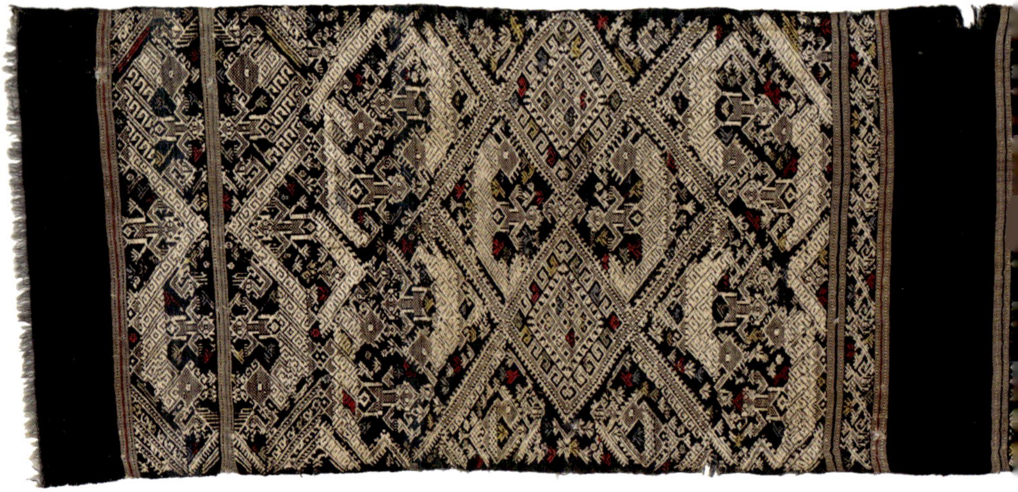

CERAMONIAL CLOTH

—

1850–1950

Laos

Silk and cotton

H. 189.5 cm × W. 40.1 cm

Gift of Museum Society Auxiliary, 1995.63

RARUNG, A DEMONIC FIGURE

—

1800–1900

Indonesia; Bali

Wood with paint

H. 59.7 cm × W. 41.9 cm × D. 25.4 cm

Gift of Thomas Murray in memory of his father Eugene T. Murray, 2000.37

—

This striking wooden statue stands in a posture common to Balinese dance: knees half-bent and slightly splayed, elbows raised to shoulder height. Bare breasts and round earplugs that were traditionally worn by Balinese women indicate her gender, but the form of a red flame rises from between her legs to mask her genitals. Matted hair, bulging eyes, and prominent fangs indicate her fierce nature.

To those familiar with Balinese culture, the figure immediately evokes Rangda, a powerful, frightening widow and witch associated with the invincible Hindu goddess Durga. Rangda appears in one of the best-known Balinese ritual dance-dramas as the black magic-wielding opponent of a lion-like creature called Barong Ketet. Like this sculpture, the costume that the performer representing Rangda would wear emphasizes her shaggy hair, demonic facial features, and extremely long fingernails.

Graveyards (where in Bali bodies are buried before they are exhumed for cremation) are home to dangerous beings (*leyak*), and Rangda is considered queen of these powerful practitioners of black magic. Tourist literature describes Rangda as the epitome of evil, who brings illness, destruction, and death, but Balinese interpretations are more nuanced. Rangda is a powerful being capable of both benevolence and malevolence.

A close examination of this statue reveals some characteristics not associated with this terrifying goddess and suggests it represents a different character. The figure's hair is black and her breasts are not pendulous, indicating a younger person than the widow. At the base of the statue, letters in faded Balinese script faintly spell out the word "Rarung," the name of Rangda's apprentice, who is sometimes called her daughter.

—*NR*

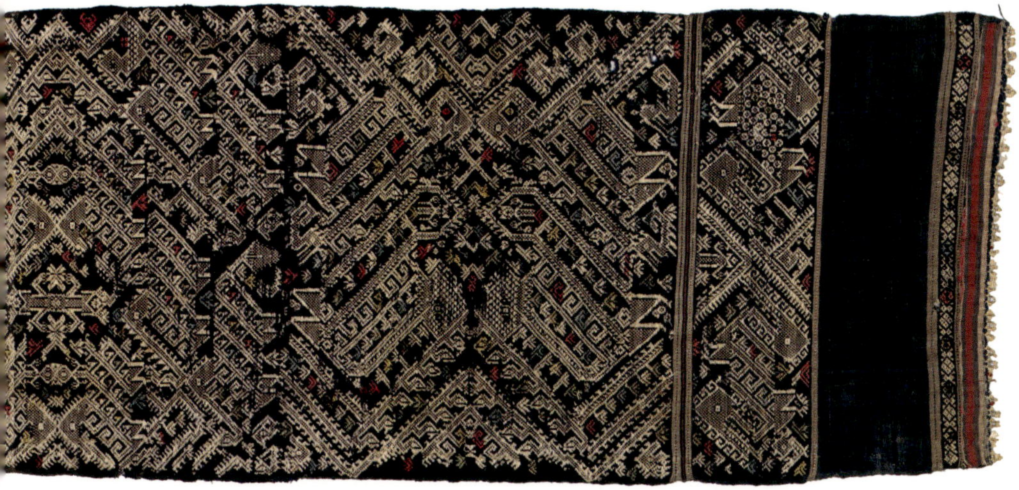

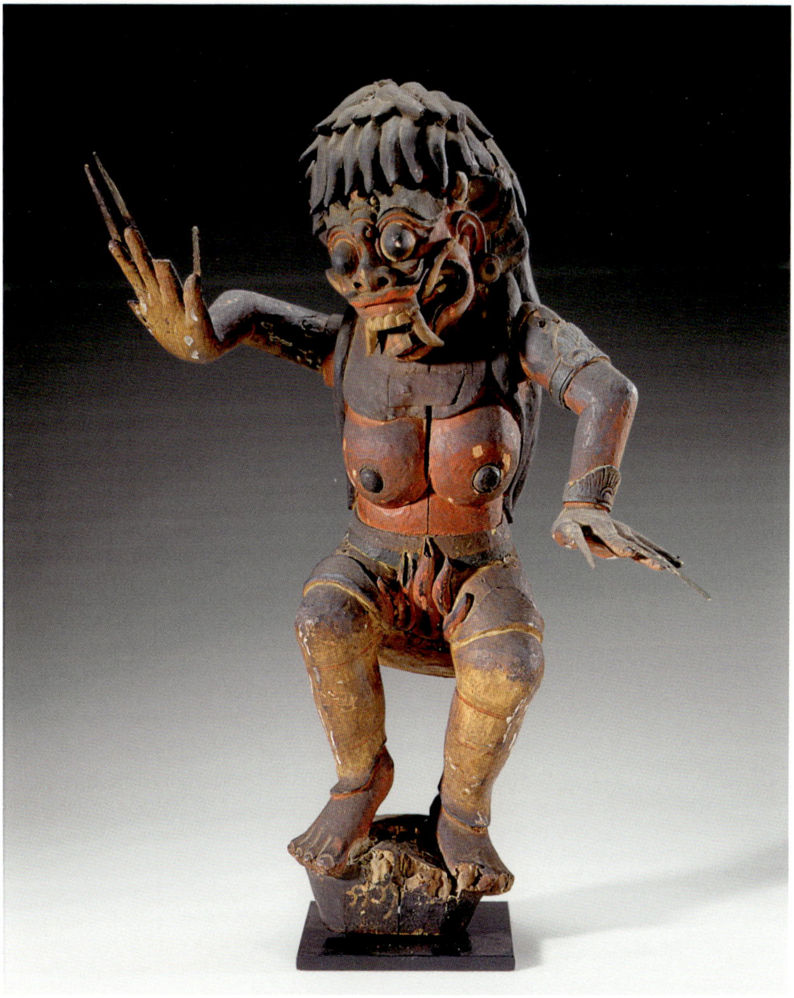

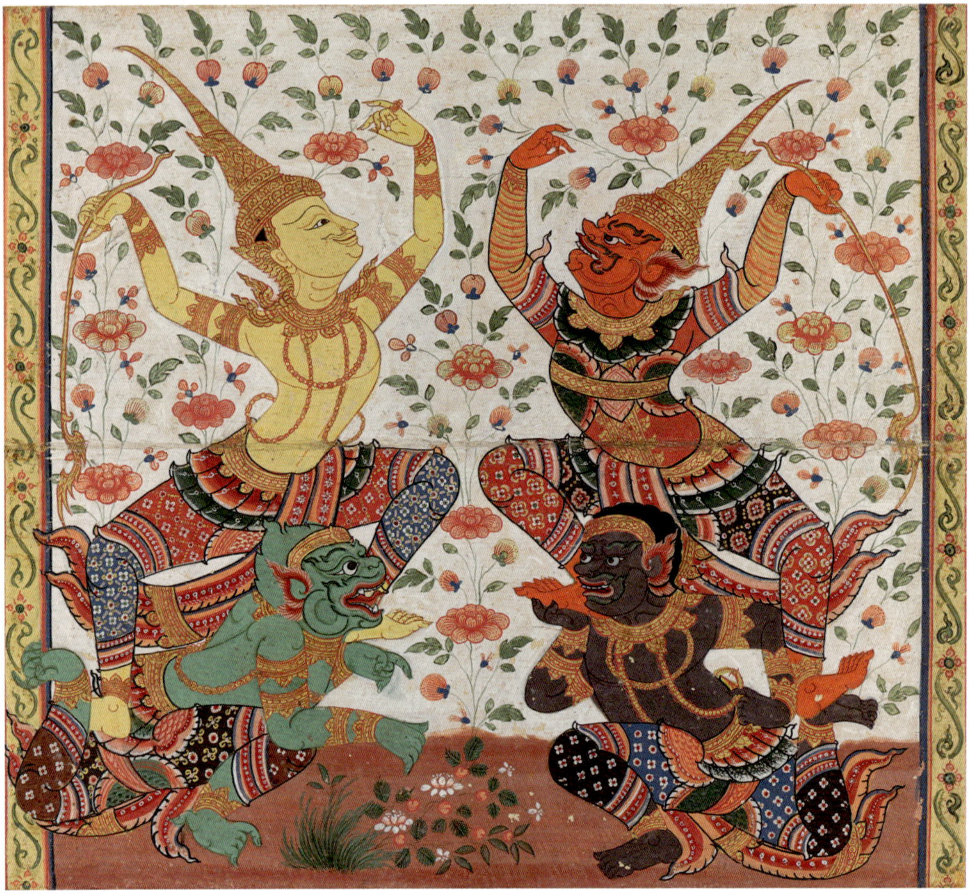

MANUSCRIPT WITH SCENES OF COMBAT FROM THE THAI VERSION OF THE EPIC OF RAMA (DETAIL)

approx. 1800–1840

Central Thailand

Opaque watercolors and gold on paper

H. 22.2 cm × W. 49.5 cm × Th. 6.3 cm

Gift from Doris Duke Charitable Foundation's Southeast Asian Art Collection, 2006.27.9

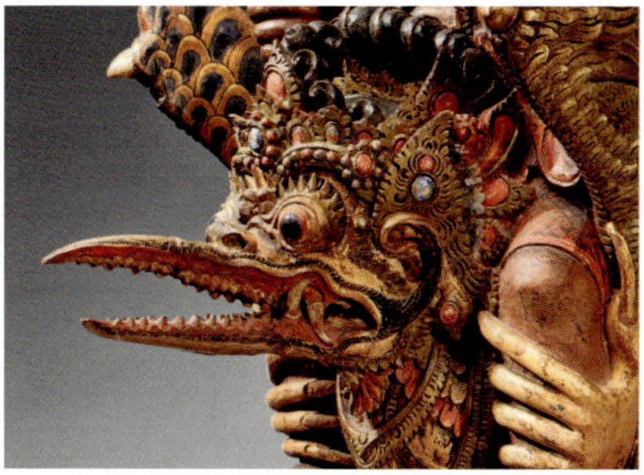

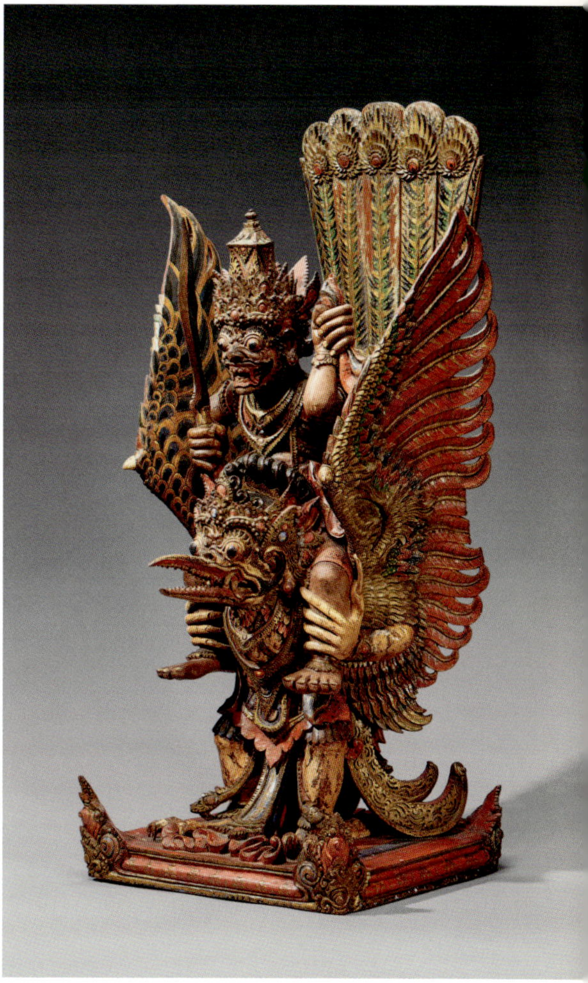

THE DEMON KING RAVANA RIDING A MYTHICAL BIRD

1800–1900
Indonesia; North Bali
Wood with paint and gilding
H. 96.5 cm × W. 46.4 cm × D. 45.7 cm
Acquisition made possible by the Connoisseurs' Council and the estate of K. Hart Smith, 2010.18.2

Ravana, a demon king from the epic Ramayana, sits on his fierce mount, Wilmana. In the epic, Ravana abducts Sita, wife of the hero Rama, and takes her away on his chariot. The name "Wilmana" may be a corruption of the Sanskrit word *vimana*, which means "flying chariot for the gods." In Javanese and Balinese, the word *wil* means a demon or evil spirit. The confusion of these words may have led to the interpretation of Ravana's mount as a winged demon in Indonesia.

Dutch museum collections contain many Balinese images of Ravana and Wilmana, indicating the popularity of the subject. It is rare, though, to find an example as large and intricately carved as this one, which most likely dates from the nineteenth century.

How statues such as this one were used is not known. Architectural elements shaped like winged creatures sometimes served as a base for the pillars supporting the roof of a pavilion. When used in such a manner, these statues often contained space for a beam. Since this example lacks that feature it was likely a decoration for a royal palace.

—*NR*

MASTERPIECE

CROWNED AND BEJEWELED BUDDHA IMAGE AND THRONE

approx. 1860–1880

Myanmar (Burma); Mandalay area

Wood and iron, with lacquer, gilding, and mirrored glass

H. 345.4 cm × W. 208.3 cm × D. 172.7 cm (throne);

H. 50.8 cm × W. 41.9 cm × D. 27.9 cm (Buddha image)

Gift from Doris Duke Charitable Foundation's Southeast Asian Art Collection, 2006.27.17 and 2006.27.1.a-.t

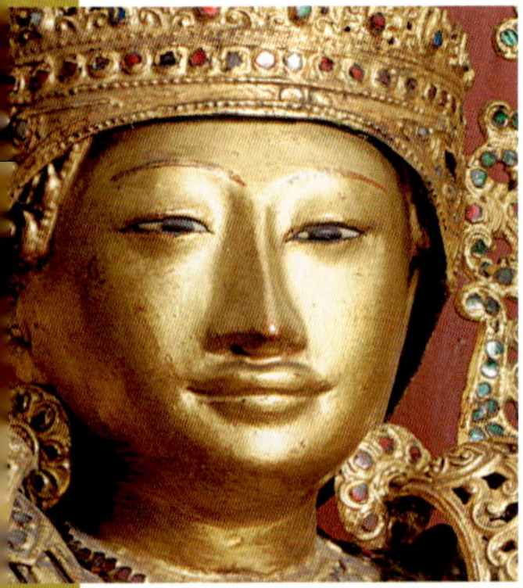

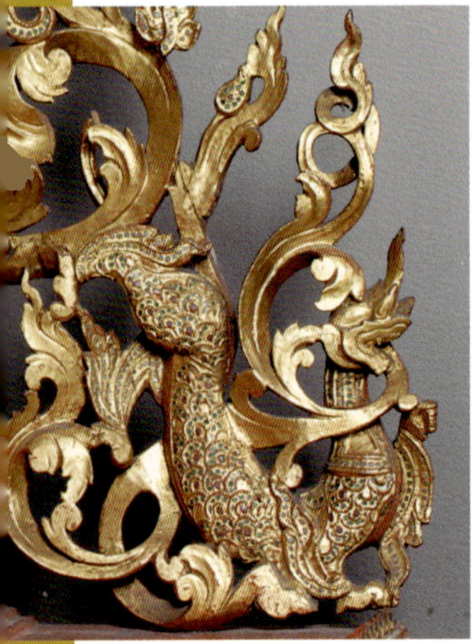

A presumptuous king named Jambupati once attempted to display his superiority to all the other kings of the world. In response, the Buddha manifested himself enthroned in a magically created palace, adorned with magnificent royal finery, to teach Jambupati that the grandeur of buddhahood vastly outshines that of earthly kingship. The Buddha then preached to Jambupati of the emptiness of riches, the inevitability of suffering, and the impermanence of all things.

This tale has been known in Myanmar and neighboring countries for several centuries, and perhaps considerably longer. It may well have been in the minds of those who created and worshiped before this elaborate shrine with an image of the Buddha in the attire of a king. (Kingly Buddha images have other meanings and associations in other cultures and periods, however.)

The shrine shares many features with the royal thrones of old Myanmar. For example, the lower part has tiers stepping inward to a sort of waist and then stepping outward again, creating an hourglass shape. The lower tiers refer to the vast system of increasingly high mountain ranges that are thought, in Buddhist cosmology, to make up the world. They culminate in Mount Meru, the central axis of the system. The upper tiers refer to higher and higher heavens above.

Such an elaborate throne and Buddha image would have been an important fixture of a nineteenth-century Myanmar Buddhist temple, and similar ones can still be seen in temples today.

The original crown of this Buddha image disappeared long ago. The one the image now wears was made in traditional techniques and style in 2002 by U Win Maung, an expert artisan in Mandalay, Myanmar.

—*FMcG*

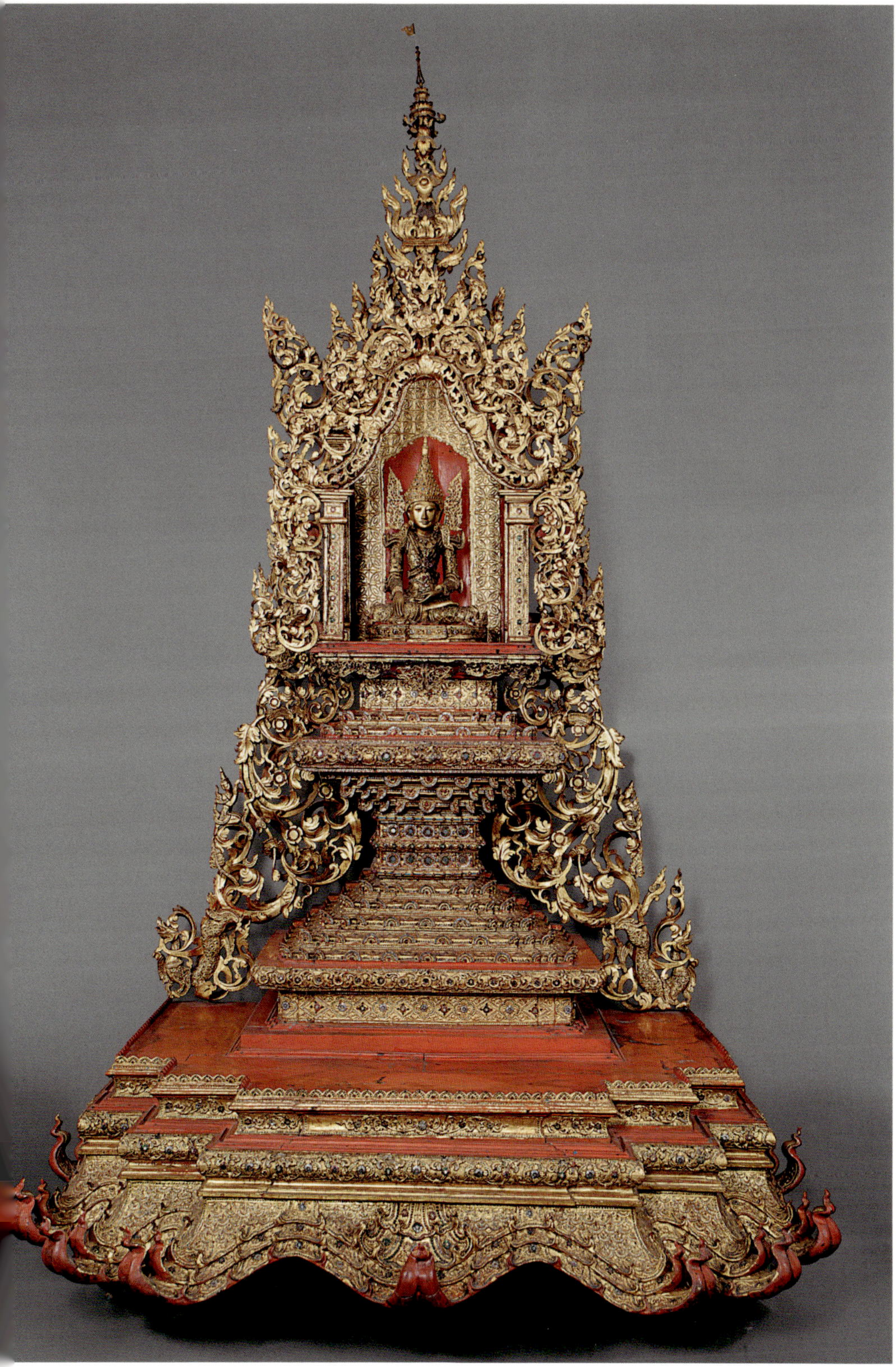

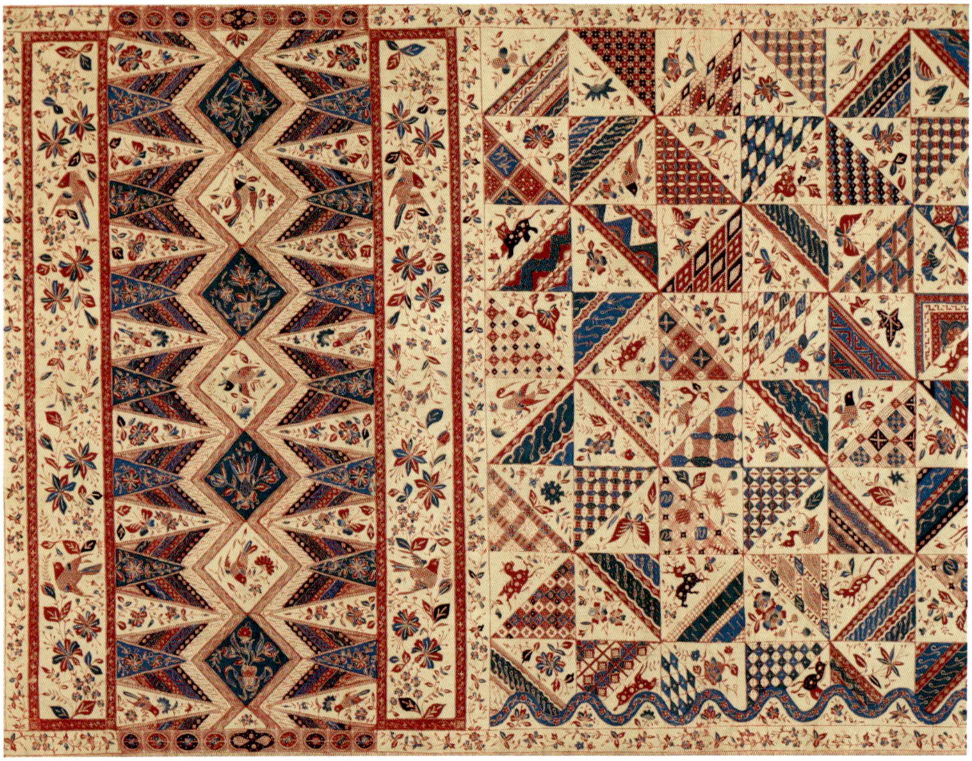

SARONG (DETAIL)

approx. 1890–1915
Indonesia; north coast of Java
Cotton
H. 123.8 cm × W. 103.5 cm
Gift of Joan and M. Glenn Vinson, Jr., 2018.109

The pattern of this remarkable batik textile is called *tambal*, a word that means "patch" or "repair" in Indonesian. The motif may have been adapted from actual patchwork fabrics, composed of fragments of valuable textiles and once worn by both priests and royalty in Java. Each square pairs a triangle featuring a schematic design with a triangle featuring a plant or animal motif.

Whatever the origin of the pattern, the textile is a tour de force for the artist, demonstrating her skill at hand drawing in wax dozens of unique designs. The color palette as well as the depictions of animals suggest connections with Chinese communities on the north coast of Java.
—*NR*

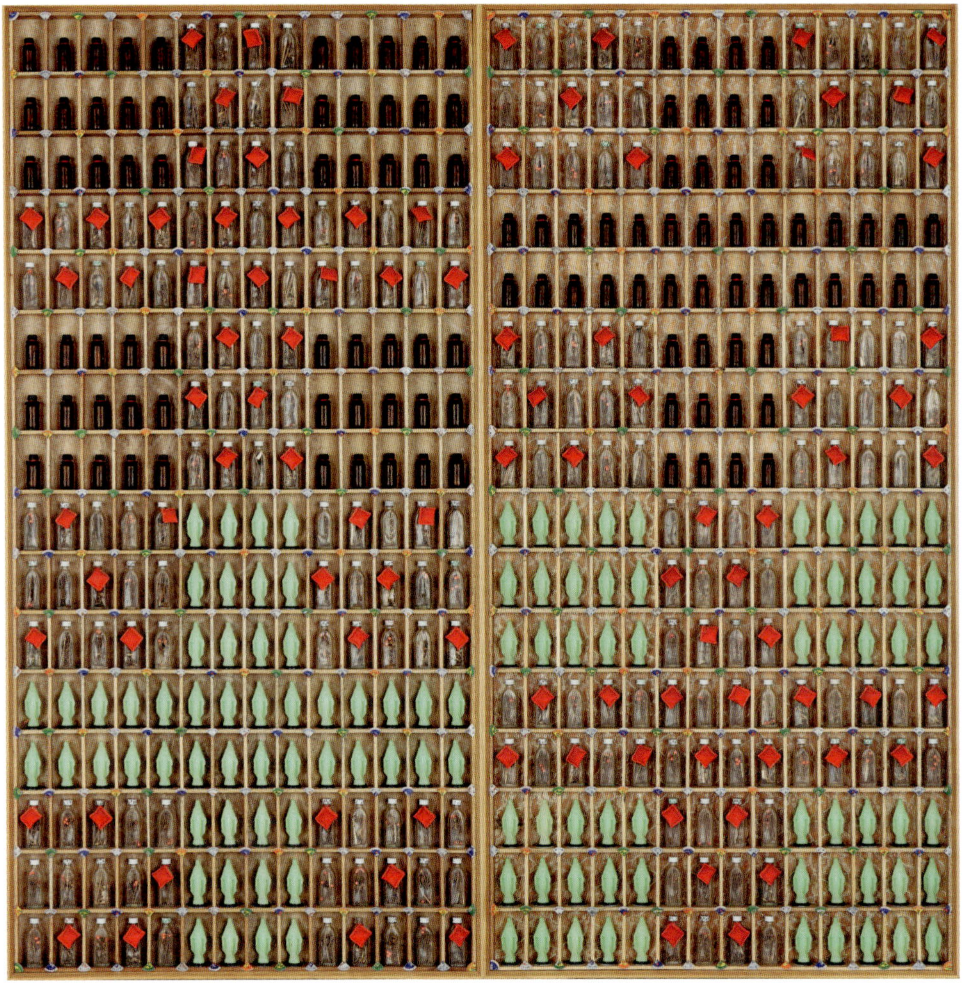

EVERYTHING IS SACRED #1

2009

By Norberto Roldan (Filipino, b. 1953)

Wood, glass, plastic, metal, and cotton

H. 182.9 cm × W. 182.9 cm × D. 6.4 cm

Acquisition made possible by the San Francisco-Manila Sister City Committee (2014–15), Therese Francia Martin, Catherine Cheung and museum funds, 2015.33.a-.b

RECESSION

—

2010

By Jakkai Siributr (Thai, b. 1969)

Textile, window mesh, safety pins, and amulets

H. 269.2 cm × W. 309.9 cm

Gift of Mrs. Frances Rollins, 2011.42

—

Growing up a Buddhist in Thailand, I never questioned the rituals and practices of the pious. I thought they were religious traditions that had been observed for generations. One such tradition is merit making to mark a milestone—a birthday, a wedding, a new house, or even a funeral. This usually involves Buddhist monks chanting specific mantras and laypeople making offerings in exchange.

Only after my return from a decade's study overseas did I realize that religious practice in contemporary Thai Theravada Buddhism is in fact a syncretism of animistic beliefs, ancestral worship, and astrology, as well as Brahmanical influences. Superstition is such an integral part of Thai religious life that it is responsible for our current social, political, and cultural instability.

Recession attempts to counter these issues in our hybridized religion in which materialism, hypocrisy, and quick fixes to karma are rampant. Instead it points to Buddhism's true principle as a nonsuperstitious religion. It urges Buddhists to practice the five precepts (avoiding harm to living creatures, stealing, sexual misconduct, lying, and taking intoxicants) as moral guidelines and to cultivate mindfulness that will eventually lead to spiritual enlightenment.

Intricate motifs form an outline of the Buddha image on the wall. It marks the presence and absence of the Buddha all at once. The absence of the Buddha suggests the Buddhist notion of void while its implied presence is a gentle reminder of Buddhist principles.

A closer inspection reveals that the constituents, cut from mesh, are Pali language mantras, several of the many I chant daily as part of my morning meditation. These floating "words" are delicately connected with safety pins, and among them numerous amulets with depictions of the most revered monks are entwined.

Amulets and statues depicting the Buddha image or teacher were originally meant as reminders of the Buddha's teachings. But today's amulets have become protective talismans, lucky charms, and collector's items.

The Buddha's image of *Recession*—which is there and not there—suggests the fragility of Thai Buddhism in this modern world. It hopes to remind museumgoers and the Buddhist faithful alike that our obsession with rituals and objects needs to be pared down. Being mindful of the Buddha's teaching will lead us to that spiritual path.

—Jakkai Siributr is one of Southeast Asia's leading contemporary artists working primarily in the textile medium.

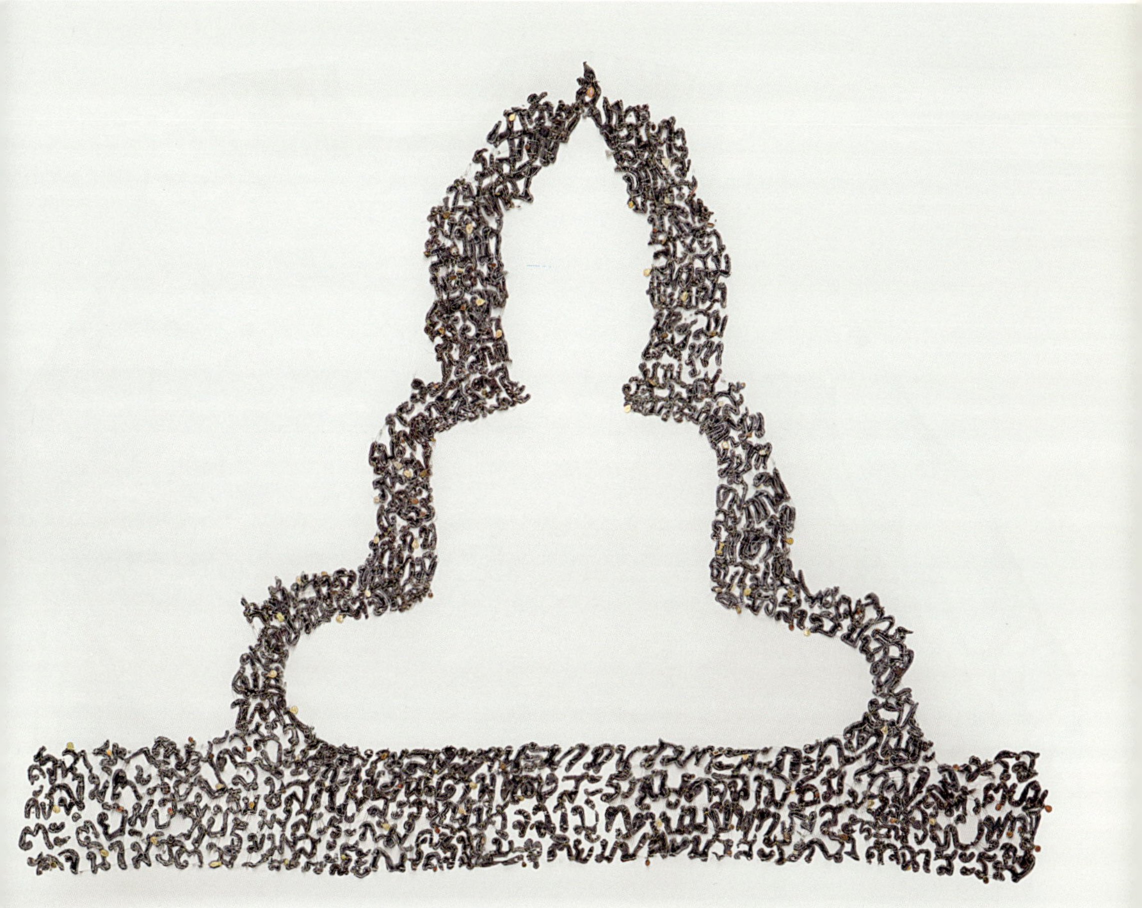

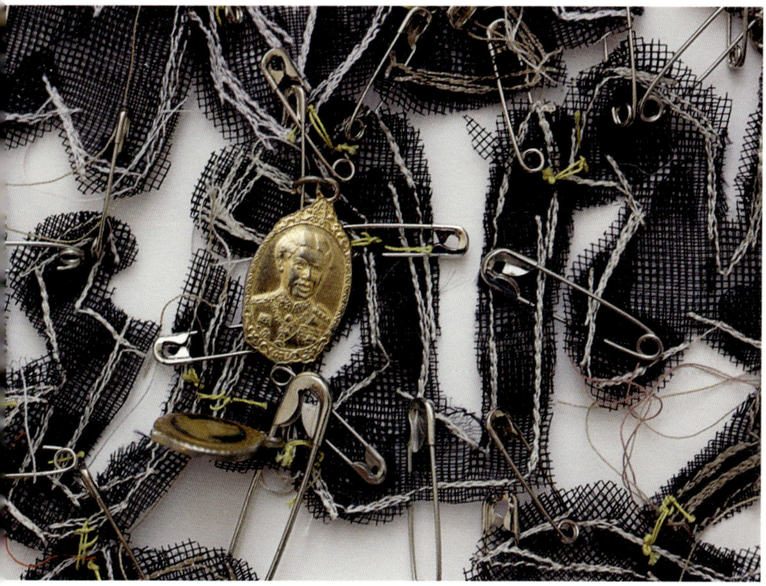

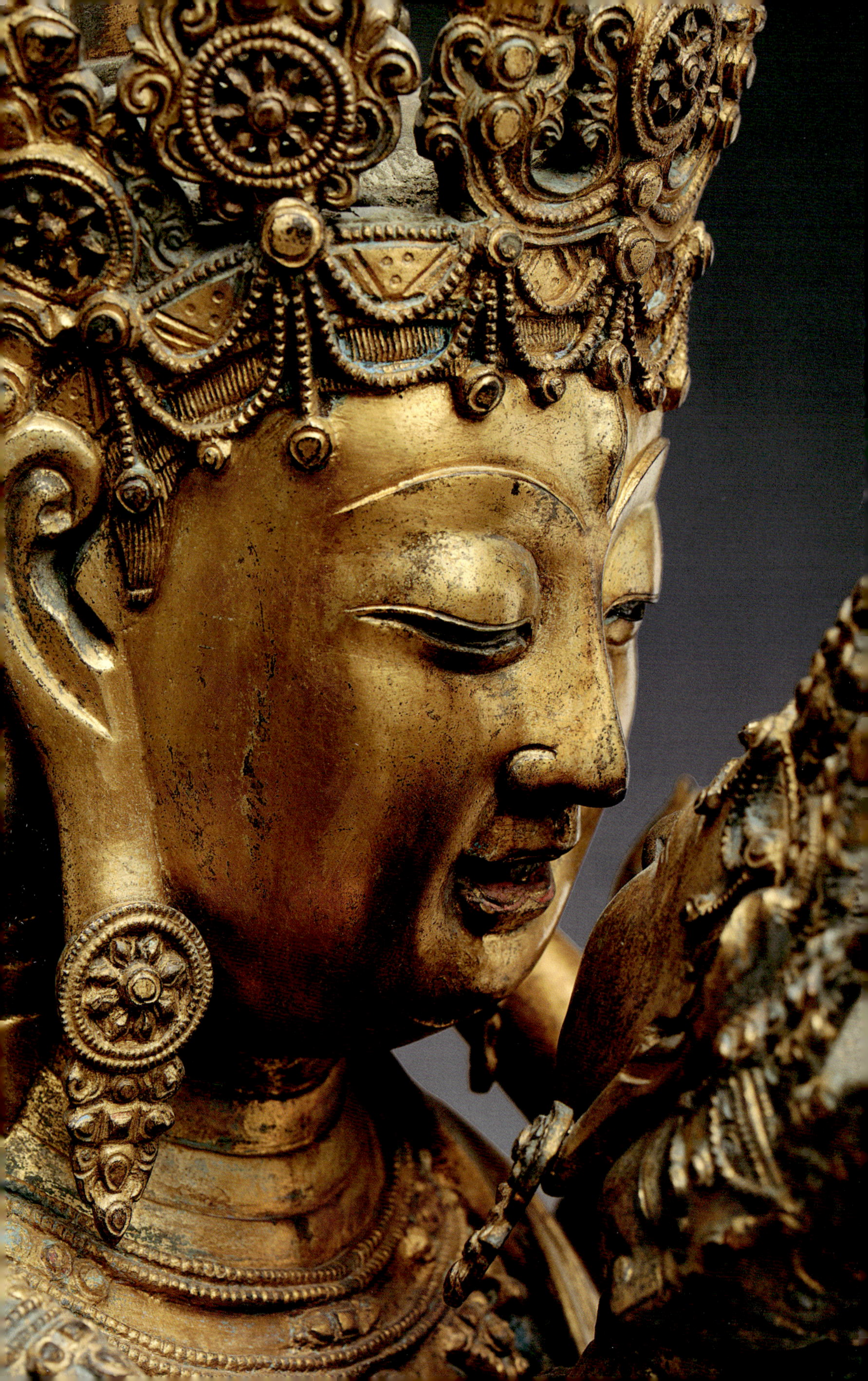

THE HIMALAYAS AND THE TIBETAN BUDDHIST WORLD

THE BUDDHIST LAMA TASHIPEL

1210–1273
Tibet; Taklung Monastery
Colors on cotton
H. 27.9 cm × W. 21 cm (image); H. 59.1 cm × W. 35.9 cm (overall)
Gift of Marsha Vargas Handley and the Connoisseurs' Council, 2013.19

During the thirteenth century a controversy over succession rocked the Buddhist monastery of Taklung in central Tibet. In its wake, the displaced former abbot Onpo departed to found his own monastery at Riwoche in eastern Tibet. He took with him some sacred objects, which he reconsecrated upon his arrival at Riwoche. This *thangka* painting, according to an inscription on its reverse, is one of the objects he took.

From the center of this *thangka*, the lama Tashipel, who founded the monastery at Taklung in the twelfth century, rests his back on a scrolled green cushion characteristic of the late Indian Pala style of *thangka* painting. Tashipel faces us directly, a posture previously reserved for Buddhas alone. Above him is his lineage of teachers, including Indian yogis, Tibetan lamas, and, second from the left, the cosmic Buddha Vajradhara, who is thought to have authored the tantric texts. Below Tashipel is a row of protective deities. These figures appear amid rainbow-colored crystalline staves that suggest mountain caves.

Several figures along the sides of Tashipel's throne depict events and beings from his life as a visionary. Among them are red Vajrayogini in the center right; to the left opposite, Vajrayogini embraces her blue consort Chakrasamvara. Similarly, white Avalokiteshvara sits above Vajrayogini on the right, while the historical Buddha Shakyamuni, surrounded by four disciples, balances the composition on the left.

Beneath these meditation deities is something entirely unexpected: two more images of Tashipel—to the right with a yellow hat, to the left without one. These are not Tashipel's only additional appearances, for beneath the lotus on which Tashipel sits are five more tiny images of the great lama. Each of these peeks out from a window at Taklung Monastery; the two golden stupas to the left belong to Tashipel and to his guru Phagmodrupa, who in this painting sits, diminutive, just above the large central image of Tashipel. The multiple appearances of Tashipel on this painting refer to his Buddha-like ability to be simultaneously present in multiple space-time locations.
—*JD*

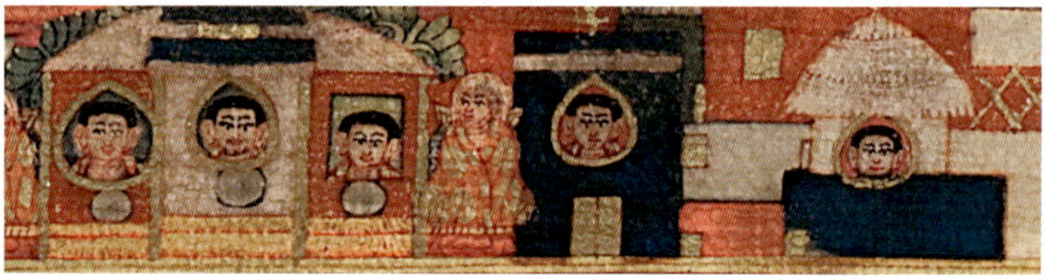

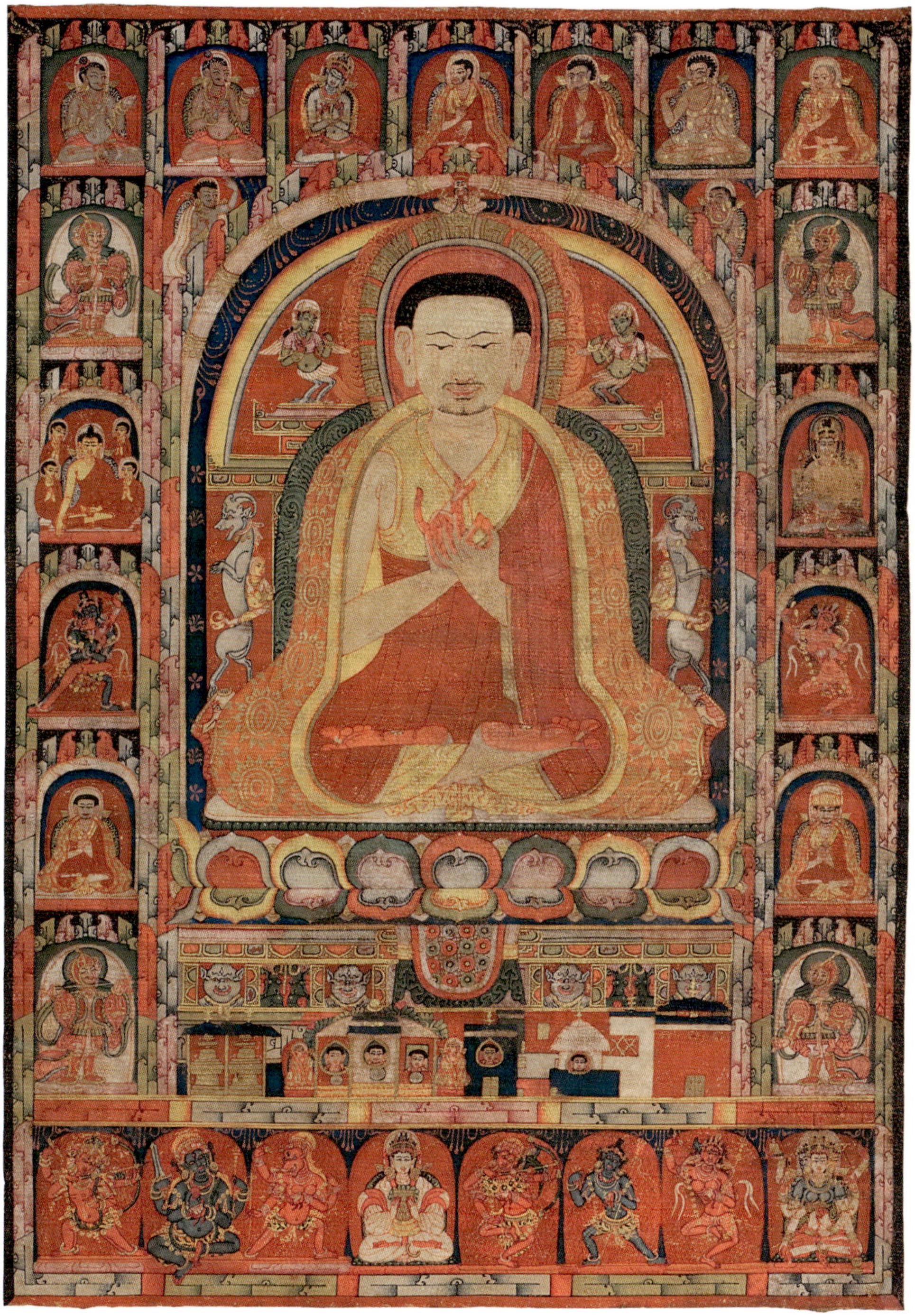

THE BON DEITY KUNZANG AKOR

1300–1400
Tibet
Copper with gilding
H. 19.1 cm. × W. 15 cm × D. 8.3 cm
Museum purchase, B87B1

The Bon tradition of Tibet is a religious system whose practices focus on shamanic phenomena. These practices include initiatory ordeals, meditative travel, and spiritual healing. Widely viewed as comprising Buddhism and indigenous Tibetan religions, Bon accordingly exhibits many visual, philosophical, and practical similarities with Vajrayana Buddhism. It can therefore be difficult to differentiate Bon sculptures from Buddhist ones.

The Bon deity Kunzang Akor presents a number of parallels to Buddhist gods. In this sculpture, he sits in lotus position atop a double lotus base in good Buddhist fashion. Moreover, with his hands folded in meditation and missing his typical crown, it would be easy to mistake Kunzang Akor for the historical Buddha Shakyamuni.

However, this rare example of early Bon bronze work supplies several clues to the figure's identity. Kunzang Akor, unlike Shakyamuni, is no monk. Instead, he is dressed in sumptuous jewelry. On the center of his chest is the Tibetan transliteration of the Sanskrit syllable "A," which Kunzang Akor embodies. On the lotus above Kunzang Akor's right shoulder, the artist has created a characteristic geometric swastika, literally a "good luck charm" in Sanskrit. Based on an ancient Indian symbol for the path of the sun through the sky, the swastika in Bon artwork substitutes for the Buddhist ritual object (*vajra*), of which it is an analogue in terms of its swiftness and indestructibility. The lotus above Kunzang Akor's left shoulder would have originally held a water pot, but it is now missing.

While Bon practitioners claim that their scriptures were composed in the pre-historic past, there are no records of these scriptures until the eleventh century—not long before this sculpture was cast. In this respect, the Bon scriptures are similar to the *terma* or "treasure text" tradition of the Nyingma or Ancient Order of Tibetan Buddhism, which appeared historically at almost the same time. But instead of purporting to be compositions of the Buddhist lama Padmasambhava, as do the Nyingma texts, the Bon considered their texts to be translations from the mysterious language of the lost kingdom of Zhang-zhung, deep in the desert to the north. Both the Nyingma and the Bon traditions have provided rich sources of religious innovation in Tibet.

—JD

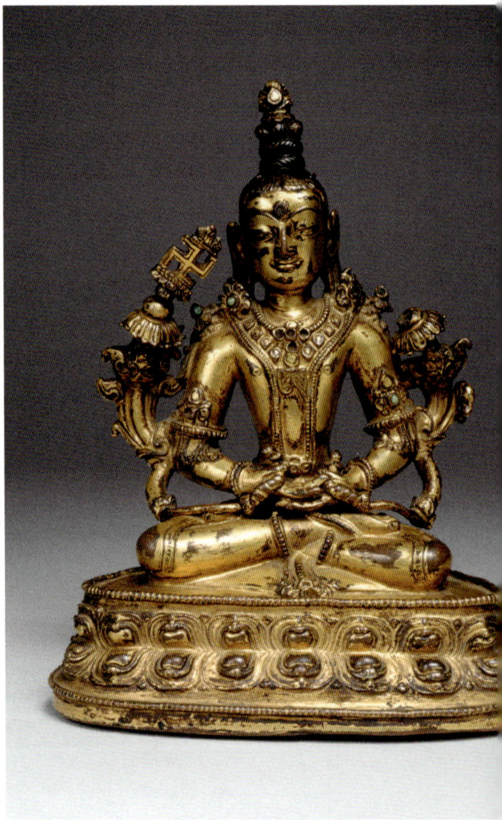

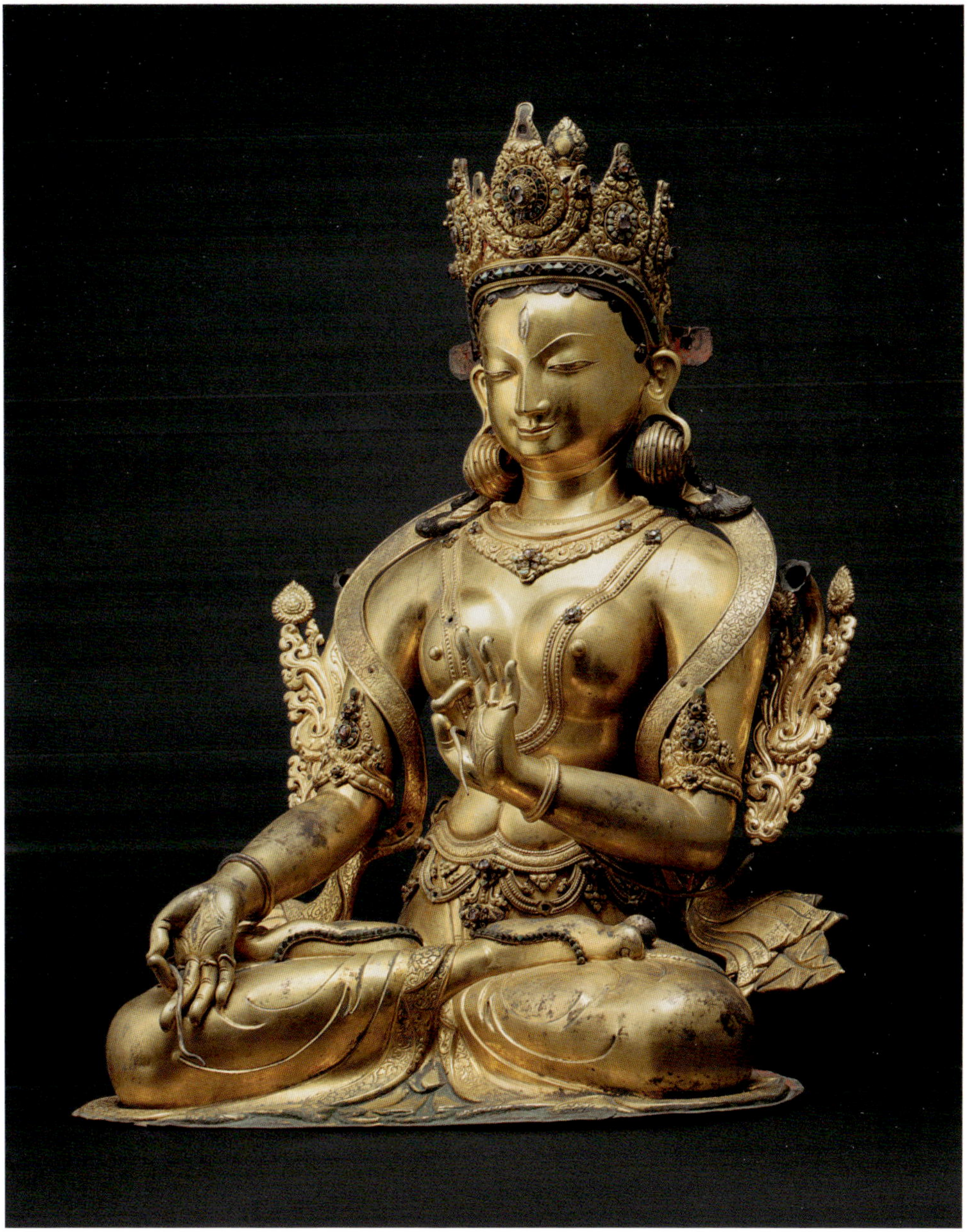

THE BUDDHIST DEITY WHITE TARA

approx. 1400–1500

Nepal

Copper with gilding, turquoise, lapis lazuli, other gemstones, and glass

H. 54.6 cm × W. 43.2 cm × D. 31.8 cm

The Avery Brundage Collection, B60S22+

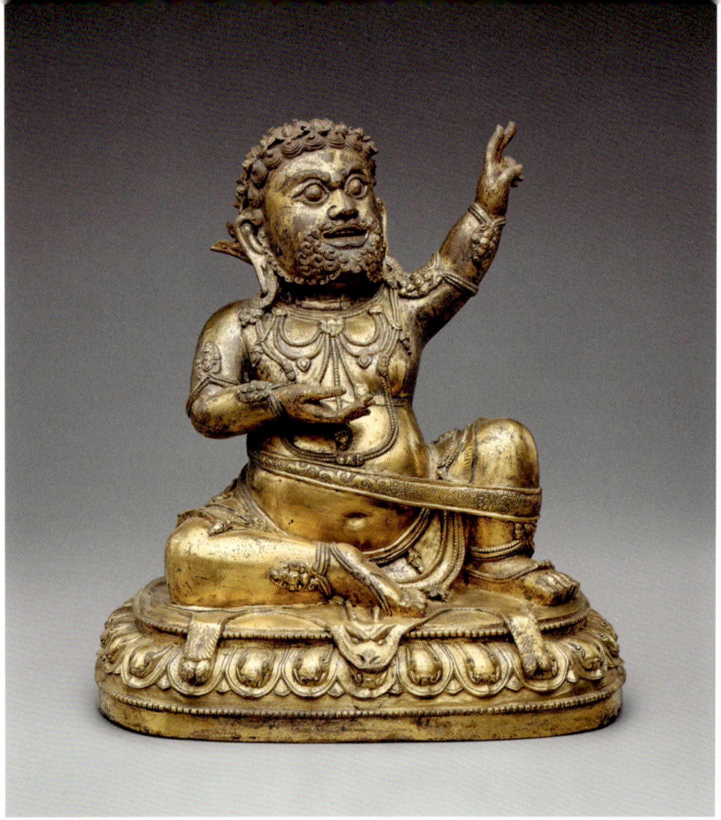

THE BUDDHIST ADEPT VIRUPA

—

approx. 1400–1450
China; Beijing
Ming dynasty (1368–1644)
Bronze with gilding
H. 26.7 cm × W. 25.4 cm × D. 16.5 cm
The Avery Brundage Collection, B62B20

—

Seated on a deerskin, his paunch barely contained by his yoga strap, the adept Virupa leans back at his ease. His wide-eyed smile is justified; Virupa, whose name translates as "Mr. Repulsive," has just attained enlightenment and is now enjoying his freedom. Recently, he had been chief abbot at the great north Indian monastery of Nalanda. Now, however, he has resigned and is at last free of his institutional obligations.

Although a lifetime meditator, Virupa had but a few nights ago given up his spiritual quest, going so far as to throw his rosary of meditation beads (*mala*) into the latrine in frustration. That very night, however, the meditation deity Vajrayogini appeared to him in a dream; she proclaimed that his enlightenment was imminent, and that he ought to retrieve his beads from the latrine and return to meditation. Heeding the words of the fierce red Vajrayogini, Virupa climbed into the latrine, found his rosary, and was that very night enlightened. The next morning, he resigned his monastic post, put flowers in his hair, and left the monastery to become an independent teacher.

Traveling north across the plains of Bihar, Virupa found himself thirsty—for beer. He stopped at a tavern and began to consume prodigious amounts of alcohol. When the innkeeper asked for payment, Virupa promised to pay his bar tab as soon as the sun set. In this sculpture, we see Virupa using his magic powers (*siddhi*) to freeze the sun in the sky so that he might continue to fill his skull bowl—now missing from Virupa's right hand—indefinitely. The symbolism of this scene has been characterized as that of "crazy wisdom" espoused by Buddhist teachers who taught that all convention was bondage. The Sakya order of Himalayan Buddhism counts Virupa as their founding Indian master.

—JD

THE BUDDHIST DEITY GUHYASAMAJA

approx. 1400–1500
China, Beijing
Ming dynasty (1368–1644)
Bronze with gilding
H. 66 cm × W. 45.7 cm × D. 31.7 cm
The Avery Brundage Collection, B64B23

Guhyasamaja means "secret union," and this sculpture of just such a union embodies many symbolic secrets. Among the most important of these secrets, the two figures in sexual embrace represent wisdom and compassion—the two components of the Buddhist enlightened state—in dynamic balance.

Originally, the large male Guhyasamaja's central hands would have held the bell of emptiness and the symbolic thunderbolt of means. His other hands would have held symbols corresponding to four Buddhas: the wheel of Vairochana, the lotus of Amitabha, the gem of Ratnasambhava, and the sword of Amoghasiddhi. Thus this image embodies the universe as symbolized by the five cosmic Buddhas, but clothed in sexual imagery.

The text from which Guhyasamaja is derived features the transgressive language and imagery characteristic of the coded Buddhist "twilight speech." In Tibetan practice as codified by the lama Tsongkhapa, Guhyasamaja is classified as a "father tantra," while Chakrasamvara is a "mother tantra" (see page 103). In father tantras like that embodied in Guhyasamaja, practices center on manipulation of the internal winds and channels that compose the subtle body. Mother tantras, in contrast, focus on realizing bliss within the central channel of the subtle body.

The secret union embodied in Guhyasamaja implicitly echoes an important relationship that held for centuries between the monks of Tibet and emperors of China. During the reigns of the Yongle and Xuande emperors (1403–1435), for example, Chinese court artisans cast high-quality bronzes like this both as presents to the high monks of Tibet and for their own personal use. This exchange of religious goods and ideas reaffirmed an ongoing relationship between certain rulers of China and the Vajrayana Buddhism practiced by the lamas of Tibet.

—JD

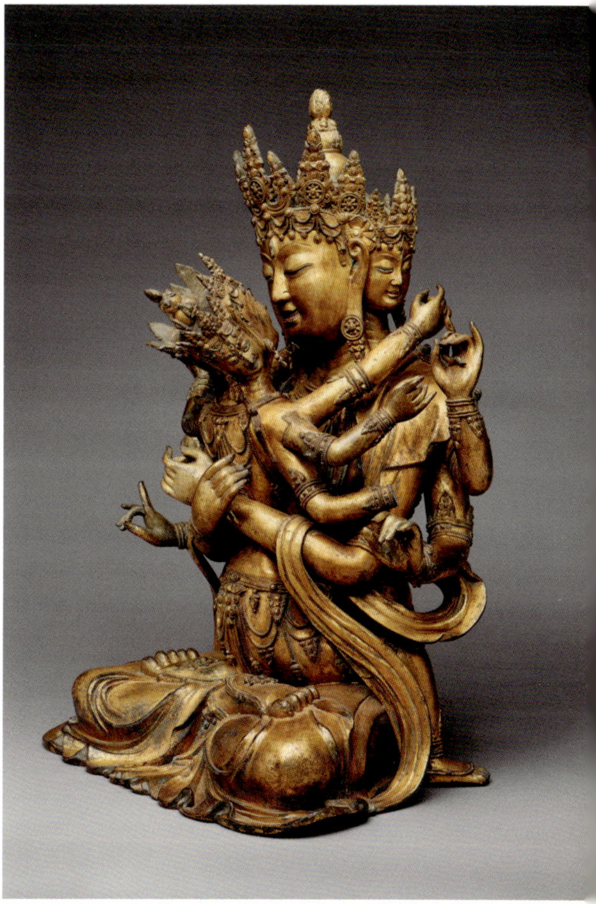

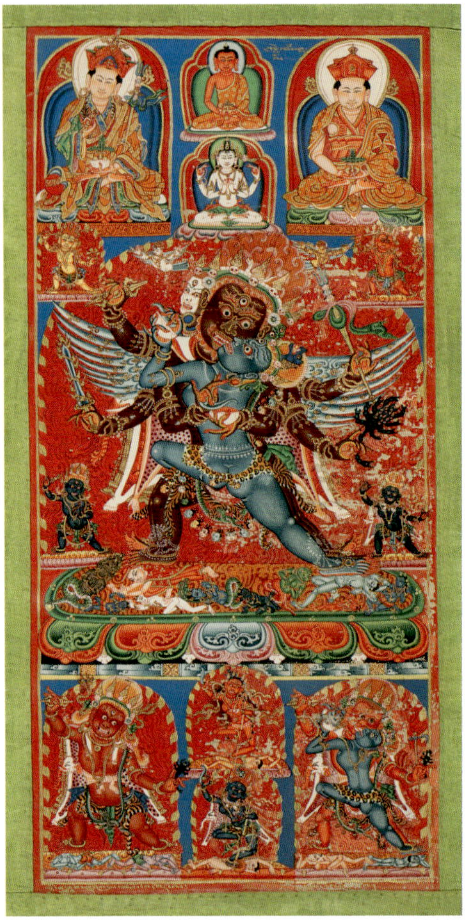

THE LAMA PADMASAMBHAVA AS GURU DRAKPOCHEY

—

approx. 1475–1525
Tibet
Colors on cotton
H. 27.3 cm × W. 13 cm (image);
H. 52.7 cm × W. 24.2 cm (overall)
Gift of the Connoisseurs' Council, 1992.344

—

One traditional translation of *thangka* is "flat body," and this *thangka* features Padmasambhava, the Precious Teacher, Guru Rinpoche. Head tilted and bearing his trident (*khatvanga*), Padmasambhava sits in multicolored robes and characteristic hat at the top left of this *thangka*. According to traditional Tibetan histories, Padmasambhava was an Indian sorcerer from a northwestern region of the subcontinent called Oddiyana. In the ninth century Padmasambhava transmitted Vajrayana Buddhism to Tibet.

Guru Drakpochey, the Great Fierce One at the center of this painting, is a visionary body imagined by Padmasambhava in meditation. Note the black scorpion consuming the human corpse on the right side of the painting, and the flayed elephant skin behind it; this fierce imagery indicates Drakpochey's ability to overcome such negative forces and personality defects as neurotic inhibitions and compulsions.

On the back of this *thangka*, a golden inscription praises the *Lotus Skull Rosary*. This is the text from which the visualization of Guru Drakpochey derives, and its composition is attributed to Padmasambhava. Calligraphed on a brilliant orange stupa, the golden text in "headless" (*umey*) Tibetan cursive script links the painting to a corpus of works associated with the monastery of Riwoche in eastern Tibet.

The *Lotus Skull Rosary* did not appear in public until the fifteenth century, when it was "rediscovered" by the lama at the top right of the *thangka*. Dressed in ornate robes and bearing a vase, he is Pema Lingpa, a lama who became a key cultural hero of his birthplace, Bhutan. Here, Pema Lingpa wears the telltale red hat of a treasure-finder or *terton*. Such treasure-finders rediscovered texts that Padmasambhava hid in the ninth century. They were hidden in order to survive an impending period of sociopolitical chaos, only to be rediscovered centuries later, by just the right people at just the right time. Executed during the sixteenth century in a manner that intentionally adopts fourteenth-century stylistic features to depict a ninth-century lama, this painting may itself embody the fundamental principle of the text: that it should survive intact despite the passage of time.

—JD

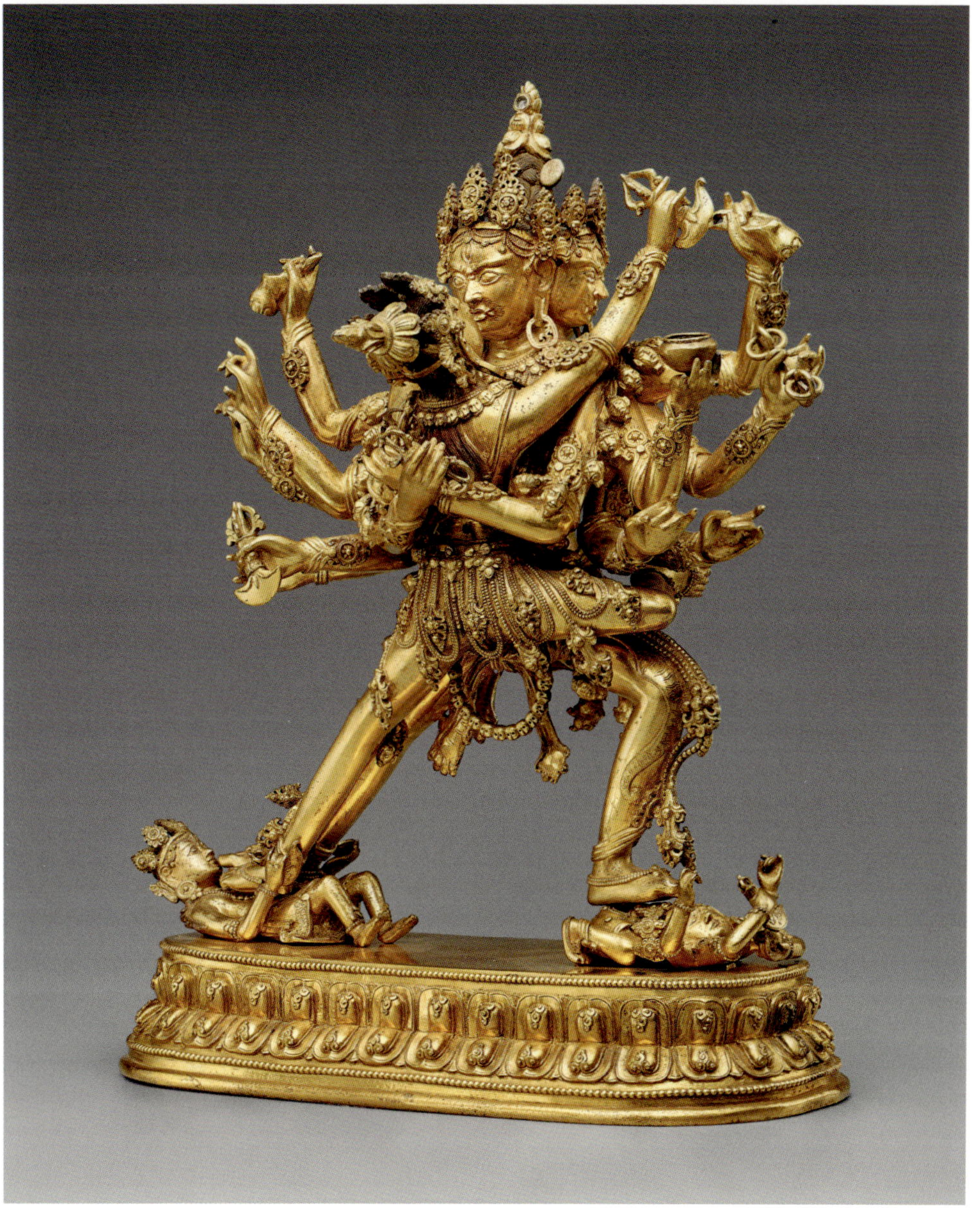

THE BUDDHIST DEITY CHAKRASAMVARA

approx. 1600–1700

China

Ming (1368–1644) or Qing dynasty (1644–1911)

Bronze with gilding

H. 30.5 cm × W. 25.4 cm x. D. 11.4 cm

The Avery Brundage Collection, B60B179

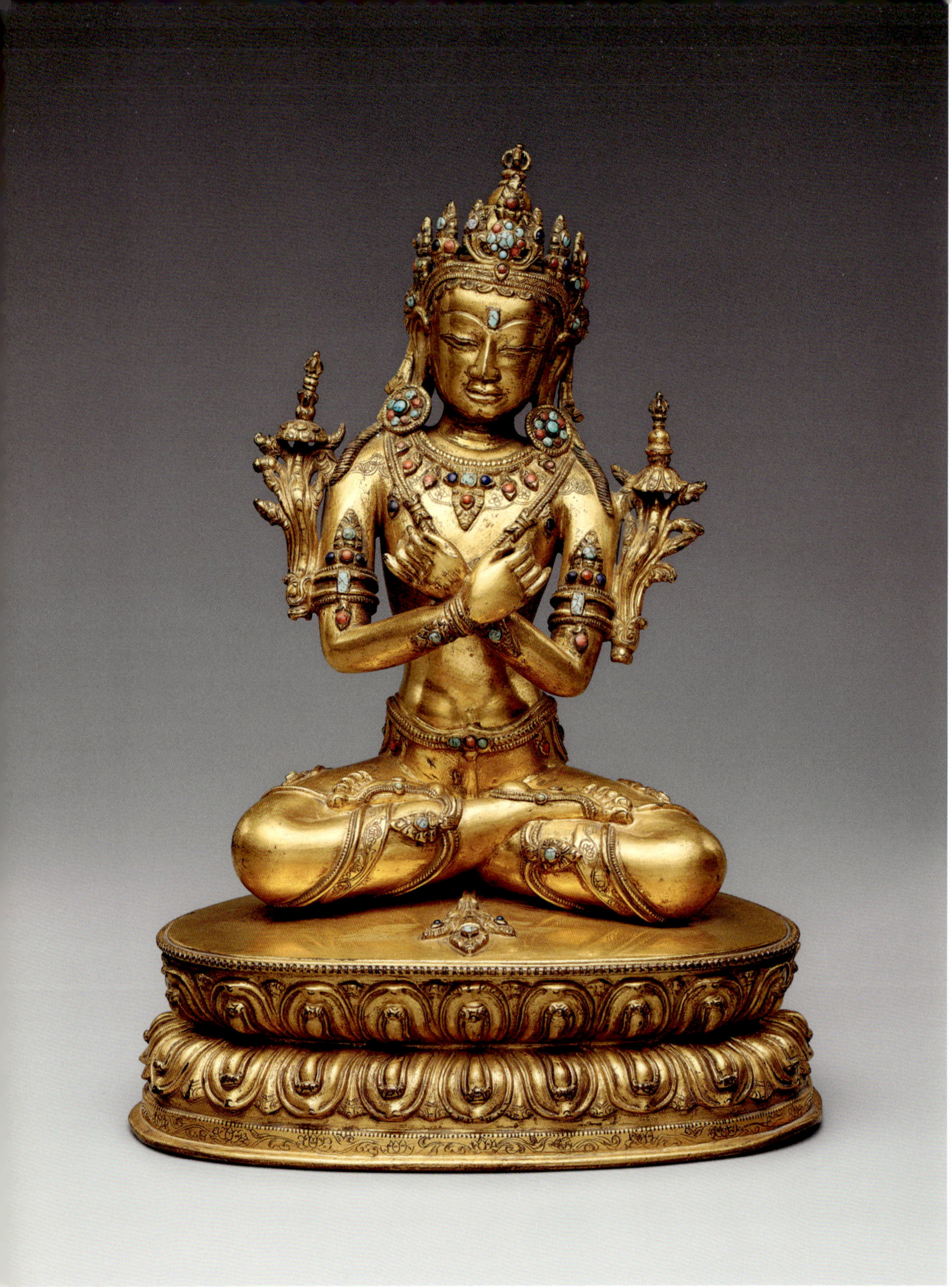

THE BUDDHIST DEITY VAJRADHARA

1500–1600

Tibet

Bronze with gilding and inlaid turquoise, coral, and lapis lazuli

H. 30.5 cm × W. 23.5 cm × D. 15.9 cm

The Avery Brundage Collection, B60B165

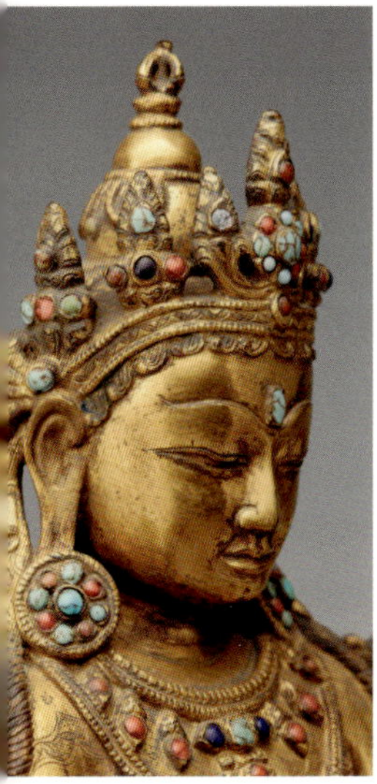

Over the course of a millennium in India, the conception of what it meant to be a Buddha, literally an "awakened one," grew and expanded. At first, "Buddha" simply referred to the historical figure Shakyamuni. Then, as others practiced the dharma and experienced enlightenment (nirvana), they concluded that, given the infinite temporal scope of the Buddhist cosmos, Shakyamuni could not be a unique being. Other beings must have discovered and realized enlightenment—so there must be other Buddhas in other places or times, however distant they might be. Thus, even in the early Pali texts, the first known Buddhist scriptures, a series of seven human Buddhas was posited.

Under the influence of Mahayana (Great Vehicle) texts, these other Buddhas then began to proliferate into a large number of "cosmic" Buddhas. Each cosmic Buddha was thought to oversee his own universe, each with its own particular characteristics. At this point, Buddhist thinkers began to ask themselves a basic but crucial question: where did all these multifarious "cosmic" Buddhas come from?

One answer to this question was that there was a primordial Buddha from whom all others had emanated. Vajradhara, the "holder of the thunderbolt," is one form of the original, primordial Buddha. In this sculpture, Vajradhara can be identified by his crossed forearms, which make the power-projecting posture called *vajra-hum-kara* (a term that refers to the thunderbolt-like syllable "hum" that Vajradhara embodies). Two lotuses on Vajradhara's shoulders support a thunderbolt and a bell. The thunderbolt on his right shoulder represents the male principle of strategic spiritual action (*upaya*) as well as the compassion with which such actions must be applied. The bell on his left shoulder symbolizes the female principle of emptiness (*shunyata*) realized by wisdom.

The artist who created this fine bronze sculpture decorated it with tiny pieces of turquoise from Tibet, coral from Italy, and lapis lazuli from Afghanistan. Note the precise bilateral symmetry according to which these semiprecious stones have been applied to Vajradhara's gilded body; the turquoise at his third eye occupies the central axis, while lapis and coral symmetrically flank the turquoise. The finely incised patterns around Vajradhara's neck and below his lotus seat further reveal the manifold skills of the artist.

—JD

THE LAMA BUTON RINCHEN DRUP

By Khyenrab Jamyang (Tibetan, active 1650–1700)

Colors and gold on cotton

H. 88.9 cm × W. 61.6 cm (image); H. 166.7 cm × W. 96.5 cm (overall)

The Avery Brundage Collection, B60D38

Iridescent halo shimmering behind him, the lama Buton Rinchen Drup smiles out from deep empty darkness. In the fourteenth century, Buton organized the Buddhist canon into scripture (Kanjur) and commentary (Tenjur) from his home monastery of Shalu in southwestern Tibet. He also established guidelines for creating mandalas (meditation maps in the form of visionary palaces) that inform Tibetan Buddhism to this day. Buton was an inclusive thinker who drew ideas from many meditative and artistic traditions. Lamas from many different Tibetan Buddhist orders are arrayed along each side of his throne. This painting is stylistically inclusive, incorporating elements of Tibetan, Nepalese, and Chinese traditions.

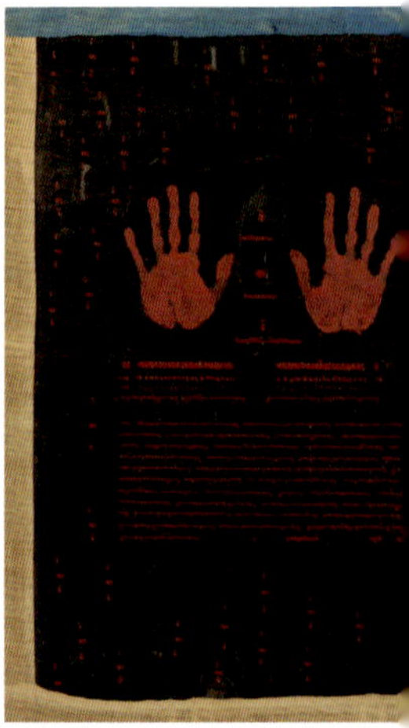

The reverse of the painting bears a series of inscriptions unique in Tibetan art both for their completeness and for their superb calligraphy. In the center of the dark surface, Buton's ghostly shadow hovers between two cinnabar handprints. The anonymous owner of these hands likely penned the veritable Rosetta stone of Buddhist sacred script that appears below them. Here, a standard Buddhist consecration phrase appears in four different forms, in formal *landza*, flowing *siddham*, standard Tibetan *uchan* ("with heads") script, and cursive Tibetan *umey* ("without heads") script.

In every script, the text reads the same: "The Buddha has explained the cause of all things that arise from a cause. He, the Great Monk, has also explained their cessation." This phrase succinctly summarizes the fundamental thought of the Buddha, which led to his enlightenment. Indeed, it transforms the object on which it is inscribed into a virtual stupa, which is itself the visual emblem of the mind of the Buddha.

If this painting is a virtual stupa, a Buddhist reliquary, just whose relics does it contain? The reverse of the painting reveals the answer. Here, several occurrences of the three-syllable sequence *om ah hum* (body, speech, mind) appear. When juxtaposed with painted images on the front of the *thangka*, we see that these syllables have been written at the brows, throats, and hearts of the figures represented on the front. What principle is behind this peculiar pattern?

The syllables behind each figure are traces of an important Vajrayana (esoteric) Buddhist rite of consecration. Lamas use this procedure to "seal" a being into its representation. Such consecration procedures are thought to preserve the presence and the power of the being a painting virtually contains, just as a stupa might be thought to contain the physical relics of the Buddha.

—*JD*

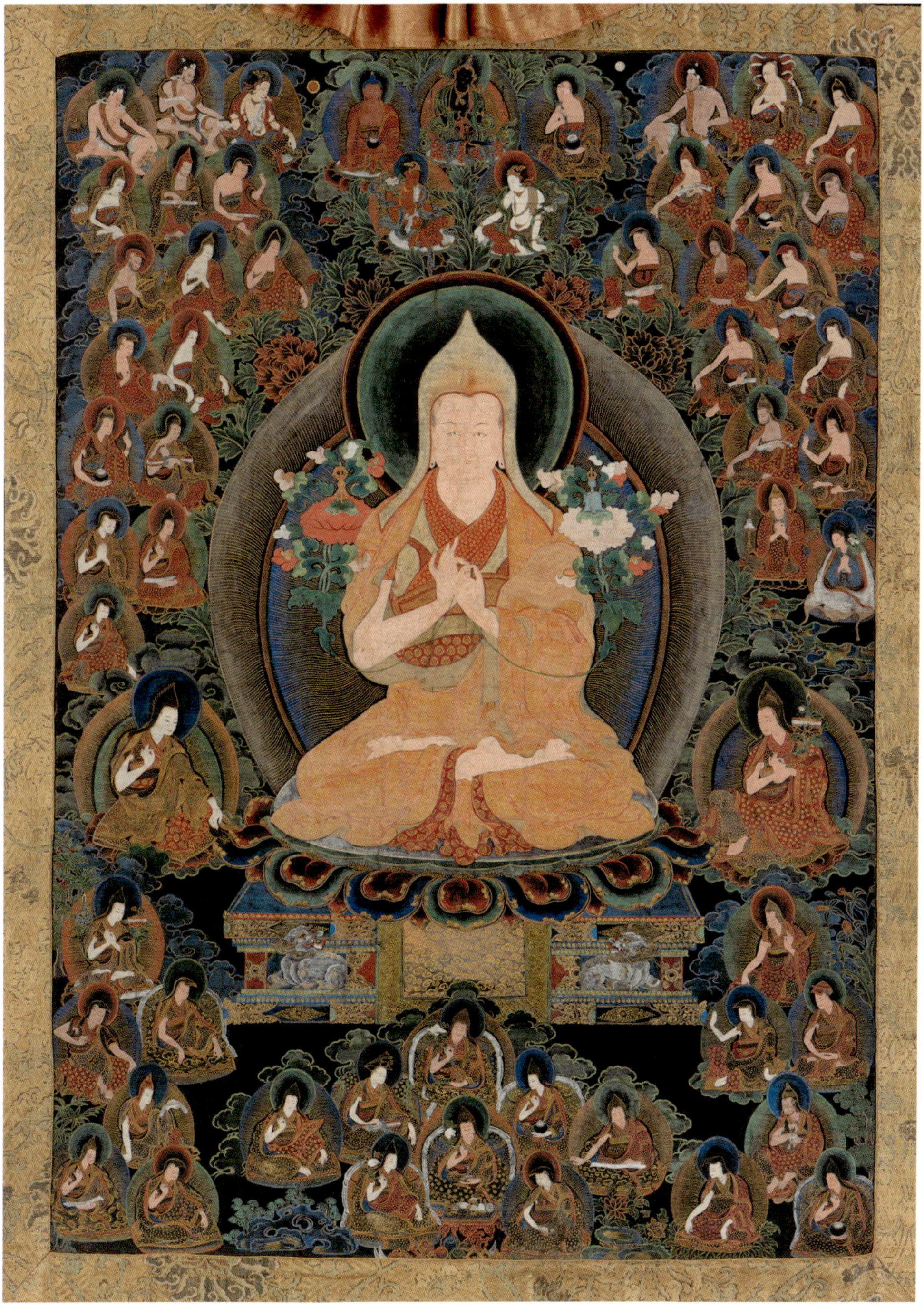

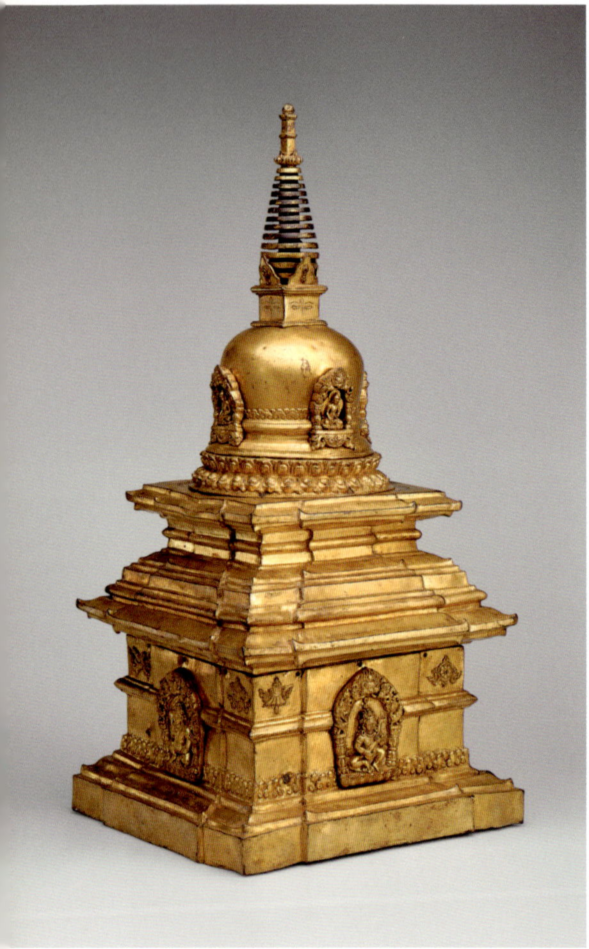

SVAYAMBHU STUPA

1700–1800
Nepal
Copper with gilding
H. 52.7 cm × W. 25.4 cm × D. 25.4 cm
The Avery Brundage Collection, B60B212

This gilded sculpture is a symbolic replica of the Svayambhu (Self-Born) Stupa, a monumental Buddhist reliquary in Kathmandu, Nepal. The most important monument of Nepalese Buddhism, it is called "self-born" because it is thought to have appeared from a lotus blossom; since lotus flowers bloom on dark ponds without visible means of support, they are the symbol par excellence of self-existence in South Asian imagery.

According to the Nepalese story, an ancient Buddha once planted a lotus seed in a lake in the Kathmandu valley. The seed grew into a self-born lotus flower; its petals appear just beneath the central dome on this sculpture. Then, a five-colored beam of light spontaneously emanated from the lotus. Each color corresponded to one of five directional Buddhas: blue Akshobhya (The Unshakeable) in the east, yellow Ratnasambhava (Jewel-Born) in the south, red Amitabha (Infinite Light) in the west, green Amoghasiddhi (Unfailing Attainment) in the north, and white Vairochana (The Effulgent) in the center.

The above account corresponds with what we see on this stupa. Each of four Buddhas appears on a visible face of the cube atop the dome. Although their characteristic colors are not used here, each Buddha can be identified by a specific symbol and hand gesture: a symbolic thunderbolt appears above Akshobhya, who touches the earth; a jewel above Ratnasambhava, who makes the gift-giving gesture; a lotus above Amitabha, who folds his hands one atop the other in meditation; and two crossed ritual objects (*vajras*) above Amoghasiddhi, who holds up his right hand in the "no-fear" gesture. The fifth Buddha, Vairochana, looks out with half-closed eyes from the four sides of the cube atop the dome.

The earliest Buddhist stupas were created to contain the relics of the historical Buddha Shakyamuni, his disciples, or even his teachings. This stupa, however, did not come to the Asian Art Museum of San Francisco with its consecration deposit intact. For this reason, when the museum moved to the Civic Center, Bhutanese lamas reconsecrated the sculpture. They included in the new consecration deposit traditional herbs, sacred texts, and a wooden central axis. After the ceremony, they resealed the stupa; the original seal, which includes the crossed *vajras* of Amoghasiddhi, is now displayed underneath the stupa. When consecrated and sealed, the stupa retains the power of the objects it holds inside. Since the spiritual potencies it contains cannot, in Buddhist thought, leak out of a stupa, the benefits of objects sealed within are theoretically available to worshipers forever.
—*JD*

THE BUDDHA SHAKYAMUNI AT MOUNT MERU

approx. 1700–1800
Tibet
Colors on cotton
H. 99.4 cm × W. 65.1 cm (image)
The Avery Brundage Collection, B60D13+

The central figure depicted in this *thangka* presents a great mystery. He looks like the historical Buddha Shakyamuni, but he is painted in actual gold rather than the typical saffron. The golden hue represents the Buddha's merit (*punya*), but the golden richness of the image also generates merit for the donor who commissioned it. Moreover, the setting is not northern India but some other locale. What then does this painting depict?

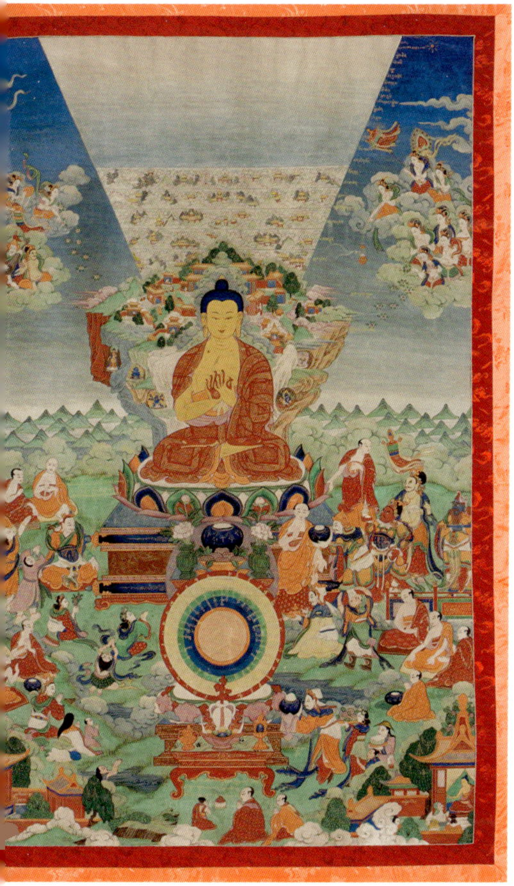

The first clue is that the Buddha is surrounded by the guardians of the four directions; they typically appear in images of the cosmos. A second lies in the painting's background, a series of mountain peaks that exhibit a slight curvature and represent a range called Chakravada. These mountains surround the Buddhist cosmos like a circle. A third clue lies behind the Buddha. It is the base of Mount Meru, center and summit of the cosmos. Meru's four directions are clearly labeled with their traditional red, blue, white, and yellow colors. Finally, note the heavenly realms that fan out above the Buddha. These represent different realms attainable through different levels of meditation. The earthly realms below, on the other hand, feature a number of figures making offerings to the Buddha. What is the significance of this peculiar configuration?

According to Tibetan cosmology, imagery that features Mount Meru at the center, with the heavenly realms stacked above it and part of the semicircular chain of mountains behind, represents the entire universe. This imagery plays a key role in the ritual called the "mandala offering." In this ritual, one offers a model of the entire universe to all the Buddhas—and this model, as it turns out, takes precisely the form seen in this painting, whether the model is offered physically or meditatively envisioned.

Such offerings generate merit, which can then create positive effects on individual experience. For example, negative emotions subside, and positive conditions for meeting appropriate teachings and teachers arise. In this way, one creates the conditions necessary for enlightenment. And this kind of traditional Tibetan *thangka*, which reveals the importance of making merit in the process of realizing enlightenment, is like a rare jewel, for it reminds us of the effects of making offerings to benefit all sentient beings—offerings which, like bread cast upon the water, come eventually back to us.

—*Pema Namdol Thaye is a master of traditional Tibetan arts and the author and illustrator of several books, including* A Guided Tour of Hell: A Graphic Memoir.

MASTERPIECE

THE BUDDHIST DEITY SIMHAVAKTRA, A *DAKINI*

China; Beijing or vicinity, Hebei province
Qing dynasty, reign of the Qianlong emperor (1736–1795)
Dry lacquer with inlaid semiprecious stones
H. 142.2 cm × W. 66 cm × D. 30.5 cm
The Avery Brundage Collection, B60S600

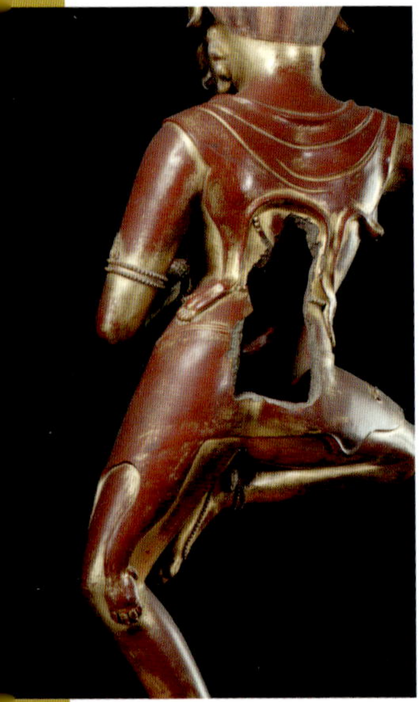

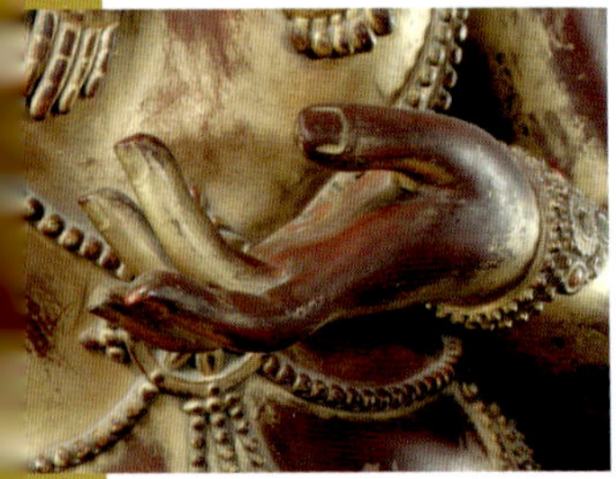

Simhavaktra means "lion-headed," and a *dakini* is a "sky-walker" in Himalayan Buddhism—an inhabitant of the atmosphere. Like many sculptures created for the practice of Vajrayana Buddhism, this Simhavaktra is packed with religious and philosophical symbolism. The third eye in the middle of her forehead is open to suggest that she sees the true nature of reality. She wears human skin that symbolizes the veil of illusion stripped away from perception during the process of meditation. Her jewelry—two bracelets, two anklets, and a necklace—is fivefold, a reference to the five kinds of knowledge that lead to enlightenment. Simhavaktra's flaming hair symbolizes her fierce determination to overcome all superficial appearances and obstacles to enlightenment.

Dakinis like Simhavaktra are known in the Himalayas as guardians of treasure. They perform this function in two ways. First, they guard Tibetan magical texts known as *terma* (treasure). These texts were created by the lama Padmasambhava in the ninth century. They were then hidden to survive a prophesied "age of fragmentation," during which Buddhism would be persecuted and endangered, and were meant to be rediscovered after that age passed.

This Simhavaktra sculpture is a treasure guardian in a second, more strictly physical sense, for she guards a secret consecration deposit in her body. For decades this sculpture was thought to have been robbed of this deposit, due to a prominent gaping hole in her back. Simhavaktra received another examination in 2013, when the Asian Art Museum acquired a borescopic camera that allowed conservators and curators to explore her interior. By threading the camera up through her shoulder and into her muzzle, museum staff confirmed that the treasures contained in Simhavaktra's consecration deposit had not been rifled and were still intact. From a ritual perspective, then, she is just as alive today as when she occupied a Vajrayana monastery in the Himalayas more than two hundred years ago.

—JD

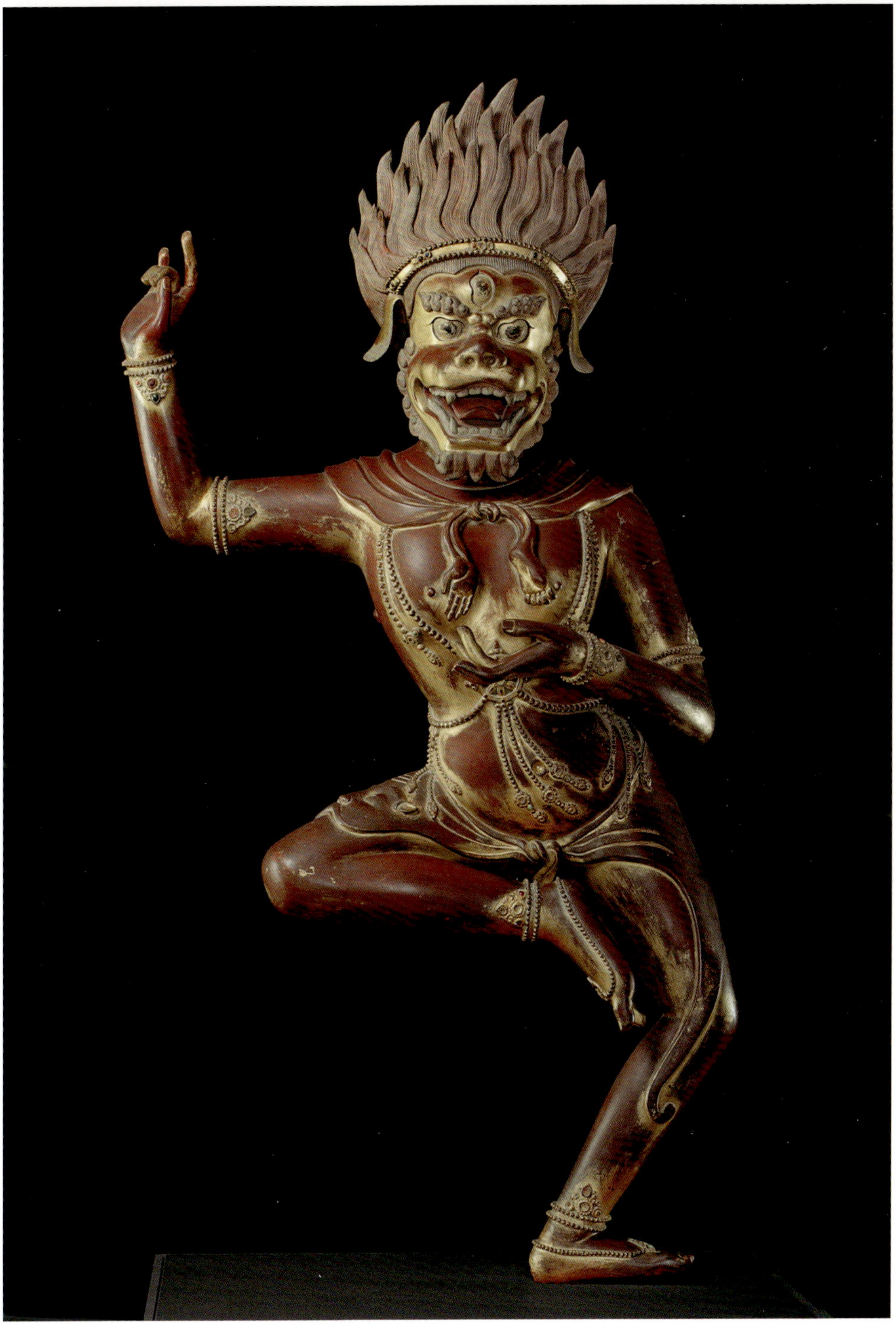

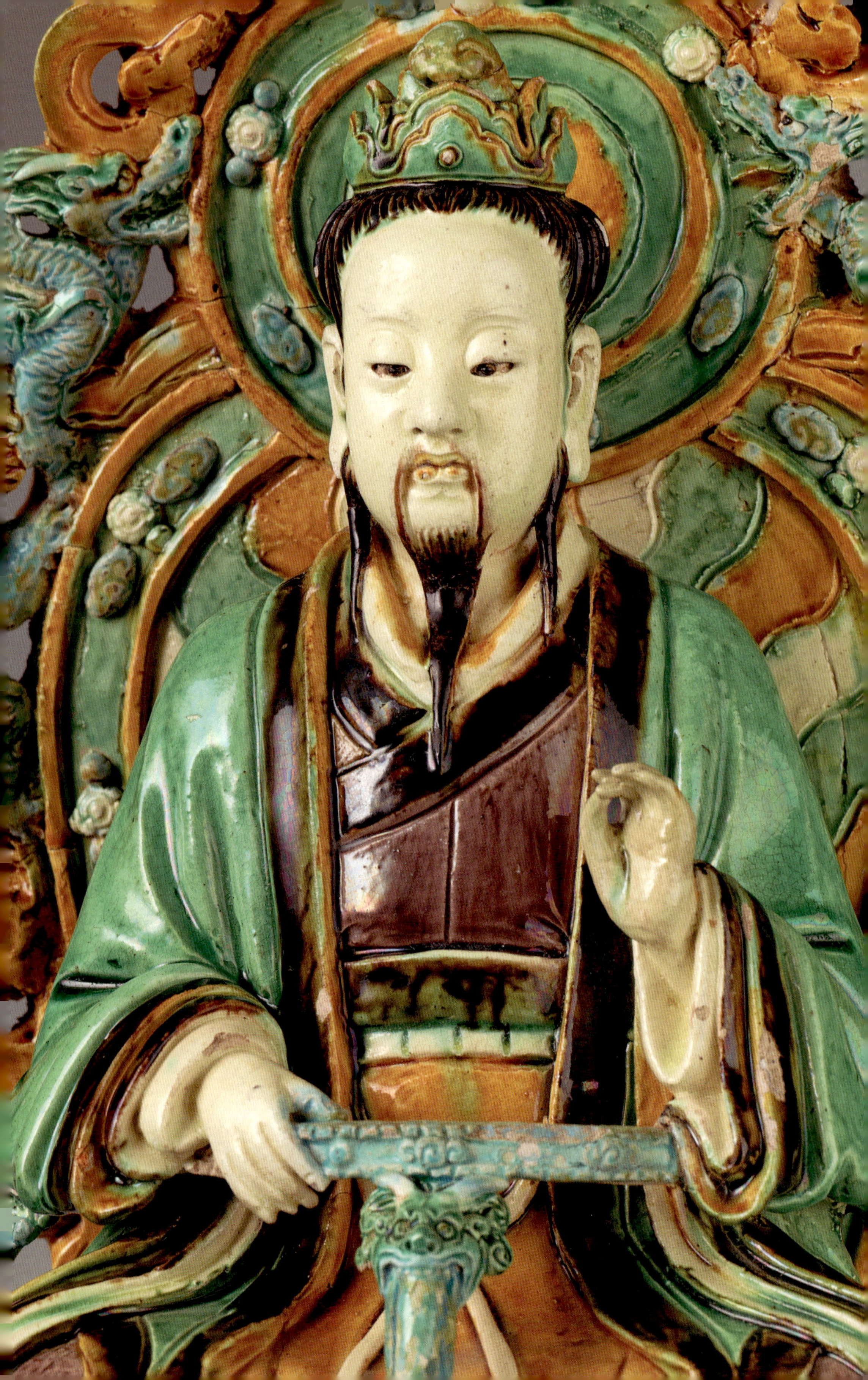

CHINA

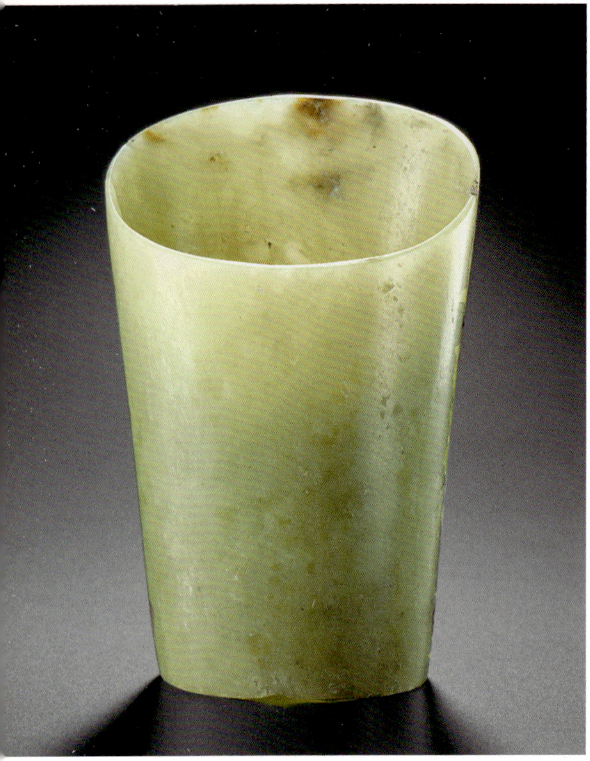

ORNAMENT IN THE SHAPE OF A HOOF

4000–3000 BCE

China; Liaoning province

Neolithic period, Hongshan culture (approx. 4700–2900 BCE)

Nephrite

H. 15.2 cm × Diam. 8.6 cm (at widest point)

The Avery Brundage Collection, B60J226

In Chinese, the term "jade" (*yu*) refers to a wide range of fine minerals, including nephrite, jadeite, and other hard stones in mostly green, yellow, or gray colors. Jade has been venerated for its beauty, purity, rarity, and durability for thousands of years.[1] Ancient Chinese people created jade objects that simulated practical tools and weapons, such as disks (*bi*), axes (*fu*), and blades (*dao*). Many of these were made as ceremonial objects symbolizing power and wealth, and thus they were frequently found in prehistoric burials, hoards, shrines, and other sites.

Situated in the Liao River basin and representing one of the oldest Neolithic traditions in northeastern China, the Hongshan culture was known for its construction of large stone worship sites, such as altars and temples. It also developed a distinctive jade culture reflected in its characteristic jade wares, such as a pig-dragon pendant and this horse-hoof-like tube.

The function of horse-hoof objects is still open to debate. Some scholars suggest that because they were often found in graves close to the heads of the deceased, they were hair ornaments indicating status or privilege. Others suggest they were cult objects exclusively owned by high-ranking tribal priests who used them to facilitate communication between the supernatural and human realms.

—*FJZ*

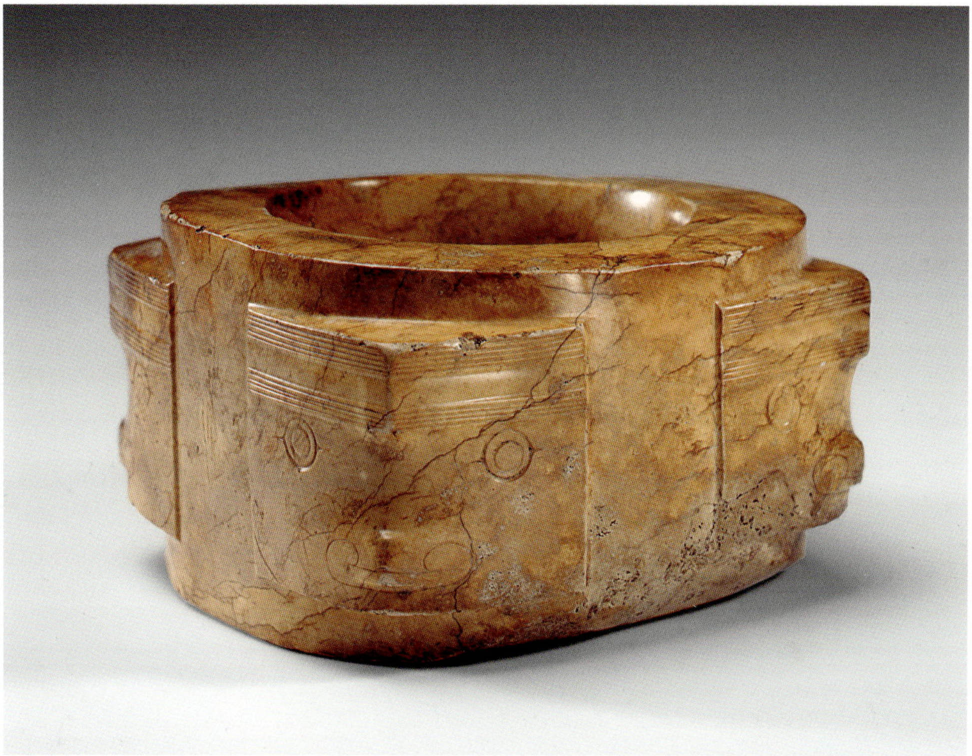

RITUAL OBJECT (*CONG*)

China; Jiangsu or Zhejiang province

Neolithic period, Liangzhu culture (approx. 3400–2200 BCE)

Nephrite

H. 5.7 cm × W. 9.2 cm × D. 9.2 cm

The Avery Brundage Collection, B60J603

Located in the lower reach of the Yangtze River, the Liangzhu culture had an advanced jade industry. The discoveries of rich carvings from its cemeteries and ritual sites prove that jade played an important role in Liangzhu society. Its people used quartz sand and other abrasives to cut, grind, and engrave jade into various shapes for ceremonial and personal use. Despite the technological difficulty of this time-consuming process, jade art reached new heights in Liangzhu and profoundly affected the Neolithic cultures of neighboring regions.

Among the jade disks, beads, plaques, and tubes unearthed from Liangzhu, the two most popular shapes are the *cong* (square blocks with cylindrical inner tubes) and the *bi* (perforated disks). According to the ancient ritual text *Rites of Zhou*, a brown *cong* symbolized the square earth while a green *bi* represented the spherical heaven.[2] This short *cong* with a polished surface is decorated with monster-like masks with round eyes. Some *cong* have additional tiers and more schematic surface decoration, showcasing the skillful craftsmanship of jade carving in prehistoric China. This object type later spread to other regions in China, possibly because of its enigmatic form of religious significance.

The irresistible qualities of jade continued to fascinate in the millennia that followed the Liangzhu. Worshiping the magical power of jade, Chinese people frequently used jade articles as personal tokens, household ornaments, and even burial goods. Jade also became the favorite stone of the perfect gentleman, and Confucian scholars believed it embodied the five human virtues—benevolence, righteousness, courtesy, wisdom, and integrity.

—*FJZ*

THREE-PRONGED PLAQUE WITH ANIMAL-MASK DESIGNS

China; Jiangsu or Zhejiang province

Neolithic period, Liangzhu culture (approx. 3400–2200 BCE)

Nephrite

H. 3.8 cm × W. 6 cm × D. 1.3 cm

Gift of Chauncey Peter Lowe, 2001.31

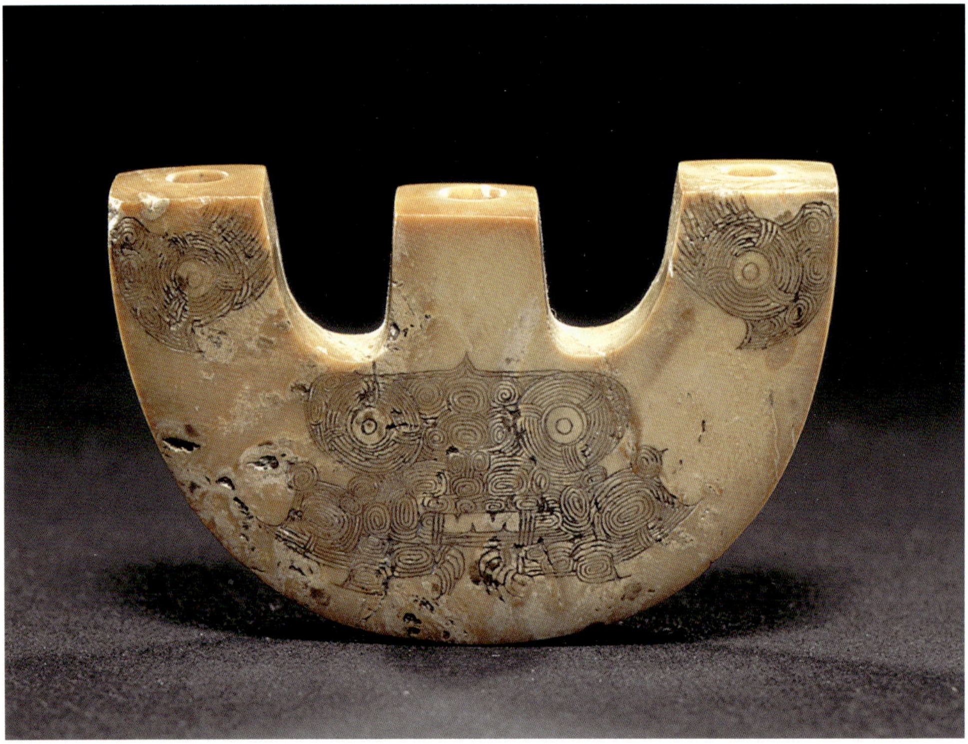

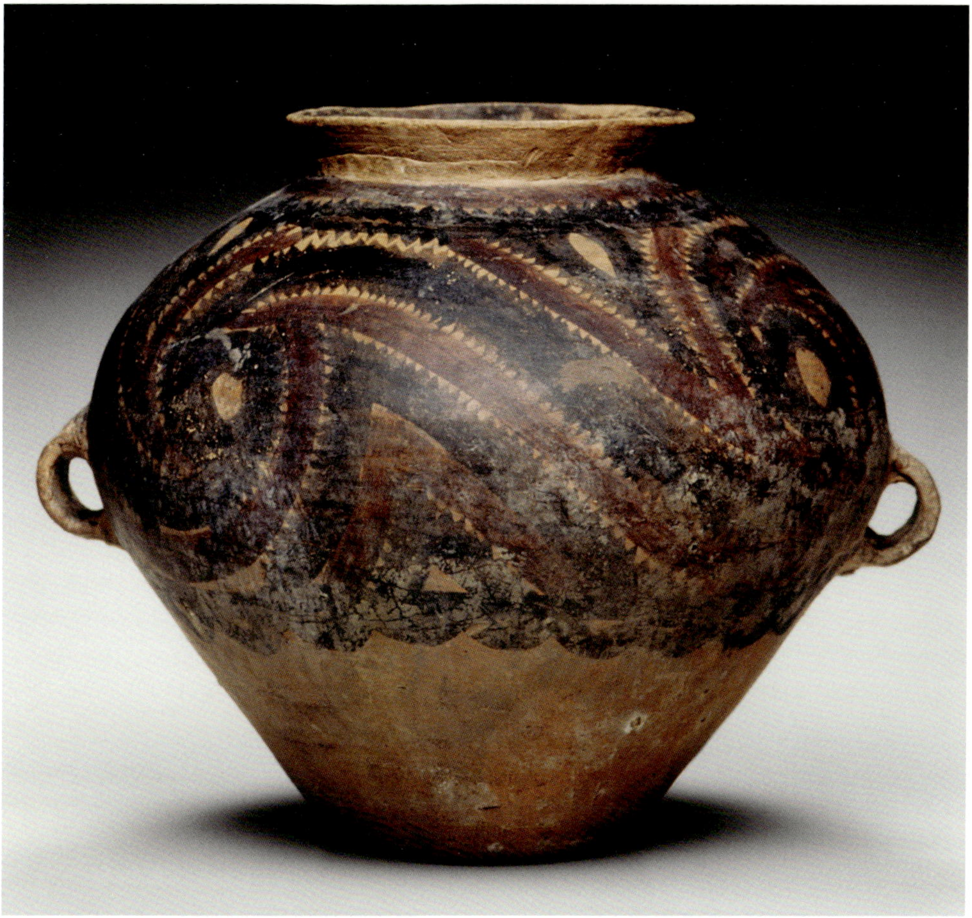

DOUBLE-HANDLED JAR

China; Gansu province
Neolithic period, Majiayao culture (approx. 3300–2000 BCE)
Earthenware with painted decoration
H. 24.1 cm × W. 21.6 cm
The Avery Brundage Collection, B60P1836

This funerary jar comes from the Majiayao culture in the Gansu and Qinghai provinces of northwestern China. This agrarian society, probably a regional subset of the Yangshao civilization, had connections with other early civilized societies in the Central Plains of China during the late Neolithic period (approx. 3000–2000 BCE).

There were two major types of pottery in Neolithic China: unpainted black clay pottery from the coastal region of the east and red clay pottery with painted patterns from central and northwestern China. The decoration of painted pottery often features geometric, floral, and zoomorphic patterns in dynamic and bold lines of brown and black mineral pigments.

This painted pottery is a typical Majiayao vessel, which was handcrafted by stacking coils of clay into a round body before firing. Its dark orange color contrasts with the dense decoration on its upper part. The ornament is not a realistic representation of animals or birds but wavelike alternating brown and black lines formulating concentric swirls. Boldly painted encircling designs and dynamic spirals such as this convey a rhythmic energy that supplements the robust shapes of large Majiayao jars, urns, and basins.
—*FJZ*

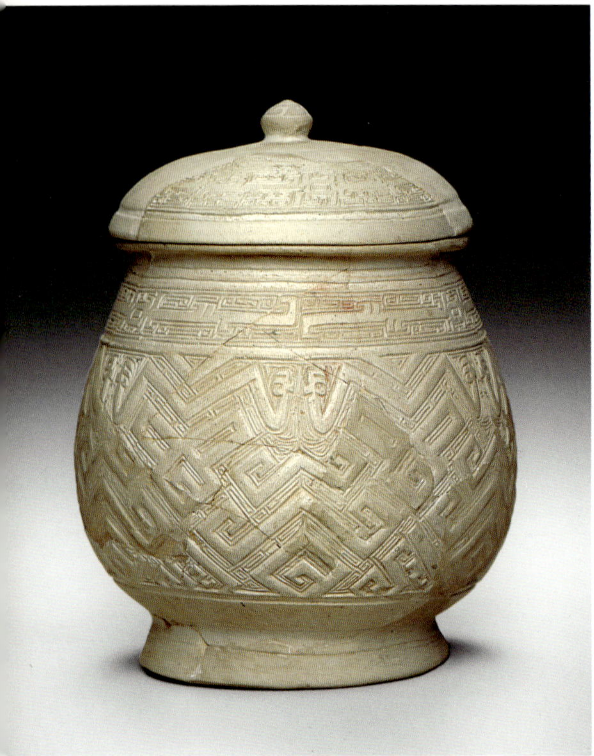

In both shape and design, the production of white earthenware occurred in sync with that of bronze wares. Both were in demand by Shang aristocrats who used them as altar vessels for holding sacrifices of food or wine. This piece corresponds in style to a common type of Shang bronze art, and the principal decoration on its body is worked in intaglio. Its series of triangular patterns consists of stylized zoomimic bodies and claws. Motifs on the lid and around the neck of the vessel echo Shang bronze décor, with simple dragons in profile against a spiral ground.

At Yinxu in Henan province, in central China, hundreds of late Shang white-earthenware vessels—including this jar—were discovered in the 1900s. This lidded jar offers significant information about early Chinese ceramic production. Scientific analysis shows that Shang white earthenware is composed primarily of kaolin clay with oxides of silicon, aluminum, and iron, which are necessary for the high-temperature vitrifying that results in the vessel's hardness. This earthenware required a firing temperature of 1,000°C, higher than the 850–950°C required for other earthenware.

—*HL*

LIDDED JAR WITH DESIGN OF DRAGONS

1300–1050 BCE
China; Henan province
Shang dynasty (approx. 1600–1050 BCE)
High-fired ceramic with carved decoration
H. 20 cm × Diam. 21 cm
The Avery Brundage Collection, B60P538

Shang dynasty white earthenware such as this jar holds a special place in the study of ancient ceramics of the Chinese Bronze Age. The later phase of Shang-dynasty culture, celebrated for its artistic and technical achievements, is characterized by prolific production of works made of bronze, jade, and ceramics. Many of these works were made for the rituals that played a vital role in the Shang political structure. The royal pottery workshop, known as *Taoshi*, created an entirely new medium—white earthenware, a relatively inexpensive material—specifically for ritual vessels.

RITUAL WINE VESSEL (*YAYI JIA*)

approx. 1300–1050 BCE
China; Henan province
Shang dynasty (approx. 1600–1050 BCE)
Bronze
H. 75.3 cm × W. 38.1 cm × D. 31.8 cm
The Avery Brundage Collection, B61B11+

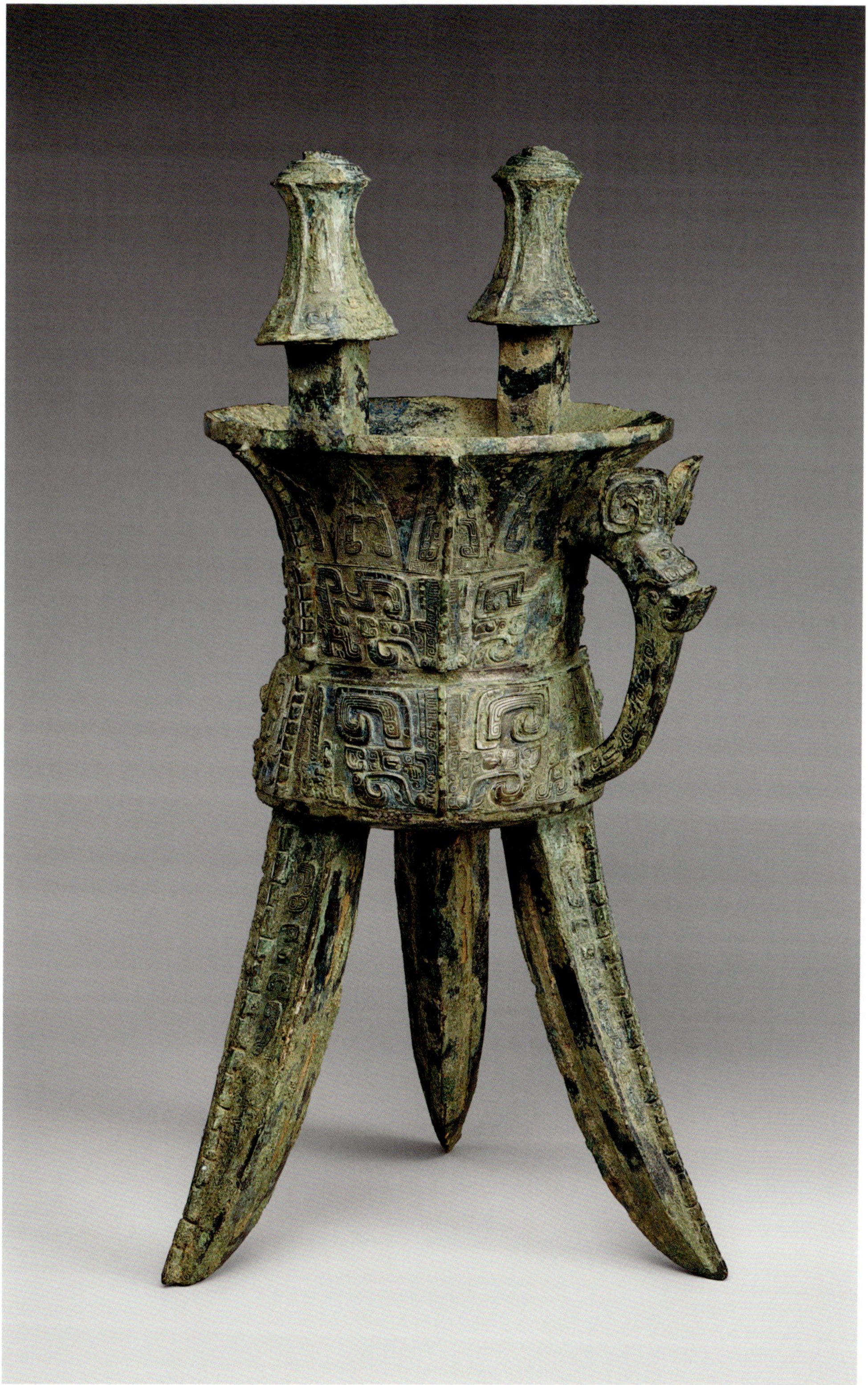

MASTERPIECE

RITUAL VESSEL IN THE SHAPE OF A RHINOCEROS

probably 1100–1050 BCE
China; unearthed in Shouzhang, Shandong province
Shang dynasty (approx. 1600–1050 BCE)
Bronze
H. 22.8 cm × W. 22.8 cm × D. 32.8 cm
The Avery Brundage Collection, B60B1+

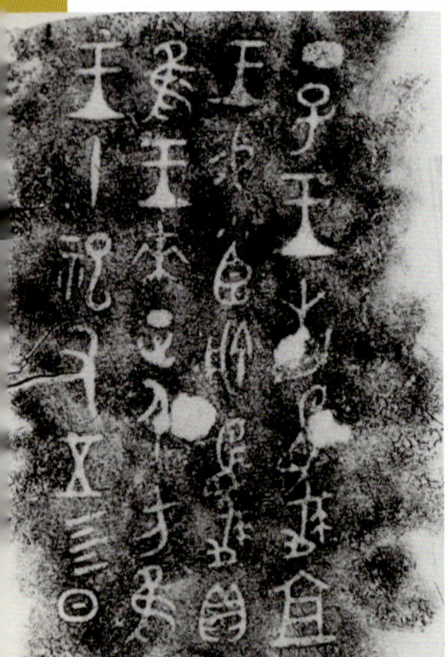

Sometime in the second half of the eleventh century BCE, a courtier at the mighty kingdom of Shang commissioned this bronze vessel, one that is among the most celebrated Chinese bronzes in the world.

This vessel is extraordinary for two reasons: its shape and its text. Animal shapes of any kind were rare among Bronze Age Chinese vessels, but this one is unique, portraying a rhinoceros in the flesh. Though measuring only nine inches tall, the beast is lively and powerful, with features portrayed with a straightforward, natural charm. Its drooping body is heavy and plump, imparting a very tactile appeal; its legs are stout and splayed, conveying vividly the great weight they carry; its skull appears like a powerful locomotive with two horns. The bronze caster attentively depicted the teeth and the puckered hide, odd-numbered toes, and stubby tail. The extended ears indicate that the rhinoceros is in a state of high alert. One detail the caster omitted, however, is the genitals of the beast; we do not know its sex.

The fact that the rhinoceros has two horns suggests a Sumatran rhinoceros, which probably roamed the land of China three millennia ago. The rhinoceros's belly is exaggerated to accommodate a rounded cavity, which makes it a vessel. The vessel would originally have had a lid, one probably modeled to conform to the contours of the animal's body.

The courtier in question went into some length intimating the reason for making this extraordinary creature in an inscription in the inside bottom of the vessel. Composed of twenty-seven characters, the inscription (shown at left) may be translated as,

> *On the day* dingsi *[the 54th day of the ancient Chinese sixty-day cycle], the King inspected the Kui temple. The King bestowed upon Xiaochen [Lesser Minister] Yu cowry shells from Kui. It was the time when the King returned from the military campaign against the Renfang. It was the King's fifteenth sacrificial cycle, a day in the rong-ritual cycle.*[3]

Lesser Minster Yu apparently commissioned the rhinoceros-shaped vessel as a tangible testimony for his service to the Shang king, one that warranted a royal grant of cowrie shells, which could be used as a medium of exchange for other commodities such as metal. He took pain to document the place and time of the king's gift. Yet, he was mute on the actual accomplishment for which he was rewarded, though we can suspect it involved the military campaign. Equally mystifying was why he chose to have his vessel made in the shape of a rhinoceros, though he surely succeeded in capturing our fascination and inspiring our imagination with it.

—JX

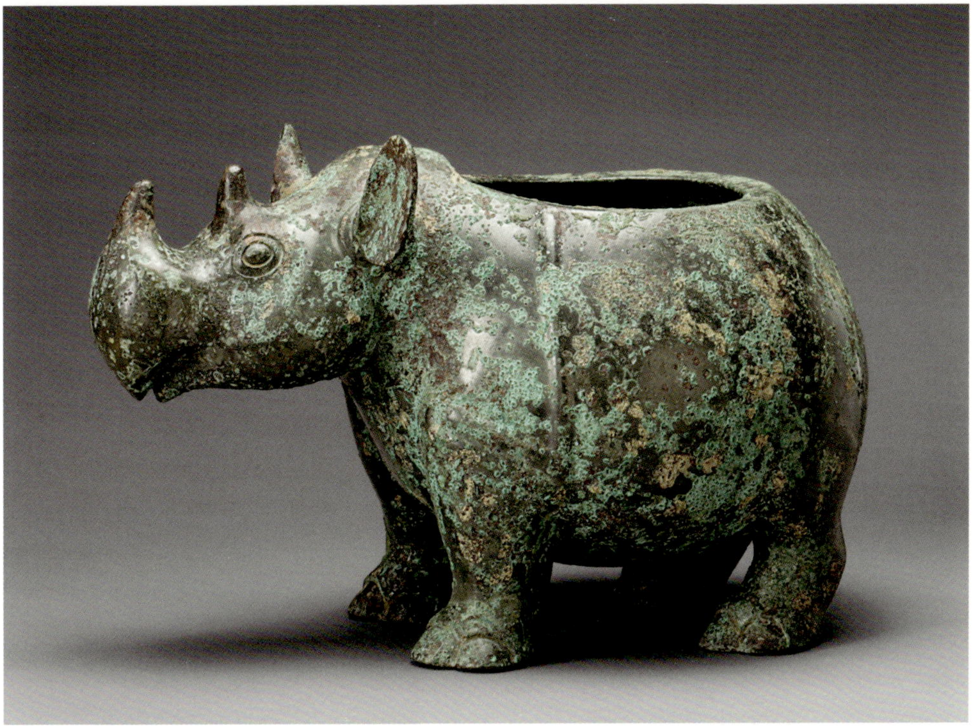

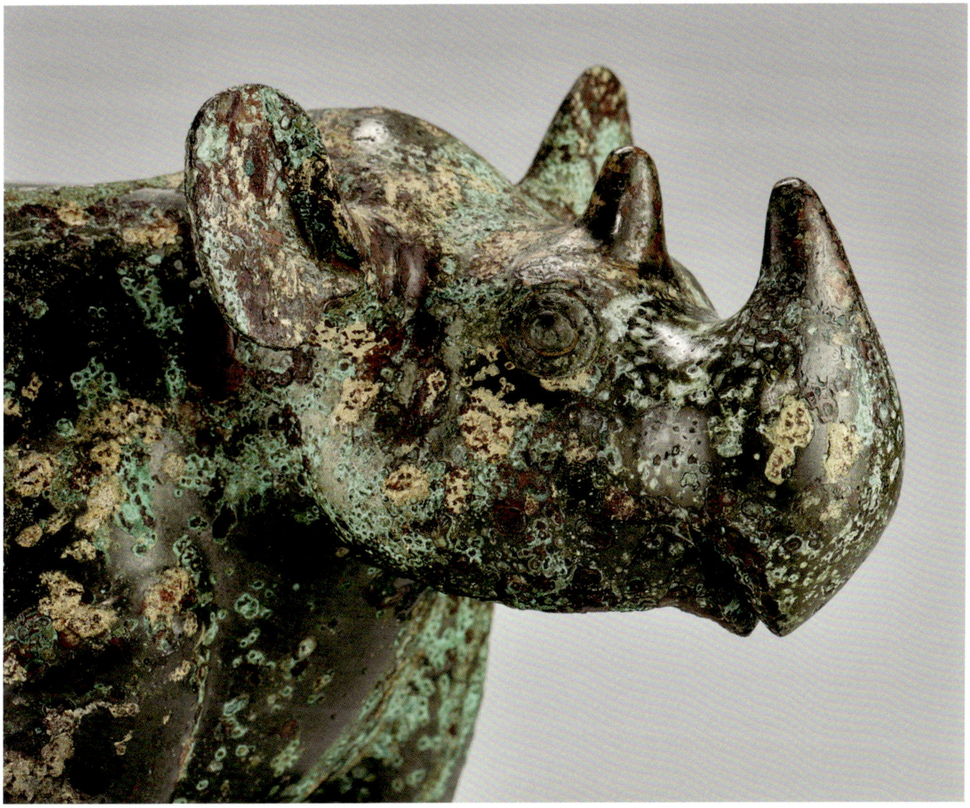

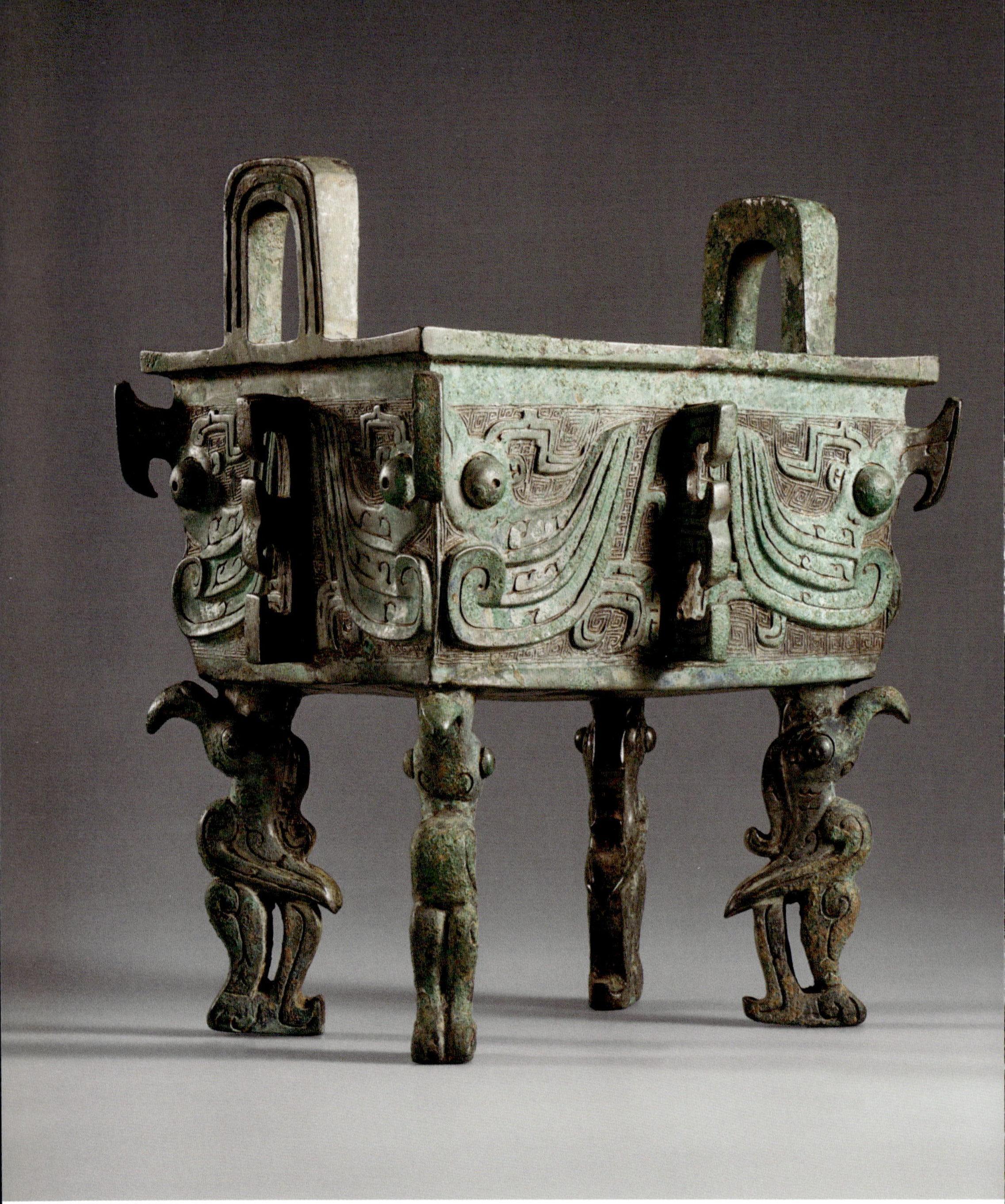

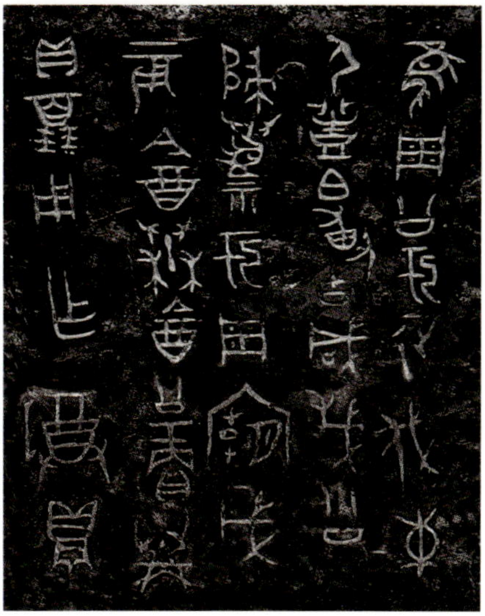

RITUAL FOOD VESSEL

approx. 1042–1021 BCE
China; unearthed in Baoji, Shaanxi province
Western Zhou period (approx. 1050–771 BCE)
Bronze
H. 25.4 cm × W. 22.9 cm × D. 16.5 cm
The Avery Brundage Collection, B60B2+

Among the more than seven hundred bronzes in the collection of the Asian Art Museum of San Francisco, this ritual vessel (the Ran cauldron) has attracted the greatest attention from scholars. This vessel is widely recognized as one of the most historically important of all Western Zhou period (approx. 1050–771 BCE) bronzes to be published since the 1950s.

This vessel is unique in both its style and inscription. Eight big-eyed, long-beaked, long-tailed, and crested birds in high relief cover the entire surface of the body, a decorative scheme that is very different from the tao-tieh motifs that appear on most late Shang (approx. 1250–1050 BCE) and early Western Zhou bronzes. Each bird is in a panel separated from the next by a central flange and faces a corner of the vessel, the beaks of each pair fusing together to form a shoe-shaped projection. The legs are formed of three-dimensional birds facing outward on the diagonal.

More importantly, the inscription, which appears on one of the inside walls and continues on to the interior base in five columns, records an important event: the thirty-four graphs reference a military campaign to the east led by the Duke of Zhou, the brother of the Western Zhou's founder, King Wu, in the first years after the Zhou's conquest of the Shang, around 1045 BCE. The Duke of Zhou, or Zhou Gong, later became a cultural hero in China and a symbol of perfect virtue and loyalty. Because of this inscription, the vessel is also called the *Zhou Gong dong zheng ding* (The Duke of Zhou's Eastern Campaign cauldron). Its other name, Ran cauldron, comes from the person, Ran, who commissioned the vessel, as mentioned in the inscription.

Ironically, the rediscovery of this vessel was also related to military action. In the 1920s, China was ruled by independent warlords, some of whom were notorious for looting ancient tombs. One of these warlords was Dang Yukun, who between 1917 and 1928 was stationed with his troops in Baoji (in Shaanxi province), an area abounding in ancient tombs. It is believed that the Ran cauldron was looted by Dang and his troops at the Daijiawan cemetery nearby.[4]

—Tianlong Jiao is Josef de Heer Curator of Asian Art at Denver Art Museum.

RITUAL WINE VESSEL WITH LID (*JI FA GONG*)

approx. 1100–1000 BCE

China; Henan province

Shang dynasty (approx. 1600–1050 BCE) or Western Zhou period (approx. 1050–771 BCE)

Bronze

H. 31.8 cm × W. 38.1 cm × D. 13.3 cm

The Avery Brundage Collection, B60B1004

A heavy lid follows the undulating profile of the rim of this gravy-boat-like vessel. A grinning bottle-horned dragon head covers the front while a tao-tieh (the face of a mythical animal) is at the rear. The tao-tieh has horns in the form of dragons and a beak that juts out over a massive loop handle. The upper part of the handle resembles a gargoyle with horns like those of the tao-tieh. The gargoyle devours a beaked bird, whose neck and wings form the rest of the loop (a hook hanging from the loop is a tail plume). The body of the vessel is divided horizontally into three zones, which are divided into compartments by vertical flanges. Crested birds fringed with barbs occupy these compartments. Their beaks and claws are shaped to match the barbs. The birds are executed in moderately high relief, their smooth surfaces set off by a ground pattern of fine spirals.

The matching inscriptions that are cast inside the body and the lid follow a standard formula well established in China's late Shang period (1200–1050 BCE). The text reads, "The second son Ji [or Qi] Fa made this vessel for offerings to his cultured father Ding." This is followed by two characters that are official titles of Ji Fa. An almost identical *gong* in the Princeton University Art Museum has the same dedicatee—"cultured father Ding"—but does not mention the patron's name or title except for a graph that means "the fourth son."[5] Recent excavations in north China at Anyang, the last capital of the Shang dynasty, in particular excavations of casting debris at foundry sites, have shown that local casters experimented with a wide variety of designs during the last few generations of Shang rule, including designs quite close to this and the Princeton *gong*.[6] The two vessels are thus likely to have been cast at Anyang toward the end of the Shang period, probably by two brothers. The Princeton *gong* is said to have been found, however, far to the west of Anyang, in the Wei River Valley. Recent discoveries in this valley suggest that many vessels found there were plundered from Anyang by the Zhou conquerors.[7]

—Wang Haicheng is Mary and Cheney Cowles Endowed Associate Professor of Art History at the University of Washington.

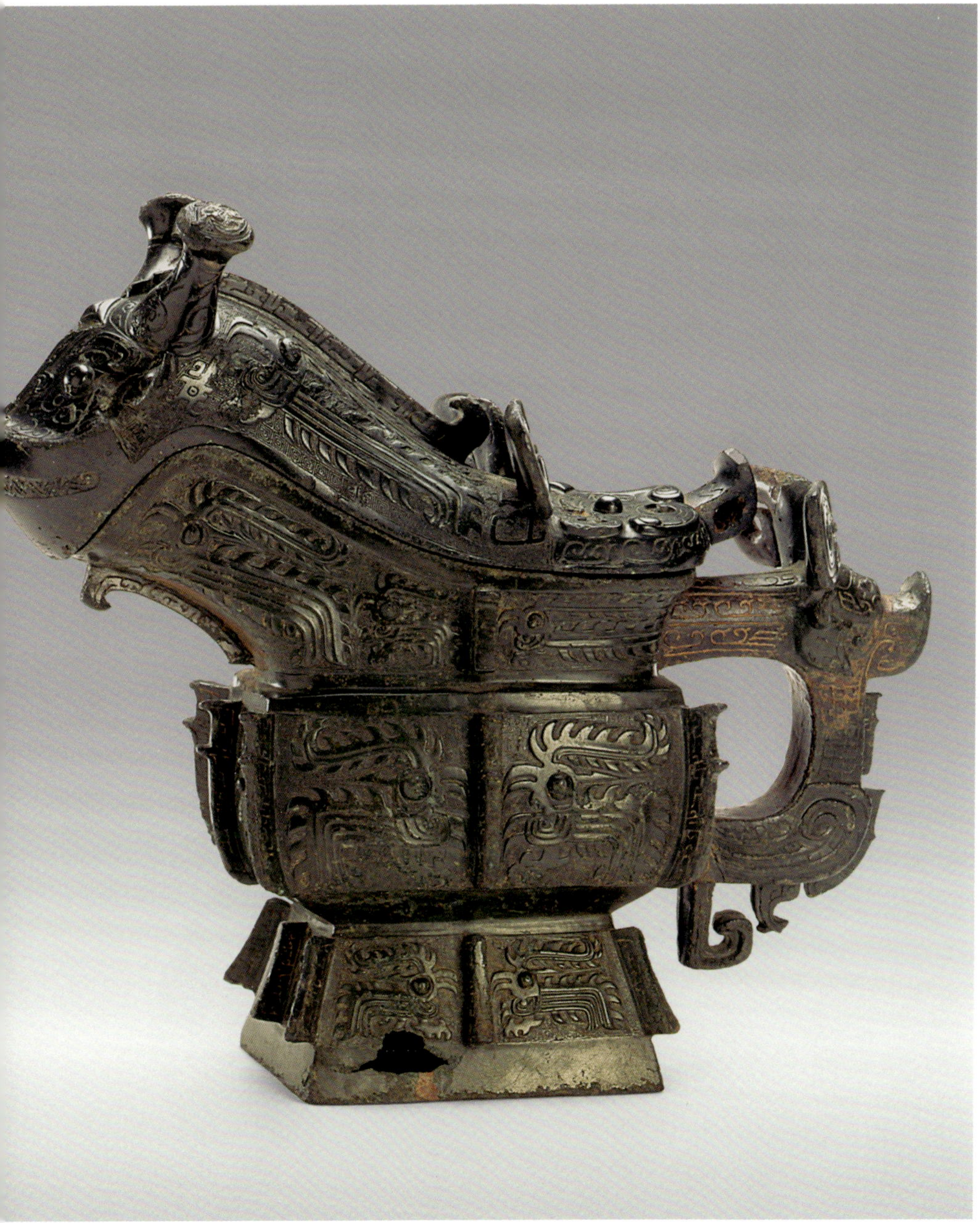

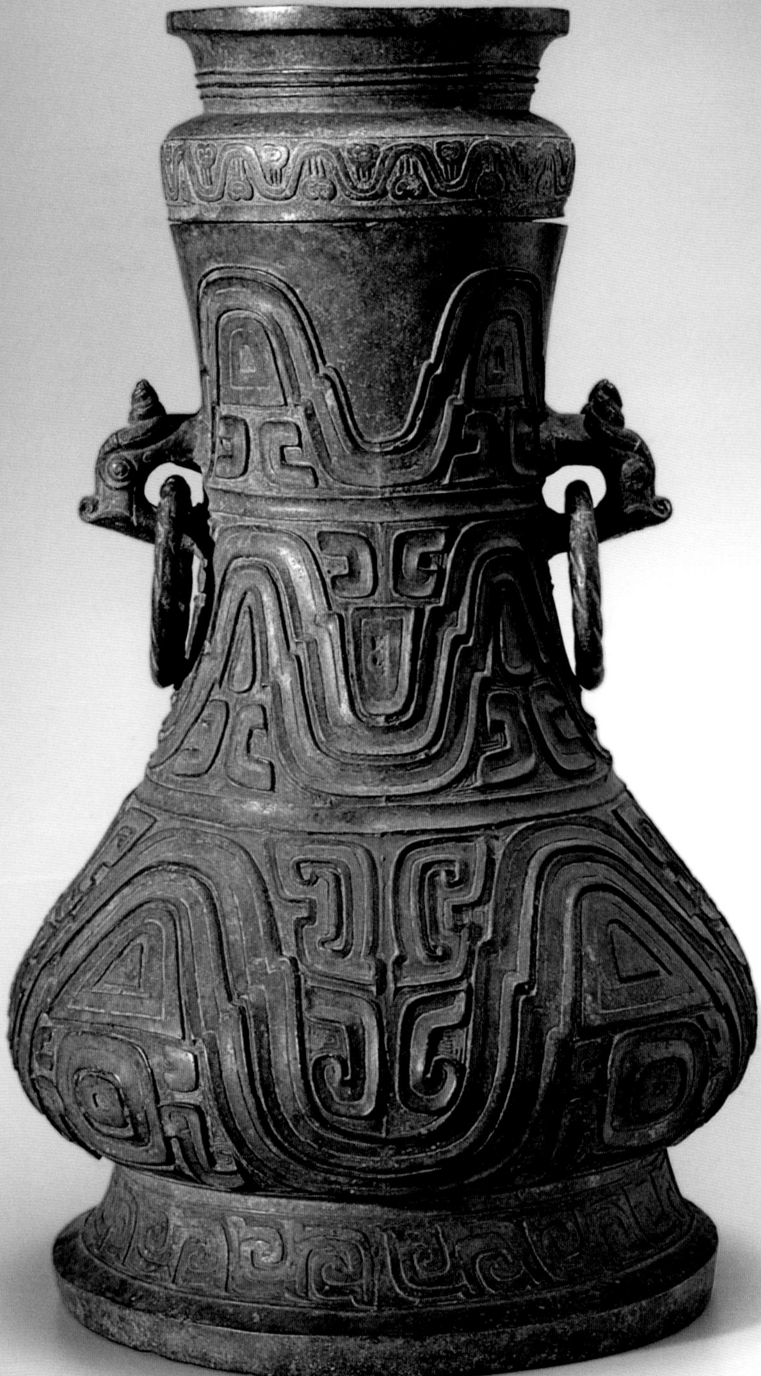

RITUAL WINE VESSEL (*FAN JU SHENG HU*)

—

approx. 900–850 BCE
China
Western Zhou period (approx. 1050–771 BCE)
Bronze
H. 61 cm × W. 36.8 cm × D. 19.7 cm
The Avery Brundage Collection, B60B972

—

The most striking impression of this stately vessel is the horizontal movement of bold waves around a shape that seems to be sagging under its own weight. The static and compartmented schemes of decoration seen on earlier Chinese bronzes have given way here to a design that flows uninterrupted. The strips that form the waves, doubled in the two lower registers but single on the neck, have raised edges and dished centers. In the two lower registers the crests and troughs are filled by variously shaped elements that have the same dished form. These fillers obstruct the flow of the waves but give a uniform texture to the surface of the vessel. In the register on the neck the troughs are left empty, strengthening the movement of a wave that, because of its smaller size, might otherwise seem too subdued. The lid has a miniature wave around its lower edge and a coiled dragon inside its cup-shaped handle. The ring foot carries a band of recumbent-S shapes, and the rings interlocked with the loop handles have rope-like patterns.

A twenty-nine-character inscription (shown at right) is cast inside the lid, which reads: "It was in the twenty-sixth year, the first period of the tenth month, on the day *jimao*, Fan Ju Sheng had this bridal *hu* cast for the dowry of his eldest child, Meng Ji X. May sons and grandsons forever treasure and use it."

This *hu* bears one of the earliest inscriptions that explicitly mention casting a bronze vessel as dowry; it says that the bride's father cast the vessel for her. Some scholars identify this man, Fan Ju Sheng (nephew of the Ju branch of the Fan lineage), with the minister Fan Sheng (nephew of the Fan lineage) named on a bronze now in the Nelson-Atkins Museum.[8] The Fan lineage ruled a region in southeast Henan in central China. It allied by marriage with the Zhou royal house in neighboring Shaanxi. The bride mentioned in this inscription did not marry into the royal house, however, but into the Meng lineage, so her father addresses her as Meng Ji X, calling her by the lineage name of her betrothed (Meng), then the name of her own clan (Ji), and finally by her personal name (X, a graph whose reading is uncertain).

—*Wang Haicheng is Mary and Cheney Cowles Endowed Associate Professor of Art History at the University of Washington.*

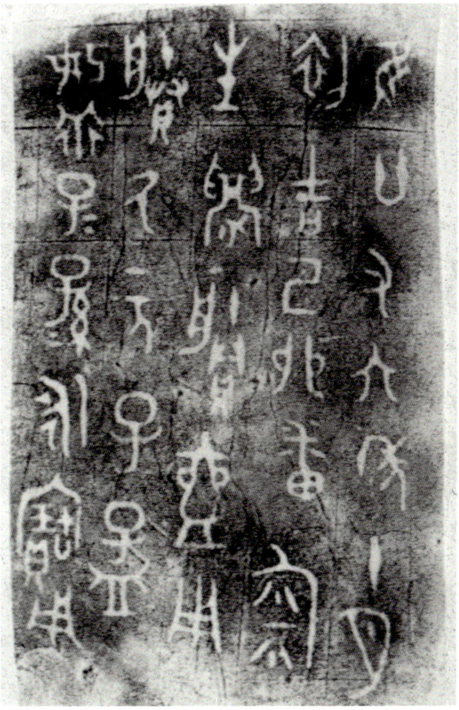

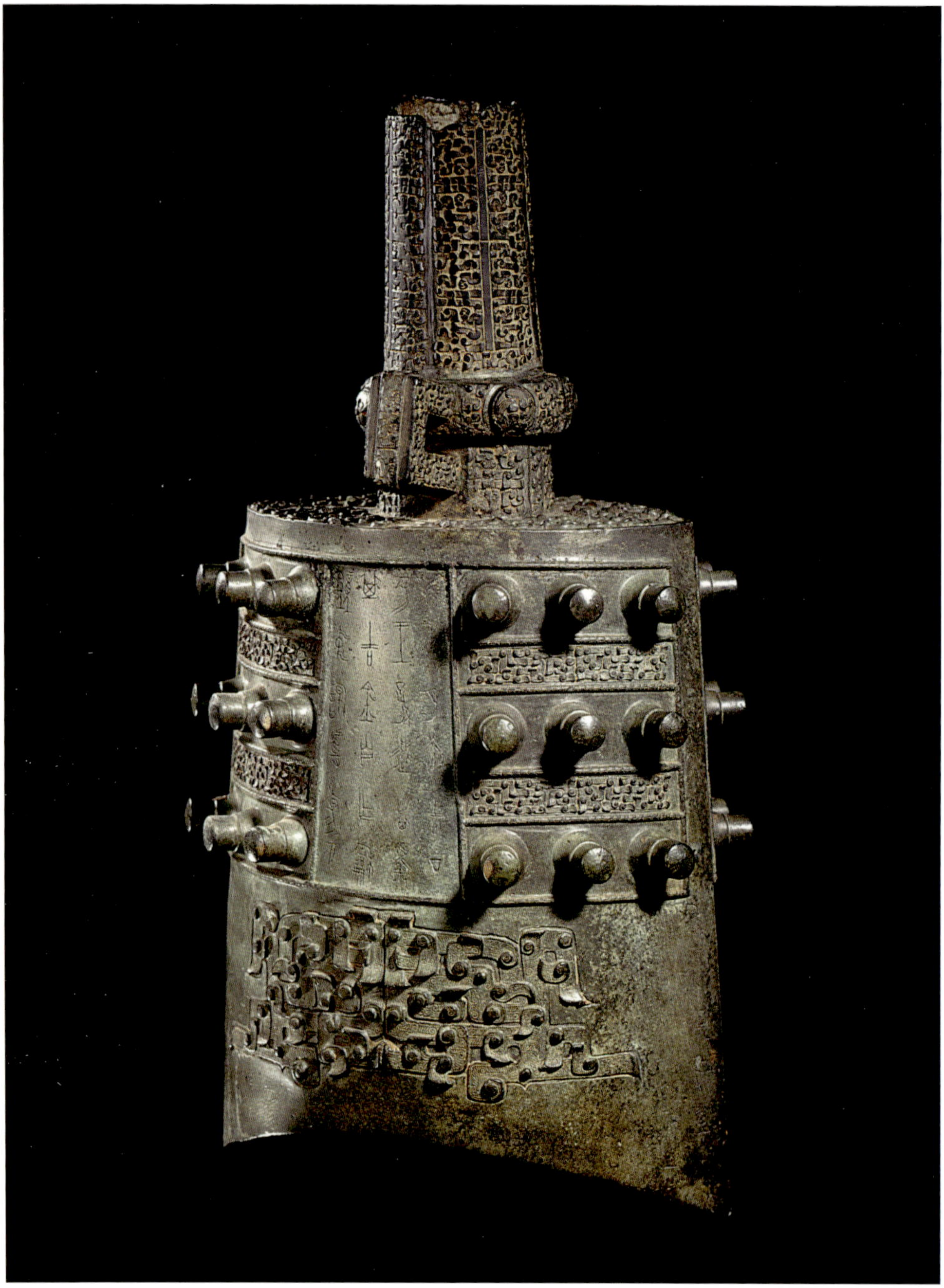

RITUAL BELL (*WANGSUN YIZHE YONGZHONG*)

—

approx. 550 BCE
China
Eastern Zhou period (770–256 BCE)
Bronze
H. 58.4 cm × W. 27.9 cm × D. 22.2 cm
The Avery Brundage Collection, B60S552

—

Ancient Chinese bell sets were not like Western carillons, large bells played from the top of a tower. Rather, they were smaller bells displayed on a rack and played as one instrument—the most spectacular one—in the musical ensemble of a ruler's or nobleman's court. Unlike a Western bell, which is circular in cross section, a Chinese bell has an almond shape that gives it acoustic properties very suitable for making music. Its sound dies away quickly, so melodies played on a tuned set are not muddled by lingering notes. Moreover, it can produce two distinct pitches depending on where it is struck: one pitch is made by striking a mallet on the central axis and another, higher pitch by striking at a point near the side. In the Eastern Zhou period (770–256 BCE) bell founders normally aimed for an interval of a minor or major third between the two pitches.

The bell has a U-shaped loop near the bottom of its tubular shank. Suspended by this loop from the horizontal bar of a rack, it would hang at a slant, making its strike points conveniently accessible to the player. The massive knobs, eighteen on each side of the bell, originated as small decorative bosses on bells five hundred years earlier. Modern acoustic studies have shown that the knobs affect the bell's sound, helping to make its two pitches more distinct by damping higher partials, but whether the bell founders understood this is unknown. The rows of knobs alternate with horizontal panels filled with a pattern of comma-shaped curls. The same pattern covers the shank and top of the bell. The curls originated as miniaturized dragon wings, joints, and snouts, although here they are more stylized. They appear again on a larger scale in the panel just above the mouth of the bell, and here an imaginative viewer can still glimpse bits of dragons.

A 113-character inscription tells us that Wangsun Yizhe, a member of the royal family of the southern state of Chu, commissioned this set of bells for sacrifices and banquets. Some scholars have identified Yizhe with a son of King Zhuang (reigned 614–591 BCE) named Prince Zhuishu. The prince was appointed chancellor of state (*lingyin*) during the reign of his nephew King Kang (reigned 560–545 BCE) but executed the next year, in 550 BCE.[9] A set of very similar bells unearthed from a Chu princely tomb has been dated to 548 BCE, agreeing with our proposed date.[10]

—Wang Haicheng is Mary and Cheney Cowles Endowed Associate Professor of Art History at the University of Washington.

PENDANT WITH DESIGN OF TWO DRAGONS

—

China
Warring States period (approx. 475–221 BCE)
Nephrite
H. 7 cm × W. 11.8 cm × D. .3 cm
The Avery Brundage Collection, B60J681

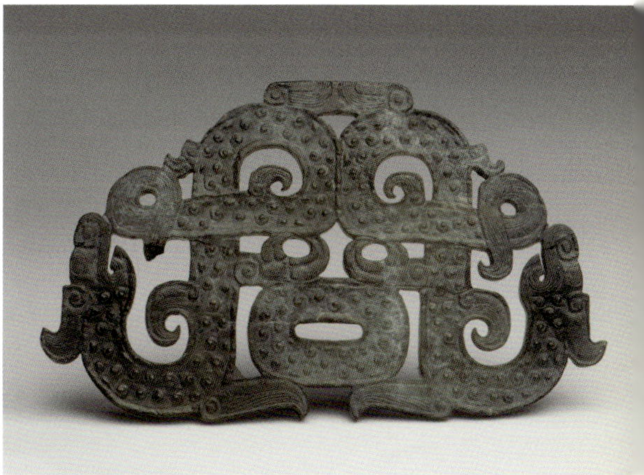

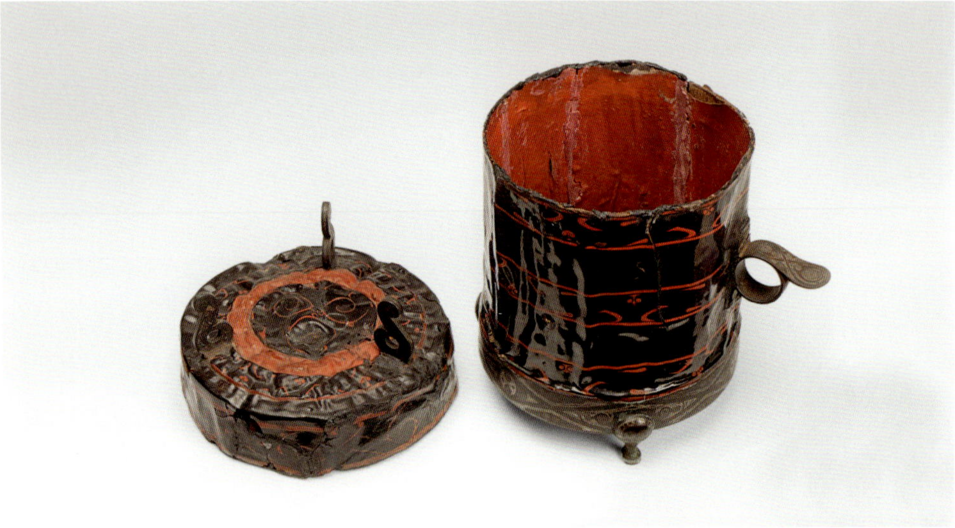

LIDDED VESSEL WITH DESIGN OF CLOUDS AND PHOENIXES

278 BCE
China; Chu culture, Hunan province
Warring States period (approx. 475–221 BCE)
Lacquer on wood and bronze fittings with inlaid silver
H. 17.8 cm × W. 12.4 cm × D. 12.1 cm
The Avery Brundage Collection, B60M286.a-.b

This wine vessel is the only known lacquer work with an inscription dating from 278 BCE, the year the central Chinese state of Qin conquered the Chu state in central south China. The artistic configuration, in a quintessentially Chu style, was long a specialty of lacquer craftsmen in the Chu region. The interior of the vessel is coated in red, while the exterior is painted with red designs on a dark brown background. The principal motifs, alternating spirals with fine whirls, represent heavenly clouds or the *qi* spiritual energy associated with the constellations, which are known in ancient astrology as the Twenty-Eight Lunar Mansions. The side wall of the lid is painted with mythical phoenixes, a prominent design in Chu art.

The lacquerware is highly prized because of its rare, technically challenging design, which features metal pieces holding the lacquer parts together. The cylindrical form of the body's core and the lid's side wall were first formed with thin sheets of wood. They were then attached to the base and the lid's top, both made of thick layers. After the entire piece was lacquered, the metal fittings—three S-shaped ears, a loop-shaped handle, and a lower band set on three legs—were respectively affixed on the lid, the body, and the lower portion. Not only did the metal fittings stabilize the entire lacquer work, they also created a decorative aesthetic. Their silver inlays represent stylized cloudy whirls in figure eight and diamond patterns.

The inscription presents a historical account of this vessel made for Queen Dowager Xuan (died 265 BCE), a native of the Chu region and mother of King Zhaoxiang (died 251 BCE) of the Qin state. Her cross-state marriage was probably arranged as a political alliance between Qin and Chu. Upon the accession of the young Zhaoxiang in 307 BCE, Xuan appointed her brother to be the military commander-in-chief and began a political campaign to suppress neighboring kingdoms. In a series of successful battles, the Qin forces seized the heartland of the Chu in 278 BCE, forcing the Chu to move its capital east. Queen Dowager Xuan likely commissioned this piece in celebration of acquiring her hometown under the Qin's territory.

—*HL*

MONEY TREE

probably 100–200
China; Sichuan province
Eastern Han period (25–220)
Bronze with glazed earthenware base
H. 175.2 cm × Diam. 50.8 cm (overall)
Gift of the Connoisseurs' Council, 1995.79.a-.dd

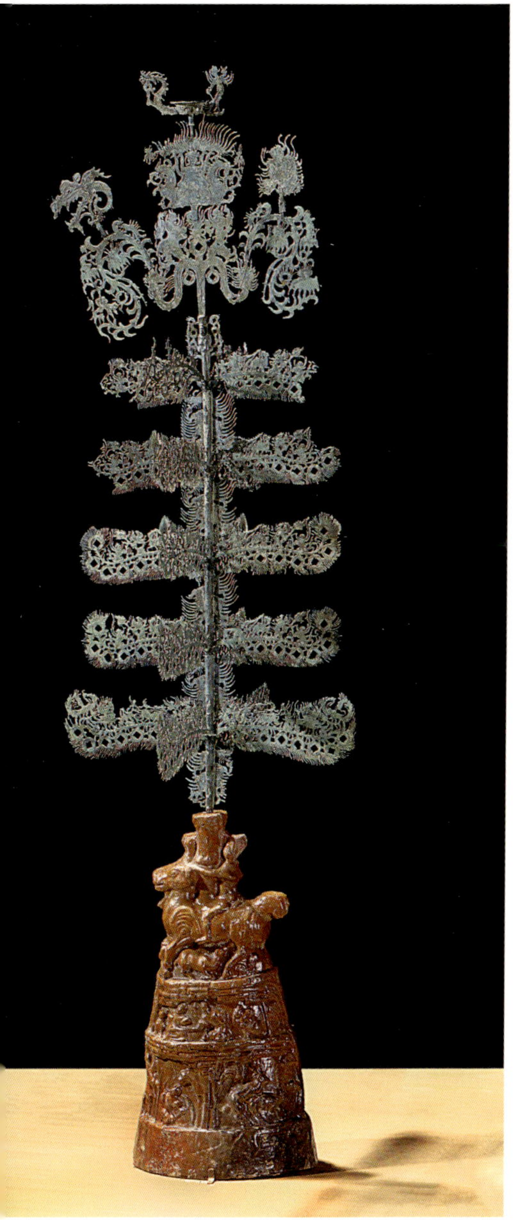

A money tree was a burial object characteristic of Sichuan and neighboring regions in southwestern China. Its popularity lasted from the start of the Eastern Han period to the end of the Three Kingdoms period (221–265). Possibly originating from a myth of money-growing trees, it reflects an indigenous Chinese belief about an immortal world full of wealth, abundance, and eternal brightness. It also carried a prevailing wish for people of all walks of life to obtain good fortune and reach pleasant paradise in the afterlife.[11]

This early Chinese funerary object shows an interesting melding of representations of Daoist and Buddhist motifs and forms. Under a canopy lifted by a flying dragon and a winged immortal, the Queen Mother of the West (Xiwangmu) sits on her unique dragon-tiger throne. At the top, two warriors guard the entrance to heaven, just above a small seated Buddha. Numerous figures from unidentified stories of immortality appear on the top of the tree branches, while rows of *wuzhu* coin replicas, like fruits from a tree, grow beneath the branches.

When Buddhist iconography was first introduced to southwestern China, the figures of Xiwangmu and the Buddha often appeared together, possibly because they both came from the West. It was believed that Xiwangmu, one of the most prominent deities in Han mythology, dwelled on the mythical Kunlun Mountain, the gateway to paradise that connected heaven and earth, and the place where souls of the deceased would be brought before ascending to heaven.

The glazed earthenware base features a man riding a large ram above a bell-shaped foundation. This probably symbolizes that the animal is carrying the deceased up through the tree on a spiritual journey to paradise, where deities and immortals reside. Because the pronunciation of ram (*yang*) is like that of luck (*xiang*), rams were a popular auspicious animal, and their images often appeared in murals or wall reliefs in Han-dynasty tombs.

—*FJZ*

MASTERPIECE

BUDDHA DATED 338

China; Hebei province

Later Zhao kingdom (319–351)

Bronze with gilding

H. 40 cm × W. 24.1 cm × D. 13.3 cm

The Avery Brundage Collection, B60B1034

This sculpture is the earliest known dated Buddha object produced in China, with an inscription on its base mentioning the year 338. This year, which is five hundred years after Buddhism was transmitted from India to China, makes it an important milestone in the development of Buddhist art in China. This is among the largest bronze sculptures to have survived from its period.

The style of this work was influenced by Buddhist sculptures from the ancient region of Gandhara, which included parts of modern Pakistan, Afghanistan, and northwestern India. The figure's arrangement, with legs crossed beneath, set symmetrically on a rectangular pedestal, is modeled after Indian sculptures brought to China via the Silk Road. However, this Buddha's overlapping, inward-facing palms are adopted from a formal Chinese gesture of reverence.

The inscription on the back of the base attributes this sculpture to the Later Zhao, a small state founded by the Jie. A non-Han Chinese people from Central Asia, the Jie controlled China's Central Plain during the fourth century. The state's rulers regarded the Indian monk Fotudeng as their principal religious counselor and military adviser in the campaigns they undertook to extend their territory and authority. Fotudeng had settled in the Central Plains in 310, preaching the Buddhist faith and seeking converts. He inspired Shi Hu, the third king of the Later Zhao, which may have prompted the ruler to commission this dignified statue. In 338, Shi Hu captured more than forty cities in the Central Plain. This sculpture was produced the same year, likely because the king believed the Buddha was miraculous and worshiped him to achieve a blessing of victory.

Since gold was scarce and expensive in ancient China, it was often imitated with bronze thinly coated in gold, which gave the metal greater resistance to tarnishing. The Chinese use of gold on bronze goes back more than two thousand years and was applied using a technique known as "mercury gilding." The gilded surface is produced by applying a paste-like mixture of gold and mercury on the bronze. The bronze is heated on a charcoal fire to evaporate the mercury, leaving the gold bonded to the surface. This gold surface is then burnished with a hard, smooth metal or stone tool to make it more compact and shiny. The gilding over the entirety of this large Buddha, much of which has been preserved, makes the sculpture one of the most accomplished of its time.

—*HL*

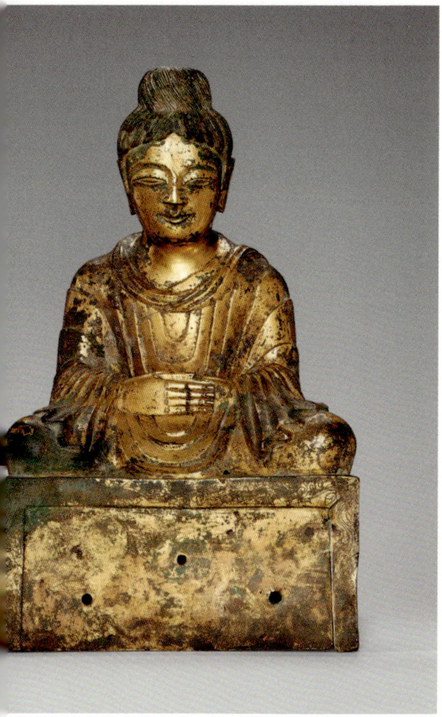

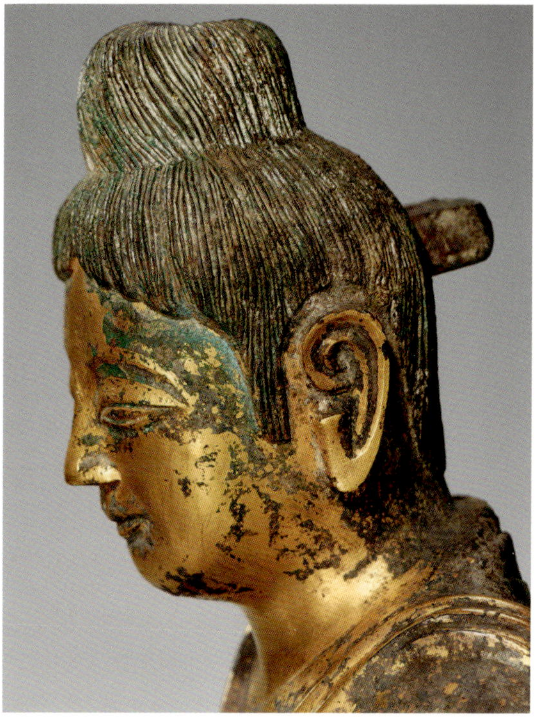

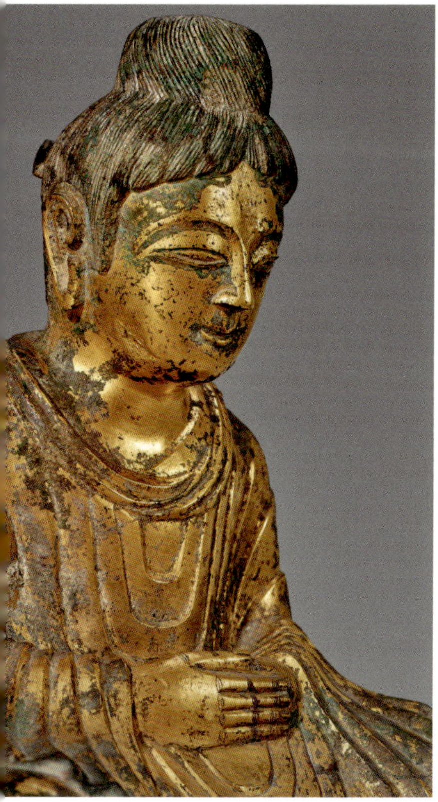

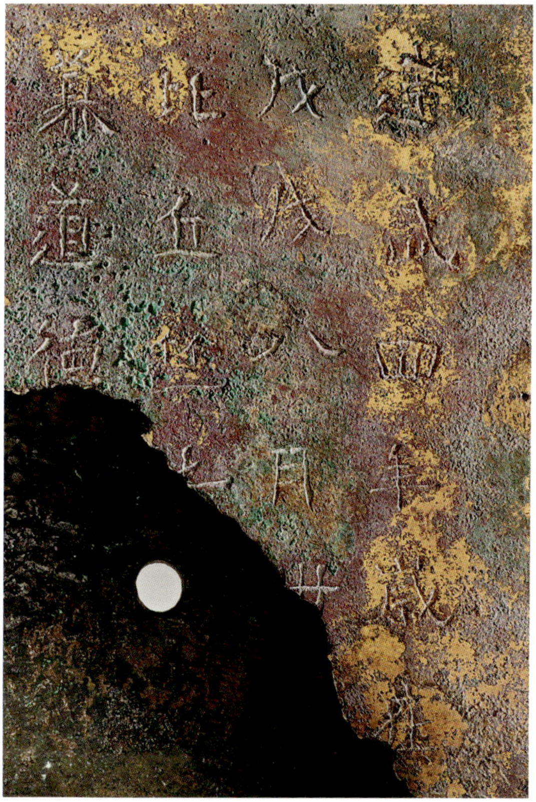

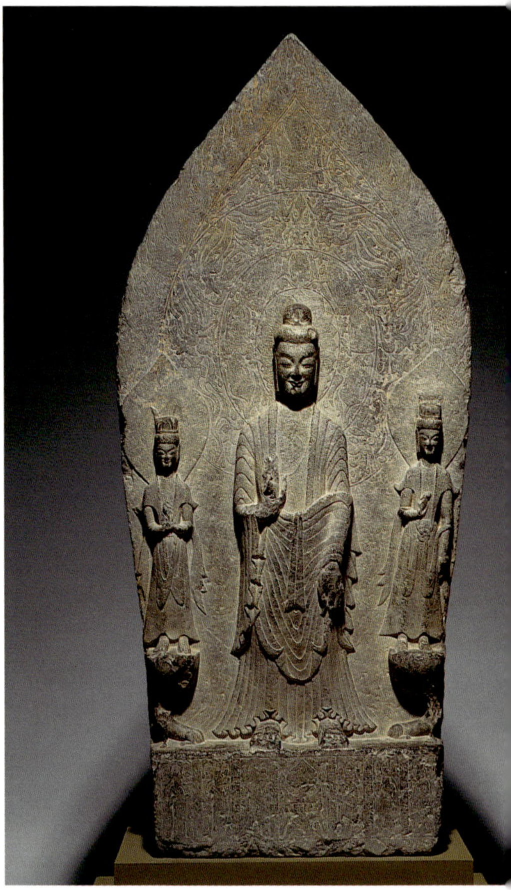

STELE OF THE BUDDHA AND TWO BODHISATTVAS

533
China
Northern Wei dynasty (386–534)
Limestone
H. 170.2 cm × W. 76.2 cm × D. 25.4 cm
The Avery Brundage Collection, B60S44+

Soon after their conquest of northern China, rulers of the Northern Wei dynasty (386–534) became devout Buddhists and eagerly pursued the paradise of the afterlife. Under imperial support, Buddhism began to grow quickly. Tremendous resources were spent on lavishly decorated temples, pagodas, and grottoes throughout the state. The widespread admiration of the Buddha resulted in fascinating portrayals of the Buddhist world in durable mediums such as metal and stone.

This limestone stele is representative of a typical sculptural style of the late Northern Wei dynasty, when Buddhist art reached its apex. Carved in smooth, symmetrical lines, its images of Buddhist figures have slender bodies, narrow faces, long eyebrows, and Chinese-style robes. The figures' so-called "archaic smiles" and the fishtail-shaped drapes of their robes characterize the Northern Wei style, which creatively adapted imported Indian prototypes to meet native Chinese preferences.[12]

This work shows, in addition to the graceful aesthetics, the complexity of iconography of Northern Wei Buddhist art. Its front combines sculpture and images rendered in both low relief and incised lines. A standing Buddha is flanked by two bodhisattvas on animal-supported lotus pedestals before a flame-shaped body halo. The backdrop is divided into five sections and shows different buddhas along with heavenly beings in the Buddhist paradise. Six male patrons from the Zhao family are carved onto the base of the stele. They all wear official-looking headdresses and robes and stand in three-quarter-view poses below canopies.

The back of the stele includes additional incised imagery. Its central scene shows a meditating Buddha seated in a canopied niche and flanked by the bodhisattva Manjushri and sage Vimalakirti, who are debating the Buddha's doctrine. Birds, flowers, and flying celestial nymphs (*apsarases*) appear in the air and surrounding areas, while images of various donors and devotees fill in six rows below. The inscription on the bottom states the date of the stele, 533.
—*FJZ*

HEAD OF BODHISATTVA MAHASTHAMAPRAPTA (DASHIZHI)

China; Xiangtangshan
Northern Qi dynasty (550–577)
Limestone
H. 88.9 cm × W. 48.3 cm × D. 43.2 cm
The Avery Brundage Collection, B60S32+

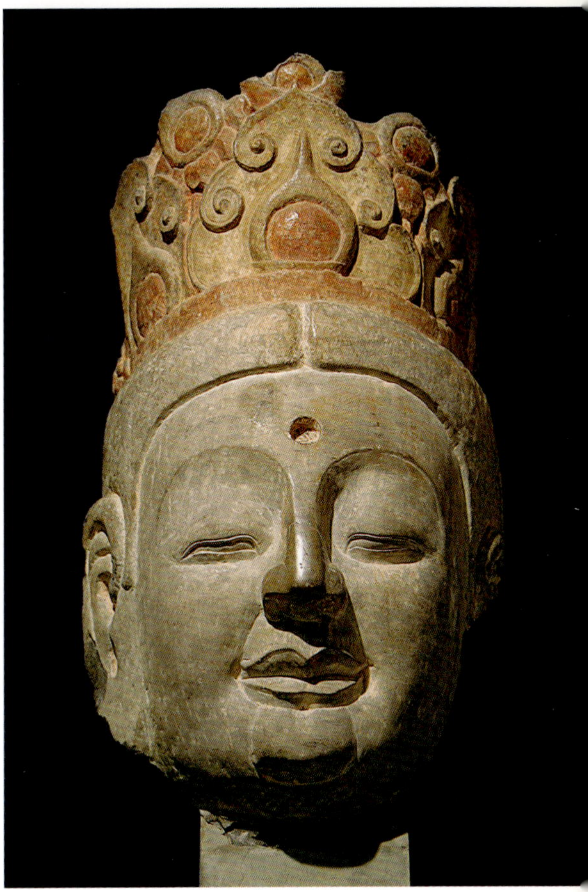

Bodhisattvas are sages who gave up the opportunity of reaching enlightenment to help human beings. Because they maintain connections to worldly possessions, they are often depicted with elaborate headdresses and beautiful jewels. Viewed facing a temple altar, Mahasthamaprapta (Dashizhi) stands on the left of Amitabha, the celestial Buddha who presides over the Western paradise. Avalokiteshvara (Guanyin), the bodhisattva of compassion, stands on the right of the Buddha. The three constitute the holy triad of Amitabha's Pure Land, a Buddhist paradise.

This sculpted head is probably from bodhisattva Mahasthamaprapta, who often wears a headdress with a central ornament of a vase. He has a rounded face with a full jaw, showing a peaceful and pleasant look of meditation. His youthful appearance and smooth contours are typical of merciful bodhisattvas of the period. A dot on his forehead called the *urna* is one of the thirty-two marks of the Buddha that denote his greatness. This piece was purportedly severed from a tall statue in the rock-cut cave temples at Xiangtangshan, in China's northern Hebei province. These caves were sponsored by the ruling house of the short-lived Northern Qi dynasty (550–577), who were pious Buddhist devotees.

At that time, influence from Gupta-period India (approx. 320–550) impacted Buddhist art in northern China, which probably resulted in the roundness of Buddhist statues and the richness of their embellishments. The new treatments of facial features and garments are very different from the flatness and linear quality seen on earlier Buddhist sculpture of the previous Northern Wei dynasty.

—*FJZ*

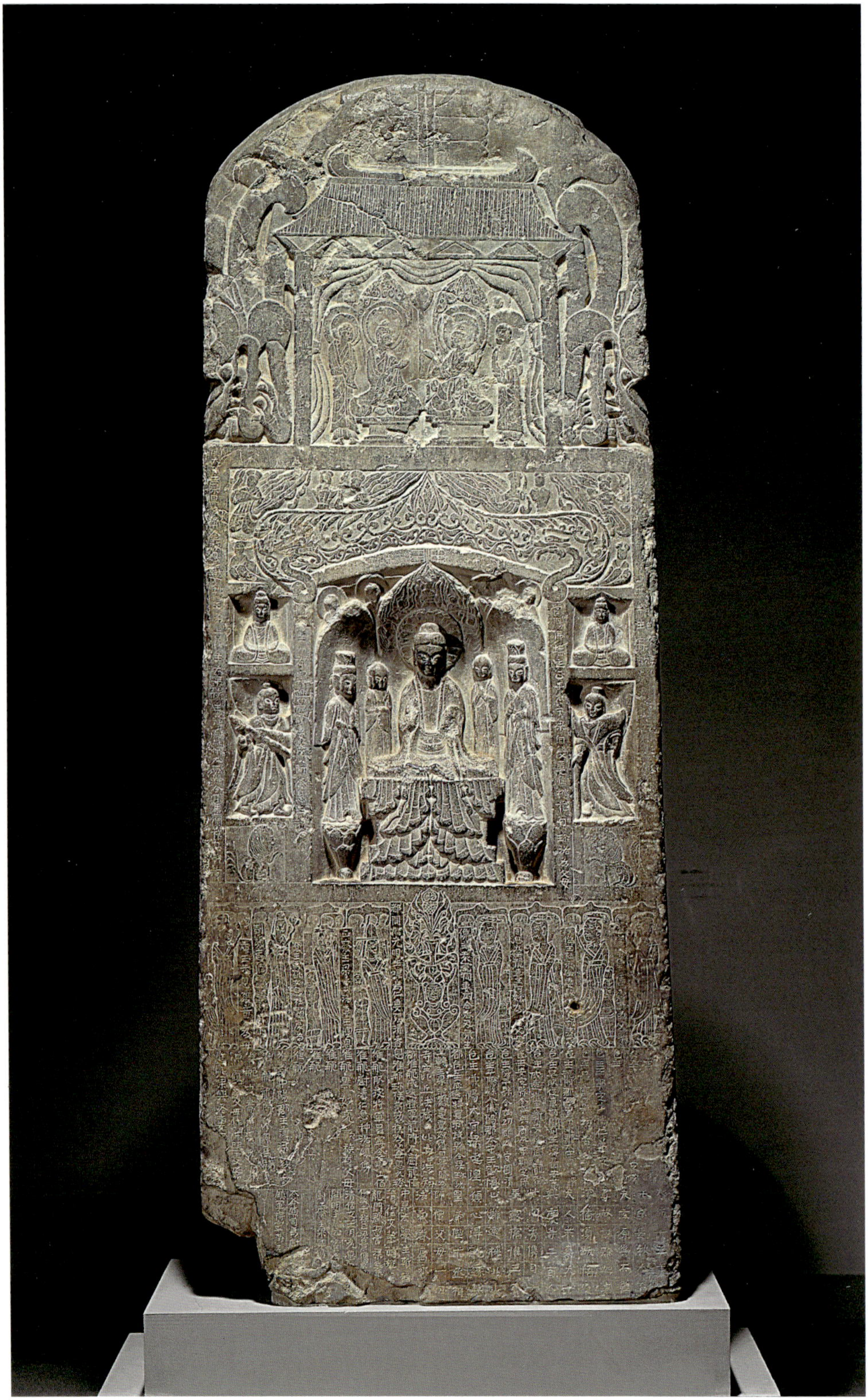

BUDDHIST STELE

549
China
Western Wei dynasty (535–557)
Limestone
H. 170.2 cm × W. 67.3 cm × D. 26.2 cm
The Avery Brundage Collection, B62S2+

This stone stele, carved in three bands with stylized, sixth-century relief, was once erected outside a monastery in central China. It includes depictions of several Buddhist deities and a long list of their human devotees, as well as inscriptions conveying devotion to and wishes for blessings from these deities.

A stele carved with this type of relief sculpture is known as a votive stele. Votive steles reflect the fifth-century Buddhist practice of producing devotional statues and steles to be set on the grounds of pagodas and temples. The composition of these steles, which places deities above human figures to represent their hierarchy, attempted to engage ordinary people with Buddhist beliefs. Steles commonly included pledges for wishes, which usually contained the date the stele was made, names of donors who pooled their resources to commission the piece, and the name of the person to whom the stele was dedicated. Supplications varied and included wishes for prosperity and peace for country and family, the passage of ancestors to heaven, and the cure of beloved sick ones.

The principal image in the central niche is the Buddha Shakyamuni seated on a draped pedestal, accompanied by the disciples Ananda and Kashyapa in monks' attire. Standing next to them on lotus buds are the bodhisattvas Avalokiteshvara (Guanyin) and Mahasthamaprapta (Dashizhi). On each side of the niche is a small depiction of the Buddha Amitabha above a demigod holding a long-handled weapon.

The top band, with a two-headed dragon arching along the border, illustrates the debate between the wealthy layman Vimalakirti (at viewer's left) and Manjushri, the bodhisattva of wisdom, attended by a monk. Their encounter is described in a sutra that is valued by Chinese Buddhists because it demonstrates how a layperson can participate in a discussion of Buddhist doctrine on equal terms with a bodhisattva—a perfected being.

The lower part of the stele is incised all around with names of devotees, their posts, and family members. Eight prominent district magistrates and regional governors from regions in China's Central Plain are registered, along with their portraits. The inscription also contains the date, 549. The rear of the stele presents a standing Buddha with two monk attendants in the central niche. They are surrounded by four rows of twelve meditating Buddhas seated in niches.

—*HL*

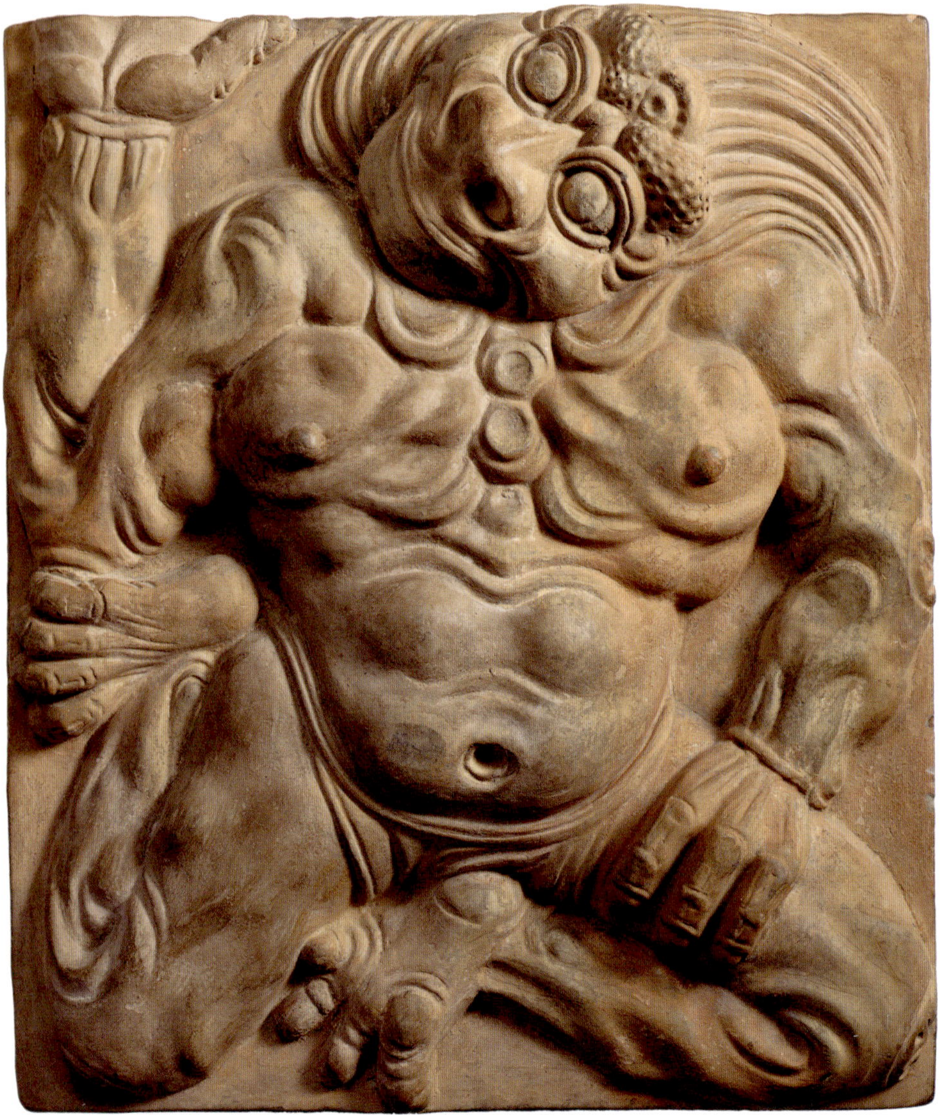

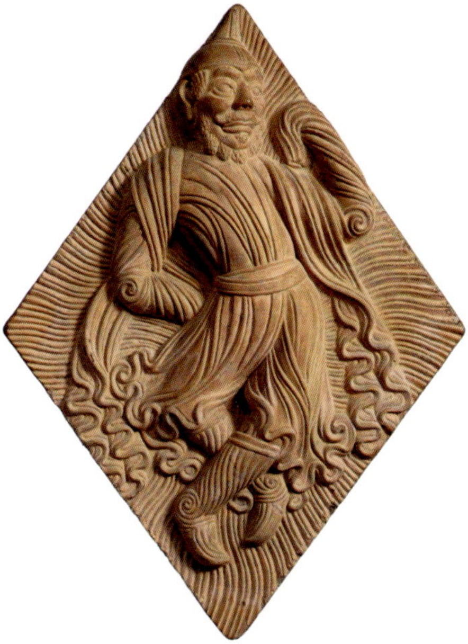

BRICK TILES WITH DESIGNS OF A MONSTER AND A CENTRAL ASIAN DANCER

approx. 860–870
China; Xiuding temple, Anyang county, Henan province
Tang dynasty (618–907)
Terra-cotta
Monster: H. 43.2 cm × W. 36.8 cm × D. 10.8 cm, dancer: H. 64.8 cm × W. 48.3 cm × D. 9.5 cm
The Avery Brundage Collection, B60S56+ and B60S74+

These brick tiles, part of a set of eight in the collection of the Asian Art Museum, are among the most magnificent architectural fragments to have survived from Xiuding, an ancient Buddhist temple near Anyang in Henan province. On the temple site, a single-story, brick pagoda stands in front of the main hall. This square-shaped construction, 9.3 meters high with each side measuring 8.3 meters, held three Buddhist statues. It survives in its original setting with a few remnants of brick tiles on its outer walls. The images on these bricks consist of mythical creatures, monsters, and Central Asian entertainers. They express a fusion of elements of Chinese and non-Chinese cultures and reflect the political alliances that resulted from the Tang empire's expansion to Central Asia.

These bricks were part of architectural segments used to decorate the walls of the pagoda. Massive bricks depicting as many as seventy-two subjects were hand molded or pressed, creating impressive and dramatic high-relief images that are among the most accomplished of their time.

The Xiuding temple was subsequently known as the Red Pagoda, since its entire surface was originally painted red. It was rediscovered by archaeologists in 1961 and designated one of China's National Important Historical Heritage sites in 1982. The temple has endured being demolished, restored, and expanded throughout an extraordinary history of more than a thousand years. The inscriptions carved on stone steles and architectural structures around it narrate the temple's fascinating story. This includes its erection by the monk Zhang Meng in 494, its subsequent demolition ordered by the royal family of the Zhou state in 576, and its official restoration from the seventh through sixteenth centuries.

One of the reconstructions, which took place sometime between 860 and 870, was especially significant. Emperor Yizong (reigned 860–874) of the Tang dynasty appointed the county governor Zheng Dang to carry out the task, likely with financial support from his administration. Zheng sought to rebuild the temple in a contemporarily fashionable style. The temple reconstructed under Zheng was a large expansion to the original one, and its decorations reveal a Tang-period style.
—*HL*

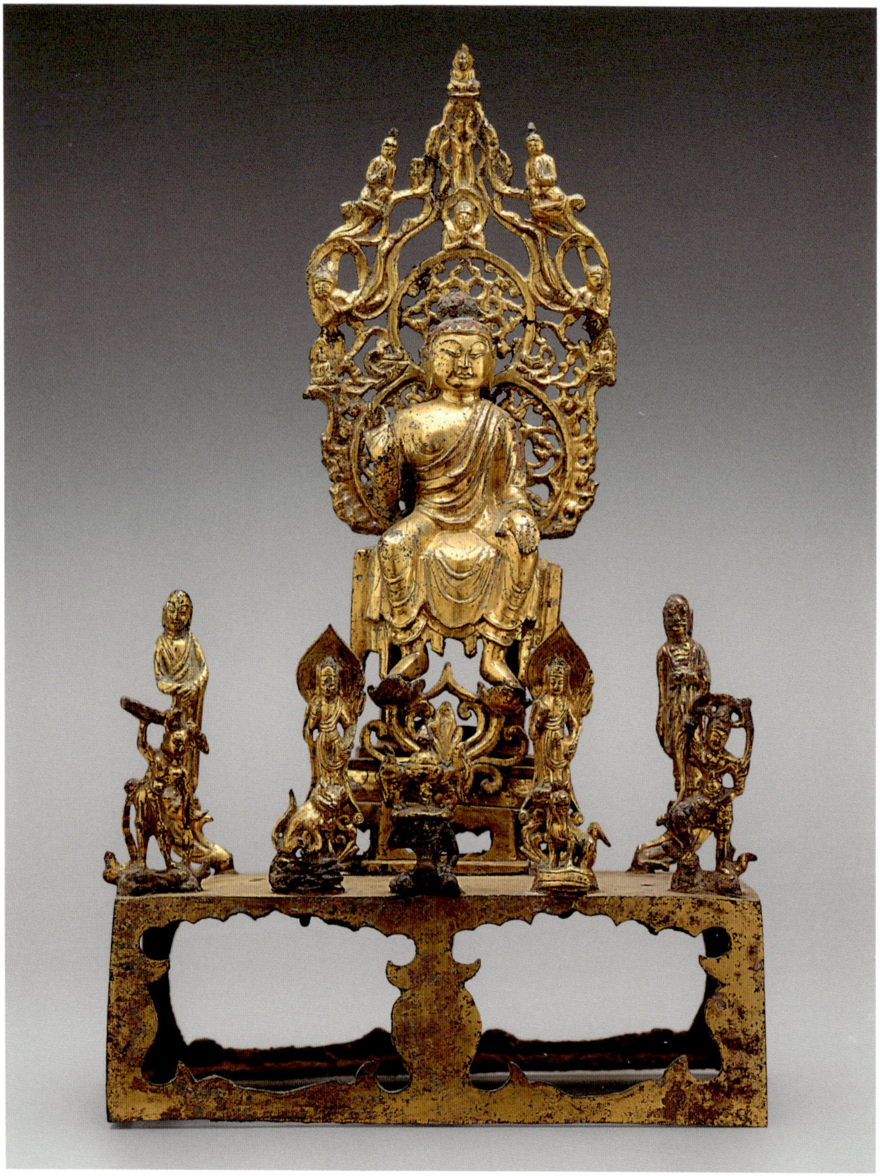

A BUDDHA, PROBABLY MAITREYA, FLANKED BY BODHISATTVAS AND ATTENDANTS

—

approx. 650–750

China

Tang dynasty (618–907)

Bronze with gilding

H. 31.1 cm × W. 19 cm × D. 13.3 cm

The Avery Brundage Collection, B60B8+

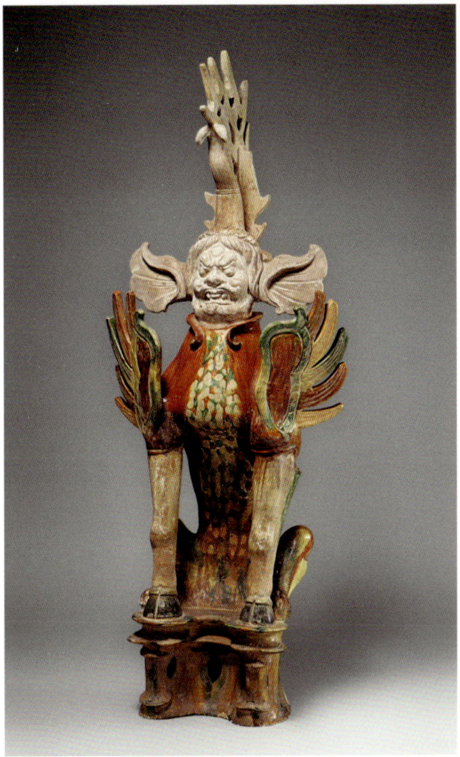

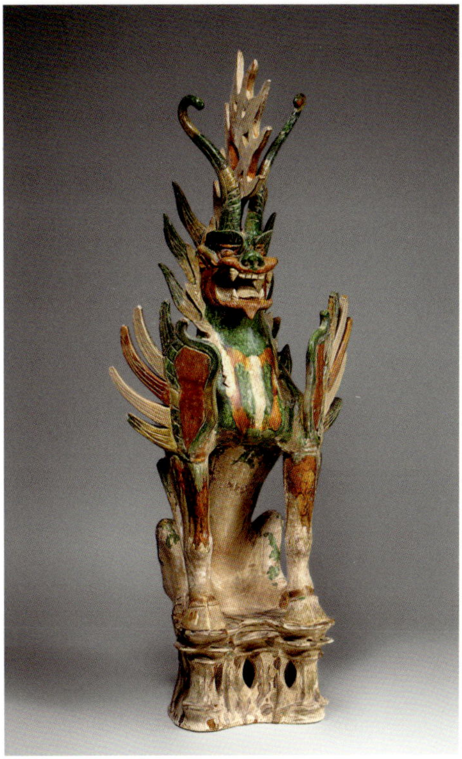

TOMB GUARDIANS

—

approx. 690–750
China
Tang dynasty (618–907)
Earthenware with multicolor glazes
Left: H. 104.5 cm × W. 41.3 cm × D. 40.6 cm;
right: H. 100.6 cm × W. 40 cm × D. 40.6 cm
The Avery Brundage Collection, B60S51+ and B60S52+

—

First appearing in the Zhou dynasty (approx. 1050–256 BCE), sculpted tomb guardian beasts were common in Tang-dynasty (618–907) tombs of the wealthy and powerful. Often imagined as mythical monsters standing on mountain rocks, these creatures looked ferocious, with bulging eyes, long upturned horns, protruding fangs, double wings, and flaming crests. They were often paired with imposing portrayals of heavenly kings to dutifully guard tombs and protect the deceased from unwelcome ghosts and looters.

Earthenware tomb guardian figures were finished with various techniques. Some had colorful glazes applied before the second firing, and others were directly ornamented with slips and pigments. This set of tomb guardians, one with an animal face and one a human face, represents the best-known stylistic advancement of ceramic production during the heyday of the Tang dynasty—the *sancai* glaze technique. This term refers to the glaze's three dominant, mineral-based colors: iron oxide for amber, copper oxide for green, and cobalt for blue. After the first firing of the clay body, glaze was applied for the second low-temperature firing to create brilliant colors. *Sancai* glaze was often bold and vigorous, especially in kilns near Luoyang in China's central Henan province.

—*FJZ*

HEAD OF THE BUDDHA

approx. 700–750

China; Leigutai cave, Longmen, Henan province

Tang dynasty (618–907)

Limestone

H. 66 cm × W. 43.2 cm × D. 30.5 cm

The Avery Brundage Collection, B60S38+

Despite its large scale, this head of the Buddha is sensitively rendered and finely finished, with great care given to details. The curly hair formed by floral-shaped whirls, the fullness of the cheeks, the sharply chiseled eyebrows and eyelids, and the thick, full, and round mouth are distinctive characteristics of Buddhist statues at the time. They suggest the influence of Indian Buddhist art.

This head is of great historical value. It was once attached to the principal figure in the central cave in the Leigutai site at Longmen, Henan province, in central China. The Longmen site, with 2,345 caves and more than 100,000 statues, was built over several centuries. The workmanship and proportions of this head display clear mastery of the art of sculpture during the eighth century, the golden age of the Tang dynasty, during which time Buddhist art reached its zenith.

The Longmen site was established under the early imperial patronage of Buddhism, headed by the Northern Wei emperor Xiaowen (reigned 471–499). In 494, he selected Longmen (about thirteen miles south of his capital of Luoyang) as one of the primary imperial sites to express patronage of and devotion to Buddhism. Xiaowen began to honor the Buddha by building shrines into cliffs, and there he dedicated large caves to himself and his ancestors.

The second phase of Longmen was launched during the Tang dynasty by Empress Wu Zetian (reigned 684–705). In 672 Wu reassigned an enormous amount of money from funds allocated for her cosmetics to build the great image of Vairochana, the Buddha known as the Effulgent One, in Longmen. However, after the court's persecution of Buddhism beginning in 845, construction rapidly dwindled. Decades after Wu Zetian, imperial patronage continued the cave construction in Longmen. Longmen was designated a UNESCO World Heritage site in 2000.

—*HL*

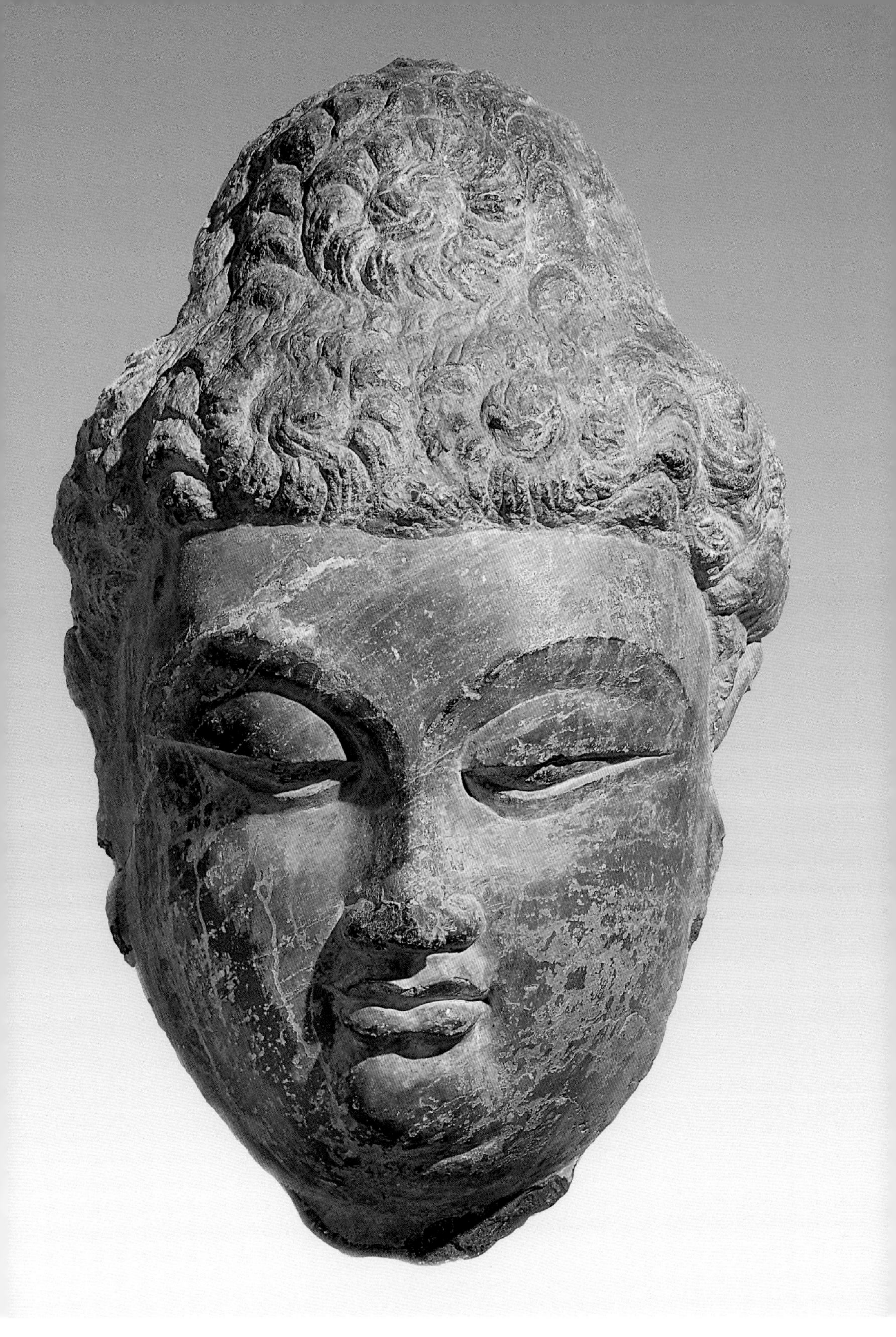

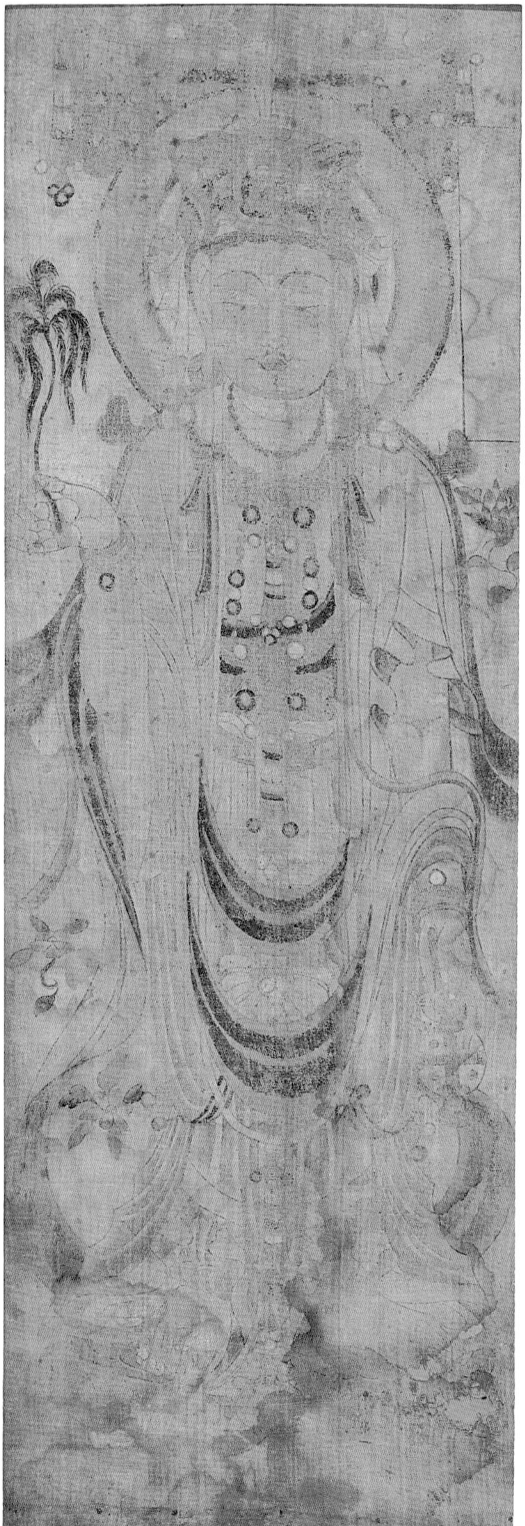

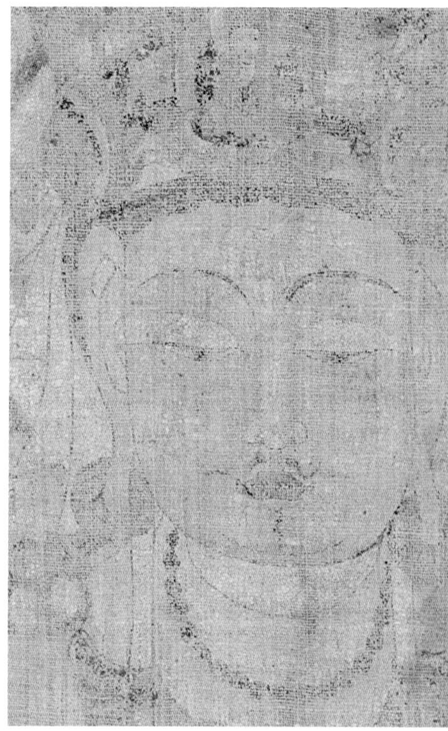

THE BODHISATTVA AVALOKITESHVARA (GUANYIN) WITH WILLOW SPRIG

approx. 800–900
China; Dunhuang, Gansu province
Tang dynasty (618–907)
Colors on ramie bast fiber
H. 161.3 cm × W. 50.8 cm (image)
The Avery Brundage Collection, B62D10

In 1900, by a stroke of good luck, the Daoist priest Wang Yuanlu and his assistant discovered a hidden cave inside the Mogao Caves, filled floor to ceiling with textile hangings, paintings, manuscripts, and sutras dating as early as the fourth century CE. The trove included this painting of the bodhisattva Avalokiteshvara (Guanyin in Chinese). The Mogao Caves, famous for their Buddhist shrines, sculptures, and wall paintings, are in Dunhuang, situated in Gansu province in northwestern China, where the two main branches of the Silk Road converge. Dunhuang was the major hub for travelers from China to the west and from Central Asia to China. The treasures were hidden in this cave sometime during the Song dynasty (960–1279), possibly as a precaution against the encroaching Western Xia army, and were forgotten.[13]

Although Wang Yuanlu and his assistant were careful about the discovery, foreign treasure hunters soon heard about it. Aurel Stein (1862-1943), a Hungarian-British archaeologist, came in 1907 and again in 1914 and "persuaded" the Daoist priest to sell him truckloads of manuscripts and paintings. These were later divided between the Indian and British governments and are now housed in the National Museum in New Delhi and the British Museum in London. Stein was soon followed by the French Sinologist Paul Pelliot (1878–1945), who came to Dunhuang in 1908. Pelliot purchased ten truckloads of manuscripts from Wang.[14] Many of these treasures ended up in the Guimet Museum in Paris, but Pelliot kept some for himself. After his death, his wife sold this painting.

The painting, which has suffered severe water damage, was executed on ramie bast fiber on a white ground. Avalokiteshvara, the bodhisattva of compassion, is shown standing upright with each of his feet supported by a lotus blossom. His raised right hand carries a sprig of willow, with which he sprinkles the nectar of life from the bottle he holds in his right hand. The bodhisattva wears a red and green robe and a crown adorned with the seated image of his spiritual father, the Buddha Amitabha. His hair is fashioned into a chignon except for two long locks, knotted at the shoulders, that flow down his arms. A halo surrounds his head, and a tasseled hanging appears above him. He is richly adorned with thick circular earrings, a necklace, and an elaborate jeweled pendant on his chest. This early representation of Avalokiteshvara depicts him wearing a thin moustache and goatee. From the Song dynasty on, Chinese images show this deity as female.

—Terese Tse Bartholomew is former curator of Himalayan Art and Chinese Decorative Art at the Asian Art Museum of San Francisco and author of the book Hidden Meanings in Chinese Art.

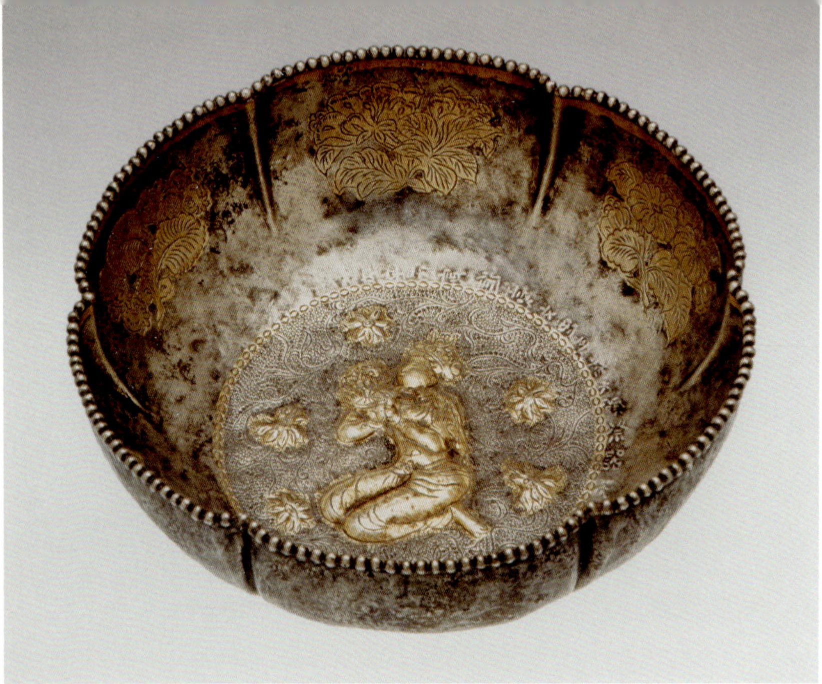

TRIBUTE BOWL

1026
Northern China
Liao dynasty (916–1125)
Silver with partial gilding
H. 3.9 cm × Diam. 13.2 cm
Gift of the Shorenstein Fund, 1990.206

This inscribed silver bowl is dedicated to a prominent historical figure, Yelü Longyun (born Han Durang, 941–1011). Longyun, a Han Chinese official, won the trust and admiration of the young widowed Empress Xiao (953–1009). With her direct patronage, Longyun, through great adversity, contrived to inspire loyalty and valiance among her administration and army.

Given glory and power higher than any subject and even princes, Longyun was granted the surname "Yelü" from the Qidan royal clan, as well as honorable titles including Chief Minister of the Xuanhui Northern Court, which was the central government of the Liao dynasty. His special privileges included exemption from bowing in front of the throne during the emperor's audience, a hereditary mansion called Wenzhong (Literary Faith), and personal guards equal in scale to that of the imperial guard. Emperor Shengzong (reigned 982–1031) treated Longyun with greater dignity than anyone else in the Liao court. The emperor once got out of his chariot fifty steps from Longyun's tent and made a courteous gesture towards him.

In 1011, Longyun died of a sickness contracted in a battle against Korea. The lavish funeral ceremony sponsored by the court culminated in a posthumous temple built near the royal graves. Fifteen years later, in 1026, Emperor Shengzong appointed a Han Chinese official and a few senior staff members to oversee the Xuanhui Southern Court, the liaison with the Northern Court. These new officials, probably in remembrance of Longyun's spirit, commissioned this bowl dedicated to the Wenzhong mansion.

The surface ornamentation, including flowers and beads, on this bowl is derived from Tang-period prototypes. At the center is a kneeling devotee of Longyun, surrounded by scattered blossoms, offering a flower pot with two hands. The six-lobed wall borders are composed of three kinds of stylized flowers in alternation. The craftsmanship is extraordinarily fine and represents a radical departure from conventional relief ornamentation of its era. Complex methods of its metalworking involved gilding, engraving, repoussé, and beading.

—*HL*

VESSEL (*ZUN*) IN THE SHAPE OF A DUCK

China

Song dynasty (960–1279)

Bronze with inlaid silver and gold

H. 24.8 cm × W. 33 cm × D. 35 cm

The Avery Brundage Collection, B60B14

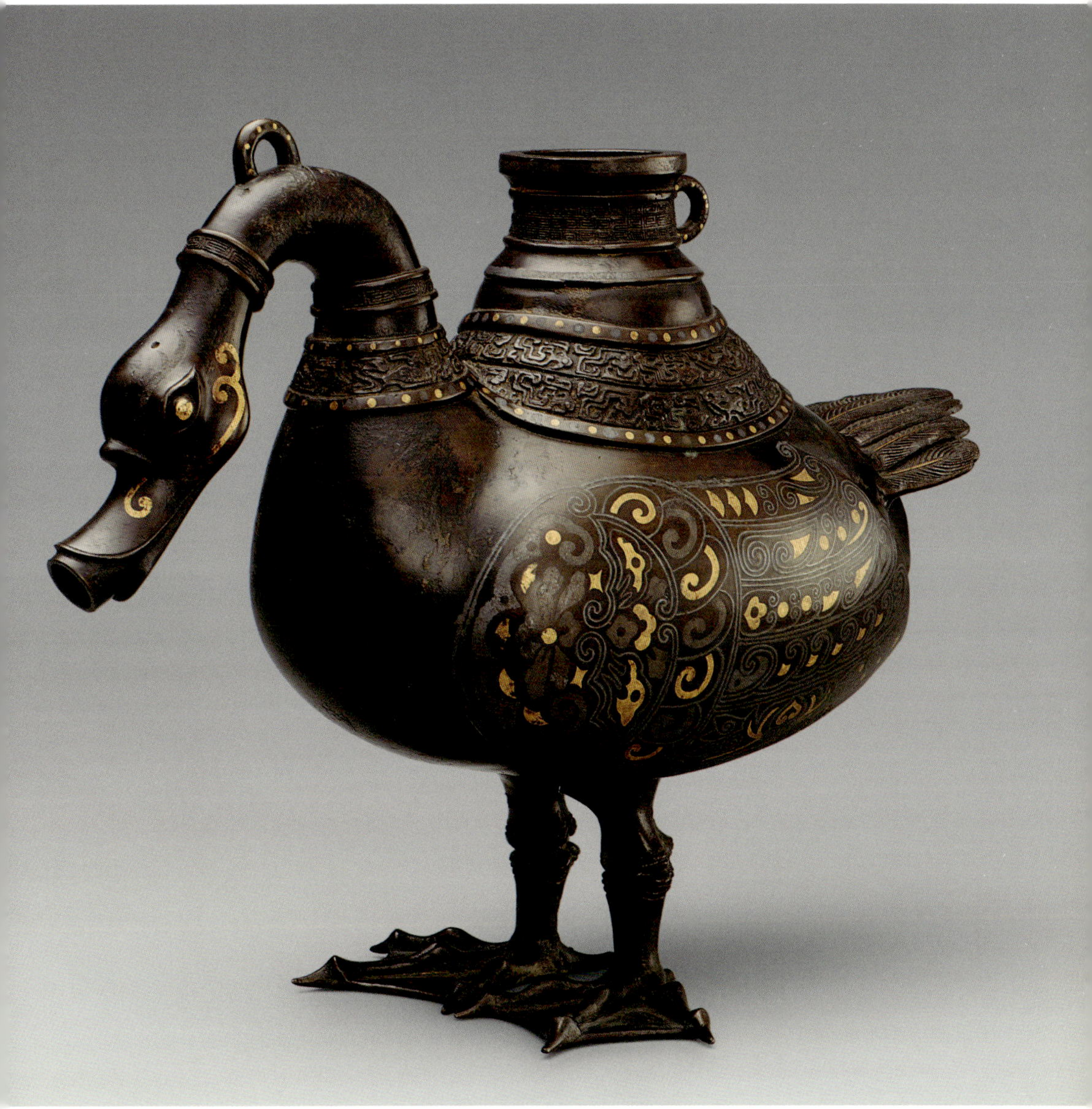

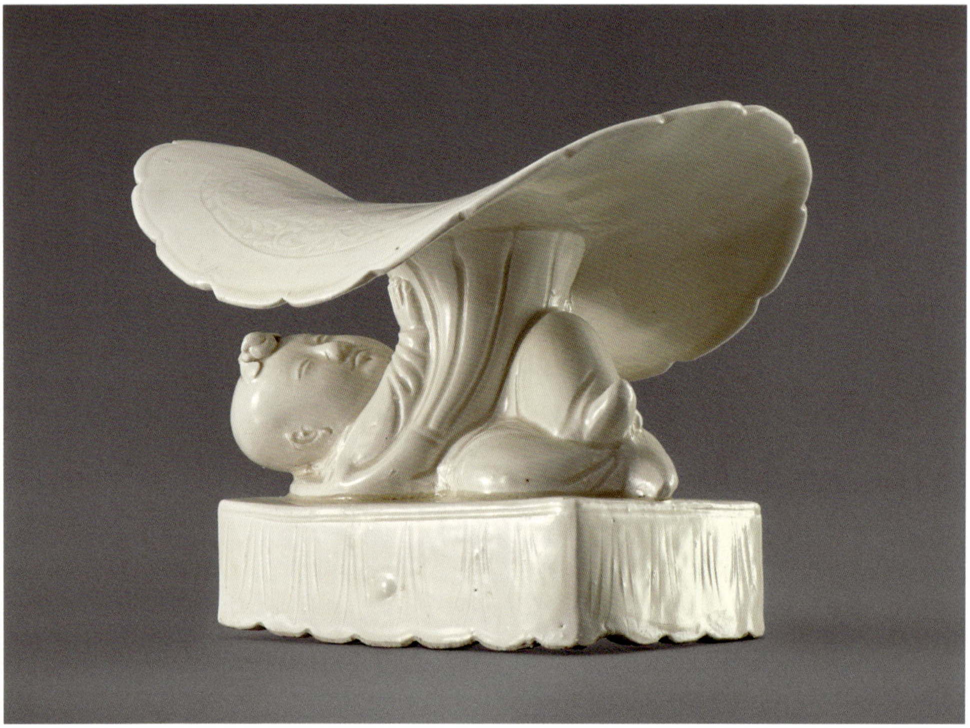

PILLOW IN THE FORM OF A BOY AND A LOTUS LEAF

—

approx. 1050–1127
China; Hebei province
Northern Song period (960–1127)
Porcelain with white glaze (Ding ware)
H. 8.3 cm × W. 20.3 cm × D. 16.5 cm
The Avery Brundage Collection, B60P1351

—

This pillow uses a lively sculptural treatment to both please its users and convey good wishes. Its rendering of a plump boy under a lotus leaf indicates a traditional desire for male heirs and family prosperity. The Chinese character for "lotus" (*lian*) is a homonym of the character for "succession." Thus, chubby toddlers with lotuses signify giving birth to many healthy boys. In addition, lotus's other Chinese name, *he*, sounds like the character for "union" and so suggests the marriage of a man and a woman.[15]

The subject of lotus-bearing boys, including those lying beneath a lotus leaf or carrying a lotus stem, has thrived in China since the tenth century. It frequently occurred in the forms of ceramic objects, surface decoration, relief carving, woodblock prints, scroll paintings, and murals, constituting one of the most appealing pictorial subjects of the time. Various ceramics decorated with motifs of plants and toddlers provided an ideal format to express auspicious wishes and became popular products in many kilns throughout Song and Yuan China.

This pillow with a milky porcelain body is an outstanding product of Ding ware from Hebei province in northern China. One of the best specimens of its kind, this elaborate pillow was finely sculpted and would have been a favored item in a wealthy household. The curvature of the headrest and the folds of the curtained platform suggest the maker's interest in achieving a design for practical use and naturalistic beauty. Ding-ware works featuring ivory white glazes and elegant forms were highly influential in Song art and copied by kilns in many other regions, constituting an important fashion in the visual culture of the time.[16]

—FJZ

VASE WITH DESIGN OF SCROLLING PEONIES

—

China

Northern Song period (960–1127)

Porcelain with sgraffito decoration (Cizhou ware)

H. 48.6 cm × Diam. 19.1 cm

The Avery Brundage Collection, B60P161

—

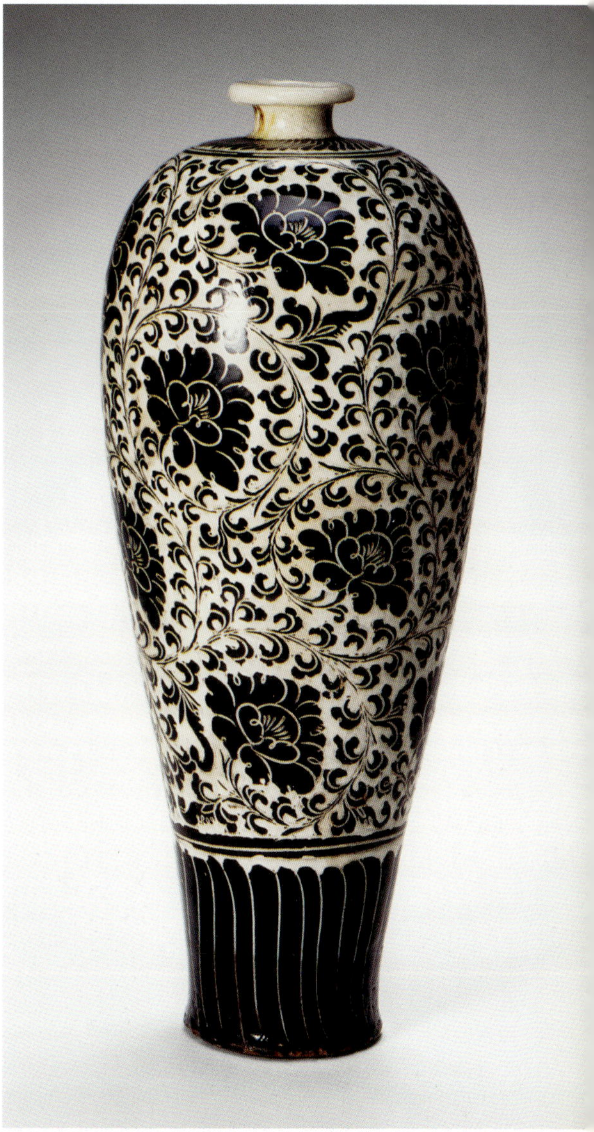

This vase's perfect *meiping* (plum vase) body, unusually large size, and finely executed decoration establishes its rarity and places it among the most refined Cizhou pieces in existence. Its design of scrolling peonies, a symbol of both prosperity and nobility, was achieved by "white-glaze black sgraffito," a rare and highly valued decorative technique on Cizhou wares. First, the clay body was covered with white slip. Then, black slip, made from iron pigments, was added on top. Using painted, incised, or impressed designs on the body as an outline, the artist delicately carved away sections of black slip to reveal the white slip below. Finally, the vessel was coated with transparent glaze.[17]

Cizhou wares—commercial ceramics originally produced at kilns in Ci county, Hebei province in China's Central Plains—were made for non-elite patrons for everyday use. They included a multitude of tablewares and vessels, and their characteristic contrasting dark and light colors became so popular that the production of Cizhou wares expanded countrywide, and regional variations became evident. Decorative techniques quickly evolved and varied from their original form—pieces with painted decorations—to encompass impressed, incised, marbled, and sgraffito designs, such as this work.[18]
—*DCh*

MASTERPIECE

THE BODHISATTVA AVALOKITESHVARA (GUANYIN)

approx. 1100–1200
China
Song dynasty (960–1279)
Wood (paulownia) with pigments
H. 132.1 cm × W. 106.7 cm × D. 63.5 cm
The Avery Brundage Collection, B60S24+

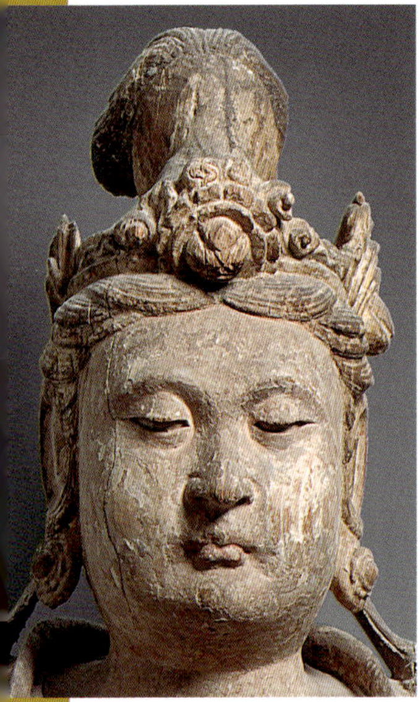

Seated in the pose of "royal ease," this deity is known as the "Water-Moon Guanyin" (Shuiyue Guanyin). He was believed to reside on an isolated isle named Potalaka in the mythical South Sea, sitting in contemplation as the moon reflected in the water. The reflection metaphorically refers to the illusory and temporal nature of all phenomena in the human world—a subject upon which Buddhist believers meditate.[19] Guanyin is also known as the bodhisattva of compassion. His benevolence and power of salvation made him one of the most popular deities in traditional China.

Here, Guanyin is dressed as an Indian prince in a fluid garment with crossed sashes, scarves, and a necklace on his bare chest. He rests his right hand on a bent knee and holds his left in a gift-granting gesture. This impressive statue indicates that the finest sculptures of the Song-Yuan period were carved out of wood and covered with gesso and pigments (which have worn away from this piece). The sculptor's graceful rendering of the face contributes to the confidence and calmness of this deity and fluently presents his mercy over the suffering of humans.

Beginning in the middle Tang dynasty (618–907), portrayals of Guanyin—often including delicate, soft modeling of his face, torso, and hands—assumed an ambiguous gender identity. Guanyin is always shown with a calm, gentle, and benign face (traits that could be considered feminine), yet it is different from the stereotypical female faces on secular statues. Such images are thought to have attracted female devotees, who believed worship of Guanyin would help them bear sons and bring prosperity to their families.

This statue was probably removed from a temple altar, where Guanyin was believed to sit on a rocky base in an elaborate grotto setting. Chinese Buddhist monasteries of the eleventh century often contained richly illustrated murals and gilded figures. The fabulous integration of architecture, mural, and sculpture into the visual and ceremonial programs of monasteries characterized new heights of Buddhist art in the Song-Yuan period.[20]

—*FJZ*

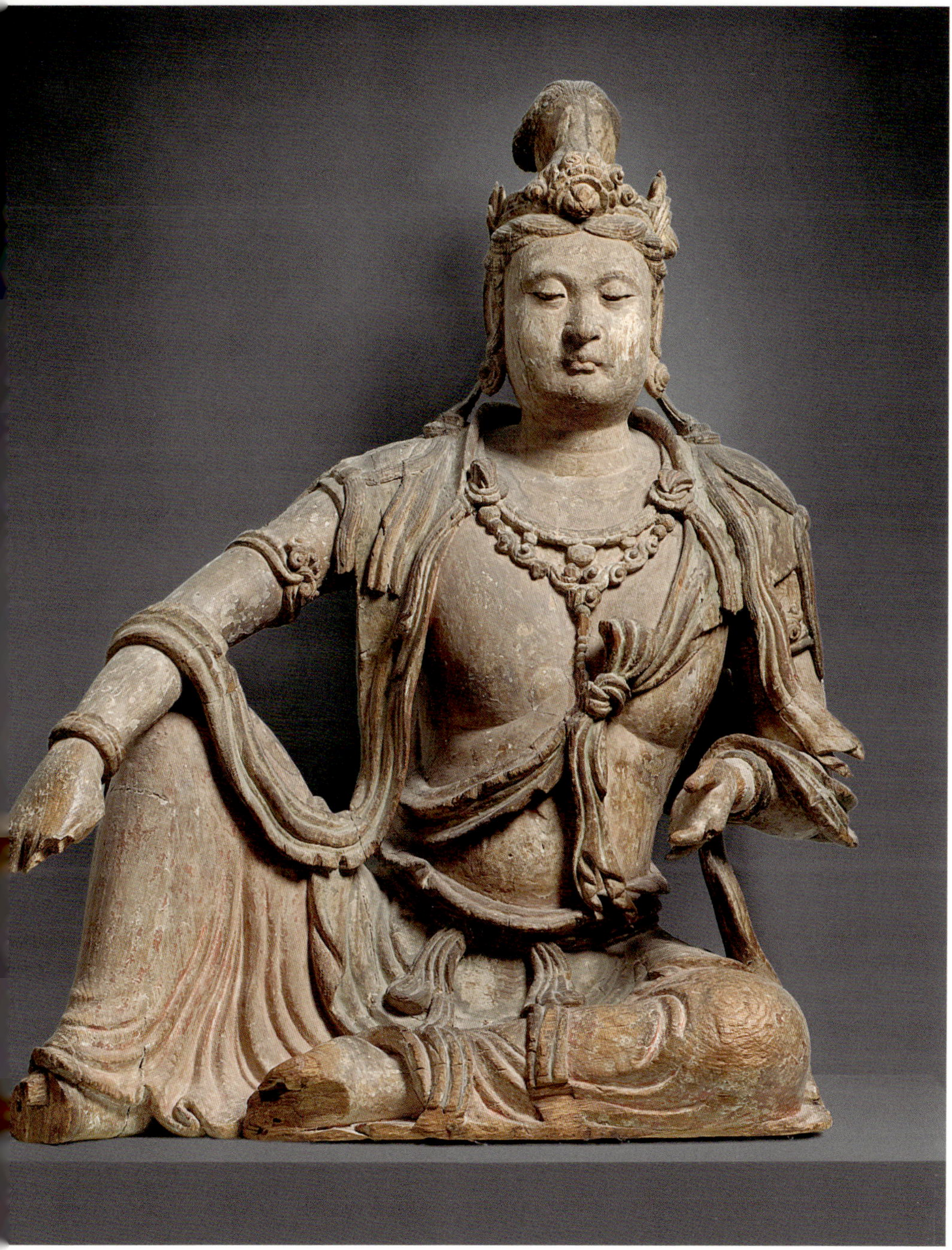

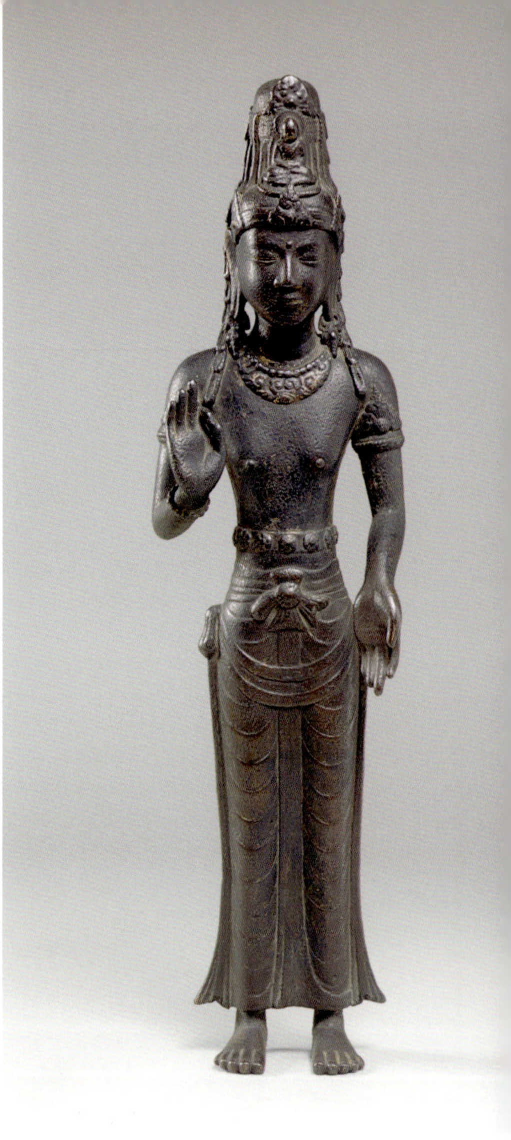

THE BODHISATTVA AVALOKITESHVARA (GUANYIN)

China; Yunnan province

Dali kingdom (937–1253)

Bronze with gilding

H. 44.5 cm × W. 11.8 cm × D. 7.6 cm

The Avery Brundage Collection, B60S34

This sculpture of Acuoye Guanyin (Sanskrit: Ajaya Avalokiteshvara, meaning "invincible Avalokiteshvara") depicts a slender figure wearing a high crown and a tightly fitting lower garment, his bare upper torso decorated with jewels. He holds his hands in common gestures, with the *vitarka* mudra of religious discussion on the right and the *varada* mudra of mercy granting on the left. He can be identified by the distinctive diadem on his crown, which shows an image of his spiritual father, the Buddha. Since the late Tang dynasty (618–907), worship of bodhisattvas and arhats (Buddhist spiritual beings) such as Guanyin gained popularity in China, and artistic portrayals of them thrived throughout the vast land.

It was believed that Avalokiteshvara, under the guise of an Indian monk, spread Buddhism in the Nanzhao kingdom (738–937) in modern China's southwestern Yunnan province. Because this monk successfully predicted the ascension of the first king of Nanzhao under Buddhist protection, the Acuoye Guanyin became the patron saint of the royal clan of Nanzhao. Bronze statues of this deity in a rigid, forward-facing stance thrived in the succeeding Dali kingdom (937–1253). This unusual, slender form of Guanyin worshiped by rulers of Yunnan shows a strong regional identity different from that in the central kingdoms of China, reflecting the distinctive religious, political, and cultural contexts of Yunnan.

Because Yunnan sits at the crossroads of India, Vietnam, and Tibet, its esoteric Buddhist art borrowed elements from South and Southeast Asia. Yunnanese possibly adopted some prototypes from Champa in central and southern Vietnam or Srivijaya in Sumatra, Indonesia.[21] Yet, it is also possible that the characteristic form and style of Acuoye Guanyin seen in this work originated in Yunnan and then affected religious portrayals in other regions.[22]

—*FJZ*

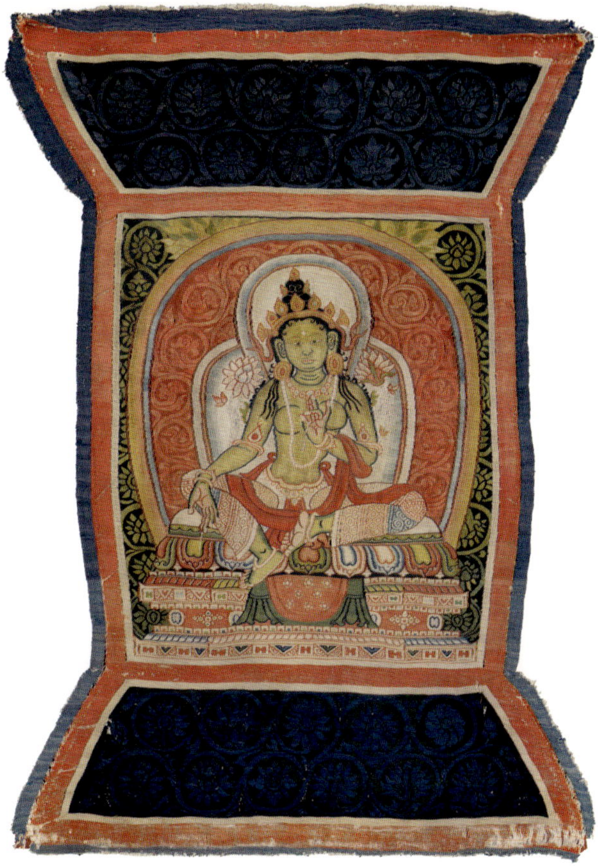

THE BUDDHIST DEITY GREEN TARA

—

1200–1250
China
Xi Xia kingdom (1038–1227)
Slit-silk tapestry (*kesi*)
H. 23.2 cm × W. 19 cm (image); H. 43.8 cm × W. 30.48 cm (overall)
Museum purchase, City Arts Trust Fund, 1992.59

—

One of the most important aspects of esoteric Buddhist thought is its emphasis on female imagery. In its most basic mandala (a virtual palace that is visualized in meditation), each of five directional buddhas has a specific female counterpart called a "wisdom" (*prajna*). Green Tara, shown here, is the wisdom of the active green Buddha Amoghasiddhi of the north, which underscores her role as active bodhisattva of compassion. Further emphasizing her active nature, Green Tara's right arm is extended in the gesture of gift giving, while her right foot virtually steps out of the tapestry. Tapestries such as this are superb tools for esoteric Buddhists to practice visualization, since their different textures, piles, and modes of production create a series of planes that give a semblance of dimensionality.

This tapestry comes from the lost Tangut kingdom of Xi Xia in northwest China. When Khara Khoto, the capital of the kingdom, was breached by Genghis Khan in the thirteenth century, some of its art treasures survived in a series of stupas, which are hemispherical reliquaries enshrining the sacred remains of enlightened beings. A number of these stupas were excavated by Russian archaeologists in 1907, and today the bulk of the material from the lost kingdom of Xi Xia lies in the State Hermitage Museum in Saint Petersburg, Russia.

—JD

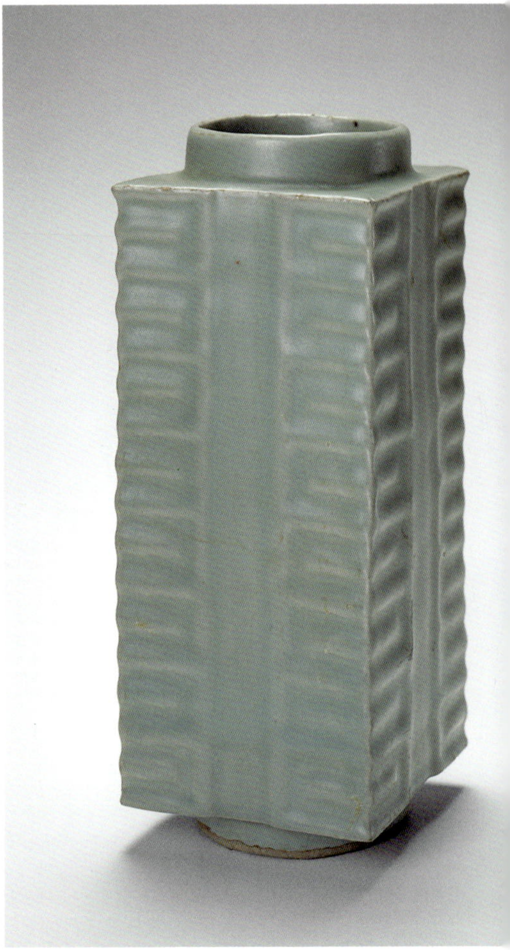

VASE IN THE SHAPE OF A RITUAL OBJECT (*CONG*)

China; Zhejiang province
Southern Song period (1127–1279)
Stoneware with celadon glaze (Guan ware)
H. 26.4 cm × Diam. 10.2 cm
The Avery Brundage Collection, B60P1444

Its simple, soft bluish-green color, its relatively large and thin surface crackles, and the unglazed edge of its foot ring characterize this vase as Guan ware, an official ceramic of the Southern Song period (1127–1279).[23] Celadon wares such as this, ranging in color from pale blue to earthy green, were held in the highest esteem in Northern Song (960–1127) official Ru kilns. Their crackles, although a technical flaw due to the different cooling temperatures of the ceramic body and the glaze, were appreciated for their ability to catch light, which accentuated Guan ware's resemblance to jade.[24] When the ruling elite lost their northern territory to invaders, they established official kilns closer to their new southern capital. The resulting Southern Song official Guan wares, such as this vase, emulated their northern celadon predecessors.

The formation, regulation, and use of multiple kiln sites contributed to the development of ceramic production during the Song dynasty, a time noted for its adherence to classic Confucian traditions and reverence of the past. These beliefs permeated daily life and heavily influenced both the functionality and modest aesthetics of artwork of the time.[25] Appreciation for antiquities and visual harmony of color and shape is evident in the use of shapes originally seen in much earlier ritual jade and bronze forms, and the lustrous, mostly monochrome glazes of the period's ceramics.

The geometric shape of this *cong*—a strikingly rigid rectangular tube with cylindrical center—is one that has existed since the Neolithic period. Some of the most elaborate *cong*, originally carved in jade, have stylized animal masks etched on their corners (see the ritual implement on page 115). Later iterations of the *cong* in different materials have simplified this decoration, as in the alternating surface ridges seen here. Though its shape remained popular for ceramics through the Song dynasty and can still be seen today, the function of the *cong* changed, and its ritual aspect was gently phased out and replaced with more decorative uses, such as a flower vase.

—*JC*

TEABOWL STAND

approx. 1200–1300

Southern China

Southern Song period (1127–1279) or Yuan dynasty (1271–1368)

Lacquer on wood

H. 8.4 cm × Diam. 18.4 cm

Museum purchase, B76M3

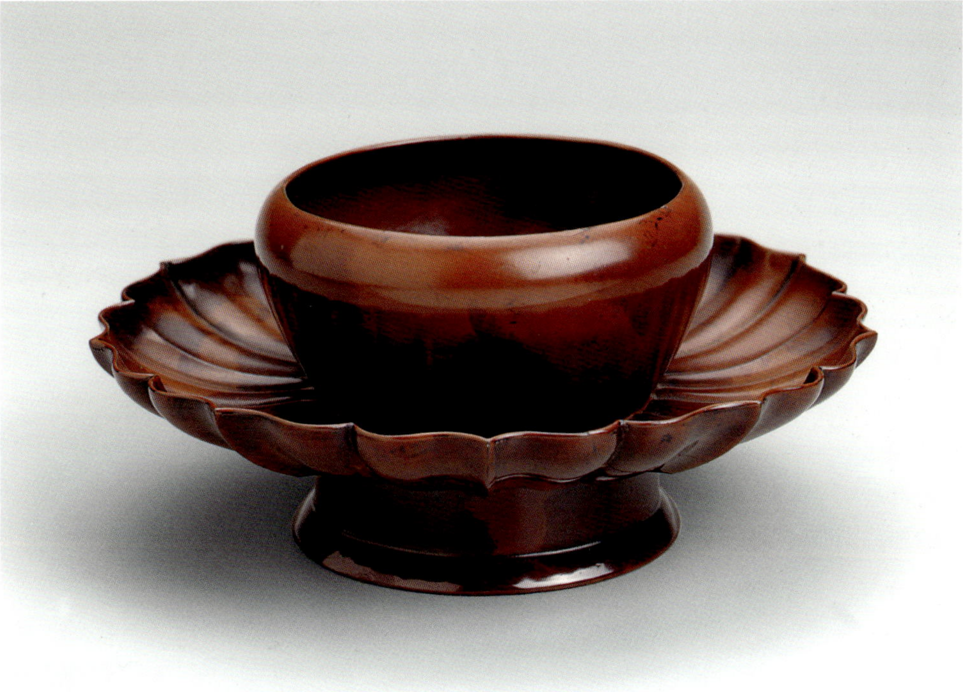

TRAVELERS AMONG VALLEYS AND PEAKS

—

1200–1300

China

Jin (1115–1234) or Yuan dynasty (1271–1368)

Hanging scroll; ink and light colors on paper

H. 106.7 cm × W. 40 cm (image)

The Avery Brundage Collection, B66D1.a

—

In this mountain scene, the natural world is shown in all its splendor. The towering, vertical composition, the suggestion of perspectival depth, and the inclusion of small figures of travelers defined a style cultivated by artists of the Northern Song court (960–1127). Song painting marked a new era in brushwork technique. The use of brush and ink came to be crucial in judging painting, to the detriment of subject, inspiration, and mood.

The systematized style of Song painting inspired later generations of artists. As seen in this painting, created a century later, an unknown artist follows Song models. The painting's carefully executed brushwork, which resulted from studying Song techniques, expresses different rock textures, water, and foliage.

For thousands of years the veneration of mountains was a central practice in Chinese rituals for entreating the blessings of heaven, and it found expression in material culture, including paintings. Song dynasty artists, in particular, used landscapes to convey an intimate connection between humans and nature. In their works, people have a small and often minimal presence, as though subordinate to the supreme power of nature. To accommodate the Song emperors' fascination with mountains, considered sacred in Daoist philosophy, court painters created large-scale, monumental landscapes. Many of these either were made from sketches of famous mountains or were works done in a studio with imaginary settings.

The Song landscapes were conventional models for both court artists and individual painters throughout Chinese history. Even when China was under Jurchen, Mongol, or Manchu rule, its non-Chinese leaders appreciated, collected, and studied Song paintings. Their patronage tightly bound the practice of court painters to Song models. At the same time, individual artists did their best to compete with court painters—their stylistic and commercial rivals. This landscape painting could have been completed by a court painter, professional painter, or scholar-painter, although the absence of a signature suggests that it was not made for an emperor.

The importance of this painting has long been acknowledged by elites and connoisseurs, as can be seen by its accompanying scroll. Its three critiques, written from the late sixteenth to early nineteenth century, attribute this painting to one of the early Song masters, Fan Kuan (active late tenth–early eleventh century). Many subsequent scholars, however, believe that the brushwork in this piece shows that it was a later work, probably from the Jin or Yuan dynasty, inspired by Fan Kuan and other Song masters.

—*HL*

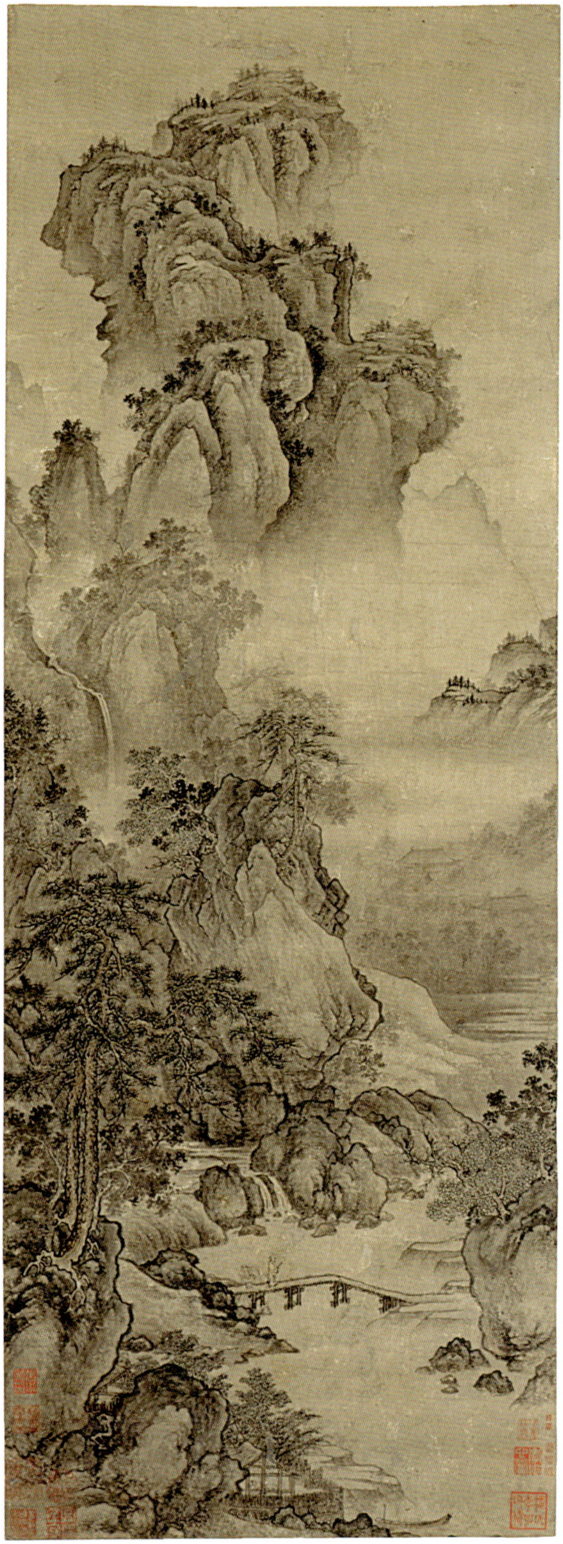

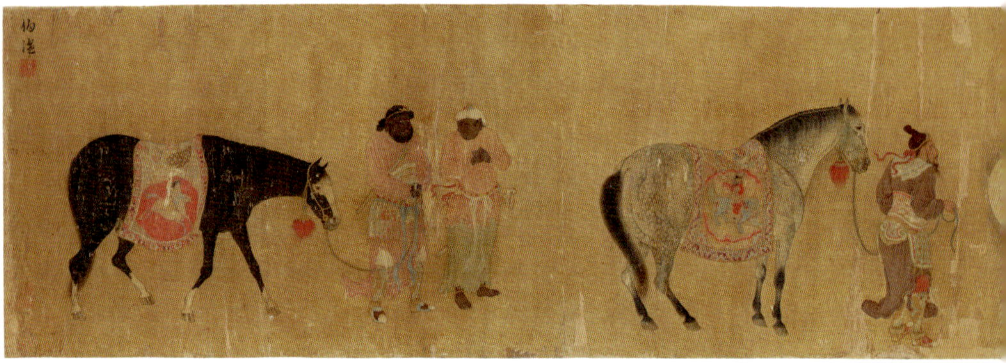

TRIBUTE BEARERS

Attributed to Ren Bowen (Chinese, 1254–1327)
Yuan dynasty (1271–1368)
Handscroll; ink and colors on silk
H. 34.9 cm × W. 221.6 cm (image)
The Avery Brundage Collection, B60D100

The multiethnic procession in *Tribute Bearers* is characteristic of the Yuan dynasty, when China's Mongol rulers employed diverse groups as officials, experts, and craftspeople. The parade is led by a barefoot, dark-skinned dwarf who carries a lion sculpture in a jewel-strewn basin on his head. Two senior emissaries follow; one holds an incense burner with wisps of smoke curling upward from its lid. Both balding envoys wear golden, jeweled diadems and hoop earrings. One may represent an Indian or Southeast Asian, while his companion and other figures with prominent long noses and full beards probably indicate central or western Asian groups. The mixture of ethnicities continues in the figures of sword-carrying guardsmen and grooms; one attendant holds a pennant with "Presenting Tribute" figured in gold characters. Dark-skinned attendants are similarly represented in a well-known painting in the collection of the National Palace Museum, Taipei: Liu Guandao's *Kublai Khan Hunting* of 1280.

The principal tribute offering comes last, in the form of three stallions, likely prized breeds from Central Asia. Ren Bowen, the painter of *Tribute Bearers*, is usually identified as a grandson of Ren Renfa (1255–1328), a Yuan-dynasty official and expert in irrigation engineering who was also a renowned specialist in horse painting.[26] The horses in this painting follow Ren Renfa's manner of closely observed muscular anatomy and sensitive rendering of mouths and eyes. Their colorful saddle blankets are decorated with panels of youths riding canine, feline, and equine mounts.

The subject of *Tribute Bearers* dates to the Tang dynasty (618–907 CE), as noted in a colophon on this painting written by the eminent Ming painter Wen Zhengming (1470–1559). The many sinuously fluttering scarves and hair ribbons likely refer to other conventions of ancient figure painting. Another early feature appears in the concentric drapery folds on the torsos of the last two attendants, linked to the imported style of a late seventh-century painter from the Central Asian oasis state of Khotan. *Tribute Bearers* manifests not only distant historical references but also the richness of Yuan-dynasty material and cultural diversity.

—Richard Vinograd is Christensen Fund Professor in Asian Art at Stanford University.

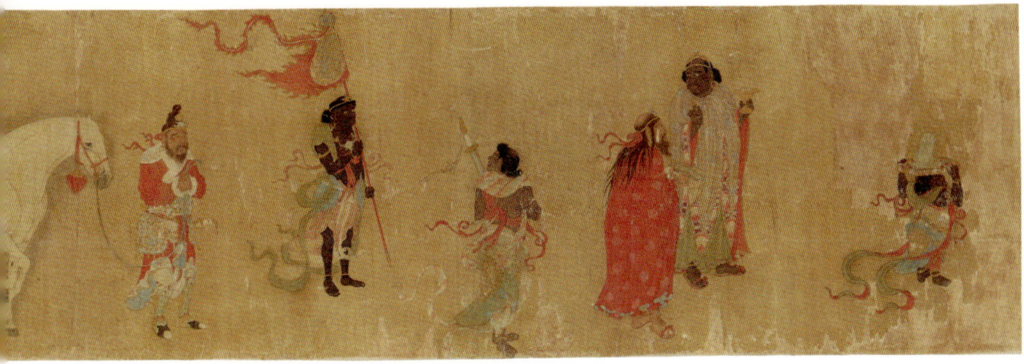

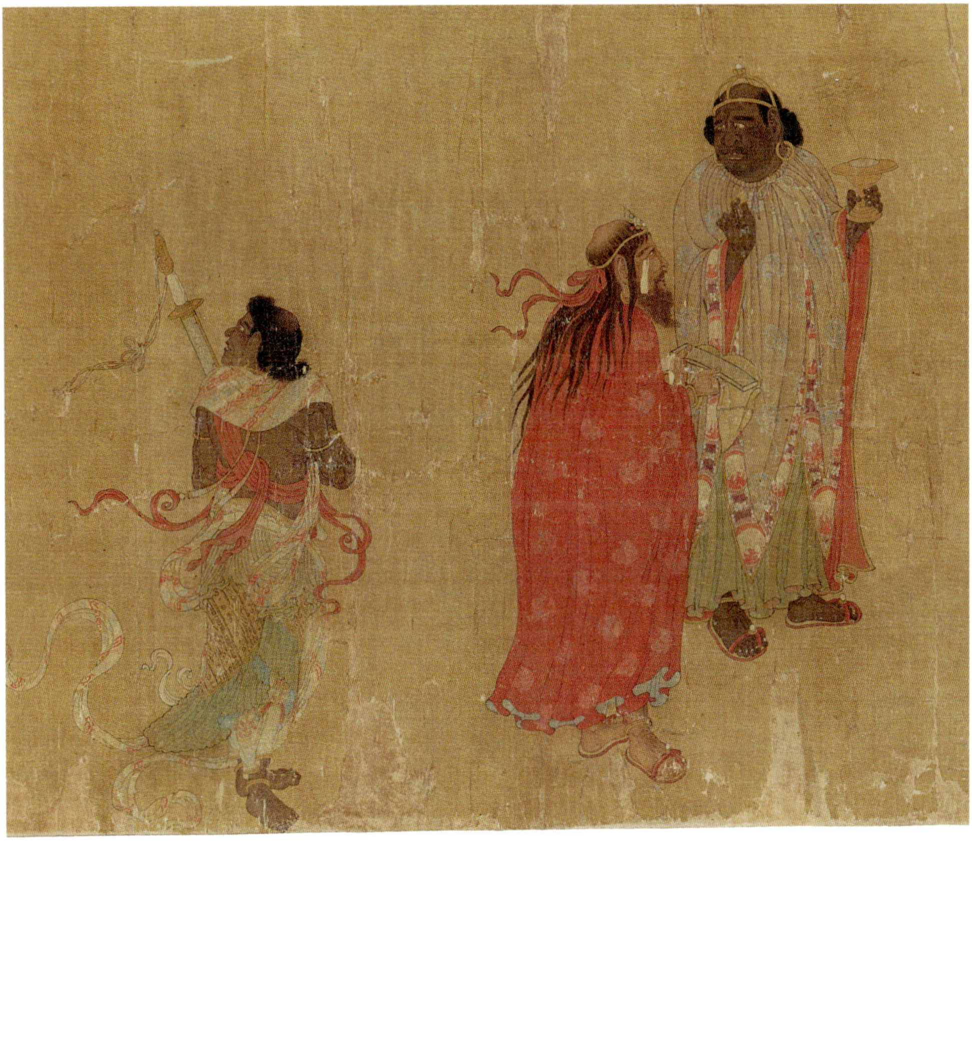

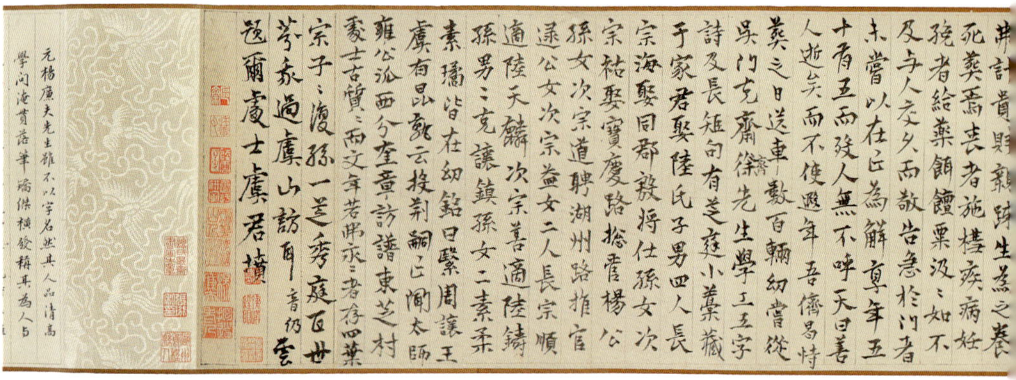

EPITAPH FOR YU DEZHANG

1369

By Yang Weizhen (Chinese, 1296–1370)

Yuan dynasty (1271–1368)

Handscroll; ink on paper

H. 25.4 cm × W. 141.6 cm (image)

Gift of the Tang Family in memory of P. Y. and Kinmay Wen Tang, 1992.63

Written on paper or silk, or carved on a stone stele, an epitaph offers important information about both its writer and the person to whom it is dedicated. It tells about their work and social lives, education, and leisurely pursuits, which increases our understanding of the intellectual lives of elites in an imperial era.

This work by Yang Weizhen, an acclaimed academician at the Yuan court, celebrates the life of Mr. Yu (posthumous name Dezhang, 1301–1355), a relatively unknown country gentleman from Changshu in Jiangsu province on China's southern coast. With a clear structure, Yang unfolds this narrative epitaph, beginning

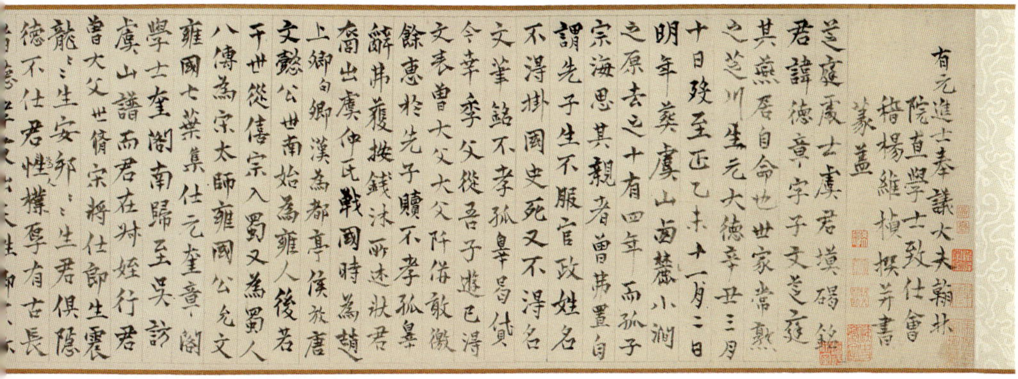

with a family tree tracking the prominent posts held by Yu's ancestors. Yang's text looks at Yu's decades-long involvement in his hometown and sums up Yu's fascinating story. It describes Yu's virtues of simplicity and kindness, how he demonstrated filial piety, how he treated his countrymen equally regardless of social status, and how he offered financial support to the poor and sick. It tells how Yu's reputation extended far beyond his hometown, as hundreds of chariots joined his funeral procession to show reverence and send off Yu's coffin. Yang writes about Yu's family members then ends with a lyrical piece expressing the human spirit and devotion to Yu's noble soul.

Here the calligrapher, in a long handscroll, delivered an innovative composition combining narrative prose with the classical form of rhapsodic poetry. Yang offers a personal retrospective in running script, a calligraphic style he occasionally practiced. Appropriate for a solemn epitaph, the characters flow together legibly and are consistent in size. The writing glides through Yang's skillful control of the brush, fluidly executed strokes, and evenly laid out structure as he composes characters within columns marked by vertical lines.

The Shaoxing-born Yang Weizhen achieved an advanced degree at the civil service examination in 1337 and made his reputation in Zhejiang, in southeastern China, as a talented writer and Confucian scholar. After serving the local administration as a minor official, Yang secluded himself in the mountains and refused an invitation to work for the government. His calligraphy was considered slender and pleasant, yet forceful.

—HL

PLEASURES OF FISHING IN A RIVER IN THE MOUNTAINS

Attributed to Sheng Mao (Chinese, active 1310–1360)
Yuan dynasty (1271–1368)
Hanging scroll; ink and colors on silk
H. 170.2 cm × W. 103.5 cm (image)
Museum purchase, B69D10

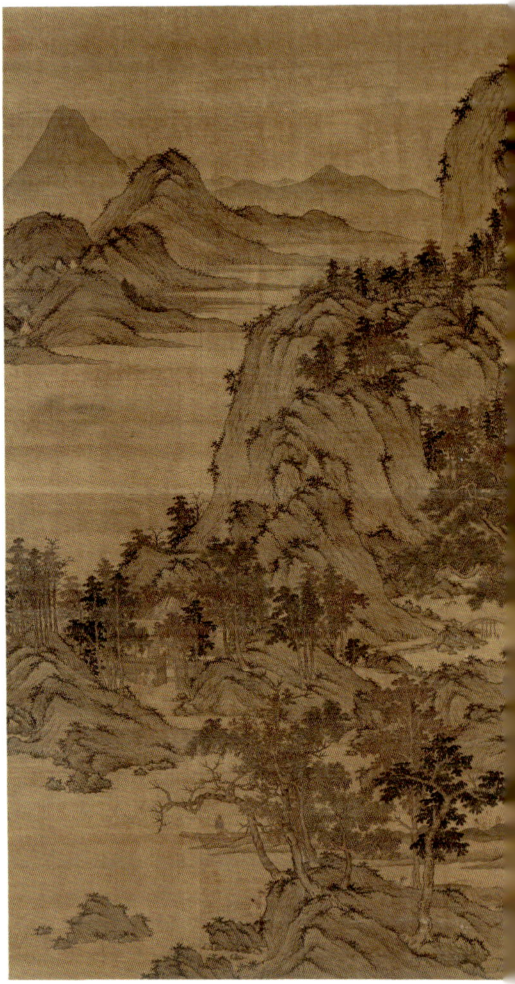

The appeal of this painting, attributed to the Yuan artist Sheng Mao, lies in its portrayal of tasteful and charming mountain villages in summer. Sheng aimed to capture the rustic life and activity of country dwellers in a narrative way, arranging his subjects in a succession of diagonal planes from bottom to top. The foreground of the painting shows fishermen holding rods and casting offshore, while others gather for drink and food. The middle ground depicts two men returning to a mountain villa; a fisherman carries a basket on his shoulder while a woodcutter hoists a bundle of kindling. Inside a thatched house, a woman stands by the door as if to welcome the men. The top of the painting shows mountaintops absent of figures.

This monumental work represents a significant and enduring theme in Chinese visual art in which art is bound with literature, specifically to the written works of scholars. This is traditionally referred to as the literati school. Idyllic subjects, as seen in this landscape, are often related to the poetry of Wang Wei (701–761), a prominent scholar-official at the Tang court known as Right Minister. From time to time, Wang retreated from service at the court into the mountains in China's northwestern Shaanxi province. He hints at this in his painting and poetry series on twenty scenic spots, *Wangchuan Retreat House*. The series was acclaimed by many renowned poets, who praised it as poetry that embodies painting, and painting that conveys poetry. Wang's work inspired numerous writers and artists over the centuries, continuing to today. Resulting scenes of fishing, practicing music, collecting water chestnuts, and entertaining eccentric guests by the river have been painted and engraved by Chinese artists for centuries.

The fisherman's life became a popular subject during the Yuan dynasty, when many educated Han Chinese refused to serve the Mongol-ruled court and lived in seclusion from city and society. Through painting fishermen's lives, artists conveyed the spiritual ideal of a peaceful life free of political corruption.

—*HL*

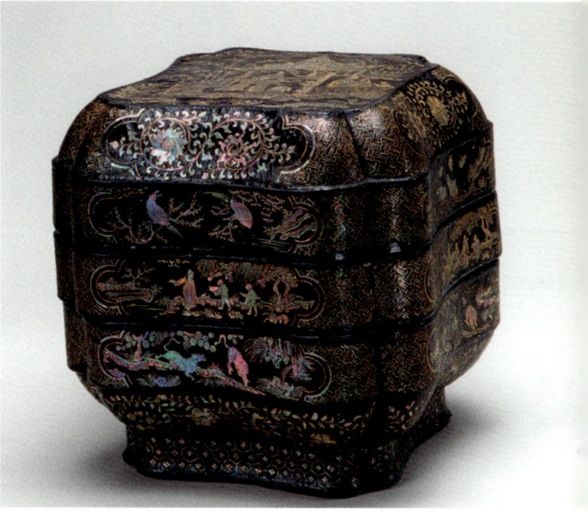

TIERED BOX

China
Yuan dynasty (1271–1368)
Lacquer with inlaid mother-of-pearl
H. 20 cm × W. 21 cm × D. 21 cm
Gift of the Asian Art Museum Foundation, B77M21.a-.c

This three-layered container is both a piece of expert craftsmanship and a reflection of its owner's wealth and social status. Its elaborate design and fine execution are understandably rare, given the fragility and delicacy of its material. Such a container was used to hold small precious objects, yet it was also a work of art intended for display. When it was made during the fourteenth century, literati painting and scholars' objects were fashioned in an opulent manner. The literati ideal was to paint a narrative depiction that contained a miniature world of men and nature. Reactions to literati painting appeared rapidly in artworks made of other mediums. To meet the general desire for technically challenging work, craftsmen mastered the art of transforming paintings into three-dimensional form on utensils and furniture through lacquer, mother-of-pearl, gold, silver, and pigments.

In southern China, where lacquerwares flourished for thousands of years, one special, complicated technique for achieving this ideal involved applying lacquer, marquetry, and mother-of-pearl to create a depiction on a wooden or bamboo core. This filling-and-inlaying technique was documented in the sixteenth-century text *Record of Lacquer Decoration* (*Xiushi lu*). This tiered box was crafted with this technique and is among the few known examples of such multilayered containers. It was likely made by lacquer master Hu Zhaogang from Jiangxi province in southeast China. The principal motif atop its lid depicts educated elites reciting poetry, drinking, and strolling in a mountain-and-river landscape. Around the middle section of the box, they enjoy a party by a river, accompanied by a covered zither, a sword, books and painting scrolls, and a board game. The decorative setting includes landscape vignettes and auspicious birds and beasts framed by bouquets of flowers and brocade patterns.

The fluidity of this box's lobed shape is secondary to the stunning marquetry of mother-of-pearl that decorates its surface. Its execution required eight to twelve procedures. The most time-consuming step was to break the mother-of-pearl into countless small particles, each about .04 to .1 mm thick, and to lay them out one by one to create a design on lacquer. The surface was then coated with more layers of lacquer and carefully polished, after the coating dried, to reveal the mother-of-pearl depiction. Color pigments such as gold or silver might be applied beneath each piece of mother-of-pearl, which would add a dazzling glow to the surface.

—*HL*

VASE WITH DESIGN OF DRAGONS AMID CLOUDS

—

China; Jingdezhen, Jiangxi province

Ming dynasty, reign of the Hongwu emperor (1368-1398)

Porcelain with copper decoration under glaze

H. 47 cm × Diam. 22.2 cm

The Avery Brundage Collection, B60P1235

—

This porcelain vase, with its unique form and decoration, announced an era in the late fourteenth and early fifteenth century when red dominated decorations in porcelain. It was made for Zhu Yuanzhang (1328-1398), a Chinese monk and rebel leader who defeated the Mongols and founded the Ming dynasty. The red dragons on this vase were particular to Zhu's story. Following his early victories in southeast China, Zhu followed the advice of fortune tellers and built temples in Nanjing. There he set up sacrificial altars dedicated to the dragon and phoenix. In so doing, he was following an ancient belief in the fundamental cosmic forces of the negative and positive polarities of yin and yang. Alone or paired, these entities symbolized dynastic virtue and were employed to legitimize the emperor's power. A number of porcelain pieces decorated with the dragon and phoenix were produced in the famous kilns of Jingdezhen, part of Zhu's territory, for the altars in his temple.

Based on the fortune tellers' words regarding his fate and his communal relationship with the cosmic elements, Zhu chose "Hongwu"—meaning "great force"—for his reign name. "Hong" is a homonym for red and a synonym for his family name, "Zhu," also meaning red color. Zhu linked the red to the "red phoenix," the god of the south, under whose protection he defeated the Mongols. The color red, therefore, played an essential role in Ming court art.

Two types of red were produced in ceramics: overglaze iron-red and underglaze copper-red. The latter was difficult to achieve because at high temperatures the red color would easily burn out or become dark, as seen in this vase. The rarity of underglaze-red wares has resulted in a small number of surviving works. This piece is one of only two known examples of its type; a matching piece is in the Shanghai Museum. The form of this vase was based on the traditional bronze vessel *hu* from the late Bronze Age. Its pear-shaped body and handles in the shape of mythical animal heads carrying rings exemplify the *hu*.

—*HL*

LIDDED BOX WITH CARVED FLOWER DESIGNS

—

China

Ming dynasty, reign of the Yongle emperor (1403-1424)

Lacquer

H. 8.3 cm × Diam. 24.1 cm

The Avery Brundage Collection, B60M309.a-.b

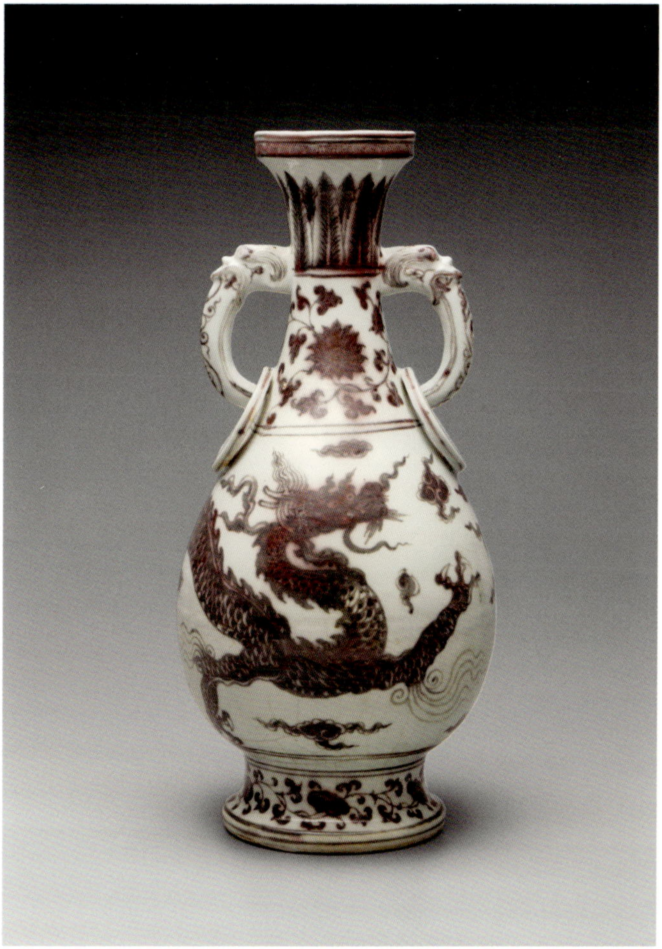

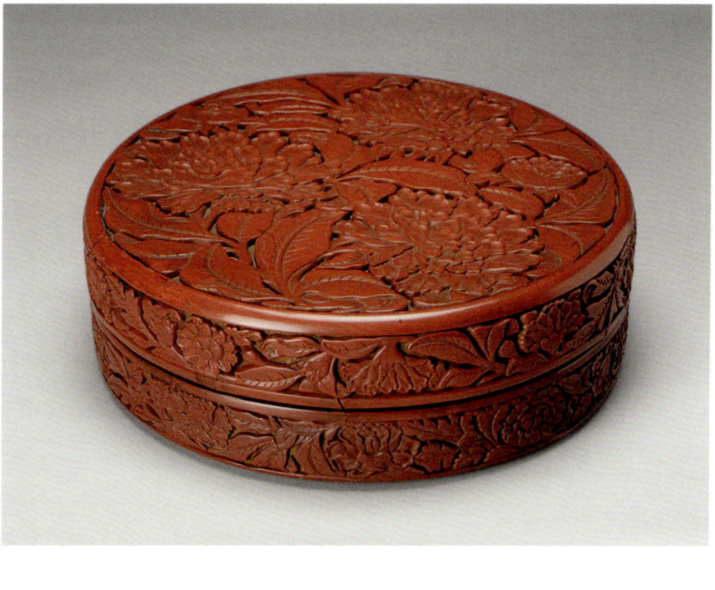

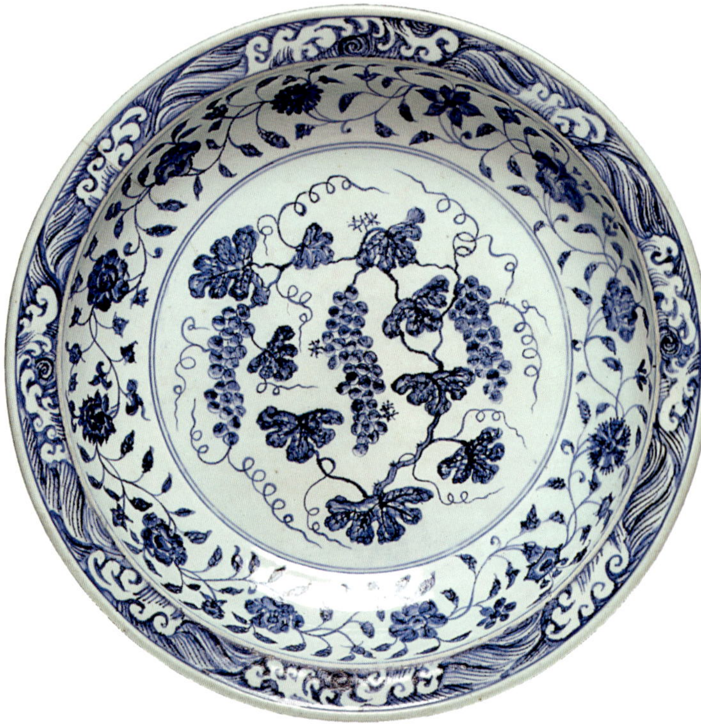

PLATE WITH GRAPE DESIGN, INSCRIBED WITH THE NAME OF THE MUGHAL EMPEROR SHAH JAHAN

China; Jingdezhen, Jiangxi province
Ming dynasty, reign of the Xuande emperor (1426–1435)
Porcelain with underglaze blue decoration
H. 7.6 cm × Diam. 37.5 cm
The Avery Brundage Collection, B65P6

This blue-and-white Ming-dynasty dish belonged to Shah Jahan (ruled 1628–1658), the Mughal emperor of India most famously known as the patron of the Taj Mahal in Agra. The emperor clearly valued this dish when it came into his collection, as he had his name and the year of its acquisition inscribed on it. The text, on the side of the foot, in Persian, says "Shah Jahan, son of Jahangir Shah, 1054 AH (1644 CE)."

Chinese porcelains made at commercial kilns were traded as luxury goods at various centers in the Islamic world from at least the ninth century. They are prominently featured in paintings made for Persian rulers and nobility during the 1400s. By the 1600s the Persian Safavid shahs and Turkish Ottoman sultans became leading collectors of Chinese ceramics. Their royal collections (preserved today at the shrine of Shaykh Safi in Ardabil, Iran and at the Topkapi Palace Treasury in Istanbul, Turkey) are the two most important collections of Chinese ceramics outside China. This dish is among the rare examples that attest to Mughal emperors' interest in Chinese porcelains.

—*QA*

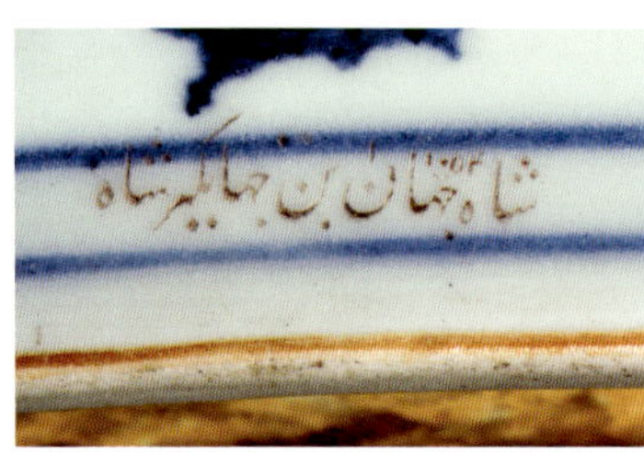

JAR DEPICTING A CELEBRATION OF LONGEVITY BY DAOIST IMMORTALS

—

approx. 1450–1464
China; Jingdezhen, Jiangxi province
Ming dynasty, reign of the Jingtai emperor (1450–1456) or reign of the Tianshun emperor (1457–1464)
Porcelain with underglaze blue decoration
H. 35.9 cm × Diam. 36.8 cm
The Avery Brundage Collection, B60P90

—

This wide-mouthed, broad-shouldered, porcelain jar was made at the kilns in Jingdezhen, a porcelain center in southeastern China. It dates to the Ming dynasty, though its shape harkens to Neolithic-era earthenware. The jar lacks an imperial mark, which suggests it was made at a time when the Ming court decreased its patronage of porcelain; this coincided with the reigns of the Jingtai and Tianshun emperors (1450–64). Despite the decrease in imperial porcelain production, Ming records document court orders for Jingdezhen porcelain as gifts and ceremonial items in 1459 and 1464.[27] This jar may have been produced for such diplomacy. Or it may be evidence of the kilns searching for new markets and patrons.

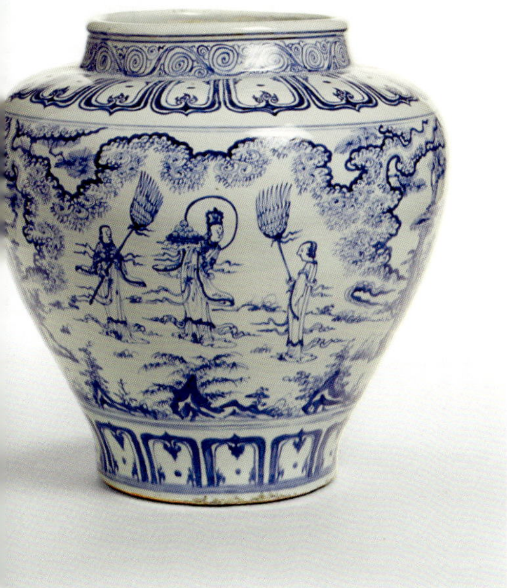

Bordered by three decorative friezes, the main motif consists of eight immortals (*xian*) from the Daoist pantheon. Swirls of stylized clouds link the various figures into one imaginary realm dominated by themes of eternity. A crane, a towering pine tree, and a prancing deer—all icons of longevity—also inhabit the blue-and-white surface. One scene depicts the most famous of ancient female immortals, Queen Mother of the West (Xiwangmu). Behind her lavish headdress is a cobalt-painted halo. Fanned by two attendants, she holds a platter of peaches, a suggestion of the peach tree growing in her place of eternal residence, Kunlun Mountain.[28] On the opposite side of the jar, a scene depicts three people playing *weiqi*, a board game similar to chess. One figure holds a mangled wooden stick that identifies him as Wang Zhi, who wanders in the mountains looking for firewood and encounters two men playing the game. After some time, one of the players looks up and remarks that Wang's wooden ax handle has rotted. At that moment, Wang realizes he is in the realm of the immortals.

Other figures on the jar engage in playing music, drinking wine, and merrymaking. Together, the jar's pictorial elements convey the hope for longevity and immortality. As an embodiment of well wishes, the jar would have played a significant role in court diplomacy or in temple rituals.
—Ellen Huang is Curatorial Fellow of Asian Art at Stanford University, Cantor Center for the Visual Arts.

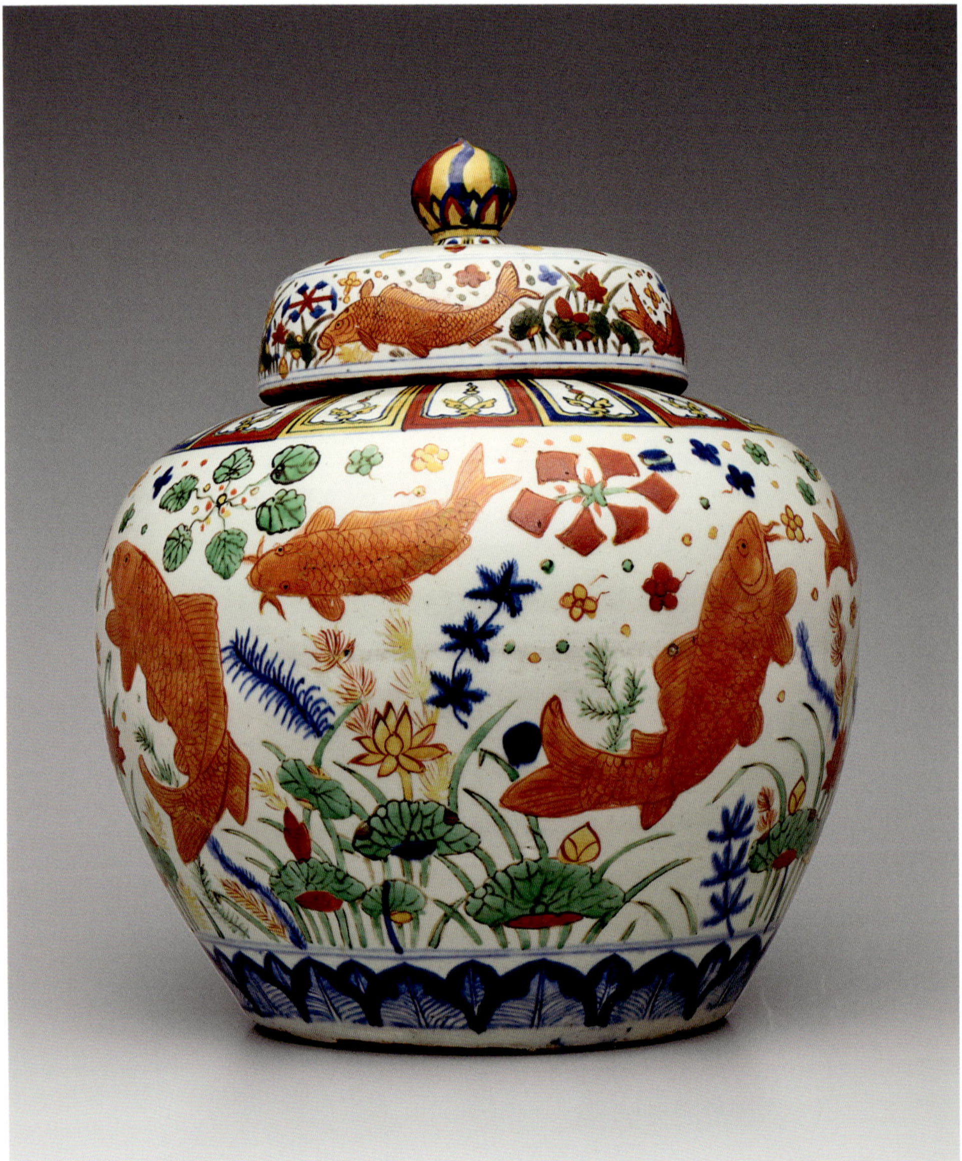

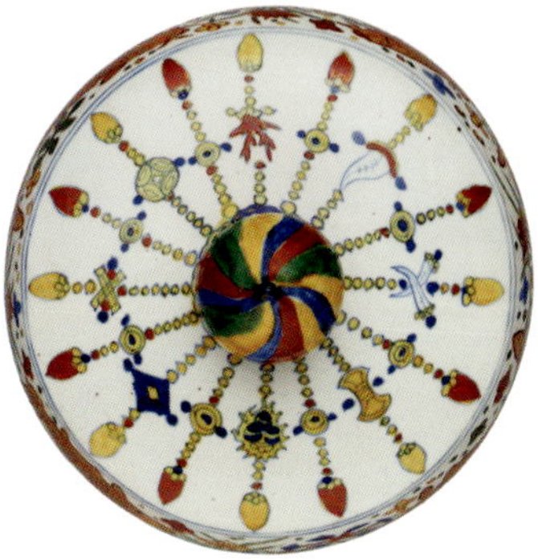

MASTERPIECE

LIDDED JAR WITH DESIGN OF A LOTUS POND

China; Jingdezhen, Jiangxi province

Ming dynasty, reign of the Jiajing emperor (1522–1566)

Porcelain with underglaze cobalt and overglaze multicolor decoration

H. 49.5 cm × Diam. 40 cm

The Avery Brundage Collection, B60P78+

During the Jiajing period of the Ming dynasty, potters at the imperial workshop mastered a refined execution of clay, design, and decorative colors, as seen in this precious fish jar. Fish are among the most favored iconography in celebrating the New Year, as the word in Chinese is a homonym for *abundant* and *plentiful*. The motif of fish in a lotus pond, symbolic of eternal prosperity, was popularized during the thirteenth and fourteenth centuries and became an iconic symbol of the imperial ceramic workshop in Jingdezhen, in southeast China, in the fifteenth century. Here it appears on a jar from the sixteenth century.

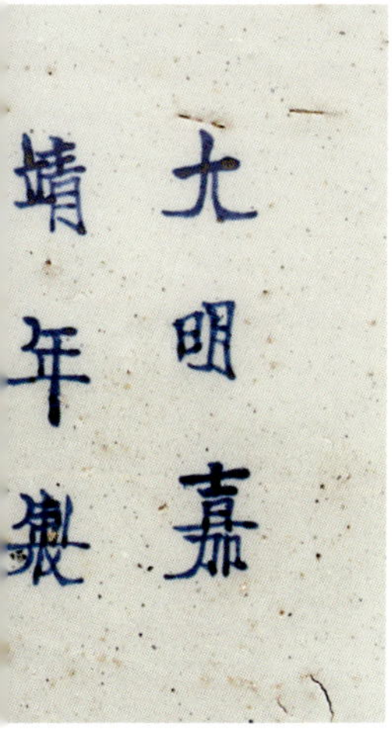

Round jars were especially suitable for presenting the fluid world of fish in a lotus pond. This motif was executed by Jingdezhen potters in underglaze red, underglaze blue, or a combination of underglaze blue with overglaze multicolor decorations known as *wucai*, which can be translated as "five colors." The decoration required, in general, two firings. A portion of the pottery body is painted in blue cobalt, after which a clear glaze is applied. The glazed vessel is fired once at a high temperature, and then additional enamels are painted over the glaze for the second low-temperature firing.

The Jiajing imperial workshop produced many large-sized jars. This example is decorated with bright, dense, and subdued colors rendered with strong contrasts. The potters experimented with mixing finely ground minerals such as iron, copper, or cobalt to obtain a broad variety of hues, enriching the possibilities of color and design. The scene depicted on this lidded jar is rendered exuberantly, with seven tones in overall harmony. New color hues are evident in the attenuated greens and overlapping oranges and reds. The cobalt blue, rather than being used in a typical manner for thin outlines in underglaze, was applied in bold washes to complement vigorous overglaze enamels.

—*HL*

DAOIST CELESTIAL WORTHY

approx. 1500–1644
Northern China
Ming dynasty (1368–1644)
Stoneware with multicolor glazes
H. 132.1 cm × W. 54.9 cm × D. 33 cm (overall)
The Avery Brundage Collection, B70P4.a-.f

This three-color (*sancai*) glazed sculpture consists of four sections: statue, body halo, lotus-dragon support, and two-tiered hexangular platform. It represents a member of the Three Pure Ones, the Daoist triad of supreme power. He is depicted as an immortal with a long beard, elongated earlobes, and a serene expression, and his hair is gathered into a bun-shaped headdress. Seated on a lotus pedestal, he rests one of his hands on an armrest and gestures with the other.

As the manifestation of ultimate celestial energy, the Three Pure Ones are usually portrayed as elderly sages holding divine objects associated with their individual roles. Judging from his posture and headdress, this Daoist figure is probably Yuanshi Tianzun (Celestial Venerable of the Original Commencement), the first of the Three Pure Ones. He is often depicted holding a pearl representing the creation of the universe from void and chaos. The second of the triad is Lingbao Tianzun (Celestial Venerable of the Numinous Treasure), who holds a scepter (*ruyi*) signifying authority and order. Daode Tianzun (Celestial Venerable of the Dao and Its Virtue) was later added to the Three Pure Ones during the Tang dynasty, and he always has a fan to spread the Daoist doctrine.

Many workshops in Ming-dynasty Shanxi were well known for their production of wall tiles, statues, and vessels in *sancai* glazes. A representative of the era's *sancai* ware, this double-fired statue was probably made in such a glazed-tile workshop. Although prefabricated molds of the components were used to reduce cost and increase efficiency of production, this kind of large work assembled after firing was no less expensive than similarly sized wood or stone statues carved out by individual hands.[29] To attract more patrons, many workshops that mainly produced architectural components en masse also chose to pursue artistic quality and hired skilled sculptors to make refined products with vivid ornamental details.

—*FJZ*

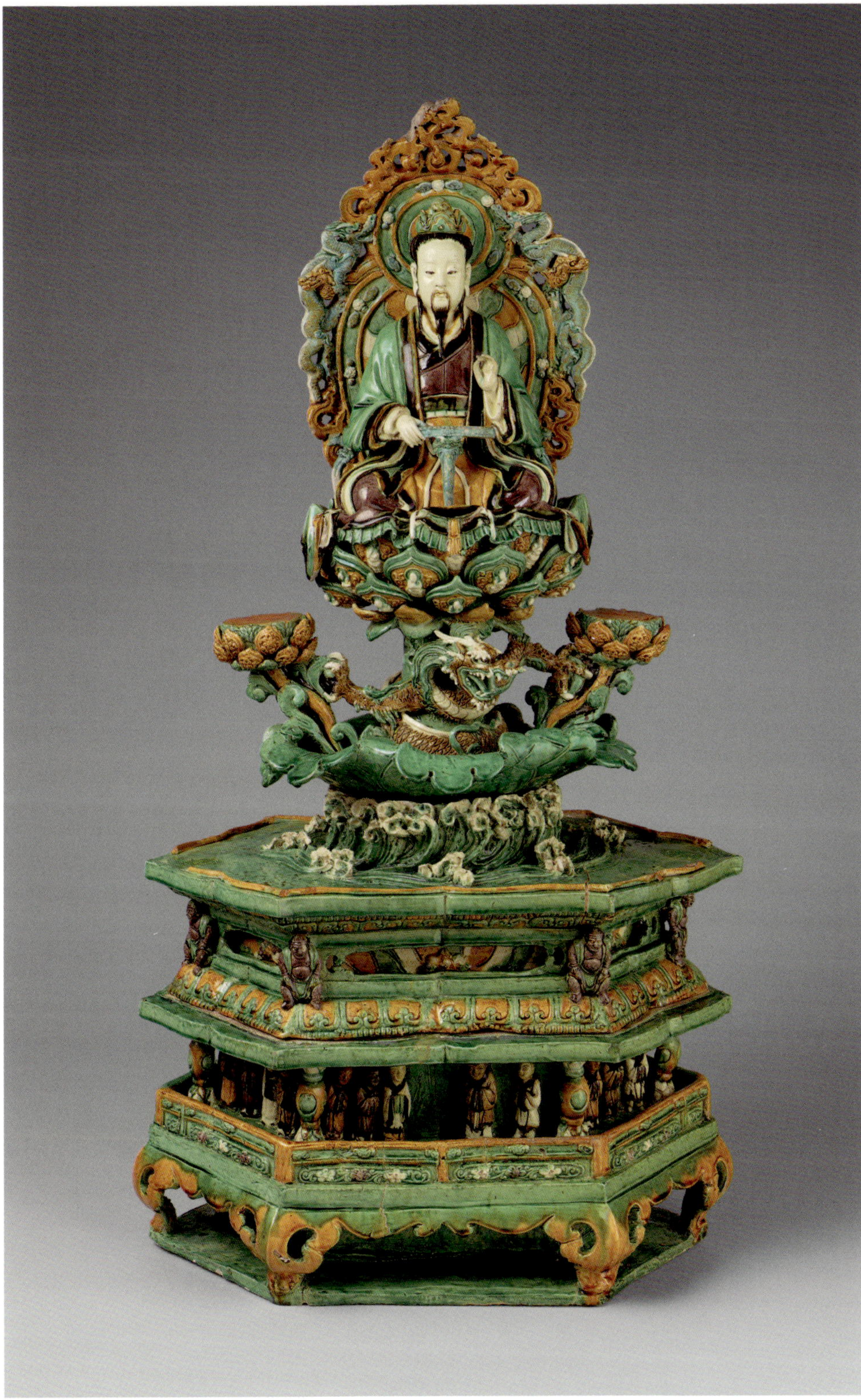

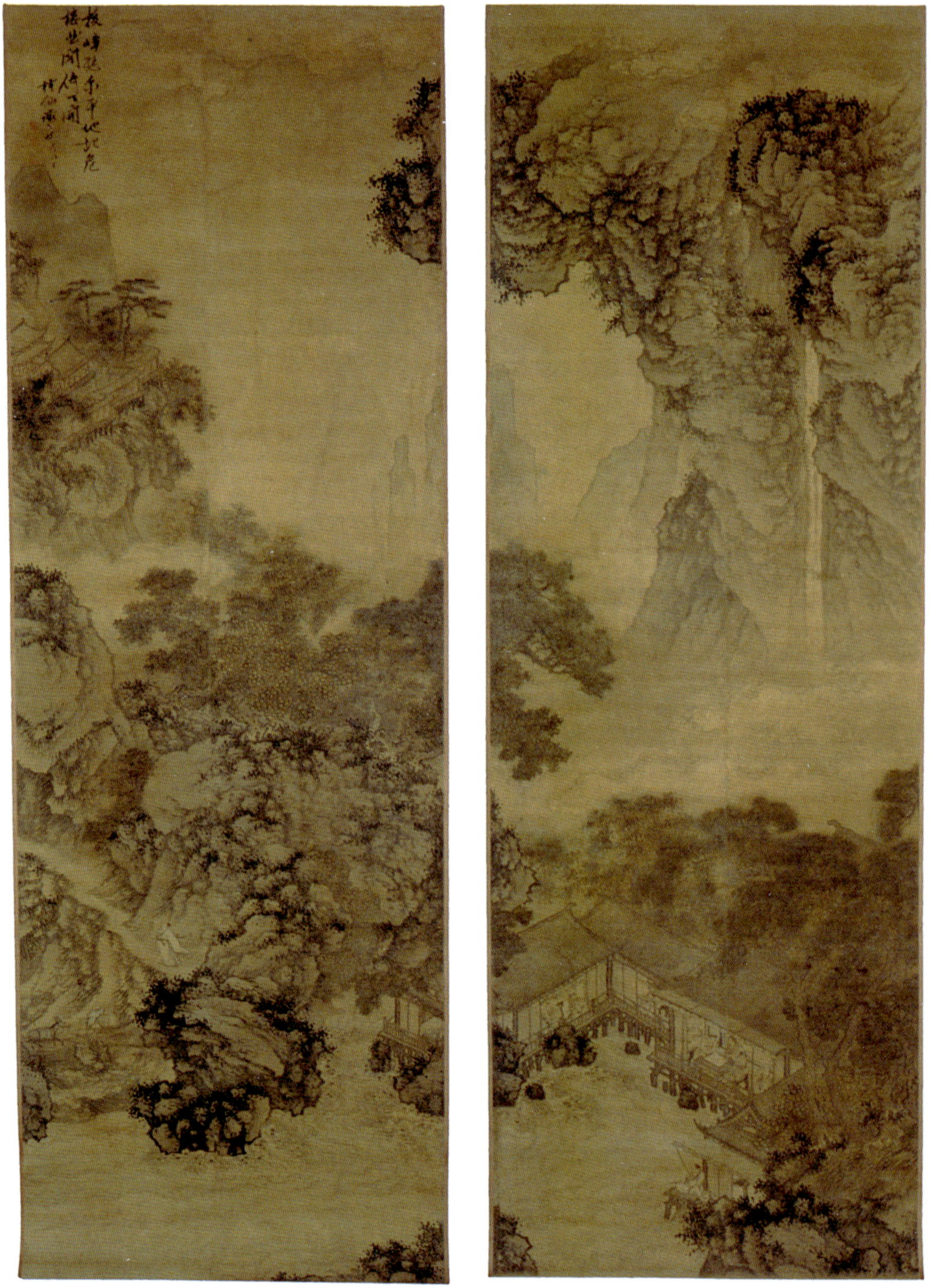

SCHOLARS IN A WATERSIDE VILLA

By Xie Shichen (Chinese, 1487–1567)
Ming dynasty (1368–1644)
Pair of hanging scrolls; ink and colors on paper
H. 243.2 cm × W. 83.8 cm (each image)
Gift of the Tang Family in memory of P. Y. and Kinmay Wen Tang, 1992.64.a-.b

A native of Suzhou, Xie Shichen associated with amateur scholar-painters of the Wu School. This group pursued the literati spirit of self-expression and used individualistic styles in their calligraphic strokes and ink play. He possibly studied the work of Shen Zhou (1427–1509), a leading Wu School artist who commanded versatile styles of earlier Yuan masters in his landscape painting. After several unsuccessful attempts to pass the civil service examination, Xie gave up his pursuit of a governmental position and launched a professional career as a painter in his forties. To cater to his patrons, he sometimes incorporated stylistic, decorative elements of the professional court painters into his landscapes. Xie also depicted famous sites and topographic scenes that he observed in his travels in nature.

This pair of scrolls shows the peaceful and rustic life of recluses in remote mountains—a popular subject for scholars and officials involved in the network of social obligations and political affairs. On the right scroll, some literati are fishing, drinking, and playing a board game in a villa by the water. Beyond the villa are towering peaks with a waterfall cascading from a high cliff. On the left scroll, a white-robed gentleman walks along a trail that leads to a pavilion complex hidden in the distant mountains. The artist inscribed a couplet in semicursive script, which reads, "Screen-like mountain peaks and suspending waterfalls rise from a flat ground; perilous towers and multistory pavilions rest on opening hills."

The large size of the painting suggests that it was intended for display in a large hall at the residence of a wealthy patron. Xie originally painted intimate scenes in soft ink tones, but became more interested in bold brushwork and large compositions to present the monumental look and awe-inspiring atmosphere of deep mountains. His love of travel and association with friends won him fame among scholar-officials of the time, for whom Xie's peaceful landscapes provided solace and served as desirable collectibles.

—*FJZ*

PINE LODGE AMID TALL MOUNTAINS

approx. 1590–1620
By Wu Bin (Chinese, 1573–1620)
Ming dynasty (1368–1644)
Hanging scroll; ink on paper
H. 308 cm × W. 98.4 cm (image)
Gift of the Avery Brundage Collection Symposium Fund and the M. H. de Young Memorial Museum Trust Fund, B69D17

The spectacular pinnacles of Wu Bin's *Pine Lodge amid Tall Mountains* rest upon a slender foundation, conveying a dynamic effect of perilous balance. The unusual height of the scroll—just over ten feet tall—and proportions of the central peak suggest monumentality. Such forms are also reminiscent of rocks displayed in Ming-dynasty residential gardens or on tables in scholars' studios. The implied alternation between the colossal and the human, or even miniature, scale lends a provocative ambiguity to the painting. This enigmatic quality might fall under the esthetic of *qi*—the novel, rare, or unusual—that figured so prominently in late-Ming art and letters.

Wu Bin had a long association with the late Ming official and painter Mi Wanzhong (1570–1628), a connoisseur and collector of rocks and the owner of a famed Beijing garden compound decorated with large-scale arrangements of curiously shaped stones. Mi appreciated the values of earlier painting from the Northern Song period (960–1127). These qualities included monumentality and illusionistic rendering of surface textures, volume, and atmosphere—all abundantly demonstrated in this painting, with its angular faceted surfaces interrupted by pockets of mist. Wu Bin's imposing painting may have been designed with these kinds of taste and interest in mind and was suited for the residences of men of means—aristocrats, high officials, or the emerging group of merchant literati. His signature is accompanied by a couplet written in seal script, quoted from a poem by Du Fu (712–770):

My whole life I've lived out of the way, my ramshackle gate remote;
In the fifth month the river runs deep and my thatched pavilion is cold.[30]

The couplet is from a longer poem of thanks to an official patron for his visit to Du's cottage, and so Wu's citation is likely an elegantly indirect, literary acknowledgment of his unidentified sponsor. The recipient of the painting might be suggested at the lower left of the painting by the red-robed, bearded, and capped figure sitting within the large timber-frame cabin of a pleasure barge, calmly surveying a scene of natural or otherworldly significance.

—Richard Vinograd is Christensen Fund Professor in Asian Art at Stanford University.

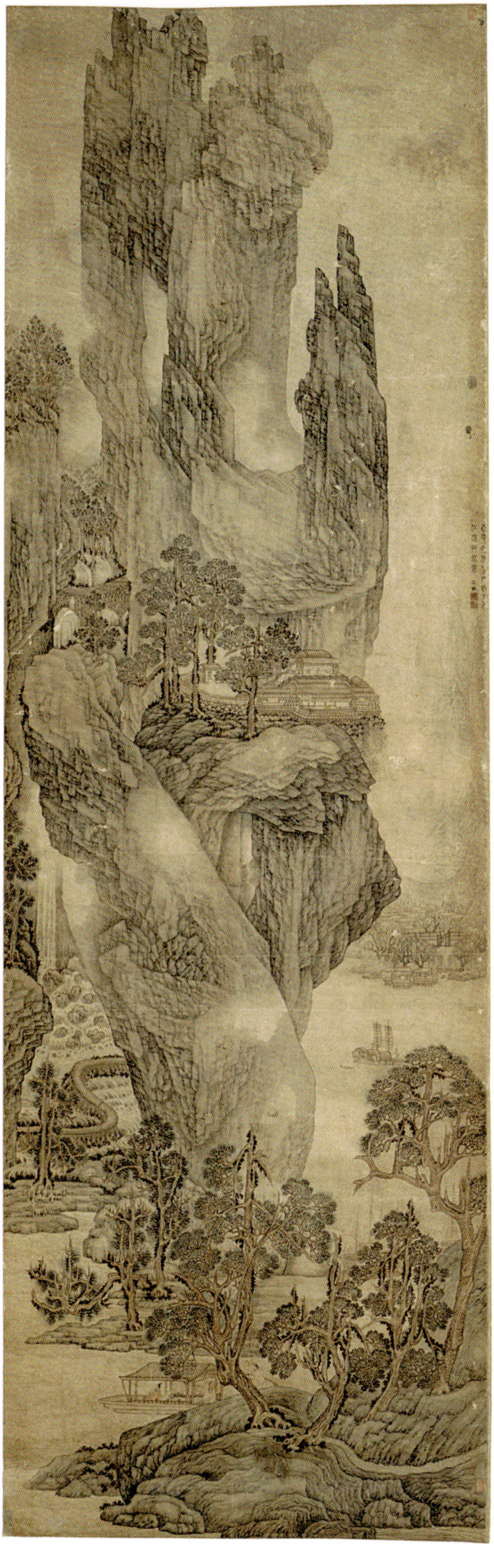

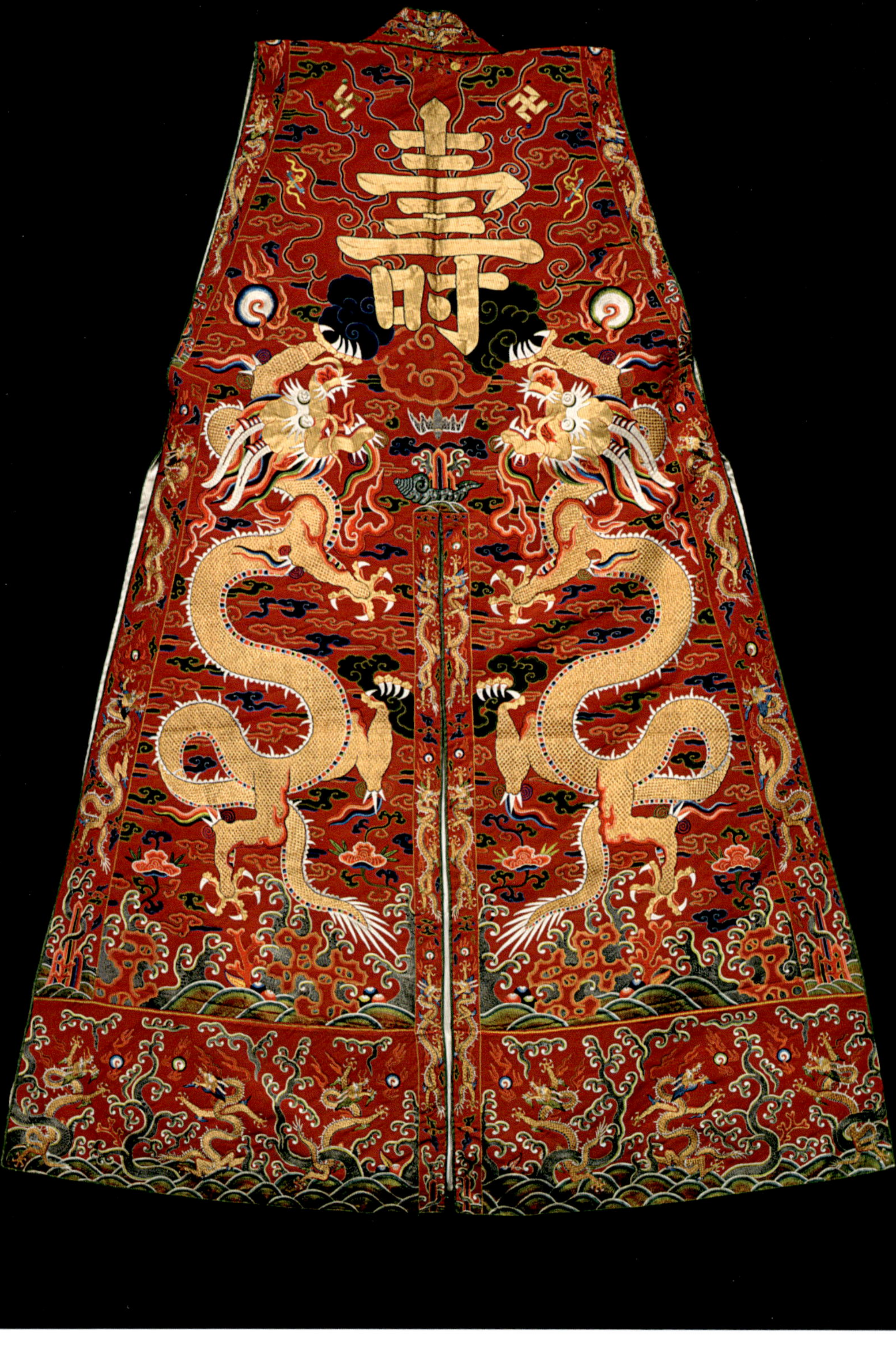
壽

IMPERIAL COURT OVERVEST

1595
China
Ming dynasty, reign of the Wanli emperor (1573–1620)
Silk satin with silk, silver, and gold embroidery
H. 139.7 cm × W. 111.8 cm (at hem); W. 43.2 cm (at shoulder)
Museum purchase, City Arts Trust Fund, 1990.214

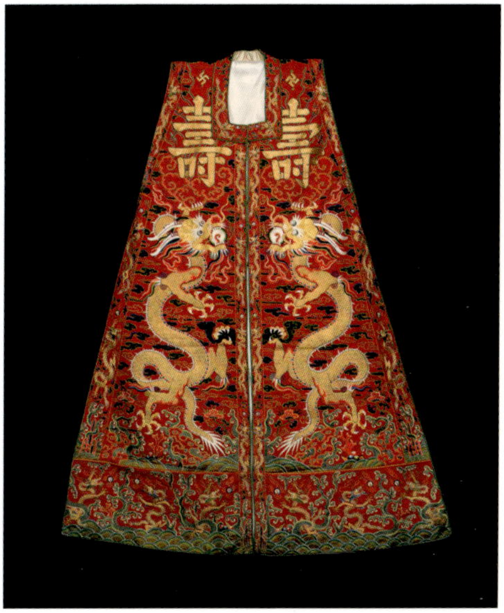

The red of this vest was an auspicious color for Ming rulers, for their family name, Zhu, and the name *red* share the same character. Here two golden dragons, rising from rocks and waves strewn with jewels, coral branches, and the fungus of immortality, ascend toward a sky filled with wish-granting clouds. Smaller dragons decorate the front (shown at right) and side seams and the collar. White horns, eyebrows, and whiskers and rainbow-colored hair characterize these dragons of the Wanli reign period (1573–1620). Their bodies are embroidered with gold scales, with a white spiky ridge along their backs. Biting flaming pearls between their fangs, the dragons grasp red wish-granting clouds, which in turn support a golden longevity character, from which mists rise and enclose a swastika. The swastika *wan*, a pun for "ten thousand," is paired with the longevity character *shou* to make up *wanshou* or "ten thousand longevities," a term that was used only to honor emperors and empresses of China on their birthdays.

An embroidered inscription inside the lapel reads, "Made on the fifth day of the eleventh month, twenty-third year of the reign of the Wanli emperor [equivalent to December 5, 1595]. Length four feet and one inch, two *liang* [slightly more than two ounces] of silk floss [for padding]." The wording of the inscription and the measurements and weight of the silk floss is identical to those embroidered on the emperor's robes excavated from Ding Ling, the tomb of the Wanli emperor, in Beijing.[31] December fifth, the date of the inscription, was two days before the fiftieth birthday of the most powerful woman of the period, the Empress Dowager Li, the Wanli emperor's mother. Whether this elegant embroidered vest was made for the Empress Dowager or for the Wanli emperor to wear on her birthday remains a mystery.

This vest's history after the Ming period cannot be documented. It is said that the vest had been found in an English collection and that its previous owner wore it as an opera cape. The white lining probably was put into the robe during that time. White, a sign of mourning in China, would not have been used to line an imperial garment.

—*Terese Tse Bartholomew is former curator of Himalayan Art and Chinese Decorative Art at the Asian Art Museum of San Francisco and author of the book* Hidden Meanings in Chinese Art.

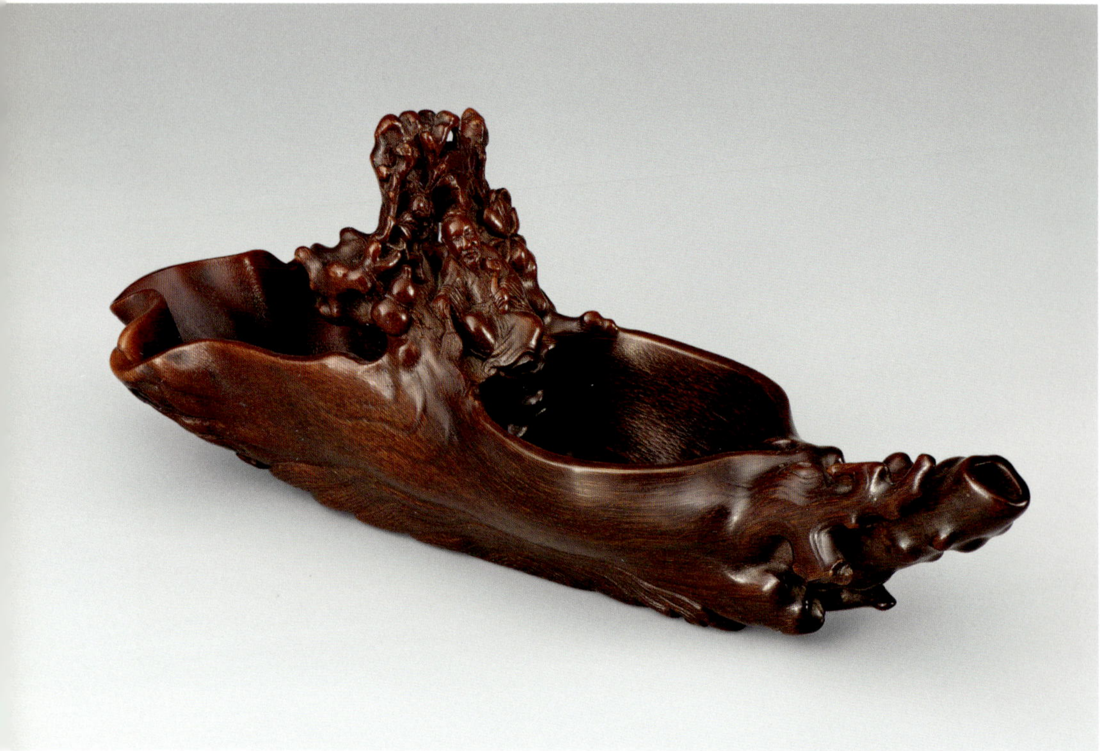

WATER DROPPER IN THE SHAPE OF AN IMMORTAL ON A BOAT

China
Ming dynasty (1368–1644)
Rhinoceros horn
H. 9 cm × W. 23.1 cm × D. 9.1 cm
Transfer from the Fine Arts Museums of San Francisco, Gift of Sanford Lowengart, B68M9

We know from the Asian Art Museum's own bronze ritual vessel in the shape of a rhinoceros (see page 120) that as early as the Shang dynasty (approx. 1600–1050 BCE) rhinoceroses held powerful supernatural significance in China. Rhinoceros horns functioned as drinking vessels, perhaps because of a belief in the horns' healing properties. The *Shennong Bencaojing* (The Divine Farmer's Materia Medica, approx. 250 BCE) mentions rhinoceros horn in powdered form as a cure for colds; the late-Ming medicinal compendium *Bencao gangmu* by Li Shizhen (1518–1583) defines rhino horns as a panacea.

Rhinoceros horns have a natural inner cavity bored through to the very tip. This lends to their use as containers. The horn is not a true bone but rather partially matted hair, similar in substance to human nails and composed of fibrous bundles of keratin. This enables it to be shaped by first softening it in heated water.

After softening, carvers created the shape of this water dropper by fashioning the material into the form of a hollowed-out log. After forming the log shape, skilled carvers, who by the late-sixteenth century were based in the commercially vibrant city of Suzhou, adorned the log to create the scene. Flowering branches serve as a boat for a bearded scholar holding a cane. The subject likely draws from third-century tales of the search for immortality, during a craze of elixirs of longevity. This water dropper thus fulfills desires for longevity and health in both its pictorial content and material.

—Ellen Huang is Curatorial Fellow of Asian Art at Stanford University, Cantor Center for the Visual Arts.

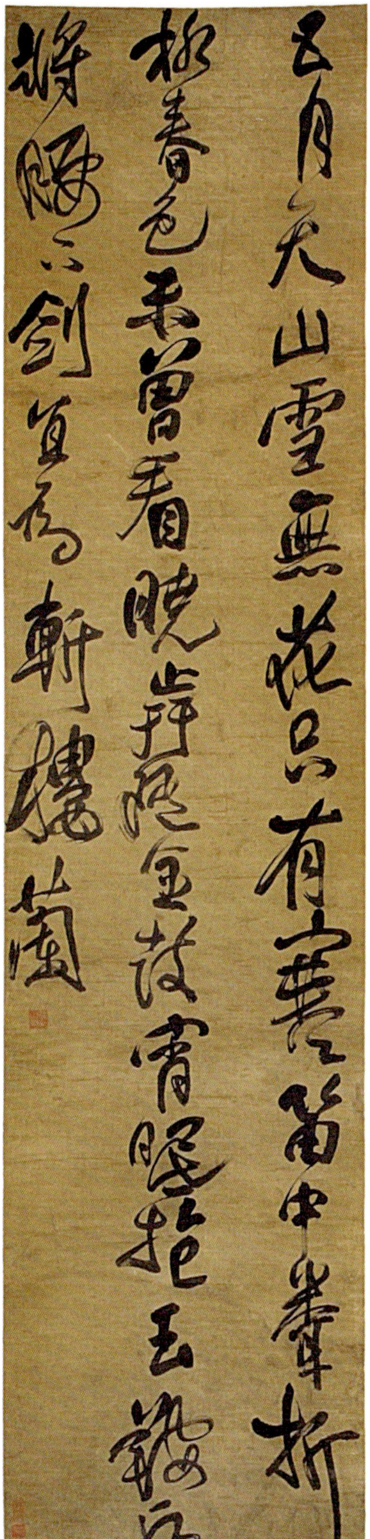

POEM BY LI BAI IN SEMICURSIVE SCRIPT

By Fu Shan (Chinese, 1606–1684)
Ming (1368–1644) or Qing dynasty (1644–1911)
Hanging scroll; ink on silk
H. 199.1 cm × W. 47.3 cm (image)
The Yeh Family Collection, 2012.69

Fu Shan, one of the most original and creative calligraphers of the 1600s, quotes a poem here by the Tang-period poet Li Bai (701–762) to indirectly express his faith and loyalty to his Han Chinese identity. During the late Ming dynasty, when mainland China was invaded by the Manchu from the northeast, Fu hid himself in a deep cave. He remained there underground for more than twenty years, until the new government, under the Qing, stabilized. He later gave up his service at the Qing court and fled to northwestern China, where he remained in self-imposed exile through 1652.

The poetry of Li Bai, who won acclaim as the "Sage of Tang Poetry," resonated with Fu Shan. In several compositions, Li advocated for the Tang defeat of minority tribes to maintain peace and sovereignty in the territory. This poem, which represents Li's patriotism, swings from a description of the scenery around the Heavenly Mountain, Tianshan (in Xinjiang, northwest China), to a lyrical hymn on the life of soldiers preventing attacks by hostile tribes. Here Li references the Han-dynasty general Huo Guang (died 68 BCE), whose army defeated the king of the ruling Loulan state around the Heavenly Mountain. These eight five-character lines, written in running script, read:

The fifth month saw snow around Heavenly
Mountain,
No flowers, only chill.
Snapping willows can be heard in the flute's song,
Spring colors yet to be seen.
Fighting at daybreak follows the metal drum,
Sleeping at night holding a jade saddle.
Wishing to pull the sword hanging at my waist,
Wanting only to cut off Loulan.

—*HL*

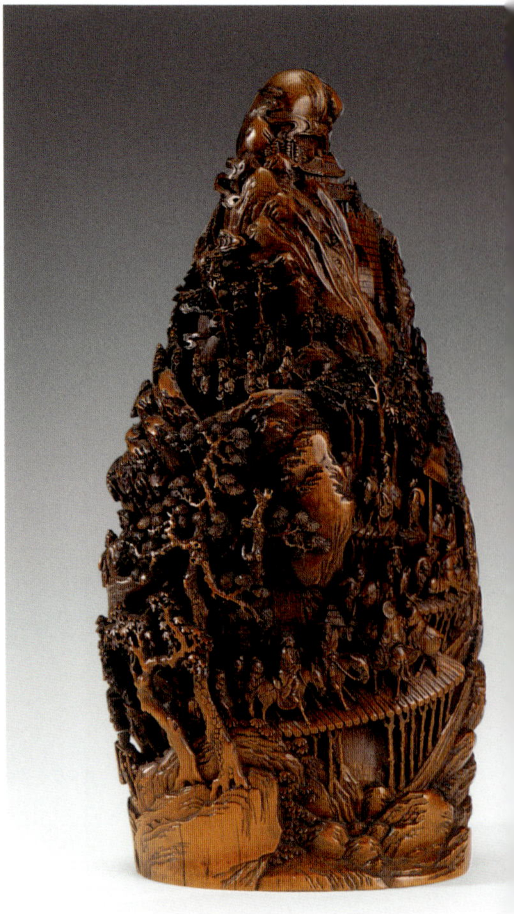

MOUNTAIN SCENE

China
Qing dynasty (1644–1911)
Bamboo root
H. 35.6 cm × Diam. 15.2 cm
The Avery Brundage Collection, B62M85

Bamboo objects have often decorated a Chinese scholar's studio. During the Ming dynasty (1368–1644), bamboo carvers in Jiading, in China's central coastal Jiangsu province, produced brush containers made from bamboo stalks, and boxes, cups, and other decorative objects from bamboo roots. As time passed the size of these bamboo carvings tended to increase, as seen in this large mountain scene, which is carved from an entire bamboo root placed upside down. The bamboo root is dense and hard, and fine details can be carved into it.

This piece depicts travelers on a steep path winding through sheer precipices and overhanging rocks, up to the gate of a city wall located on top of a mountain. Many travelers are seen on the steep paths—some riding, others minding loaded mules, others on foot struggling with cargo on bamboo poles. The paths wind along cliffs and forests of pines, deciduous trees, and bamboo.

One side of the sculpture shows a *zhandao*, a plank road built along the face of the cliff, supported by tree trunks slotted into holes cut into the mountainside. Plank roads are associated with Sichuan province, a southwestern area known for its mountainous terrain. In the fourth and third centuries BCE, the state of Qin built this type of road between Shaanxi and Sichuan provinces. Chinese paintings that portray the Tang emperor escaping into Sichuan province in the eighth century CE—such as the "Emperor Minghuang's Journey to Shu" in the National Palace Museum, Taipei—show such roads.[32]

Along the path are pavilions where the travelers rest and a stable with a feeding trough for animals. A smaller path leads down to a stream where mules, guarded by young servants, slake their thirst. Other mules, having reached their destination, enter the narrow passageway to the city gate. The top of the mountain, wreathed in clouds, rises above the city.

—Terese Tse Bartholomew is former curator of Himalayan Art and Chinese Decorative Art at the Asian Art Museum of San Francisco and author of the book Hidden Meanings in Chinese Art.

THOUSAND TREES ON AZURE PEAKS IN THE STYLE OF DONG YUAN

—

1668
Wang Jian (Chinese, 1596–1677)
Qing dynasty, reign of the Kangxi emperor (1662–1722)
Hanging scroll; ink on paper
H. 217.5 cm × W. 95.9 cm (image)
Museum purchase, B69D2

—

This landscape by Wang Jian, a minor scholar-official and artist serving at the Manchu Qing court, focuses on the theme of seclusion in remote mountains. Wang used his knowledge of mountains, water, buildings, and the human figure to blend nature and humanity in a compact landscape. He earned fame for his enchanting and refined landscapes, inhabited only sparsely by humans. In the foreground here, two men dressed in typical Confucian robes sit alone. One is in a thatched house near a crude bridge, and the other is behind hills in a cottage among trees. A few clusters of dwellings, which hide in valleys or hug the edge of cliffs, suggest the lodgings of mountain dwellers. The figures are small and lightly rendered, and their activities, such as observing the water or quietly meditating, are simple. A pleasant sense pervades the landscape and the humble activities of its inhabitants.

Wang's thoughtful arrangement, with water winding upward into narrow streams that gradually blend into white clouds, conveys nature's vast scale. The artist used soft strokes and dark dots to depict the curving ranges of overlapping hills. He employed a brush technique established by some of the great masters during the eleventh and twelfth centuries. The untouched areas, which effectively form white clouds floating around valleys, are also characteristic of a classical scholarly style.

Wang Jian's pictorial composition was rendered in a classical manner developed by an early master, Dong Yuan (died 962). Dong tended to formalize natural features in monumental compositions, arranging cloudy hills and dense foliage along zigzagging waters, a composition known as the so-called dragon path. Wang noted his inspiration in a poetic inscription at the top of this painting:

Uncountable clouds float from deep and shallow mountains
Clouds so plentiful that one cannot know the depth of the mountains
Too remote to attract humans to come and go
Excuse [the master] for brushing out a picture to poetry
Where a thatched cottage once opened towards green peaks
The year wushen [1668], second month of spring
After the manner of Beiyuan's [Dong Yuan's] brush, Wang Jian

—*HL*

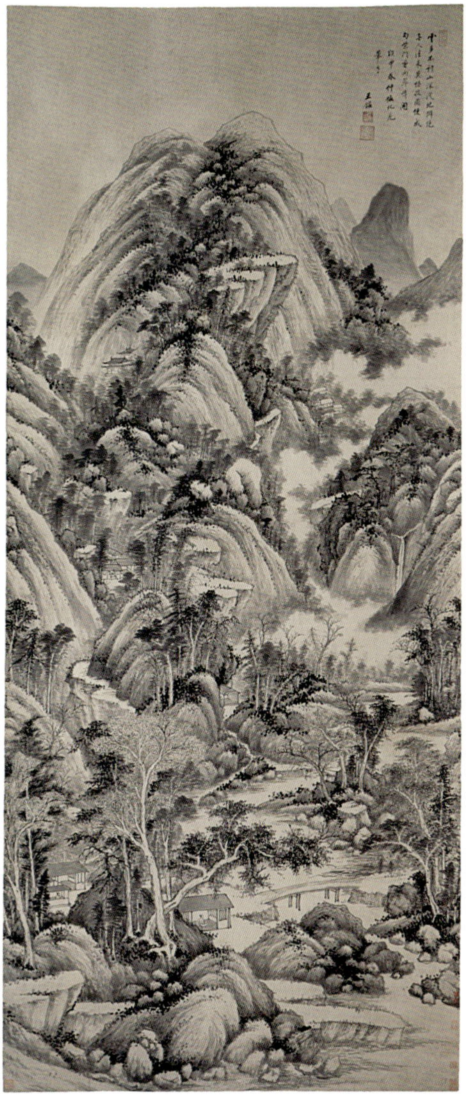

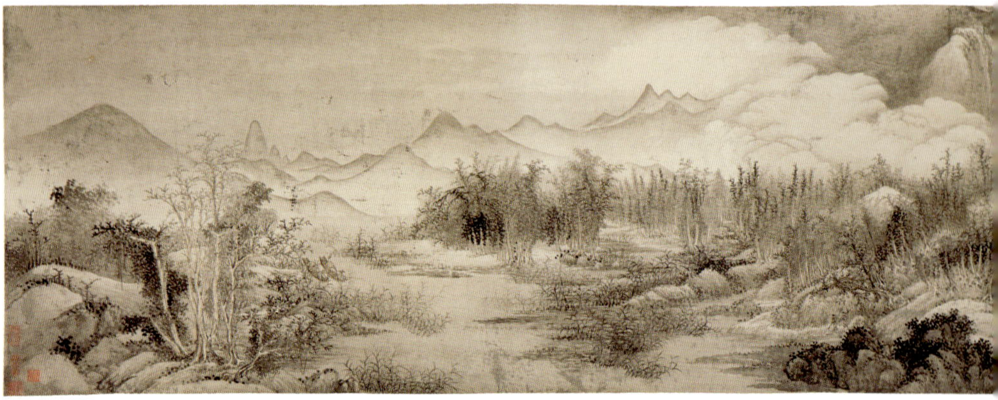

SUMMER MOUNTAINS, MISTY RAIN

1668

By Wang Hui (Chinese, 1632–1717)

Qing dynasty, reign of the Kangxi emperor (1662–1722)

Handscroll; ink on paper

H. 43.1 cm × W. 246.4 cm (image)

Gift of the Tang Foundation, presented by Leslie, Martin, and Nadine Tang in celebration of Jack C. C. Tang's sixtieth birthday, B87D8

The placid rhythms of rounded hills and rolling clouds in Wang Hui's handscroll offer little hint of its underlying purpose: to solicit the support of one of the most influential art patrons of the day, Zhou Lianggong (1612–1672). The painting accompanied a lengthy colophon by Wang Shimin (1592–1680), a mainstay of the Orthodox school of painting and theory who advocated the emulation and authority of the past as aesthetic guides for contemporary painting. His text, equal parts introduction and promotion, praises Wang Hui's talent in copying old-master painting in the most extravagant terms.

The colophon served as a practical kind of career protection for Wang Hui, still an emerging professional artist in his mid-thirties, but already recognized as a prodigy. Earlier in the 1660s, Wang Hui had arranged a letter of introduction to Zhou Lianggong from another scholar-official patron. He was clearly interested in the broader exposure that Zhou—as a Qing-dynasty official, patron, collector, and biographer of contemporary artists—could bring him.[33]

Summer Mountains, Misty Rain was thus a pivotal work in terms of Wang Hui's patronage situation and artistic approach. Yet the calculated ambition of his careerist agenda should not overshadow the subtlety of his pictorial achievement.

At the beginning of the scroll, to the right, formations of birds in flight trace branch-like patterns in the sky above the shore of a stream and silhouettes of misty mountains. Toward the end of the scroll two woodcutters make their way along a path by the water's edge; farther on a pair of anglers turn to converse from adjacent boats. Both episodes could convey, in the most restrained way, something of Wang Hui's situation as an artist on the move and his desire for supportive companionship.

The vibrant textures and atmospheric softness of the more monumental central section of hills, clouds, and trees display Wang Hui's brilliant technical range, which also allowed him to emulate diverse ancient styles with ease. These talents brought a local professional artist into the innermost circles of the scholar-official cultural elites.

—Richard Vinograd is Christensen Fund Professor in Asian Art at Stanford University.

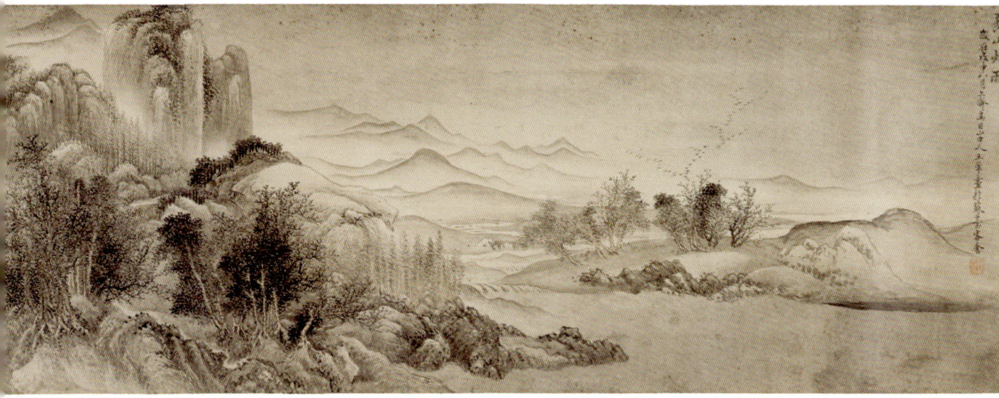
夏山烟雨

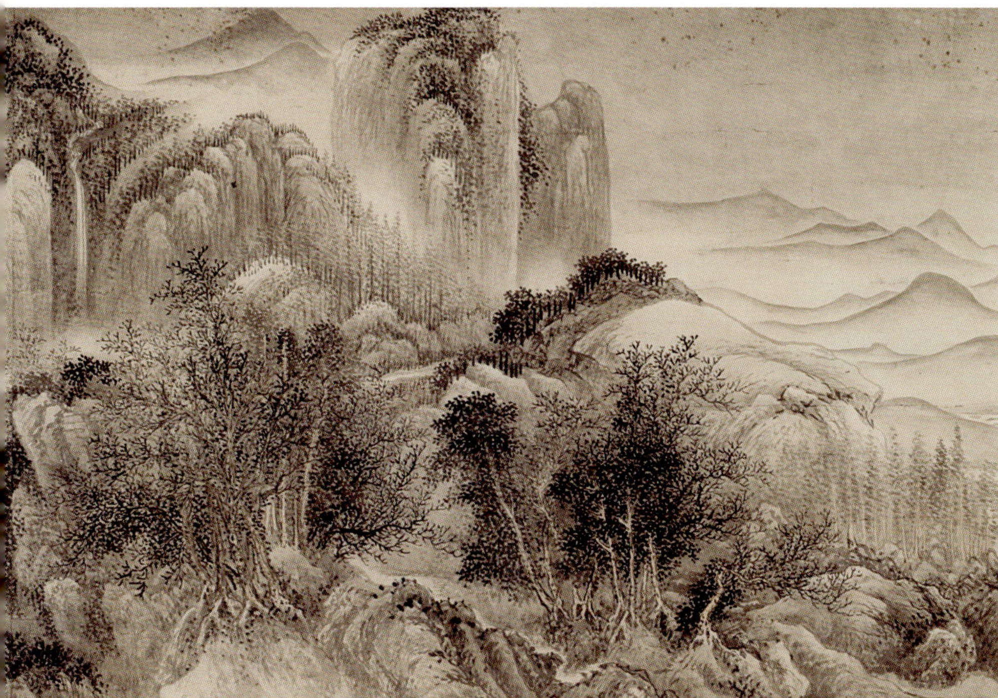

PROSPERITY IN AN IMPERIAL PALACE

1670

China

Qing dynasty, reign of the Kangxi emperor (1662–1722)

Lacquer on wood with enamel decoration

H. 274.3 cm × W. 55.9 cm (each panel)

Transfer from the Fine Arts Museums of San Francisco, Gift of the de Young Museum Society, B69M52

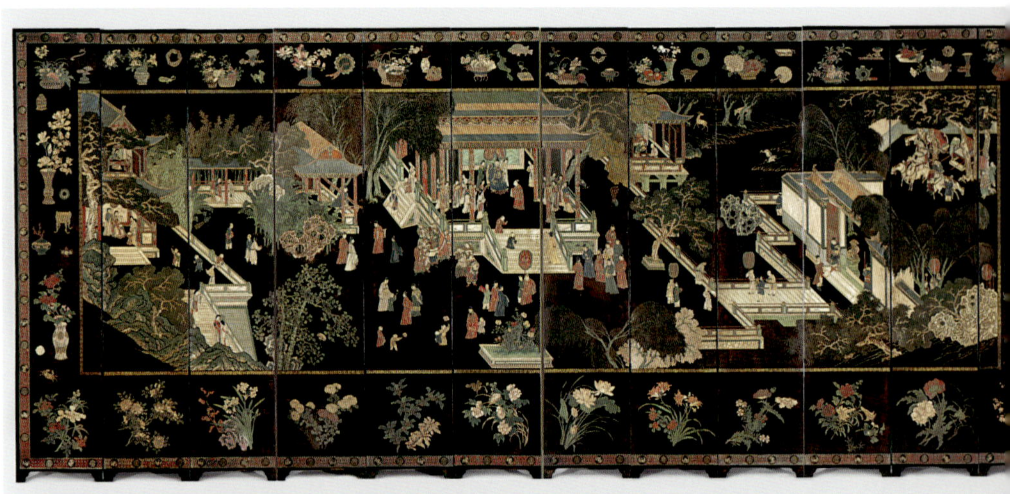

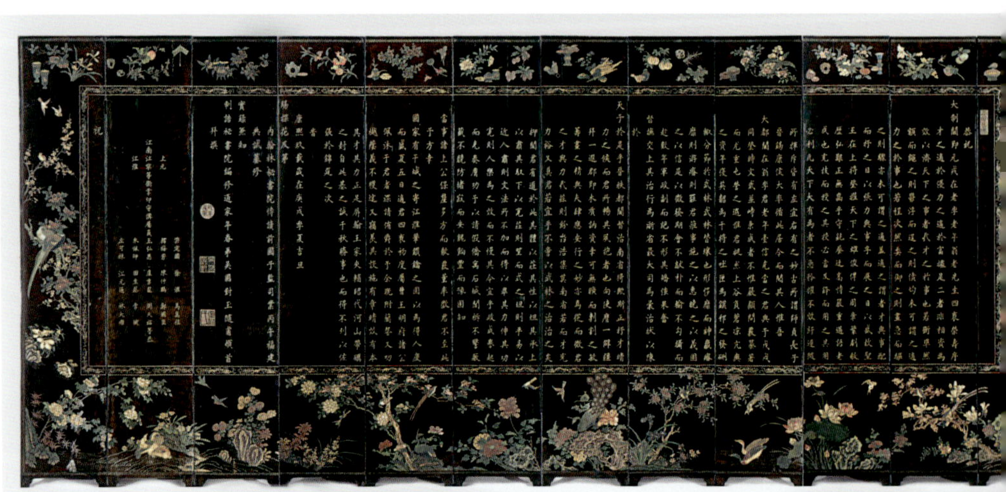

MALLET VASE WITH SCENE OF WARRIORS

China; Jingdezhen, Jiangxi province

Qing dynasty, reign of the Kangxi emperor (1662–1722)

Porcelain with overglaze multicolor decoration

H. 74.9 cm × Diam. 23.5 cm

The Avery Brundage Collection, B60P1237

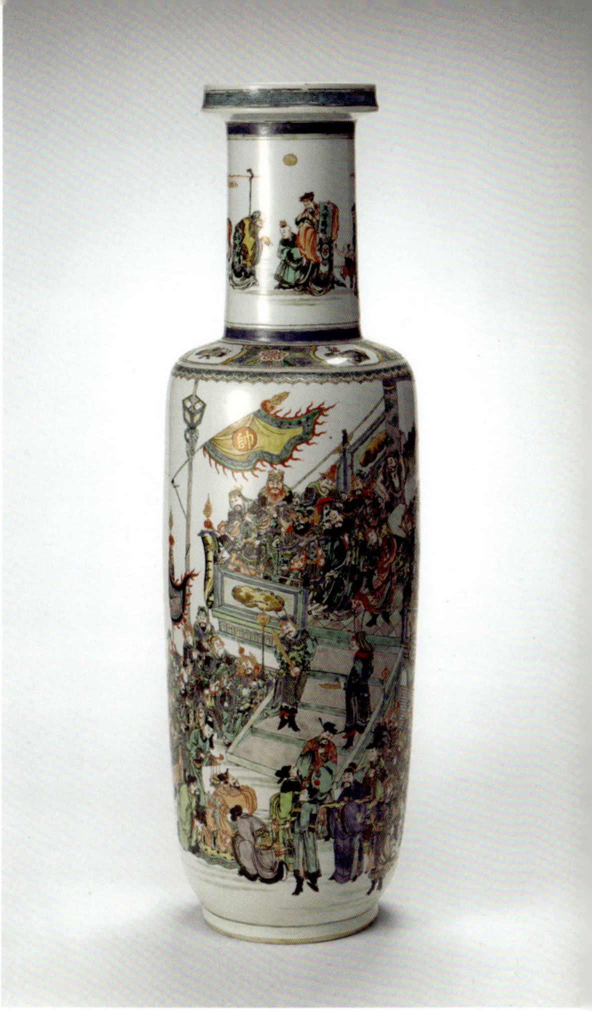

This vase is a large porcelain work dated to the late seventeenth century or early eighteenth century, when the porcelain industry revived in Jingdezhen under the sponsorship of the Kangxi emperor. Its spacious surface expanse provides a perfect white canvas to magnify the decorator's technique and facility with colors. Fifty warriors and six mythological figures populate the main body and neck. With skillful virtuosity, the artist has employed enamel colors to great effect, creating subtle shades and fantastic hues in more than ten tones. Generally, overglazed porcelain necessitated multiple separate firings, which only emphasizes the technical planning involved in creating this vase.

Looking closely, viewers will discern the dominant use of a vivid black to outline foliage, figures' apparel and accoutrements, and the central architectural structure. Using black outlines in pictorial scenes on porcelain was likely inspired by the explosion of illustrated prints and fiction that enjoyed widespread circulation in the late-Ming era. Green enamels were added on top of the black enamel lines. These served not only to deepen the shade but also to seal the black enamel onto the porcelain surface.

The cylindrical form of the vase enabled a generous amount of narrative action to be depicted on a continuous surface. The neck shows the god of longevity, Shoulao, with a peach and deer, both symbols of immortality; two boys running around the god of happiness; and a god who holds a banner with the phrase, "Tian Guan bestows happiness" (*Tian Guan Ci Fu*). The subject on the vase's main body draws from a legendary tale of the bravery of the patriotic Yang family, who fought against northern forces during the eleventh century. An emperor clothed in ornate robes grants a seal to the Yang family, represented by a kneeling general dressed in red. To the left of the general are six women, presumably the women of the Yang family, who successfully defended the Song dynasty against the Tangut peoples of the northwest. The reference to this story of dynastic loyalty—coupled with the amount of technical expertise necessary for the creation of this exciting decoration—celebrates the rule of the Qing dynasty emperor, Kangxi. His quelling of the rebellion of the Three Feudatories (1673–1681) offered a reason to extol loyal resistance.

—Ellen Huang is Curatorial Fellow of Asian Art at Stanford University, Cantor Center for the Visual Arts.

HANGING SCREEN WITH SCENE OF AN ELEGANT GATHERING

—

China

Qing dynasty, reign of the Qianlong emperor (1736–1795)

Lacquer

H. 78.7 cm × W. 111.8 cm

The Avery Brundage Collection, B60M40+

—

This hanging screen is one of the most important surviving works of carved multicolor Chinese lacquer from the eighteenth century. The screen's impressive size and its lavish carving would have made it a luxury lacquer in vogue among aristocratic circles. It was likely produced to decorate the Qing palace in Beijing and depicts a traditional theme—an elegant gathering of elites—beloved by Manchu emperors.

The narrative unfolds from the right foreground upward in a zigzag path: an old scholar with a staff crosses a bridge, likely to join seven others around a pavilion. The pavilion is surrounded by water, small islands, and a fishing boat, extending seemingly endlessly toward remote lands. Continuing further along, a scholar writes with a brush on a tall rock by a plantain; behind the rock, two people play a board game while an audience looks on. Through winding corridors, a scholar sits inside a pavilion making ink with an inkstone; another walks towards balustrades at the front, observing the lotuses floating in the lake; along the side balustrades an elder unfolds a scroll. Nine young boys serve their masters by carrying items, serving wine, or making tea.

—*HL*

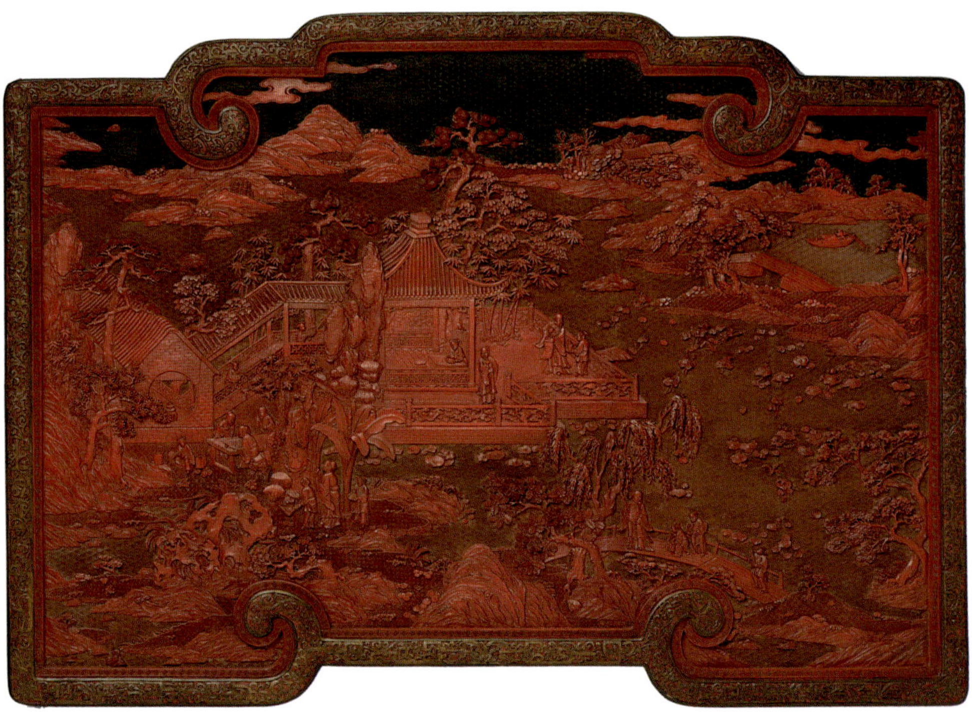

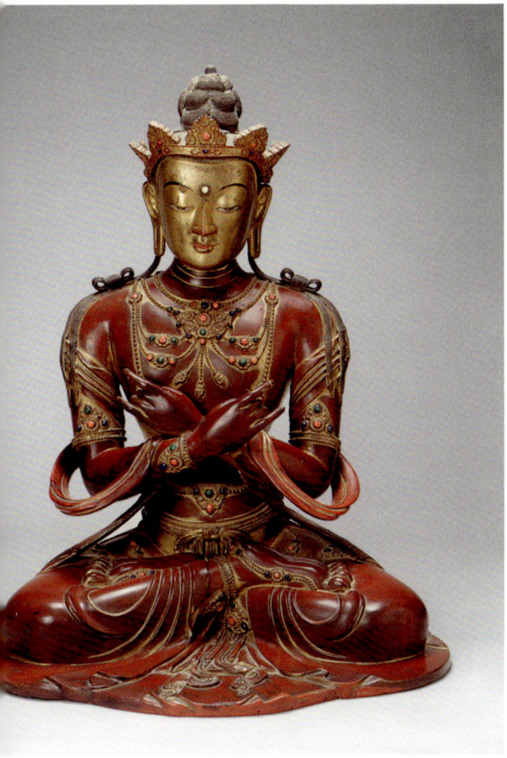

THE BUDDHIST DEITY VAJRADHARA

China; possibly Chengde, Hebei province
Qing dynasty, reign of the Qianlong emperor (1736–1795)
Hollow dry lacquer with inlaid semiprecious stones
H. 78.7 cm × W. 59.6 cm × D. 48.3 cm
The Avery Brundage Collection, B60S81

This sculpture of the Buddhist deity Vajradhara is a Qing imperial work made of lacquer and elaborately painted in gold and decorated with semiprecious stones. Coiffed and bejeweled, it has a Tibetan aesthetic. It was executed with methods rarely employed in Chinese lacquerware. The jewelry was created from a mix of cement and lacquer that was applied over the hollow lacquer body. The entire work was then coated with layers of red lacquer, out of which spaces were carved and cut to hold colorful, semiprecious materials including coral, malachite, and lapis lazuli. Gold paint was used to highlight jewelry, textiles, and Vajradhara's face.

Vajradhara can be identified by his crossed hands, which are held in the *vajrahumkara* mudra, or the gesture of highest energy. These hands would hold his attributes, which are now missing: the thunderbolt, representing the male principle of fitness and action, and the bell, which symbolizes the feminine principle of wisdom. Vajradhara wears the five-leafed crown of a bodhisattva.

Lacquered pieces of this size are rare. Intended to be placed in a temple, such a piece would have adorned the Tibetan temples of Beijing or of the imperial Mountain Villa for Summer Retreat in Chengde, about 250 kilometers northeast of Beijing. Tibetan Buddhism was one of the primary and fundamental practices of the Manchu-ruled Qing court. The Qianlong emperor (reigned 1736–1795) granted the Inner Mongolian-born Changkya Rolpai Dorje (1717–1786), a spiritual leader of the Geluk school of Tibetan Buddhism, the role of state preceptor to supervise religious affairs countrywide. Qianlong commissioned enormous Buddhist lacquerware, paintings, textile, and furniture. His interest in lacquer led to improved facilities at the imperial lacquer workshop in the capital Beijing. There, most works, likely including this example, were created by skillful artisans assembled from all over the country, sometimes under the supervision of Tibetan monks.

—*HL*

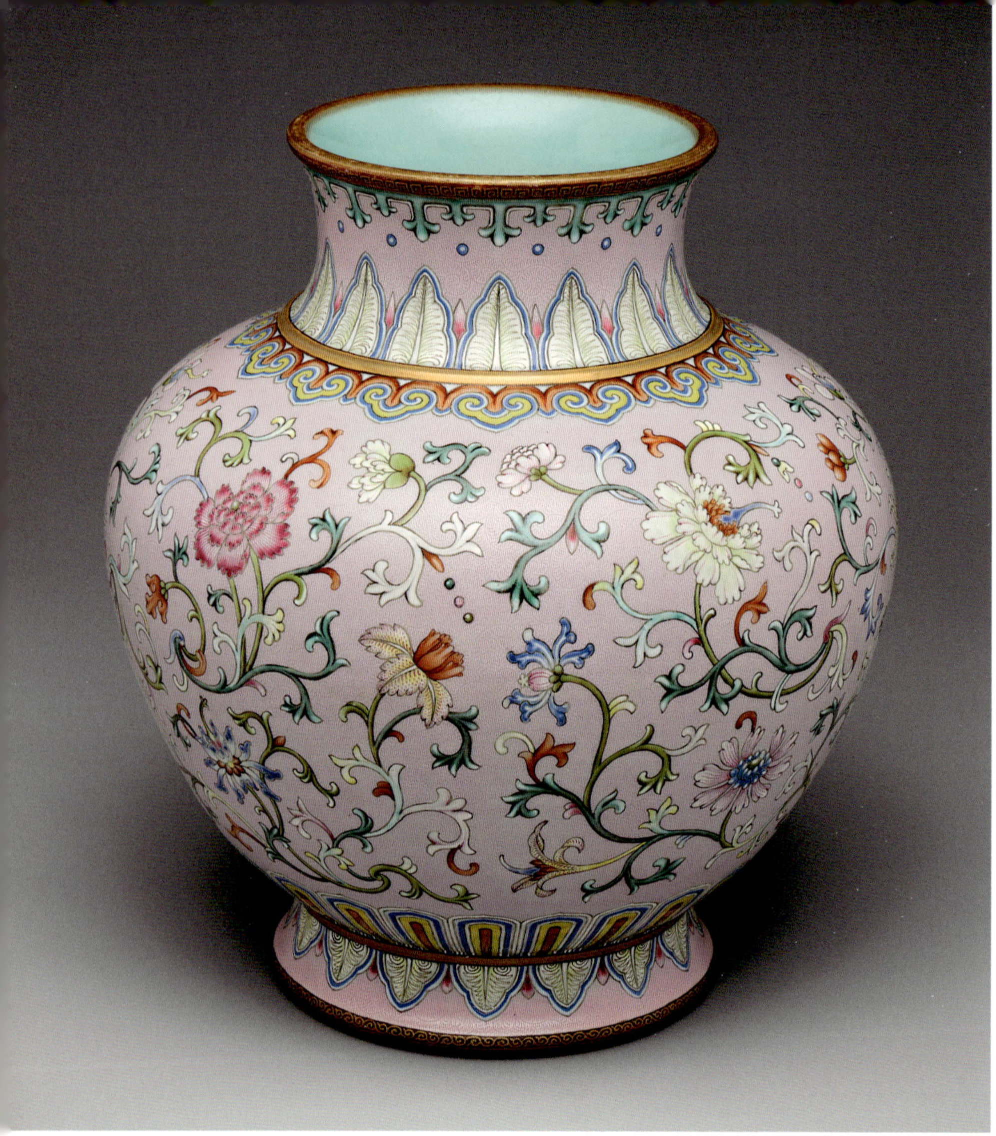

VASE WITH FLORAL SCROLLS

China, Jingdezhen, Jiangxi province

Qing dynasty, reign of the Qianlong emperor (1736–1795)

Porcelain

H. 26.7 cm × Diam. 24.1 cm

The Avery Brundage Collection, B60P15

This vase is emblematic of the flamboyance and technical accomplishments of ceramics produced during the reign of China's Qianlong emperor (1736–1795). Its innovative color palette—called *famille rose* ("pink family") in Western scholarship and *yangcai* ("Western colors") or *falangcai* ("enamel colors") in Chinese—was achieved with colloidal gold and a lead-arsenic tinting agent; both were introduced from Europe in the 1720s.

The design is remarkable for its association with textile patterning, specifically to Rococo aesthetics popular in Europe during the eighteenth century. The incised pattern on the vase's ground has been identified by Chinese scholars as "brocade ground" (*jin di*) and the floral design as "adding flowers on brocade" (*jin shang tian hua*), suggesting the vase resembles a sumptuous brocaded silk with embroidered flowers.[34] Other visual similarities to Rococo textiles include a palette of pastel colors, primacy of sinuous lines, and asymmetrical floral elements.

—*DCh*

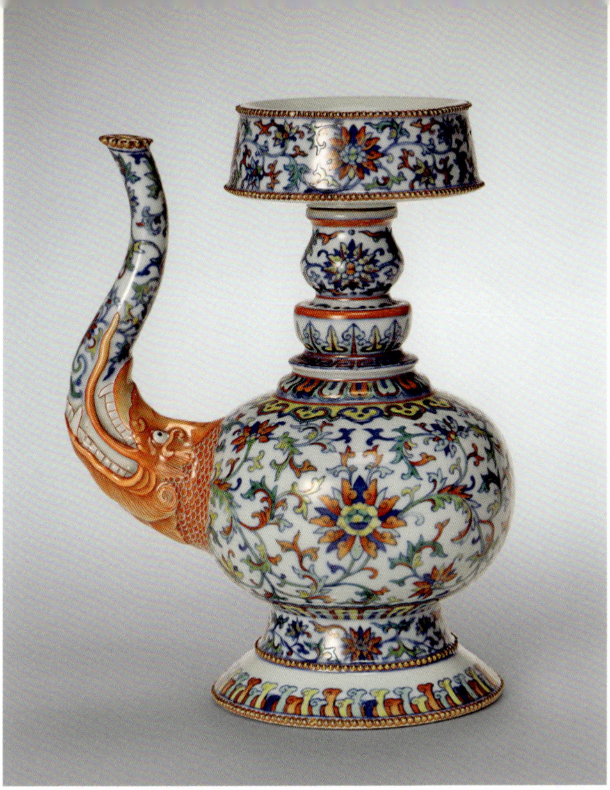

RITUAL POURING VESSEL

China; Jingdezhen, Jiangxi province
Qing dynasty, reign of the Qianlong emperor (1736–1795)
Porcelain with underglaze blue and overglaze multicolor enamel decoration
H. 19.7 cm × W. 15.2 cm × D. 14.9 cm
The Avery Brundage Collection, B60P2298

This lavishly decorated vessel—one of a set of four in the collection of the Asian Art Museum—exemplifies the Chinese porcelain industry's golden era under the patronage of Manchu rulers. With its striking, dramatic colors, it was certainly among the most impressive porcelain wares displayed on shelf, cabinet, or altar in the Qing palace. During the eighteenth century, China expanded its exchanges with many parts of the world, and its court art—including porcelains—developed alongside this. Ambitious and expensive porcelain manufacturing practices were undertaken in part due to adopting industrialized technology from the West. One result was the creation of new color enamels, inspired by European glass brought to the Qing court by Jesuit missionaries.

Examples of such novel colors in this vessel include the subdued lemon yellow, named "watery yellow"; light blue, "sky-blue"; and light green, "watery green." These overglaze colors, along with bright coral, orange, and green, fill in designs outlined in underglaze blue. Overglaze and underglaze were intended to be competing colors, or *doucai*. The *doucai* color scheme was an earlier innovation from the reign of the Ming emperor Xuande (1426–1435). It was often employed for Tibetan Buddhist ritual vessels during that time. The earliest known surviving example, a stemmed cup with *doucai* decoration, is preserved in the Sakya Monastery in Tibet.

The shape of this vessel, with a curving spout and no handle, was inspired by a type of metalware used to pour water in Tibetan Buddhist temples. The exterior of the vessel is hand-painted with lotus scrolls, echoing the stylized lotus designs on luxurious gold and silver objects of the eighth century. The elephant-head-shaped spout reflects the form of a drinking horn—rhyton—that originated in Greece and came to China on the Silk Road during the Tang dynasty (618–907).

—*HL*

BOWL AND DISH WITH SCENE OF WESTERN FIGURES IN A RURAL EUROPEAN LANDSCAPE

China

Qing dynasty, reign of the Qianlong emperor (1736-1795)

Enamel on metal

Bowl: H. 6.3 cm × Diam. 14.6 cm; dish: H 3.2 cm × Diam. 14.5

Museum purchase, B67M2.a-.b

This wine set is an outstanding example of painted metalware made in the eighteenth century. It adapts the Rococo style that once piqued the curiosity of the Manchu emperor Qianlong. Of all Manchu sovereigns, Qianlong was best known for transforming traditional court arts into unprecedented and lavish displays of imperial splendor. His court supported and regulated a centralized system to experiment with new art forms in both style and technique. Court artisans produced magnificent objects now often considered by connoisseurs and scholars to be the high point in the history of Chinese decorative arts. The designs of some of these works—including this delicate enameled metalware—were inspired by elaborate European fabrics and paintings.

This bowl-and-dish set is a fine example of a subject adopted directly from European art. Three painted panels capture a delightful moment enjoyed by Western-style figures in a rural European landscape. The two panels—repeating on the dish and one side of the bowl—celebrate an autumn grape harvest at a winery. A man raises a wine glass, while beside him his lady companion holds a basket of grapes on her arm. The couple gazes at a bunch of grapes presented by a fellow worker who kneels in front of a large grape barrel. The second panel portrays a rural couple dancing in the fields, along with a canine companion, in an idyllic country landscape with cottages in the distance.

The borders framing these panels consist of floral motifs. Their array and colors are foreign to Chinese porcelain, although their content—composed of the rose, peony, lotus, apricot, and melon—is based on Chinese elements. The complex color tones ranging from pink to crimson, from cerulean to alizarin crimson, are aesthetic interpretations of, and responses to, European tastes. These vessels, with their impressive portrayals and delicate rendering, might have been painted by a Western artist. A number of European Jesuit missionaries and artists were involved in making and handling new enamels, in collaboration with the Qing imperial workshops, from the late seventeenth to the late eighteen century.

—*HL*

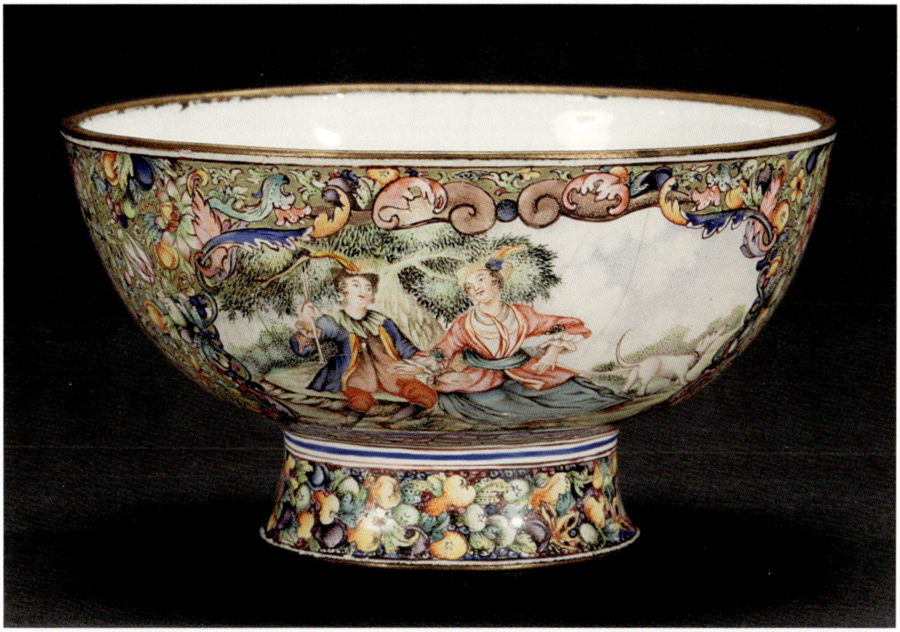

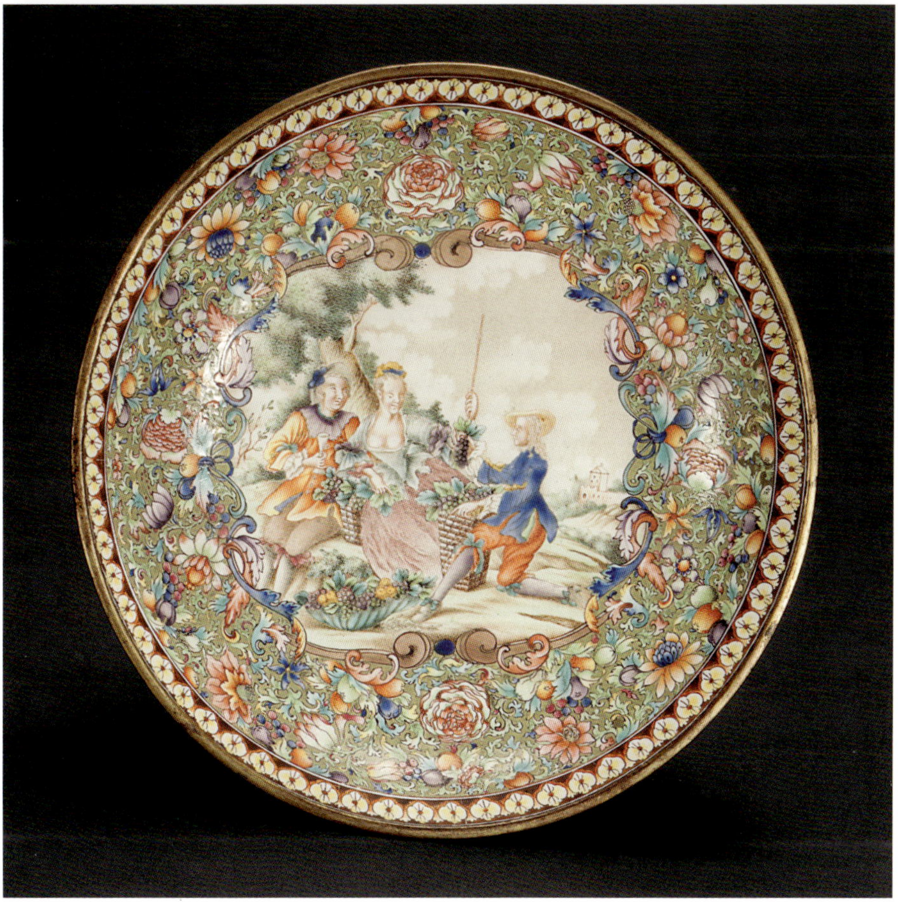

EMPEROR'S DRAGON ROBE

approx. 1700–1750

China

Qing dynasty, reign of the Qianlong emperor (1736–1795)

Silk satin with silk embroidery

H. 39.1 cm × W. 196.8 cm

Transfer from the Fine Arts Museums of San Francisco, Gift of Mr. and Mrs. Budd Rosenberg, B82M1

When the Manchus came to power during the Qing dynasty, they made changes to the roomy imperial robes that were worn by the Ming who preceded them. This Qing-dynasty robe reflects the Manchu's nomadic origin by being tailored for ease in riding horses. It is tight fitting and has cuffs to protect the wearer's hands and slits on its sides, front, and back.

This semiformal robe known as *jifu*, or "auspicious attire," was worn during occasions such as birthdays, banquets, and weddings. The robe's bright shade of yellow, together with its five-clawed dragons, could be worn only by the emperor himself. According to the sumptuary laws listed in *Collected Regulations and Precedents of the Qing Dynasty*, the emperor's robe should have a total of sixteen five-clawed dragons. Eight front-facing dragons should appear on the front, back, and two shoulders of the robe; the front and back of the collar; and on the two sleeve cuffs. Eight additional dragons should be shown in profile; these were to appear four on the bottom half of the robe, one on the under flap, two on the left and right sides of the collar, and one on the lapel.[35] The dragons on this robe are in strict accordance with these regulations.

Here golden dragons appear in the sky scattered with five-color auspicious clouds, together with longevity medallions and red bats. Red (*hong*) bats (*fu*) are rebuses for *hongfu qitian* or "blessings as vast as the sky." On the hem are rocks and waves, standard motifs symbolizing unity within China and wishes that the dynasty reign forever. Red *lingzhi* fungi sprout from a central rock; this fungus of immortality bestows long life as well as fulfills all wishes. Scattered among the waves are colorful jewels, bells, coral, halberds (*ji*), and stone chimes (*qing*). The latter two pun with *jiqing*, or auspicious. This dragon robe is an excellent example of Chinese embroidery techniques. Its satin stitch and gold couching produce a shimmering effect. Tiny French knots fill the dragon's white claws, a technique commonly known as "blind stitch" or "forbidden stitch."

—Terese Tse Bartholomew is former curator of Himalayan Art and Chinese Decorative Art at the Asian Art Museum of San Francisco and author of the book Hidden Meanings in Chinese Art.

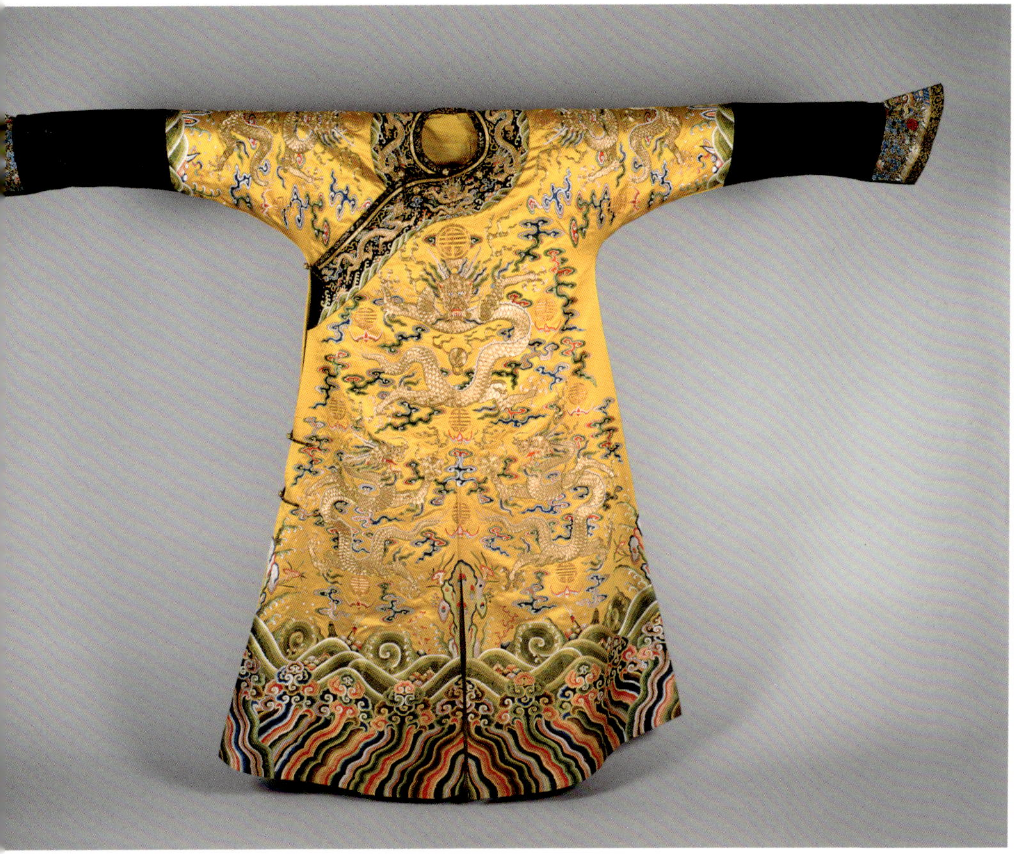

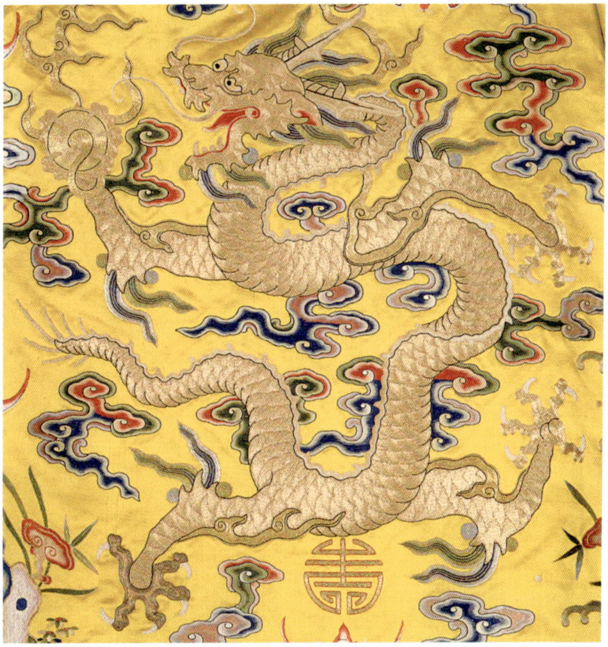

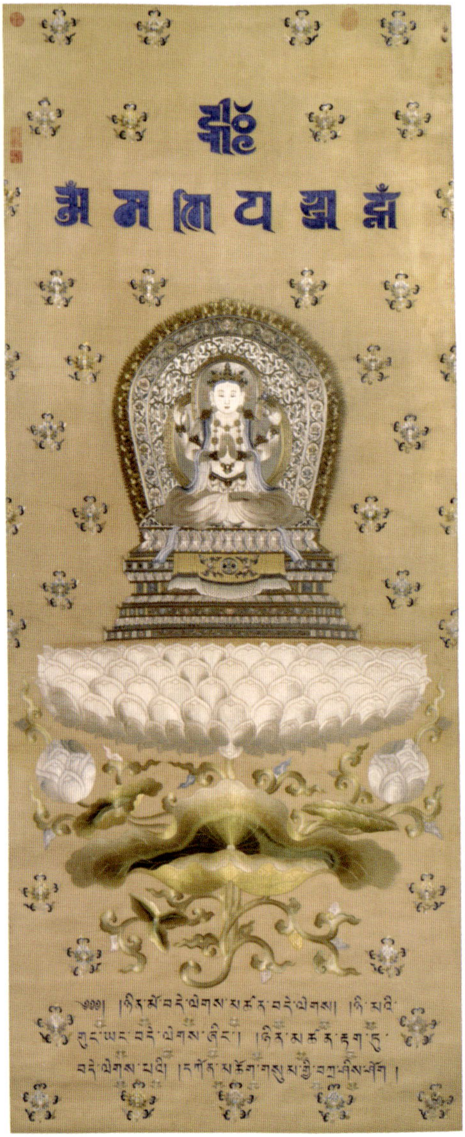

THE BODHISATTVA AVALOKITESHVARA OF THE SIX SYLLABLES

approx. 1758
China
Qing dynasty, reign of the Qianlong emperor (1736–1795)
Silk with embroidery
H. 209.6 cm × W. 86.7 cm (image)
Gift of the Walter and Phyllis Shorenstein Fund, 1989.4

The seated deity with four arms—respectively holding prayer beads (upper left), lotus (upper right), and a wish-granting jewel (front hands)—is the bodhisattva of compassion, commonly known as Avalokiteshvara (Guanyin in Chinese). With its symmetrical composition, subdued color scheme, and intricate embroidery, this work shows the high level of textile crafts attained by the artisans who worked on commissions for the Manchu emperor Qianlong (reigned 1736–1795). His passion for Buddhist artworks led to the expansion of the weaving industry and improvements in handcrafted textiles. Enormous fabric workshops were devoted exclusively to works for Qianlong. With his personal involvement, the Imperial Workshop provided textile workshops nationwide with paintings or drawings as iconographic models for textiles.

Unlike some contemporary embroidered textiles that used paint with embroidery, this scroll uses hand embroidery to represent all its elements—from the deity to his lotus throne, the Tibetan language to the floral patterns. The choice of alternating single-color threads with multicolored ones, each of which was dyed with graduating shades of blue, yellow, or white, gives the image a vibrant yet serene quality.

Avalokiteshvara sits on a lotus pedestal as shimmering lotus blossoms shower down around him. The word embroidered in blue on top, reading *hri*, represents the spiritual father of Avalokiteshvara. Embroidered on the bottom is a Tibetan poem. This was, and still is, the standard poem incorporated into presentation scarves (*kata*) for Tibetans from the eighteenth century to the present:

May you be blessed with good fortune in the morning,
May you be blessed with good fortune at night,
May you be blessed with good fortune at noon,
May your days and nights always be blessed with good fortune,
May you ever be blessed with the good fortune of the Three Jewels.

—*HL*

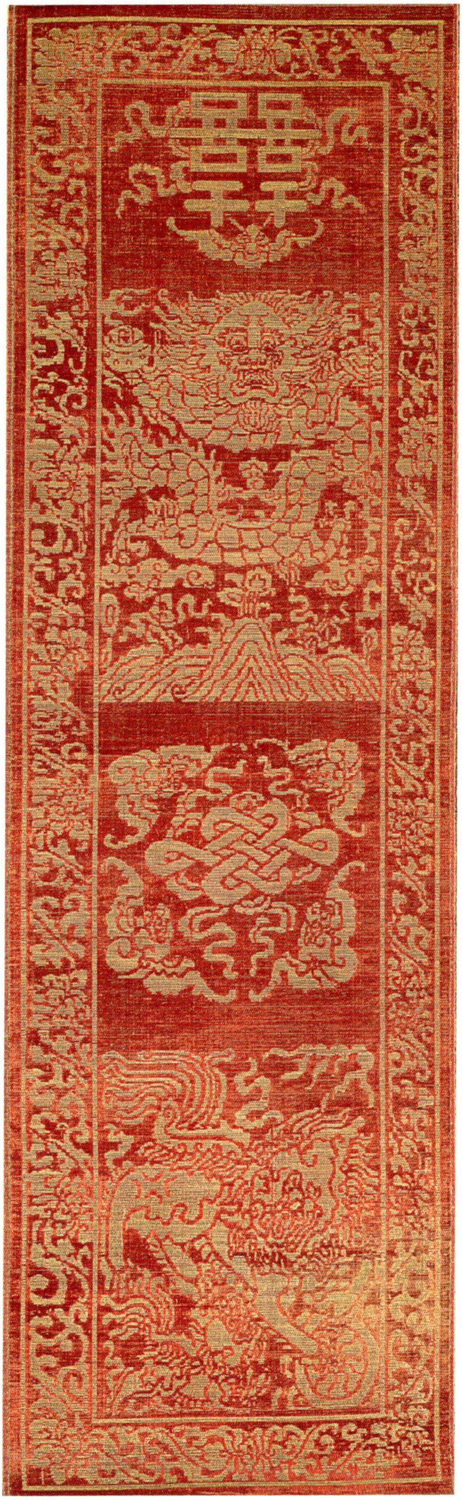

VELVET CHAIR COVER WITH STYLIZED AUSPICIOUS SYMBOLS

probably 1750–1911

China

Qing dynasty (1644–1911)

Silk and cotton velvet, voided, with supplementary gilded wefts

H. 325.1 cm × W. 50.8 cm

The Avery Brundage Collection, B69M8.a

LOTUS

1964

By Chang Dai-chien (Zhang Daqian; Chinese, 1899–1983)

Ink on paper

H. 192.4 cm × W. 101.3 cm (image)

Partial and Promised Gift of Tim Dattels and Kristine Johnson, R2002.2.28

The artist Chang Dai-chien noted, "[The ancient philosopher] Laozi said: 'Procure the essence, and transcend the phenomena.' This state is hard to attain. Images barely emerge out of an elusive haze—that's close enough."[36] This painting embodies Chang's ambitions to go beyond the form of the lotus to get at its essence. In his characteristic "splashed ink" brushwork, lotuses seem to materialize out of a gray nebula of ink wash to produce an evocative and atmospheric effect.

Chang Dai-chien is among the most intriguing figures in twentieth-century Chinese art. He was born in Sichuan in southwest China into a family of artists and became a prolific and immensely talented painter and calligrapher, a masterful forger, a connoisseur, and a collector. In the 1920s he immersed himself in the traditions of Chinese literati artists, studying and copying masterworks, then spending months as a Buddhist monk near Shanghai and at Mount Huangshan. He always wore the long robes and wispy beard of a Confucian literatus. Despite his focus on Chinese art and literature, he was international in his scope and reach: he studied textile dyeing in Japan at the age of eighteen, traveled to Korea in the 1920s, and exhibited his paintings in Paris as early as 1933. In the early 1940s, during the Second Sino-Japanese War (1937–1945), Chang migrated inland to catalogue the paintings at the Dunhuang Buddhist cave temples.

Chang spent the following decades traveling extensively, including to Nice, France, in 1956, where he met with Pablo Picasso. He lived in Argentina, Brazil, and Carmel, California, before settling in Taiwan in 1978. In each of these locations, he built homes replete with classical Chinese gardens.
—KGO and DCh

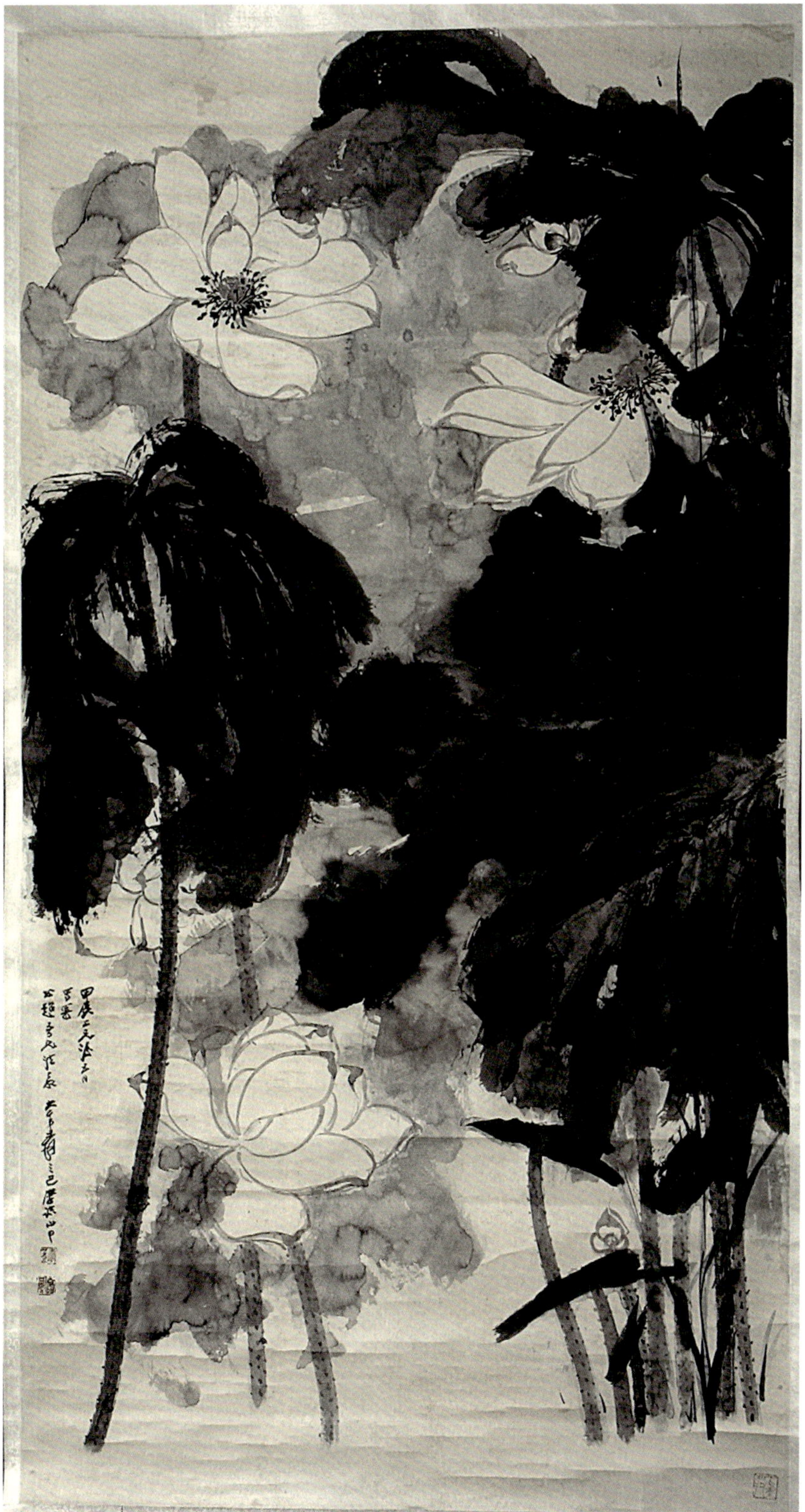

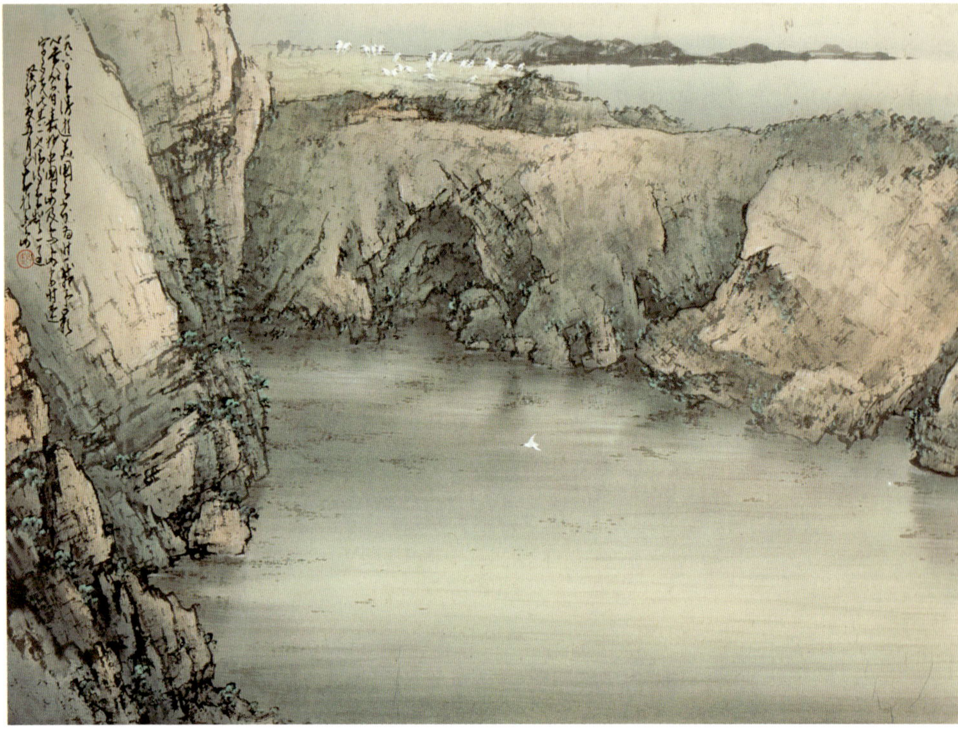

CHINA COVE, CARMEL, CALIFORNIA

1963

By Chao Shao-An (Chinese, 1905–1998)

Ink and colors on paper

H. 61.6 cm × W. 84.5 cm (image)

Collection of Master Chao Shao-An, 1992.238

This scene of the California seashore is one of a few landscapes by Chao Shao-An, a renowned twentieth-century bird-and-flower painter. Chao was a late representative of the Lingnan school, a modern artistic movement that aimed, through subject matter and stylistic choices, to establish a distinct regional identity. The school originated in Guangdong and Hong Kong in southern China. In landscapes, many Lingnan-school artists like Chao sought to record nature without idealizing it; their pictures are naturalistic and faithful to the scenes they depict. They attempted to adopt, whether in landscape or bird-and-flower painting, a realistic approach, because they found it most appropriate and suitable to their project of forging an original, indigenous identity.

This work is based on a series of seashore scenes—a prevailing subject of Lingnan artists—that Chao Shao-An sketched during the summer of 1960. Chao demonstrated his ability to organize and structure the rocky coasts with various brushstrokes and with differentiated colors. He applied textured strokes with solid ink to gray-shaded rocks, and he mixed blue paint, green paint, and black ink to make diluted washes to represent water along the seashore. The atmospheric effects are achieved through Chao's use of opaque white paint that accentuates the seabirds.

—*HL*

WHICH IS EARTH? NO. 7

1969
By Liu Guosong (Chinese, b. 1932)
Hanging scroll; ink and colors on paper
H. 137.2 cm × W. 64.8 cm (image)
Gift of the artist, 2003.51

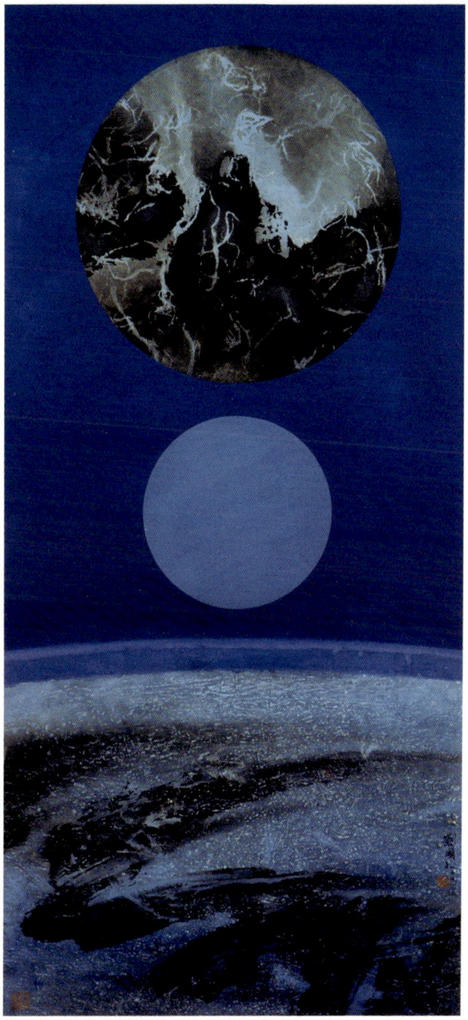

Liu Guosong began his art studies in China under traditional ink-painting (*guohua*) masters and calligraphers including Pu Ru (1896–1963). Later, as a university student in Taiwan, Liu shifted his interest to abstract oil painting, particularly Color Field painting and Abstract Expressionism. His own innovative style came out of experiments in which he sutured together elements from each tradition.

In the late 1950s, Liu began to purposefully address the issue of merging Eastern and Western art. He worked primarily in oil on canvas, but applied plaster to the fabric's surface to allow him to incorporate ink into his compositions. After a few years, he returned to ink painting on paper. He produced rough, thick paper with a high cotton content that could stand up to large splashes of ink applied with very large brushes. In this painting, as throughout his career, Liu Guosong grapples with modernization within longstanding cultural and artistic traditions. In 1968, a year before this work was made, photos of the earth and moon taken on the Apollo 8 mission became widely available. For Liu, these arresting, pervasive, and iconic images from space provided a counterpoint to his work at the time. HIs quasi-abstract, ink-on-paper paintings featured starkly perfect circles in a limited, bold color palette. He derived these circles from round paper lanterns, the type hung for moon viewing during the Mid-Autumn Festival. This type of resonance between traditional and contemporary media and subject matter is recurring and powerful in postwar art of the Chinese diaspora.

—*KGO*

MYTHOS OF LOST DYNASTIES, FORM H-16

1998
By Gu Wenda (Chinese, b. 1955)
Ink on paper
H. 95.9 cm × W. 58.4 cm
Gift of the Yiqingzhai Collection, 2013.27

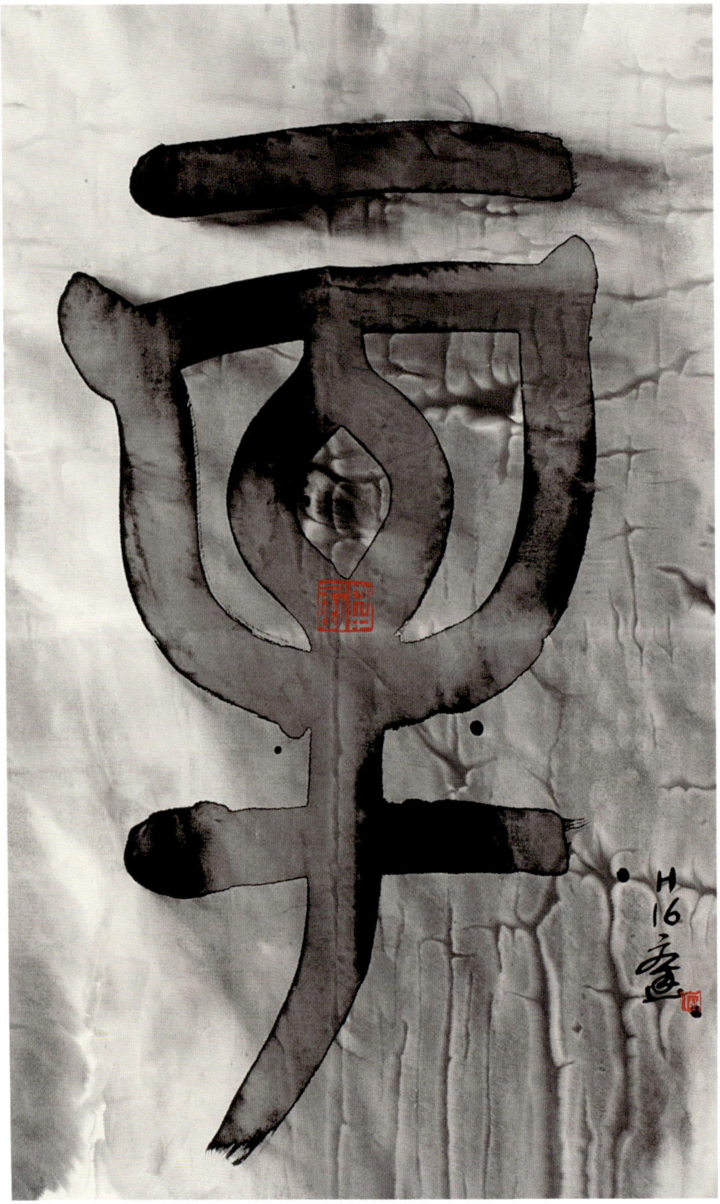

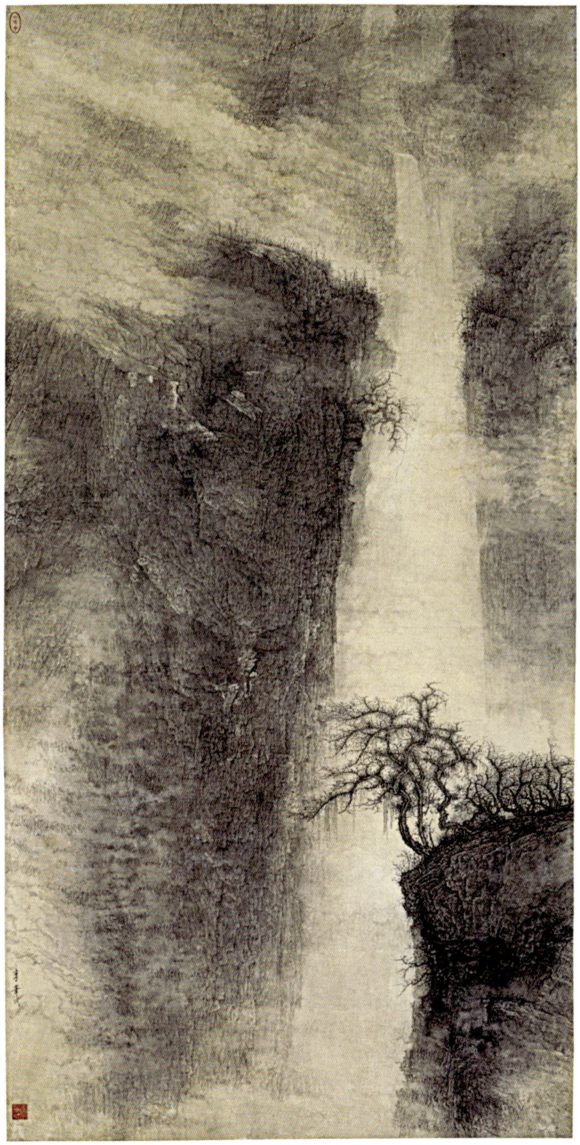

CLOUDY PEAKS AT DAWN IN SPRING

1999

By Li Huayi (Chinese, b. 1948)

Hanging scroll; ink and colors on paper

H. 141 cm × W. 72.4 cm (image)

Gift of Susan and Ian Wilson, 1999.10

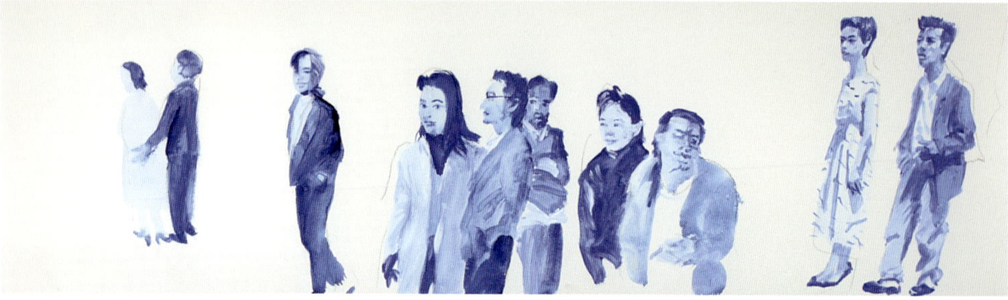

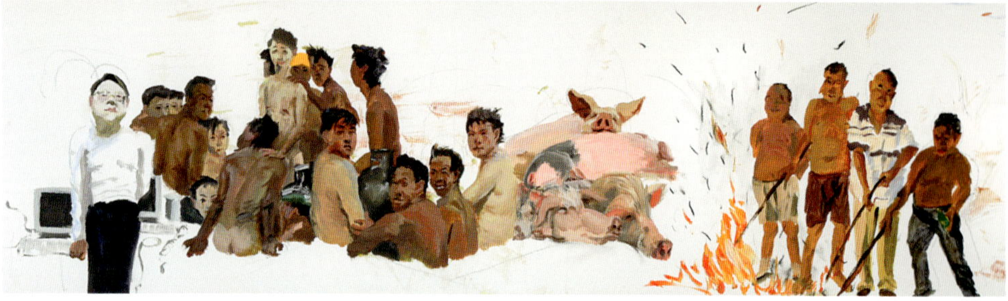

RIVER (DETAILS)

—

2005–2006

By Liu Xiaodong (Chinese, b. 1963)

Acrylic on paper

H. 36 cm × W. 941.7 cm

Gift of Bo Dan, 2006.18

—

This nine-meter painting uses a handscroll format but defies a traditional narrative story arc. Instead, the artist uses the pictorial space to depict fragments of scenes from his life. The painting references ninety-two figures and compositions from other paintings created over the course of Liu's career. Liu repaints these characters and scenes but executes them with minimal brushstrokes and a different color palette, distilling the forms and gestures even further. These are reassembled and set adrift in a work created at a time of great change in China, which included rapid economic growth and development, the building of the massive Three Gorges Dam, and the lead-up to the 2008 Beijing Olympics.

The artist created this scroll for his 2006 Asian Art Museum exhibition, *The Three Gorges Project: Paintings by Liu Xiaodong*. Liu has been a seminal figure in Chinese contemporary art since the 1980s and a leader of the New Generation painters who came to prominence immediately after the Tiananmen Square Massacre of 1989. Rather than focusing on theory and philosophy, these artists drew on their training in academic oil painting to capture details of ordinary moments and common people in a style called Cynical Realism. Liu has stated, "In life, I'm a realist. Therefore, I believe art ought to be realistic.... These objective phenomena themselves radiate a brilliance. I insert the 'contents' from my heart into them."[37]

—*KGO*

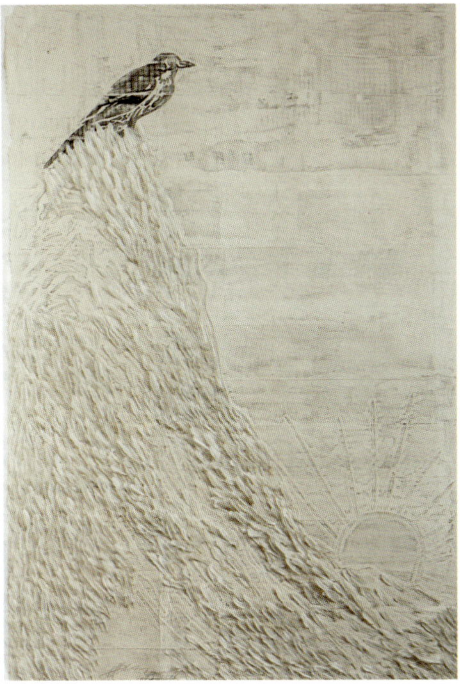

TUI BEI TU NO. 36

—

2007

By Zhang Huan (Chinese, b. 1965)

Woodblock print (ink on handmade paper) and feathers

H. 365.8 cm × W. 251.5 cm × D. 12.7 cm

Gift of Ms. Dominique Lévy, 2016.160

—

This work by the avant-garde contemporary artist Zhang Huan depicts an unusual landscape composition of a mountain, bird, and sun based on an illustration from the book *Tui Bei Tu*. That enigmatic, seventh-century, prophecy book of images and poems takes its title from another illustration in the volume, a "picture of pushing the back." Comprising Tang dynasty cosmological interpretations of the classic text *Yi Jing*, the book was banned by the Chinese Communist Party in the mid-twentieth century as a superstitious relic of China's "four olds"—old customs, culture, beliefs, and habits. In the 1990s, when Zhang moved from Henan in central China to Beijing for graduate study at the Central Academy of Fine Arts, *Tui Bei Tu* was a popular text. It was available at bookstalls and secondhand stores and was seen as an interesting alternative to both official propaganda and the rhetoric of reform-era economic liberalization.

Each illustration in *Tui Bei Tu* uses visual puns to prophesize major dynastic shifts or other political downfalls. As with most astrological predictions, their meaning is anything but clear. In the case of Zhang's interpretation here, a rising sun sits at the base of a mountain, and a closed-beaked bird stands in profile at the top. Creating this work at a monumental scale, and incorporating feathers with the woodblock print, Zhang enlarged an image that would typically appear in a small, cheaply printed, handheld volume.

The monumentality of the scale of Zhang's work, measuring more than 3.5 meters high, serves to further complicate the already-strange composition. The printed lines depicting the sun and its rays appear faded and at times hard to distinguish from the mottled, cloudy background, and the bird's body clearly reveals the imperfections and irregularities of the handmade paper. The mountain shape is eerily embellished with the addition of white feathers applied in a seemingly unmeditated, imprecise manner. The unrefined craftsmanship gives the entire work texture and a sense of motion.

Is the bird heralding the dawn of a new era, or are the textured mountain and bleached-out sunrise signs of a discombobulated world where expectations are turned on their heads? The inscrutable ambiguity of *Tui Bei Tu* fits perfectly with Zhang Huan's work, which is subtly critical of Chinese society or policies while appearing abstract or apolitical.

—*KGO*

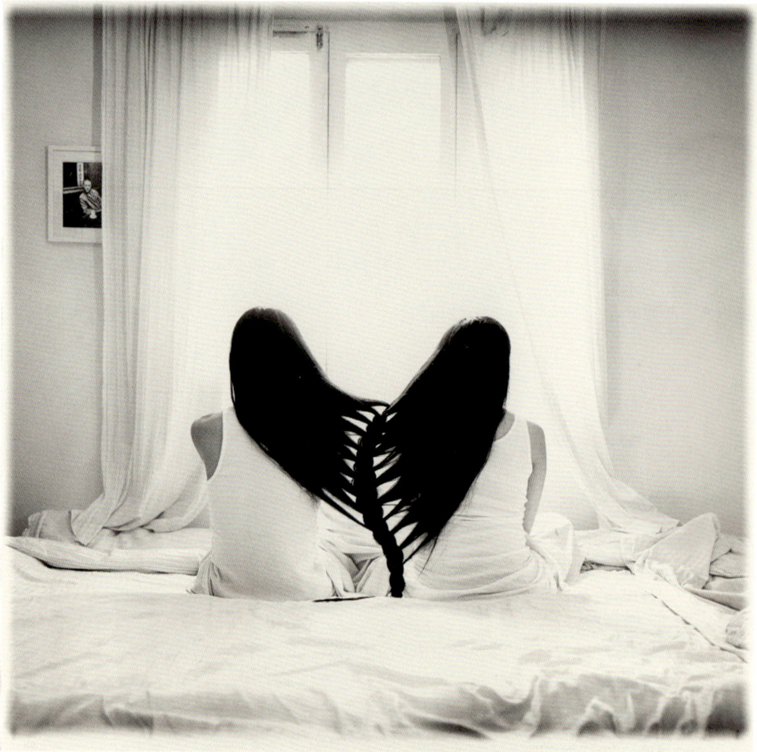

UNTITLED, NO. 25

—

2008

By RongRong & inri (Chinese, b. 1968, and Japanese, b. 1973)

Gelatin silver print

H. 127 cm × W. 19.5 cm

Gift of Jack and Susy Wadsworth, 2013.15

—

Partners and artistic collaborators since 2000, RongRong & inri work in the realm of creative photography. They experiment and innovate within traditional black-and-white darkroom techniques and compose intimate, ambiguous images that seem both mundane and surreal, featuring themselves and their children in natural or man-made settings. In this photograph the two artists appear with their backs to the camera, their long hair braided together. Their bodies are set in a spare interior defined by white curtains, white bedsheets, bright light flooding in through tall windows, and a small black-and-white photograph from which a figure stares out. In this work, like in many of their photographs, the two are portrayed as deeply intertwined and practically indistinguishable. The figure in the small photograph is hard to identify as one artist or the other, as are the two figures in the center of the composition.

RongRong came of age in the early 1990s in the experimental artists' community called the Beijing East Village, where his photographic practice often intersected with the performance art of fellow artists Ma Liuming, Zhang Huan, and Zhu Ming. Inri graduated from the Nippon Photography Institute in Tokyo in 1994 and worked as a portrait photographer for the *Asahi Shinbun* newspaper for several years before embarking on her solo practice. The two met in 1999 at an exhibition in Tokyo then married and began their joint Beijing-based practice the following year. They founded the Three Shadows Photography Art Centre, China's first contemporary art center dedicated to photography, in 2007. Their ongoing work centers on issues of intimacy, the self, and the body in a changing world.

—*KGO*

ENDED SEASON

—

2011

By Zheng Chongbin (American, b. China, 1961)

Ink and acrylic on paper

H. 207 cm × W. 718.8 cm

Museum purchase with exchange funds from the estate of K. Hart Smith with additional funds from the Clarence Shangraw Memorial, 2012.5

—

Zheng Chongbin's art combines his rigorous study of ink painting and figure painting with his deep appreciation for nature, light, and materials. His recent works, including *Ended Season*, use traditional ink and rice paper (*xuanzhi*) as well as white acrylic paint. This keeps his compositions grounded in the black-and-white palette of literati ink painting but also breaks many fundamental rules of that tradition. Zheng abandons conventional brushwork, which leaves large areas of the paper untouched, and instead covers most of the surface in paint or ink. He relies on the controlled but unpredictable interactions between ink, acrylic, water, and paper to create abstract works. His ink and paint interact to create forms that resemble trees, rivers, blood vessels, fractals, or galaxies, but his paintings remain purely abstract. While his work is informed by that of many Western abstract painters, including Franz Kline, Richard Diebenkorn, Mark Rothko, and Clyfford Still, it is devoid of the expressive color, texture, and gestures that characterize their work.

Zheng Chongbin grew up in China during the Cultural Revolution (1966–1976). He began studying art in Shanghai's youth culture clubs in the late 1970s and also undertook private study. He was admitted to the prestigious Zhejiang Academy of Fine Art (now China Academy of Art), and he and his classmates became the leaders of China's '85 New Wave art movement. Zheng taught at the academy for several years before moving to California in 1989 to study installation, performance, and conceptual art at the San Francisco Art Institute. He currently lives and works in San Francisco and Shanghai, exploring painting, video, and spatial constructions informed by his diverse interests in phenomenology, perception, Chinese classical painting, and California Light and Space art. In his words, "[The seventeenth-century master] Shitao implores us: 'On a simple piece of paper, bring about a complete metamorphosis; Let light shine forth through Primordial Confusion.' Whether I can 'transform' myself and 'shine forth' light to break open time and space replete with life is all determined by ink, through ink, and with ink."[38]

—*KGO*

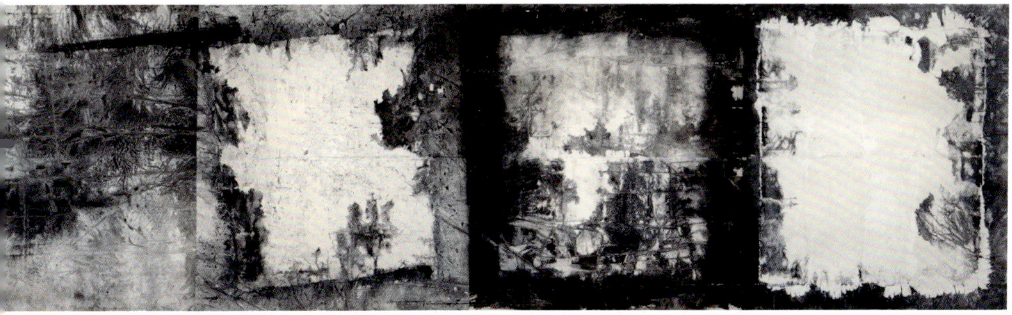

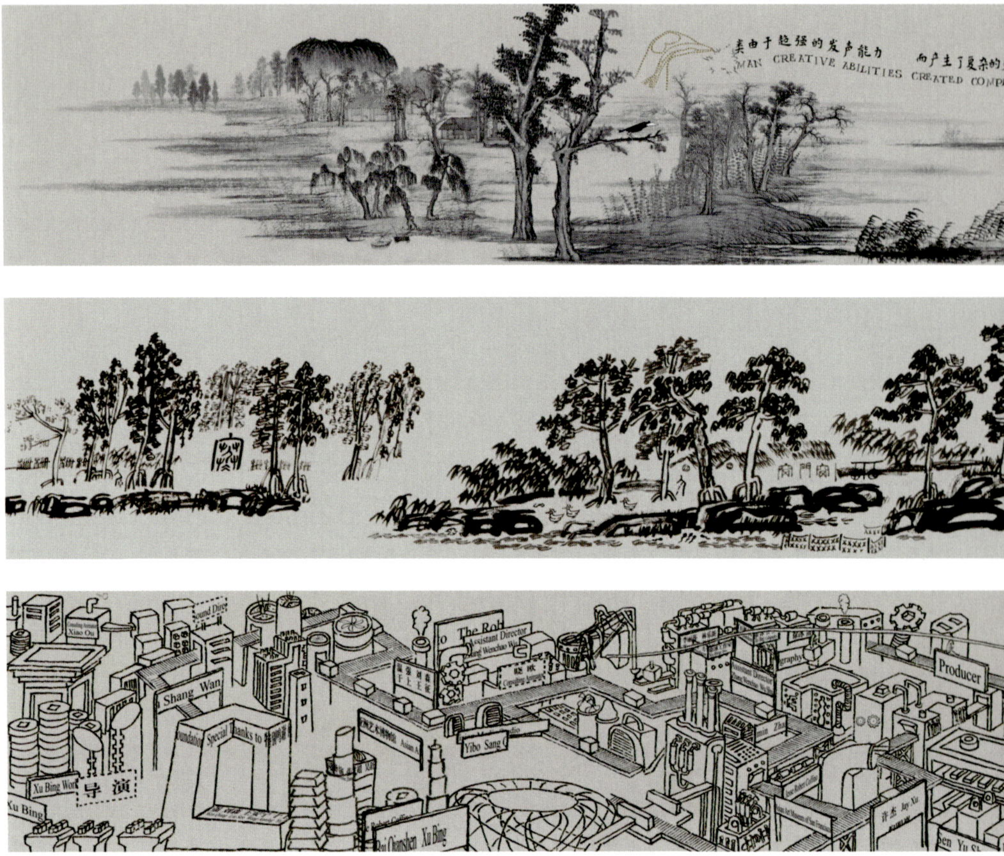

MASTERPIECE

THE CHARACTER OF CHARACTERS (DETAILS)

2012

By Xu Bing (Chinese, b. 1955)

Five-channel digital animation installation with sound, 15 min.

Dimensions variable

Acquisition made possible by The Robert H. N. Ho Family Foundation, 2013.20.1-.2

Xu Bing is renowned for his artistic explorations of the role of language in human life. *The Character of Characters* is a playful yet profound narrative executed in animation. It touches on such varied subjects as the genesis of writing, the connection between Chinese calligraphy and painting, the role of copying in art and society, and the trust native Chinese readers place in symbols, including

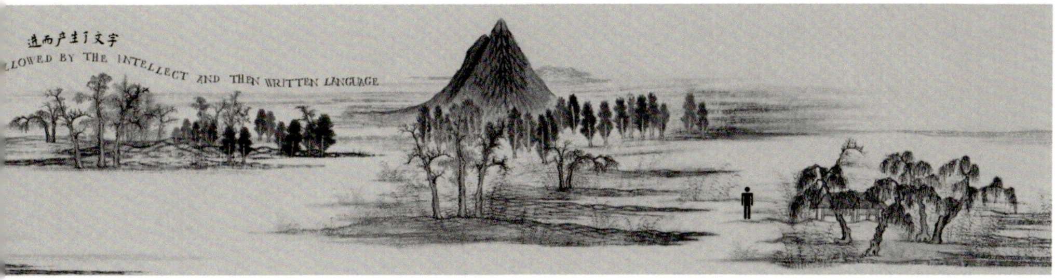

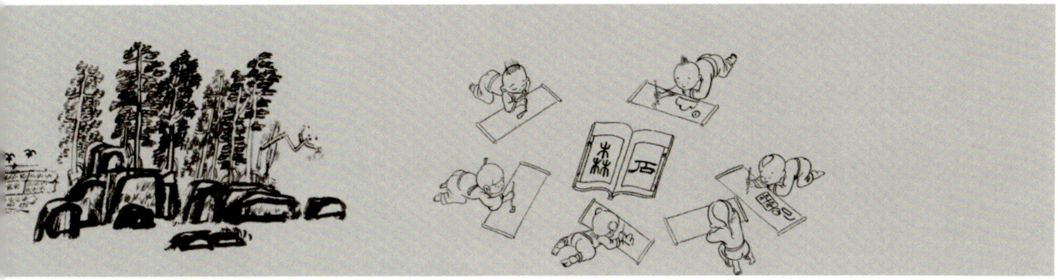

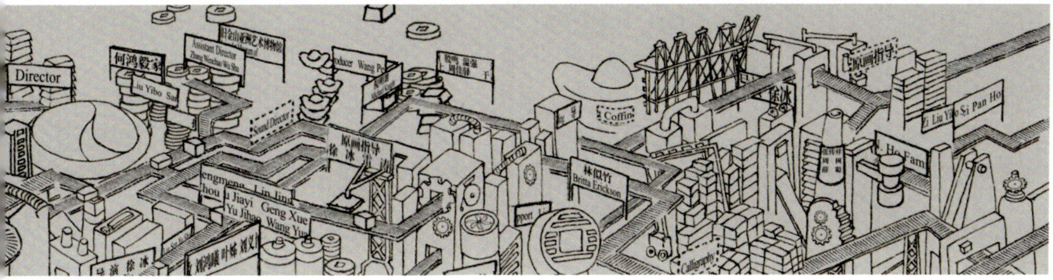

their current love affair with name-brand luxury goods. The animation moves fluidly from topic to topic, from drawing to diagram to text. Xu created *The Character of Characters* in response to Zhao Mengfu's horizontal scroll *Sutra on the Lotus of the Sublime Dharma*, a work from the late thirteenth or early fourteenth century.

Words and symbols have always been central to Xu's work. This is due in part to his facility with writing from a young age during the Cultural Revolution, a time when language, like art, was used for very specific political purposes:

> As a child, I was taught by my father, who had me trace characters every day; later, this became a habitual activity for me....Yet in all that time, I had never done any calligraphic creation, for tracing characters was simply a means of practicing writing....I had never felt it was art. But this bit of craftsmanship was put to use during the Cultural Revolution: 'Pick up your brush to use as a weapon.'...My class status was not good, but my characters were; consequently, with some difficulty I became a useful person—a 'character-writing tool' within the 'machine of the whole revolution.'[39]

Born in Chongqing, Sichuan province, in southwest China, Xu Bing earned a bachelor's degree in printmaking from the Central Academy of Fine Arts (CAFA), Beijing, in 1981, followed by an MFA in 1987. He was a leading figure in China's '85 New Wave and moved to the United States in 1990. He currently lives and works in New York and Beijing.

—*KGO*

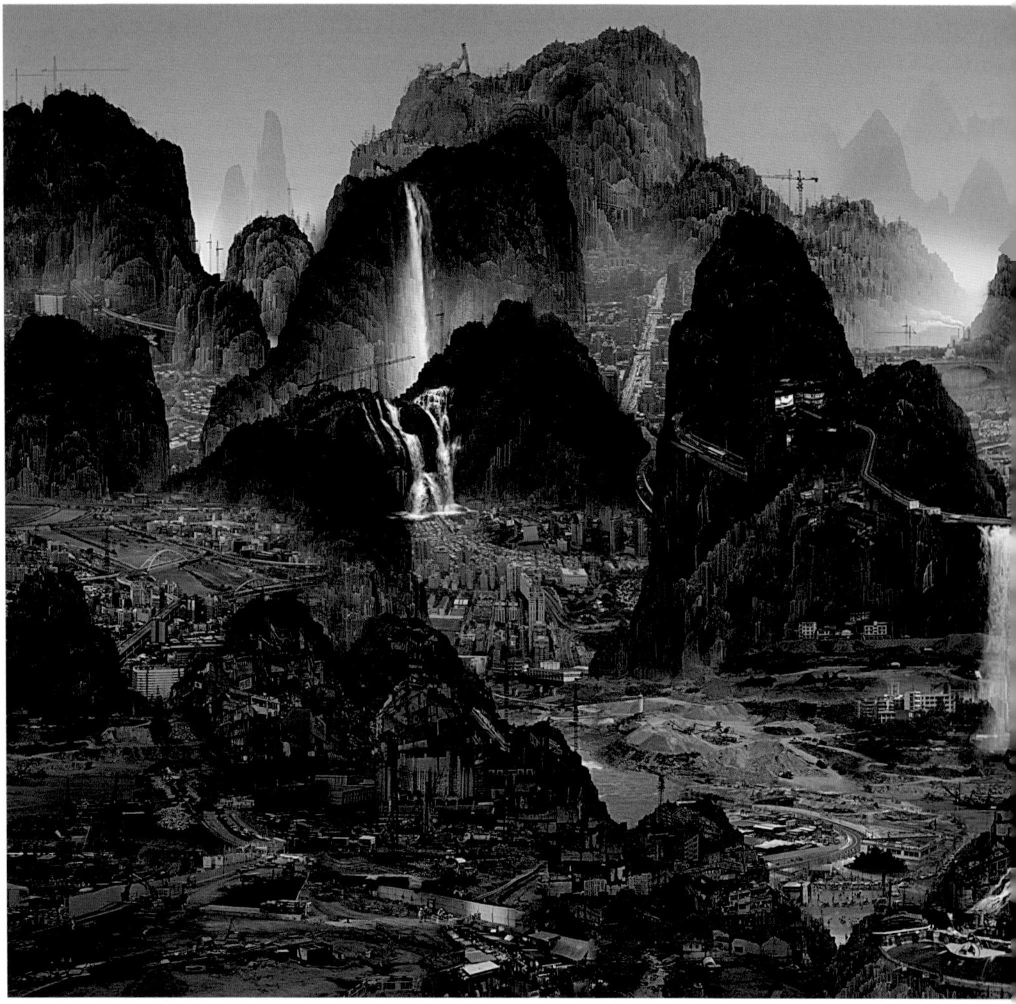

THE NIGHT OF PERPETUAL DAY

2013

By Yang Yongliang (Chinese, b. 1980)

Four-channel HD video with sound, 8:32 min.

Acquisition made possible by Gorretti and Lawrence Lui, with additional funding from Richard Beleson, 2014.14

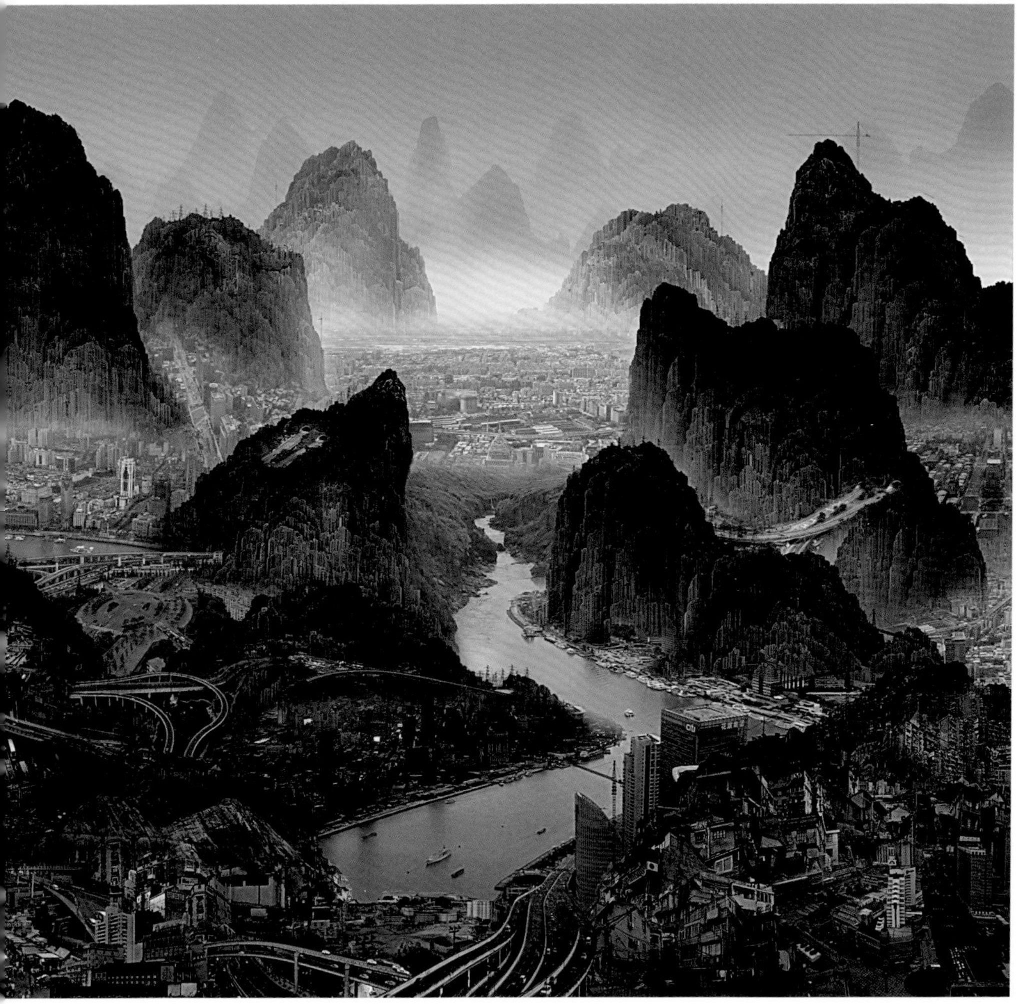

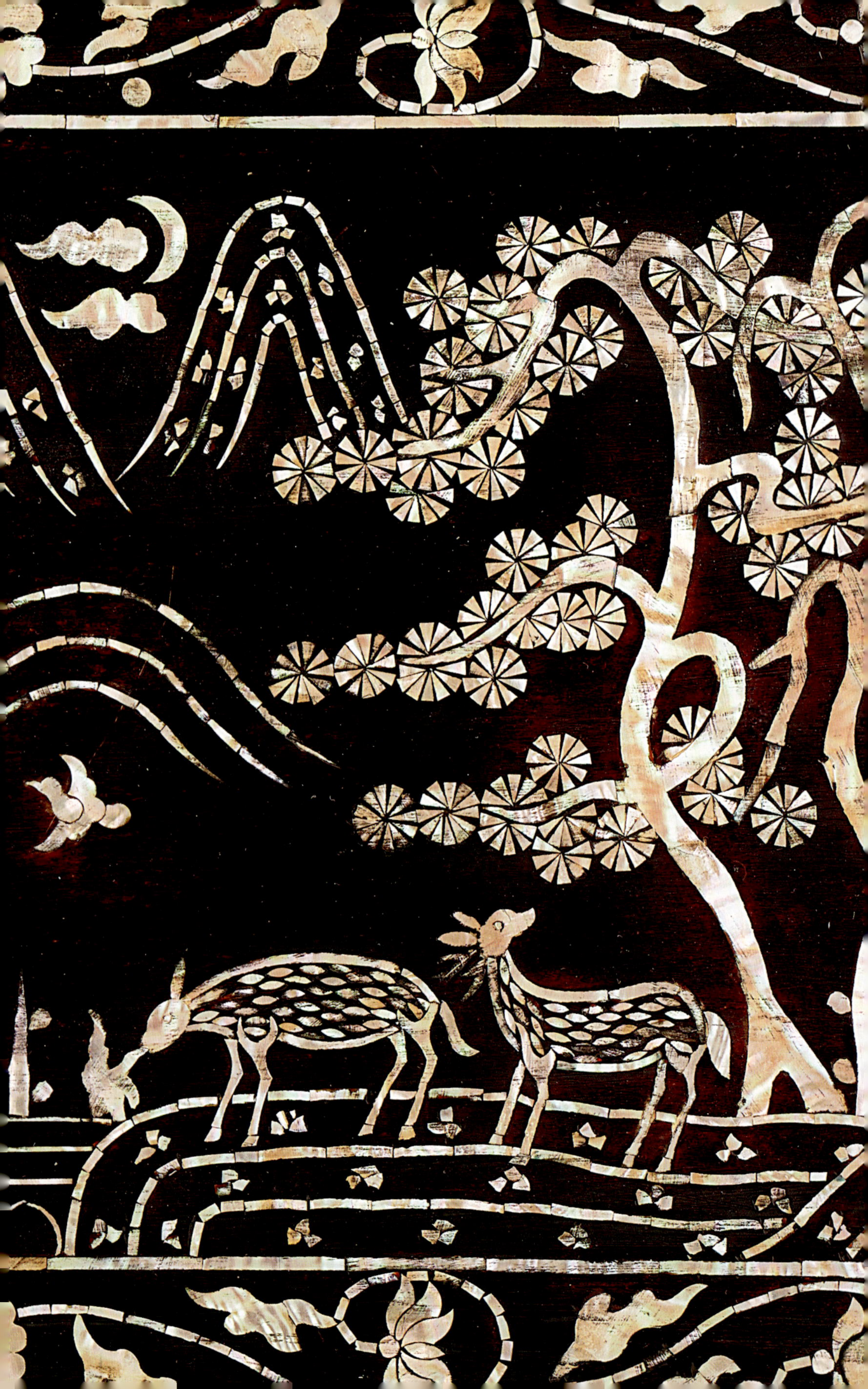

KOREA

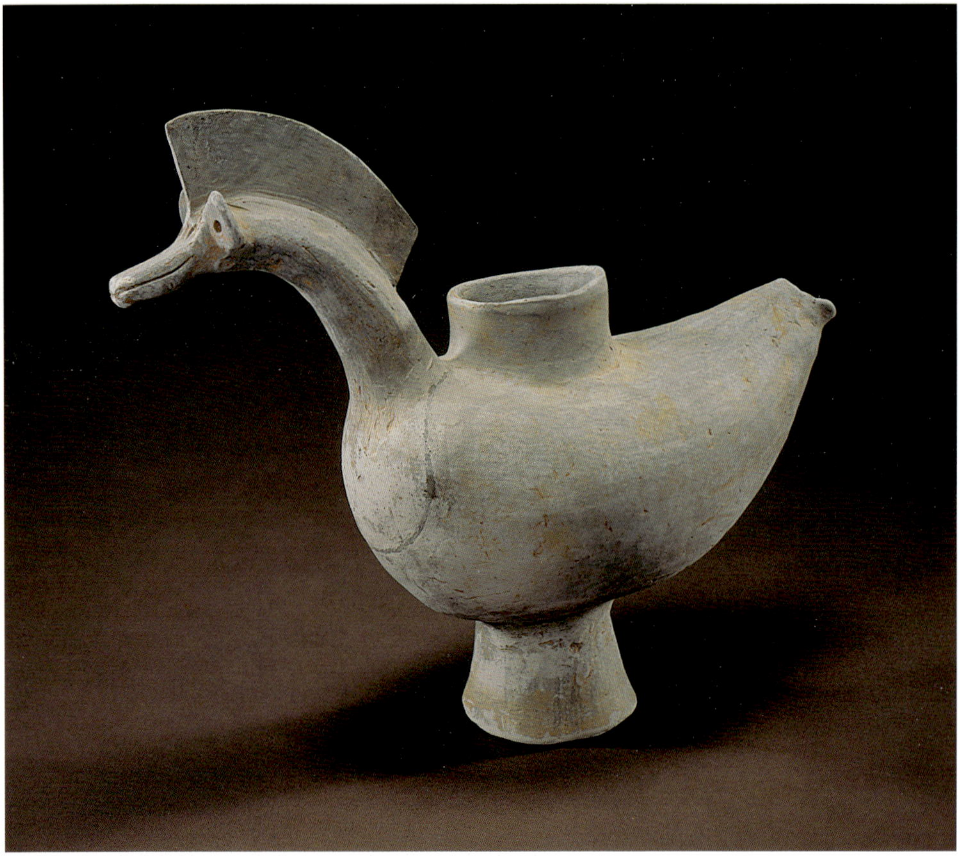

VESSEL IN THE SHAPE OF A DUCK

approx. 300

Korea; ancient region of Gaya

Earthenware

H. 30.5 cm × W. 38.1 cm × D. 16.5 cm

The Avery Brundage Collection, B63P13+

This duck-shaped vessel with openings in its back and tail likely held water or wine for ritual purposes. Its natural form—with long erect neck and crest-like feathers on its head—is accentuated by large, wide-set eyes. The slight upward curve of its beak offers a whimsical expression, as if it knowingly holds all the answers to life and beyond. Duck-shaped vessels such as this have been excavated from tombs near the Nakdong River in the southwestern part of the Korean peninsula, which was part of the Gaya Federation (42–562 CE) during the Three Kingdoms period (57 BCE–668 CE). They were most likely used at funerals to guide the spirit of the deceased to the afterlife and then buried with the deceased.

According to ancient Korean folk beliefs, birds were revered as auspicious creatures that blessed villages with good harvests, peace, and prosperity. They were also viewed as messengers to the spirit world because they traversed between the Heavens and the Earth. A third-century Chinese text, *Sanguozhi* (Records of the Three Kingdoms), states that during funerals the Eastern foreigners (people from the Korean Peninsula) "use large bird feathers to send off their dead, the intent being to allow the deceased to fly upward."[1] Remnants of this belief still exist today and can be seen as figures of birds sitting atop tall wooden posts guarding the entrances of traditional Korean villages.

—*HMY*

BUDDHA ON LOTUS-SHAPED PEDESTAL

—

approx. 700–800

Korea

Unified Silla dynasty (668–935)

Bronze with gilding

H. 47.3 cm × W. 32.8 cm × D. 18.4 cm

The Avery Brundage Collection, B65B64

—

This refined statue captures the quintessential style of the eighth century, the most creative and prolific period of Buddhist art on the Korean peninsula. During the Unified Silla period (668–935), court patronage made possible imposing Buddhist temples, impressive statues, magnificent rituals, and the finest monastic scholarship. At the same time, individual devotees from aristocratic families found their own way to express their faith. Exquisite bronze statues of modest size proved particularly useful for their private devotional practice. The large number of small gilded bronze icons of a standing Buddha, found in museum collections inside and outside of Korea, was typically used in this type of setting. This standing Buddha is one such example and one of the largest of its kind.

This statue consists of a one-piece standing Buddha and a separately cast lotus pedestal atop an ornate base. Two pegs beneath the Buddha's feet are inserted into the two perforations on the top of the lotus pedestal to securely mount the Buddha.

The disproportionately large head bears a square face with arched eyebrows, downcast eyes, a well-defined nose, a small mouth, and long earlobes, all of which contribute to its solemn expression. The fleshy face is topped by regularly spaced snail-shell curls and a relatively high *ushnisha* (a cranial protuberance signifying transcendental wisdom). The broad shoulders, expansive chest, slender waist, and protruding abdomen are covered by a clinging garment patterned with raised drapery folds. The symmetrical U-shaped lines of drapery repeated on each leg reveal the contours of the thighs. The mudra (a symbolic hand gesture) suggests either a variation of *abhaya mudra* (the gesture of dispelling fear) and *varada mudra* (the gesture of granting a wish), or perhaps an early form of the welcoming mudras of Amitabha (Buddha of Infinite Light). While a mudra typically defines a deity's qualities and identity, here it does not clarify whether the Buddha is Amitabha or Shakyamuni.

On the back of the Buddha are two projections originally intended to affix a large aureole (a painted halo surrounding an entire body). There also remain two casting holes on the back. One round hole on the head and another large hole on the body indicate the locations where spacers between the casting mold and the core were removed, and through which the clay of the casting core was removed. The statue is essentially hollow inside. This manner of using casting holes is unique to Korean bronze images.
—Sunkyung Kim is an independent scholar researching and teaching Buddhist Art.

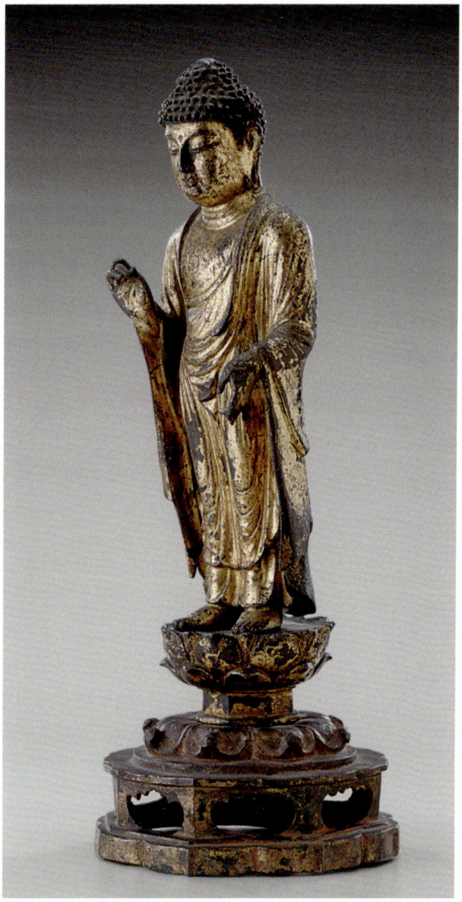

MASTERPIECE

EWER WITH LOTUS-SHAPED LID

approx. 1050–1150
Korea
Goryeo dynasty (918–1392)
Stoneware with celadon glaze
H. 24.4 cm × Diam. 16.5 cm
The Avery Brundage Collection, B60P123+.a-.b

The color, glaze, and even the beautiful surface cracks of this ewer represent the pinnacle of Korean celadon production. The form is also delightful, as it balances the elegance of the lotus leaves on the lid with the simplicity of the cylindrical body, while it harmonizes the softness of the leaves with the sharpness of the body. It is truly a timeless masterpiece that amply demonstrates the aesthetic sensibilities of the Goryeo dynasty (918–1392).

The precision of the ewer's craftsmanship and the high quality of its glaze, clay, and firing techniques indicate that this masterpiece was created for the elite circles of early twelfth-century society. The glaze covers the bottom of the base and the inside of the ewer's body, signifying that it was fired with extreme care. The clean foot ring and even application of glaze all over its surfaces imply that the artisans placed the ewer on its own in a single sagger, a box-like clay container that protects the ceramic during firing.

The ewer's form and the color of its glaze are comparable to the celadons discovered in the tomb of King Injong of Goryeo (1109–1146), which are now in the collection of the National Museum of Korea. These Injong celadons are a landmark in the history of Korean ceramics, considered to exemplify the transcendent beauty of early twelfth-century plain celadons without any surface decorations, and this ewer has equal quality to those.

Interestingly, this ewer is almost identical to one owned by the Leeum, Samsung Museum of Art in Seoul, though the knob of this ewer, lower and simpler in form, is a modern repair. The perfect celadon color and excellent form of both ewers indicate that they were made in a similar period, when a set of celadon wares was created to be buried in the tomb of King Injong. The set and the two ewers exemplify the finest Goryeo celadon wares, which were the envy of contemporary Chinese connoisseurs. Taiping Laoren, a Chinese expert active in the thirteenth century, compiled a list of objects that he considered the most highly valued. Under the category of celadon, he wrote that the exceptional color of Goryeo celadon was the "best under heaven."
—*HKH*

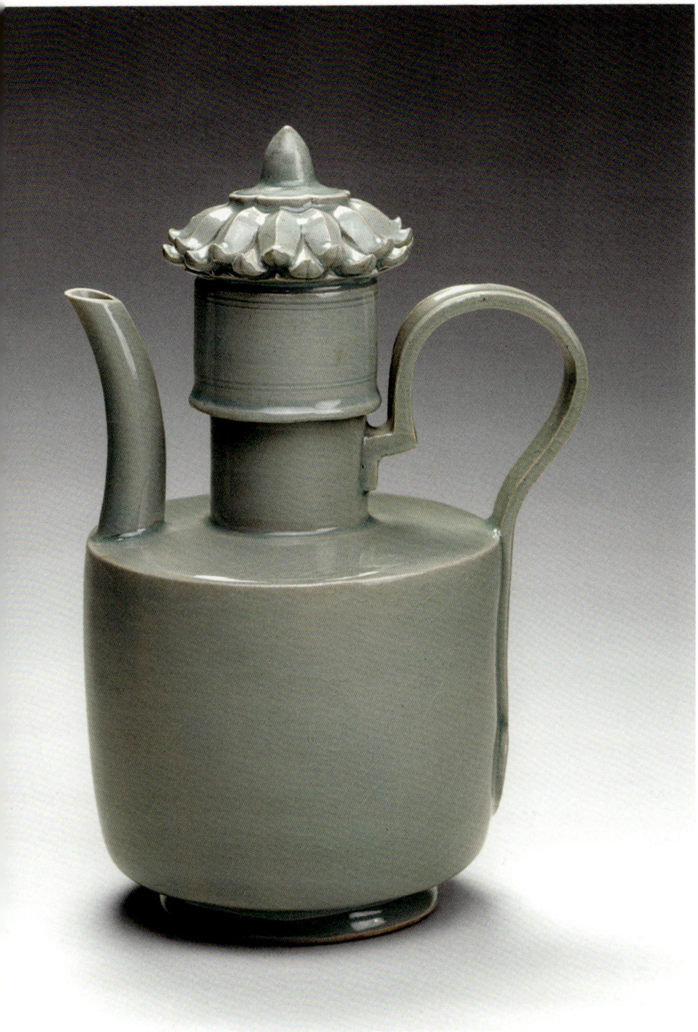

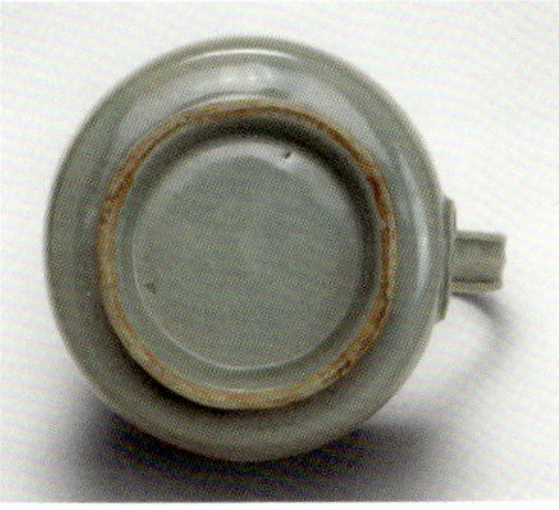

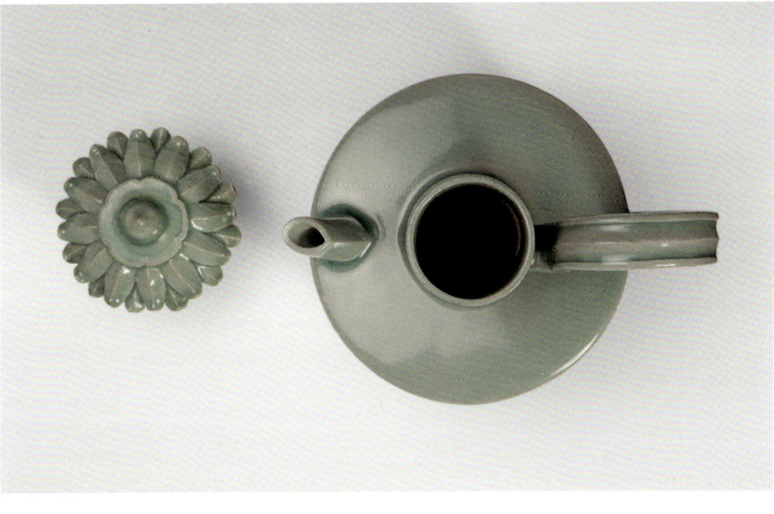

THE BUDDHA AMITABHA WITH THE EIGHT GREAT BODHISATTVAS

approx. 1350–1390
Goryeo dynasty (918–1392)
Hanging scroll; ink, colors, and gold on silk
H. 151.1 cm × W. 88.7 cm (image)
The Avery Brundage Collection, B72D38

This painting represents the Buddha Amitabha seated on a high throne, flanked by two groups each of four bodhisattvas. The transparent halos and the large circular aureole of the Buddha are delicately outlined in gold. His hands, with the thumbs touching the middle fingers, make the preaching gesture. The eight bodhisattvas face each other in three-quarter or frontal view. They can be identified by their attributes.

On the right from the top: Vajrapani holding a single-pronged ritual object (*vajra*); Maitreya with a five-pointed crown, holding a fully opened lotus; Manjushri holding a sutra manuscript, symbolizing wisdom; and Avalokiteshvara, with a Buddha seated in meditation in the center of his crown. In his right hand Avalokiteshvara holds a bottle of water meant for purification.

On the left from the top: Samantabhadra holding a sword, in the same manner as Vajrapani holds the *vajra* (both attributes are weapons to eliminate ignorance); Kshitigarbha, the only bodhisattva not to have a crown, wears a monk's headscarf and holds a jewel that serves to dispel darkness; Sarvanivarana Vishkambhin, holding a scepter (*ruyi*); and Mahasthamaprapta with a flaming jewel in his crown and another in his right hand.

This image of Amitabha with the eight great bodhisattvas is based on the *Sutra of the Eight Great Bodhisattvas*, translated into Chinese by Amoghavajra (705–774).[2] The painting's bold style demonstrates that it is a product of the fourteenth century. The rise of popularity of belief in Amitabha in the second half of the Goryeo dynasty (918–1392) made it possible to create this iconography. Goryeo monarchs and aristocrats maintained private prayer halls for worship and meditation. The relatively small size of this hanging scroll suggests that it was intended for use in worship or ceremony in such a prayer hall.

—Youngsook Pak is professor emeritus at SOAS University of London and an independent researcher.

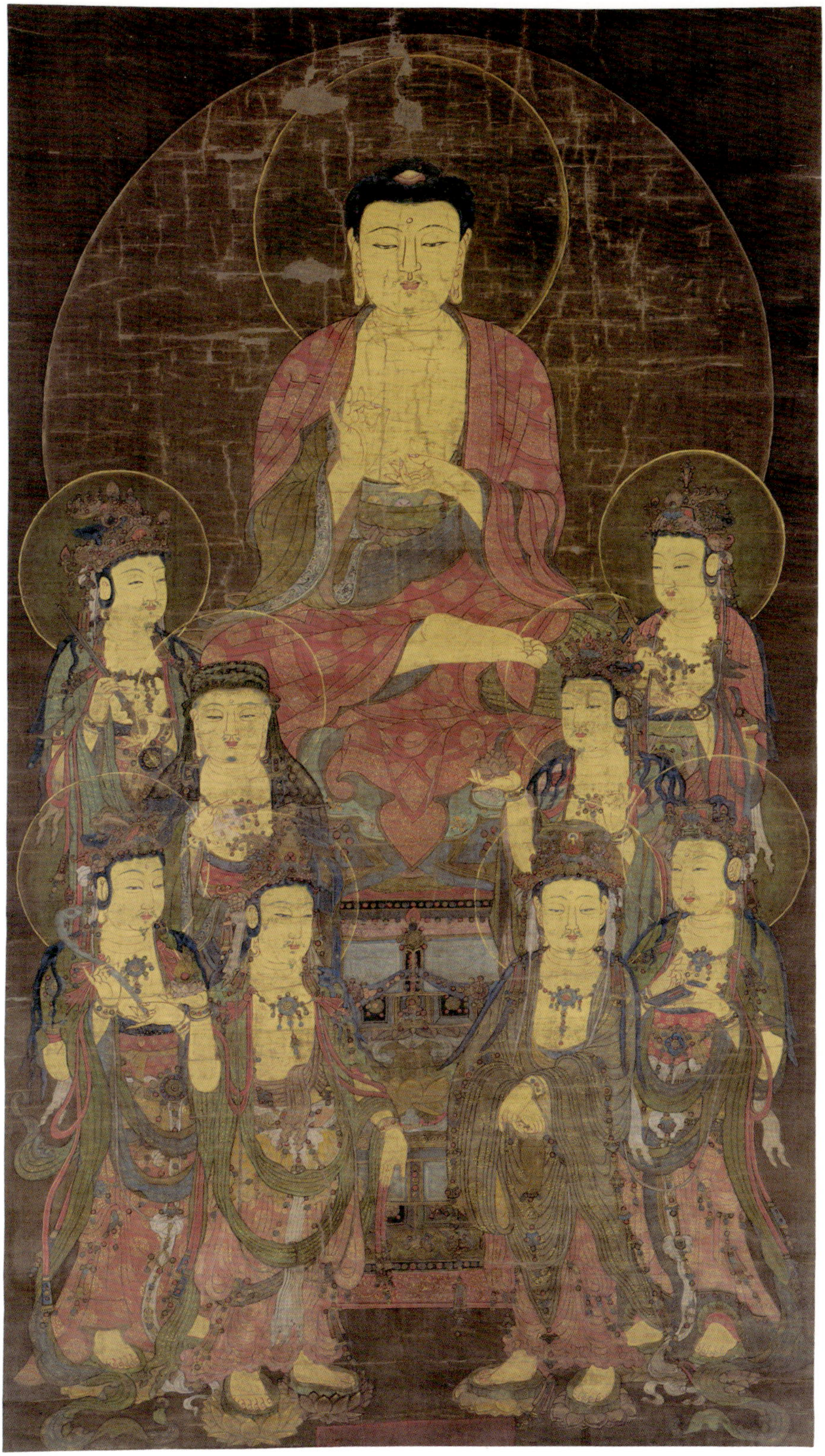

FLASK WITH PEONY DESIGN

—

1400–1500
Korea
Joseon dynasty (1392–1910)
Stoneware with incised and sgraffito slip decoration under clear glaze (buncheong ware)
H. 20.6 cm × W. 18.1 cm × D. 14.6 cm
Gift of Ms. Kyong Brotherton in honor of her husband, Joseph Brotherton, 2016.118

—

FLASK WITH LEAF DESIGN

—

1400–1500
Korea
Joseon dynasty (1392–1910)
Stoneware with incised and sgraffito slip decoration under clear glaze (buncheong ware)
H. 22.4 cm × W. 16.8 cm × D. 14.1 cm
Gift of Ms. Kyong Brotherton in honor of her husband, Joseph Brotherton, 2016.117

—

"Simple," "rough," "unobtrusive," and "grand" are just a few words that artists and art historians have used to describe the beauty of Korean buncheong ware. Buncheong are ceramics with distinct rough gray bodies embellished with white slip and transparent glaze. They were produced during the first two hundred years of the Joseon dynasty (1392–1910).

The clay and glaze of buncheong ceramics are similar to those of Goryeo celadon, but buncheong are less refined and coarser than their predecessors. At the beginning of the Joseon dynasty, buncheong shared surface designs with Goryeo celadon; however, they soon diverged from the earlier tradition. This shift responded to dynastic, religious, and philosophical changes in Korean society and also reflected the aesthetic tastes of its makers and consumers. Produced in kilns throughout the Korean peninsula, buncheong ceramics were made for all social classes. They ranged from upper-class ritual vessels to everyday wares of common people.

The buncheong tradition was gradually replaced by porcelain production and came to an end with the Japanese Invasions of Korea (Imjin War 1592–1598). It was rediscovered in the early twentieth century by descendants of Korean potters who had been forcibly relocated to Japan during that war. Potters in both Korea and Japan soon realized the creative potential behind an artistic heritage that was nearly lost by war and displacement.

Art historian Ko Yu-seop (1905–1944) coined the term *bunjang hoecheong sagi* (gray-green ceramics decorated with powder, and abbreviated to buncheong) to describe the type. The white slip of buncheong ware serves as a canvas for various designs. Examples include these flasks with leaf and peony designs, respectively featured on round and lightly flattened bodies. Both are decorated with bold and abstract figures captured in a lively manner by sgraffito. The artisan first applies white slip, then incises the design before scratching out the area surrounding the design to reveal the clay body underneath. Rendered in contrasting colors and abstract outlines, the final design is startlingly modern. Many of the characteristics that we might associate with modern and contemporary art—such as abstraction and minimalism—are expressed and highlighted in buncheong ceramics.
—*HMY*

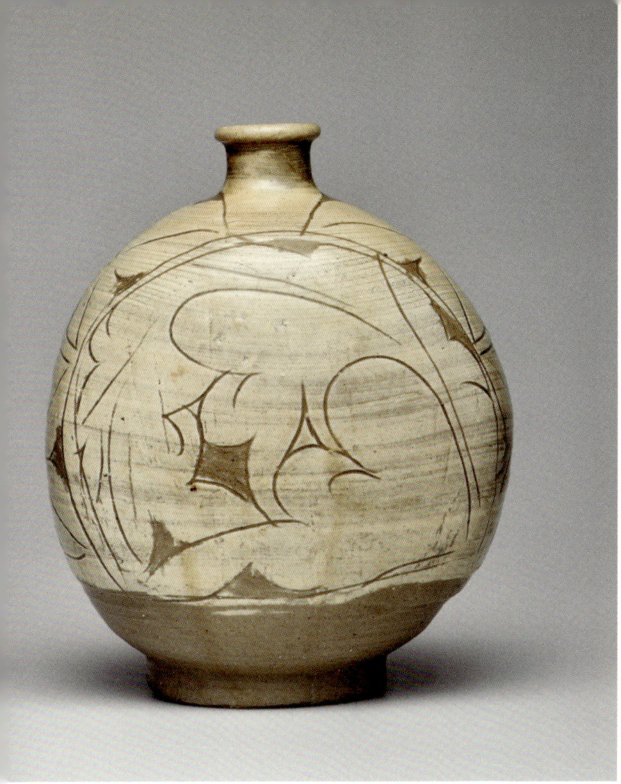

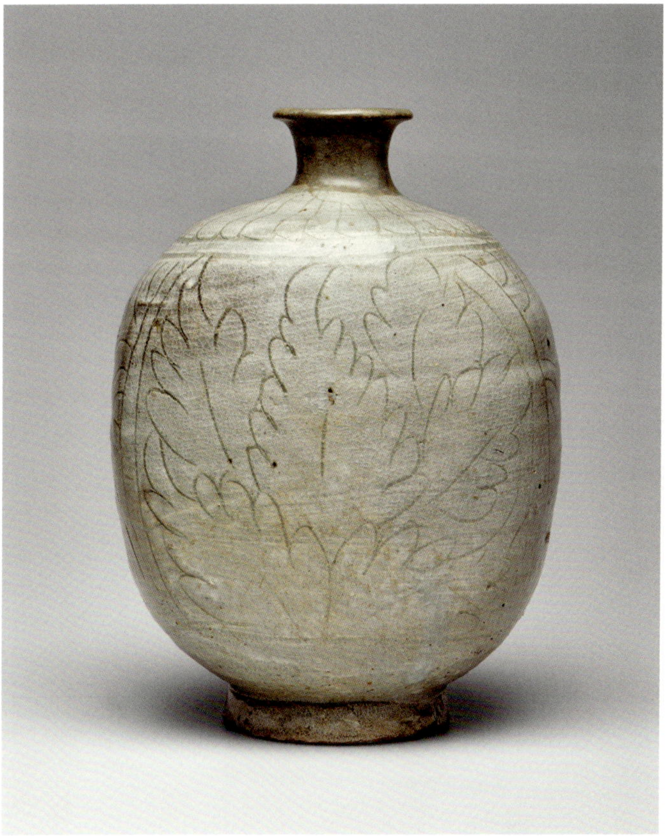

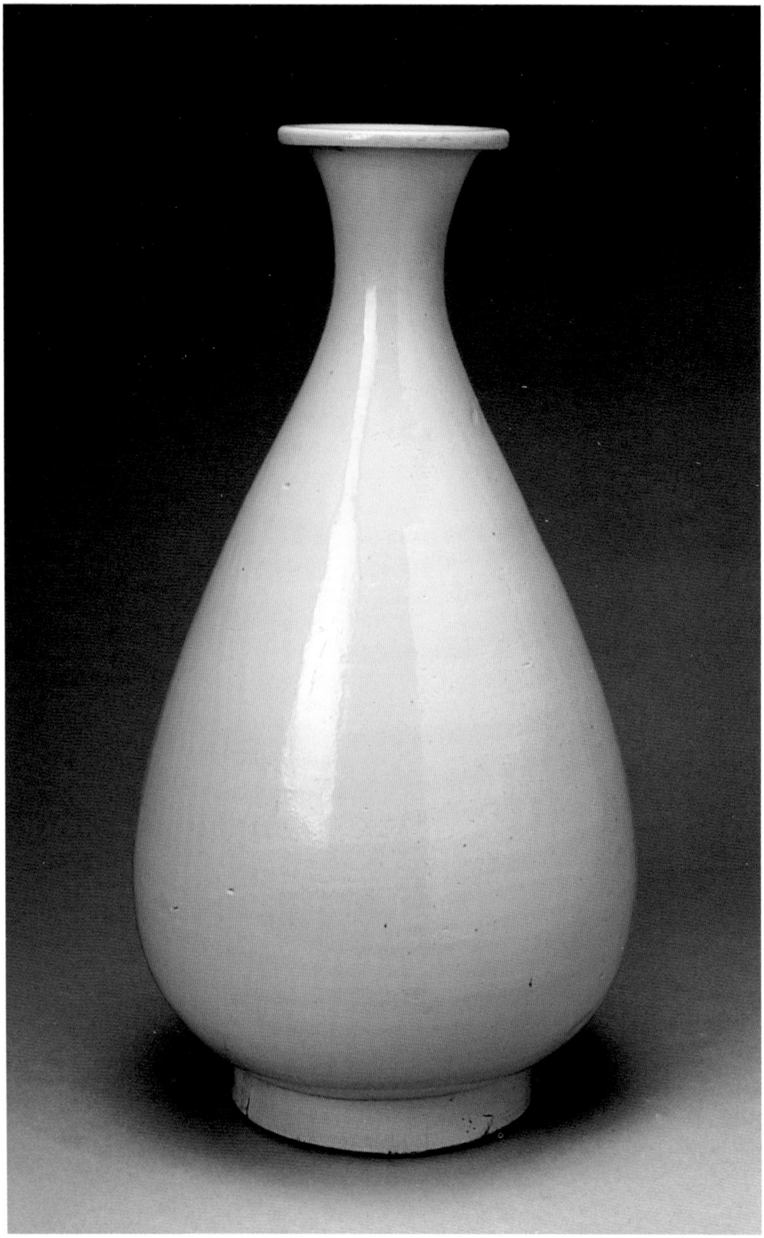

BOTTLE

1400–1500
Korea
Joseon dynasty (1392–1910)
Porcelain with clear glaze
H. 37.2 cm × Diam. 19.4 cm
The Avery Brundage Collection, B72P2

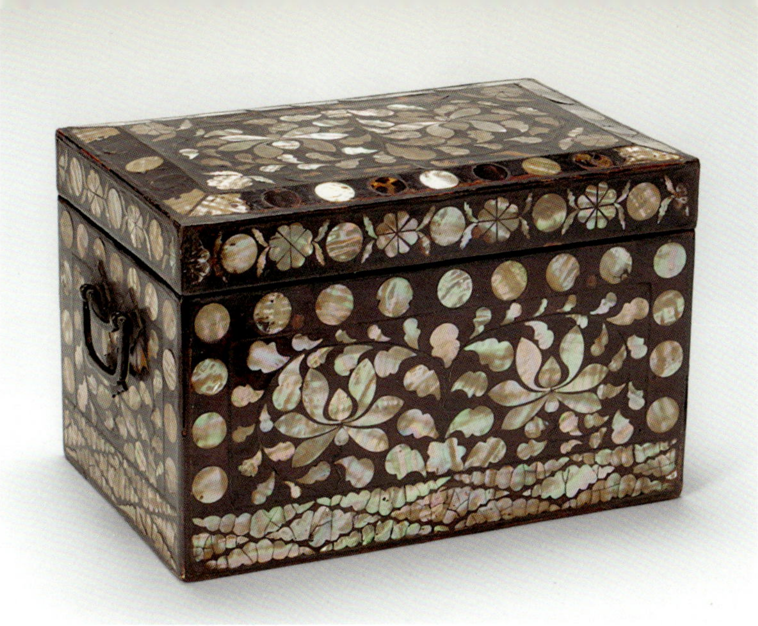

BOX WITH LOTUS MOTIF

1500–1650
Korea
Joseon dynasty (1392–1910)
Lacquer on wood with inlaid mother-of-pearl, tortoiseshell, and brass wire, and metal fittings
H. 20.6 cm × W. 33 cm × D. 21.6 cm
Gift of the Christensen Fund, BL77M46.a-.b

During the Joseon dynasty (1392–1910), mother-of-pearl lacquerwares were made not only for the Korean upper class but also as special products for annual tributes to Chinese imperial families. According to the historical records, Joseon kings sent two mother-of-pearl boxes to China every year after 1482. This rectangular box, with its fine and rare decorations of lotus flowers, might have been one of those made for royal families during the mid-Joseon period.

The outer surface of this box is decorated with mother-of-pearl, tortoiseshell, and brass wire. The use of these materials with mother-of-pearl was developed during the Goryeo dynasty (918–1392) and reappeared during the mid-Joseon period. The main pattern on this box is the lotus flower. On its top, two lotus flowers of bright mother-of-pearl are centered in a black lacquered surface. Twisted brass wires and small mother-of-pearl pieces surround the main flowers like vines with leaves. The sides of the box are also decorated with lotus flowers and roundel motifs, while the bottom features a wide band with a lozenge pattern made of cracked mother-of-pearl pieces. This cracking technique, called *tabal-beob*, could be used to cover broader and bigger patterns more easily than previous techniques.

The inside of this box is wholly lined with yellow silk woven with gold and colored thread. The main pattern of this silk shows five-colored clouds and four-colored dragons with large jaws. Such auspicious motifs were used only on works made for the upper class. The use of high-quality, patterned silk in this box is a rare and precious example among mother-of-pear lacquerwares of the Joseon dynasty.

However, more than twelve boxes nearly identical in dimension and design to this one are known to exist, including one example in the collection of the National Museum of Korea. The other similar boxes are not yet fully researched, but some of them might have been made during the same period. According to the historical record, in January 1505 Yeonsan-gun (1476–1506; reigned 1494–1506), the tenth king of Korea's Joseon dynasty, ordered 150 mother-of-pearl lacquer boxes to be made. This box and its matches could have been mass-produced during Yeonsan-gun's reign.

—Kyeongmi Joo is a specialist in Korean craft art and a lecturer at Chungnam National University.

MASTERPIECE

MOON JAR

1650–1750
Korea
Joseon dynasty (1392–1910)
Porcelain with clear glaze
H. 45.7 cm × Diam. 45.7 cm
The Avery Brundage Collection, B60P110+

Moon jars appeared in the eighteenth century and began to disappear in the early nineteenth century. Their exact function is not known, but it seems they were used either to store grain or to display flowers. Some scholars believe that they were made instead for appreciation and decoration; during the Joseon dynasty (1392–1910), the simplicity and elegance of moon jars would have satisfied the tastes and aesthetics of Confucian scholars.

Moon jars were made in two separate sections, that were then joined, leaving seam marks. Their shapes are less than perfectly round, and they have an uneven glaze on their surface. Although all moon jars have similarly undecorated surfaces and round shapes, each jar has its own peculiar character, and this specific example has attracted many Korean connoisseurs and artists since the 1980s, when moon jars came to be widely celebrated. In the early twentieth century, these jars were not widely admired, even in Korea, and only a small group of connoisseurs and collectors esteemed their naturalistic aesthetic. Bernard Leach (1887–1979), known as the father of British studio pottery, was an early convert to the beauty and naturalism of Korean ceramics, and Yanagi Soetsu (1889–1961), a Japanese connoisseur during the Japanese colonization period, published many essays on the appreciation of Korean pottery, including Joseon whitewares.

Contemporary artists have captured the Korean-ness, subtle individual beauty, and living quality of moon jars in their works. One example is Koo Bohnchang (b. 1953), who wrote about his own art based on Joseon whitewares in this book (see page 235).

—*HKH*

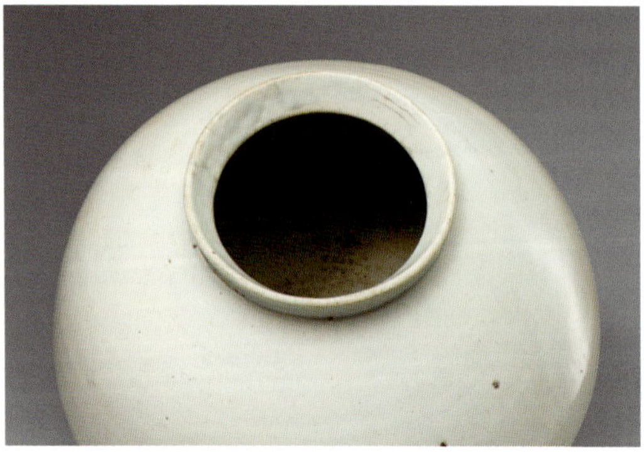

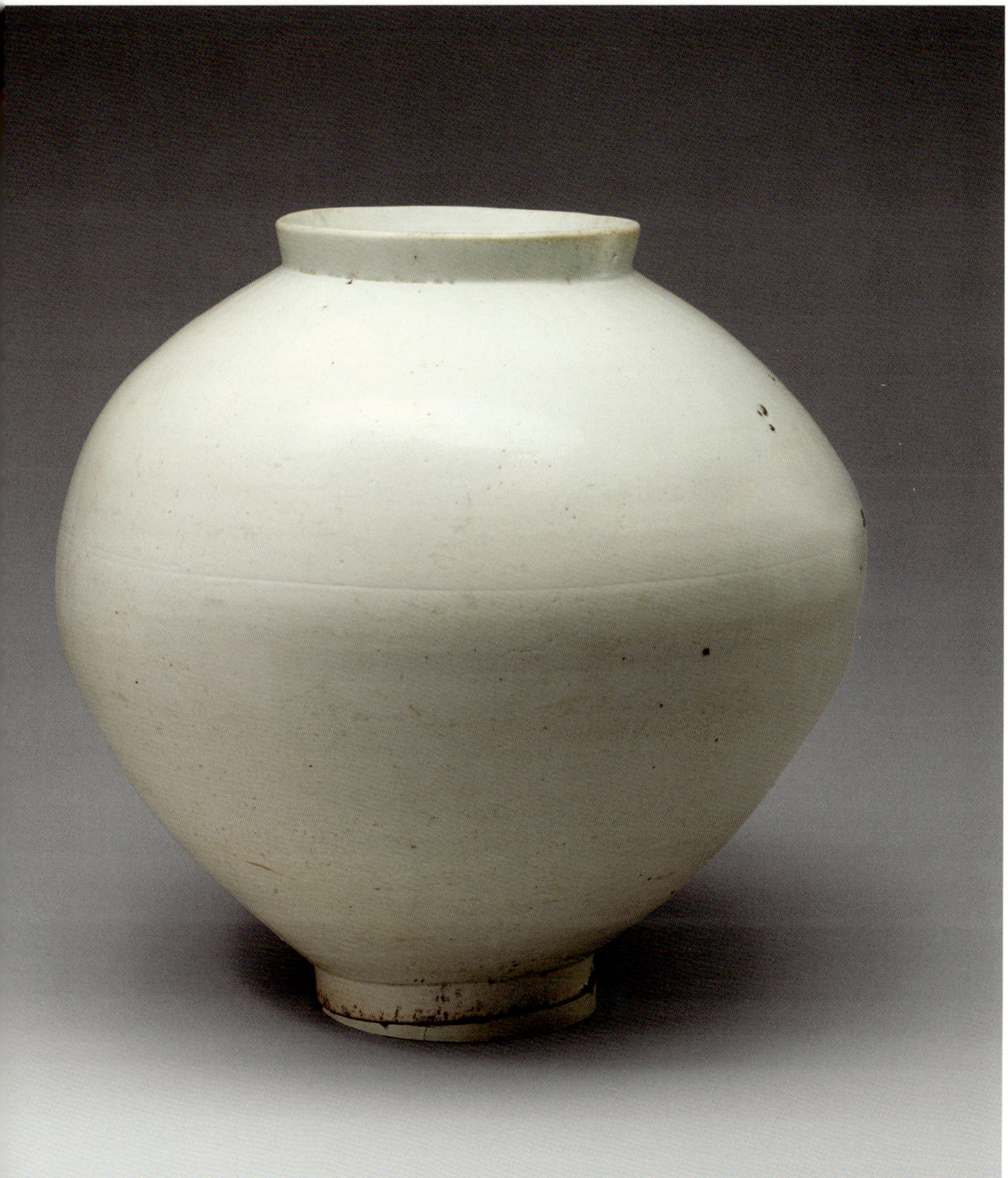

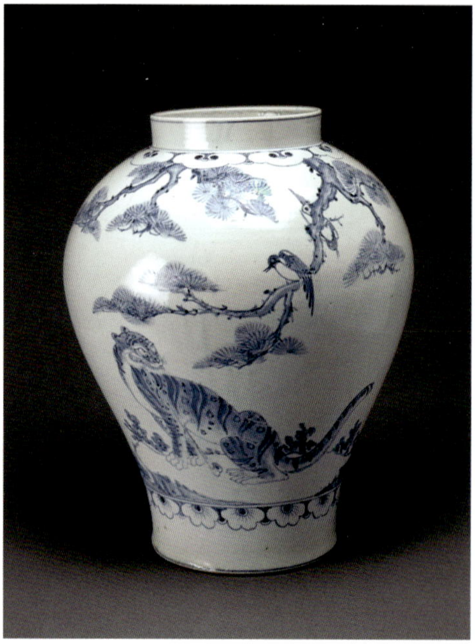

JAR WITH TIGER AND MAGPIE DESIGN

1700–1800
Joseon dynasty (1392–1910)
Porcelain with cobalt decoration under glaze
H. 40.6 cm × Diam. 33 cm
Gift of Mr. Namkoong Ryun, 2001.9

The tiger-and-magpie imagery used on this large jar was a very popular subject in folk paintings throughout the Joseon dynasty (1392–1910). To ring in the New Year many Korean families hung colorful paintings of the tiger and magpie on their walls to ward off misfortune and to be blessed with happiness. While magpies were considered to be harbingers of good news, tigers have always been the most important animal in Korea. The tiger is featured in Korea's foundation myth, is believed to serve the Mountain God (Sansin) as a messenger, and is a protector from evil and harm.

This jar is decorated with the tiger-and-magpie theme on both sides. On one side a magpie on a pine branch and a tiger on the ground appear to be conversing with each other. On the other two magpies are pictured sitting on a pine branch. One seems to be conveying an urgent message to the tiger, who looks up with a surprised expression. This tiger holds a long smoking pipe in its mouth. Korean children's stories used to begin with the phrase, "Once upon a time, long, long ago, when the tiger smoked a pipe."[3] It is easy to imagine the court painter who decorated this porcelain jar at the official kiln in Gwangju, Gyeonggi province, being inspired by this phrase to add a touch of whimsy to his work.

Korea's eighteenth-century kings, Yeongjo (reigned 1724–1776) and Jeongjo (reigned 1776–1800), expressed their concerns over the luxury-loving trend that was sweeping through the country.[4] At the time, porcelain wares decorated with cobalt under the glaze were becoming increasingly popular, and the two kings' concern was presumably prompted by the fact that cobalt was an expensive import from Arab countries via China. However, despite the repeated royal cautioning, it became fashionable among people to own as many porcelain wares with underglaze cobalt, commonly known as the blue-and-white wares, as they could afford. Unlike the simply decorated blue-and-white wares made during the fifteenth and sixteenth centuries, those made during the seventeenth and eighteenth centuries—such as this work—incorporated new designs such as landscapes with figures and various motifs from folk paintings.

—Kumja Paik Kim is former curator of Korean art at the Asian Art Museum of San Francisco.

VIEW OF NONG'EUN VILLA FROM YUKGANG HILL

approx. 1740

By Jeong Seon (Korean, 1676–1759)

Joseon dynasty (1392–1910)

Hanging scroll; ink and colors on silk

H. 29.2 cm × D. 28.6 cm (image)

Acquisition made possible by Dr. and Mrs. David Buchanan, 2000.42

This hanging scroll by Jeong Seon depicts a private estate in Seoul, quietly nestled among trees and mountains, with a stream running to the left. In the foreground, three men and an attendant sit atop a hill overlooking the estate. According to the inscription written by Jeong's friend, the painting depicts the Nong'eun Villa viewed from Yukgang Hill in Seoul. Yukgang Hill was a popular gathering site for poets during the eighteenth century. Jeong signed the painting with his pen name, Gyeomjae, and included two square intaglio seals reading "Jeong" and "Seon."

This painting falls under the genre of "true view" landscape painting in Korea, which Jeong is credited as pioneering. This style encompassed scenery that was genuine to actual Korean landscapes and represented topographies that were culturally significant. Prior to the eighteenth century, Korean landscape painting depicted imaginary landscapes conceived by the artist and derived from Chinese models or Classical Chinese sites. However, during the second half of the Joseon dynasty (1392–1910), the Practical Learning (Silhak) school was formed in response to the abstract and metaphysical teachings of neo-Confucianism. By using realistic approaches to solve social problems, Silhak scholars called for the reexamination of social structure, land reformation, and Korea's national identity and culture. This ignited an interest in native history and geography, which manifested in widespread travel to scenic sites throughout Korea.

Jeong Seon—who was influenced by Silhak—broke away from previous conventions and traveled throughout Korea painting real scenic sites of landscapes and mountains. This painting is a testament to the artist's keen eye and versatile oeuvre in "true view," in which he produced not only monumental, iconic landscapes but also private, intimate scenic views—all of which still exist today in Seoul.

—*HMY*

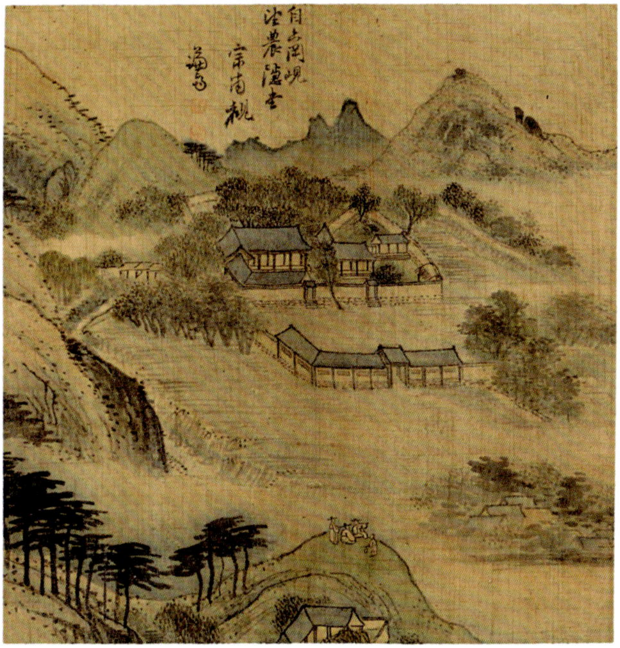

READING DESK WITH "TEN SYMBOLS OF LONGEVITY" MOTIF

1750–1850

Korea

Joseon dynasty (1392–1910)

Lacquer on wood with inlaid mother-of-pearl

H. 26.7 cm × W. 54.6 cm × D. 27.9 cm

Museum purchase, 2016.37

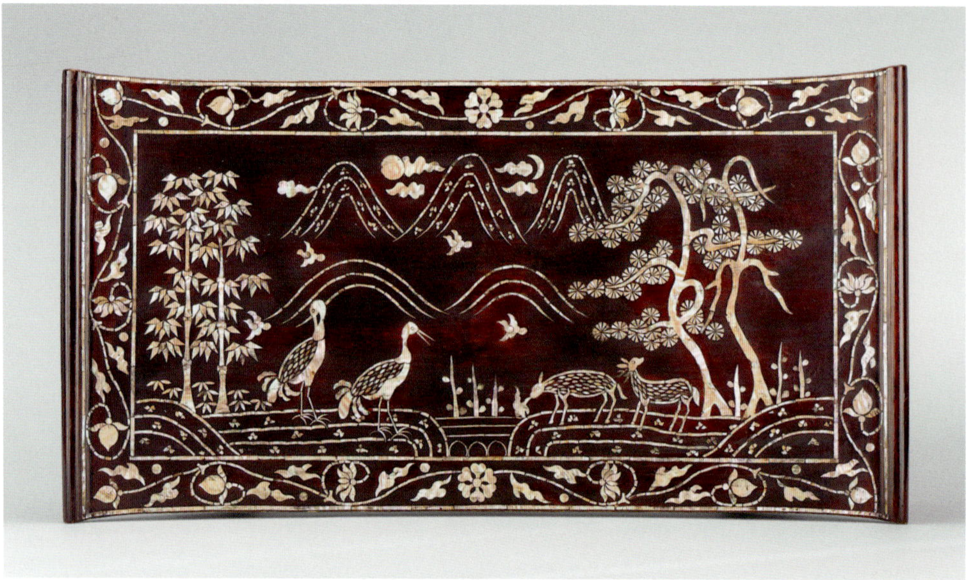

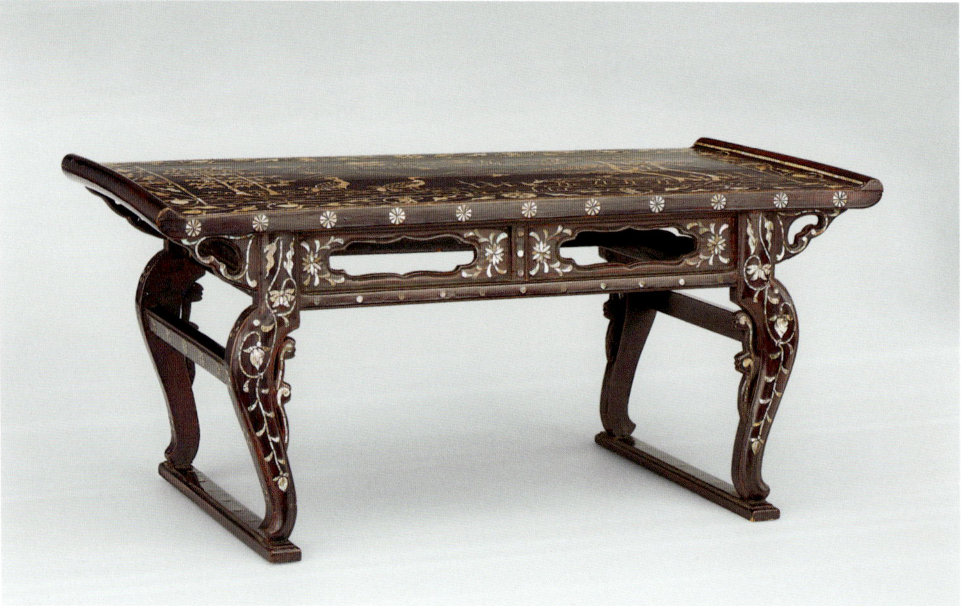

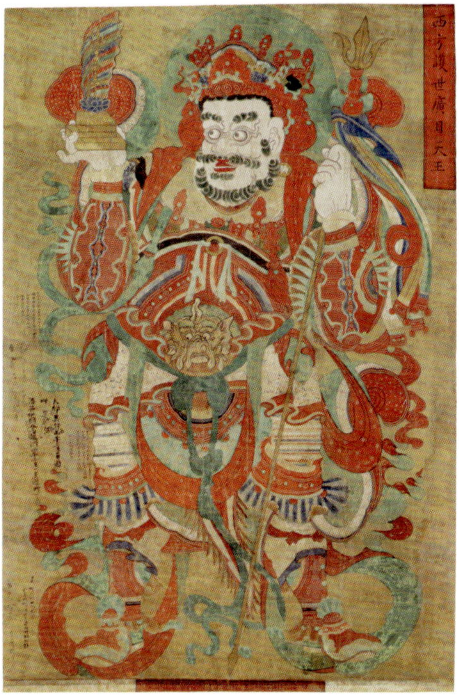

GUARDIAN KING OF THE WEST (GWANGMOK CHEONWANG)

approx. 1796–1850
By Jiyeon and others (Korean)
Joseon dynasty (1392–1910)
Ink and colors on linen
H. 294.6 cm × W. 194 cm (image)
Gift of the Museum Society Auxiliary and the Connoisseurs' Council, 1990.2

The Guardian King of the West (Korean: Gwangmok cheonwang; Sanskrit: Virupaksha) is one of the four heavenly kings who protect the cardinal directions in Buddhist cosmology. As in this huge painting, he usually holds a spear in his left hand and, in his right, a thunderbolt resting on a lotus throne that is encircled by rays of light. In Buddhist temples, paintings of the Four Guardian Kings were often hung behind sculptures of the same figures. They are the first beings that visitors would see when entering a temple, and they were meant to ward off evil spirits and to help visitors prepare to enter the Buddhist world.

The inscription at the upper right reads, "The Heavenly King who sees all and protects the western direction of the world." Judging from several markings written in Classical Chinese and Korean in its lower part, this painting once belonged to Songrim Temple, a subtemple of the Donghwa Monastery in the city of Daegu in southeastern Korea. Some Buddhist devotees who viewed this painting long ago wrote their names and the date in the bottom-left corner, both as commendations and as graffiti. In the red inscription box on the bottom, there is the list of names of artists—including monk painters such as Jiyeon—who participated in creating this painting.

The British Museum owns paintings of the Guardian King of the South and the Guardian King of the North that are similar to this painting. Both of those have Classical Chinese and Korean markings written by viewers. Some of those markings confirm that the British Museum paintings are also from Songrim Temple. Further studies will shed light on all three of these paintings from Songrim Temple as well as on our general understanding of producing huge paintings of Buddhist Guardian Kings during the Joseon dynasty.

—*HKH*

CALLIGRAPHY COUPLET

approx. 1830–1850

By Kim Jeonghui (Korean, 1786–1856)

Joseon dynasty (1392–1910)

Hanging scrolls; ink on paper

H. 143.5 cm × W. 26.7 cm (each image)

Gift of Arthur J. McTaggart, conservation made possible by Korean Art and Culture Committee, 1997.25.1

Kim Jeonghui's calligraphy is bold and decisive, yet carefully controlled. Kim (pen name Chusa) was a Renaissance man of the nineteenth century and one of the most eminent figures in the history of Korea. He was a prominent scholar with numerous followers, an upright politician who was exiled several times, an astute connoisseur with a grand art collection, and an art critic and artist. He was interested in new calligraphic trends in China. Yet he is known for having created his own style of calligraphy, called "Chusa" style, which was not only highly influential in Korea but also respected by contemporaneous Chinese and Japanese scholars. The artistic circle of Kim Jeonghui has been called the "Chusa School," and it included mainstream artists in the nineteenth century. Heo Ryeon, whose rock paintings are discussed in this book (see page 232), was one of the sincere followers of Kim.

The couplet in Classical Chinese is a two-lined poem with the same number of characters in each line:

In my writing, meaning and composition follow no method;
In this aging heart, there ever exist poems.

As is typical of couplet poems with this limited structure, the two lines here have a similar grammatical order and they rhyme with each other. This verse with seven characters per line is written in semicursive script and exhibits Kim's thoughts on literature and life. Although the couplet is not dated, its content and calligraphic style suggest that it was made in Kim's later years. The two rectangular seals on the left line are Kim's. The upper seal is read as *the seal of Kim Jeonghui*. The bottom is read as *Wandang*. Wandang is his other pen name.

In 2011, these scrolls were conserved in Korea and given new mountings. Before the work was treated, it had several horizontal creases as well as contaminated areas and water damage. In addition, the back of the paper had begun to disintegrate. After the treatment, a new mounting adopted an appropriate proportion and format suitable to a nineteenth-century Korean calligraphy work.

—HKH

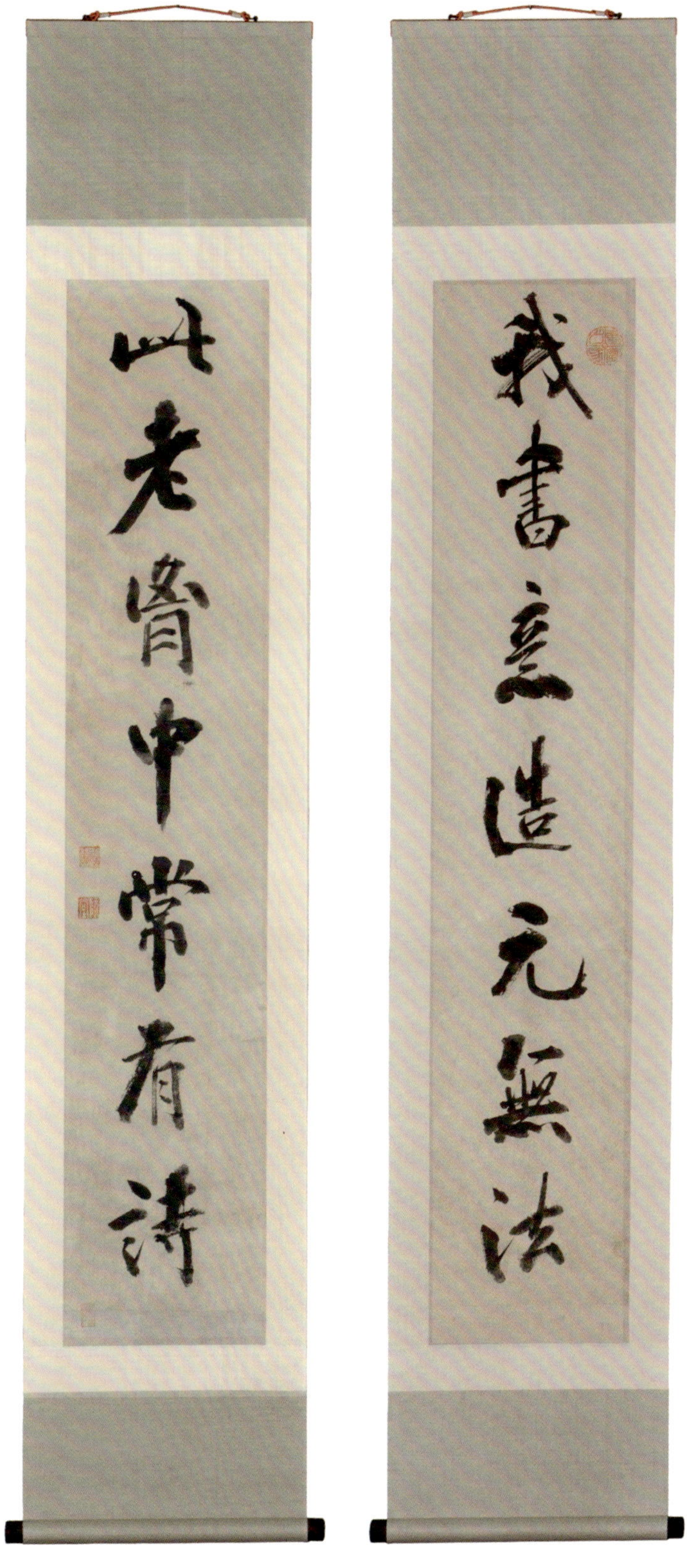

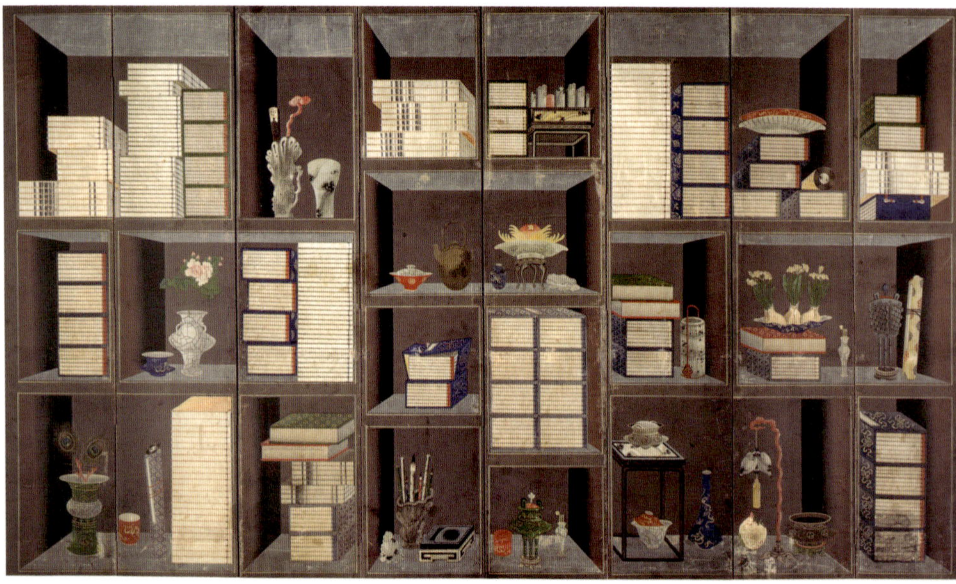

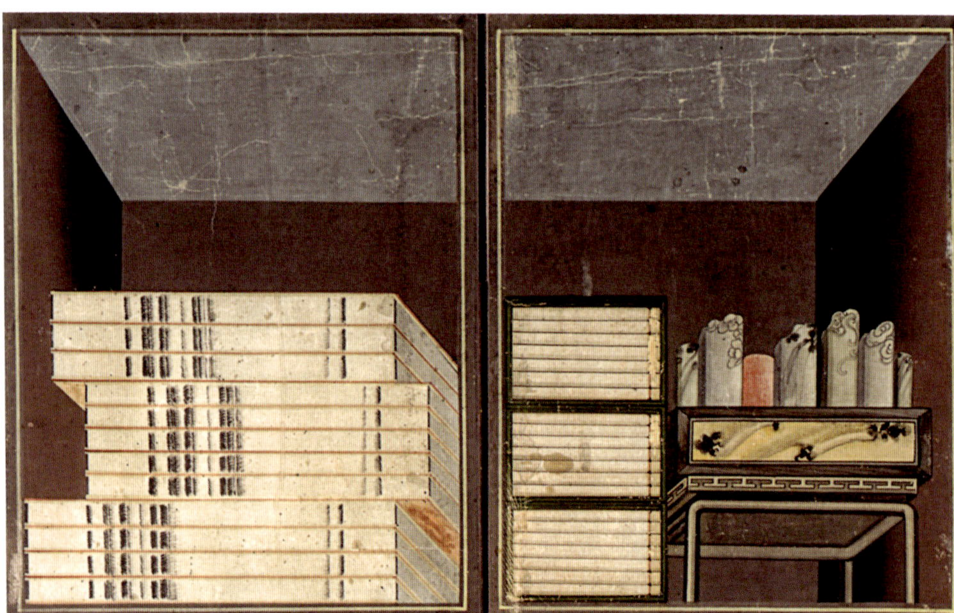

BOOKS AND SCHOLARS' POSSESSIONS (*CHAEKGEORI*)

approx. 1860–1874

By Yi Eungrok (Korean, 1808–after 1874)

Joseon dynasty (1392–1910)

Eight-panel folding screen; ink and colors on paper

H. 164.5 cm × W. 33.9 cm (image)

Acquisition made possible by the Koret Foundation, the Connoisseurs' Council and Korean Art and Culture Committee. Re-mounting funded by the Society for Asian Art, 1998.111

This is the only *chaekgeori* screen in the United States by Yi Eungrok, grandson of Yi Jonghyeon, the founder of the *chaekgeori* genre. *Chaekgeori* are paintings of books and appurtenances on folding screens, used for interior decoration during the latter part of the Joseon period (1392–1910).

In 1986, Gari Ledyard, professor of history at Columbia University, invited me to look at a *chaekgeori* at the C. V. Starr Library. I hastened to New York to find eight hanging scrolls mounted in Japanese silk needing to be restored and remounted—not the expected folding screen.

Determining the identity of the artist and the sequence of the panels proved to be difficult. I recalled a similar ten-panel *chaekgeori* screen in its original mounting at the National Museum of Korea, and I used its symmetrical composition as a model. Unlike most Korean paintings, these works included seals of the artist's name—Yi Eungrok, then an unknown artist—as objects in the painting, not imprints.

In addition to investigating two paintings by Yi Eungrok, painted in 1864 and 1866, I had been trying to learn more about works by two other *chaekgeori* artists: Yi Hyeongnok (active 1827–1863) and Yi Taekkyun (active 1873–1874). Professor Ledyard introduced me to Edward W. Wagner, the founder of Korean Studies at Harvard University. His research led to a breakthrough on the identity of all three painters. He obtained the Hanyang Yu clan genealogy, revealing that all three artists were one and the same, Yi Jonghyeon's grandson! It is believed that the painter changed his name to bring better luck.

Because the Columbia scrolls needed a good deal of money for remounting, and the C. V. Starr Library had no suitable place to display them, the library decided to de-accession them and use the proceeds for Korean studies. Columbia wanted the restored screen to stay in the United States, and art dealer Suzanne Mitchell agreed to broker it for a very modest fee.

Of the seven paintings known to exist by the three identities of Yi Jonghyeon's grandson, six are in Korea. That the Asian Art Museum ended up with the only one in the United States is a result of exhaustive research involving many scholars, dedicated fundraising on the part of the museum, and a little bit of luck.

—Kay E. Black was a research consultant to the Asian Art Department of the Denver Art Museum and has published many essays on Korean art.

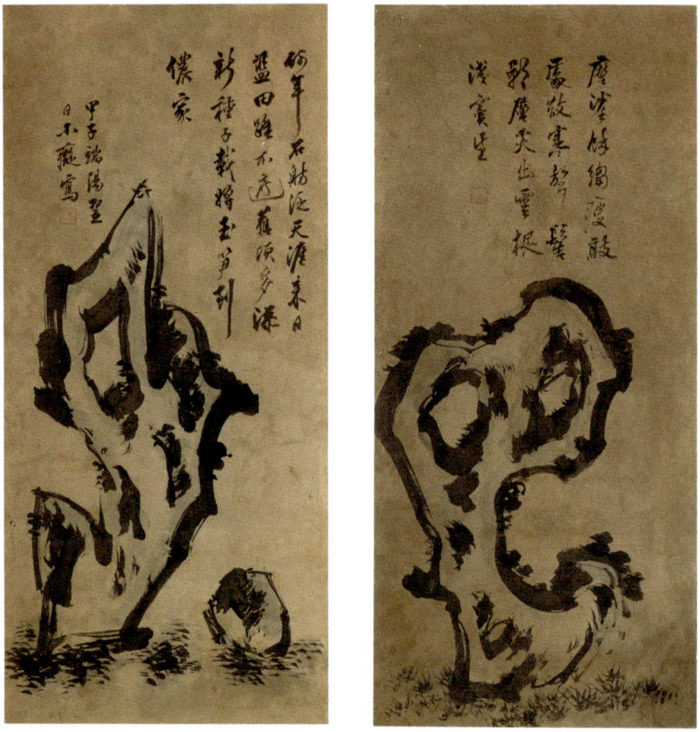

ROCKS

—

1864

By Heo Ryeon (Korean, 1808–1893)

Korea

Joseon dynasty (1392–1910)

Ink on paper

Left: H. 100.6 cm × W. 46.4 cm (image); right: H. 101 cm × W. 46.4 cm (image)

Gift of Ms. Kyong Brotherton in honor of her husband, Joseph Brotherton, 2016.116.1-.2

—

Rocks were favored subjects of scholar-artists during the Joseon dynasty (1392–1910). They were seen, symbolically, as objects that transcended the fragile and inconstant nature of human beings. A rock image could be interpreted as a symbol of the ideal Confucian gentleman scholar, facing difficulties but remaining resilient. Therefore, the subject matter was especially popular during challenging times. During the nineteenth century, when Korea was in political turmoil, rocks were often depicted to express scholar-artists' beliefs and uprightness.

Heo Ryeon's strong brushstrokes and unconventional composition animate the rocks in this pair of paintings. The painter wrote a poem on each scroll regarding the spirit of a true gentleman during hardship. He dated the paintings as 1864, the year he returned to his hometown of Jindo, an island in southwest Korea, and built the Studio of Cloud Forest Mountain (Unrimsanbang). The bold brushstrokes and vividly rendered rocks of this work are exemplary of Heo's style during his later period.

Heo Ryeon was a poet and calligrapher as well as a painter who studied under Kim Jeonghui (1786–1856; see page 228). Kim, one of the greatest artists and theorists in the history of Korea, praised Heo's artistic skills, declaring that "no artist living east of Amnok River [between China and North Korea] comes close to him." King Heonjong (reigned 1834–1849) commissioned Heo to produce many court paintings. Although most of Heo's landscape and plum blossom paintings exist, relatively few rock paintings survive.

—HKH

WRAPPING CLOTH (*BOJAGI*)

—

1950–1960
Korea
Silk
H. 38.1 cm × W. 35.3 cm
Gift of Mr. and Mrs. Edward K. Kang, 1993.7

—

The makers of *jogakbo*—*jogak* means *pieces* and *bo* means *wrapping cloth*—expressed their creativity and emotion with small silk pieces, despite the limitation of the colors and shapes of the fabric with which they worked. Artistic intention is one of the important concepts in modern art. That is why works such as this remain significant and are highlighted today as contemporary fabric art embodying objective aesthetics.

Collecting fabric pieces, ironing, and hand sewing are all time-consuming processes. Particularly, hand sewing is an endless repetition of simple motions. Wrapping-cloth makers concentrate on this motion and empty their minds; only then can they make countless tiny and dense stitches. The traces of needle and thread are the same as those of a handwritten diary. There is a melding of the maker's soul with the work during the time that that it takes to complete it. This imbues *jogakbo* with the thoughts of its maker.

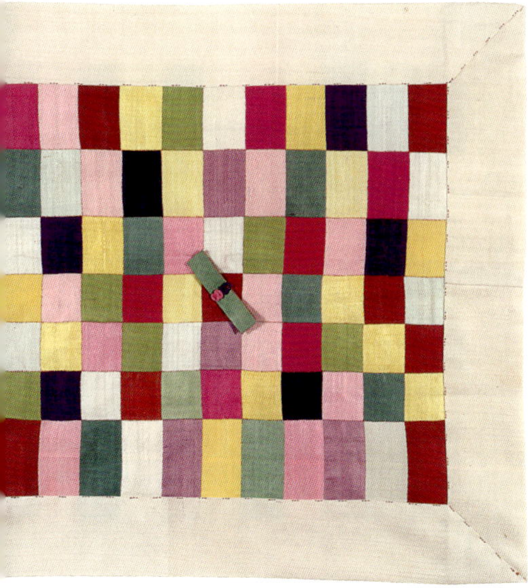

When I stand in front of this work, I can imagine the memories of the artist involved in the process of making it. It is not just a beautifully created silk *jogakbo*; I can see a life story of days and nights working on it.
—*Miran Lee is a* bojagi *and textile artist.*

Growing up in Korea, I hardly paid attention to *bojagi*—Korean wrapping cloths—because of their abundant presence. *Bojagi* were used as wrappers, covers, or storage for objects in daily life, special occasions, and religious rituals.

During the rigidly Confucian society of the Joseon dynasty (1392–1910), women were confined to the inner court of their house. Making *bojagi* was one of the few creative outlets they were permitted, and women poured their artistry into stitching to create beautiful pieces. The act of making *bojagi* carries wishes for the well-being and happiness of its recipient. This labor of love and prayers imbued *bojagi* with a memory of affection.

Jogakbo, patchwork *bojagi* such as this example, embody the philosophy of recycling, as the cloths are made from fabric remnants. Well-considered arrangements of shapes and colors give *bojagi* modern and abstract compositions and show Korean women's creative sensibility.

Today *bojagi* gets attention as a unique form of textile art. The art form is expanding its mediums from fabrics to include fiber, paper, wearable art, architecture, and installations. I hope to continue to find more artistic connections that reflect *bojagi* in our contemporary society.
—*Youngmin Lee is a* bojagi *artist.*

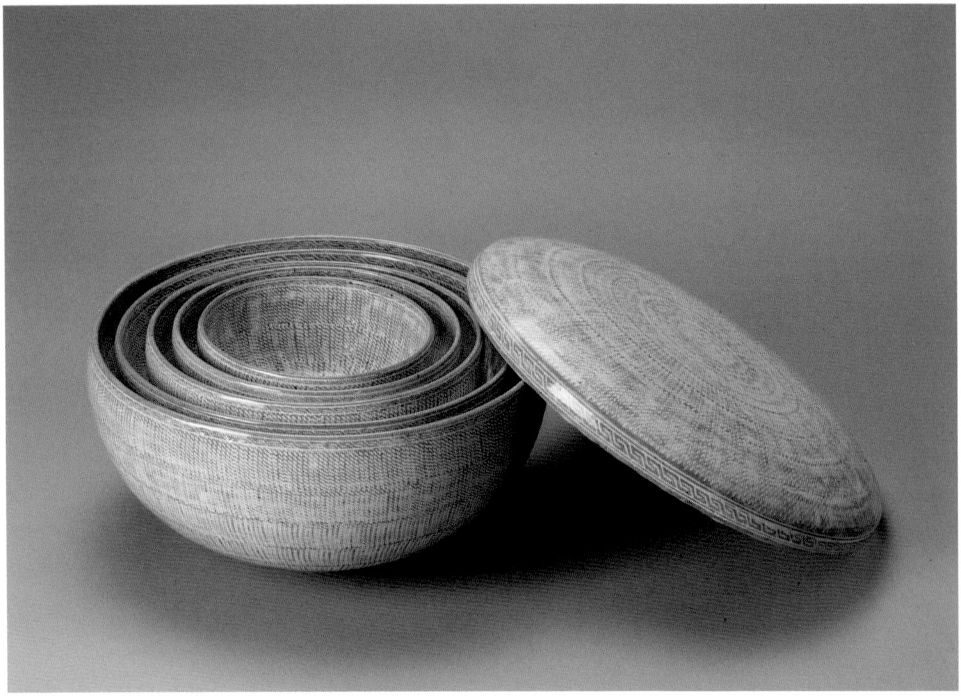

BOWL SET

approx. 1980–2000

By Park Young-sook (Korean, b. 1947)

Korea

Set of five nested bowls with lid; stoneware (buncheong ware)

H. 15.2 cm × Diam. 31.5 cm (overall)

Gift of the artist, 2010.310.a-.f

I first saw this covered nest of bowls in the early 1990s. I was strolling through the Insadong neighborhood of Seoul, stopping at antique shops and art studios, and discovered a small gallery displaying Park Young-sook's ceramics. I liked her work immediately.

Park's work at that time—including this set—was mostly glazed earthenware in shapes and decoration inspired by fifteenth-century buncheong wares, traditional Korean stoneware with white slip. She was very knowledgeable about early buncheong wares, which she used for tea at home.

While the references to buncheong wares in her work were evident, Park made works that were entirely contemporary and fresh in feeling and effect. The individual bowls and cover here have fifteenth-century precedents, but the large scale of the pieces, their concentric nesting, and fine finish are new. Her technical skills are evident in the perfect shaping of these bowls and the evenness of the stamped overall design and the gray-green celadon glaze.

Park makes some very large ceramics and these make a strong impact. And her shapes can be dramatic. Her work can be described as "expressive." The result are ceramics that, while related to the past, are emphatically part of the present.

—Frank S. Bayley III is a collector and friend of the artist Park Young-sook.

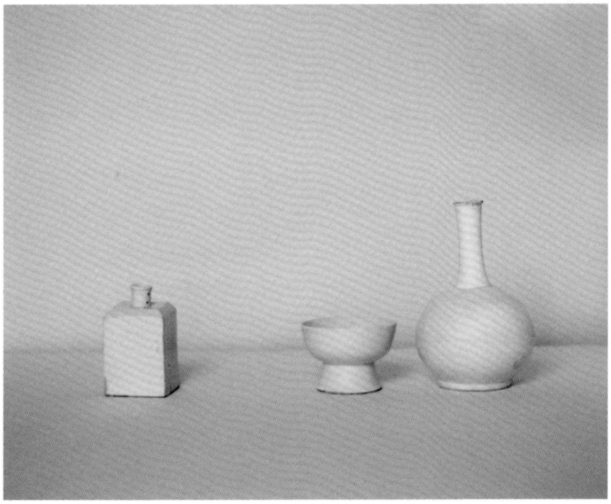

AAM 010

—

2011

By Koo Bohnchang (Korean, b. 1953)

Inkjet print on paper

H. 100 cm × W. 80 cm

Acquisition made possible by Frank S. Bayley, 2013.4

—

Whiteware, one of the most representative cultural assets of the Joseon dynasty (1392–1910), reveals its characteristics at a single glance when juxtaposed next to similar Asian ceramics. Its very essence is seemingly imperfect and naïve, unbiased and embracing beauty. Even I, born and raised in Korea, did not realize the appeal of whiteware until I turned fifty. Perhaps it is because the charm of unadorned whiteware is invisible to those who seek superficial beauty and allure.

During the Japanese colonization period in the early twentieth century, Joseon whitewares were dispersed to Japan and to many other countries. I began my work with the thought of how nice it would be to capture the soul of whiteware through photographs, even though they may not physically be returned to Korea. Since 2004, I have photographed whitewares housed in sixteen museums within my country and abroad.

The Asian Art Museum of San Francisco is a renowned museum housing some of the most representative Asian artworks. I always had an interest in the museum, but it was not until 2013 that I finally obtained permission to photograph whitewares from its Korean collection. Although each piece came into the museum through a different route, they all felt familiar to me—they had sat in silence for a long time, as if they had been waiting for me.

I was amazed to find these whitewares with different functions and uses in harmony, like old friends. The square bottle, round bottle, and cup were displayed in the same space, creating an atmosphere where they seemed to be in conversation with one another. To express Confucian virtues of the Joseon dynasty, which made a point to conceal one's inner desires, I used soft light so the lines and forms of the whitewares were not too strongly visible. And by focusing on specific sections of the ceramics, I tried to give them a fantastical quality, almost as if they were floating. The purpose of photographing the Korean whitewares was to accurately depict their shape and texture; however, I tried to capture the hidden presence found within them.

The whitewares I photographed in San Francisco are greatly appreciated by countless visitors in this faraway country of Korea. A portion of their essence is captured in my camera and will continue to emit the joy of encountering them to many people in the home country that they left a hundred years ago, or perhaps only decades ago. *—Koo Bohnchang is a photographer (text translated by HMY).*

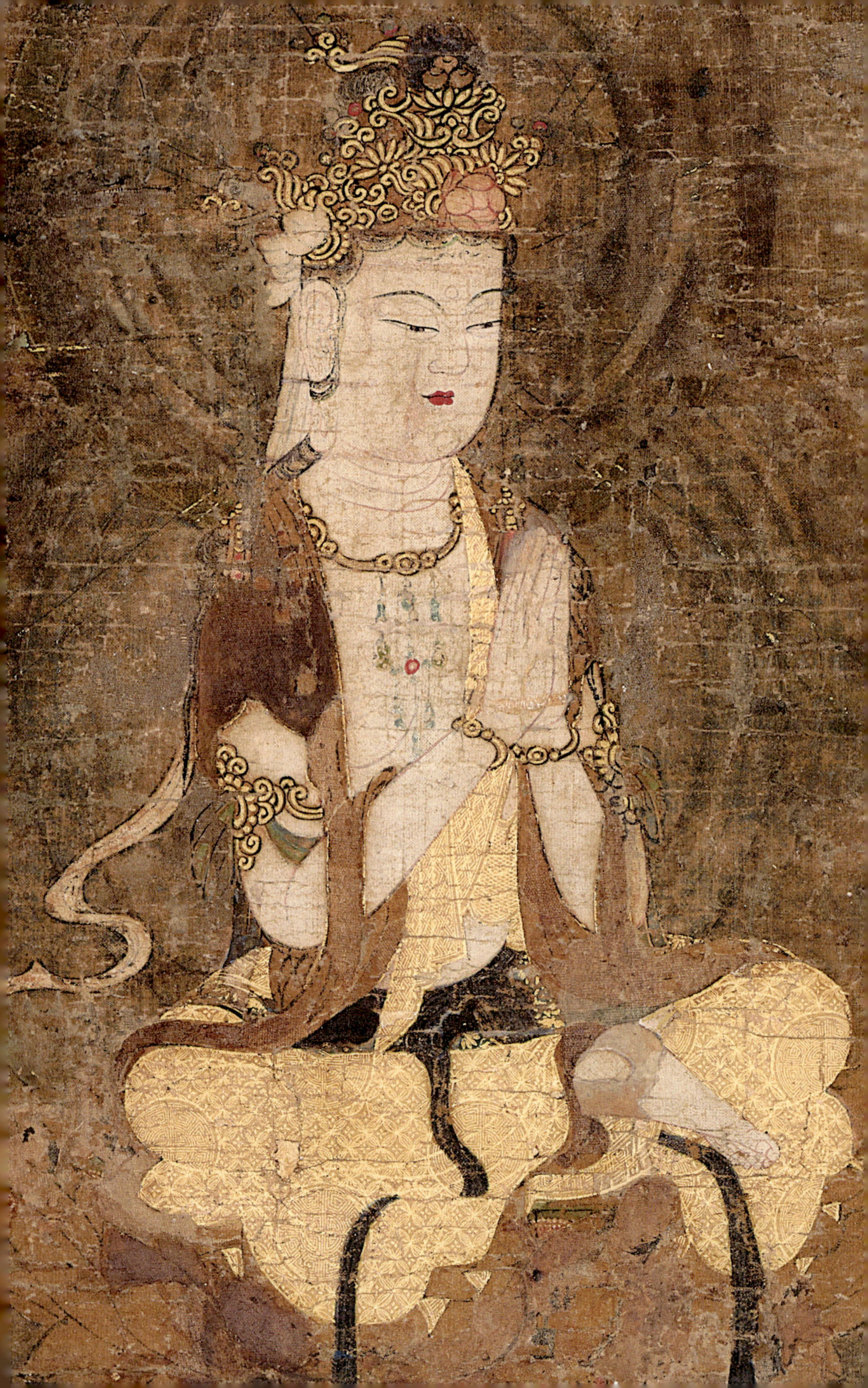

JAPAN

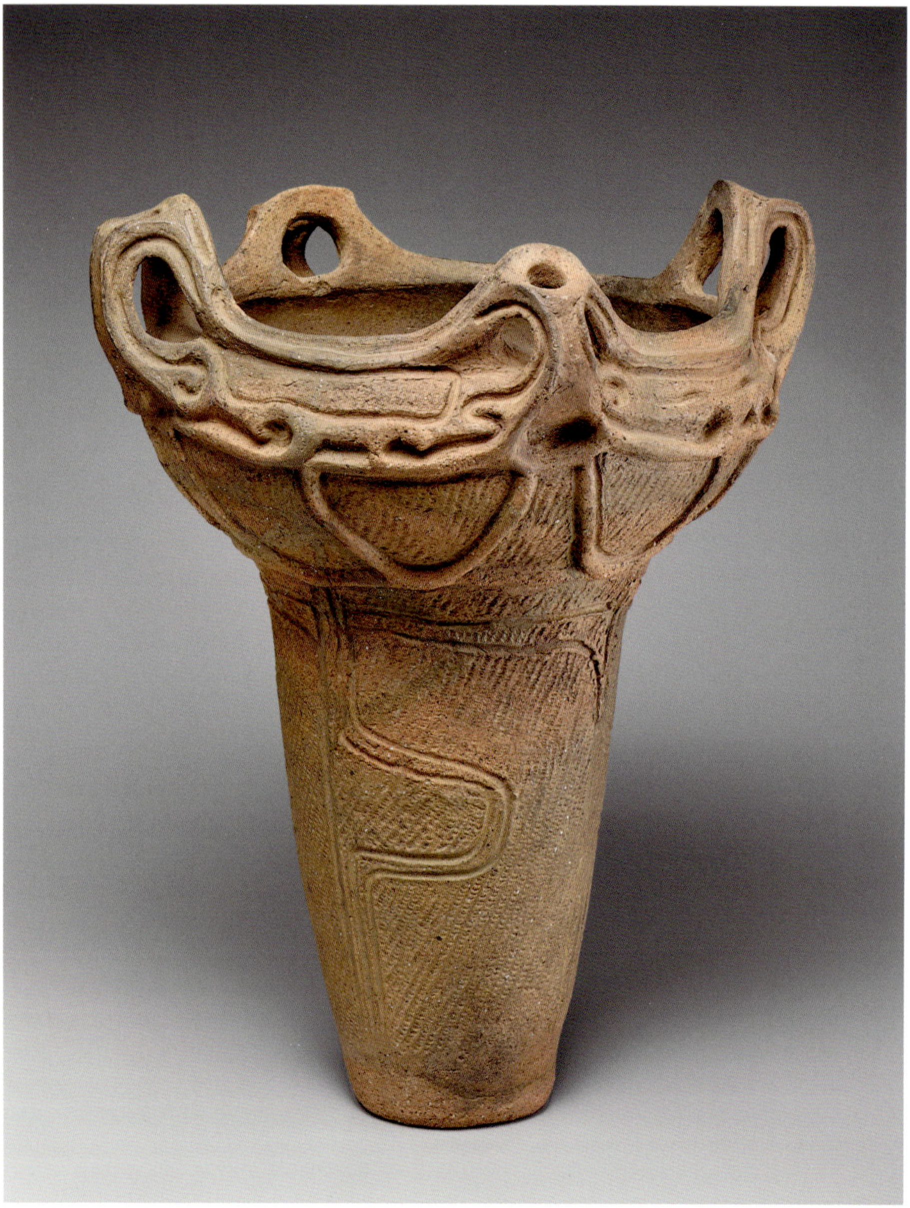

JAR WITH HANDLE-LIKE ORNAMENTATION

3000–2000 BCE

Japan; Kanto region

Jomon period (10,500–300 BCE)

Earthenware

H. 45 cm × Diam. 36.8 cm

The Avery Brundage Collection, B60P932

BELL-SHAPED RITUAL OBJECT (*DOTAKU*)

100–200

Japan; Oiwayama, Koshinohara, Yasu, Shiga prefecture

Yayoi period (300 BCE–250 CE)

Bronze

H. 62.2 cm × W. 30 cm × D. 24.1 cm

The Avery Brundage Collection, B60B14+

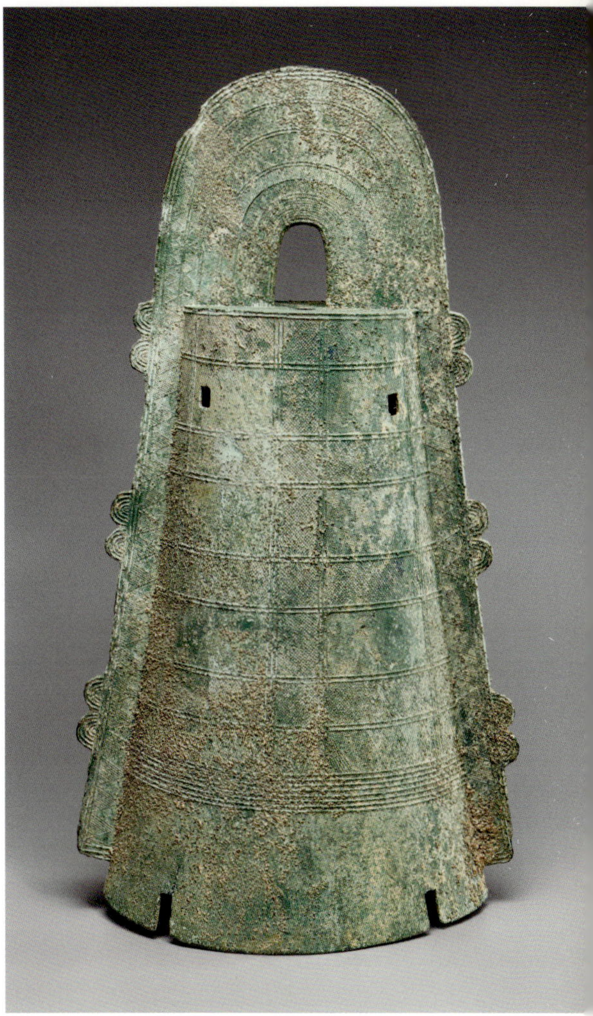

In 1881, two teenage boys accidentally discovered a group of fourteen *dotaku*, bell-shaped bronze ritual objects, on Oiwayama, a hill in Shiga prefecture. Standing an impressive 62.2 cm tall, the Asian Art Museum *dotaku* was part of this find. The largest example excavated from the site, a massive, 134.7-cm-tall *dotaku*, is now housed at the Tokyo National Museum. Another ten *dotaku* were unearthed at Oiwayama in 1962, bringing the total to twenty-four.

Many *dotaku* were interred together, on their sides, nestled one within another in an intentional act of respect or protection. Why were they buried, and with such care? In the absence of written records, the answers remain elusive. Scholars believe people of the Yayoi period (300 BCE–250 CE) used *dotaku* in communal rituals tied to agricultural production. Though details of their function remain obscure, the scale and ornamentation of the Oiwayama *dotaku* attest to their status as important ceremonial objects. With large, well-balanced forms, fine decoration, and relatively thin walls, they are the products of dedicated resources and skill, using the advanced casting technology of the later Yayoi period.

Like others from the site, this example has a hollow, conical form of oval cross section, surmounted by a flat, semicircular handle that continues in thin flanges protruding from each side of the body. Six double-hemisphere ornaments project from the flanges; three more once adorned the handle, but are missing today. The decoration continues in raised intersecting crosshatched bands that frame eight panels on each side. The lowest panels are filled with sawtooth patterns, which are repeated on the flanges and in bands on the handle. Notches and holes in the top and sides were used to connect parts of a clay mold during casting.

—*LWA*

FOOTED JAR DECORATED WITH MINIATURE JARS AND ANIMAL HEADS

500–552
Japan
Kofun period (250–552)
Stoneware with natural ash glaze (Sue ware)
H. 45.7 cm × W. 27.9 cm × D. 27.3 cm
The Avery Brundage Collection, B60P537

This vessel's complex, sophisticated form is characteristic of the wares made for ritual purposes in Japan's late Kofun period (250–552). Pieced together from multiple wheel-thrown parts, it has a spherical body set on a high, flaring base perforated with geometric openings. The cutouts are arranged in three bands divided by rows of incised lines; two rows of rectangular slits, aligned one above the other, alternate with triangles in the lowest zone. Above the swelling body, the jar's neck flares outward. The lip is indented, with a thinly potted, upright rim that suggests that the jar was once covered by a separate lid, now lost. Perched on the shoulder are four miniature jars with animal heads between them.

Vessels of this type are known as Sue ware. They were fired in the first climbing kilns, or *anagama*, to be built in Japan. The sloping floor of the *anagama* kiln allows heat to travel upward from a firebox at its base. The potters making Sue ware were able to achieve firing temperatures over 1,000°C, which hardened the clay and gave it the characteristic blue-gray color seen here. (Reddish pottery for everyday use, called Haji ware, was also made during the Kofun period.) The yellowish streaks and green rivulets that run down one side of this vessel were caused by natural kiln ash that fused and vitrified during firing.

Similar footed jars, also of gray stoneware, were made in Korea during the fifth and sixth centuries. At the time when this work was made, there were frequent contacts between Japan and Korea by sea. Both the forms and technical knowledge used in making Sue wares are thought to have been transmitted from Korea by immigrants or through trade. The Gaya Federation, at the southern end of the Korean peninsula, was close to Japan, and Gaya likely provided models for vessels like this one.[1] This is but one example of Japan's close ties to its neighbor in the sixth century; in 552, Buddhism was officially introduced to Japan by monks from Baekje in southwest Korea.
—*LWA*

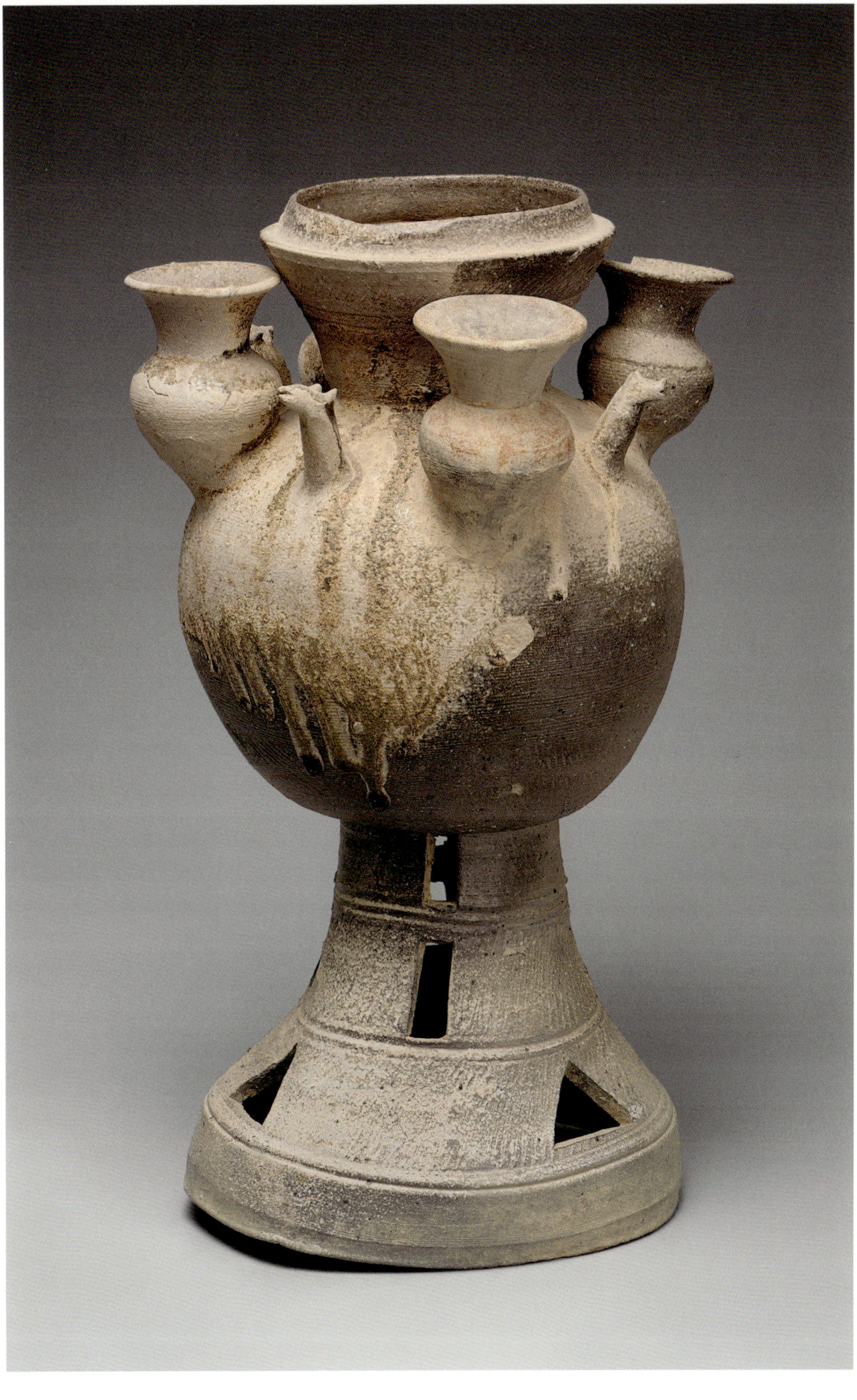

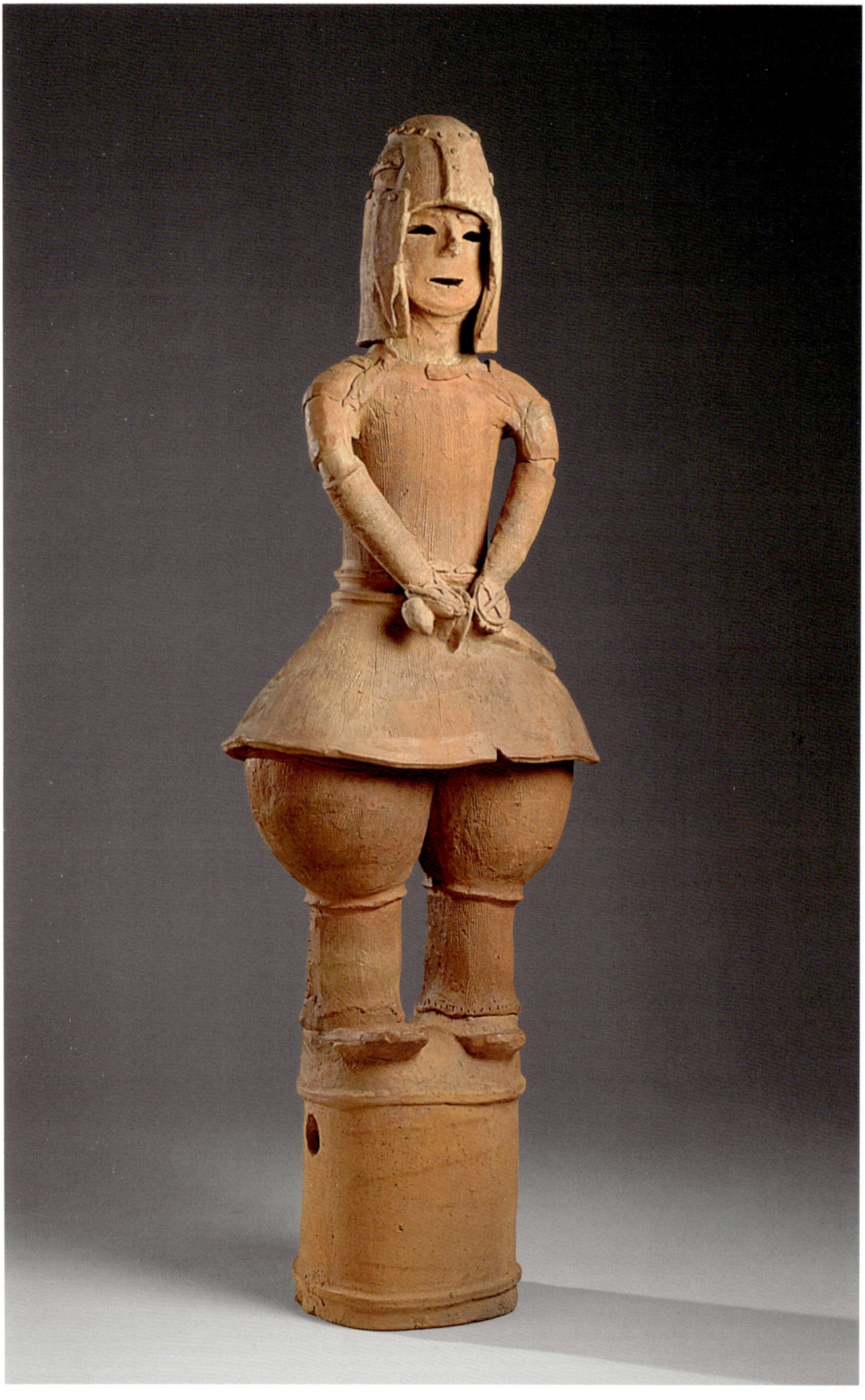

HANIWA IN THE FORM OF A WARRIOR

—

approx. 500–552
Japan; Fujioka, Gunma prefecture
Kofun period (250–552)
Earthenware
H. 120.7 cm × W. 41.9 cm
The Avery Brundage Collection, B60S204

—

This warrior, made of low-fired clay, stands at attention, poised as if preparing to draw his sword. His armor and weaponry match similar armaments buried within tombs during Japan's sixth century. A riveted keeled helmet sits on his head, while plated shoulder guards and gauntlets protect his tube-like arms. The warrior's body is draped in a suit of sleeveless lamellar armor, which flares into a wide armored skirt below his belted waist. Below the skirt he wears oversized pantaloons, gathered by a sculpted cord at the knee. In contrast to the detailed treatment of his equipment, his facial features are rendered in an elegant expedience: crescent-shaped holes form his eyes and a captivating smile, a triangular projection fashions his nose, and thin strips of clay delineate his eyebrows.

Lamellar-clad ceramic warriors drawing their swords have been found at several mid-sixth-century Japanese tombs in the Kanto region of Honshu. Their standardized military equipment and simple facial features enabled their mass production, which was likely performed by a single workshop operating within Gunma prefecture.[2] Figures like this are known as haniwa, a term used for the remarkable tomb sculptures produced during Japan's Kofun period (250–552).

The name Kofun is derived from the practice of constructing funerary mounds, termed *kofun* (literally "old tomb"), for Japan's social elite. The most impressive *kofun* date to the third through fifth centuries and take the form of enormous keyhole-shaped mounds. Early tombs of this era featured rows of cylindrical haniwa arranged around a central burial pit. In later tombs these works encircled the terraced sides of *kofun*, and by the mid-fifth century sculptures shaped as humans—such as warriors, shamanesses, and entertainers—began to appear. Rows of haniwa, sometimes numbering in the hundreds or thousands at larger *kofun*, circumscribed tomb mounds to serve as a demarcation, separating and protecting the sacred area of the grave from the outside world, and as means of displaying the wealth and authority of the deceased. At some tombs, haniwa were positioned to create elaborate dioramas, which have been variously interpreted as depicting funerary rituals or the journey of the dead to the afterlife.

The detailed emphasis on this haniwa's weaponry and armor suggests that the sculpture is important as a representative warrior rather than as an individualized portrait. Given the lack of Kofun-era texts, however, the specific ritual significance of this grinning warrior remains a mystery.[3]

—Carl Gellert is a PhD candidate at the University of California, Berkeley, studying prehistoric and early Japanese art.

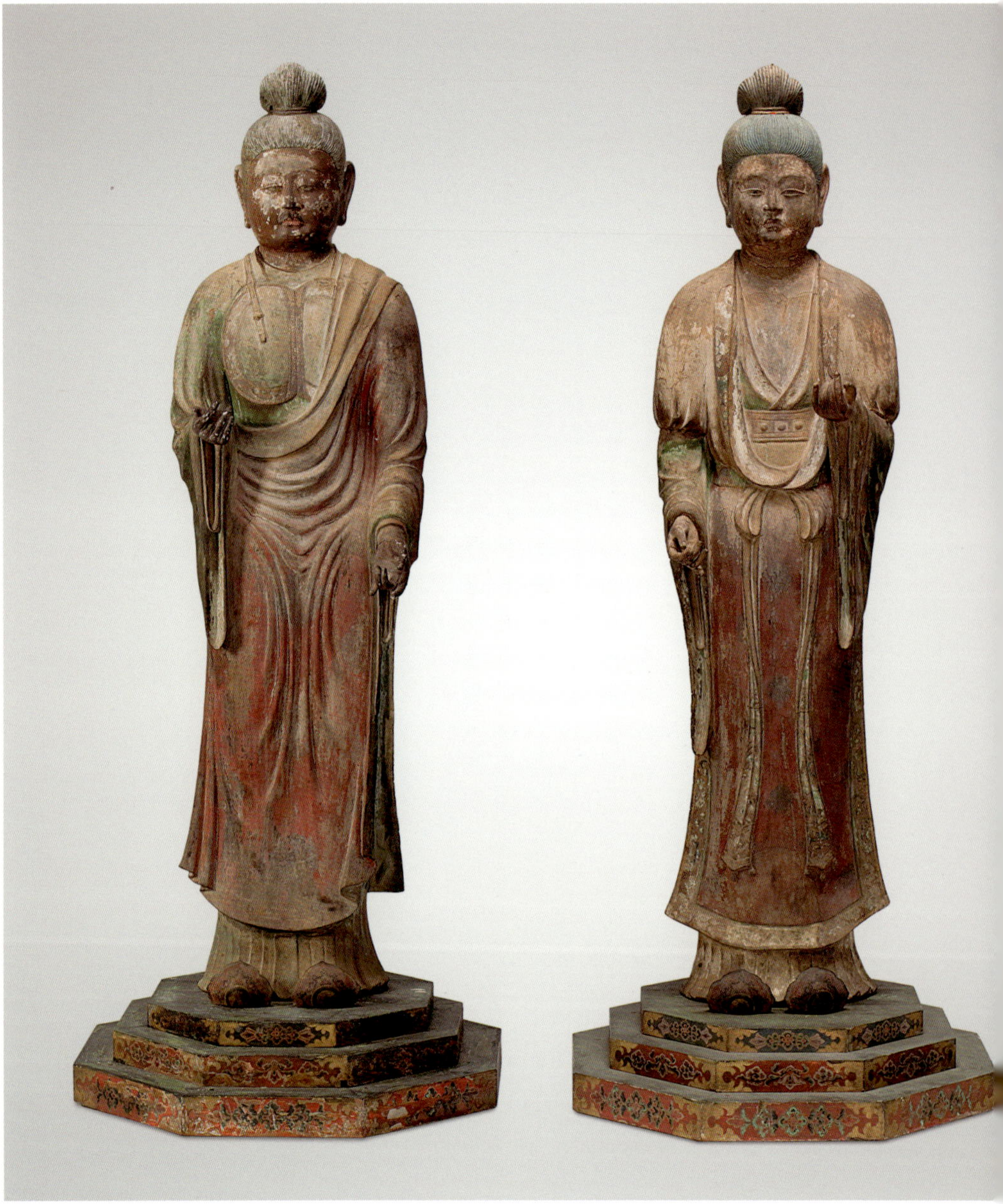

MASTERPIECE

THE DEITIES BRAHMA AND INDRA (BONTEN AND TAISHAKUTEN)

approx. 730–750
Japan; Nara
Nara period (710–794)
Hollow dry lacquer
The Avery Brundage Collection, B65S12 and B65S13

Brahma and Indra are Hindu gods who were incorporated into Buddhist mythology as attendants of the Buddha. In Japan, where they are known as Bonten (right) and Taishakuten (left), the pair typically appear as attendants to Shakyamuni (Shaka), the historical Buddha. The statues shown here were made in the eighth century, when iconographic and stylistic models from China were carefully followed in Japan's capital, then located at Nara.

The hollow dry lacquer technique used to make the statues involved creating a clay core around wooden supports, then layering lacquer-coated hemp cloth on the damp surface. Once dry, the lacquer shell was cut and the clay core removed. The surfaces were detailed using a lacquer and sawdust paste, then the entire surface was painted. This laborious method produced durable yet lightweight works with naturalistic modeling and color. Yet perhaps because of its expense, the technique was abandoned after about a hundred years, making such sculptures rare today.

Modern records about this pair go back to the early 1900s, when Kofukuji, a prominent Nara temple, sought to raise funds for temple repairs by selling some of its treasures. Masuda Takashi (1848–1938), a wealthy industrialist and collector, acquired the statues, heavily damaged at the time. By 1927 the pair had been expertly restored using the dry lacquer method. The Masuda family kept them until 1965, when Avery Brundage (1887–1975) acquired them for the museum.[4] Scholars have debated the degree to which the modern restoration preserves the original appearance of the statues. Most recently, scientific testing and study have raised the possibility that the statues' heads, which are missing (Taishakuten) and heavily damaged (Bonten) in a photo from the time of the Kofukuji sale, might have been restored in part with original fragments from the statues, separately preserved at the temple. Further research is necessary to confirm these findings.

Our dating of the statues is based on similarities to a notable set of hollow dry lacquer statues (the eight devas and ten disciples) made for Kofukuji's West Golden Hall between 733 and 738, and a much larger dry lacquer Bonten and Taishakuten pair owned by Todaiji temple in Nara and dating to the mid-eighth century.

—*LWA*

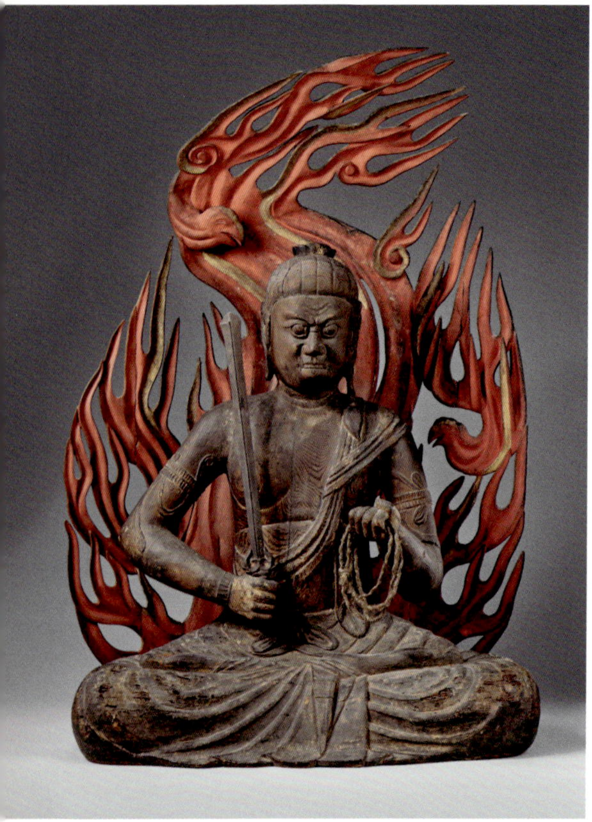

THE BUDDHIST DEITY ACHALA VIDYARAJA (FUDO MYOO)

1100–1185
Japan
Heian period (794–1185)
Wood with colors
H. 151.1 cm × W. 105.4 cm × D. 58.4 cm (figure with flames)
The Avery Brundage Collection, B60S146+

Why does this Buddhist figure, unlike the many Buddha and bodhisattva figures depicted in calm repose, appear angry? While this fierce image seems contradictory to Buddhist teachings, he is not a personification of evil. His aggressive appearance symbolizes his ability to ward off iniquity. He is believed to protect Buddhism and its true followers from evil forces. A sword in his right hand repels enemies and cuts through delusions, while a rope in his left binds evildoers who would block the path to enlightenment.

Achala Vidyaraja (Japanese: Fudo Myoo), whose name means "the immovable one," sits in front of a halo of swirling fire with which he burns down all obstacles and cleanses away evil. The heads of Garuda (Karura), fire-breathing mythical birds, emerge from the fire; their outstretched wings are expressed by the flames. Fudo's long hair is pulled to his left in one bundle before his left shoulder. His eyes are wide open and his sharp fangs protrude upward from the corners of his mouth.

As one of the Five Great Kings (Godai Myoo), Fudo is a manifestation of the central cosmic Buddha Mahavairochana (Dainichi), an idealization of the truth of the universe. Fudo is the principal deity invoked during the fire ritual called *goma*. Like his flaming halo, the consecrated fire set alight during the ritual spiritually cleanses believers, allowing them to attain tranquility and harmony. This ritual is still performed today at temples such as Toji in Kyoto.
—*YM*

SEATED AMITABHA BUDDHA (AMIDA NYORAI)

approx. 1150–1185
Japan
Heian period (794–1185)
Wood with lacquer and gilding
H. 88.9 cm × W. 73.6 cm × D. 78.7 cm (figure); H. 67.3 cm × W. 109.2 cm × D. 111.8 cm (base)
The Avery Brundage Collection, B60S10+

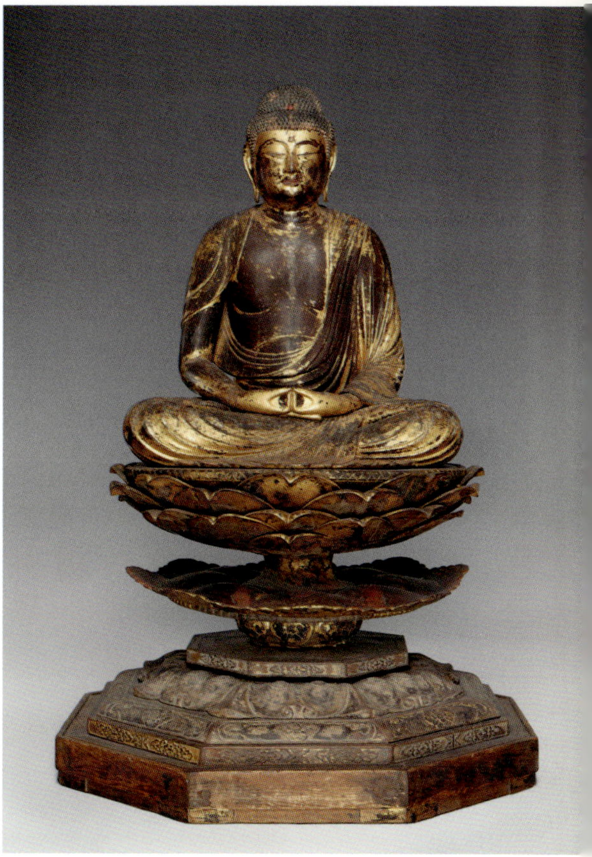

Seated on a tiered lotus pedestal, Amida, Buddha of Infinite Light, folds his hands in the gesture of meditation. His expression is tranquil, his eyes partially closed in contemplation. This peaceful and reassuring image embodies Amida's compassion and his promise of escape from suffering.

Faith in Amida was popularized in tenth-century Japan through the writings of the monk Genshin (942–1017), who taught that meditation and repetition of Amida's name would ensure a devotee's rebirth in the Pure Land, also known as the Western Paradise. For most people, the alternative to salvation by Amida was to remain in the cycle of rebirth in the Six Realms, whose lowest levels were described by Genshin in frightening, lurid detail.

As devotion to Amida flourished, there was great demand for image halls as ritual settings for Pure Land worship. These halls, which were built at large temples and on the grounds of private villas, were equipped with gilded statues of Amida, often accompanied by other images of his heavenly entourage. In one well-documented case, the surviving eleventh-century Byodoin (Phoenix Hall), a magnificent gilded Amida was surrounded by colorful decorations and vivid paintings of Amida's descent to earth to transport devotees back to the Pure Land. Written accounts from the Heian period (794–1185) suggest that some worshipers died holding cords attached to the hands of Amida images, a deathbed ritual detailed in Genshin's writings.[5]

The statue shown here was created using the joined wood method (*yosegi zukuri*), in which parts of the body were carved separately and joined. Perfected by Jocho (d. 1057), the sculptor of the Byodoin Amida, the technique was transmitted through several generations of followers. Though this statue adheres to prototypes established by Jocho, its compact proportions and slanted eyes, the method of joining blocks at the center (*shochu hagi*), and the fact that separate curls of hair are attached to the head point to a late twelfth-century date. Once covered from head to toe in gold leaf, the flaking surfaces now reveal a dark lacquer underlayer.
—*LWA*

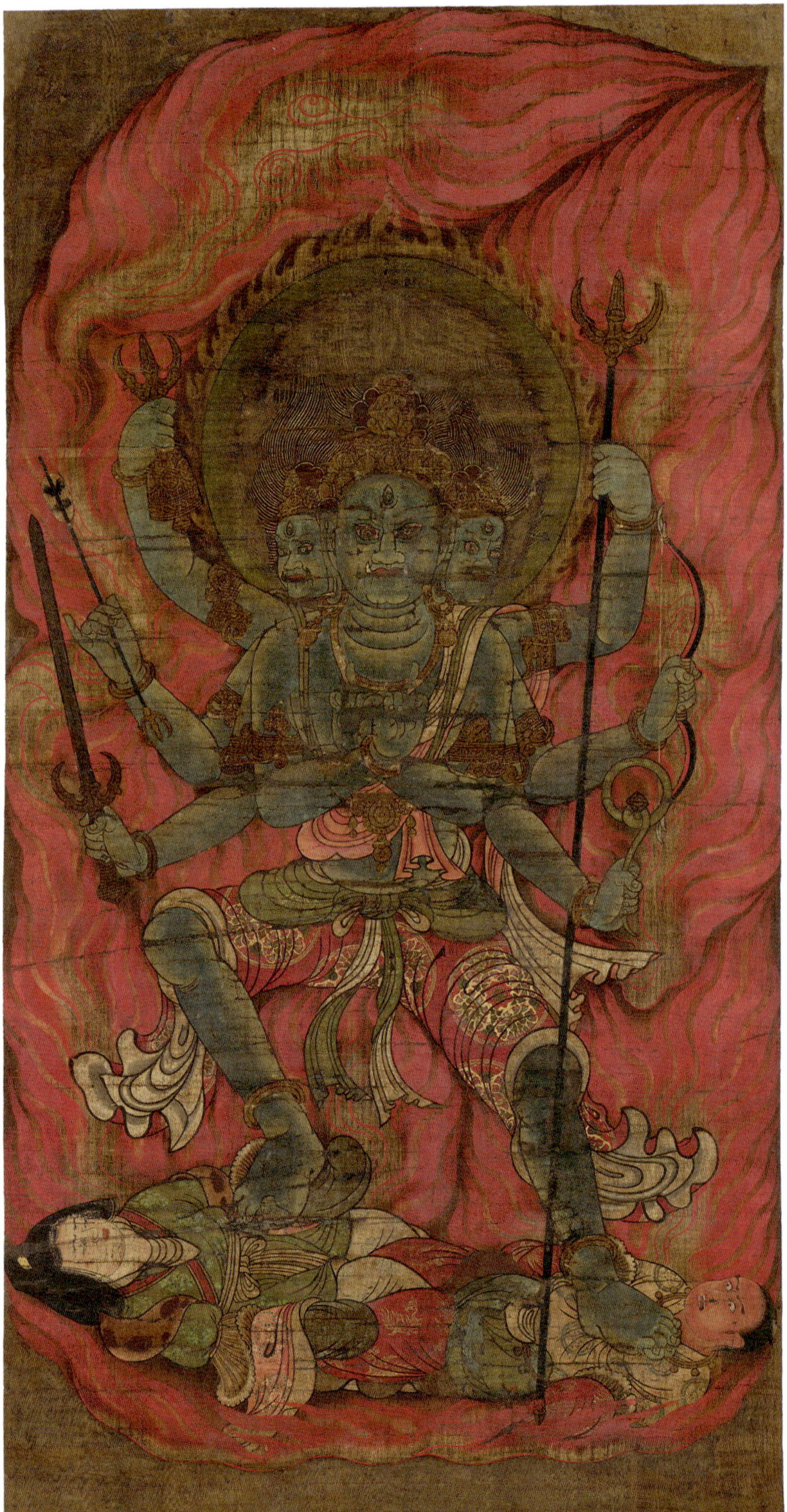

THE BUDDHIST DEITY TRAILOKYAVIJAYA (GOZANZE MYOO)

1250–1300

Japan

Kamakura period (1185–1333)

Hanging scroll; ink and colors on silk

H. 107.3 cm × W. 57 cm (image)

Gift and Purchase from the Harry G. C. Packard Collection Charitable Trust in honor of Dr. Shujiro Shimada; The Avery Brundage Collection, 1991.57

A multiheaded god with an angry expression, violent weapons in his many hands, squashes two bodies underfoot, surrounded by red-hot flames. The imagery in this seven-hundred-year-old Japanese painting is clear. This deity is aggressive and armed to the teeth, and he stands on top of two others to subdue them. The flames tell us this is a dangerous place to be. Anyone viewing this image can grasp the basic story behind it.

The painting was made during a time when Buddhist and Hindu ideas were intricately intermingled. This multiarmed figure is the wrathful form of Vajrapani, a guardian of the Buddha, who subjugates the rival tradition, here embodied by the Hindu deity Shiva and his consort. In Japan, this deity is called Gozanze Myoo (Sanskrit: Trailokyavijaya). His name means "Victor of the Three Realms"—earth, air, and heaven. The painting may have helped Buddhist practitioners visualize themselves as the deity while meditating and trampling down their own limitations, such as greed or anger.

My colleague at the Asian Art Museum who has young children suggested we create a tour of all the images in our collection with bodies squashed underfoot. We could just hear kids exclaiming, "Feet are gross!" This universal symbol of insult and brash conquest exists in about fifteen artworks currently on view at the museum. Next time you find yourself at a museum, see how many you can spot.

—*DCl*

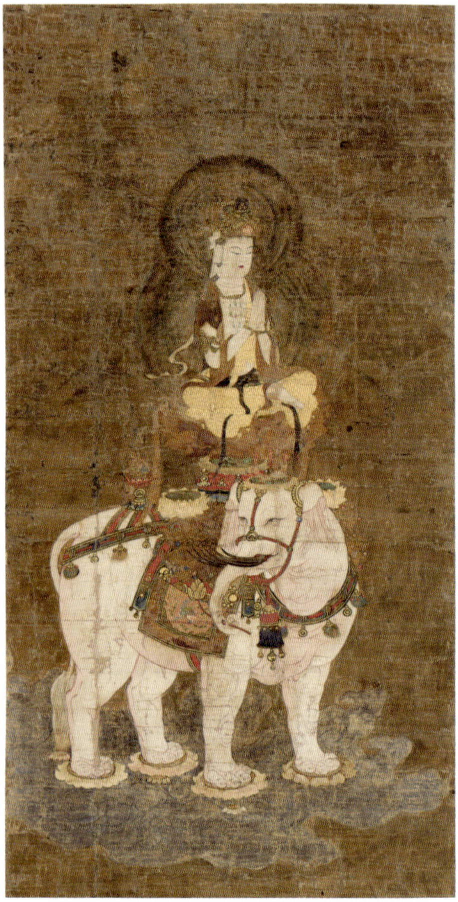

THE BODHISATTVA SAMANTABHADRA (FUGEN BOSATSU)

—

1200–1300
Japan
Kamakura period (1185–1333)
Hanging scroll; ink, colors, and gold on silk
H. 71.1 cm × W. 36.8 cm (image)
The Avery Brundage Collection, B66D2

—

The bodhisattva Samantabhadra (known in Japan as Fugen) is here shown in his role as protector of those who honor the Lotus Sutra, one of Mahayana Buddhism's most influential texts. Seated on a lotus pedestal, Fugen descends to earth on the back of a cloud-borne elephant. The scriptural source for this image comes from Chapter 28, added to the sutra by adherents of the Tendai sect:

> Whether that person is walking or standing, if he reads and recites this sutra, then at that time I will mount my six-tusked kingly white elephant and with my multitude of great bodhisattvas will proceed to where he is.[6]

The elephant's six tusks represent the six perfections, or paramitas, mentioned in the Lotus Sutra and other texts.[7] Fugen's radiance is expressed through the golden light that emanates from his body, by his gold jewelry, and by the intricate cut-gold-leaf (*kirikane*) patterns that embellish his robes. Fugen's right-facing orientation suggests that this might be the surviving left-hand scroll of a triptych with the Buddha Shakyamuni (Shaka) at center and bodhisattva Manjushri (Monju) at right. If so, the iconography is unusual: other intact triads typically show Fugen holding a lotus rather than with hands clasped in prayer, as seen here.

Stylistic features place this painting in the Kamakura period (1185–1333), when faith in the Lotus Sutra was strong among Japan's elite. The sutra includes women among the beings with potential to attain buddhahood, and aristocratic women were among its fervent devotees. Fugen is pictured in numerous paintings of the time, both alone and surrounded by women in Chinese- or Japanese-style court costumes: the Ten Rakshasi (Ju Rasetsunyo, or "ten demons"), who are revered as guardians of adherents to the Lotus Sutra. Scholar Miya Tsugio speculates that women may have sponsored such paintings "as an outgrowth of their particular interest in the sutra."[8] Was female veneration of Fugen a factor behind the popularity of paintings like this one? What role did such images play in the religious life of women? We look to future scholarship on the role of women in Buddhism to provide answers to these important questions.

—*LWA*

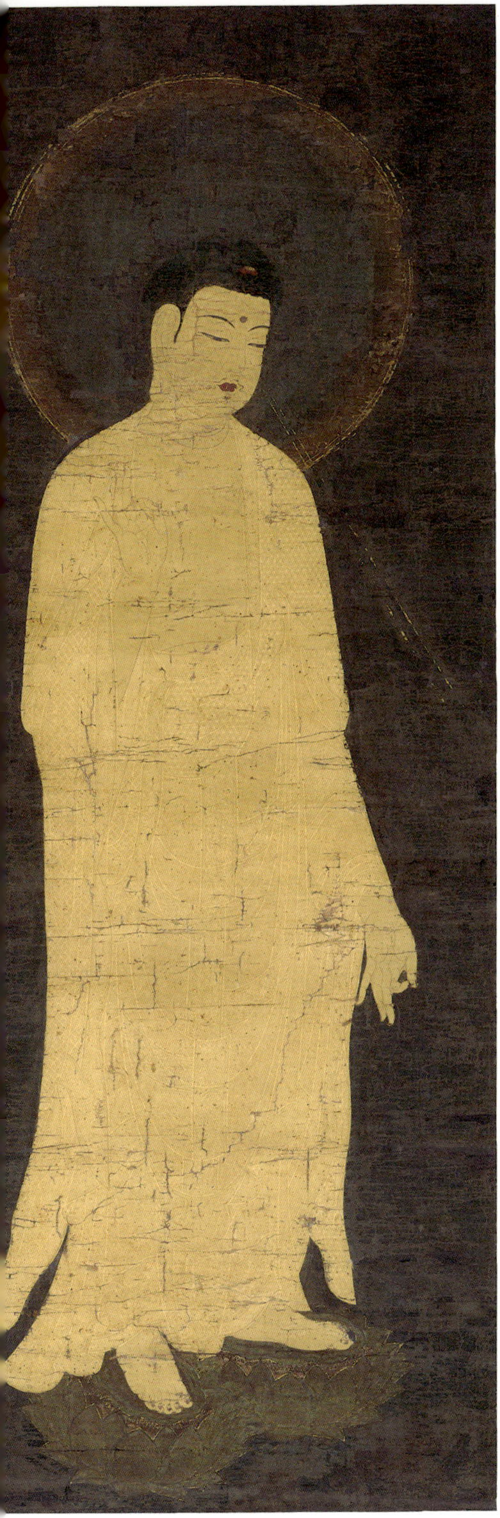

THE DESCENT OF THE BUDDHA AMITABHA (AMIDA)

1300–1400

Japan

Kamakura (1185–1333), Nanbokucho (1333–1392), or

Muromachi period (1392–1573)

Hanging scroll; ink, colors, and gold on silk

H. 98.1 cm × W. 38.7 cm (image)

The Avery Brundage Collection, B64D7

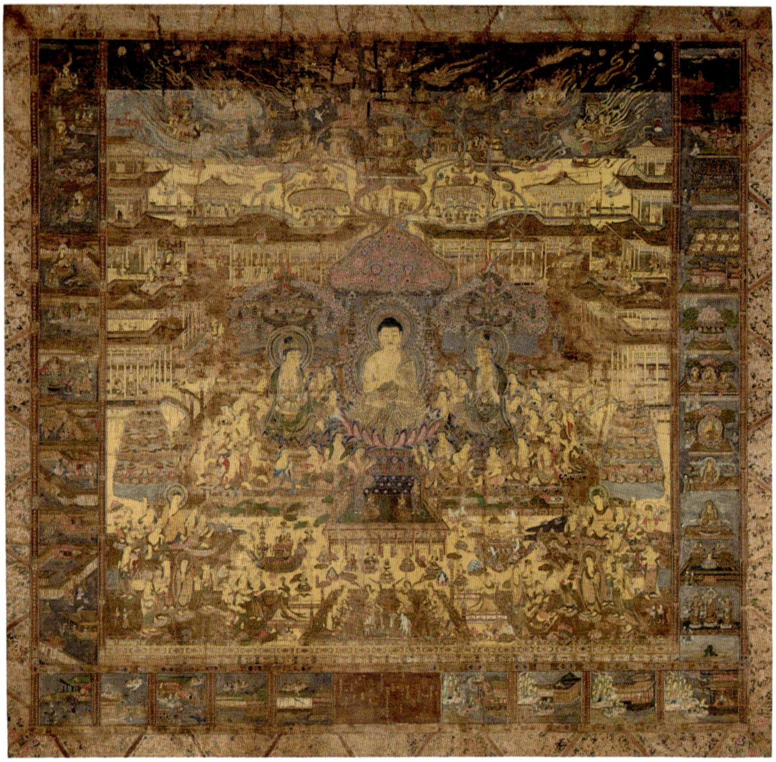

TAIMA MANDALA

1300–1400
Japan
Kamakura (1185–1333), Nanbokucho (1333–1392), or Muromachi period (1392–1573)
Hanging scroll; ink, colors, and gold on silk
H. 178.1 cm × W. 169.9 cm (image)
The Avery Brundage Collection, B61D11+

Pure Land Buddhism offers the promise of salvation to those devoted to the power of the Buddha Amitabha, known in Japanese as Amida. The Taima mandala, a type of painting closely associated with the Japanese Pure Land school, enables devotees to visualize the moment of salvation and to learn about the practices leading to birth in Amida's Pure Land, also known as the Western Paradise.

In the mandala's central court, a majestic assembly awaits the faithful. Amida is the largest figure; seated on a lotus pedestal, his hands form the gesture of teaching. Flanking Amida are the bodhisattvas Avalokiteshvara (Kannon) and Mahasthamaprapta (Seishi), accompanied by other sacred beings. In the foreground, Amida is manifest in additional seated and standing figures ready to welcome and preach to the faithful.

Intricate gold decorations, a pair of jeweled, seven-tiered trees, and food served by bodhisattvas in a palatial Chinese-style building convey the magnificence of Amida's paradise. Dancers accompanied by heavenly musicians

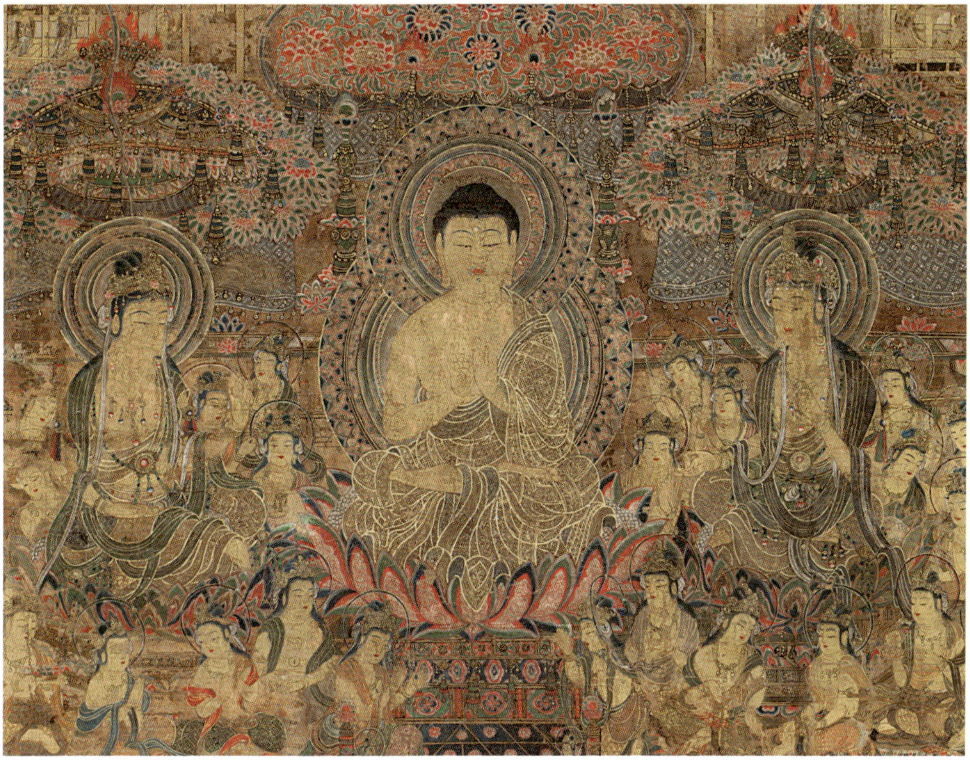

perform on a stage at center foreground. Almost lost within this splendor are the tiny figures of reborn devotees, who appear directly before Amida on a terrace and in the golden pond below.

On three sides of this assembly, bands of smaller scenes illustrate teachings on faith in Amida and a set of sixteen "contemplations" that enable the devotee to visualize his domain. Arranged at the bottom are the last three contemplations, further subdivided into the nine levels of birth. Several scenes show Amida's descent to earth to greet the dying.

Scriptural authority for this imagery resides in two major Pure Land texts, the Muryojukyo (Sutra of Measureless Life) and the Amidakyo (Sutra of Amida). A third sutra, the Kan Muryojukyo (Sutra of Visualization of the Buddha of Measureless Life) provides the basis for the outer courts. The Chinese monk Shandao's commentary on the latter text informed the overall organization in one central and three outer courts.

The pictorial source for this composition was a Tang dynasty Chinese woven mandala housed at Taimadera, a temple in the ancient city Nara. It is said that the tapestry languished unnoticed for hundreds of years, until a disciple of Honen, founder of the Pure Land sect, "rediscovered" it in the early 1200s. Seen as giving tangible form to Honen's teaching, the weaving was copied for use in Pure Land rituals. In addition to exquisite hand-painted versions, countless woodblock-printed copies were made and distributed, spreading faith in Amida far and wide.

—*LWA*

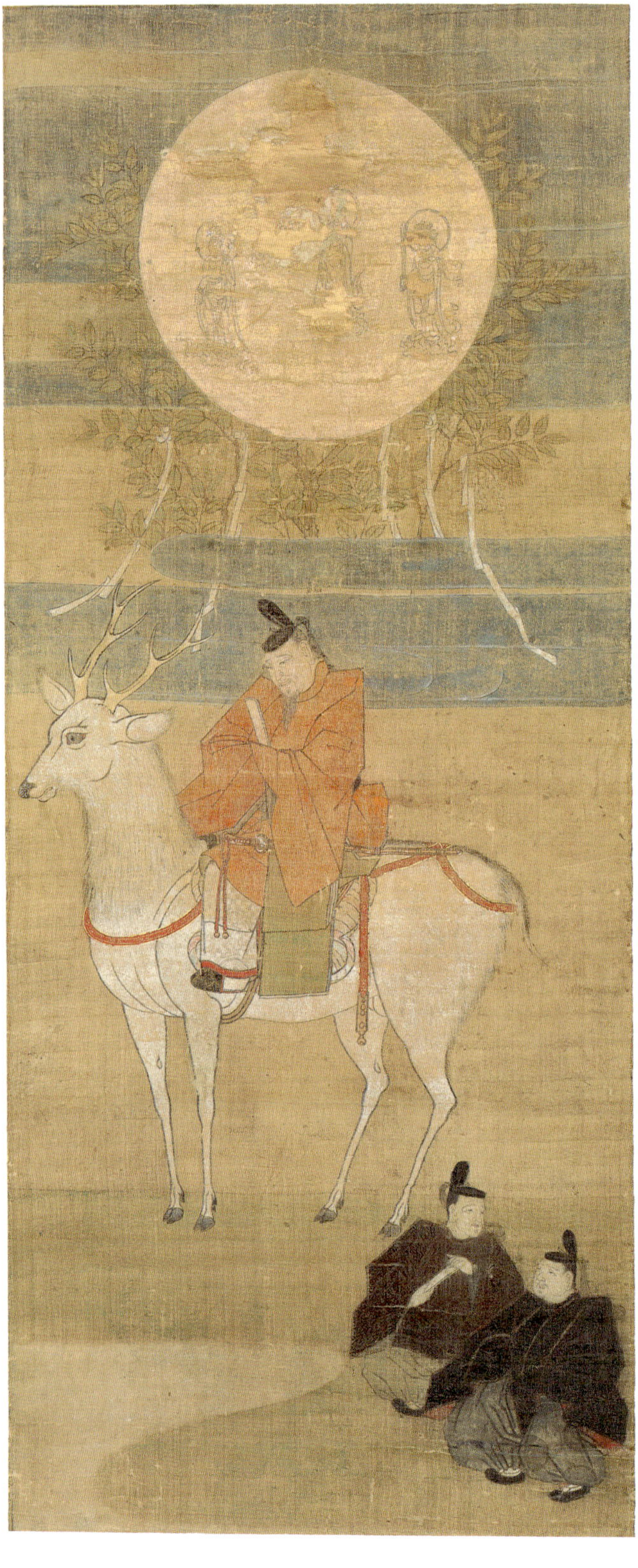

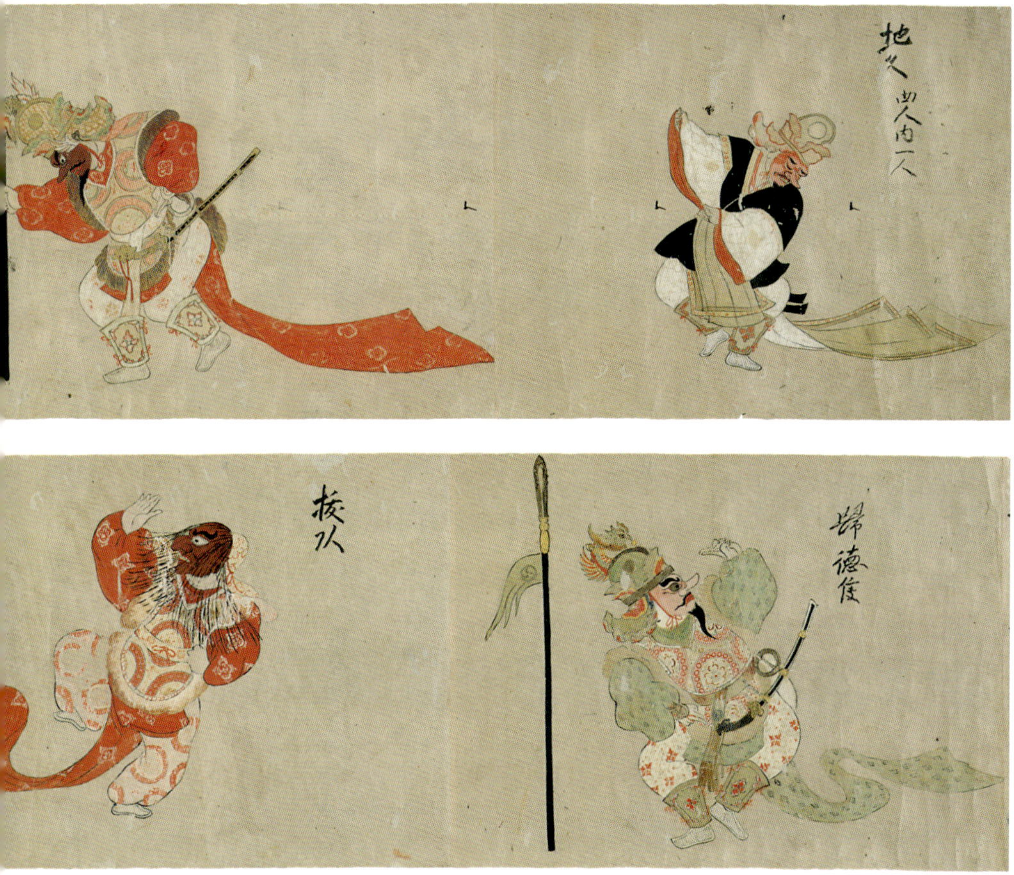

LEFT

DEPARTURE FROM KASHIMA

1300–1400

Japan

Kamakura (1185–1333), Nanbokucho (1333–1392), or Muromachi period (1392–1573)

Hanging scroll; ink and colors on silk

H. 92.8 cm × W. 39.3 cm (image)

Gift and Purchase from the Harry G. C. Packard Collection Charitable Trust in honor of Dr. Shujiro Shimada; The Avery Brundage Collection, 1991.58

ABOVE

BUGAKU DANCERS

1408

By Abe no Suehide (Japanese, 1361–1411)

Muromachi period (1392–1573)

Handscroll; ink and colors on paper

H. 28.2 cm × W. 419 cm (image)

Gift and Purchase from the Harry G. C. Packard Collection Charitable Trust in honor of Dr. Shujiro Shimada; The Avery Brundage Collection, 1991.60

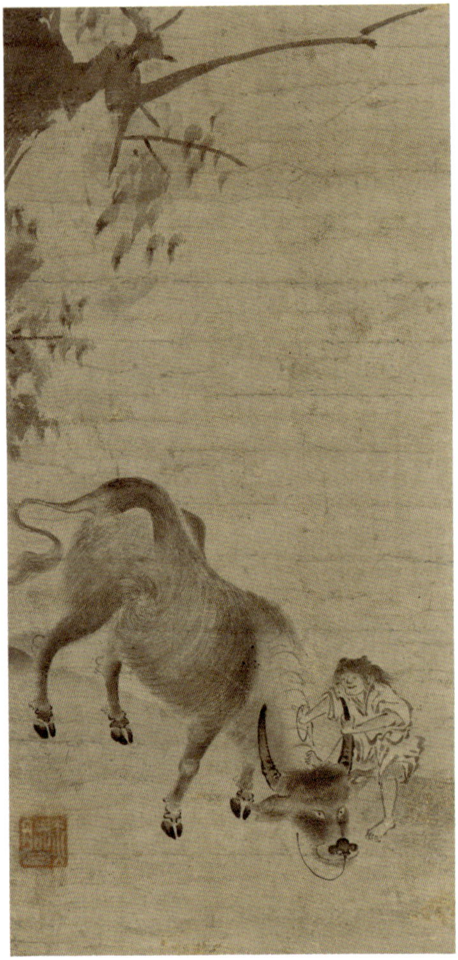

CATCHING THE OX

—

By Sekkyakushi (Japanese), active approx. 1400–1450

Muromachi period (1392–1573)

Hanging scroll; ink on paper

H. 47.9 cm × W. 23.2 cm (image)

Transfer from the Fine Arts Museums of San Francisco, Gift of Ney-Wolfskill Fund, B69D46

—

With all his strength, a boy grasps the horn of an unruly ox. Struggling, he steps on its neck, trying to push its head to the ground and gain control. The image expresses the Zen Buddhist teaching that enlightenment is attained through struggle. The animal represents the unenlightened state, in which the mind rampages like a wild ox. The ox also represents desire, while the boy taming the ox symbolizes self-discipline.

This is the fourth scene of a series called the "Ten Ox Pictures." The paintings represent the ten steps of awareness progressively leading closer to enlightenment. The series typically begins with the scene of a boy searching for his ox in the wilderness and ends with him entering a city with an ox that has been tamed. The Zen ox-herding pictures, first illustrated in China during the Northern Song period (960–1127), became popular among Japanese Zen practitioners by the mid-fourteenth century. These paintings visualize the Zen doctrine and provide the followers with an easy, explanatory analogy for complex ideas.

Through the centuries, many variations of the "Ten Ox Pictures" have been made. This scene, "Catching the ox," was based on a twelfth-century edition written by the Chinese monk Kuo'an. The name of the scroll's artist, Sekkyakushi, means "red-legged person." He was a pioneer of Zen ink painting and a member of the studio of Zen monk Mincho (1351–1431) of Tofukuji temple in Kyoto.

Sekkyakushi illustrated the fifth scene of this series, "Herding the ox," in a work that now belongs to the Metropolitan Museum of Art. As he created more than one set of ox-herding paintings, further research is necessary to determine if the paintings from the Asian Art Museum and the Met once belonged to the same set. While they are not signed, they both bear Sekkyakushi's square seal. The artist painted the hoofs and the knees of the oxen and a whirlpool-like pattern on their fur in a manner similar in both works. In both paintings, he used light and dark ink to create a sense of volume. Scholars conjecture that the Asian Art Museum's painting is slightly smaller than the Met's because it has been trimmed in recent remounting.

—*YM*

STORAGE JAR

1400–1500

Japan; Shiga prefecture

Muromachi period (1392–1573)

Stoneware with natural-ash glaze (Shigaraki ware)

H. 54 cm × Diam. 53.3 cm

The Avery Brundage Collection, B66P38

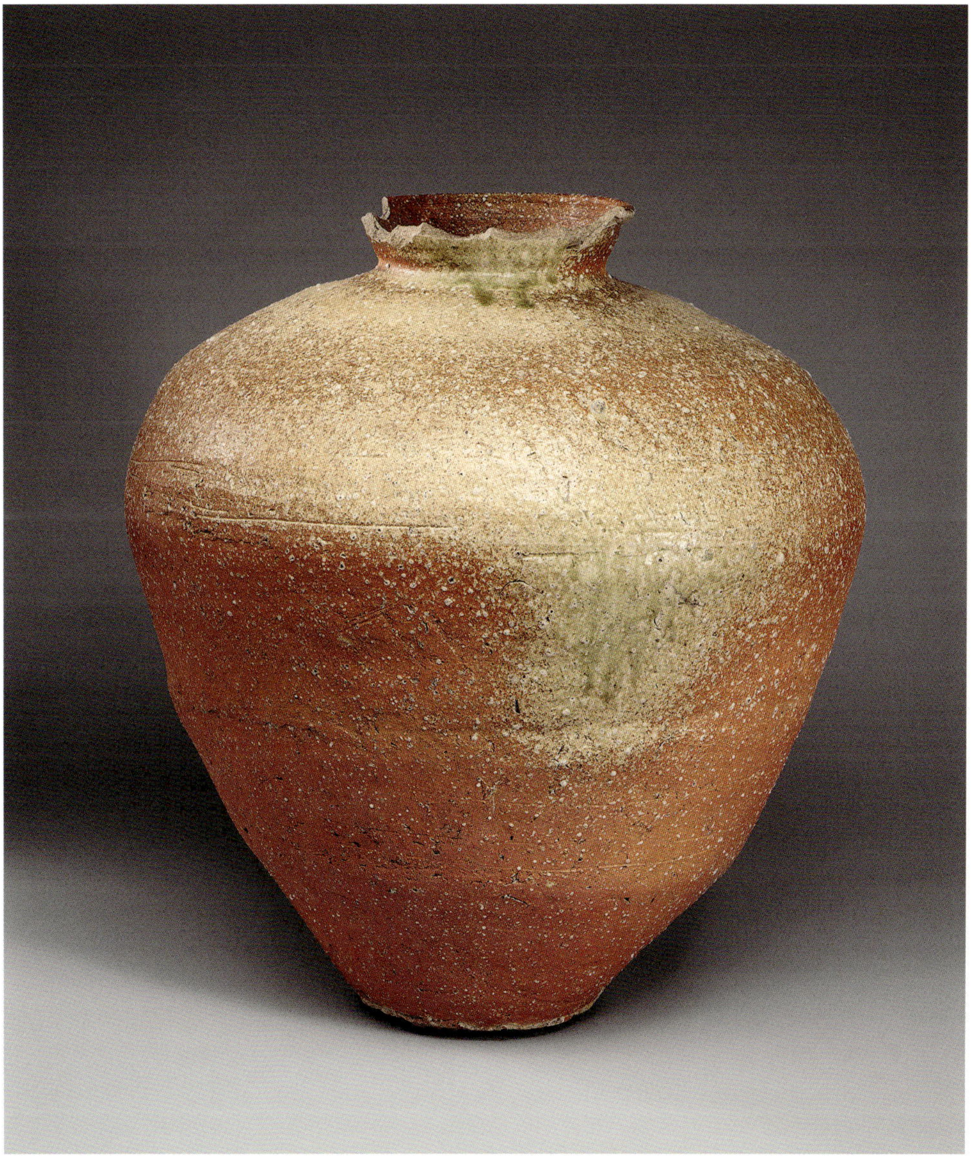

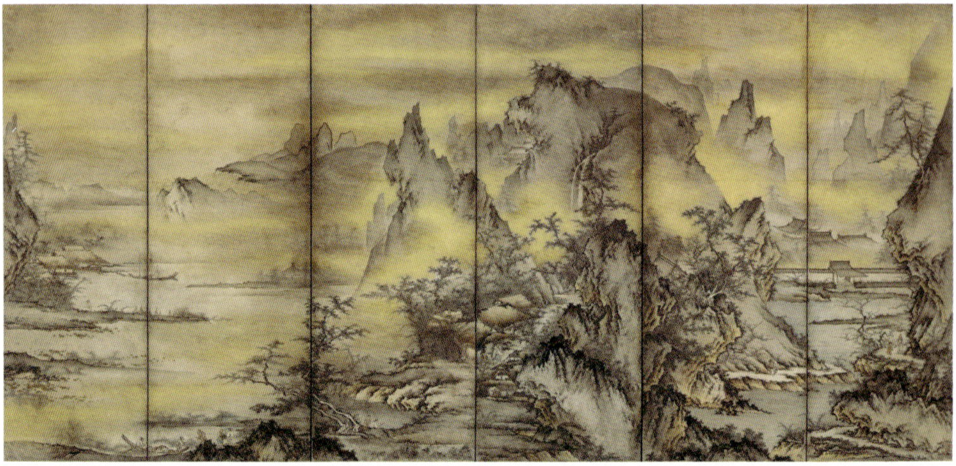

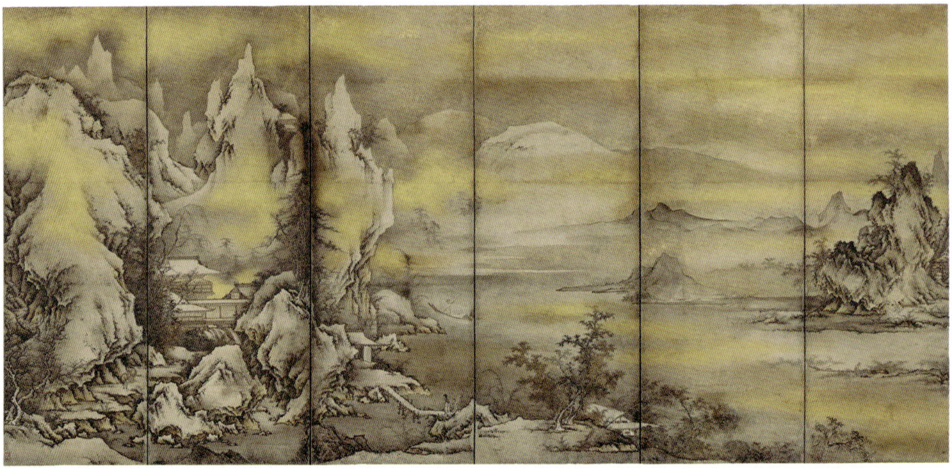

LANDSCAPE OF THE FOUR SEASONS

By Shikibu Terutada (Japanese, active mid-1500s)

Muromachi period (1392–1573)

Pair of six-panel folding screens; ink and colors on paper

H. 153.7 cm × W. 325.1 cm (each image)

The Avery Brundage Collection, B60D48+ and B60D49+

BIRD WITH LONG TAIL FEATHERS

By Kano Yosetsu (Japanese, active approx. 1500–1575)
Muromachi period (1392–1573)
Hanging scroll; ink and colors on paper
H. 47.2 cm × W. 44.6 cm (image)
Gift of Mr. and Mrs. Walter Shorenstein, B76D6

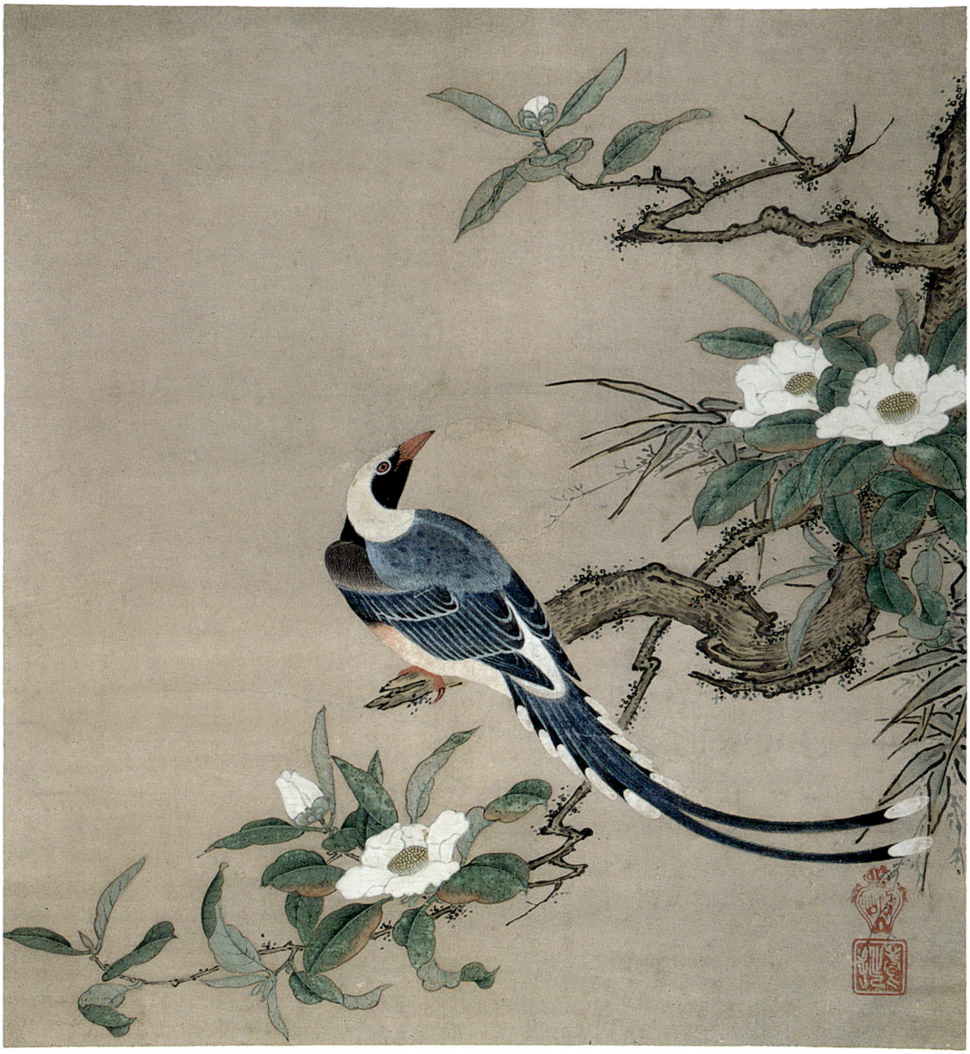

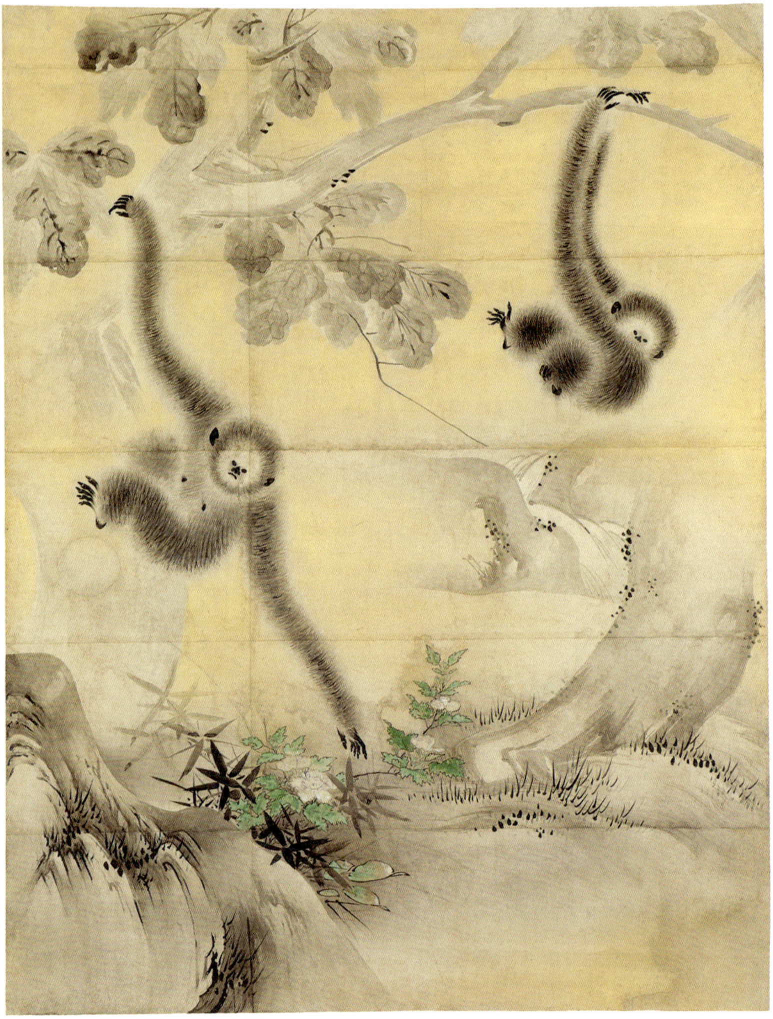

GIBBONS PLAYING IN OAK TREES

approx. 1585–1595

By Kaiho Yusho (Japanese, 1533–1615)

Momoyama period (1573–1615)

Pair of hanging scrolls; ink and colors on paper

H. 177.5 cm × W. 138.4 cm (each image)

Gift and purchase from the Harry G.C. Packard Collection Charitable Trust in honor of Dr. Shujiro Shimada; The Avery Brundage Collection, 1991.62.1 and 1991.62.2

Native to China, gibbons were known to sixteenth-century painters in Japan from imported literary and artistic sources. One highly influential model was a monochrome ink painting of a gibbon mother with her offspring by the Chinese monk Muqi (approx. 1210–after 1269). Brought from China and housed at the Kyoto Zen temple Daitokuji, Muqi's painting was studied and imitated in Japan from the fourteenth century. In Zen circles, pictures of gibbons reaching down to grasp the moon's reflection in water were appreciated as metaphors for the unenlightened mind and its delusions. Warriors may have prized gibbon paintings in the belief that monkeys had the power to protect their horses.[9]

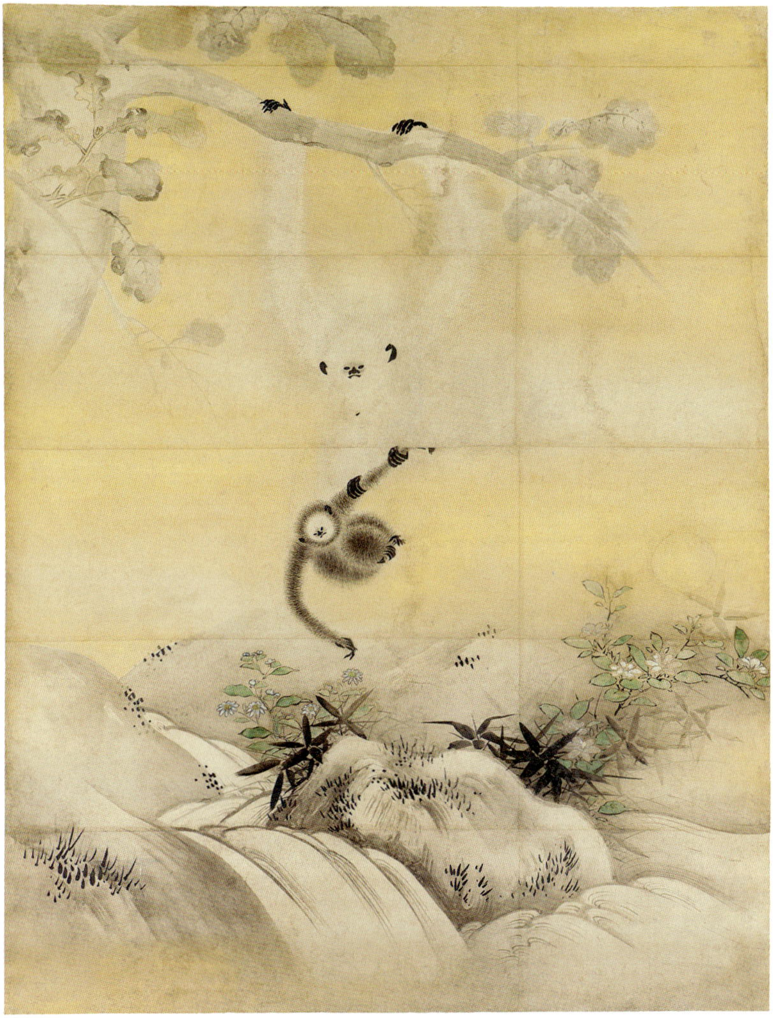

The paintings shown here are now mounted as a pair of hanging scrolls, but traces of repairs where metal door pulls were removed suggest that they were once part of a set of sliding door panels. In contrast to the quiet, austere imagery of Muqi's painting, here four lively and agile gibbons move among oak trees and colorful plants on the banks of a cascading stream. Legs braced against a tree trunk, the gibbon on the left (in the left image) snakes one long arm toward bamboo leaves on the ground. A second gibbon swings from a branch nearby, its body curled into a ball. At right, a white gibbon grips the arm of a black juvenile tightly in its feet as the little one stretches down toward the asters that grow below.

Kyoto National Museum curator Yamamoto Hideo recently identified these unsigned scrolls as early works by Kaiho Yusho, a major ink painter active during the Momoyama period (1573–1615). As evidence, he points to traits familiar from Yusho's work, such as the manner of painting the stream and its environs, the technique of leaving portions of the tree trunks unpainted, the application of colored accents in an otherwise monochromatic setting, the method of weaving together light and dark in bamboo leaves, and the colliding forms of the stream's waves.[10]

—*LWA*

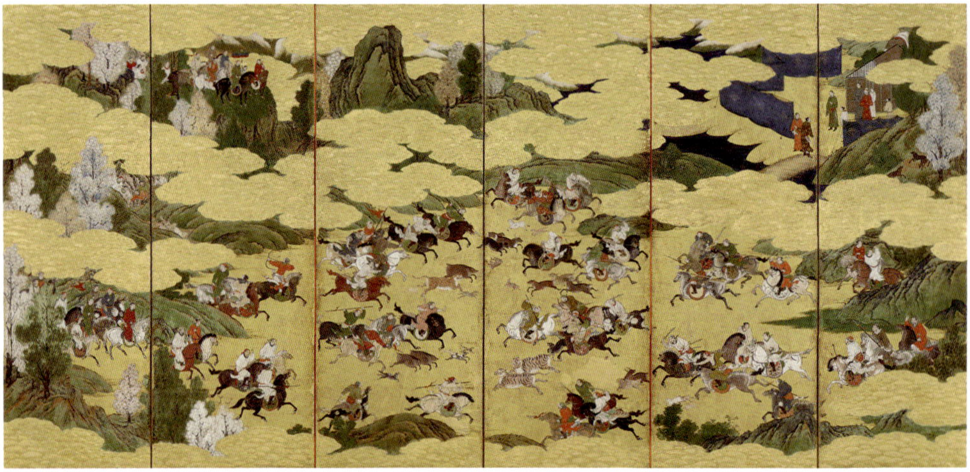

TATARS PLAYING POLO AND HUNTING

Attributed to Kano Soshu (Japanese, 1551–1601)
Momoyama period (1573–1615)
Pair of screens; ink, colors, and gold on paper
H. 166.4 cm × W. 348 cm (each image)
Museum purchase, B69D18.a-.b

In this magnificent pair of lavishly gilded folding screens, an artist of Momoyama period Japan has depicted exotic scenes from a faraway land. The painter has divided the composition into two distinct scenes. On one screen several mounted "Tatars"—nomadic peoples who once dominated northeast Asia beyond China's northern frontier—chase a menagerie of tigers, bears, deer, and other animals in a frenzied hunt. The other screen presents Tatars on horseback playing a spirited match of polo under the watch of a canopied chieftain holding court at his yurt.

Screen paintings of Tatars manifest what has been aptly phrased a "fracture of meaning" in which Chinese literary or pictorial themes were completely transformed in Japan. The source for the Tatars screens was undoubtedly the "Eighteen Songs of a Nomad Flute," a set of poems that recount the sad story of Cai Wenji, a Han-dynasty Chinese woman who was kidnapped by the nomadic Xiongnu people and ransomed from her captors a dozen years later. Chinese

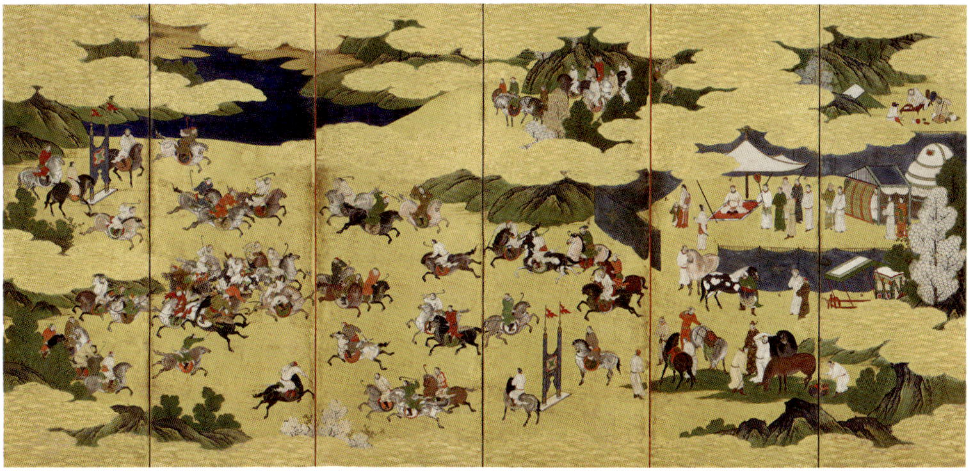

handscrolls illustrating the "Eighteen Songs" include depictions of the nomads hunting; these probably provided the source for the displays of horsemanship featured in these and other portrayals of Tatars.

Although equestrian skills dominate most Tatars screens, vestiges of Cai Wenji's tragic story appear in the present pair. The woman who peeks out of her tent near the seated chieftain probably represents Wenji. The children nearby may represent her half-Han children, from whom she must choose to part. Another group of figures nearby, identifiable as Han Chinese by their dress and black hats, probably depict the emissaries who have arrived to pay Wenji's ransom.

Surviving examples and records indicate that Tatars were a popular pictorial subject in sixteenth-century Japan. The works shown here, considered the finest example of screen paintings of Tatars, have been attributed to Kano Soshu (1551–1601), head of the Kano school of painters in the 1590s. Japanese samurai encountered firsthand the people and customs of northeast Asia during feudal lord Toyotomi Hideyoshi's invasion of Korea in 1592, when the general Kato Kiyomasa (1561–1611) launched an attack on the Jurchens on Korea's northeastern border. Tatars screens may commemorate Japan's attempts at overseas conquest during this period. The Kano-school painter's command of subtle details, rendered in self-assured brushwork, together with the screens' fascinating mixture of literary and historical references, make them a masterpiece of Momoyama period painting.

—Matthew McKelway is Takeo and Itsuko Atsumi Professor of Japanese Art History and Director of the Mary Griggs Burke Center for Japanese Art at Columbia University.

PORTRAIT OF TOYOTOMI HIDEYOSHI

1599
Japan
Momoyama period (1573–1615)
Hanging scroll; ink and colors on silk
H. 90.7 cm × W. 37.8 cm (image)
Gift and Purchase from the Harry G. C. Packard Collection Charitable Trust in honor of Dr. Shujiro Shimada; The Avery Brundage Collection, 1991.61

This portrait is among the finest of the roughly twenty extant depictions of the great warlord Toyotomi Hideyoshi (1537–1598). Superbly executed, it shows Hideyoshi seated with a ceremonial fan in his right hand and his left fist clenched. He wears white silk socks and sits cross-legged on raised mats like those used by emperors. Beside Hideyoshi rests a long, embellished sword indicating his status as a ruler. His headgear, white coat, and loose trousers are the formal garments of a high-ranking noble, representing his status as an imperial regent (*kanpaku*). Emperor Go-Yozei (1571–1617) allowed Hideyoshi to use a simplified version of the imperial paulownia crest as the Toyotomi family crest. The ink landscape with a large paulownia tree behind him suggests an imperial connection, thus further legitimizing Hideyoshi's rule.

It was customary in Japan for people close to the deceased to commission commemorative portraits of their loved ones. The commissioner of this portrait was Yakuin Zenso (1526–1600), a Tendai Buddhist priest and Hideyoshi's physician. Zenso had gained Hideyoshi's confidence and was his companion during his military campaigns. The inscription was done by Saisho Jotai (1548–1607), the ninety-second abbot of Shokokuji. He was the head administrator of all Zen priests in the hierarchy of the Five Mountain (Gozan) Temples. Jotai worked closely with Hideyoshi and became one of his political advisers; he showed his gratitude by inscribing the painting.

Because Japanese portraits functioned as instruments of mortuary rituals, they were often commissioned just prior to the monthly commemoration (*gakki*) of the deceased's death. Accordingly, many paintings of Hideyoshi were dated the eighteenth day of the month, as he died on the eighteenth day. The date Zenso dedicated this portrait—the eighteenth day of the fourth month, 1599—was an extremely important one, as it was the day Hokoku Jinja (Shrine of the Prosperous Country) in Kyoto was dedicated to the deified Hideyoshi. In accordance with the Shinto custom of deifying influential leaders, Hideyoshi was venerated with the name Hokoku Myojin (The Bright Deity of the Prosperous Country), and his spirit was invited to reside in this new shrine building on this day.

It is perhaps no coincidence that the dedication of the shrine and the inscription of the portrait occurred on the same day. While it is unclear whether the portrait was present at the dedication ceremony, Zenso was surely inspired to initiate this project with this date in mind.

—*YM*

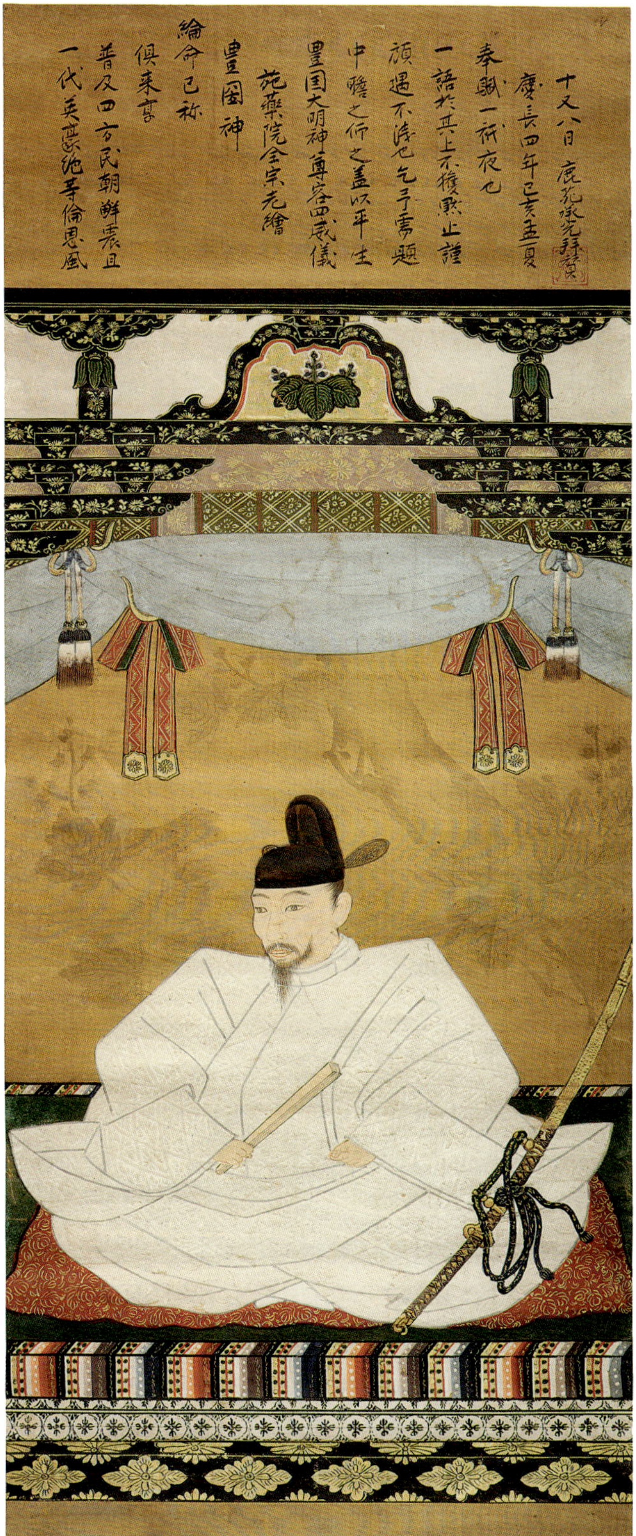

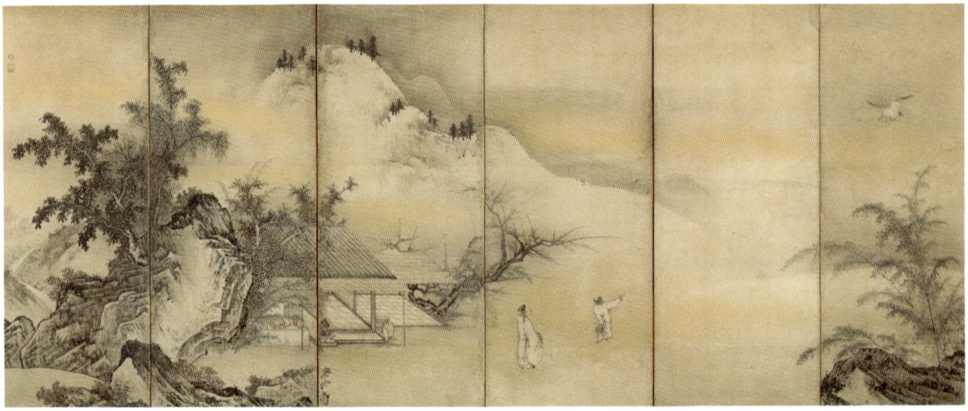

LANDSCAPE WITH THE POETS TAO YUANMING AND LIN HEJING

—

By Unkoku Togan (Japanese, 1547–1618)

Momoyama period (1573–1615)

Pair of six-panel screens; ink and colors on paper

H. 147 cm × W. 358 cm (each image)

The Avery Brundage Collection, B60D73+ and B60D74+

—

This pair of screens depicts two well-known Chinese poets in landscape settings. The right screen shows Tao Yuanming (365–427) and the left includes Lin Hejing (967–1028). By placing the poets in similarly painted landscapes, Unkoku Togan made a connection between them even though they lived centuries apart. These two men symbolize the idealized hermit lifestyle, which has been a favorite Zen Buddhist subject in ink painting since Japan's Muromachi period (1392–1573).

Tao Yuanming gazes at Mount Nanshan in Shaanxi province from his hut while enjoying wine. In retirement, Tao moved to the country to seek his true nature. This screen depicts the scene described in his most famous poem on the subject of chrysanthemums.

Lin Hejing led an ideal life of seclusion in the Gu Mountains behind West Lake in Hangzhou. He kept a crane as his companion and loved plum trees. In this screen, a child servant points to a crane in flight, which symbolizes the auspicious bird on which Daoist immortals ride through the sky. Plum trees, symbols of refined character, are found by the buildings on the left section of the screen.

The Japanese painter Togan trained in Kyoto under Kano Eitoku (1543–1590) or Eitoku's father, Shoei (1519–1592). He then became the official painter for the feudal lord Mori Terumoto (1553–1625). Terumoto ordered Togan to copy a landscape handscroll by the great Japanese painting master and Zen monk, Sesshu Toyo (1420–1506). Terumoto was so impressed by the copy that he gave Togan the original scroll and

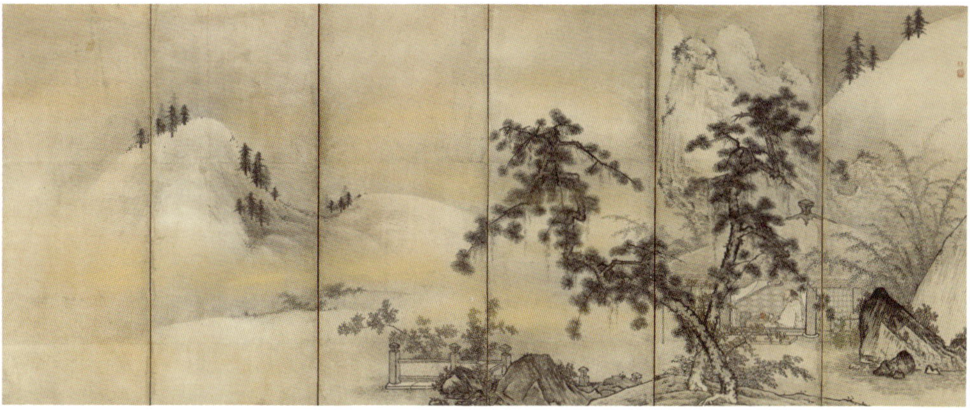

allowed him to live in Sesshu's former studio. The rocks and trees portrayed in this pair of screens are inspired by Sesshu.

Togan was born as Hara Jihei, the second son of the lord of Nogomi Castle in Hizen province (today's Saga prefecture). He later changed his name to Unkoku Togan to honor Sesshu. Togan took "Unkoku" from the name Sesshu gave to his studio, and he took the "To" in "Togan" from Sesshu's religious name, "Toyo." After mastering Sesshu's painting techniques, Togan became one of the leading painting masters of the Momoyama period (1573–1615) and established the Unkoku painting school, which continued for more than 260 years until 1868.

This pair of screens was once in the Imperial Household Collection. They were left as a bequest from Dowager Empress Shoken (1849–1914) to Prince Fushimi Hiroyasu (1875–1946) in 1914.[11]
—*YM*

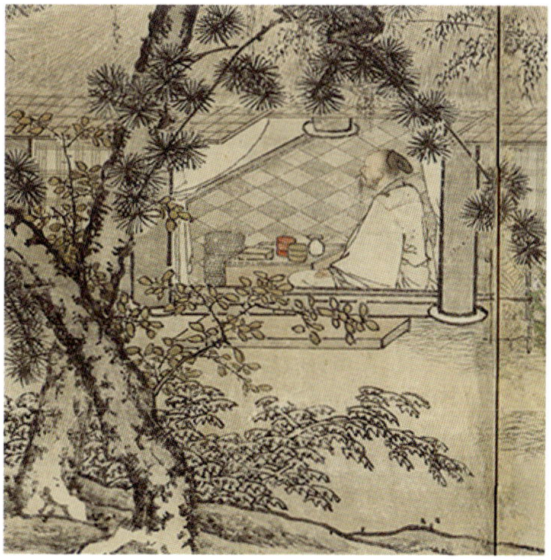

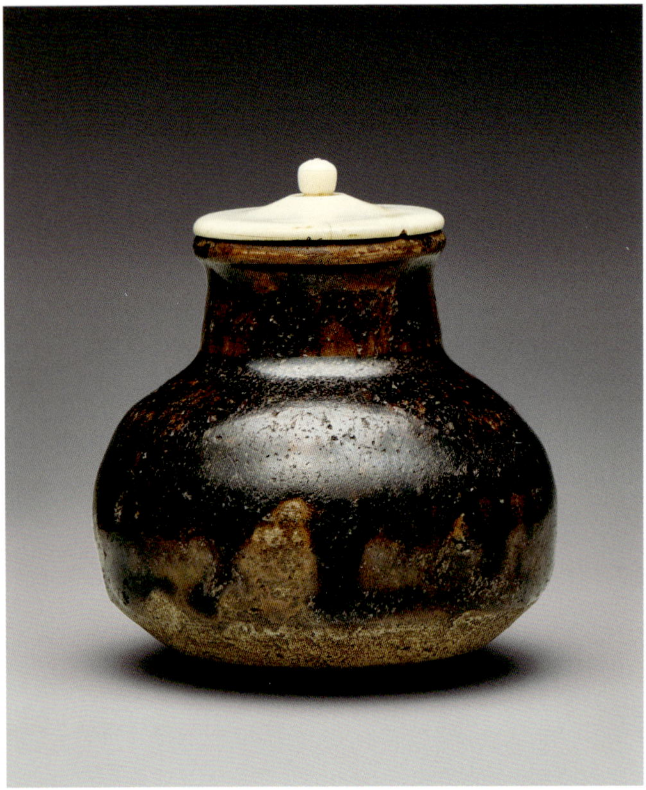

POWDERED TEA CONTAINER (*CHAIRE*)

—

Japan; Aichi prefecture

Momoyama period (1573–1615)

Stoneware with iron-oxide glaze and ivory lid (Seto ware)

H. 5.1 cm × Diam. 5.5 cm

Transfer from the Fine Arts Museums of San Francisco, B85P11

—

DISH WITH HANDLE

—

Japan; Gifu prefecture

Momoyama period (1573–1615)

Stoneware with iron-oxide decoration and copper-oxide glaze (Mino ware, Oribe type)

H. 15.2 cm × W. 22.5 cm × D. 20 cm

The Avery Brundage Collection, B64P34

—

These two vessels exemplify key aspects of premodern Japanese ceramics created in the orbit of *chanoyu*, a prominent cultural practice that centered around a host's preparation and guests' consumption of tea as well as around appreciation of its requisite objects. A *chanoyu* object deemed excellent was not only beautiful (according to the standards of its day), but also useful. The powdered tea container shown here is a characteristically small jar used exclusively to hold ground tea leaves, at the ready for the host to whisk into hot water in a bowl. Placed within arm's reach of the host, the container was, despite its small size, a prominent actor at a *chanoyu* gathering. The handled dish held food for the modest repast that was part of a full tea gathering or perhaps for a celebratory meal.[12] Neither vessel was an all-purpose, everyday item, but served a distinct function at a special occasion.

Appearance greatly mattered in these objects. Both eschew polished regularity, and each explores a distinct aesthetic. The jar is round and sheathed in dark brown glaze; the dish is roughly square and covered with varied kinds of ornament. The jar celebrates the natural

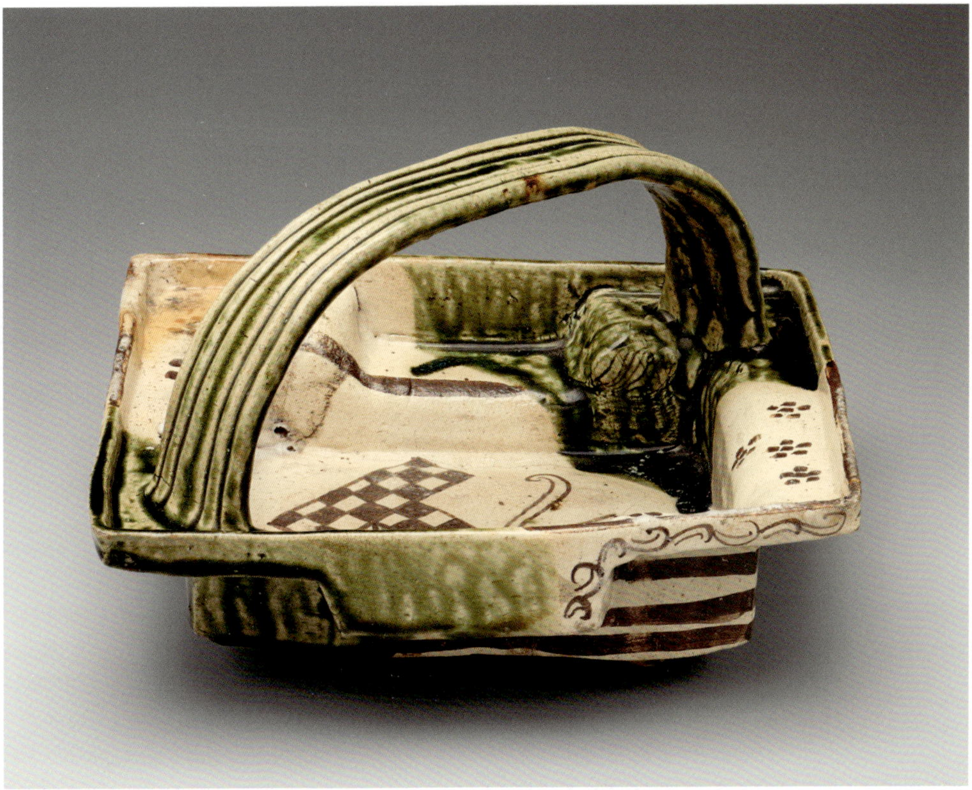

possibilities of glaze that flowed when it was liquid, as seen in the visible drips, and vitrified into glossy permanence in the high heat of the kiln. Its makers well understood those properties and contrived to leave the bottom portion of the jar uncovered, its rough clay visible. The dish incorporates similar glaze effects in the copper-green that covers the handle, overflows the outer wall, and pools inside at two corners; but on the broad expanse of the flat interior it also includes deliberate, hand-painted iron-oxide designs of abstracted plum blossoms and geometric checkerboard patterns intersected by organic vegetal forms. These decorations would be revealed, bit by bit, as the food arranged on top of them was removed.

The two vessels were created by differing potting techniques to achieve their respective round and rectilinear shapes. The jar was thrown on a rotating wheel, its potter making use of centripetal force to create its near symmetry, fluidly pushing and pulling the clay to create the distinctive bulbous body and tall-necked contour. Then, he cut the jar from the lump of clay with a string to produce the flat base. (A carved ivory lid was added to complete the tea container.) The creator of the dish, in contrast, draped thin slabs of clay over a prepared square mold cut into sharply angled stepped tiers. He then pinched the arching handle, which was formed separately and etched with deep lines, into place.

The two vessels speak to different traditions. The powdered tea container is rooted in Chinese precedent. Its shape and glaze would have been admired for their practiced evocation of small jars long imported from China and appropriated for use in *chanoyu*. The dish explored novel shapes and applications of glaze and figural decoration that were valued for their experimentalism. Together the two vessels show Japan's long-term exploration of continuity and inventiveness.

—Andrew M. Watsky is Professor of Japanese Art History and Director, P. Y. and Kinmay W. Tang Center for East Asian Art at Princeton University.

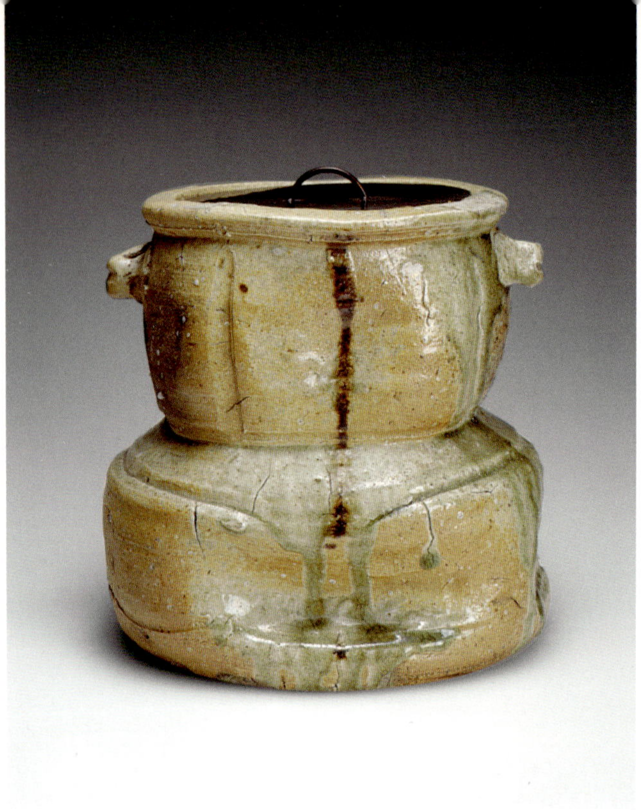

FRESHWATER JAR

Japan; Mie prefecture
Momoyama period (1573–1615)
Stoneware with natural-ash glaze and lacquered wood lid (Iga ware)
H. 19.7 cm × Diam. 19.7 cm
Museum purchase, B68P4

Cool water from this jar (*mizusashi*) is used to replenish a kettle during the making of powdered green tea. Often the first utensil carried into the tearoom during a Japanese tea gathering, this vessel sets the tone for the host's selection of utensils used on a particular occasion. At the close of the gathering, the host would take clean water from this jar to rinse the teabowl.

This type of pottery, called Iga ware, was made in Iga province (today's Mie prefecture). While Iga ware was produced as early as the eighth century, it became important during the sixteenth century with tea practitioners' increasing preference for a rustic aesthetic. This jar reflects the taste of famous tea masters like Furuta Oribe (1544–1615) who saw beauty in imperfection. Many Japanese feudal lords and tea masters preferred the rustic appearance of Iga, and they commissioned deliberately distorted wares. They also appreciated cracked clay surfaces and did not consider them to be flaws. This jar was first wheel thrown and then intentionally distorted to make it irregular in shape.

Ashes from a wood fire fell onto the jar and were transformed by high heat into a glassy green glaze. This glaze is difficult to control, and its drips are mostly accidental. However, experienced potters could foresee the firing effect and control the glaze to a certain degree. In order to achieve the desired result, potters carefully placed ceramic wares into steep-sloping kilns and controlled the temperature to manipulate the firing environment. The firing temperature of Iga ware was as high as 1,300°C (2,372°F), which caused the clay to become vitreous (glass-like) and therefore watertight.

The thin, elegant lid is made of a piece of wood coated with multiple layers of black lacquer. It was probably not made by the potter but was custom made by a lacquer craftsman.

—*YM*

DISH WITH PLANT DESIGN

Japan; Gifu prefecture

Momoyama period (1573–1615)

Stoneware with iron-oxide decoration under glaze (Mino ware, E-Shino type)

H. 8.3 cm × Diam. 27.9 cm

The Avery Brundage Collection, B66P37

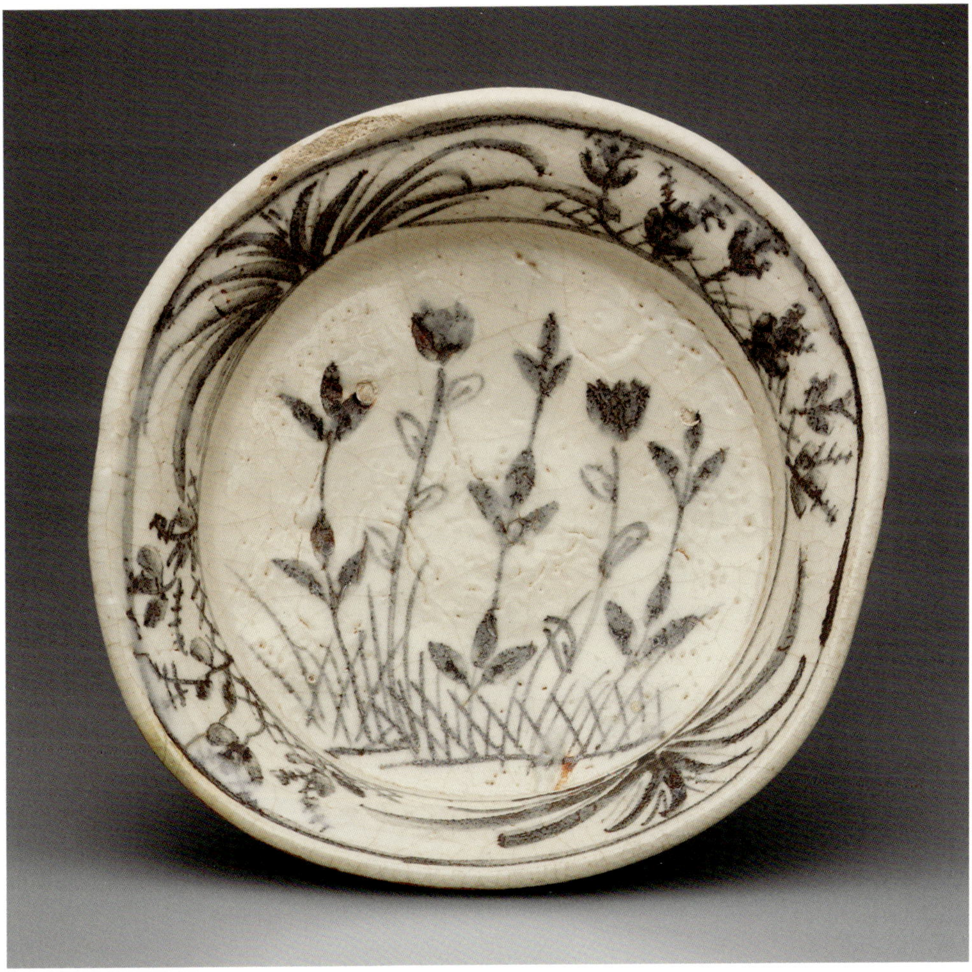

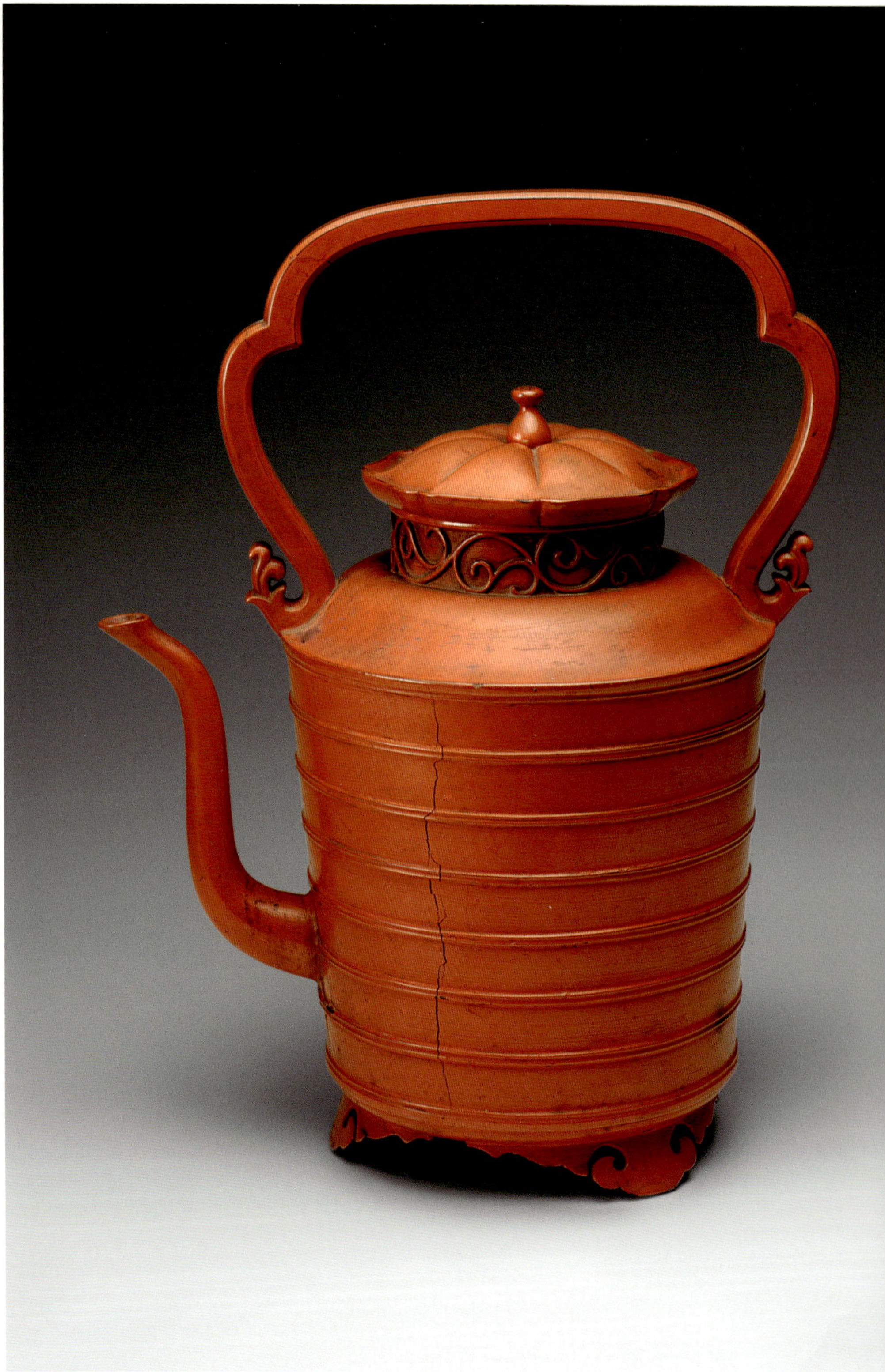

POURING VESSEL

approx. 1600–1650

Japan

Momoyama (1573–1615) or Edo period (1615–1868)

Lacquer on wood

H. 35.6 cm × W. 27.9 cm × D. 20.3 cm

The Avery Brundage Collection, B60M1+.a-.b

This red-lacquered pouring vessel is a type called Negoro ware. Fine Negoro lacquers are characterized by their elegantly created forms, which are made of wood and reinforced with linen. Many coatings of black lacquer build up a durable body, which is covered by an often-single-coat finish of red lacquer. Over years of use, the red coat gradually wears away, revealing the black undercoat, particularly at edges and corners. People in Japan appreciated this naturally aged look and did not consider the wear as a flaw. In particular, tea masters preferred the imperfection, and they often used Negoro wares for their tea gatherings. This vessel represents a new appreciation for simplicity and rusticity as aesthetic qualities in Japanese art that began in the fifteenth century.

Negoro ware was named after a temple complex. The Negoro temple was established in Kii province (present-day Wakayama prefecture) in 1288. Initially, this type of lacquerware was made primarily for use by the monks living there. After the warlord Toyotomi Hideyoshi's troops destroyed the temple in 1585, artisans continued to make Negoro wares elsewhere. Eventually, the term *Negoro* came into general use for all lacquer of this style. The inscription "Konzoin" on this vessel's base suggests that it was made for a temple by that name—perhaps a subtemple of the Negoro temple.

This vessel shows the influence of Chinese designs, such as a lobed lid, decorative ends of the handle, and cloud-shaped feet. Elegantly shaped lacquerware such as this demonstrate the remarkable skills of Japanese lacquer artists.

—*YM*

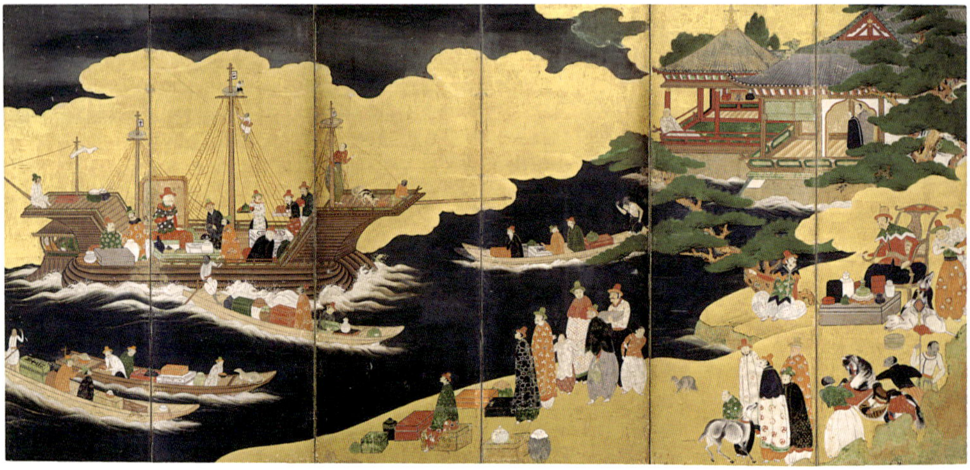

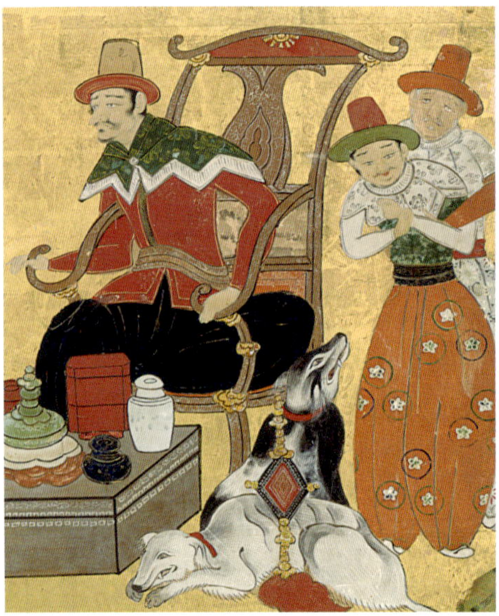

ARRIVAL OF A PORTUGUESE SHIP (*NANBAN* SCREENS)

approx. 1620–1640

Japan

Edo period (1615–1868)

Pair of six-panel folding screens; ink, colors, and gold on paper

Left: H. 147.6 cm × W. 320 cm (image); right: H. 147.6 cm × W. 316.2 cm (image)

The Avery Brundage Collection, B60D77+ and B60D78+

The scenes depicted in this pair of folding screens recall the excitement of Japan's first encounters with visitors from Europe. Portuguese traders arrived in Japan in 1543, followed by the Jesuit missionary Francis Xavier in 1549. On Japan's southern island, Kyushu, local warlords vied to offer ports for ships that brought silk and other valuables from China in exchange for silver, a prized commodity recently located in Japan. The Jesuits profited alongside the traders, converting thousands of Japanese to Christianity by the century's end.

Fascination with the Portuguese quickly gave rise to a genre known as Southern Barbarian (*nanban*) art. The term, derived from the Chinese *nanman*, refers to people from outside Japan's borders, specifically Europeans. The first of this pair of seventeenth-century *nanban* screens

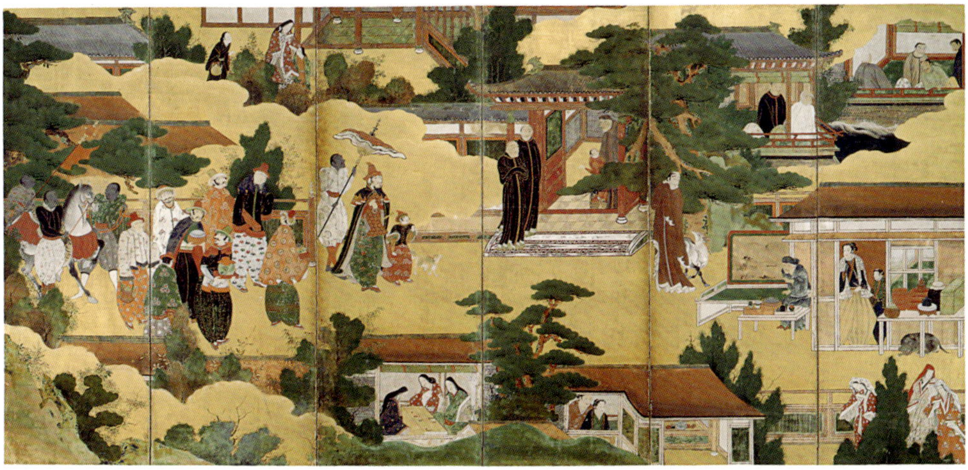

shows a ship's captain and his retinue parading through a city that is likely Nagasaki, the primary port for overseas trade. Two priests greet the traders at their mission, while nearby a grizzled man prepares tea, and a youth in European-style clothes waits near a display of imported goods. The subject of the other screen, the annual arrival of the Portuguese carrack, shows launches carrying goods to and from the shore, where a well-dressed trader waits in an elaborately carved chair. At the upper right, missionaries observe the scene from two buildings, one with a cross on its roof.

The foreigners' appearance and possessions are depicted with care. There are men with long-nosed, hirsute faces and some with dark skin. They sport novel costumes like balloon-legged trousers (bombachas), capes, and peaked hats. Some escort exotic animals, presumably breeds new to Japan: a prancing horse, dogs, and a goat. Others carry luxury imports: Chinese lacquered trays and boxes, some no doubt containing prized silks, and ceramic jars holding teas or spices unavailable in Japan.

There is evidence that elite Japanese coveted Portuguese accessories like jewelry, buttons, and crucifixes along with all the other curiosities represented in these screens. One missionary wrote in 1594 of a warlord and his followers who were

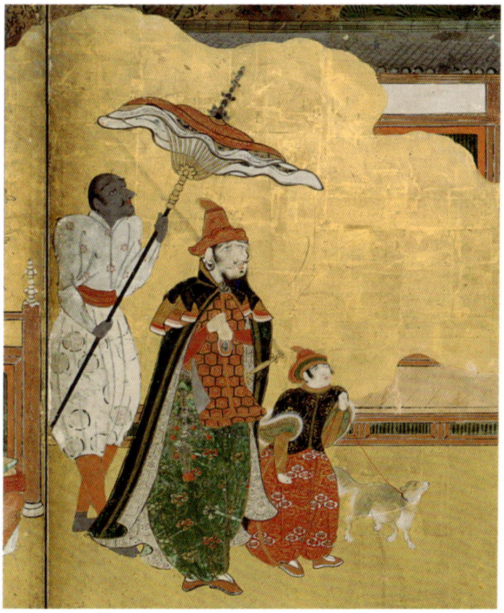

"often attired in the Portuguese style." A picture from the late 1500s shows European-style hats for sale in Kyoto; many tea enthusiasts owned Chinese jars like those carried in the screens. The fashion for things Portuguese ended abruptly in the early 1600s, however, when the Jesuits, suspected of endangering the stability of the new Tokugawa regime, were unceremoniously expelled from Japan.
—*LWA*

JAR WITH DESIGN OF BIRDS ON A LOQUAT BRANCH

mid-1600s

Japan; Saga prefecture

Edo period (1615–1868)

Porcelain with cobalt decoration under glaze (Hizen ware)

H. 27.9 cm × Diam. 22.9 cm

The Avery Brundage Collection, B64P37

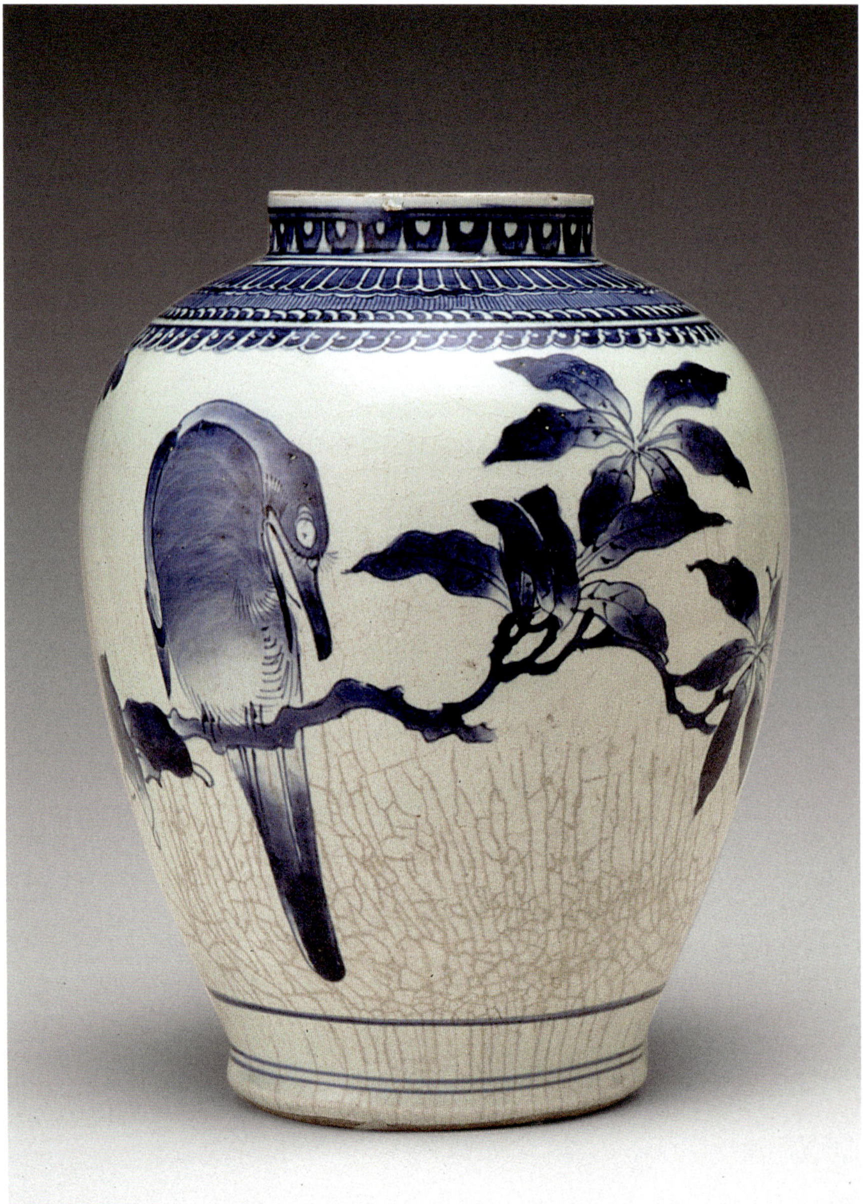

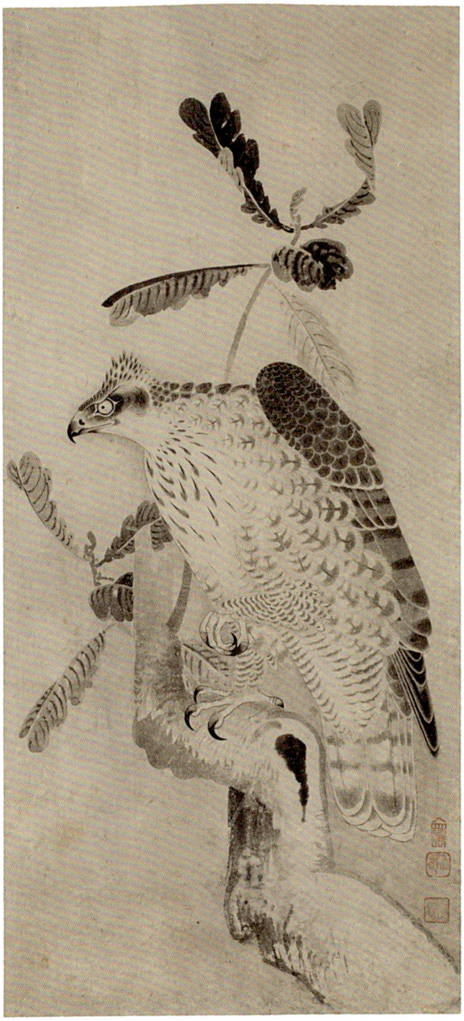

HAWK ON OAK TREE

By Soga Nichokuan (Japanese, active mid-1600s)
Edo period (1615–1868)
Hanging scroll; ink on paper
H. 119.4 cm × W. 55.7 cm
The Avery Brundage Collection, B60D18

This is not just a generic bird of prey. The pale eyes, the crest, the vertically streaked breast, and the horizontally barred leg feathers reaching all the way to the feet are all characteristics of a *Kumataka* (Japanese mountain hawk-eagle, *Nisaetus nipalensis orientalis*), the largest raptor traditionally trained by Japanese falconers. All these details are difficult to observe in a bird in the wild; the model for this painting was a trained hunting hawk, but the artist chose not to include the jesses (leather leg straps) and bell that would have revealed this.

The behavior shown here can be observed in a trained hawk or a wild one. At rest the hawk stands straight upright, balancing on one foot, with the other foot closed and tucked up under its breast feathers. But as soon as it spots prey, it constricts the pupils of its eyes for a better view and begins to lean forward into a more horizontal position. At the same time its crest and hackles rise. The raised foot is lowered to grasp the perch, and the wings are pulled back and up, all in preparation for launching. Here the artist skillfully captured this moment of transition, from relaxed watchfulness to intense interest, just before the attack.

—*MF*

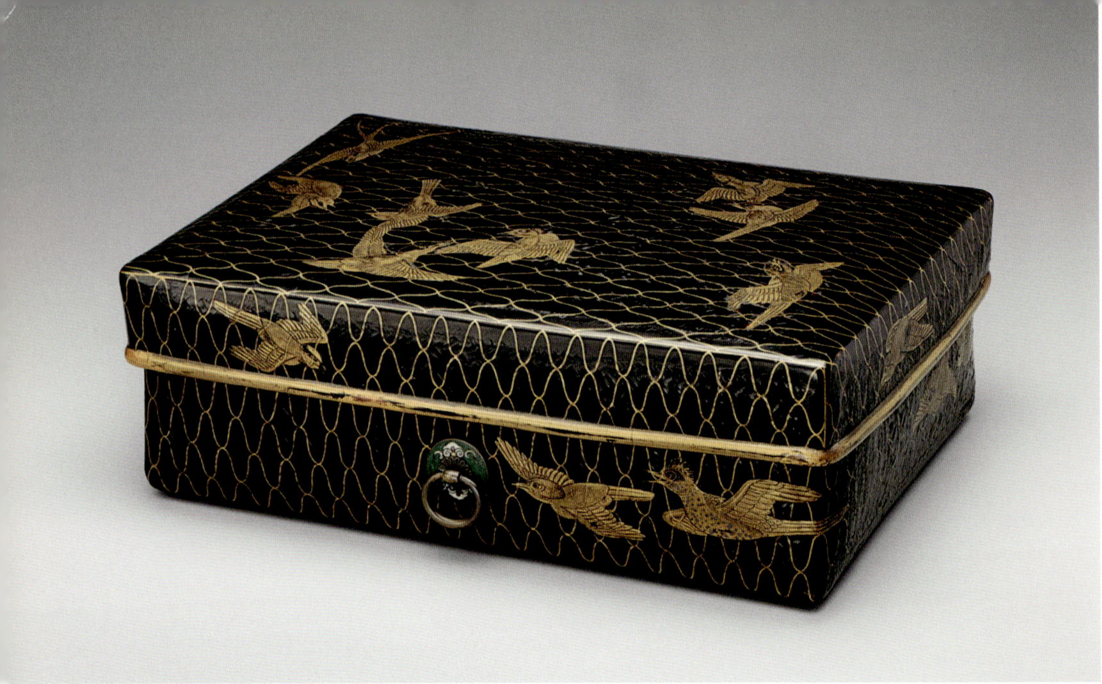

BOX FOR WRITING PAPER

approx. 1615–1800

Japan

Edo period (1615–1868)

Lacquer, gold, and silver on bamboo with metal fittings

H. 10.2 cm × W. 30.5 cm × D. 21.6 cm

The Avery Brundage Collection, B60M162.a-.b

This exquisite lacquered stationery box (*ryoshibako*) was once part of a writing set including implements for calligraphy: ink stone, water dropper, and brushes. The box is made of interwoven bamboo coated with multiple layers of lacquer. The intricate pattern of the bamboo weave can be still seen under the lacquer. It is decorated with a motif of flying birds confined behind a net, or in an aviary—a popular motif in seventeenth-century Japan. The work is a fine collaboration between an artisan who wove the box and a lacquer artist who embellished it.

This box shows three Japanese lacquer decoration techniques: *hiramaki-e* (flat sprinkled metal design), *takamaki-e* (raised sprinkled metal design), and *kirikane* (finely cut metal foil). The ornate technique of *maki-e* can be traced back to at least the late eighth century. In the *hiramaki-e* process, shown here in the netting, an artist first paints a design with lacquer. While the lacquer is still wet and acts as an adhering agent, metallic powder, often gold, is sprinkled on the design. When the decoration is raised to some thickness, it is called *takamaki-e*. Here, some parts of the birds were painted with a mixture of lacquer and charcoal powder to increase the thickness of the design and to create a sense of volume. In the *kirikane* technique, seen in the square patterns on one of the birds, small pieces of sheet silver are carefully applied on the *maki-e* surface. The interior of the box was elegantly finished with plain black lacquer. On two sides of the box, a cloisonné fitting originally held silk cords for tying the box together.

In all lacquer objects, regardless of type, a resinous sap coating preserves the core material and allows for decoration. The material for lacquering is extracted from lacquer trees (*Toxicodendron vernicifluum*), which is the same genus as poison oak. The sap is collected by cutting the bark of the tree and scraping off the milky white sap, which is later colored with materials such as pine soot and the mineral cinnabar. Lacquer hardens in a humid environment by curing rather than drying. One thin coat hardens overnight. The toxic properties of lacquer limit its use to specially trained, highly skilled artisans.

—*YM*

PLATE WITH FERN DESIGN

1650s–1660s

Japan; Saga prefecture

Porcelain with overglaze enamel decoration (Hizen ware, Aode Kutani type)

H. 6.7 cm × Diam. 40.3 cm

The Avery Brundage Collection, B64P31

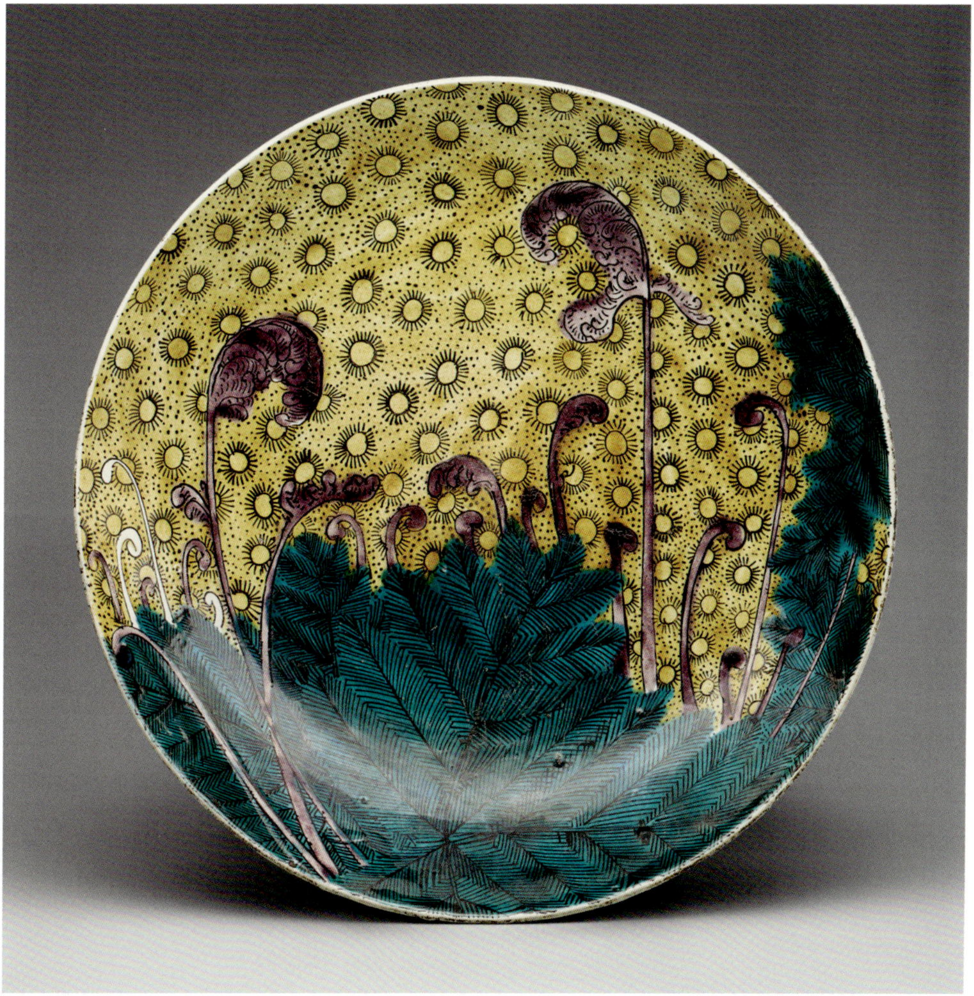

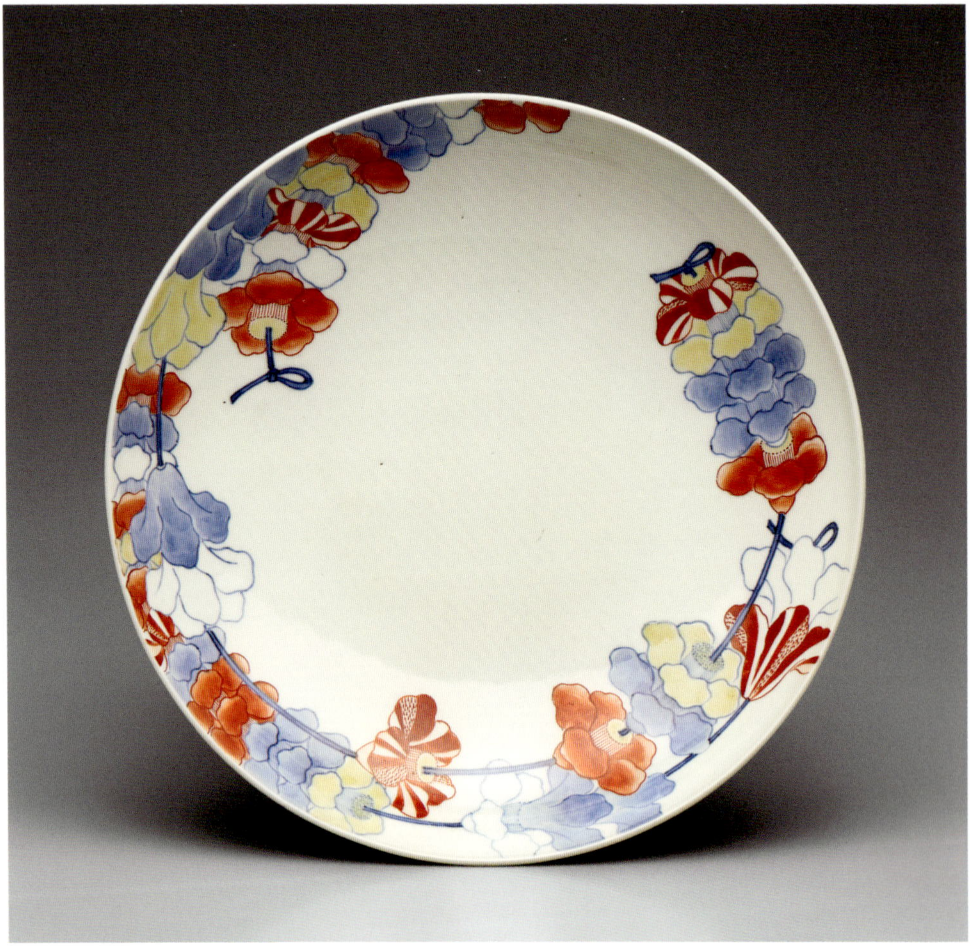

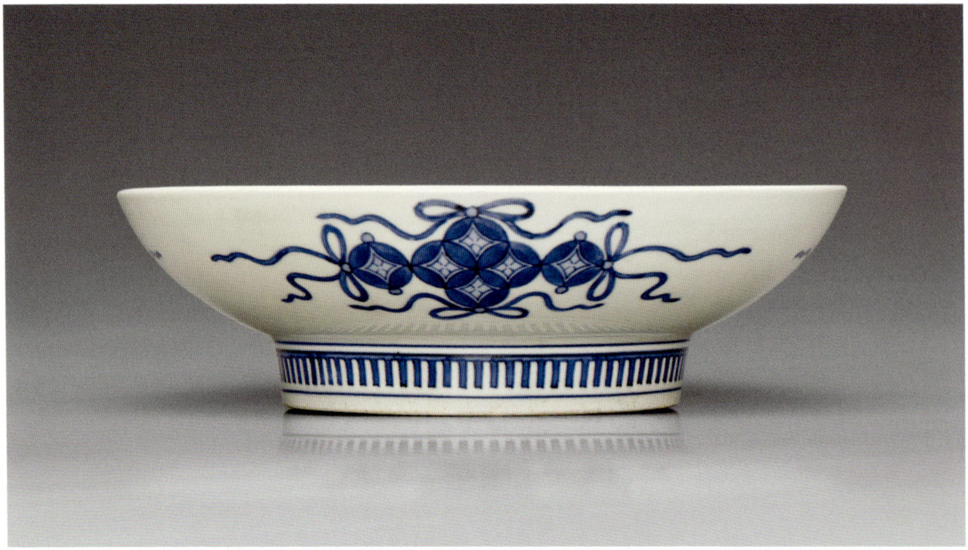

DISH WITH DESIGN OF A GARLAND OF CAMELLIAS

—

1690s–1720s

Japan; Saga prefecture

Edo period (1615–1868)

Porcelain with underglaze cobalt and overglaze enamel decoration (Nabeshima ware)

H. 5.7 cm × Diam. 20.3 cm

The Avery Brundage Collection, B60P46+

—

Camellias strung on a cord and arranged in a circular band wrap around the rim of this small dish. The elegant design in an underglaze blue was enhanced with light red and yellow overglaze enamels. Tasty food placed in the middle of the dish would have been beautifully framed by the flowers. Six coins tied with ribbon decorate the back, while an evenly painted comb-tooth pattern covers the foot.

This type of dish is called "Nabeshima ware" after the provincial governor who controlled the kiln in present-day Saga prefecture. These refined porcelains were made exclusively for the Nabeshima ruling clan to use not only as tableware but also as diplomatic gifts to the shogun and feudal lords. They were never sold for mass consumption due to this special function. Because the sophisticated production techniques of Nabeshima ware were well protected, craftsmen from other areas could not copy them, making these refined porcelains special and desired. In order to maintain their high quality and to prevent leaking their secret techniques, carefully selected craftsmen lived and worked in a secluded area. The Edo-period craftsmen who worked there were well compensated and, in some cases, even allowed to wear a short sword, a privilege typically reserved for the samurai class. If you visit the Nabeshima kiln today, you realize how isolated the area is as you travel through a small road into the mountainous valley. There is only one place to enter and exit out of the valley.

The development and production of Nabeshima ware reflected the political and economic situation surrounding the area. Because the Nabeshima clan had aligned with a defeated clan at the Battle of Sekigahara in 1600, it needed to prove its loyalty to the victorious Tokugawa shogun by offering rare and distinguished tributes. Initially, the Nabeshima lord presented imported porcelain from Jingdezhen, China, because it was considered the best. When political chaos in China caused a shortage of this porcelain, Nabeshima craftsmen were encouraged to produce high-quality porcelain themselves.

—*YM*

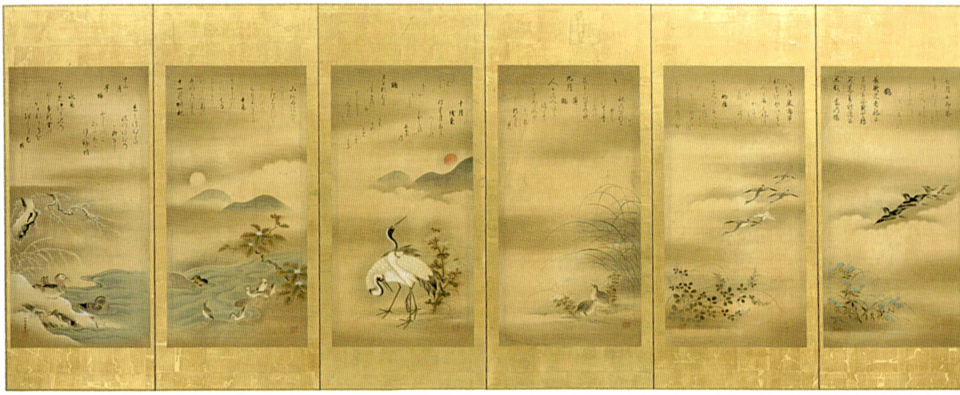

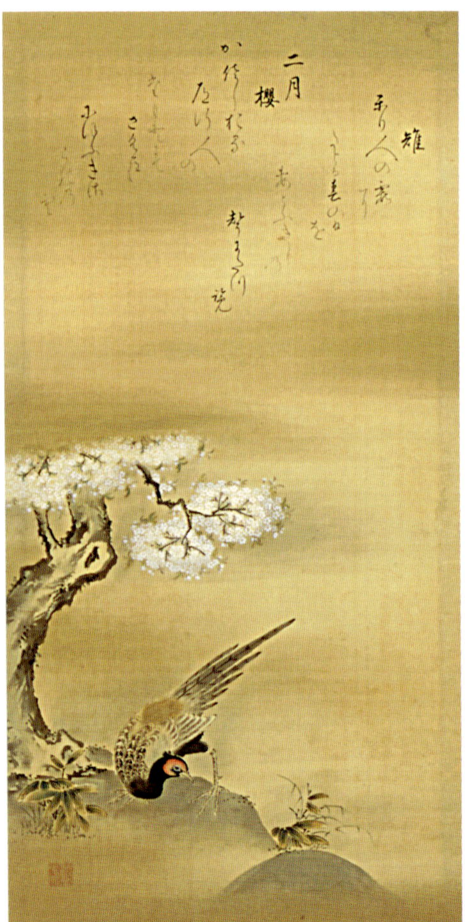

FLOWERS AND BIRDS OF THE TWELVE MONTHS

1703

By Yamamoto Soken (Japanese, 1683–1706)

Edo period (1615–1868)

Pair of six-panel folding screens; ink and colors on silk

H. 113 cm × W. 44 cm (each panel)

The Avery Brundage Collection, B60D82+.1-.2

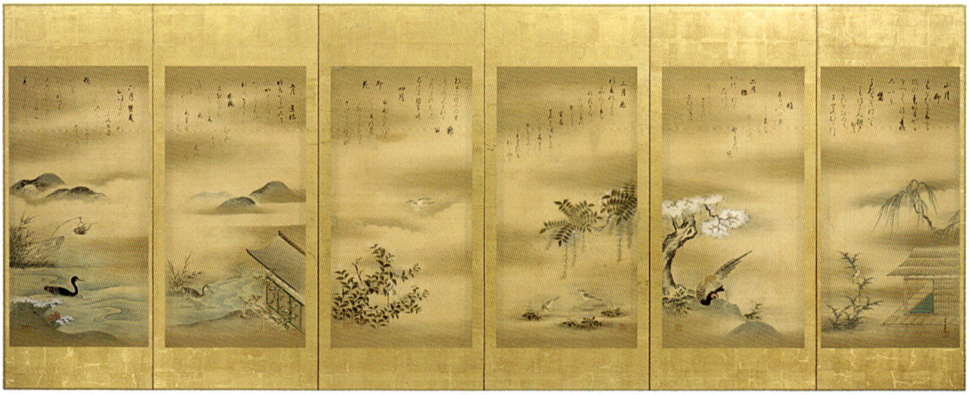

The subject matter for these screens is based on a set of verses by one of Japan's most celebrated poets, Fujiwara Teika (1167–1241). Teika's twenty-four poems feature a flower and a bird for each month of the year. In 1703, twelve members of the imperial court inscribed Teika's famous poems at the top of the screens' twelve panels, with each courtier writing two poems per panel. For example, the second month (second panel from the right on the right-hand screen) is represented by poems featuring cherry blossoms and a pheasant:

Even the sleeves of travelers who broke off cherry blossoms
to decorate their hair have caught the scent that fills this spring sky.

Searching through the spring day's mists,
the hunter goes where he hears the cry of the pheasant for his mate.[13]

Below the inscriptions, the painter Yamamoto Soken evoked the passage of the months by placing each bird and flower pair within scenes that move from early spring at the far right to deep winter at the far left. Rolling hills in some of the panels recall both the environs of Kyoto and the traditions of court painting. Within this imagined space, delicate blossoms and carefully posed birds mirror the refined sensibilities of court society.

Research by Endo Motoko, a curator at the National Institutes for Cultural Heritage, Tokyo National Museum, has revealed that these screens were commissioned as a gift from Emperor Higashiyama (1675–1710) to Matsudaira Nobutsune (1666–1717), the shogun's personal deputy (Shoshidai) in Kyoto.[14] The choice of theme, with its deep roots in traditions linking court poetry and painting, and the carefully arranged examples of courtly calligraphy combine to assert the authority of the court and its deep cultural heritage.

—*LWA*

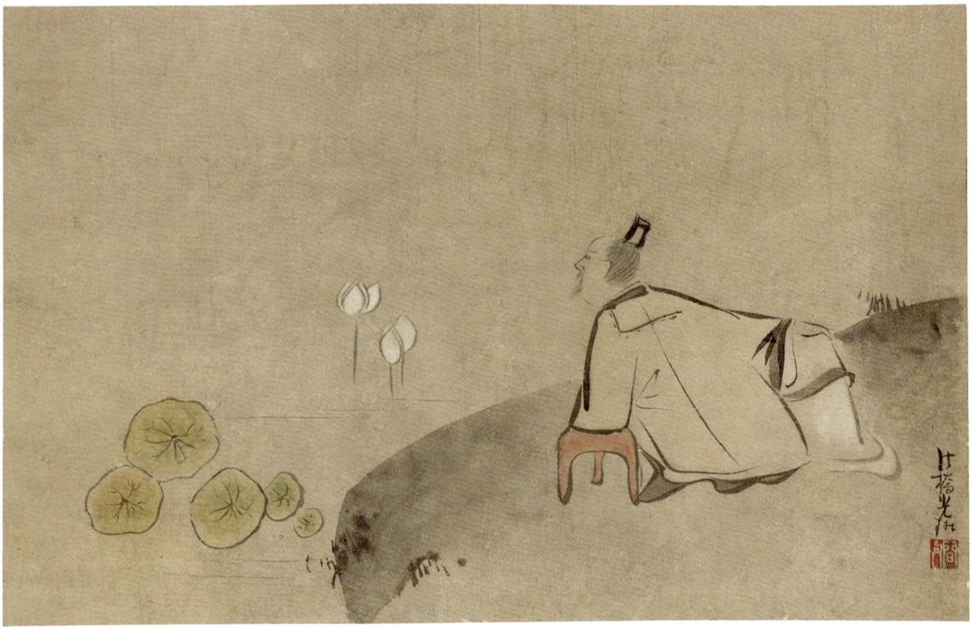

ZHOU MAOSHU ADMIRING LOTUSES

approx. 1704–1716
By Ogata Korin (Japanese, 1658–1716)
Edo period (1615–1868)
Hanging scroll; ink and colors on paper
H. 34.8 cm × W. 56.1 cm (image)
Museum purchase, B76D1

The subject of this charming painting is Zhou Maoshu (1017–1075), a Chinese scholar admired in Japan for his love of flowers. His voluminous white robe, peaked cap, and pose with one elbow resting on an elegant red lacquered armrest suggest his status as a cultivated gentleman. Lotuses, a flower associated with virtue, blossom in the water nearby.

The painter is Ogata Korin, the foremost practitioner of the style known today as Rinpa. The word *Rinpa* itself combines the second character, *rin*, from Korin's name and the character *ha* (also read as *pa*), meaning "school." Korin's sensual visual language is all curves: teardrop-shaped flower petals, undulating lines that flow around the scholar's robe, and a rounded mound of earth, executed in a graded ink wash without the use of outlines. Details of the clothing and setting are abbreviated or eliminated, leaving a shorthand arrangement of elements like the flat, repeated disks of the lotuses' leaves balanced in a dreamlike, abstract composition.

Clues to the date of this painting include the square red seal, also found on one of Korin's few dated works, a portrait of his patron painted in 1704. Korin's fame in the century after his death was such that his known works were carefully documented by other artists. A sketch of this painting appears in the *Sumiyoshi-ke koga tomecho*, a record of old paintings kept by the Sumiyoshi painting school. The sketch appears on a page bearing the date Bunka 9 (1812).[15]

—*LWA*

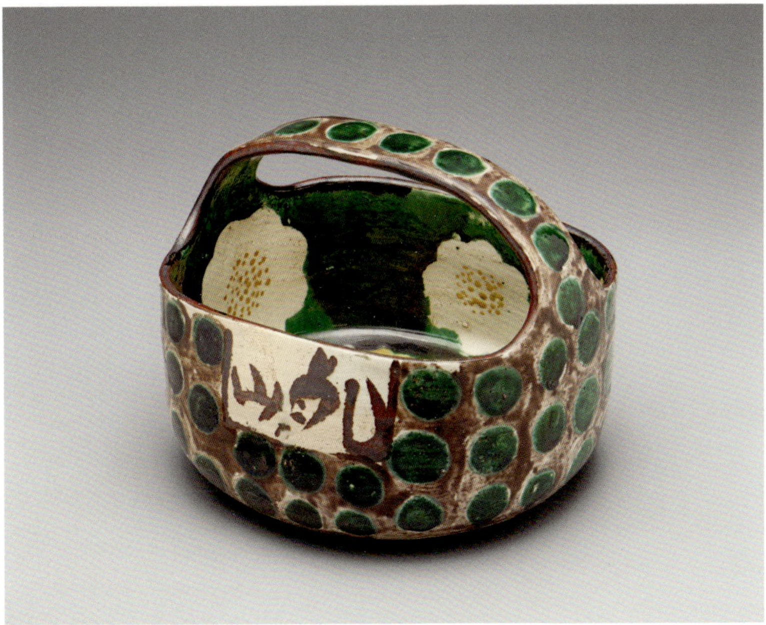

BOWL WITH HANDLE

approx. 1712–1731
By Ogata Kenzan (1663–1743)
Edo period (1615–1868)
Stoneware with white slip and overglaze enamels
H. 14.3 cm × W. 18.1 cm × D. 17.1 cm
Transfer from the Fine Arts Museums of San Francisco, Gift of the Ney-Wolfskill Fund, B69P32

This bowl was made for serving food during tea gatherings, where its striking design would have enhanced the delicacies on offer. Camellias, a winter flower, brighten the interior; ten white, yellow, and eggplant-colored blossoms with colorful dotted anthers stand out against a deep green background. On the exterior big green disks march across a ribbon-like handle and proceed down the sides, and a sprawling signature announces the artist's name: Kenzan.

Ogata Kenzan's novel ceramic designs sprang from his background as the son of a successful textile merchant in Kyoto. Like his brother and sometime collaborator, Ogata Korin (1658–1716)—one of the most inventive painters of his day (see page to the left)—Kenzan was attuned to the sophisticated, two-dimensional visual language of Edo-period textile design. In this case, the potter used paper stencils of the kind used to pattern fabrics to shape the stylized blossoms in the bowl's interior and the disks that dot the outside. The designs are colored with a combination of white slip and glaze.

Kenzan had legions of followers and imitators, a fact that has spurred debates about the authenticity of surviving works inscribed with his name. A similarly shaped bowl preserved in the Hatakeyama Memorial Museum of Fine Art collection in Tokyo has camellias in the interior and white disks on the exterior inscribed in red with characters for good fortune. The scholar Oka Yoshiko identifies the dot patterns on both bowls as water droplets. She has argued that Kenzan designed bold, decorative works like these during the period when his studio was located at Nijo Chojiyacho in central Kyoto, before his move to Edo (Tokyo) in 1731.[16]

—*LWA*

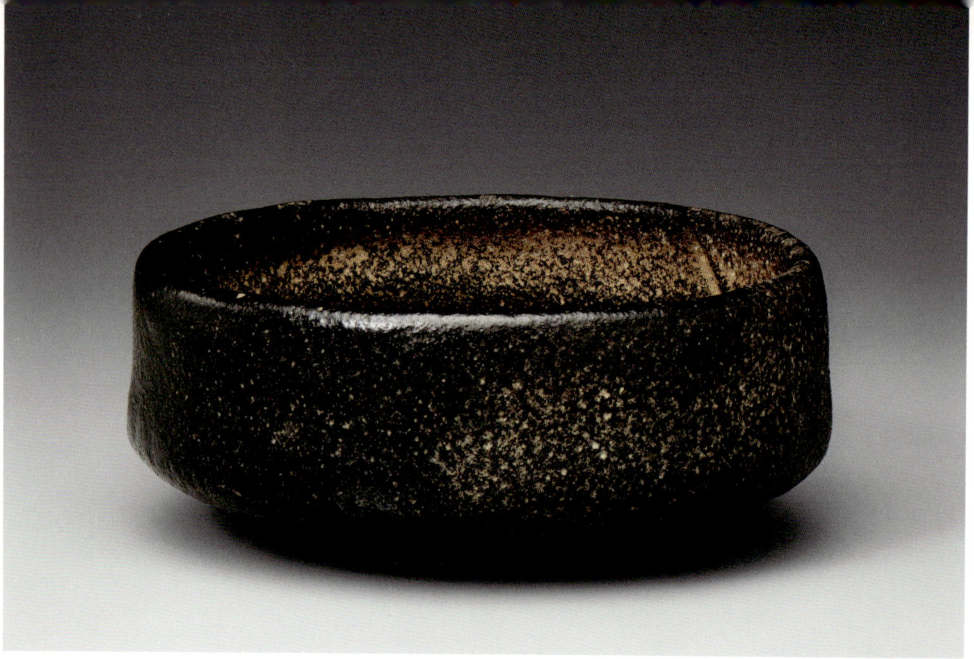

SUMMER FESTIVAL MUSIC (NATSUKAGURA)

Attributed to Raku Sonyu (Japanese, 1664–1716)
Edo period (1615–1868)
Earthenware with glaze (Raku ware)
H. 5.5 cm × Diam. 14 cm
Gift of William S. Picher, B76P5

At first glance, its uneven shape seems spontaneous; but in fact this teabowl is carefully considered, with a form and size that fits comfortably into two hands and a smooth lip for drinking green tea (*matcha*). The teabowl looks heavy, but it is surprisingly light. During the hot summer months, hosts of tea gatherings often choose shallow teabowls such as this one to quickly dissipate the heat of the tea. Compared to high-fired teabowls, this type of low-fired teabowl, called Raku ware, does not conduct as much heat. This makes it ideal for serving hot tea. The bowl's black glaze would also enhance the color of *matcha* inside it. As opposed to being wheel thrown, Raku teabowls are traditionally molded by hand before being fired one at a time in small cylindrical kilns.

The term *Raku* refers to glazed teabowls made by the Raku family of Kyoto, and by extension to similar wares made by other potters. The history of Raku ware goes back to Raku Chojiro (1516–1592), the son of a roof-tile maker. Sen no Rikyu (1520/2–1591), a famous tea master, purportedly requested Chojiro to create teabowls suitable to his austere and rustic tea aesthetics.

The Raku family has continued to produce teabowls in Kyoto since the 1500s. It has worked in close relationship with the three Sen families (the three major schools of Japanese tea practice that followed Rikyu) for generations. Today, Raku Kichizaemon XV (b. 1949) continues the Raku ware tradition. His craft has been a closely guarded family secret with unchanged basic techniques passed down to the present day.

This black teabowl is attributed to Raku Sonyu (1664–1716), the fifth-generation Raku family potter. Before it was sent to the United States, this vessel previously belonged to Nintokusai (active 1801–1826), the tenth-generation grand master of Urasenke, one of the three Sen schools of tea. Nintokusai named the bowl *Natsukagura* (Summer Festival Music). It is a common practice that an artist, owner, or tea master give poetic names to tea utensils. Naming indicates that tea practitioners consider a piece a one-of-a-kind artwork rather than a utilitarian tea vessel. When given by a well-respected person, these names could significantly increase the value of the objects.

—*YM*

COURTESAN IN A ROBE DECORATED WITH CALLIGRAPHY

By Baiyuken Katsunobu (Japanese, active approx. 1704–1716)
Edo period (1615–1868)
Hanging scroll; ink and colors on paper
H. 88.6 cm × W. 41.9 cm
The Avery Brundage Collection, B60D119

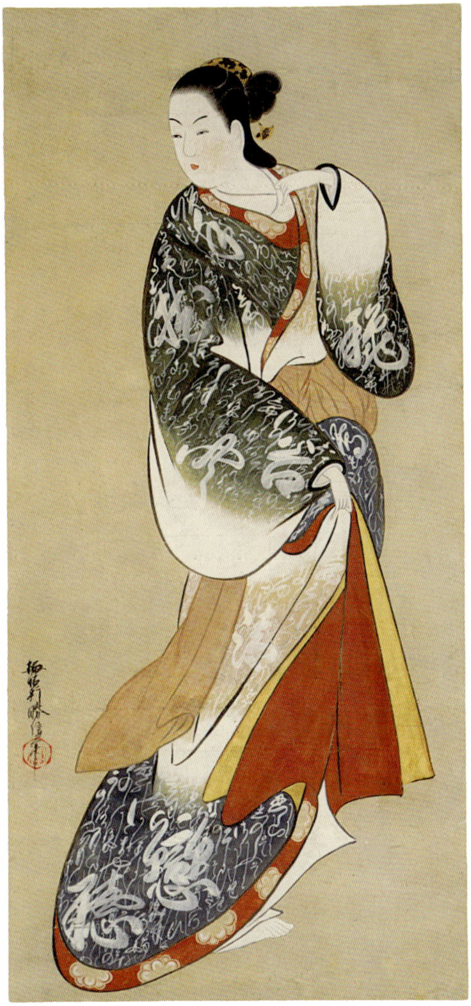

A statuesque beauty lifts the front edge of her robe, revealing red and white underlayers and a glimpse of bare toes. Her other hand grasps the edge of her lapel, calling attention to the powdered white skin of her neck. Her pose, with head turned coyly away from the viewer, creates a graceful S-curve accentuated by her billowing sleeves. Loosely tied at the front, the light brown sash of her robe trails behind, giving the figure a sense of slight forward motion.

Eighteenth-century paintings of alluring courtesans were valued as mementos of dalliances in urban pleasure quarters and as items of fantasy for the uninitiated. In addition to having such desirable traits as a pale complexion, small mouth, and delicately shaped ears, the courtesans are invariably shown modelling fashionable attire.[17] Mimicking a popular style, the painter Baiyuken Katsunobu frequently dressed his subjects in robes decorated with flowing script. Here bold characters are superimposed over smaller cursive writing, using language typical of poems on the seasons and love: "year" (*toshi*) is visible on her right shoulder; "pine" (*matsu*), "cold" (*samui*), and "suffering" (*kurushii*) on her right sleeve; "autumn" (*aki*) on her left sleeve; "hear" (*kiku*) and "love" (*koi*) on her hem; and "wave" (*nami*) faintly legible at the center of her skirt. The sweeping, curvaceous outlines of the costume, also characteristic of Katsunobu's work, reinforce the sensual nature of his subject.
—*LWA*

BODHIDHARMA (DARUMA)

approx. 1750–1768
By Hakuin Ekaku (Japanese, 1685–1768)
Edo period (1615–1868)
Hanging scroll; ink on paper
H. 122.7 cm × W. 55.9 cm (image)
Gift from The Collection of George Gund III, 2016.82

Hakuin Ekaku is arguably the most influential figure in the history of later Zen Buddhism. He is admired for having revitalized the Rinzai sect of Zen through teachings expressed in many writings published during his lifetime. In the latter half of his life, Hakuin traveled far and wide and used lectures, sermons, paintings, and calligraphy to convey Zen insights to a broad cross section of the populace. A self-taught artist, he used ink in a direct and vital way, depicting familiar figures from Zen lore, landscapes, and, occasionally, genre subjects.

One of Hakuin's favorite subjects was Bodhidharma, the first patriarch of Zen Buddhism. Following established conventions, he represents the monk from the shoulders up, with a large, balding head and bulging, lidless eyes. A popular legend attests that Bodhidharma, known in Japan as Daruma, cut off his eyelids to prevent himself from falling asleep while meditating. Here, a powerful curving line defines the edge of Daruma's monk's robe, underscoring the fixity of his resolve. Shaggy eyebrows, unkempt beard, and a bulbous nose allude to the patriarch's origins on the Indian subcontinent, whence he brought Zen teachings to China.

The portrait successfully conveys the intensity of Daruma's spiritual quest and the inward concentration required for enlightenment. Above the portrait Hakuin enjoined viewers to take up a similar quest with the inscription, "Pointing directly at the human heart, see your own self to attain buddhahood." Mitigating the seriousness of this message is the somewhat cartoonish quality of the image, with its exaggerated features and unpolished style. This playful spirit helps to disarm the viewer and offers a means to communicate complex, abstract principles to ordinary people.

—*LWA*

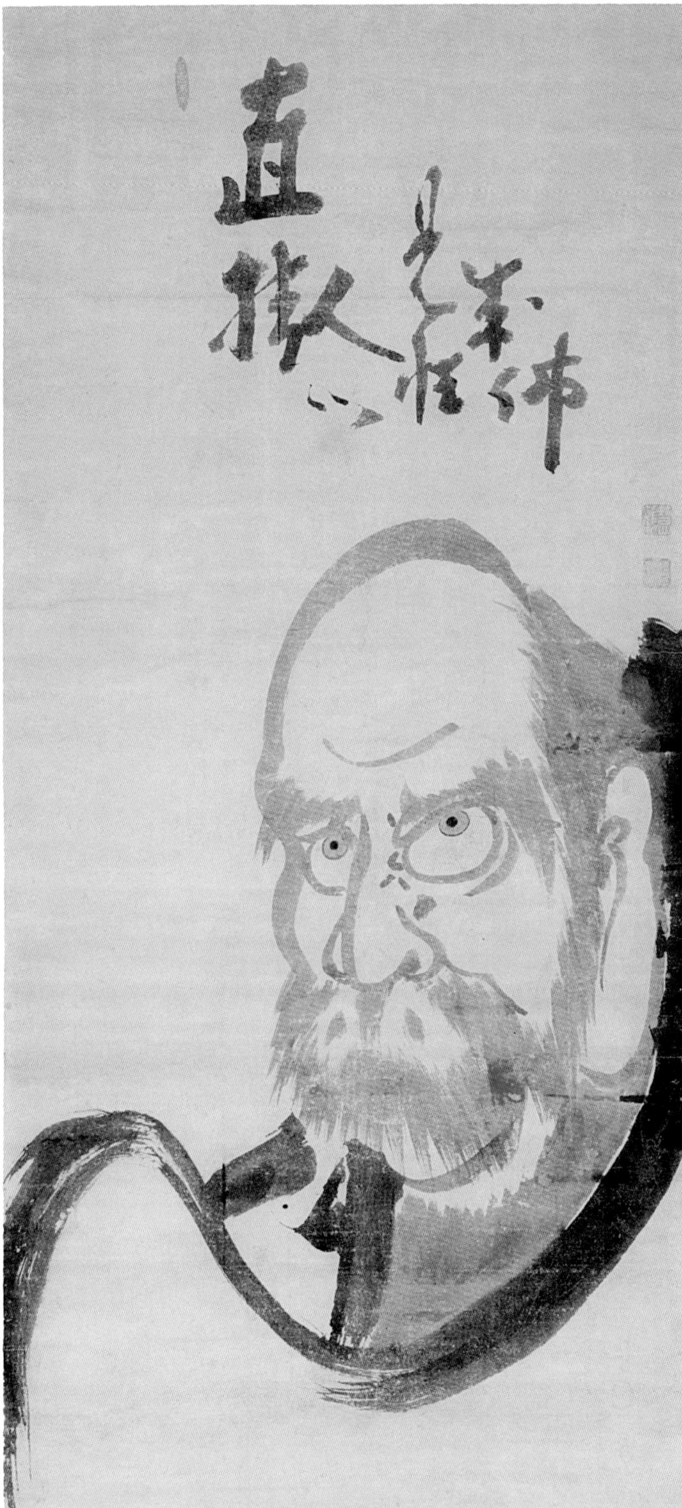

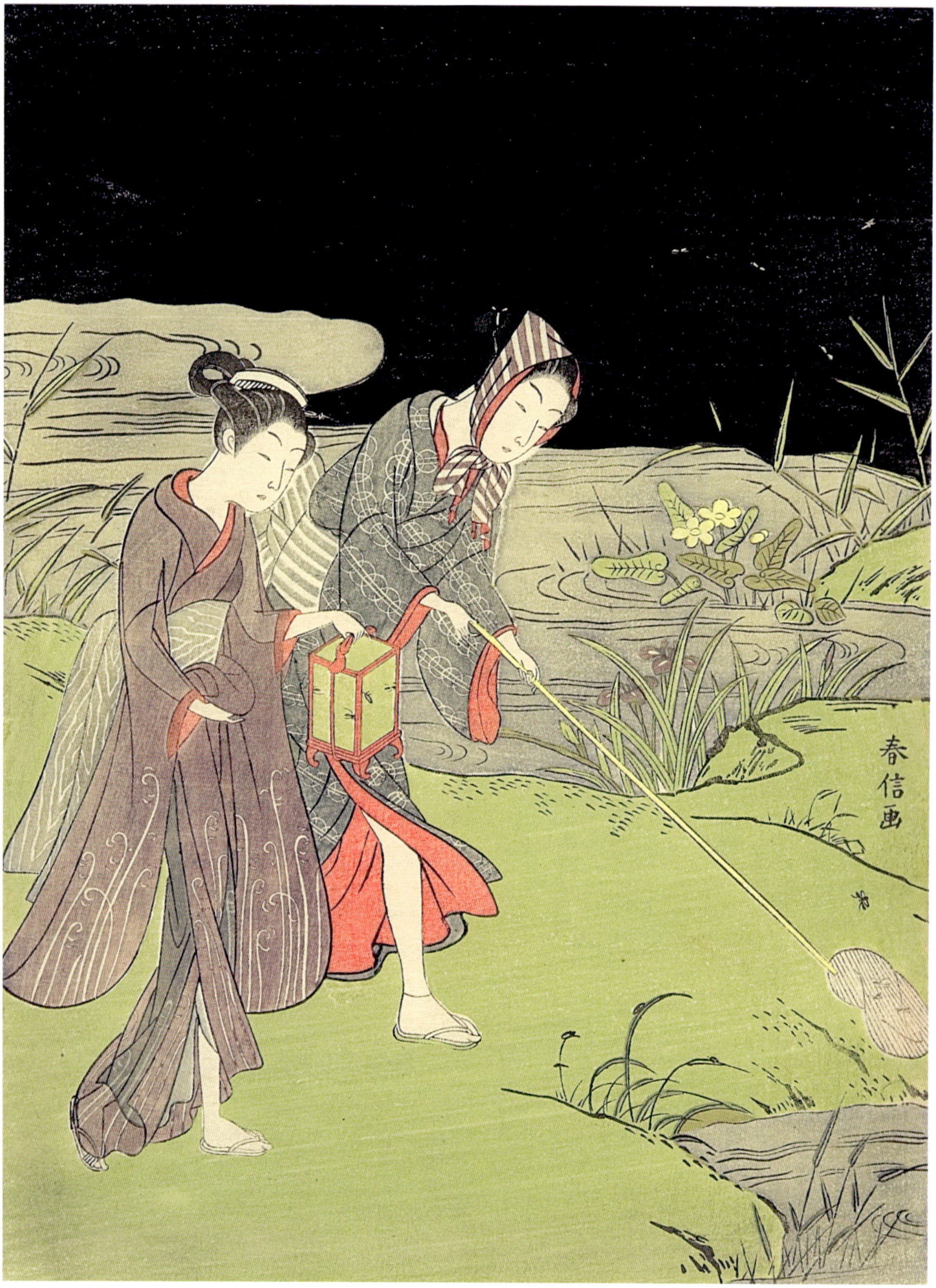
春信画

HUNTING FOR FIREFLIES

1767–1768

By Suzuki Harunobu (Japanese, approx. 1725–1770)

Edo period (1615–1868)

Woodblock print; ink and colors on paper

H. 26.7 cm × W. 20.3 cm

Gift of the Grabhorn Ukiyo-e Collection, 2005.100.29

Fireflies glow above a stream on a hot summer evening. A young couple engages in firefly hunting, a popular leisure activity of short summer nights. At first glance, both show youthful innocence, but this print hints at more guilty pleasures.

Throughout history, Japanese poets composed many poems about fireflies, which symbolize burning desire. When this print was made, catching fireflies referred to love affairs, as fireflies produce light from their lower abdomens during twilight to attract mates. Eighteenth-century viewers would have also associated the designs on the figures' kimonos with love affairs. The geometric pattern on the young man's robe at the right is known as *kuruwa tsunagi*, which has the double meaning of "joined circles" and "joined pleasure quarters." His companion wears a long-sleeved kimono decorated above the hem and on the sleeves with a fern (*Pteridium aquilinum*) pattern. This motif shows tightly curled fern fronds that are not yet fully developed but that are fresh and edible at this stage. This motif may simply symbolize youthfulness, but it may also suggest that the wearer of the kimono is ready to be sexually consumed.

Woodblock prints from the Edo period (1615–1868) are known as ukiyo-e (pictures of the "floating world"). Originally a Buddhist term used to describe the impermanence of the human world, the concept of floating world (*ukiyo*) later became secularized. Ukiyo-e printmakers often took their themes from the transient or everyday world and focused on leisure activities such as love affairs, theater, and sumo wrestling. This full-color print of a young couple was produced by making impressions from a set of woodblocks. This type of print is called "brocade pictures" (*nishiki-e*) because the effect is thought to resemble a colorful silk brocade. Picture calendar designs made in 1765 by the artist of this print, Suzuki Harunobu, are thought to be the earliest multicolor prints in Japan.

—*YM*

PINE, BAMBOO, AND PLUM

By Maruyama Okyo (Japanese, 1733–1795)
Edo period (1615–1868)
Pair of six-panel folding screens; ink and color on paper
H. 164.5 cm × W. 363.8 cm (each image)
The Avery Brundage Collection, B60D55+ and B60D56+

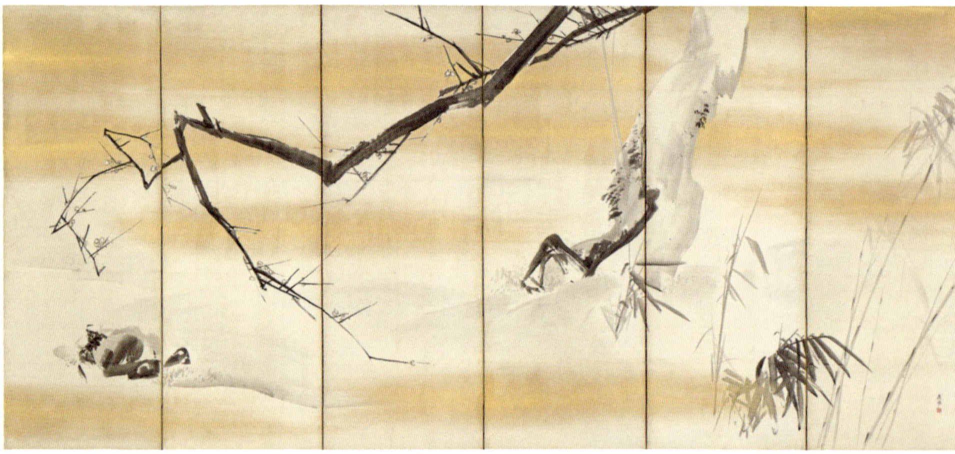

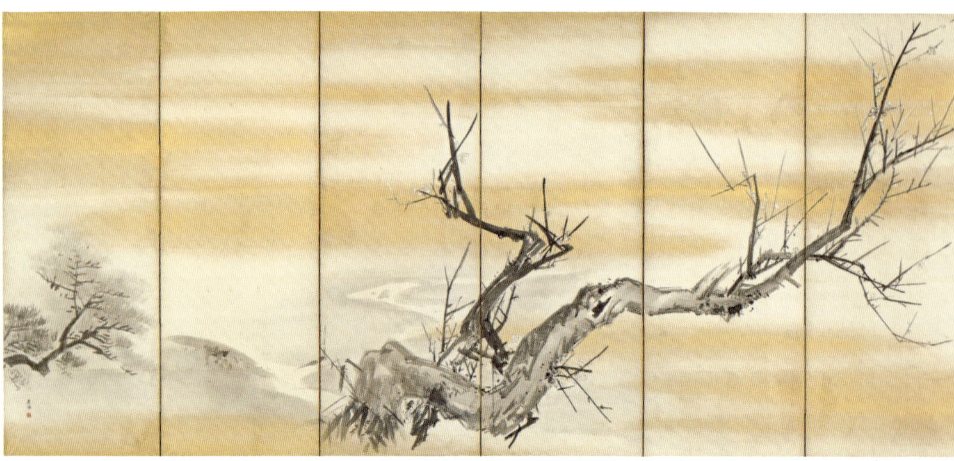

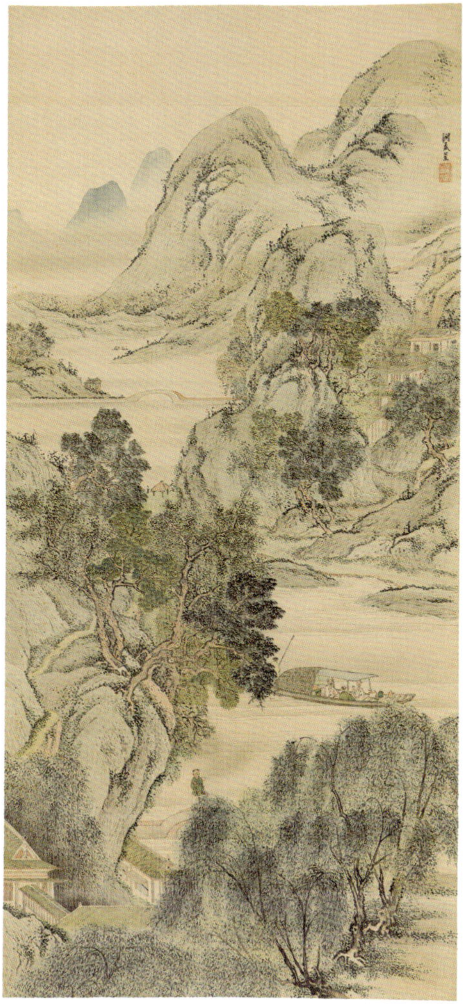

WEST LAKE IN SPRING

approx. 1777
By Yosa Buson (Japanese, 1716–1783)
Edo period (1615–1868)
Hanging scroll; ink and colors on silk
H. 133.2 cm × W. 62.5 cm (image)
Gift and Purchase from the Harry G. C. Packard Collection Charitable Trust in honor of Dr. Shujiro Shimada; The Avery Brundage Collection, 1991.80

In the midst of towering mountains and expanses of still water, a small figure on a bridge beckons us to join him in his beautiful paradise. A friendly-looking figure such as this is common in Yosa Buson's (1716–1783) landscape paintings. He stares out at us just as we gaze into the rich landscape. He guides us to enjoy this imagined world with its boat full of Chinese scholars out for an afternoon on West Lake in Hangzhou.

This famed location in eastern China inspired Chinese poets and artists for many centuries before Buson created the scene, yet it was a location to which the painter could never travel. When this work was made, Japan's borders were closed and travel was possible only through the vicarious means of painted images and written accounts.

Buson created this work around 1777, when he had settled in Kyoto and was actively painting for his growing circle of patrons.[18] In earlier years he had studied Chinese poetry and philosophy, including the literature of the eleventh-century poet Su Shi, whose works featured West Lake. Undoubtedly, Buson saw many Chinese paintings and read other poetry that celebrated this place. By the time he was sitting down to create this landscape, Buson's imagination held a host of specific signs that most any Japanese patron interested in or even perhaps desperate to travel to China would immediately understand.

The placid waters that wend their way through the painting would transport the patron to this often-imagined place. Buson and other painters known today as the literati or Nanga (southern painting) school artists created Chinese subjects, scenes, and poetry among many other things. They painted and wrote in a language that was simultaneously Japanese and based on Chinese precedents and prototypes. This view of West Lake is an image of China made for and in Japan.
—*RM*

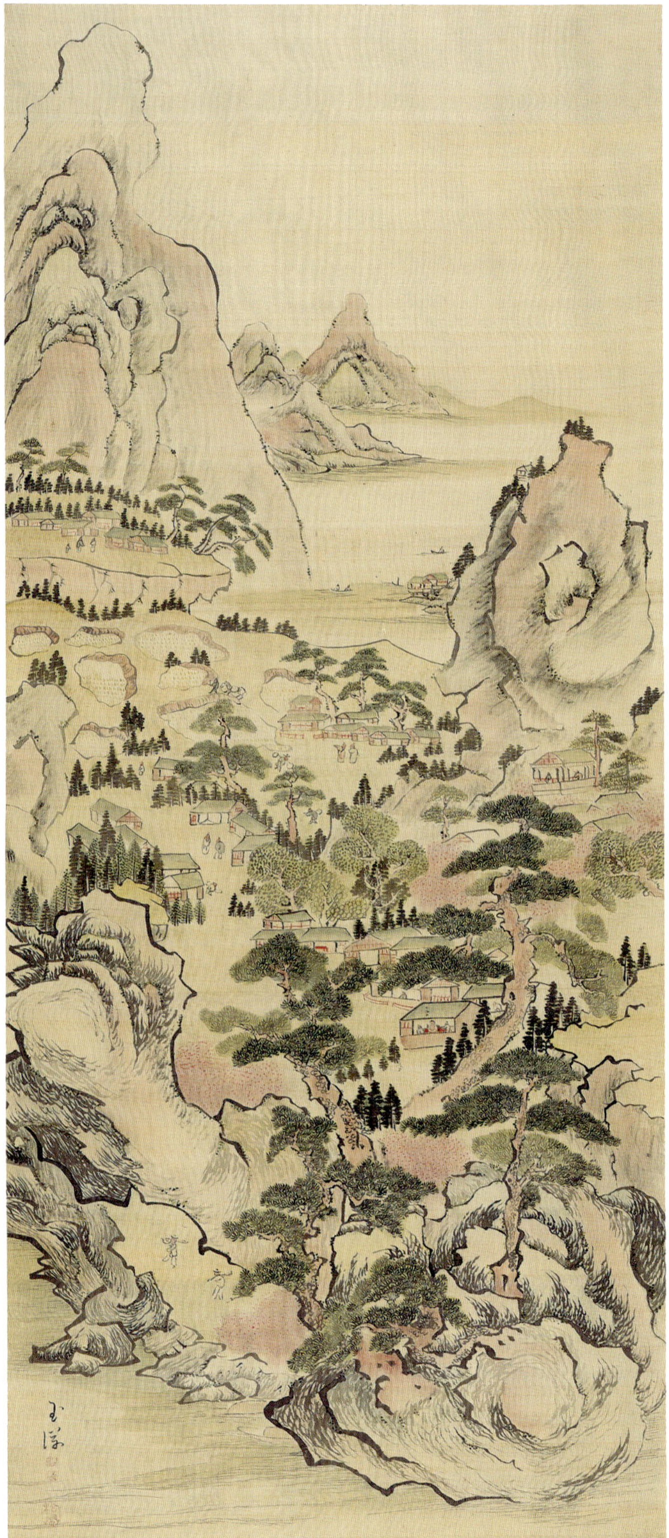

PEACH BLOSSOM IDYLL

—

approx. 1750–1784
By Tokuyama Gyokuran (Japanese, 1728–1784)
Edo period (1615–1868)
Hanging scroll; ink and colors on paper
H. 111.7 cm × W. 49.5 cm (image)
Museum purchase, B76D3

—

How do you picture utopia? One of China's most famous poets, Tao Yuanming (365–427), supplied a lasting vision in his tale "Peach Blossom Spring." The story recounts a fisherman's discovery of an idyllic village cut off from the rest of the world. Centuries later, the Japanese artist Tokuyama Gyokuran reinterpreted the centuries-old theme, picturing fanciful, tilting peaks that rise above a clearing dotted with houses, trees, and fields. In the foreground two men enter a jagged portal through large boulders that line the shore. Clouds of stippled pink blossoms mark the setting as the mythical "peach blossom village."

Gyokuran invites us to linger, using vibrant washes of yellow and pink to suffuse the scene with warmth. Rippling texture strokes—known as "ox-tail wrinkles"—animate the rocks, and heavily accented outlines energize the scene with jagged twists and turns. Amid these lively surroundings, the village is a zone of calm, an orderly arrangement of houses and trees on a level plane. There the inhabitants, in small groups and pairs, enact a convivial yet tranquil existence.

Other elements emphasize the otherworldly nature of this fabled setting. Gyokuran had a penchant for strangely distorted rock formations that look like giant oyster shells dragged from the sea. She carefully plots figures, houses, and trees in diminishing scale as they proceed up the page, then undermines the effect of recession with patterned trees and craterlike rice paddies that resist gravity, floating freely in space.

These touches are in keeping with the mission of Japan's literati painters, who aspired to balance personal expression with conventions derived from paintings by Chinese scholar-officials. Famous in her time, Gyokuran was married to the celebrated literati painter Ike Taiga (1723–1776). Taiga reportedly filled two handscrolls with landscape motifs for Gyokuran to use as painting models. A number of these archetypes appear in this painting, where they are recombined, distorted, and reimagined in a unique variation of her husband's style. Like her mother and grandmother before her, Gyokuran was also a serious poet. Her method of reusing compositional elements in new configurations is said to resemble the time-honored practice of allusive variation (*honka dori*) in court poetry.[19] Gyokuran's goal, in poems or painting, was to be inventive while honoring tradition. Her vision of this utopian world articulates this principle of creative refreshment in visual form.

—*LWA*

SUNRISE ON NEW YEAR'S MORNING

approx. 1795
By Eishosai Choki (Japanese, active approx. 1780–1810)
Edo period (1615–1868)
Woodblock print; ink, colors, and mica on paper
H. 38.1 cm × W. 25.1 cm
Gift of the Grabhorn Ukiyo-e Collection, 2005.100.84

This print comes from an untitled series of beauties of the four seasons. The woman who pauses to glance back across the sea toward a brilliant red sunrise is out to greet the auspicious first sunrise of the New Year, as is customary in Japan. The mica sprinkled over the black sky evokes the iridescence of the early morning light.

The blossoming pheasant's-eye plant placed on the basin signals the time of the year. During the Edo period (1615–1868), these yellow flowers were sold in flower pots as New Year's decorations. The plants persevere through the cold weather and blossom around the lunar New Year in the early spring. Pheasant's-eye in Japanese is *fukujuso*, which means "plant of good luck and longevity." Its alternative name, *ganjitsuso*, means "New Year's Day plant."

The figure's outer robes fall open, exposing her red undergarment, while her soft green sash is loosely tied in front. Her slightly disheveled appearance suggests that the woman hastily came out of her bed chamber to catch the first sunrise of the year. With her right hand tucked warmly inside her garment, she reaches her left arm out to cover her shoulder against the cold morning air. Her kimono's design with vertical stripes, based on imported South and Southeast Asian textiles, became popular in Japan in the mid to late eighteenth century. The multistriped inner robe and simple pinstriped outer robe represent the essence of understated Edo chic.

Japanese woodblock prints such as this one were produced rapidly, inexpensively, and in large numbers during the Edo period. They were affordable arts for the middle class, such as merchants. Similar to a fashion magazine today, these prints were created quickly to reflect seasonal changes and fashion trends. With its nearly perfect color preservation, this print is one of the best surviving examples of the prints of Eishosai Choki, who was known for his depictions of beautiful, stylish women.

—*YM*

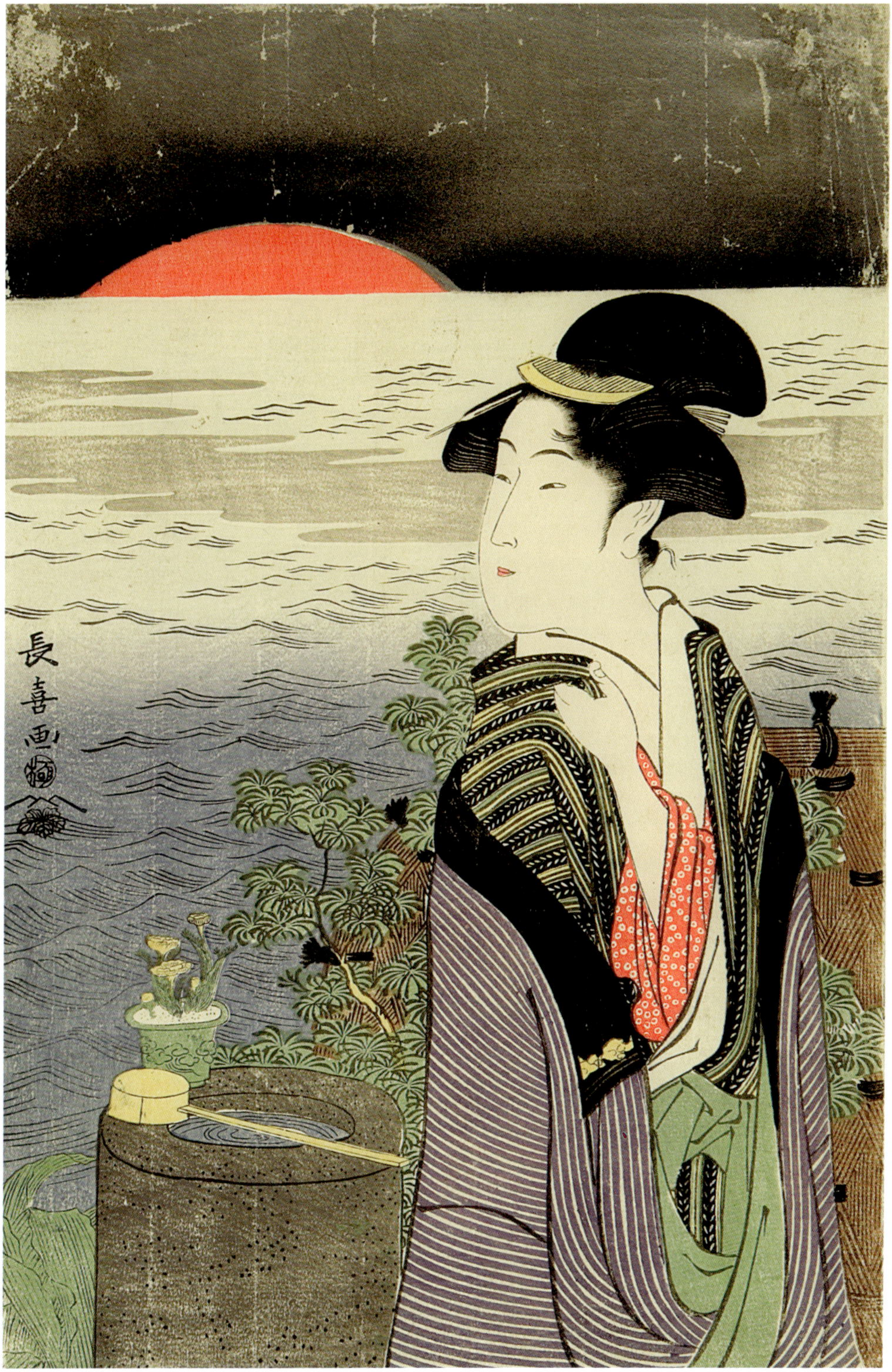
長喜画

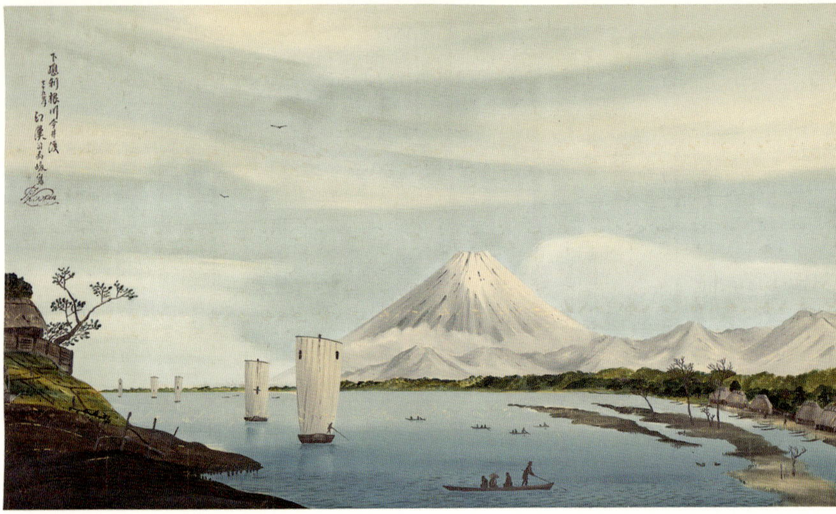

MOUNT FUJI VIEWED FROM THE IMAI FERRY ON THE TONE RIVER, SHIMOSA PROVINCE

—

1812

By Shiba Kokan (Japanese, 1747–1818)

Edo period (1615–1868)

Hanging scroll; oil on silk

H. 57.7 cm × W. 98.5 cm (image)

Gift of Junkichi Mayuyama, B66D18

—

This view of the traditional subject of Mount Fuji is an example of so-called mud painting (*doro-e*), a Japanese medium the artist Shiba Kokan concocted in order to reproduce the effect of European oil paintings. The depiction of the blue sky with soft, white clouds, the diminution of scale of the sailboats as they recede into the distance, and the use of three-dimensional shading derive from Western painting.

In the 1630s, the Japanese government imposed strict regulations on trade with the West. Only the Dutch were allowed to trade through Dejima, a man-made island in Nagasaki. Although foreigners were not allowed to enter the mainland, Western goods still flowed through Dejima into Japan. Western art provided Japanese artists with fresh perspectives and challenged them to find new ways to express themselves.

Kokan was one of the most versatile and adventurous artists of his time. He learned about Western science and art from the limited number of books and other materials then available in Japan. In 1799, he published *Discussion of Western Painting* (*Seiyo gadan*), which praises Western art for its techniques of realistic representation. He admired Western naturalism attained through shading and color gradation. In this painting, Kokan signed his name in the Latin alphabet.

The inscription on the upper left states: "Ferry at Imai on the Tone River in Shimosa Province. Portrayed by Shiba Kokan, a seventy-five-year-old man." For some unknown reason, the artist began to add nine years to his actual age when he reached sixty-two. Therefore, he inscribed this painting in 1812 when he was sixty-six years old. Another odd fact is that he sent out his own death notice five years before he actually died. One theory to explain his strange behavior is that Kokan was influenced by a fable written by Zhuangzi, a Chinese Daoist philosopher from the fourth century BCE. The story suggests that if one follows an instruction given by a wise man, he can progressively improve himself every year. In the eighth year, he did not understand death and did not understand life. However, in the ninth year, he could finally penetrate "the profound mystery."[20] Kokan perhaps hoped to achieve enlightenment by adding nine years to his age and experiencing his virtual death by sending out the death notice.

—*YM*

SECLUDED RIVER, ROCKS, AND STREAMS

1812–1817
By Uragami Gyokudo (Japanese, 1745–1820)
Hanging scroll; ink on paper
H. 110.8 cm × W. 61.9 cm (image)
Gift from The Collection of George Gund III, 2016.56

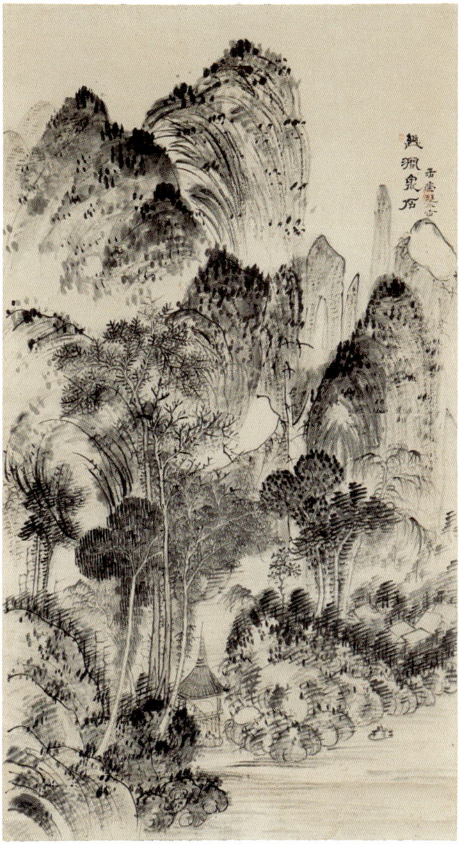

Uragami Gyokudo was known in his day as a poet, calligrapher, and especially as a musician, playing and composing new music for the Chinese seven-string *qin*. This instrument for centuries has been especially beloved by poets and sages; its soft, low tones are suitable for meditation or for playing for a close friend. Halfway through his life, Gyokudo gave up his samurai-official position and began wandering through Japan, carrying his *qin*. It was in these years that he painted the landscapes that at the time were appreciated only by a small circle of literati. Now the situation is reversed; Gyokudo is highly appreciated as a painter, while his music is almost completely forgotten. Yet it was his *qin* music that gave him a unique approach to painting.

On the *qin*, the same note may be played by different means, on different strings and plucked or flicked with different fingers. As a result, what may sound like the same note is never the same, always showing slight tonal differences. Similarly, in Gyokudo's calligraphy of his title and signature, there are similar strokes, such as the swelling and diminishing horizontal or diagonal lines moving to the right. On close viewing, however, these too vary in the length, width, and angle. Examination of the title and signature reveal that Gyokudo applied the same approach of varying similar strokes in his calligraphy.

In his paintings, Gyokudo seems to repeat brushstrokes many times—horizontal dashes with an upward thrust, downward curving parallel lines, washes of different tones of gray, and clusters of dots—but they are all slightly different in tone, form, and rhythm, creating his powerful personal style. Humanity is represented only by a waterside pavilion, sandwiched tightly between two landmasses that seem to vibrate with pulsating energy. But wait—there are also a few roofs barely to be seen, almost smothered by the horizontal dashes that indicate foliage. Most notable are the larger trees and mountains that surge upwards; they are built up by layers of overlapping wet and dry, dark and light, short or longer strokes of the brush in different tonalities of ink, accented and reinforced by black dots. Mastering these techniques allowed Gyokudo to create a counterpoint of overlapping rhythms that evokes an almost unnerving vision of nature. For anyone who has been through a hurricane, tornado, or earthquake, this vision is not unfamiliar; it emboldened Gyokudo to express his understanding of the elemental forces that abide and endure behind everyday life in the natural world.

—Stephen Addiss is a scholar-artist with extensive publications on East Asian painting, calligraphy, and poetry.

TRAVELING PRIEST

—

By Minko (Japanese, 1736–1816)
Edo period (1615–1868)
Netsuke; wood
H. 3.5 cm × W. 3.8 cm × D. 3.7 cm
The Avery Brundage Collection, B70Y202

—

ZHONG KUI (SHOKI), THE DEMON QUELLER, PUSHING DEMONS INTO A PICKLING TUB

—

1800–1900
By Gyokko (Japanese)
Edo (1615–1868) or Meiji (1868–1912) period
Netsuke; ivory
H. 4.4 cm × W. 3.5 cm × D. 2.8 cm
The Avery Brundage Collection, B70Y122

—

THREE MONKEYS PLAYING WITH DEER

—

1800–1900
By Ikkosai (Japanese)
Edo (1615–1868) or Meiji (1868–1912) period
Netsuke; ivory with inlaid horn and staining
H. 3.9 cm × W. 3 cm × D. 4.1 cm
The Avery Brundage Collection, B70Y1250

—

Attached to the end of a silk cord, netsuke were fashion accessories for men of the Edo period (1615–1868). These small sculptures are not only visually intriguing but also practical. Netsuke were used as toggles to secure small personal objects such as carrying cases (inro) and tobacco pouches. Because kimonos did not have pockets, Japanese men hung personal items from a cord slipped under a sash (obi) and secured with a netsuke. A fine and functional netsuke would be compact, light, durable, and smooth without any sharp edges that could damage a kimono.

Assembling a thematically consistent set of netsuke and inro was a fashionable activity during the Edo period. A good ensemble would have been a fun source of conversation among friends who often sought new and interesting designs. To meet the demand, netsuke carvers chose a wide variety of subjects, including the animals, ghosts, and humans shown here. They executed their designs in great detail and often with humor, and created work out of ivory, wood, walrus tusk, bamboo, walnut, ceramic, and other materials.

Small found objects such as gourds, seashells, stones, and pieces of wood were initially used as toggles. Because of this, the Edo Japanese originally treated netsuke as purely functional objects and did not consider them works of art. This might explain why there is no extant primary record of the birth and development of netsuke, even though images of netsuke can be found as far back as the seventeenth century. Gradually, netsuke evolved to the sophisticated miniature sculptures we know today. Some carvers signed their names on their work, showing that they considered them more than utilitarian objects.

People appreciated the craftsmanship, diverse subject matter, and playful nature of netsuke. But in the late nineteenth century, when Japanese men began to wear Western-style clothing with pockets, netsuke lost their importance and declined. These carefully carved miniature sculptures later became an obsession for collectors all over the world. The Asian Art Museum's netsuke are one of its visitors' most beloved collections. More than 1,600 netsuke are in the collection, and over a hundred are on display at any given time.

—*YM*

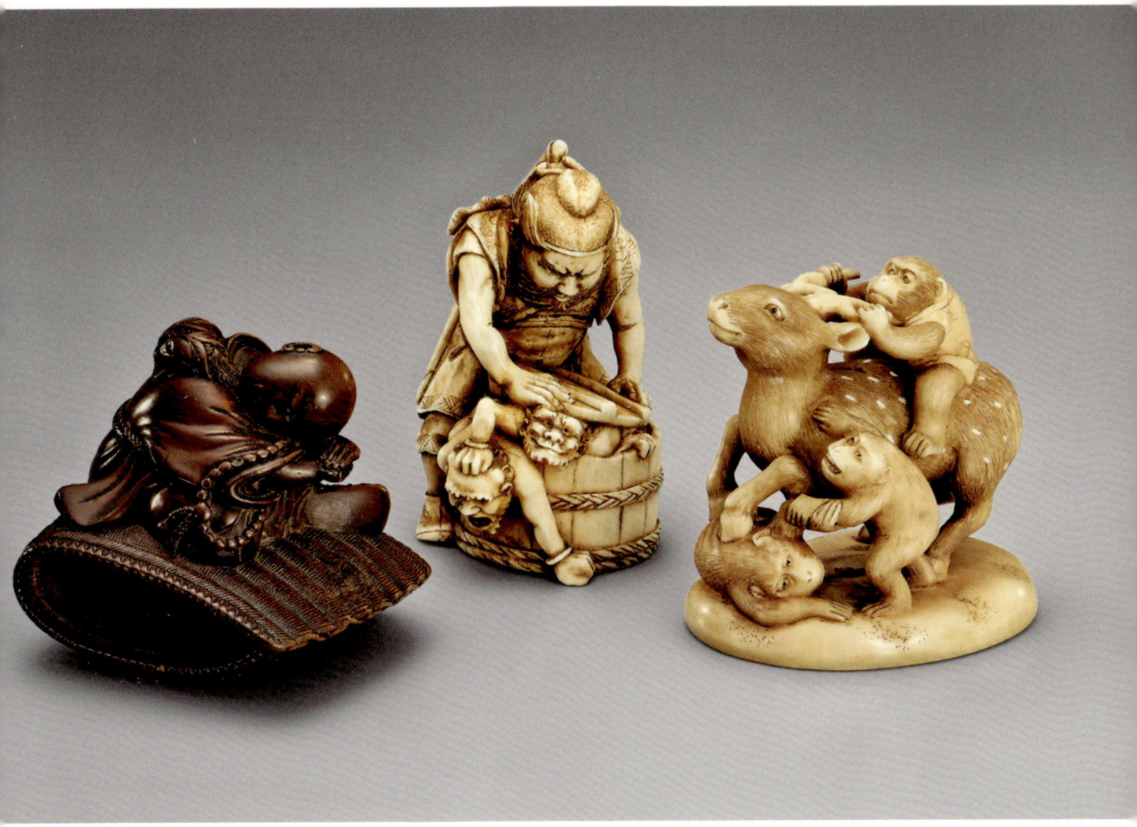

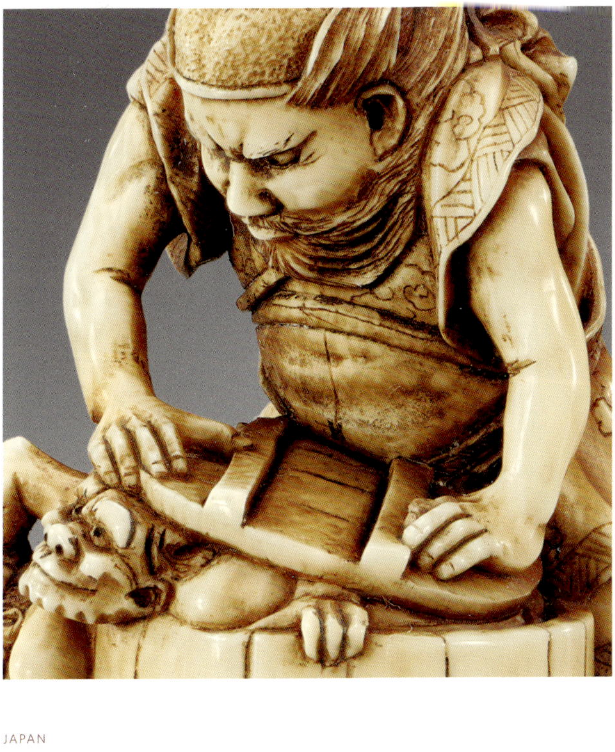

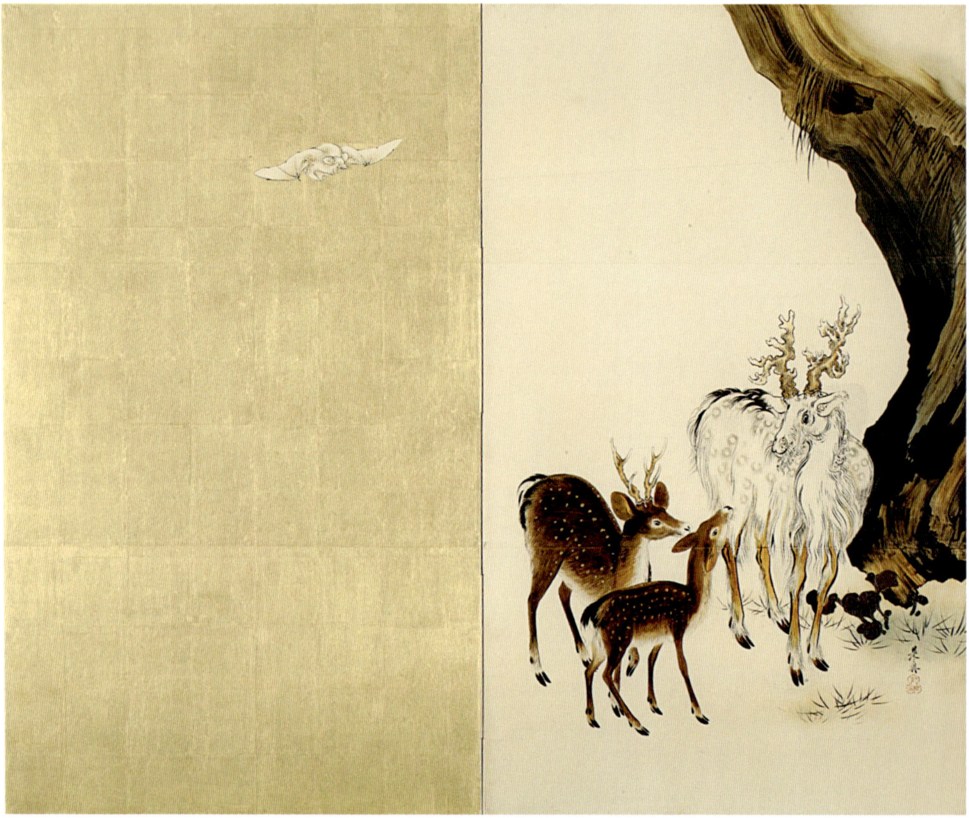

DEER AND BAT

approx. 1872–1891
By Shibata Zeshin (Japanese, 1807–1891)
Meiji period (1868–1912)
Two-panel folding screen; lacquer and gold on paper
H. 136.2 cm × W. 165.7 cm (image)
The Avery Brundage Collection, B60D59+

BOXES WITH DESIGNS OF WILDFLOWERS GOING TO SEED

By Shibata Zeshin (Japanese, 1807–1891)

Edo (1615–1868) or Meiji period (1868–1912)

Lacquer on wood

Left: H. 11.6 cm × W. 12.8 cm × D. 10.2 cm; right: H. 4.7 cm × W. 9.6 cm × D. 7.2 cm

The Avery Brundage Collection, B60M3+ and B60M4+

Their muted color and diminutive scale might make you miss these boxes—the larger one is less than twelve centimeters wide—but they reward close looking. Their maker, Shibata Zeshin, trained in the studio of a master lacquer artist, Koma Kansai II (1767–1835). Zeshin perfected ingenious techniques that played with perception, including tricking the eye to make lacquer look like other materials, from bamboo to metal. He used one such method to make these boxes resemble *shibuichi*, a brown-gray alloy of copper and silver traditionally used to decorate sword guards. The effect was achieved by applying powdered charcoal and tin dust to a wet lacquer surface.[21]

Zeshin used this dark background as the foil for an ethereal design of springtime flowers. Rendered in monochrome, the effect is extremely subtle, like a garden glimpsed in evening shadows. No showy cherry blossoms here; instead Zeshin focuses on humble wildflowers: dandelions, milk vetch, shepherd's purse, horsetail, and violets. Their flowers spent, the fluffy dandelion heads are partly scattered; the vetch and violets bear seedpods instead of blooms.

These delicate motifs form a single composition that wraps the walls of each box and extends onto the lid, orienting the motifs in space. On the larger box, a single butterfly hovers in the "air" on the lid, while a second butterfly waits, hidden on the signed underside of an inset tray. The execution is spectacularly refined: leaves and stems are rendered in slight raised relief, textured with naturalistic details, and the dandelion seeds and butterfly are delicately etched into the wet lacquer. The spare composition, painterly touch, and sensitive handling of natural motifs are evidence of Zeshin's training in the studios of Suzuki Nanrei (1775–1844) and Okamoto Toyohiko (1773–1845), two artists affiliated with the Kyoto-based Shijo painting lineage, as well as his interest in haiku poetry.

—*LWA*

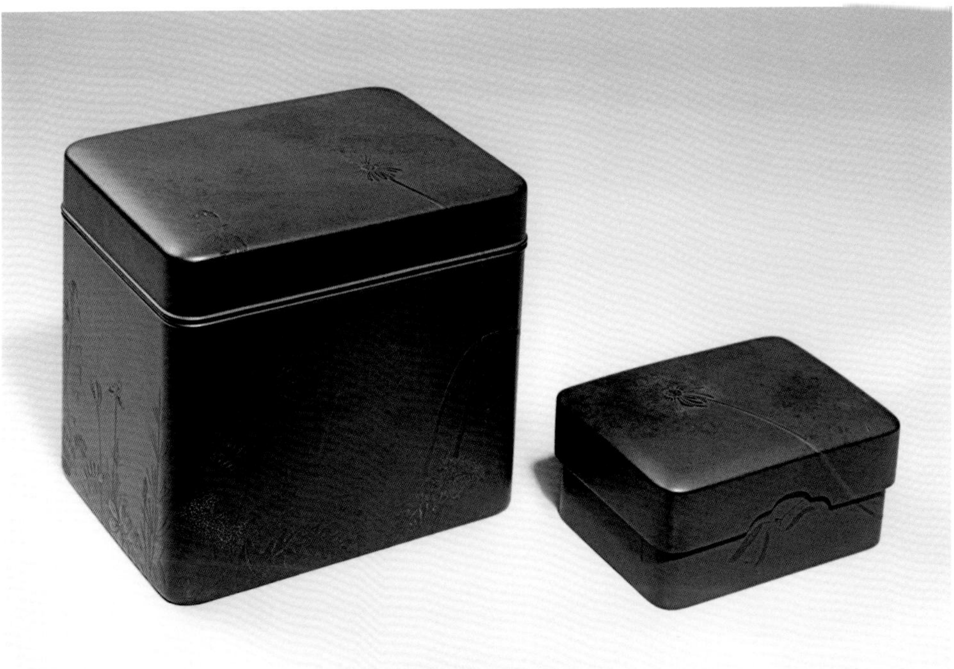

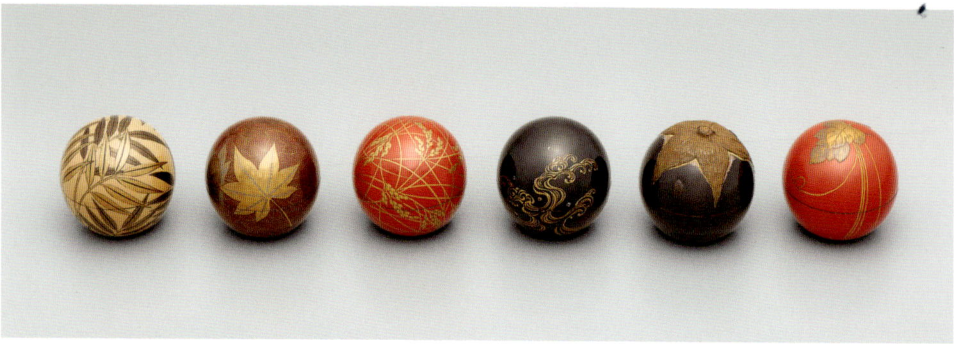

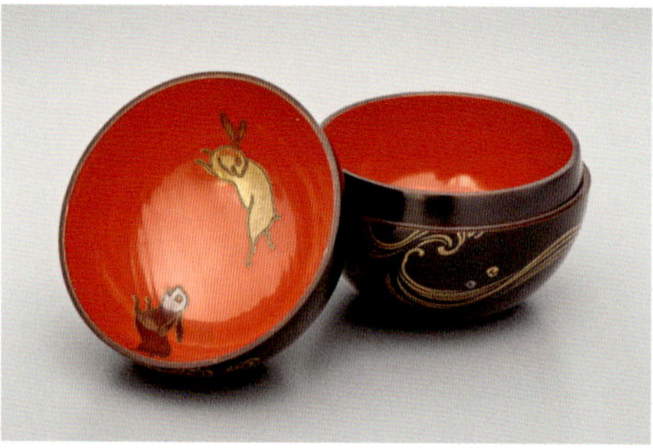

SET OF TWELVE INCENSE CONTAINERS

Lacquered by Suzuki Hyosaku I (Japanese, 1874–1943) and decorated by twelve *maki-e* artists
Taisho period (1912–1926)
Lacquer and metal on wood
Diam. 5.1 cm (each)
The Avery Brundage Collection, B60M295.a-.l

January: Embroidered Ball by Koda Shuetsu (Japanese, 1881–1933)
February: Jewel by Uehara Shunko (Japanese, 1877–1948)
March: Willow by Yuasa Kagyo I (Japanese, 1875–1952)
April: Cherry Blossom by Domoto Gosaburo (Japanese, 1889–1964)
May: Saxifrage by Uono Jisei (Japanese, 1883–after 1953)
June: Thunder by Inai Gyokuho I (Japanese, 1876–1930)
July: Star Festival by Koda Katei (Japanese, 1886–1961)
August: Eggplant by Yamada Rakuzen I (Japanese, 1874–1939)
September: Wave by Miki Gyokushin (Japanese, 1881–1944)
October: Rice Plant by Okamoto Shoho (Japanese, active approx. 1910s)
November: Autumn Leaves by Kamisaka Yukichi (Japanese, 1886–1938)
December: Maianthemum Japonicum by Toshima Kofu (Japanese, 1882–1956)

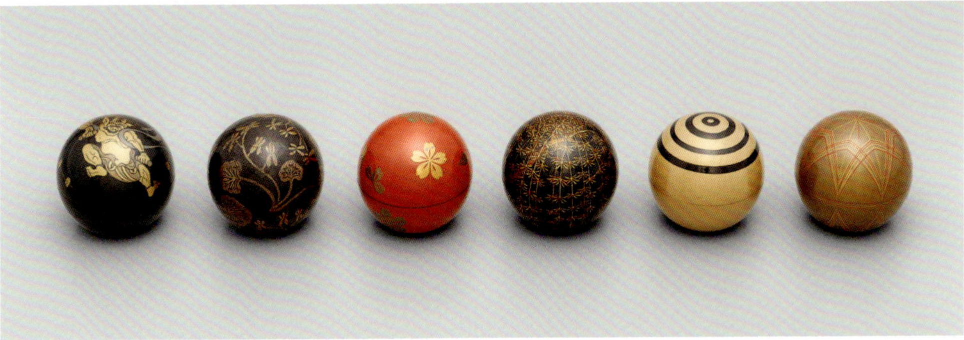

In this unique project, Suzuki Hyosaku I (1874-1943), a leading lacquer artist, collaborated with twelve lacquer decorators to create a set of twelve incense containers (*kogo*). Suzuki applied base lacquer on twelve incense containers and then asked fellow artists to decorate them. Each artist chose a motif to symbolize a specific month of the year. For example, the container for January simulates a toy ball called *temari*, which was made from a cotton core wrapped decoratively with silk thread. Historically, girls played with these balls on New Year's Day. Another container, for the month of June, bears the depiction of the thunder god, who represents the early summer storms during the rainy season. He is encircled by a ring of drums that he beats to create thunder.

Some of the containers, such as the one for September, are decorated not only on the outside but also inside. The month of September is traditionally associated with a beautiful full moon in the clear autumn sky. The artist did not include the moon on the container; instead, he applied a wave motif on the exterior and playfully hid two lunar hares inside. Japanese folklore mentions a hare living on the full moon. Here the combination of waves and hares derives from the *noh* play *Chikubushima*, which describes the moonlight reflected on water as "waves above which hares fly." From this, hares frolicking over waves became a symbol of the beautiful moonlight. When the lid of this container is opened, the combination reminds us of the harvest moon.

The division of labor in this project and other lacquerwares between those who applied the base lacquer and the decoration has been common for centuries in Japan. In this case, all the artists were from the Kyoto area and were closely associated with Suzuki. Some were brothers of each other, some were teachers and their students, and others were related through marriage. Kyoto has long been a prestigious center of lacquer production. These twelve incense containers represent the highest technical and aesthetic achievement in Japanese lacquer.
—*YM*

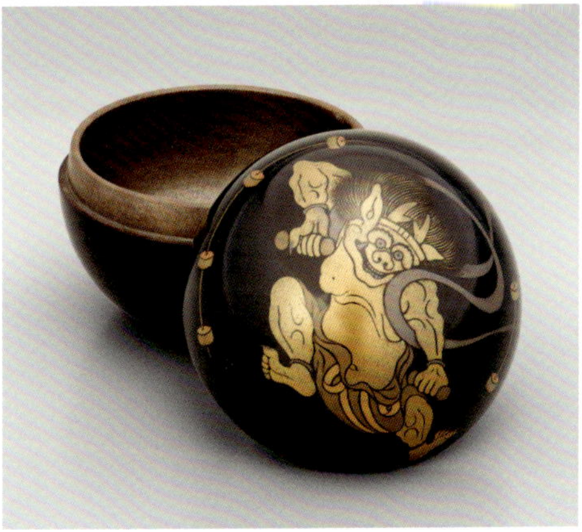

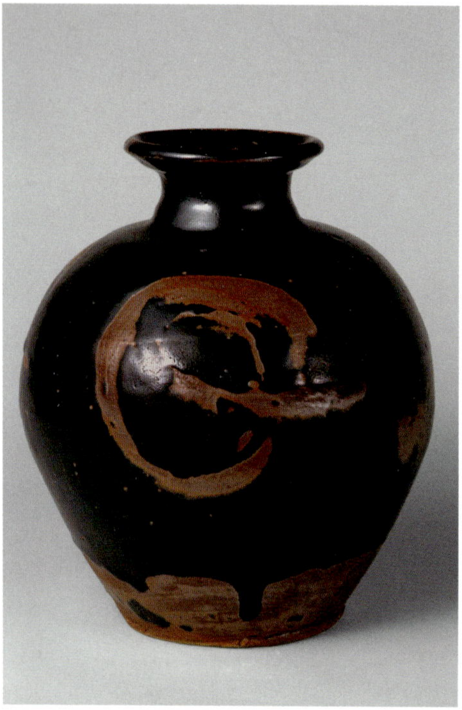

VASE WITH CALLIGRAPHIC DESIGN

1950–1960
By Hamada Shoji (Japanese, 1894–1978)
Stoneware with glaze
H. 27.9 cm × Diam. 25.4 cm
Gift of June and William Vredenburg, 1991.96

This round vase with a short neck, flat flaring mouth rim, heavy black glaze, and wax-resist decorations on two sides is typical of Hamada Shoji's simple, bold ceramic style of the 1950s. Hamada's elegant calligraphic designs were created in harmony with the rustic simplicity of the stoneware that they decorated. This modest but beautiful vase is a good example of the Mingei (folk craft) style and its reverence for simple proportions and an earthy color palette. Hamada was one of the most significant Japanese artists of the twentieth century and a key figure in the founding and promotion of the Mingei movement in the 1920s. This movement centered on the aesthetic of rustic simplicity found in everyday utensils. Through Mingei, work made by anonymous craftsmen over the centuries became inspiration for modern craftspeople to create new work.

Despite its local, rustic flavor, the Mingei movement was quite international in scope. Hamada and other artists founded this movement with the scholar and critic Yanagi Muneyoshi (1889–1961). They were inspired by the natural, intuitive approach to the arts Yanagi discovered through the writing and art of William Blake (1757–1827) and the poetry of Walt Whitman (1819–1892). They also exalted the simple beauty of traditional ceramics from Korea and crafts from Okinawa as well as ceramics from many parts of Japan.

In the early 1920s, Hamada worked closely with the British studio potter Bernard Leach (1887–1979), joining him in Cornwall to set up the Leach Pottery Studio. In 1924, Hamada returned to Japan to establish his own studio in the village of Mashiko, Tochigi prefecture, north of Tokyo, which is still the epicenter of Mingei ceramic production. He was designated a Living National Treasure in 1955. In addition to his identity as a leading Mingei artist, Hamada was a teacher and mentor for younger artists, and he became director of the Japan Folk Art Museum in Tokyo in 1962. Artistic training and public education were both important components of the Mingei movement.

—*KGO*

SHIMMERING OF HEATED AIR (KAGERO)

approx. 1969
By Shono Shounsai (Japanese, 1904–1974)
Bamboo, rattan, and copper alloy
H. 34.9 cm × Diam. 35.6 cm
Lloyd Cotsen Japanese Bamboo Basket Collection, 2006.3.836

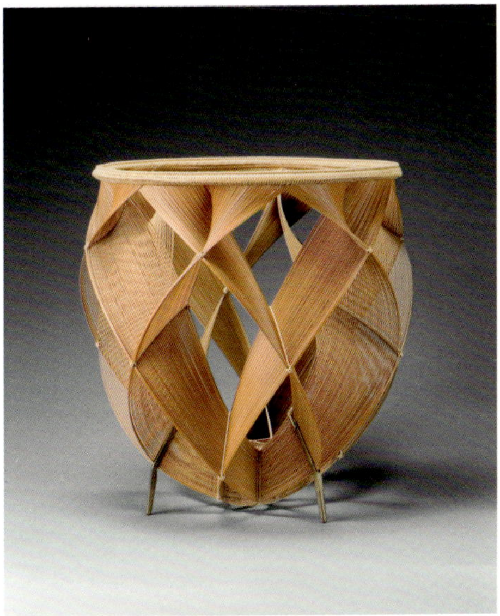

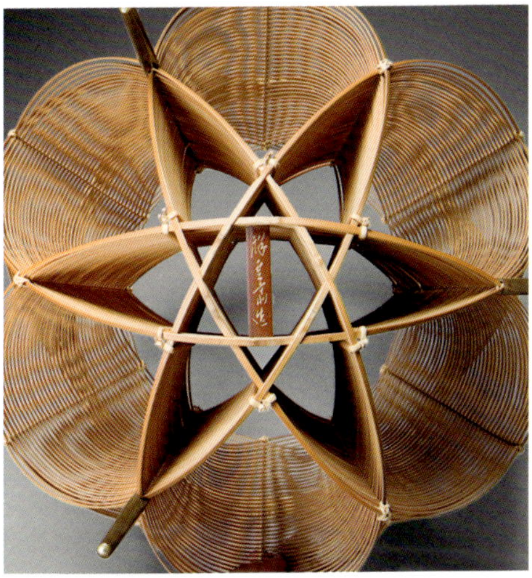

Shono Shounsai (1904–1974) was born in Beppu city, Oita prefecture, Japan's heartland for bamboo crafts. He began making woven bamboo baskets in the 1920s and successfully submitted many works to the annual Japan Fine Arts Exhibition (Nitten) in the 1940s and early 1950s. In 1953, his Nitten submission was a neotraditional, intricately woven round basket. This basket was rejected, which prompted him to rethink his approach to the art and craft of basketry. From that point on he was committed to pushing the genre and his own capabilities.

Shounsai began creating dynamic pieces that expressed motion. This included a series inspired by ocean waves that used very thin strips of bamboo in parallel construction and exploited the flexibility of the material. His 1958 Nitten entry was very similar to this work created in 1969 (both are entitled *Kagero*). The 1958 work, which used an open construction of interwoven ovals, marked Shounsai's transition to a more contemporary style.

In addition to pushing limits and experimenting with bamboo-weaving techniques, Shounsai explored the expressive possibility of using single bamboo sheets in place of woven strips, inspired by the extreme simplicity in thought and action associated with the practice of Zen Buddhism. He eventually selected sections of bamboo that required minimal cutting or carving. In this way he removed the decorative elements from his practice and allowed the material to speak for itself. Shounsai was designated a Living National Treasure in 1967.

—*KGO*

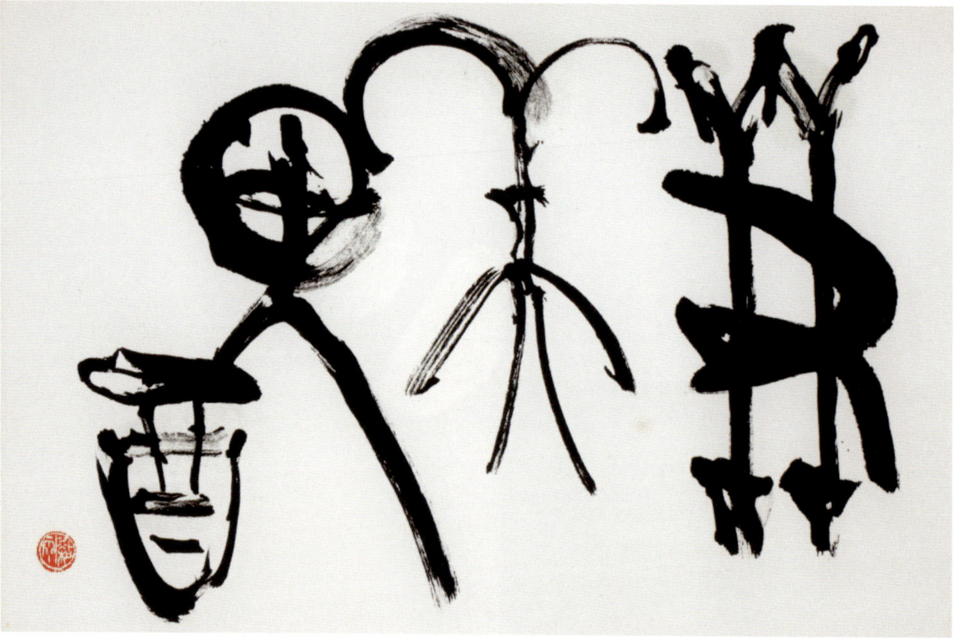

BOTH BEAUTIFUL AND UGLY (KENBISHU)

—

1977
By Aoyama San'u (Japanese, 1912–1993)
Ink on paper
H. 45 cm × W. 69.1 cm (image)
Gift of the Aoyama family, 2016.95

—

Aoyama San'u was a lifelong student of Chinese and Japanese calligraphy, a dedicated collector, and an educator of calligraphers and connoisseurs. He taught at Daito Bunka University and also took on private pupils. For thirty-seven years beginning in 1956, he published a monthly periodical, *Kindai shodo gurafu*, that greatly contributed to the popularization of Chinese and Japanese calligraphy in the postwar period.

As a young man, San'u studied Chinese calligraphers of the Wei (220–265), Jin (265–419), and Tang (618–907) dynasties under the tutelage of Oike Seiran (1899–1977). In his early thirties, he began studying with Nishikawa Yasushi (1902–1989) and became very influenced by Ming and Qing dynasty (1368–1911) calligraphers, including Wu Changshi (1844–1927) and the late-Qing-dynasty Stele School. In 1975, he encountered the work of Dong Qichang (1555–1636) at the National Palace Museum in Taipei, which informed much of his later work.

This piece is an excellent example of work done in the artist's late sixties and seventies that examines the raw vitality and energy of calligraphy as well as specific historical referents. Referencing the dualistic concepts present in Daoist and Buddhist philosophy often explored in Chinese calligraphy, *Both Beautiful and Ugly* incorporates archaic characters with bold, modern brushstrokes. To elaborate on the simple brevity of San'u's piece, consider this Daoist musing attributed to the legendary Chinese emperor Huangdi:

> *Some things are called beautiful and others ugly,*
> *But this is an abuse of words.*
> *Everything is impermanent.*
> *Something that is now beautiful*
> *Will metamorphose into something ugly,*
> *And that which is ugly will become beautiful.*[22]

—KGO

FLOWER BASKET WITH CIRCULAR FAN CONSTRUCTION

approx. 1997

By Hayakawa Shokosai V (Japanese, 1932–2011)

Bamboo and rattan

H. 20.3 cm × Diam. 33 cm

Lloyd Cotsen Japanese Bamboo Basket Collection, 2006.3.809

Hayakawa Shokosai V was born into the lineage of Osaka- and Kyoto-based artists who, beginning in the mid-nineteenth century, transformed the craft of basketry into the art of sculptural bamboo. His great-grandfather Hayakawa Shokosai I (1815–1897) was the first artist to sign his bamboo baskets. These vessels, created in the style of Chinese tea utensils and flower baskets, were popularized in conjunction with the Edo-period (1615–1868) interest in Chinese literati and the practice of the *sencha* (whole leaf) tea gathering.

Designated a Living National Treasure in 2003, the artist studied under his father Hayakawa Shokosai IV, who had studied under his father Hayakawa Shokosai III. "When I was young I was so enamored of my ability to bend bamboo to my will and make a vessel, but it had no beauty or life....I began to make art when I gave bamboo its voice in what I was doing."[23]

This low, handle-less basket is an example of a sophisticated simplicity that highlights the natural beauty of the material. Constructed using double-layered carved pieces, tapered at the ends and thicker in the middle, it is modern and minimal, while at the same time it draws on the Hayakawa family's signature plaiting and knotting techniques.

—*KGO*

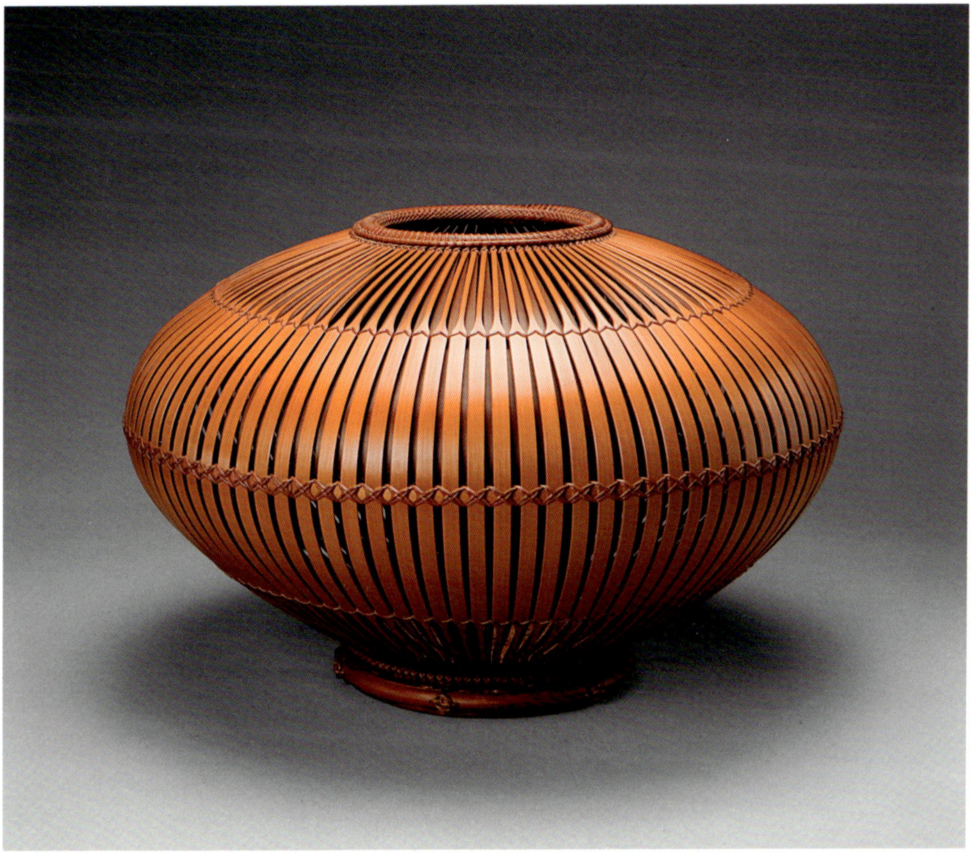

UNTITLED MV-1014

—

2010

By Akiyama Yo (Japanese, b. 1953)

Stoneware with distressed surface

H. 38.1 cm × W. 54.3 cm × D. 42.2 cm

Gift of Paul and Kathleen Bissinger, 2016.96

—

Akiyama Yo approaches ceramics by focusing on the material properties of clay. He considers his work's primordial connection to the earth and its core and the chemical changes that occur when clay meets a kiln's fire. In the artist's words, "There is always a yearning or longing for the primordial at the root of my way of thinking.... Ten years ago I came across the word '*arche*,' which covers a primordial state, fundamentals, and origins in Greek, and became all the more aware that this was an indispensable point of view and the axis of my thoughts in producing works."[24]

Akiyama studied ceramics in the mid-1970s at the Kyoto City University of the Arts. After completing his degree, he felt that he still had not discovered an approach to clay that was truly his own. Rather than focusing on his studio practice, he spent the next three years working in a home for children with special needs, introducing them to clay and seeing the way they would spend endless hours exploring the material.

Akiyama had a breakthrough when he realized his fascination with the rugged surface that results from clay splitting, cracking, and fissuring when fired. He has since experimented with the distressed surface of clay at large and small scales, as shown in this work from his *Untitled* series. *Untitled MV-1014*, like all of Akiyama's work since the mid-1990s, is made of pigmented stoneware clay that achieves a dark, sometimes completely black color. The artist patinated the surface with a mixture of iron filings and vinegar, giving it a rusty finish reminiscent of raw metallic ore and igneous rock.

—*KGO*

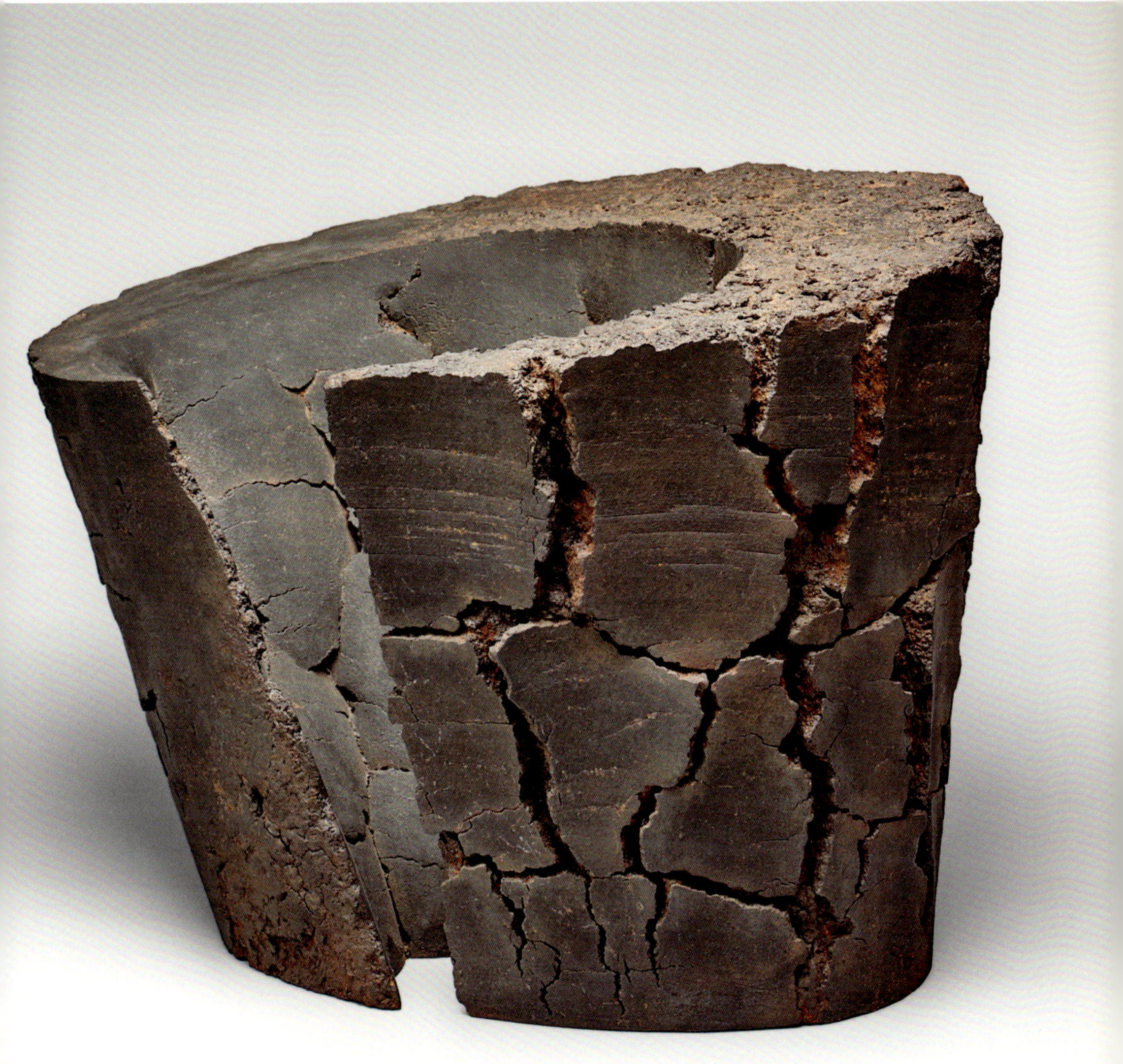

NOTES

PERSIAN WORLD

1 Translation by Manijeh Bayani.

2 Martina Rugiadi, "Carved Marble in Medieval Ghazni: Function and Meaning," *Hadeeth ad-Dar* 34 (2011): 9.

3 Translation by Oliver Watson.

SOUTH ASIA

1 Stella Kramrisch, *Manifestations of Shiva* (Philadelphia: Philadelphia Museum of Art, 1981), 3.

2 Wladimir Zwalf, "Background to a Buddha," *The British Museum Society Bulletin* 41 (1982): 8–9, quoting a pamphlet by the engineer E. B. Harris published in London in 1864.

3 All quotations are from Padma Kaimal, *Scattered Goddesses: Travels with the Yoginis* (Ann Arbor, MI: Association for Asian Studies, 2012).

4 Adapted from the ancient Buddhist text Nidanakatha, in Henry Clarke Warren, *Buddhism in Translations: Passages Selected from the Buddhist Sacred Books* (Cambridge, MA: Harvard University Press, 1896), 80–81.

5 Susan L. and John C. Huntington, *Leaves from the Bodhi Tree: The Art of Pāla India (8th–12th Centuries) and Its International Legacy* (Dayton, Ohio: Dayton Art Institute in association with the University of Washington Press, 1990), 105.

6 Indira Viswanathan Peterson, *Poems to Śiva: The Hymns of the Tamil Saints* (Princeton: Princeton University Press, 1989), 11; wording slightly adapted.

7 Stuart Cary Welch, *India: Art and Culture, 1300–1900* (New York: Metropolitan Museum of Art, 1985), 27.

8 Jayadeva, *Love Song of the Dark Lord: Jayadeva's Gitagovinda*, ed. and trans. Barbara Stoler Miller (New York: Columbia University Press, 1977), 107–14.

SOUTHEAST ASIA

1 Inscription of Thvar Kdei, translated and slightly adapted from Georges Coedès, ed. and trans., *Inscriptions du Cambodge* (Paris: École française d'Extrême-Orient, 1954), 6:136–37.

2 Adapted from *The Ramayana of Valmiki: An Epic of Ancient India*, vol. 6: *Yuddhakanda*, Robert P. Goldman, Sally J. Sutherland Goldman, and Barend A. van Nooten, trans. (Princeton: Princeton University Press, 2017), 286, 54:16.

3 Henri Parmentier, *Inventaire descriptif des monuments čams de l'Annam* (Paris: E. Leroux, 1909), 1:182; Jean Boisselier, *La statuaire du Champa: recherches sur les cultes et l'iconographie* (Paris: École française d'Extrême-Orient, 1963), 275–77.

4 Zhou Daguan and Peter Harris, *A Record of Cambodia: The Land and Its People* (Chiang Mai, Thailand: Silkworm Books, 2007), 51, 77–78.

CHINA

1 Rene-Yvon Lefebvre d'Argencé, *Chinese Jades in the Avery Brundage Collection* (San Francisco: Asian Art Museum of San Francisco, 1977), 9.

2 Li Xueqin, ed., *Shisanjing zhushu: Zhouli* (Beijing: Beijing University Press, 1999), 18:561.

3 Translated by Jay Xu.

4 This text is excerpted from Tianlong Jiao, "The 'Archaeology' of Two Ancient Chinese Bronzes in the US," *Orientations* 48, no. 4 (July–August 2017): 74–75.

5 Jessica Rawson, *Western Zhou Ritual Bronzes from the Arthur M. Sackler Collections* (Washington, DC: Arthur M. Sackler Foundation, 1990), 2:117. The reading of the graph as "the fourth son" is by Cao Dazhi, personal communication.

6 Robert Bagley, *Shang Ritual Bronzes in the Arthur M. Sackler Collections* (Washington, DC: Arthur M. Sackler Foundation, 1987), 295–309. For Anyang foundry remains, see Li Yung-ti, "The Anyang Bronze Foundries: Archaeological Remains, Casting Technology, and Production Organization" (PhD thesis, Harvard University, 2003), 259–61.

7 For recent discoveries of Anyang bronzes in Shaanxi Baoji, see Shaanxi Sheng Kaogu Yanjiuyuan et al., eds., *Zhouye luming: Baoji Shigushan Xizhou guizumu chutu qingtongqi* (Shanghai: Shanghai Shiji Chuban Jituan, 2014).

8 Proposed by Guo Moruo and endorsed by Xu Shaohua, see Xu Shaohua, *Zhoudai nantu lishi dili yu wenhua* (Wuhan: Wuhan daxue chubanshe, 1994), 123–24. See Nelson-Atkins Museum object number 32-68/6.

9 Sun Qikang, "Chuqi Wangsun Yizhe zhong kaobian," *Jianghan kaogu* 4 (1983): 41–46; Liu Xiang, "Wangsun Yizhe zhong xinshi," *Jianghan luntan* 8 (1983): 76–78.

10 For this set, see Henan Sheng Wenwu Kaogu Yanjiusuo et al., eds., *Xichuan Xiasi Chunqiu Chumu* (Beijing: Wenwu chubanshe, 1991), 140–78; for the date of the tomb, see Li Ling, "Chushu zhi sun Peng jiujing shi shui?" *Zhongyuan wenwu* 4 (1981): 36–37.

11 Angela F. Howard et al., *Chinese Sculpture* (New Haven, CT: Yale University Press, 2006), 93.

12 City Council of Hong Kong, *Gems of Chinese Art from the Asian Art Museum of San Francisco: The Avery Brundage Collection* (Hong Kong: Hong Kong Museum of Art, 1983), 228.

13 Xie Zhiliu, "The Library Cave of the Mogao Grottoes in Dunhuang," in Shanghai Museum and the Art Gallery, The Chinese University of Hong Kong, *Cultural Relics from Dunhuang and Turfan* (Shanghai: Shanghai Museum, 1987), 9.

14 Ibid.

15 Ann B. Wicks, ed., *Children in Chinese Art* (Honolulu: University of Hawai'i Press, 2002), 11–14.

16 Li Zhiyan, Virginia L. Bower, and He Li, eds., *Chinese Ceramics: From the Paleolithic Period through the Qing Dynasty* (New Haven, CT: Yale University Press, 2010), 271.

17 He Li, *Chinese Ceramics: A New Comprehensive Survey from the Asian Art Museum of San Francisco* (New York: Rizzoli, 1996), 197.

18 He Li, "Ceramics of the Song, Liao, Western Xia, and Jin Dynasties," in Li Zhiyan, Virginia L. Bower, and He Li, eds., *Chinese Ceramics: From the Paleolithic Period through the Qing* dynasty (New Haven, CT: Yale University Press, 2010), 286.

19 Petra Rösch, *Chinese Wood Sculptures of the 11th to 13th Centuries: Images of Water-Moon Guanyin in Northern Chinese Temples and Western Collections* (Stuttgart, Germany: ibidem Press, 2007), 27–32.

20 Ellen B. Avril, ed., *Chinese Art in the Cincinnati Art Museum* (Cincinnati: Cincinnati Art Museum, 1997), 26.

21 Megan Bryson, *Goddess on the Frontier: Religion, Ethnicity, and Gender in Southwest China* (Palo Alto, CA: Stanford University Press, 2016), 33.

22 Woon Wee Teng, *The Hidden Treasures of Nanzhao and Dali Kingdoms* (Singapore: Mainland Press, 2014), 36.

23 Li He, "Problems in Song Ceramics: Redating Official Guan Ceramics in the Asian Art Museum of San Francisco," *Apollo Magazine* (March 1998): 11.

24 Mary Tregear, *Song Ceramics* (New York: Rizzoli, 1982), 132.

25 He Li, *Chinese Ceramics* (London: Thames & Hudson, 2006), 132.

26 Robert E. Harrist Jr., *Power and Virtue: The Horse in Chinese Art* (New York: China Institute, 1997), 94, 115n117.

27 Geng Baochang, *Ming Qing ciqi jianding* (Beijing: Zijincheng chubanshe, 1993), 69–70.

28 For more on Queen Mother of the West, see Suzanne E. Cahill, *Transcendence and Divine Passion: The Queen Mother of the West in Medieval China* (Redwood City, CA: Stanford University Press, 1993).

29 Eileen Hsiang-ling Hsu, *Monks in Glaze: Patronage, Kiln Origin, and Iconography of the Yixian Luohans* (Boston: Brill, 2016), 98.

30 Stephen Owen, *The Poetry of Du Fu* (Boston: Walter de Gruyter, 2016), 3:116–17.

31 Institute of Archaeology, CASS; Museum of Ding Ling; and the Archaeological Team of the City of Beijing, *The Imperial Tomb of the Ming Dynasty: Ding Ling* (Beijing: Wenwu Press, 1990), 2:251–57.

32 National Gallery of Art, Washington, DC, *Chinese Art Treasures: A Selected Group of Objects from the Chinese National Palace Museum and the Chinese National Central Museum, Taichung, Taiwan, Exhibited in the United States, 1961–1962*, (Geneva: Skira, 1961), 37.

33 Hongnam Kim, *The Life of a Patron: Zhou Lianggong (1612–1672) and the Painters of Seventeenth-Century China* (New York: China Institute, 1996), 125–34.

34 Hajni Elias, "Adding Flower to Brocade (Jin Shang Tian Hua): A Magnificent Qianlong Yangcai Vase," in *Fine Chinese Ceramics and Works of Art* (Hong Kong: Sotheby's, Hong Kong, 2014), 80–81.

35 Zong Fengying, "The Edrina Collection of Ming and Qing Imperial Costumes," in Art Museum, Chinese University of Hong Kong, *Heavenly Splendour: The Edrina Collection of Ming and Qing Imperial Costumes* (Hong Kong: Art Museum, Chinese University of Hong Kong, 2009), 24.

36 "Lotus," The Metropolitan Museum of Art, accessed September 30, 2016, http://www.metmuseum.org/art/collection/search/72796.

37 Liu Xiaodong, "Respecting Reality" ("Zunzhong xianshi"), in *Fine Arts Research (Meishu yanjiu)* 3 (1993), referenced in Wu Hung and Peggy Wang, eds., *Contemporary Chinese Art: Primary Documents* (New York: Museum of Modern Art, 2010), 162.

38 Zheng Chongbin, "My Reading of Shitao's *Remarks on Painting*," in Britta Erickson et al., *Zheng Chongbin: Impulse, Matter, Form* (Beijing: Ink Studio, 2014), 80.

39 Xu Bing, "On (1999/2000)," trans. Phillip Bloom, in Wu Hung and Peggy Wang, eds., *Contemporary Chinese Art: Primary Documents* (New York: Museum of Modern Art, 2010), 254–55. Originally published as "Guanyu 'zi' de zishu" in *Wenhua yu daode* [*Culture and Morality*] 4 (2000): 19–21.

KOREA

1 Mark E. Byington, "The Account of the Han in the *Sanguozhi*—An Annotated Translation," in Mark E. Byington, ed., *Early Korea 2: The Samhan Period in Korean History* (Cambridge, MA: Korea Institute, Harvard University, 2009), 146.

2 I introduced this painting in my paper "Koryŏ Buddhist Paintings in American Collections," presented at First International Conference of Korean Art, Asian Art Museum of San Francisco, 1977.

3 For a similar piece, see Chung Yang-mo, *Baekja* [Porcelains], Hanguk-ui Mi [Beauty of Korea] 2 (Seoul: Jungang Ilbosa, 1978), 202, plate 57.

4 Kim Yeong-won, *Joseonsidae dojagi* [Joseon dynasty ceramics] (Seoul: Seoul University Press, 2003), 312–27.

JAPAN

1 "Stand," The Metropolitan Museum of Art, accessed May 22, 2017, http://www.metmuseum.org/art/collection/search/39518.

2 Wakamatsu Ryōichi, "Jinbutsu-dōbutsu haniwa," in *Kofun jidai no kenkyū: 9 kofun III haniwa*, ed. Ishino Hironobu, Iwasaki Takuya, Kawakami Kunihiko, and Shiraishi Taichirō (Tokyo: Yūzankaku shuppan kabushikigaisha, 1992), 123–33.

3 Chiga Hisashi, "Haniwa—kofun no naka no haniwa hairetsu no hensen," in *Yamato no Kofun II*, ed. Kawakami Kunihiko (Osaka: Kinki Nihon Tetsudō, 2006), 45–55; Tenri University Sankokan Museum, *Dai 72 kai kikakuten zuroku: Haniwa dai shūgō* (Nara, Japan: Kansai bijutsu insatsu, 2014), 1–4.

4 For a detailed account of this story, see Melissa M. Rinne, "Avery Brundage's Other Olympic Prize: The Asian Art Museum's Dry Lacquer Sculptures Bonten and Taishakuten," *Lotus Leaves* 11:1 (Fall 2008): 15–25.

5 Sarah Johanna Horton, "*Mukaeko*: Practice for the Deathbed," in Jacqueline I. Stone and Marko Namba Walter, eds., *Death and the Afterlife in Japanese Buddhism* (Honolulu: University of Hawai'i Press, 2008), 41–43.

6 Burton Watson, trans., *The Lotus Sutra* (New York: Columbia University Press, 1993), 320. This passage occurs in Chapter 28, "Encouragements of the Bodhisattva Universal Worthy."

7 John M. Rosenfield and Elizabeth ten Grotenhuis, *Journey of the Three Jewels: Japanese Buddhist Paintings from Western Collections* (New York: Asia Society, 1979), 57.

8 Miya Tsugio, "Pictorial Art of the *Lotus Sutra* in Japan," in George J. Tanabe, Jr. and Willa Jane Tanabe, eds., *The Lotus Sutra in Japanese Culture* (Honolulu: University of Hawai'i Press, 1989), 80.

9 Yoko Woodson and Richard L. Mellott, *Exquisite Pursuits: Japanese Art in the Harry G. C. Packard Collection* (San Francisco: Asian Art Museum, 1994), 85.

10 Kyoto Kokuritsu Hakubutsukan, *Kaiho Yusho: Kyoto Kokuritsu Hakubutsukan Kaikan 120-shunen Kinen: Tokubetsu Tenrankai* / Kaiho Yusho: Kyoto National Museum 120th Anniversary Commemorative Special Exhibition (Kyoto: Kyoto Kokuritsu Hakubutsukan, 2017), 275.

11 Fujikake Shizuya, "Unkoku Togan hitsu Toenmei Rinnasei-zu," *Kokka* 750 (September 1954): 266.

12 For a survey of similar dishes, see Miyeko Murase, ed., *Turning Point: Oribe and the Arts of Sixteenth-Century Japan* (New York: Metropolitan Museum of Art, 2003).

13 Translated by Edward Kamens. See Edward Kamens, "The Past in the Present: Fujiwara Teika and the Traditions of Japanese Poetry," in *Word in Flower: The Visualization of Classical Literature in Seventeenth-Century Japan*, ed. Carolyn Wheelwright (New Haven, CT: Yale University Art Gallery, 1989), 30. Teika's sequence is based on the traditional lunar calendar, in which the New Year began in late January or early February.

14 Endo Motoko, "Yamamoto Soken juni kagetsu kacho-zu byobu no seisaku jijo (The Production of "Flowers and Birds of the Twelve Months" by Yamamoto Soken)" *Museum* 597 (August 2005): 7–25.

15 The album is owned by the Tokyo University of the Arts. Thanks to Frank Felton, who generously shared this information.

16 Oka Yoshiko, "Ninsei to Kenzan-sono katachi to monyō" [Ninsei and Kenzan, form and pattern], *Bujitsu Forum* 29 (2012): 91.

17 These traits are described in Ihara Saikaku's *Life of an Amorous Woman*. Cited in Melinda Takeuchi, "Seduction: Japan's Floating World," in Laura W. Allen, *Seduction: Japan's Floating World* (San Francisco: Asian Art Museum, 2015), 13n26.

18 Ogata Tsutomu, Sasaki Johei, and Okada Akiko, *Buson Zenshu*, vol. 6, *Kaiga iboku* (Tokyo: Kodansha, 1998), 250.

19 Kyoko Kinoshita, "The Life and Art of Tokuyama Gyokuran," in Felice Fisher with Kyoko Kinoshita, *Ike Taiga and Tokuyama Gyokuran: Japanese Masters of the Brush* (Philadelphia: Philadelphia Museum of Art, 2007), 45.

20 Hosono Masanobu, "Kokan to Denzen," *Nihon no Bijutsu* 232 (September 1985): 17.

21 Joe Earle, *Shibata Zeshin: Masterpieces of Japanese Lacquer from the Khalili Collection* (London : Kibo Foundation, 1997), 9–10.

22 Timothy Freke, *Taoist Wisdom: Daily Teachings from the Taoist Sages* (New York: Sterling, 2002), 20.

23 Robert T. Coffland, "My Sensei Hayakawa Shokosai V," *The Hayakawa Shokosai Lineage* (Santa Fe: Tai Gallery, 2011), 4.

24 Akiyama Yo, "Towards the Sea of *Arche*?," exhibition text for *Yo Akiyama: Towards the Sea of Arche*, presented at Musée Tomo, Tokyo, April–July 2016.

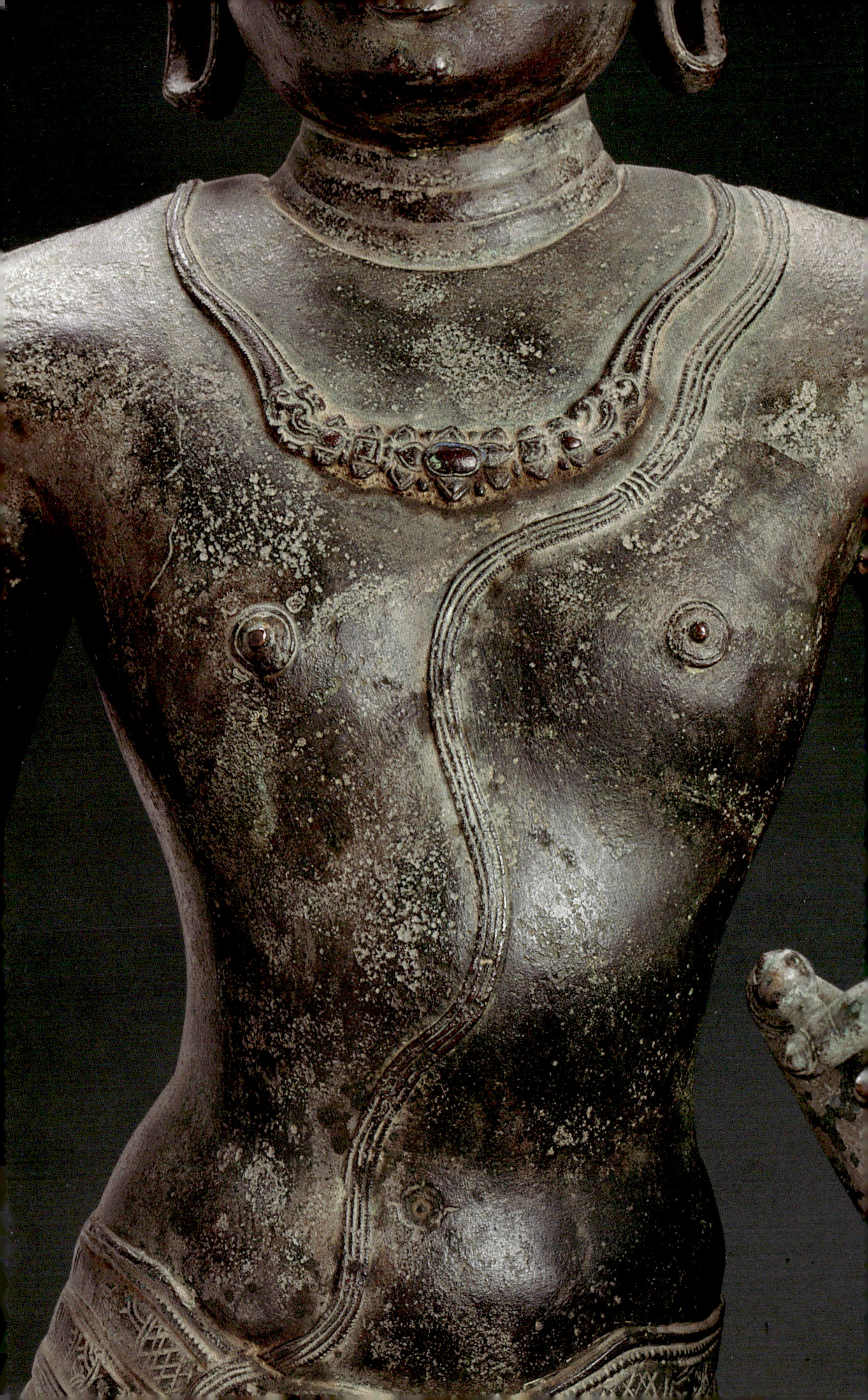

FURTHER READINGS ON THE COLLECTION

Adamjee, Qamar, Jeffrey Durham, and Karin G. Oen. *Divine Bodies: Sacred Imagery in Asian Art*. San Francisco: Asian Art Museum, 2018.

Allen, Laura W., and Melissa M. Rinne, eds. *The Printer's Eye: Ukiyo-e from the Grabhorn Collection*. San Francisco: Asian Art Museum, 2013.

Asian Art Museum of San Francisco: Selected Works. San Francisco: Asian Art Museum, 1994, 1998, 2015.

Bartholomew, Terese Tse, Mayching Kao, and So Kam Ng Lee. *The Charming Cicada Studio: Masterworks by Chao Shao-an*. San Francisco: Asian Art Museum, 1997.

Beauty, Wealth, and Power: Jewels and Ornaments of Asia. San Francisco: Asian Art Museum, 1992.

Bridge to Understanding: The Art and Architecture of San Francisco's Asian Art Museum–Chong-Moon Lee Center for Asian Art and Culture. San Francisco: Asian Art Museum, 2003.

Chan, Dany. *Flower Power: The Meaning of Flowers in Asian Art*. San Francisco: Asian Art Museum, 2017.

The Character of Characters: An Animation by Xu Bing. San Francisco: Asian Art Museum, 2012.

d'Argencé, Rene-Yvon Lefebvre. *Ancient Chinese Bronzes in the Avery Brundage Collection*. Berkeley: de Young Museum Society and Diablo Press, 1966.

———. *Bronze Vessels of Ancient China in the Avery Brundage Collection*. San Francisco: Asian Art Museum, 1977.

———. *Chinese Ceramics in the Avery Brundage Collection*. San Francisco: de Young Museum Society, 1967.

———. *Chinese Jades in the Avery Brundage Collection*. San Francisco: Asian Art Museum, 1977.

———, ed. *Chinese, Korean, and Japanese Sculpture in the Avery Brundage Collection*. San Francisco: Asian Art Museum, 1974.

———. *Chinese Treasures from the Avery Brundage Collection*. New York: Asia Society, 1968.

———. *The Hans Popper Collection of Oriental Art*. San Francisco: Asian Art Museum, 1973.

d'Argencé, Rene-Yvon Lefebvre, and Terese Tse. *Indian and South-East Asian Stone Sculpture from the Avery Brundage Collection*. Pasadena and San Francisco: Pasadena Art Museum and San Francisco Center of Asian Art and Culture, 1969.

A Decade of Collecting (1966–1976): An Exhibition Celebrating the 10th Anniversary of the Asian Art Museum of San Francisco, The Avery Brundage Collection. San Francisco: Asian Art Museum, 1976.

The Effie B. Allison Collection: Kosometsuke and Other Chinese Blue-and-White Porcelains. San Francisco: Asian Art Museum, 1982.

The Elegant Gathering: The Yeh Family Collection. San Francisco: Asian Art Museum, 2006.

Fang Zhaoling: A Life in Painting. San Francisco: Asian Art Museum, 2005.

Froom, Aimée. *Persian Ceramics from the Collections of the Asian Art Museum*. San Francisco: Asian Art Museum, 2008.

Gems of Chinese Art from the Asian Art Museum of San Francisco: The Avery Brundage Collection. Hong Kong: Urban Council, 1983.

Harding, Allison, and Forrest McGill, eds. *Gorgeous*. San Francisco: Asian Art Museum, 2014.

He Li. *Chinese Ceramics: A New Comprehensive Survey from the Asian Art Museum of San Francisco*. New York: Rizzoli, 1996.

Kakudo, Yoshiko. *The Art of Japan: Masterworks in the Asian Art Museum of San Francisco*. San Francisco: Asian Art Museum and Chronicle Books, 1991.

Kim, Kumja Paik. *The Art of Korea: Highlights from the Collection of San Francisco's Asian Art Museum*. San Francisco: Asian Art Museum, 2006.

———. *Hopes and Aspirations: Decorative Painting of Korea*. San Francisco: Asian Art Museum, 1998.

Knight, Michael, He Li, and Terese Tse Bartholomew. *Later Chinese Jades: Ming Dynasty to Early Twentieth Century from the Asian Art Museum of San Francisco*. San Francisco: Asian Art Museum, 2007.

Looking at Patronage: Recent Acquisitions of Asian Art. San Francisco: Asian Art Museum, 1989.

McGill, Forrest, ed. *Emerald Cities: Arts of Siam and Burma, 1775–1950*. San Francisco: Asian Art Museum, 2009.

Moura Carvalho, Pedro, ed. *Collected Letters: An Installation by Liu Jianhua*. San Francisco: Asian Art Museum, 2016.

Nagasaki and Yokohama Prints from the Richard Gump Collection. San Francisco: Asian Art Museum, 1981.

Ng, So Kam. *Brushstrokes: Styles and Techniques of Chinese Painting*. San Francisco: Asian Art Museum, 1992.

Rinne, Melissa M. *Masters of Bamboo: Artistic Lineages in the Lloyd Cotsen Japanese Basket Collection*. San Francisco: Asian Art Museum, 2007.

Thai Ceramics: The James and Elaine Connell Collection. Kuala Lumpur: Oxford University Press, 1993.

Woodson, Yoko, and Richard L. Mellott. *Exquisite Pursuits: Japanese Art in the Harry G. C. Packard Collection*. San Francisco: Asian Art Museum, 1994.

INDEX

A

B

C

K

L

M